In Search of Power

In Search of Power is a history of the era of civil rights, decolonization, and Black Power. In the critical period from 1956 to 1974, the emergence of newly independent states worldwide and the struggles of the civil rights movement in the United States exposed the limits of racial integration and political freedom. Dissidents, leaders, and elites alike were linked in a struggle for power in a world where the rules of the game had changed. Brenda Gayle Plummer traces the detailed connections between African Americans' involvement in international affairs and how they shaped American foreign policy, integrating African-American history, the history of the African diaspora, and the history of United States foreign relations. These topics, usually treated separately, not only offer a unified view of the period but also reassess controversies and events that punctuated this colorful era of upheaval and change.

Brenda Gayle Plummer is Merze Tate Professor of History at the University of Wisconsin at Madison and currently chairs the Department of Afro-American Studies. She is the author of *Rising Wind: Black Americans and U.S. Foreign Affairs, 1935–1960* (1996); *Haiti and the United States* (1992); and *Haiti and the Great Powers, 1902–1915* (1988). She is the editor of *Window on Freedom: Race, Civil Rights, and Foreign Affairs, 1945–1988* (2003).

In Search of Power

*African Americans in the Era of
Decolonization, 1956–1974*

BRENDA GAYLE PLUMMER
University of Wisconsin, Madison

CAMBRIDGE
UNIVERSITY PRESS

CAMBRIDGE
UNIVERSITY PRESS

32 Avenue of the Americas, New York NY 10013-2473, USA

Cambridge University Press is part of the University of Cambridge.

It furthers the University's mission by disseminating knowledge in the pursuit of education, learning and research at the highest international levels of excellence.

www.cambridge.org
Information on this title: www.cambridge.org/9781107654716

First published 2013

A catalogue record for this publication is available from the British Library

Library of Congress Cataloguing in Publication data
Plummer, Brenda Gayle.
In search of power : African Americans in the era of decolonization,
1956–1974 / Brenda Gayle Plummer.
    p.   cm.
Includes bibliographical references and index.
ISBN 978-1-107-02299-7 (hardback) – ISBN 978-1-107-65471-6 (paperback)
1. African Americans – Civil rights.   2. Decolonization – Africa.   3. United States –
Foreign relations – Africa.   4. Africa – Foreign relations – United States.   5. African
Americans – Relations with Africans – History.   6. African diaspora – History.   I. Title.
E185.615.P5435   2012
323.1196′073–dc23   2012024348

ISBN 978-1-107-02299-7 Hardback
ISBN 978-1-107-65471-6 Paperback

Contents

Figures

Introduction

In late summer 1959 two aging generals and trusted staff members met for a series of candid conversations at a medieval fortress. The generals were also presidents, and the venue, the Château de Rambouillet, was the official summer home of French heads of state. Charles De Gaulle enjoyed receiving his foreign counterparts at the chateau, whose interior, resplendent with gilt and tapestries, and exterior, lush with formal gardens, reflected the grandeur of France. "Our guests," he noted, "were made to feel the nobility behind the geniality, the permanence behind the vicissitudes, of the nation which was their host."[1]

De Gaulle's guest this time was the president of the United States, Dwight D. Eisenhower, who on arriving in Paris received a hero's welcome as the liberator of wartime Europe. While the shared experience of World War II united the two men, their talks were not limited to the past. The major powers had accepted the inevitability of decolonization by the end of the decade, but not without hand wringing. Eisenhower and De Gaulle bemoaned colonial peoples' lack of preparation for independence. As an aide recalled the discussion, Ike declared that "often we were asked for tractors when the level of the economy required the ability to handle a plow and an ox. Many of these peoples were attempting to make the leap from savagery to the degree of civilization of a country like France in perhaps ten years, without realizing that it took thousands of years to develop the civilization which we know." De Gaulle concurred. In spite of disagreement between the two as to how Western Europe might best be defended, they agreed that it was now vital that the West act in concert in handling the developing countries.[2] De Gaulle ultimately consented to a French withdrawal from Algeria and Eisenhower was the first American to be

---

[1] De Gaulle quoted in Jean Lacouture, *De Gaulle, Ruler, 1945–1970* (New York: HarperCollins, 1991), 333.

[2] Memorandum of Conversation, September 3, 1959, Declassified Documents Reference System, hereafter DDRS. Note that the separate digitized and micofiche DDRS collections do not always overlap. See also Cyrus Sulzberger, *The Last of the Giants* (New York: Macmillan, 1970), 75.

I

so informed. Ike himself had little prior knowledge of Africa, and awkward mistakes compromised his administration's efforts to conduct normal relations with the new states.

Competition between the West and the Soviet bloc underwent transition after Stalin's death, becoming less dangerous to Europeans and North Americans but more lethal to emerging nations. The great powers had difficulty accommodating the democratic aspirations of their own ethnic minorities, and while they supported majority rule in principle, they sought to maintain patterns of social and political domination in previously colonized areas.

Across the Atlantic, a more modest meeting had taken place earlier in the season, also at a special site. The former summer home of the late Robert Russa Moton, who had presided over historically black Tuskegee Institute, was nestled in the Virginia countryside. Holly Knoll in Capahosic, Virginia, possessed rustic charm and lacked the luxury of Rambouillet but, like the chateau, served a manifest political purpose. Remodeling made it a conference center "where white and Negro leadership might convene and deliberate the important and crucial issues which must be faced in a spirit of understanding and goodwill," the Phelps Stokes Fund had argued in the proposal for funding it. The discussions held at Holly Knoll were not limited to domestic civil rights issues. "Responsible Negroes" and well-meaning whites worried about the impact of U.S. race relations on foreign publics and the lack of a coherent national policy toward African states.[3]

Earlier in the decade, while the Montgomery bus boycott was making the news all over the world, a group of prominent African-American figures met secretly at Capahosic. The clandestine all-male March 1956 conclave, sponsored by the Phelps Stokes Fund and paid for by the General Education Board, addressed the worries of conservatives who felt uncomfortable with the mass mobilization and popular participation that Montgomery represented. The list of participants read like a *Who's Who* of the black establishment of a decade before, minus Dorothy Ferebee of the National Council of Negro Women (NCNW). The contemporary observer notes the marked gender exclusion, but at midcentury, many Americans participated in mass organizations in which gender separation was the norm.

Men attending the meeting included UN official Ralph Bunche; President Rufus Clement of Atlanta University; Representative William L. Dawson of Chicago; Urban League director Lester B. Granger; federal judge William Hastie; Charles S. Johnson, president of Fisk University; President Benjamin Mays of Morehouse College; Frederick D. Patterson, president, respectively, of the National Negro Business League and the Phelps Stokes Fund; Willard

---

[3] Proposal of the Phelps Stokes Fund to the John Bulow Campbell Foundation, September 1958, General Education Board Records, Phelps Stokes Fund–Holly Knoll Conference Center, Series 1.2, folder 3029, Rockefeller Archive Center, hereafter RAC; Frederick D. Patterson, *Chronicles of Faith: The Autobiography of Frederick D. Patterson* (Tuscaloosa, Ala.: University of Alabama Press, 1991), 163–4.

Townsend, head of the United Transport Workers Union; New York state rent commissioner Robert Weaver; John H. Wheeler, president of the North Carolina Mutual Insurance Company; and National Association for the Advancement of Colored People (NAACP) secretary Roy Wilkins.[4]

Conveners timed the conference to occur one day before a mass meeting on civil rights in Washington, D.C., organized by fifty-two organizations. The Capahosic gathering in contrast was "hush-hush," speculated an Associated Negro Press correspondent, because participants wanted a gradualist entente with southern moderates and sensed that the deal-making, top-down leadership that characterized their modus operandi was becoming obsolete. Roy Wilkins recalled the meeting as unproductive, but it reflected fault lines in the black freedom movement that had already become visible by the late 1950s.[5]

One of these traversed gender. The NCNW and the National Association of Colored Women's Clubs had vigorously supported civil rights mobilization beginning with the Truman years (1945–52) and beyond. They were joined in activism by sororities and such local groups as the Women's Political Council, which played a formative role in mobilizing the Montgomery, Alabama, bus boycott of 1954–5.[6] The impressive credentials of these black women's organizations did not entitle them, however, to an equal seat at the table where the shape of the coming freedom struggle was debated and where prestigious African-American men contemplated their positions vis-à-vis the newly emerging states of Africa and the Caribbean.

Capahosic gatherings were as select in their way as De Gaulle and Eisenhower's meeting. During these years, the core group consisted of African-American college presidents and, as the specific topic would dictate, various experts. Vernon Jordan, a young Howard University law student who subsequently led the National Urban League and later advised President Bill Clinton, fondly recalled Capahosic as "the equivalent of a black Bohemian Grove, a unique gathering of members of the talented tenth." In his account,

The atmosphere was very male, with conversations over poker games or while sitting on the porch drinking. We played tennis, went on long walks, and ate great Southern cuisine. I loved every minute of it. Most of these men had been at their business for many

[4] F. D. Patterson, "Report on the Capahosic Conference, March 3–4, 1956"; Associated Negro Press [ANP] dispatch, [unpublished] March 12, 1956, Claude Barnett Papers, series G, reel 3 (Frederick, Md.: University Publications of America, 1985). Hereafter CBP.

[5] ANP Press dispatch, March 23, 1956, in ibid.; General Education Board, Annual Report, 1956, p. 8, General Education Board, Phelps Stokes Fund–Holly Knoll Conference Center, Series 1.2, folder 3029, RAC; Barnett to F. D. Patterson, March 12, 1956 and June 7, 1958, and ANP dispatch, March 12, 1956, CBP, series G, reel 3; "Leaders Ask NAACP 'Go Slow,'" Roy Wilkins to Percival Prattis, March 31, 1959, Box 144-10, Percival L. Prattis Papers, Moorland Spingarn Collection, Howard University, hereafter MSC.

[6] V. P. Franklin and Bettye Collier-Thomas, "For the Race in General and Black Women in Particular: The Civil Rights Activities of African American Women's Organizations, 1915–1950," in *Sisters in the Struggle: African American Women in the Civil Rights–Black Power Movement* (New York: New York University Press, 2001), 38.

years. Wisdom, experience, and just solid information about the way the world worked was on almost constant display. I took in as much as I could.[7]

All these savants, whether commanding great powers or modest institutions, faced a world changing in ways that they could not always direct and often could not predict. Their common desire was the power to manage and modify the transitions. The heads of state wanted to inoculate themselves against the challenges to global order they believed decolonization would bring. All had a stake in the status quo. They believed in the maintenance of a world founded on core values whose unshakable stability would admit only incremental change. The black college presidents had learned to thrive in the restricted world of American segregation. In the mid-1950s, they had held anxious meetings with others from the world of black business, education, and the professions to worry about a civil rights movement that had spun beyond their control, boasting leaders they did not know and espousing goals they found threatening.[8]

In addressing the issue of decolonization, the educators, unlike Eisenhower and De Gaulle, did not think Africans were primitives who were unready for civilization. But they did want to project their own influence into the new relationship that Africans would have with the United States. They consequently signed on to the United Negro College Fund's (UNCF's) African Scholarship Program and a plan to fly African students to the United States to receive American educations at historically black colleges and universities. UNCF collaborated with the African Scholarship Program and Ithaca College's Cooperative African Scholarship Program of American Universities to solicit aid from private backers and the African-American Institute, which channeled funds to the project from the International Cooperation Administration (ICA).[9]

A September 1960 airlift from Nairobi, Kenya, carried some 250 students to New York, where they received red carpet treatment on their arrival. One of them was Barack Obama Sr., father-to-be of the future U.S. president Barack Obama. UN undersecretary Ralph Bunche, Nelson Rockefeller, New York governor Averell Harriman, Roy Wilkins, and the Reverend James Robinson, founder of the volunteer organization Crossroads Africa, scheduled meetings with the newcomers. "Everyone wanted to get in on the act," journalist Percival Prattis complained.[10]

---

[7] Tina McCloud, "'Great People' Came to Moton" (Newport News, Va.) *Daily Press*, February 16, 1997, online, accessed September 2011; Vernon E. Jordan and Annette Gordon-Reed, *Vernon Can Read! A Memoir* (New York: Public Affairs, 2001), 212.

[8] Patterson, "Report on the Capahosic Conference"; and ANP release March 12, 1956; Claude Barnett to F. D. Patterson, March 12, 1956; minutes of the June 1958 Capahosic conference, Box 4, Phelps Stokes Fund Records, Schomburg Center for Research on Black Culture, New York Public Library, hereafter SC; Roy Wilkins to Percival Prattis, 3, March 31, 1959, MSC; "NAACP Asked to Go Slow at Capahosic," *Amsterdam News*, March 10, 1957, p. 24.

[9] William J. Trent Jr., "The United Negro College Fund's African Scholarship Program," *Journal of Negro Education* 31 (Spring, 1962): 205–9; Percival Prattis to Senator Hugh Scott, August 28, 1960, Prattis Papers, Box 144–12.

[10] Ibid.; James H. Meriwether, *Proudly We Can Be Africans: Black America and Africa, 1935–1961* (Chapel Hill: University of North Carolina Press, 2002), 146–8; Herbert L. Wright to Ralph

Why were these anonymous undergraduates significant to U.S. elites? To retain their places of influence and power, the leadership had to respond to colonial unrest and to the aspirations of minority peoples by supporting models of democratic process in the likeness of the West. For France, this meant sovereignty for Algeria. For the United States, it meant disseminating American political values to African and Asian elites-in-training.

Race is fundamentally embedded in every aspect of U.S. history and culture. For most of the republic's history, devices such as segregation permitted a direct recognition of its power and provided for a system of management that only partially contained its violence. As formal segregation became steadily untenable, so did a foreign policy that hampered U.S. objectives outside Europe. Socially and culturally the United States found itself on the threshold of a new era in which its formerly – and formally – isolated subcultures began to seep into the mainstream. Racial proscription and exclusion were under attack everywhere in the world as the 1960s began. "There had never been," one scholar notes, "a decade rung in with such heady self-consciousness of high purpose."[11]

By the end of that decade, the mood had changed. Insurgents came to see the state as a barrier, rather than the guarantor of true emancipation. The rebellions of the 1960s represented the return of radical energies dormant since the early cold war era. Knowledge about race incubated in the marketplace as well as in the academy, where the prospect of economic opportunity could quicken cultural and intellectual leadership. Corporate and government interest in developing human capital in the United States and natural resources in Africa provided a fresh impetus for philanthropic support of black education and race relations projects.

Historically, framing U.S. race relations as first a southern problem, and later a domestic issue only, had blocked both global debate and external mediation. This changed when civil rights, anticolonialist, and human rights activists helped open spaces for nongovernmental actors to influence decision making; promoted contacts with foreign governments and other external agents; and, above all, explicitly linked racial reform and the United States' desired world order. Scholars have subsequently begun reconfiguring race in conventional histories.

Reconfiguration must address several key questions. As historians such as Carol Anderson, Thomas Borstelmann, and Mary Dudziak have demonstrated, national leaders in the cold war era unlinked the association commonly made between civil rights struggle and radicalism and attached civil rights to liberalism instead. Long after cold war purges neutralized the conventional Left, the desire to manage and contain insurgency continued. One must ask why. If race

Bunche, September 14, 1960, Ralph J. Bunche Papers, University of California Los Angeles (UCLA), Box 113, NAACP board. This study cites two separate collections of Bunche's papers, one at UCLA and the other at SC. Prattis to Scott, August 28, 1960.

[11] Rick Perlstein, *Before the Storm: Barry Goldwater and the Unmaking of the American Consensus* (New York: Hill & Wang, 2001), 50.

was defused as a national security issue by legislative reform, why did a militant international racial discourse emerge before the ink on the signing of the Civil Rights Act of 1964 was dry? Why did it continue long after formal civil equality had been achieved?

Independence for colonies in Africa, Asia, and the Caribbean also raises questions. The stark polarities of white versus black, colonialism versus freedom, and racism versus tolerance resonated during the late colonial era. They grew ambiguous, however, in the era of self-rule. For historian James Meriwether, the friction between the African National Congress and the Pan African Congress in South Africa, and the civil war in the Congo, were the first indications that these questions could fracture African-American opinion on African issues. Blacks in the States "were faced now with the challenge of unraveling the meanings of a fragmented, complex Africa," he wrote, without the benefit of a "ready-made cast of heroes and villains." Rather than deal with these thorny issues, they focused instead on the remaining pockets of white resistance in southern Africa that could be more readily understood in binary terms. Pinpointing racial conflict helped keep the faltering domestic civil rights coalition together and allowed African Americans to "skirt the realities and intricacies of independent Africa."[12]

The requirements of African nation-statehood meant that Americans were not the only ones who wanted either to suppress or to put a positive spin on events occurring in the United States. New governments needed U.S. aid and friendship but condemned Jim Crow to avoid censure from their constituents. They thus greeted with relief the Civil Rights Act of 1964, which at least put racial equality on the books. The law provided a way for Washington to distance itself from the racial violence that continued to wrack U.S. society and, most importantly, promised to relieve weak nations of a responsibility to confront the United States over the issue. That the national consensus on civil rights and race disseminated by federal information agencies was partly fictive did not matter, nor that ambivalence continued in policy circles. The most important consideration was that racism, while as real and destructive as ever, had been deprived of legitimacy.[13] Whatever its staying power, Washington's declared disavowal sufficed to let African leaders off the hook. Most relaxed their militant stand against U.S. domestic policies.

An assault on the notion that U.S. race relations were unique and could not be understood with reference to international experience played an important role in delegitimating racism. Comparisons to other countries resulted in an analogy that likened inner-city minority communities to colonies engaged in wars of liberation against racially different oppressors. Michael Omi and Howard Winant, in *Racial Formation in the United States,* have documented the colonial model's influence among 1960s activists who wanted to explain

[12] Meriwether, *Proudly We Can Be Africans*, 209, 229, 239–40.
[13] John David Skrentny, "The Effect of the Cold War on African-American Civil Rights: America and the World Audience, 1964–1968," *Theory and Society* 27 (1998): 272–3.

and then correct the abuses of segregation and discrimination.[14] As anticolonial struggles also had a vital cultural dimension, the recognition of the enormous power of culture to create and enforce hegemonies, and to forge national political communities out of regional ones, formed a major part of the national liberation experience. This liberationist model abetted the restoration, and in some cases, the fabrication of a national culture and constituted a critical weapon in the search for power.

The inability of African states to break through the barriers to development and stability kicked the props from under the liberationist model and the scholarship and policies predicated upon it. Even under the best of circumstances, once national liberation movements made the transition to ruling parties and state bureaucracies, the contrast between those who were majorities in their home countries and those who remained racial-ethnic minorities was plainly evident. Critics of the African states often scorned the petty bourgeois leadership, which they held responsible for many of these countries' failings. Yet once victorious, the liberation organizations hardly fared better. African peoples' quest for genuine freedom and power continued.

In spite of diaspora hopes, many African countries could not provide even rhetorical protection to overseas communities of African descent. Those hoping to effect practical Pan-African linkages, moreover, continue to face the resistance of nation-states to perceived infringements of their sovereignty. Although most countries have ratified United Nations instruments regarding human rights, many have rejected the principle that signatory status obliged them to implement these human rights provisions internally. Few are without disadvantaged minorities whose issues they wish to keep buried and off international dockets.[15]

No less important than the political changes marking the transition from colonialism to independence are the ways in which these experiences were understood. Desegregation in the United States and decolonization in Africa were both preceded by and accompanied by fundamental changes in knowledge structures that helped to normalize them. In an evolution traceable at least to the Universal Races Congress of 1911, sociobiological racism was gradually discredited, along with the political frameworks it had helped construct. A vigorous tradition of diaspora scholarship also challenged conventional racism. This learning was rooted in two branches: textual knowledge originally derived from moral suasionist antislavery literature and apologetics; and traditions preserved and communicated through the oratory of nationalist street speakers and preachers.[16] The creation of a professional, scientific African-American

---

[14] Michael Omi and Howard Winant, *Racial Formation in the United States* (New York: Routledge, 1994).

[15] Henry J. Richardson III, "Black People, Technocracy, and Legal Process: Thoughts, Fears, and Goals," in *Public Policy for the Black Community*, eds. Marguerite Ross Barnett and James A. Hefner (Port Washington, N.Y.: Alfred, 1976): 179.

[16] Brenda Gayle Plummer, *Rising Wind: African Americans and U.S. Foreign Affairs, 1935–1960* (Chapel Hill: University of North Carolina Press, 1996), 230.

history, pioneered at black colleges and universities and by lay historical societies, began to filter into the white ivy tower only when black students did, in
the mid-1960s. Conflicts over the merits and legitimacy of African-American
historiographic interpretation went to school with these students.

African and African-American studies, originally wedded, became divorced
and developed distinct paths. African studies was taken up during and after
World War II by foundations and historically white universities eager for the
United States to supplant Britain as the hub of knowledge and resources on
Africa for the Anglophone world. The field of African-American studies, in
contrast, was never wholly detachable from specific domestic political agendas.
The goals of both the U.S. civil rights movement and the wars for national liberation in sub-Saharan Africa promised a reunion of this pair in the 1960s and
early 1970s that did not wholly succeed.

The disjuncture between Third World polities and ethnic politics in the
United States proved even deeper. U.S.-based intellectuals failed to achieve clarity regarding the comparative affluence and cultural transparency of African
Americans. On the latter point, it is important to remember that no geographic
or impenetrable linguistic frontiers separated blacks from other Americans.
The boundary marked by the inner city, once touted as the borders of a colony, proved both fragile and transient as the next forty years of urban restoration, renovation, and gentrification would suggest. Just as legislative and
court-ordered integration provided blacks with some means to penetrate the
mainstream, the same reforms opened the inner life of African-American communities to the ethnographic – and entrepreneurial – gaze of others.

In spite of the unanticipated difficulties that both failures and successes
caused, the era was one of astounding creativity and imagination. Those who
had been at ease in an earlier period struggled to keep their gains and interpret
inevitable changes in ways that favored their position. Those who confronted
elites developed an arsenal of weapons to challenge their political, economic,
and cultural domination. Scholars have already addressed the competing his-
toriographies of sixties declension and achievement. This reading leans toward
the latter interpretation but suggests that the era cannot be understood simply
as a matter of insurgents against the state who managed to have parts of their
agenda incorporated into the status quo. Instead, political actors from a range
of nations, classes, and ethnicities joined in the search to define, extend, defend,
and legitimate their respective claims to power and authority.

Philosopher Cornel West has described the sixties "not [as] a chronological category which encompasses a decade, but rather a historical construct
or heuristic rubric that renders noteworthy historical processes and events
intelligible."[17] Those interested in the period have choices to make about its
intelligibility and the relation of those choices to current political and cultural

---

[17] Cornel West, "The Paradox of the African American Rebellion," in *Is It Nation Time?
Contemporary Essays on Black Power and Black Nationalism*, ed. Eddie S. Glaude Jr. (Chicago:
University of Chicago Press, 2002), 22.

battles. Sixties historiography is a major theater in which these battles have been enacted. The periodization, which includes at least part of the succeeding decade, does not pertain so much to discrete chronological intervals as to ways to construct discursive arenas where stakeholders make truth claims about what the epoch means. Those who see the era as anarchic and destructive compete with those who champion it as a period of celebration, innovation, and reform that altered the course of history for the better. Both camps, with varying degrees of consciousness and sophistication, create the decades that they want. The epoch I want is the one that helps to write, as Foucault would have it, "the history of the present."

It is easy to read the anarchy of the present into the past, emphasizing chaos as the cardinal feature of the "long" 1960s. Dissidents all over the world questioned and repudiated authority. Disruption became a daily occurrence and conventional pieties were contested everywhere. According to this interpretation, activist efforts to operate internationally succeeded only rhetorically because they failed to understand objective conditions, not only in foreign countries but in their own as well. In spite of the revitalization of conservatism in the United States during the era, popular narratives of the time continue to feature colorful exploits on the Left and among bohemians. Social history research has furthermore overly emphasized the role of college-educated youth. The study of working people, women, and other social orders during these years still presents opportunities. In the conventional story, few of the period's troublemakers had constructive plans or a lasting impact on subsequent developments. As Max Elbaum observes,

> The civil rights movement and the broad anti–Vietnam War movement have been extensively chronicled and receive much deserved scholarly and activist attention. But the dominant view even in progressive circles is that the young people who embraced revolutionary ideas after 1968 had essentially "gone crazy," and that the early "good sixties" were replaced by a later "bad sixties" characterized by political madness.

The decade was followed, it is implied, by a chastened return to realism in foreign policy and a prioritization of stability over ideology. Like *The Tragic Era*, the historian Claude Bowers's account of Reconstruction, this historiography debuts a decade that began with bright promise, closed with unrealistic expectations, and incurred certain repression.[18]

[18] Winifred Breines, "Whose New Left?" *Journal of American History* 75 (September 1988): 528–45; Jefferson Cowie, "'Vigorously Left, Right, and Center': The Crosscurrents of Working-Class America in the 1970s," in *America in the Seventies*, eds. Beth Bailey and David Farber (Lawrence: University Press of Kansas, 2004): 75–106; idem, "Nixon's Class Struggle: Romancing the New-Right Worker, 1969–1973," *Labor History* 43 (Summer 2002): 257–83; Christian G. Appy, *Working-Class War: American Combat Soldiers and Vietnam* (Chapel Hill: University of North Carolina Press, 1993); Max Elbaum, "What Legacy from the Radical Internationalism of 1968?" *Radical History Review*, no. 82 (2002): 3; Gerald J. DeGroot, *The Sixties Unplugged: A Kaleidoscopic History of a Disorderly Decade* (Cambridge, Mass.: Harvard University Press, 2008); Jeremi Suri, *Power and Protest: Global Revolution and the Rise of Detente* (Cambridge, Mass.: Harvard University Press, 2002); Allen J. Matusow, *The Unraveling*

e suggested that the desire for freer cultural expression
owerment were competing ambitions,[19] but each freedom
...er. That cultural intelligentsias and officialdom often encour-
agents forms a significant but often neglected part of the story.
.rt is the degree to which the meaning of justice and struggles for
equ. are embedded in the fabric of national history. African-American resistance to racial oppression, for example, originated in colonial times and did
not disappear after 1968. The ideological framework that civil rights, antiwar,
and anticolonial movements often shared may have been eclipsed in the dominant discourses of establishment media and policy making circles but hardly
vanished. Critics continued to challenge America's dual identity as democratic
abroad and racist at home. For those observers who root the "bowling alone"
social alienation in the discontents of the 1960s, however, dissenters' rebelliousness, their idiosyncrasies, and their refusal to compromise laid the groundwork for today's problems.[20]

Most historians do agree that combined pressures from social movements
created a "crisis of governability." In Nikhil Pal Singh's words, "By the early
1970s, scholars and pundits closely associated with official orthodoxy and the
state's interest" interpreted "the simultaneous emergence of newly assertive
groups within the domestic realm and eruptions within the established cold
war framework for managing international relations" as a threat to accustomed
patterns of dominance. Key elements failed to accept the cold war's Manichean
optic. "We can glimpse this in the international reporting of African-American
newspapers of the period," Michael Curtin writes. "Unlike the *New York
Times* or the *Washington Post*, black papers tended to be less concerned about
the Soviet challenge and instead focused on race, a central concern in foreign
policy deliberations."[21]

The African-American experience lies deeply embedded in the history of the
United States: in its founding, in the manner in which it worked out its identity as a nation, and in its activities in the community of nation-states today.

of America: A History of Liberalism in the 1960s (New York: Harper & Row, 1984); William
L. O'Neill, *Coming Apart: An Informal History of America in the Sixties* (Chicago: Quadrangle
Books, 1971); John M. Blum, *Years of Discord: American Politics and Society, 1961–1974* (New
York: W. W. Norton, 1991); Peter Collier and David Horowitz, *Destructive Generation: Second
Thoughts about the Sixties* (New York: Summit, 1990).

[19] Thomas Frank, *The Conquest of Cool: Business Culture, Counterculture, and the Rise of Hip
Consumerism* (Chicago: University of Chicago Press, 1997); John Fiske, *Reading the Popular*
(Boston: Unwin Hyman, 1989).

[20] David Burner, *Making Peace with the Sixties* (Princeton, N.J.: Princeton University Press, 1996);
Todd Gitlin, *The Sixties*, 2nd ed. (New York: Bantam, 1993); John M. Blum, *Years of Discord:
American Politics and Society, 1961–1974* (New York: Norton, 1991); Peter Collier and David
Horowitz, *Destructive Generation: Second Thoughts about the Sixties* (New York: Summit,
1990).

[21] Nikhil Pal Singh, "Culture/Wars: Recoding Empire in an Age of Democracy," *American Quarterly*
50 (13) (1998): 511; Michael Curtin, *Redeeming the Wasteland: Television Documentary and
Cold War Politics* (New Brunswick, N.J.: Rutgers University Press, 1995), 229.

Having predicated national security on the bedrock of racial domination, the state was bound to maintain the pattern. The only way out was to readjust the basic premise so that security now required racial justice in order to prevail. Foundations, educational institutions, the mass media, and the intelligentsia assisted the state in making these only partially successful modifications. Political and cultural leaders often failed to agree among themselves about appropriate strategies. Race blinkered the vision of those hoping to topple the hierarchical order as well as those seeking to preserve it.

Black challenges to white nationalism in civil society and government produced "a remapping of the world, an alternative moral geography, and a new imagined community that did not begin and end with Africa."[22] After the Civil War broke the First Republic, the nature of governance and the principal actors changed. Racist ideologies survived the transition and were incorporated into the Second Republic in the form of state and private violence against racial minorities, and the naturalization of racial rank orders in law and popular culture. The new society emerged simultaneously from the South's defeat and the national crucible of white supremacy. A reaffirmation of racism paradoxically accompanied the rise of "the Negro" to circumscribed citizenship. The United States did not expand its definition of humanity to become more liberal about race. Instead, institutions, including government, academia, and corporate capitalism, refashioned racism, which marched hand in hand with egalitarianism into the future.

Throughout most of its history, the republic's racial narratives have been framed in black and white. Little account was taken of ethnic differences among people of color. Indeed, repressing such differences supported the primacy of race as an engine of subordination. Yet, the history of radical insurgency in the United States is heavily inflected by the presence of racial others, including a dynamic Caribbean diaspora. Throughout the twentieth century, hundreds of thousands of Caribbean people were not only immigrating to metropoles, but from one metropole to another. This population movement accompanied growing resistance to colonial domination in these immigrants' homelands.

Histories specific to particular nations and transregional histories have been written, all of which can be appreciated independently of U.S. and Canadian developments. But there is also a Caribbean history not easily disentangled from larger accounts of imperialism and migration. The Black Power revolt in the Caribbean, for example, coincided with the growing realization that the politics of independence had not extended to creating equal opportunity and economic improvement for the masses of black people in the Americas. Disaffection encouraged concerted action among diaspora dissidents with common grievances against the imperialist powers. The curious liminality of the Caribbean in American perceptions clashes with the profundity of its constitutive role in the history of the hemisphere. Just as it is not possible to

---

[22] Melani McAlister, "One Black Allah: The Middle East in the Cultural Politics of African American Liberation, 1955–1970," *American Quarterly* 51 (3) (1999): 650.

write U.S. history without studied reference to African-American experience, it is not possible to write the history of African-American freedom struggles without careful examination of their intersection with Caribbean goals and aspirations.[23]

The result is a hybrid history that challenges the bounded construction of history's subfields. "The very tendency toward categorical separation," Stephan Palmié writes, "so characteristic of modern attempts to register the world in the form of multiplying binary discriminations – invariably calls forth the 'hybrids' that such schema must disperse or repress."[24] So an examination of how states, elites, and dissidents faced the challenges of the late twentieth century cannot be an African-American history or a history of U.S. foreign relations because it violates the ground rules of each genre.

African-American history, as it came to be written in the second half of the twentieth century, increasingly emphasized the primacy of local and non-elite voices. Time and resources spent on analyzing elites, some scholars felt, detracted from long overdue study of silenced and underprivileged groups. But all too often, failure to address dominant groups resulted in misunderstanding the relationship of these to ideology, policy, and those they ruled. In ascribing a fundamental autonomy to the poor and exploited, historians often fail to see how even the most geographically remote areas were never completely isolated from national trends, ideologies, and behaviors.[25] Ignoring elites leads too often to the dismissal of important information when, in sweeping repudiation of rank orders, scholars throw the baby out with the bathwater.

In spite of this problem and the commonly encountered uncritical embrace of almost all leftist formations, African-American historiography distinguishes itself by its relative expansiveness and inclusiveness. Not so with the history of U.S. foreign relations, all too often defined as inextricable from an intense focus on the state, its records, and its agents, and perceived as the only significant axis of power in the world system.

In contrast, Kristin Hoganson writes, "an important consideration in recent efforts to open up foreign relations history is the fact that power has operated in multiple registers. Yes, 'the state' has deployed it, but so have the fifty states and local governments, and so have heads of households, employers, doctors,

---

[23] For a detailed discussion of this point, see Winston James, *Holding Aloft the Banner of Ethiopia: Caribbean Radicalism in Early Twentieth-Century America* (London and New York: Verso, 1998).

[24] Stephan Palmié, *Wizards and Scientists: Explorations in Afro-Cuban Modernity and Tradition* (Durham, N.C.: Duke University Press, 2002), 52.

[25] Nancy McLean in *Freedom Is Not Enough: The Opening of the American Workplace* (Cambridge, Mass.: Harvard University Press, 2006) reproves social historians' neglect of corporate elites, 344. Similar insights derive from Bryan D. Palmer in "Rethinking the Historiography of United States Communism," *American Communist History* 22 (2) (2003): 151; Robert Vitalis, "The Graceful and Generous Liberal Gesture: Making Racism Invisible in American International Relations," *Millennium: Journal of International Studies* 29 (2) (2000). See also Nan Enstad, "Fashioning Political Identities: Cultural Studies and the Historical Construction of Political Subjects," *American Quarterly* 50 (December 1998): 745–82.

teachers, workers, tourists, celebrities, revolutionaries, and others."[26] Power resides in the state, but not exclusively, and the state itself is as much an arena of struggle over power as a stakeholder itself. To the extent that the history of foreign relations insists on the primacy of the state, it closes off important options for the examination of the past. Writing hybrid history, then, must be a negotiation among fields.

As this chapter is being written, the world press swirls with the story of Wikileaks, an organization that publishes classified government documents online. A firestorm has erupted as U.S. intelligence officials worry about the safety of their sources and methods. Sources and methods concern not only diplomats and spy agencies, but also historians. A recent trend in writing American history places considerable emphasis on multiarchival sources, which usually means only the state papers of more than one nation. Historians strive to keep up, employing graduate students and others to supply a patchwork of sketchy foreign documentation to grace themes that remain essentially U.S. history.

Some have managed to ingratiate themselves with officials in the majority of countries that do not open their archives to the public. Their sympathetic hosts peel off a dossier or two, a breakthrough for the gleeful recipient. Lack of access to indexes or findings aids, however, leaves unknown the scope or context of the shared document, and often its relationship to what policy making elites deem crucial. As Mario Del Pero sadly notes, "as a consequence and despite its many merits, the much broadcasted internationalization of U.S. diplomatic history (and of Cold War history) has far too often produced a methodological regression and the return to an orthodox form of diplomatic historiography, which consists simply of telling what a second secretary or a chargé d'affaires has said."[27]

The closer a historical epoch to the troubled present, the more reluctant the few countries that allow public access to archives have been to enact their own rules. This humbles the vast claims made for the use of state papers. In this work, the need to supplement what is *officially* available with what is available is a necessity. "Nor do the records need to be governmental – private, artistic, local, anything goes," writes Jessica C. E. Gienow-Hecht. "If some diplomatic historians scratch their heads wondering if this or that source or approach still constitutes good research, they only need to ask: to what extent does the encounter affect the agents, analysis, and course of the story? And, to what extent is the tale relevant to the American experience?"[28]

Receptivity to an array of sources is important because national archives can subtly dictate a methodology that privileges intergovernmental binary relations and occludes the circulation of ideas and activities that occur outside

---

[26] Kristin Hoganson, "Hop off the Bandwagon! It's a Mass Movement, Not a Parade," *Journal of American History* 95 (4) (2009): online.

[27] Mario Del Pero, "On the Limits of Thomas Zeiler's Historiographical Triumphalism," ibid.

[28] Jessica C. E. Gienow-Hecht, "What Bandwagon?" *Journal of American History* 95 (4) (2009): online.

the state framework. One makes a choice: Susan Strange, noting sociologist Oliver Cox's observation that "ideology is always for something," suggests that "methodology and the treatment of power is also usually for something, in that it sustains one perspective, and the prescriptions that go with it, more than rival ones."[29]

The ideological choices framing the debut and evolution of Black Power historiography provide a case in point. Jeanne Theoharis has skillfully described how some renderings of the phenomenon have linked it to the tale of decline and chaos that characterize conservative interpretations of the 1960s and early 1970s generally. Periodization plays a major role in such analyses. "In many accounts," she writes,

the Northern black struggle appears only after the Watts riot, when Martin Luther King Jr. is chastised by the young rioters and allegedly realizes that the Voting Rights Act had not solved black people's problems in the North. This version paints local and national civil rights leaders, and Rev. King in particular, as naive and out-of-touch with the gritty realities of ghetto blacks. Simultaneously, the Watts uprising is used to introduce Black Power – and through it, Black Power comes to be seen as an angry, emotional and disorganized response of underclass black communities post-1965. Cast through the misconception that sustained political action was largely absent in the urban poor North, Black Power is shown born out of fire and looting as opposed to indigenous political organizing, organic theorizing and varied tactical strategies. In short, Black Power is framed as the absence of political organizing. The Watts riot, then, often becomes a way for historians to introduce the racial struggle in the North through a declension narrative in which the movement loses its righteous drive and disintegrates amidst spontaneous violence, internecine struggles between militant, intense government repression, and white backlash.[30]

Theoharis and a number of other analysts of Black Power[31] have extended its historical arc back in time to the early twentieth century and connected

[29] Susan Strange, *The Retreat of the State: The Diffusion of Power in the World Economy* (Cambridge: Cambridge University Press, 1996), 24.

[30] Jeanne Theoharis, "Alabama on Avalon: Rethinking the Watts Uprising and the Character of Black Protest in Los Angeles," in *The Black Power Movement: Rethinking the Civil Rights-Black Power Era*, ed. Peniel E. Joseph (New York: Routledge, 2006), 30.

[31] These include Scot Brown, *Fighting for Us: Maulana Karenga, the Us Organization, and Black Cultural Nationalism* (New York: New York University Press, 2003); Rod Bush, *We Are Not What We Seem: Black Nationalism and Class Struggle in the American Century* (New York: New York University Press, 1999); Collier-Thomas and Franklin, eds. *Sisters in the Struggle*; Devin Fergus, *Liberalism, Black Power, and the Making of American Politics, 1965–1980* (Athens: University of Georgia Press, 2009); E. S. Glaude, ed., *Is It Nation Time?* eds. Monique Guillory and Richard C. Green, *Soul: Black Power, Politics, and Pleasure* (New York: New York University Press, 1997); Cedric Johnson, *Revolutionaries to Race Leaders: Black Power and the Making of African American Politics* (Minneapolis: University of Minnesota Press, 2007); Peniel Joseph, *Waiting "'Til the Midnight Hour": A Narrative History of Black Power in America* (New York: Henry Holt, 2006); Jeffrey Ogbar, *Black Power: Radical Politics and African American Identity* (Baltimore: Johns Hopkins University Press, 2004); James Smethurst, *The Black Arts Movement: Literary Nationalism in the 1960s and 1970s* (Chapel Hill: University of North Carolina Press, 2005); Kimberly Springer, *Living for the Revolution: Black Feminist*

domestic and international struggles as part of the world-historical black radical tradition. They identify the political ferment in which discussion of the best strategies and tactics for black liberation enlarged the debate and the definition of what constitutes freedom. In their renderings, Black Power radicals' rediscovered international perspective opened up theoretical and practical ground. These historians challenge the trivializing dismissal of Black Power as identity politics, maintaining that black radicals were not pursuing forms of self-actualization in their perspectives on international issues, but rather joining a larger global fight against white supremacy and imperialism. They fault scholars who have been content to focus on the eccentric or sensational aspects of the Black Power period and have not been attuned to the complexity of its politics.

Black freedom, according to convention, would be realized within the framework of the democratic nation-state, but an international Black Power movement saw in universalist Americanism a source of black people's difficulties. Kevin Gaines, describing black expatriates in Ghana, asserts that "white racism was not the only weak link in the civil rights coalition. As much as racism, the world of ... the Ghana expatriates was defined by the Cold War. African-American radicals in Ghana struggled against Cold War ideology, and the U.S. government's attempts to impose constraints on the political language and tactics of black activists and movements."[32] Nikhil Pal Singh concurs, stating that "what is most frequently targeted as the precursor of multicultural dissensus in this country today, namely the radicalization of the civil rights movement and the alliance of the student-led New Left and black power movements, was actually a more purposive and pointed affair and part of a much more complex legacy." These movements had always rejected "the cold war settlement that portrayed racism and colonialism as atavisms that were disappearing in the face of an enlightened American nationalism and internationalism."[33]

It happens, however, that in ascribing cogency to the Black Power era, historians sometimes trip themselves up by denying coherence to phenomena that do not seem to them to fit within its confines. Worse, they may diminish the worth and achievements of other activist practices, such as the integrationist demonstrations and voting rights campaigns classically associated with

Organizations, 1968–1980 (Durham, N.C.: Duke University Press, 2005); Stephen Ward, "'Ours Too Was a Struggle for a Better World': Activists Intellectuals and the Radical Promise of the Black Power Movement, 1962–1972" (PhD diss., University of Texas, 2002); Fanon Che Wilkins, "'In the Belly of the Beast': Black Power, Anti-Imperialism, and the African Liberation Solidarity Movement, 1968–1975" (PhD diss., New York University, 2001); Komozi Woodard, *A Nation within a Nation: Amiri Baraka (LeRoi Jones) and Black Power Politics* (Chapel Hill: University of North Carolina Press, 1999).

[32] Kevin Gaines, "From Black Power to Civil Rights: Julian Mayfield and African American Expatriates in Nkrumah's Ghana, 1957–1966," in *Cold War Constructions: The Political Culture of United States Imperialism, 1945–1966,* ed. Christian G. Appy (Amherst: University of Massachusetts Press, 2000), 258.

[33] Singh, "Culture/Wars," 511.

the Deep South in the 1950s and early 1960s. Not revolutionary enough, not "black" enough, and tainted by cold war liberalism's universalist assumptions, this manifestation of the movement is deprecated in order that Black Power militancy might not only shine in contrast but also take on legibility based on what it is perceived *not* to be.

At the time when Stokely Carmichael was articulating Black Power as a phrase, among the insufficiencies attributed to liberal integrationism was the lack of space it accorded to an assertive black masculinity. Recent authors have noted the interrelationship between demands for black citizenship and challenges to the gender subordination of African-American men.[34] That subordination is rooted in slavery and colonialism, where the subjection and feminization of "boys" (of various ages and nationalities) marked the triumph of Western imperialism and its racial orders. If undoing that oppression meant reclaiming for subjected men the prerogatives of the white masters, including the reinvention of the self-sufficient rational subject, their relationship to community, and especially to women, is problematic.

Just as Black Power advocates in their time all too often shrouded black women in mystifying veils of nationalist honor and respect, it is curious to see Black Power historians lauding contemporaneous women activists for manipulating the nationalist vocabulary to achieve their ends rather than challenging it.[35] One is led to mull why men are the preponderant students of this era, and why they speak of it in such strong terms of self-identification. Women historians, in contrast, appear to mark out separate spaces under the broad Black Power umbrella. Separate spheres have historically been handy devices: they provide a limited degree of female autonomy while keeping women out of men's business.

Black Power historiography has adeptly dissected cold war political culture's claims of inclusion and justice. It is thus odd to find scholars making comparably sweeping assertions for the sameness of black activism. "Black sharecroppers in Lowndes County, Alabama, urban militants in Harlem and Chicago, trade unionists in Detroit, Black Panthers in Oakland, Philadelphia, and New Haven, and female antipoverty organizers in Baltimore and Durham, North Carolina, all advocated a political program rooted in aspects of black

---

[34] Steve Estes, *I Am a Man! Race, Manhood, and the Civil Rights Movement* (Chapel Hill: University of North Carolina, Press, 2005); Christopher B. Booker, *"I Will Wear No Chain!" A Social History of African-American Males* (Westport, Conn.: Praeger, 2000); Darlene Clark Hine and Earnestine Jenkins, eds. A *Question of Manhood: A Reader in U.S. Black Men's History and Masculinity* (Bloomington: University of Indiana Press, 1999). See also Philip Brian Harper, *Are We Not Men? Masculine Anxiety and the Problem of African-American Identity* (New York: Oxford University Press, 1996); Gail Bederman, *Manliness and Civilization: A Cultural History of Gender and Race in the United States, 1880–1917* (Chicago: University of Chicago, 1995); and Joy James, *Shadowboxing: Representations of Black Feminist Politics* (New York: St. Martin's Press, 1999).

[35] Peniel E. Joseph, "The Black Power Movement: A State of the Field," *Journal of American History* 96 (December 2009): 753; Rhonda Y. Williams, "Black Women, Urban Politics, and Engendering Black Power," in Joseph, ed., The *Black Power Movement*, 97.

power ideology," Peniel Joseph declares.[36] Joseph goes on to attribute President Barack Obama's election to a changed "racial and political climate" originating in "black power's insistence on reimagining the range of America's democratic rhetoric and practice."[37] If Black Power is to mean anything, it cannot mean everything.

A sign of the times is that nuanced views of black political and cultural activity in the 1960s and 1970s are moving to the fore. Devin Fergus, for example, has questioned whether Black Power remained above the fray of U.S. political pragmatism. His work on Floyd McKissick's Soul City project for building a new town in rural North Carolina reveals the negotiations between McKissick and the Nixon White House to realize a conservative version of Black Power.[38] Fergus's claim that liberals and Black Power advocates ultimately reached an accommodation that exposed them to challenges by the New Right is supported by Cedric Johnson's research on black politics.

Johnson is interested in understanding how the democratic insurgency of the Black Power period morphed into normal politics. He works his way through an approach that supports Black Power as a complex and varied politics executed by numerous and not necessarily connected actors, rather than as a single set of historical events or rhetorical practices. He writes:

The racial unitarian views articulated by Black Power radicals and moderates alike embraced the tendency within segregation era discourse to treat African Americans as a corporate political entity. This recurrent view that black political disagreement should be handled "behind closed doors" or that blacks should "close ranks" is a repressive tendency derived from nationalist discourse that hinders the development of open, principled debate. Under this perspective, ideological or political differences among blacks were treated like lines in the sand-lacking depth and permanence. Furthermore, many activists held that such ephemeral differences were drawn by outside hands. From this logic, many concluded that political and ideological lines could be swept away with effective organization and the development of proper "black consciousness" to reveal a solid core of racial interests that connected all African Americans and, for many, all peoples of African descent.[39]

Clearly, more than one Black Power movement is discernible in the hurly-burly of twentieth-century African-American life. Their multiplicative genealogies include figures on the Right and the Left, as well as those rooted in varieties of black nationalism. They can be studied without censuring patterns of resistance that do not conform to a prescribed *style* of struggle, and without

---

[36] Joseph, "The Black Power Movement," 755.

[37] Ibid., 722.

[38] Devin Fergus, "Black Power, Soft Power: Floyd McKissick, Soul City, and the Death of Moderate Black Republicanism," *Journal of Policy History* 22 (2) (2010): 148–92; idem, *Liberalism, Black Power, and the Making of American Politics, 1965–1980*; idem, "The Ordeal of Liberalism and Black Nationalism in an American Southern State, 1969–1980," paper presented at the annual meeting of the Association for the Study of African American Life and History, Orlando, Florida, 2002.

[39] Johnson, *Revolutionaries to Race Leaders*, 88.

idealizing their respective appeal. Devin Fergus, in a chapter of his book aptly titled "Speaking Truth to Black Power," notes the ultimate pragmatism behind the practice, rather than the discourse, of Black Power politics.[40] Putative revolutionaries sought power and, like their enemies, were willing both to improvise and to make concessions in order to hold on to influence and affect public policy. If co-optation was a hallmark of insurgency's decline, cooptation was a two-way street.

Power seeking, in spite of the rhetoric, tended to leave the masses in the dust. Specific individuals among the dashiki-and-Nyerere-jacketed leadership remain the most haunting and persistent personas of the Black Power era. While the clergy-led civil rights movement in the southern states had its Big Names, it had too many participants to be reduced to a few. Black Power leaders, in contrast, stand out partly because a mass politics did not ensue from their efforts. Just as the nation-state provided the most persuasive model for the politics of developing countries, it shaped the politics of racial-ethnic minorities in the United States, predisposing them to pursue conventional strategies within traditional frames.

Of all the perspectives on the radical black insurgency of the 1960s and 1970s, none is as celebratory and idealizing as that on the Left. Wahneema Lubiano's critique of cultural-nationalist adulation of the grass roots equally applies to "culture workers," read scholars. To the extent that "black middle-class culture workers" romanticized the poor and empowered themselves by identifying with them, they created "a (generally) masculinist and heterosexist black national subject who is always working-class or poor," she writes. "Such a subject, once created, reflects his (and I use the pronoun advisedly) politically resonant glow back onto the non–working class warriors who articulate him and his agenda." The proletarian then comes "to stand in for the entire group." The working-class hero allows his creators "to avoid coming to terms with the complexity of their own class standing and its history."[41]

Radicals' statism also played a role in helping to contour the global political environment of the time. Like traditional liberals, they remained deeply enamored of the modern nation-state and the promise and limits of its emancipatory potential. Stalinism made conventional communism unpopular in the West, but in the newly independent African states, in the colonies engaged in wars of liberation, and in Vietnam, Cuba, and China, activists could discern in socialism the outlines of potentially successful societies. "Mao gave black radicals a non-Western model of Marxism that placed greater emphasis on local conditions and historical circumstances than canonical texts," Robin Kelley observed. "China's Great Leap Forward challenged the idea that the march to socialism must take place in stages or that one must wait patiently for the proper objective conditions to move ahead." Maoist thought disputed Western

[40] Fergus, *Liberalism, Black Power*, 165–95.
[41] Wahneema Lubiano, "Standing in for the State: Black Nationalism and 'Writing' the Black Subject," in Glaude, ed., *Is It Nation Time*, 160–1.

ideas about the causes of and remedies for poverty and racism. It "sought to overturn bourgeois notions of expertise." Of course, the Great Leap Forward was a colossal disaster. One wonders, then, whether an essential problem lies in the nation-state form itself.

Another strand of research on black radicalism rightly notes the connections across generations between sixties and seventies insurgency and the Old Left, links that cold war historiography had masked. For some authors, however, it is not enough to empower this unrecognized history. It is all too tempting to neglect and disparage the authentic radical demands for equality that emerged from the traditional civil rights movement's social and political practice, as if black radicalism could be retrieved from somewhere other than on the ground where people are actually struggling. Ultimately, those wishing to preserve the postwar liberal order with the United States as the center of the solar system shared a focus with those who looked to the revolutions in Asia and Africa for the key to global emancipation. All embraced the nation-state as the measure of progress and searched for power within its frameworks of possibility.

This study begins with the turn of the 1960s decade, when cold war barriers could not block the fervent hope of an end to racism and colonialism. It ends in 1974 with the issue of formal colonialism still unsettled and race unresolved as a factor in international relations. It accounts for the shift back to "normal politics." Recent scholarship has revealed the ways in which the United States and other Western powers made concessions because of the pressures exerted by peoples of African descent. We want to know now how and why those changes remained incomplete, and how and why the United States, as the dominant nation-state during the era, retained its ability to circumscribe the newly acquired power of subject peoples.

Chapter 1 of *In Search of Power* appraises the achievements and limitations of the drive for racial integration. It evaluates the impact of colonial revolt and the increasing power of nationalism in emerging states and among African Americans. The chapter also probes the growing dissatisfaction with liberal universalism that increased the appeal of leaders like Malcolm X. States, elites, and dissidents used the changing sensibilities to further their specific ends, resulting in a politics perceived by all as new.

Chapter 2 shows how middle classes were enlisted to preserve and extend a Western, and more specifically, U.S. agenda in new countries and among racial-ethnic minorities. It explores how Africa, kept out of international affairs during the colonial era, was drawn into the nuclear debate. The shock of the Sharpeville massacre in South Africa accelerated the debut of the new states on the international stage and hastened the repudiation of nonviolent direct action in favor of armed struggle. For all parties concerned – states, elites, and dissidents – the Congo crisis marked a point of no return. It became a reference point for U.S. foreign policy in Africa while reaffirming every suspicion entertained by blacks about Western motives. The same benchmarks inspired elite determination to win African hearts and minds.

A Catholic president's unprecedented election, accompanied by a newly liberal ethos originating from the Vatican, further contributed to a sense of epochal change. The confluence of civil rights insurgency in the early 1960s and a presidential administration making significant, if largely symbolic, gestures toward emerging nations encouraged an African-American foreign policy interest. This interest, discussed in Chapter 3, drew for organizational strength from existing civil rights groups. African independence also elicited a response from philanthropic institutions that identified American-style education as an effective way to influence the new countries. The UN General Assembly, formerly an expression of the political will of the United States and Western Europe, increasingly became a forum for Afro-Asian disaffection that entered into the cold war calculus as both Eastern and Western blocs courted the new powers.

By middecade, important demographic and economic change was under way in the United States, much of which was driven by federal initiative. Chapter 4 relates the restructuring of racism to the refiguring of America's "moral geography," and the creation of a new New South. Although government projects intended to mainstream African Americans and integrate the South more fully into the national economy by eradicating racial segregation, the Johnson administration's response to black interest in world affairs indicated that it was not willing either to modify racist foreign policies or to recognize African Americans as an ethnic interest group. The chapter examines the Student Nonviolent Coordinating Committee (SNCC) as an organization that became paradigmatic for the era and whose history is threaded through this narrative. Members' travel, and that of others, suggests the opportunities and limitations embedded in African Americans' increased exposure to the world Chapter 5 analyzes the resort to old-fashioned gunboat diplomacy in the Dominican Republic, where the local racial outlook held up a buckled mirror to the figuration of race in the United States. If the Great Society marked a certain innovation in managing domestic issues, in foreign affairs, conventional statecraft, including the appropriation of violent strategies to contain popular dissidence, continued to prevail. If mounting tensions over Vietnam and Southern Africa divided the civil rights leadership, in contrast, the Nigerian civil war was not legible in the cold war and racial binary terms to which most foreign policy audiences were accustomed.

Chapter 6 discusses how protest continued to pervade the national and international arenas, making it impossible to separate foreign and domestic affairs neatly. The Student Nonviolent Coordinating Committee (SNCC), which pointedly changed its name to the Student National Coordinating Committee, provides an example of the transformation and internationalization of an organization that began with specific regional aims. SNCC veterans numbered among the dissidents who envisioned foreign assistance as a nongovernmental project they could initiate on their own. Tanzania, which had replaced Ghana in Pan-Africanists' nation-building imaginary, was the target country. Willingness on the part of its government to cooperate made direct aid from the diaspora a reality. The chapter explores the internationalism of these groups and the links they established abroad. It addresses the effort to define defensible urban space and to create politically competent and culturally complete constituencies within it. Institution building included the intellectual products of activists and scholars.

The legislative successes of the U.S. civil rights movement and the partial realization of colonial independence demonstrated that these measures fell short of achieving economic democracy. Technological change contributed to widespread labor unrest at the turn of the 1970s decade. The South's incomplete transition to democracy left many behind – and hungry. Faced with a new president who owed little to the black electorate, African Americans needed to rethink conventional strategies. Chapter 7 appraises the efforts made to construct alliances and create a national black politics to draw together liberal, leftist, and black nationalist constituencies.

This task was infinitely more difficult than aiding foreign struggles, whose aims appeared more achievable. But this was deceptive: the breaches in freedom fighters' united front were not always evident to would-be diaspora participants. Chapter 8 traces the considerable effort that activists put into support of African liberation movements and the antiapartheid struggle. Resistance to the Vietnam War and to class and race oppression was fractured, with labor militancy and ethnic politics in an urban environment sometimes coalescing and sometimes clashing with international goals. The Arab-Israeli wars and the oil embargo enlarged the arena of debate about race, ethnicity, religion, and dissent. By this time, the civil rights and Black Power movements, broadcast through the world with all their visual éclat, were influencing the vocabulary through which other peoples mounted protest movements. In the academy, younger African studies scholars rebelled against outmoded orthodoxies. The chapter also reveals that the conjunction of a Caribbean Left and Caribbean black nationalism echoed the confluence of these ideologies in the United States and underscored the interdependence of North American black political thought and action.

Chapter 9 describes how the changing global economy of the mid-1970s sparked conflict over basic material issues relating to food and fuel. The United States' mission to the moon provided a striking example of the mismatch between resources and distributive justice. African development, deeply undercut by the oil embargo and the droughts of the early 1970s, came into focus again for diaspora militants when the Sixth Pan African Congress convened in 1974 and made the problematic relationship of diasporas and minorities to nation-states starker than ever.

The Conclusion summarizes an eighteen-year conversation among governmental, academic, and philanthropic elites who wished to created a post-1945 model of world democratic process in the likeness of the United States and the classes and masses who looked elsewhere for examples. In order to sell their vision to developing countries and discredit a competing communist prototype, elites had to make both substantive and rhetorical adjustments in order to maintain their own authority and the power of the state. Major innovations were the abandonment of racial segregation and the admission of African Americans to a form of citizenship.

In spite of these changes, government officialdom and conventional wisdom continued to constrain the meaning of full civil participation for black people and perpetuate older forms of domination. African Americans continued to be a "species of property" because they were assumed to have little authority in areas where decision making took place. One of these was international issues, where their efforts to weigh in were discounted by policy makers. Another was ethnic politics, nullified by the structural abandonment of cities. The terrain of participation for blacks, then, remained contradictory. African Americans were expected to identify unquestioningly with the nation and only the nation, and that was the price of their freedom. Yet, as Nikhil Pal Singh argues, "racism ... always threatens to undo a state of national belonging, since modern, civic nations have been explicitly defined in universalist terms, or precisely by relativizing and subordinating differences in the name of a national abstraction." Black citizenship in the nation-state has thus been provisional.[42]

The nation-state as a form has proven problematic for diaspora minorities. Its solidification in Asia, for example, led India and China to withdraw rights of return from their respective overseas communities in the name of defining citizenship as belonging to those who were born and live in a specific territory.[43] The transformation of revolutionary movements into governments created comparable dilemmas for those who supported revolutionary nationalism in its formative stages. Randall Robinson, founder of the African-American foreign policy lobby TransAfrica, writes:

Virtually the moment the ANC [African National Congress] became the government, it moved to collaborate with the United States and other Western donor governments in cutting off aid to nongovernmental organizations and redirecting it to the new government. Many NGOs shriveled and died. The very trade union members who had provided an indispensable pressure for change now chafed under an ANC government that consulted seriously on policy matters only with western governments and large corporations. Trade union members who had joined the new parliament began to resign in frustration.[44]

For Africa and African diasporas, national sovereignty led to justice, democratic participation, and equal opportunity only in exceptional cases. The latter-day gestural hollowness of Pan-Africanism and its increasing restriction to official delegations since 1945 further diminished the popular ability to resist hegemonic power.

---

[42] Singh, "Culture/Wars," 509.
[43] Itty Abraham, "Bandung and State Formation in Post-colonial Asia," in *Bandung Revisited: The Legacy of the 1955 Asian-African Conference for International Order*, eds. Amitav Acharya and See Seng Tan (Singapore: NUS Press, 2008), 58–64.
[44] Randall Robinson, *Defending the Spirit: A Black Life in America* (New York: Dutton, 1998), 189.

Recent history has led some scholars to reject the image of diasporas as satellites revolving around a central homeland. Population displacements on the African continent due to war, famine, and drought have cast millions adrift and muddled the distinction between core and periphery. In an era when state power has broken down, Richard Iton counsels:

The forces that both make and disrupt the virtual Africa, and encourage blacks elsewhere to internalize stigmatized notions of the 'African,' are the same pressures that make settlement unavailable elsewhere and diasporize all within and without the continent. It is in this modern matrix of strange spaces – outside the state but within empire – that naturalization and citizenship are substantively unavailable, regardless of geographical position.[45]

Dissidents continue to search for power in spite of their disenfranchisement and lack of rapport with the nation-state system. They are not always legible to that system. "Here they constitute the non-sense, the irrepresentable of historiography." They are catapulted from "history and into the mythopoeic space of arrested development and fixity vis-à-vis the forward movement of nationalism itself." Elites in their own search for power may exploit mass desires. "Popular movements are absorbed into the historically progressive trajectory of nationalism so that what is significant in them is the set of traits that lend themselves to national ends."[46] They become superfluous once these ends are achieved but can be resurrected when and where contingency beckons. The Conclusion argues that a successful emancipatory global politics must break free of its auxiliary relationship to the state.

---

[45] Richard Iton, *In Search of the Black Fantastic: Politics and Popular Culture in the Post-Civil Rights Era* (New York: Oxford University Press, 2008), 200.

[46] David Lloyd, "Nationalisms against the State," 178, in *The Politics of Culture in the Shadow of Capital*, eds. Lisa Lowe and David Lloyd (Durham, N.C.: Duke University Press, 1997).

I

A Great Restlessness

In the mid-twentieth century most African Americans belonged to a church, often Baptist. Congregations ranged from storefronts to megachurches with eleven thousand members. Ministers might exert enormous sway over churchgoers, commanding resources in the millions of dollars, living handsomely, and influencing the black vote through their sought-after endorsements. Unsurprisingly, many clerics jealously guarded their perquisites. Baptist politics were tumultuous and could be violent. A photographer for *Jet* magazine sued after a burly preacher attacked him during the National Baptist Convention (NBC) meeting in Chicago in 1952. The photographer's crime was having recorded men of the cloth "quarreling" on stage. Nearly ten years later, the dais remained a site of contestation as competing factions tried to crowd each other off the platform during the Baptist convention in Kansas City. Two men fell off the stage, with one sustaining a skull fracture and lapsing into a coma. As Taylor Branch relates it, "A staircase to the platform collapsed under the weight of the antagonists jammed on it, scattering and bruising dozens of people." The Kansas City police arrived on the scene to break up skirmishes that had erupted among the expensively tailored pastors.[1]

What would lead the purveyors of Jesus's message of peace to public brawls? The *Chicago Defender* slyly intimated that votes for Ike were for sale in the Windy City in 1956. Clergy identified as having supported Eisenhower's reelection were angered that their names were used but they had not been paid. Sums as large as $30,000 were allegedly on offer.[2]

Yet, that was only part of the story. Segregation had channeled black talent through a restricted number of filters. The ministry absorbed a disproportionate number of ambitious men who, had it not been for Jim Crow, would have found outlets for their skills in diverse occupations. Limited

---

[1] "Jet Photographer Assaulted at Baptist Convention," *Jet* 2, September 25, 1952, p. 47; Taylor Branch, *Parting the Waters: America in the King Years, 1954–63* (New York: Simon & Schuster, 1998), 502–3.

[2] "Names and Blame," *Chicago Defender*, November 10, 1956, p. 2.

opportunities made the competition all the more intense. Additionally, black Baptist leaders sought power in the context of a changing struggle for civil rights. Segregationists often spoke of the "southern way of life" as something primordial, ordained by nature, and too instinctive to be readily dismantled. It would take centuries, they insisted, for blacks to achieve the necessary civilization to function on a basis of equality with whites. Some blacks as well as whites exploited the idea, which seemed appropriate to those who claimed to believe in gradual evolution toward a desegregated society. Men like the Reverend J. H. Jackson, president for many years of the NBC, felt little need to rush matters and were in fact hostile to the growing immediatism of the civil rights movement and the emergence of unorthodox leaders like Martin Luther King Jr. who were unaffiliated with the big national organizations. Groups such as the NAACP, the Urban League, and the Congress of Racial Equality (CORE) were multiracial associations in which white liberals played important roles. None were prepared for the insurgencies from below that overtook them as the 1950s ended.[3]

Other organizations also reflected the altered environment. The National Association of Colored Graduate Nurses, for example, did not resist the tide of integration that subsumed it. The nurses' interest in foreign affairs stemmed from their participation in international medical service during World War II. Their August 1949 biennial convention "reaffirmed the UNO [United Nations Organization] as the instrument for maintenance of world peace." But the organization merged with the mainstream white Association of Graduate Nurses in 1951 and its specific racial advocacy and formal resolutions taken on international issues, ceased to exist.[4]

Judge William Hastie, addressing the nurses' final testimonial dinner, delivered what he considered a funeral oration. "For me," he told the assembled black professional women, "the passing of the National Association of Colored Graduate Nurses is a very notable occasion and essentially a specially joyful one." The group had accomplished its goals, and now there was "no longer need for a separate organization," which he called "a grand thing." Segregation as a feature of American life was disappearing and blacks needed to "throw off the psychology and habits of inferior and segregated status" and assume their rightful place in the American mainstream. "The only useful purpose of race consciousness," he reminded the nurses, "is to enable us to work together

3 Branch, *Parting the Waters*, 228, 505–7, 389, 571; and passim. A sympathetic portrayal of Jackson is found in Wallace Best, "The Right Achieved and the Wrong Way Conquered: J. H. Jackson, Martin Luther King Jr., and the Conflict over Civil Rights," *Religion and American Culture* 16 (2) (Summer 2006): 195–226.

4 Pittsburgh *Courier*, December 13, 1944; *The National News Bulletin* 4 (January 1950): 3; clippings in National Association of Colored Graduate Nurses Collection, Schomburg Center for Research in Black Culture, New York Public Library, hereafter (SC); "Negro Nurse Unit Will Disband Soon," *New York Times*, October 21, 1950, p. 15. On the decline of mass organizations generally, see Brenda Gayle Plummer, *Rising Wind: Black Americans and U.S. Foreign Affairs, 1935–1960* (Chapel Hill: University of North Carolina Press, 1996), 213.

to achieve the day when we can lose race consciousness."[5] African-American graduate nurses would no longer define themselves as an interest group. If segregation united black Americans as a group, integration would disperse them.

Not everyone was as sanguine as Hastie that workplace integration and the merging of professional clubs and associations meant genuine change. For much of the twentieth century, African Americans with a sound secondary education could take the post office examination and be ensured of reasonably stable employment if they passed it. The post office often attracted black workers who were overeducated for the jobs they held. They created the National Association of Postal Employees (NAPE), which, like the Colored Nurses, pondered the meaning of integration. President James B. Cobb, addressing a regional NAPE meeting in 1960, garnered applause when he observed that "the Supreme Court decision in 1954 has lulled us into a sense of security. We must remain alert. Many other organizations now want one big Union. They will integrate our dollars but not the opportunities."[6] Cobb recognized that the end of formal segregation had not removed the structural barriers to the full achievement of equality.

During World War II, desegregation at home and decolonization abroad had been parallel concerns of policy-aware African Americans. The cold war slowed the former and the priority given to European recovery delayed the latter. But as Europe's economy rebounded, the argument that it needed its colonies became less compelling as time went by. The major allies developed timetables for independence. U.S. officials prepared to extend limited economic and technical assistance to developing nations. Aid, the National Security Council (NSC) agreed, would gain the compliance needed to secure "strategic bases and supplies of critical material" and "lay the base for the continued association of these peoples with the free world."[7]

Washington leaders accompanied assistance to Africa with a discourse that marked the United States as an exception to Europe's past of colonial exploitation, and Americans as particularly favored by a combination of unique historical advantages. This assumed difference lent a certain cachet to African-American efforts to assert a voice in the direction of foreign affairs. Following the path of other black nongovernmental organizations (NGOs), the NBC appointed a UN observer in 1954. "We must not leave our statesmen alone to fight [the problems of the world]," the Reverend Jackson declared.

---

[5] Speech delivered by federal judge William Hastie at the Testimonial Dinner of the National Association of Colored Graduate Nurses, January 26, 1951, National Association of Colored Graduate Nurses Collection.

[6] E. Albert Norris, "Eighth District Convention," *The Alliance Leader* 20 (November–December 1960): 7.

[7] Eleanor Dulles interviewed by John T. Mason, December 6, 1965, p. 738, 739, May 23, 1967, p. 956, Eleanor Lansing Dulles interview, Columbia University Center for Oral History. Loy W. Henderson Papers, Container 5 "Africa Trips 1960," folder 2, Library of Congress, hereafter LC; Joseph C. Satterthwaite, Assistant Secretary State African Affairs, "The Role of Labor in African Development," *Department of State Bulletin*, April 13, 1959, p. 526; Office of the Director for Mutual Security, Status of U.S. National Security Programs on June 30, 1953, NSC 161, DDRS.

"The Christian church must be near them with its prayers and spiritual impact to help them make the most creative decisions for the races of mankind."[8] The claim that U.S. blacks could represent such a powerful nation validated the claims to stewardship over African peoples that some had been making since the early nineteenth century. The NBC's ascribed membership of 700,000 in Africa, Latin America, and the Caribbean was ostensibly the product of centuries of missionary work. It provides the context in which the NAACP and other conventional groups began clamoring for black inclusion in the Foreign Service and in aid distribution programs. The black middle class would interpret America to Africans and Africans to America. African-American popular culture spread across the world partly as a result of its association with this brokering role and with U.S. power generally, a phenomenon that enabled the official appropriation of that culture through the medium of propaganda agencies like the U.S. Information Agency (USIA). Government-sponsored tours by actors and musicians, artists and writers partook of a cheerful ambiguity: it was never entirely clear precisely what their performances were meant to represent and on behalf of whom they addressed foreign audiences.

This vague sense of goodwill served to camouflage the uneven development of U.S. efforts to address racism. The Housing Act of 1954, for example, passed the same year as the Supreme Court's *Brown* decision, allowed local authorities to continue separating the races in federally supported urban renewal projects even as the Court ordered schools to be desegregated. Additionally, cold war priorities could be enlisted to reaffirm the status quo. Discriminatory practices that were under fire in everyday life were revitalized whenever a national security label could be affixed to them. Colonialism benefited from the practice of invoking national security as a higher priority than freedom. This habit began shortly after World War II when the United States retained Pacific islands seized from Japan. The geostrategic importance of the Pacific Trust Territories canceled out the ideological commitment to decolonization President Franklin D. Roosevelt had declared during the war. Washington also bowed to European arguments that based postwar recovery on continued access to empire.

The narrowing of the achievement gap between the United States and the USSR took precedence over racial change as a priority. For many, the arms race provided new grounds on which to enact Jim Crow practices. Great power rivalry, especially in light of colonial independence, required better understanding of the nations becoming sovereign. Even as discriminatory practices continued, the National Defense Educational Act underwrote area studies programs, and private foundations began planning programming for Africa, Asia, and Latin America.[9]

---

[8] Arnold DeMille, "Young Cleric Stars in New Field of Church Activity," *Chicago Defender*, March 27, 1954, p. 12.

[9] Social Science Research Council (SSRC) Records, Series I, Committee Projects, subseries Africa, Box 15, RAC; Paul Tiyambe Zeleza, "The Perpetual Crises and Solitudes of African Studies in the United States." *Africa Today* 44 (2) (1997): 202.

Sputnik's call for rejuvenation had evoked a widely felt consensus on national revival, but beyond that, there was little agreement about details. Conservatives wanted a return to what they regarded as first principles of American nationhood, which included, among other political and cultural prescriptions, a reaffirmation of religion, a stricter juridical adherence to constitutionalism, and curtailment of the state's redistributive functions. While liberals addressed the malaise by promoting a broader view of government's role in effecting change, they shared with conservatives a renewed interest in education as a cold war weapon.[10] To the extent that education meant a broader view of the world and one's place in it, it served just as much to destabilize as to affirm an impeccable America whose national ideology was unquestionably correct.

If the effect of segregation was to hide African Americans from the world, and the world from African Americans, education provided a limited means of eluding this isolation. A small cultural minority escaped by leaving the United States entirely. Writers Richard Wright, James Baldwin, and Chester Himes and the painter Beauford Delaney numbered among those who sought a dignified and uncompromised life in Europe. Cartoonist Ollie Harrington remembered the consternation the phenomenon seemed to cause in the United States. "Hemingway, F. Scott Fitzgerald, all the great American writers were all in Paris at one time or another," he recalled. "But when Black expatriates sort of joined the 'fraternity,' it wasn't a very popular thing with the authorities in the United States and you can easily see why." Crossing a geographic border also meant crossing a political and psychological one. "These were really disrupting ideas which existed. Blacks had to be held in check. They had to fear white law, and that sort of thing. Living in Paris and having experiences that Blacks shouldn't have was not conducive to a smooth course towards whatever American history would finally produce."[11]

The Algerian revolution disrupted the Parisian idyll of black expatriates as French authorities began to repress people of color. James Baldwin wrote eloquently of his trumped-up arrest in Paris for the alleged theft of a bed sheet. Future African-American feminist Frances Beal arrived in Paris without prior knowledge of the Algerian conflict. She was impassively witnessing a street protest when a French police officer hit her on the head with a cape weighted with metal balls. "You can say or write anything you want over here," author

10 Patrick Allitt, *Catholic Intellectuals and Conservative Politics in America, 1950–1975* (Ithaca, N.Y.: Cornell University Press, 1993); Mary C. Brennan, *Turning Right in the Sixties: The Conservative Capture of the GOP* (Chapel Hill: University of North Carolina Press, 1995), Rick Perlstein, *Before the Storm: Barry Goldwater and the Unmaking of the American Consensus* (New York: Hill & Wang, 2001).
11 David Lionel Smith, "The Black Arts Movement and Its Critics," *American Literary History* 3 (1) (1991): 97–8; Lawrence P. Jackson, *The Indignant Generation: A Narrative History of African American Writers and Critics, 1934–1960* (Princeton, N.J.: Princeton University Press, 2011), chapter 15; James Campbell, *Paris Interzone: Richard Wright, Lolita, Boris Vian, and Others on the Left Bank, 1946–60* (London: Secker and Warburg, 1994); Oliver W. Harrington, *Why I Left America and Other Essays* (Jackson: University Press of Mississippi, 1993), 107.

Richard Wright told an *Ebony* editor, "but don't get started on France's colonies. Whoop the police will be on your neck and out you go in forty-eight hours."[12] Self-exiles found that physical escape from U.S. society did not always shield them from racism. Julius Lester, in Europe on behalf of SNCC less than a decade later, considered "French crackers" no different from Americans. The Paris intellectuals black expatriates knew were targeted for their support of the Algerian cause by a defensive French government and a virulently racist police force. Paranoia came to replace the halcyon postwar days as U.S. intelligence activities reminded those living abroad that, while they had left home, they were still on the star-spangled radar screen. "No longer are we watched by the cracker cops in the south alone," Lester wrote; "cops all over the world now watch."[13]

Of all the struggles of the period, "it was the Algerian revolution in particular," James C. Hall writes, "that had the greatest long-term impact on African-American intellectual life." The colonial struggle in general haunted the consciousness of black artists and writers in Paris. A group of them centered on the literary journal *Présence Africaine*. After the 1956 International Conference of Negro Writers and Artists, black Francophone intellectuals founded the Société Africaine de Culture (SAC). SAC concerned itself with the aesthetics and psychology of black life, and thus with the colonial condition. It quickly acquired an international reputation and a worldly roster of writers, including *Présence Africaine* editor Alioune Diop; Léopold Senghor, representing Senegal in the French senate and later heading the Senegalese government; Martinican poet Aimé Césaire; and Jean Price-Mars, Haiti's foremost intellectual.[14] SAC had the potential to mount a direct political challenge to

[12] James Baldwin, "Equal in Paris," in James Baldwin, *Notes of a Native Son* (Boston: Beacon Press, 1955), 138–58; Stephen Michael Ward, "'Ours Too Was a Struggle for a Better World': Activist Intellectuals and the Radical Promise of the Black Power Movement, 1962–1972" (PhD diss., University of Texas, Austin, 2002), p. 188; Ben Burns, *Nitty Gritty: A White Editor in Black Journalism* (Oxford: University of Mississippi Press 1996), 172–3. For the Algerian issue in Paris, see Jean-Luc Einaudi, *La Bataille de Paris. 17 octobre 1961* (Paris: Editions du Seuil, 1991).

[13] Jackson, *The Indignant Generation*, 453; Van Elteren, "The Subculture of the Beats"; James Baldwin, "Take Me to the Water," in *Collected Essays*, ed. James Baldwin (n.p.: Library of America, c. 1998), 367–9, 374–8; Tyler Stovall, "The Fire This Time: Black Expatriates and the Algerian War," *Yale French Studies*, No. 98 (2000): 182–200; Einaudi, *La Bataille de Paris*, 20–4, 81–92, 99–125; Harrington, *Why I Left America*, 108; Ollie Harrington to Percival Prattis, February 28, 1961, Percival L. Prattis Papers, MSRC; Saunders, *The Cultural Cold War*, 69. FBI, "Possible Subversives Among US Personnel in France," January 18, 1960' FBI file on Richard Wright, in the FBI's Virtual Reading Room, http://www.fbi.gov/news/stories/2005/may/foia052005. Julius Lester to Faye Bellamy and Atlanta SNCC, March 16, 1967, Series VIII, General Files, reel 52, Papers of the Student Nonviolent Coordinating Committee (hereafter SNCC Papers) (Ann Arbor, Mich.: UMI, 1994).

[14] James C. Hall, *Mercy, Mercy Me: African American Culture and the American Sixties* (New York: Oxford University Press, 2001), 79; James T. Harris Jr. to Rayford W. Logan, November 25, 1957, Rayford Logan Papers, MSRC; "Richard Wright in the 1950s: A Symposium, February 20, 1993," Occasional Paper No. 2, American Culture Studies Program, Washington University,

colonialism, but many of its contributors divorced their cultural interests from politics, in spite of the growing discomfort the Algerian crisis and other decolonization issues had begun to cause.

SAC asked Richard Wright to invite some African Americans to its 1956 Paris conference. Guests included the educators Horace Mann Bond, Mercer Cook, and John A. Davis; James Ivy, editor of the NAACP organ the *Crisis*; attorney Thurgood Marshall; and composer Duke Ellington. This group founded the American Society of African Culture (AMSAC) in 1957. Like SAC, AMSAC conceived of itself as dedicated primarily to intellectual pursuits.[15]

There was some ambiguity about AMSAC's ultimate aims: it promoted African nationalism while viewing "the great cultural contributions of man" as needing protection from "movements" whose emergence had prompted the organization's founding in the first place. The society's aestheticism masked the mounting tensions surrounding politics on the African continent, where colonial powers and settler regimes had proven intractable in their opposition to independence and majority rule. Both SAC and AMSAC in their early years had oriented African and diaspora intelligentsias away from that revolutionary ferment. AMSAC shared its New York headquarters with the Council on Race and Caste in World Affairs, which, unbeknownst to most AMSAC members, was a CIA front. The Council on Race and Caste in World Affairs merged with AMSAC in 1957 and channeled CIA funds to it.[16]

U.S. government meddling in African and diaspora affairs resulted from its conflation of antiimperialism with communism. Although Richard Wright renounced communism in the early 1940s, he appears in later FBI records as "unwittingly" supporting Red aims in France by "flirting with Titoism and Sartre-ism" and by writing for "neutralist publications." The U.S. embassy in Paris saw *Présence Africaine* as a radical journal and hoped that the "leftist tendencies" of the 1956 Black Artists and Writers Congress could "be neutralized." Efforts were made to handpick African-American participants.[17]

AMSAC nevertheless engaged many prominent members of the black cultural elite in the United States. Its activities included the creation of an African resource library, an information service, and a speakers' bureau. AMSAC set up an African visitors program that included tours of black communities in the United States, occasional secretarial service for African missions, fellowships, and artist exchange programs and cohosted events. The society published a

St Louis; Bennetta Jules-Rosette, *Black Paris: The African Writers' Landscape* (Urbana: University of Illinois Press, 1998), 5, 7, 77.

[15] Preamble, Constitution of the American Society of African Culture (AMSAC), in Logan Papers, Box 166–7.

[16] Harris to Logan, November 25, 1957, Logan Papers; Dan Schechter, Michael Ansara, and David Kolodney, "The CIA as an Equal Opportunity Employer," in Ellen Ray, William Schaap, Karl Van Meter and Louis Wolf, *Dirty Works 2: The CIA in Africa* (Secaucus, N.J.: Lyle Stuart, 1969), 54, 55.

[17] Anonymous, Re: Internal Security, April 18, 1952; U.S. Embassy, Paris to Department of State, May 3, 1956, FBI File on Richard Wright, online.

newsletter, *African Forum*, and some scholarly works, including the anthology *Africa as Seen by American Negro Scholars* and artist Elton Fax's travel book, *West African Vignettes*. It also worked outside the New York area, maintaining in Chicago ties to dozens of civic organizations, corporations, county government, churches, colleges, universities, and Jewish, Mexican, and Native American associations. AMSAC provides an example of how a clandestine government agency played an active role in scattering the seeds of a movement that it was simultaneously trying to contain.[18]

After South African police machine-gunned unarmed black demonstrators in the Sharpeville massacre of 1960, AMSAC became more political. It tried to reckon with an African revolution in Algeria, a country not deemed "black." In spite of the common theme of anticolonialism, Algeria's orientation toward the Arab world and Islam, rather than to black Africa and its myriad faiths, made it seem un-African to many black Americans. A 1959 AMSAC conference in New York failed to dislodge this impression. Even though Kwame Nkrumah had spoken of the Sahara as the "bridge that unites us," the National Liberation Front (FLN) representative in New York felt compelled to remind conference participants that Algeria's struggle was also an African one.[19]

The black organization in the United States most in touch with issues in the Muslim world, the Nation of Islam (NOI), could have broadened popular awareness of the Algerian war. The Nation's leaders, however, had closer ties to the Middle East than to the Maghreb. The Algerian revolution thus remained in the background of African-American concerns until the mid-1960s, when the writings of one of its partisans, Antillean psychiatrist Frantz Fanon, were translated into English. West Africa, the historical point of origin for African Americans and the home of indigenous leaders who were most familiar with U.S. life, provided a more accessible entry point into dialogue and action on nationalism, anticolonialism, and global race relations.

Africa held out promise for those in the diaspora who never felt entirely at home in white majority societies. Before decolonization, back-to-Africa generally meant emigration to the independent state of Liberia or Ethiopia. These countries were problematic for many would-be emigrants because both remained profoundly underdeveloped, and neither boasted a government attuned to contemporary desires for democratic freedom and economic prosperity. After 1957, Ghanaian independence revived the attractive prospect of life in a black nation. Ironically, countries like Ghana, emerging from colonialism, presented a sunnier picture of what Africans could achieve in the future than Ethiopia or Liberia, which had been sovereign throughout most of their history. Those who left American shores to live in Ghana included a number of leftists, such as W. E. B. Du Bois; his wife, Shirley Graham; and writer Julian Mayfield. Other radicals, such as William Sutherland, were pacifists and Pan-Africanists. The community at its peak in the early 1960s numbered

[18] Minutes of 4th annual meeting, June 23–24, 1961, folder 2, AMSAC Papers, SC.
[19] "New Negro Pride in Origins Found," *New York Times*, June 27, 1959, p. 2

no more than 120 persons, and although many held professional positions, their main legacy in Ghana was not their impact on Africans, but rather their meaning for African Americans attempting to envision options beyond Jim Crow strictures. Kevin Gaines, who studied this group, interprets them as having found a refuge from the political distortions U.S. ideology imposed. The expatriates' experience was "instructive," he asserts, "precisely because they defied pressure from Cold War liberals to confine their vision of black politics within the domestic realm of civil rights." They refused to let "anticommunism take precedence over their commitment to African American and African freedom" and "vehemently objected to anti-communist propaganda that portrayed domestic struggles against segregation, and African nation-building projects, as spearheaded by Soviet 'outside agitators.'"[20]

U.S. officials closely watched developments in Ghana and other countries that they linked to militant nationalism, and whose susceptibility to Warsaw Pact blandishments they feared. Washington's appointments of African-American ambassadors to sub-Saharan capitals raised African concerns that such envoys would be stalking horses for Stateside interests. Black expatriates had to take care not to jeopardize their own position as guests in their host countries by appearing to collude with espionage or subversion.[21]

These problems of trust adversely affected U.S. relations with African nations. John H. Morrow, an African American named the first U.S. ambassador to Guinea by Eisenhower, was perhaps alone among American diplomats in assessing Guinean president Sékou Touré as a nationalist rather than a communist. Courtly Howard University professor Mercer Cook found himself similarly defending Niger as ambassador a few years later. The United States had little interest in that sparsely populated desert nation. Cook was in a tough spot, journalist Enoch Waters opined. He "wants to be a working diplomat instead of a symbol," but the United States was doing little to help the desperately poor country. "Africans rate you by what you can do," Waters claimed. Faced with his government's refusal to provide substantive aid, Cook and his wife, Vashti, resorted to private fund-raising for Niger.[22]

Events were rushing past hidebound approaches to black people as social change accelerated at home and abroad. By 1959 King was well on his way to

[20] Peter Goldman, Malcolm: *The Death and Life of Malcolm X*, 2nd ed. (Urbana: University of Illinois Press, 1979), 181; Kevin Gaines, "From Black Power to Civil Rights: Julian Mayfield and African American Expatriates in Nkrumah's Ghana, 1957–1966," 259, in *Cold War Constructions: The Political Culture of United States Imperialism, 1945–1966*, ed. Christian G. Appy, (Amherst: University of Massachusetts Press, 2000). See also Kevin Gaines, *American Africans in Ghana: Black Expatriates and the Civil Rights Era* (Chapel Hill: University of North Carolina Press. 2006).

[21] William Sutherland and Matt Meyer, *Guns and Gandhi in Africa* (Trenton, N.J.: Africa World Press, 2000), 68; Franklin Williams to Jesse E. Gloster, February 2, 1966, Franklin Williams Papers, Box 25, SC.

[22] Enoch Waters to Claude Barnett, November 11, 1961, CBP, Part 2, Associated Negro Press Organizational Files, 1920–1966, reel 7.

becoming the principal spokesperson of the "Negro revolution," but not every-one agreed with his strategies. In addition to the Baptist conservatives who wished to distance the church from social activism, critics included those who adhered to a separatist black nationalism that the civil rights movement had overshadowed but not destroyed, and that scholars have yet to recover fully. "The argument of these historians is after Garvey was deposed, or deported that nothing happened," Elombe Brath, a veteran of Harlem nationalist activity, has observed. "That's not true. The movement calmly went on. And the idea was don't give these people no play, no publicity, just as they do today. Any scalawag or charlatan they could go get a live press. But people who they know are sincere or serious they don't get no play, they just evaporate." In spite of the optimism that integrationist leaders cultivated in the 1950s, and increased black middle-class mobility, black nationalist activity did not disappear but survived and gained ground during the era.[23]

Harlem remained black America's most vital nationalist site. The presence after 1951 of the UN secretariat in New York City strengthened nationalists' communications with foreign envoys and energized them politically. United African Nationalist Movement (UANM) president James R. Lawson traveled to Washington, D.C., to lobby officials for an end to helicopter sales to France, which was deploying the choppers against Algerian rebels. The UANM wanted U.S. aid to African countries to equal expenditures for Europe. The United States, Lawson and his delegation held, should advocate decolonization more aggressively and immediately unfreeze all Egyptian funds immobilized during the Suez crisis.[24]

Renewed activity was also cultural. The New York Temple of Islam, the Ethiopian Orthodox Church, and the UANM began cosponsoring a "Miss Africa Day." The winner, typically a young woman with darker skin than most black beauty contestants of the era, was crowned in front of Louis Michaux's celebrated National Memorial Bookstore on 125th Street and Seventh Avenue. "Mr. Micheaux's bookshop ... prided itself on having or being able to get a copy of any book written by a black person since 1900," writer Maya Angelou recalled. It was a vibrant period for Harlem. "One Hundred and Twenty-fifth Street was to Harlem what the Mississippi was to the South, a long traveling river always going somewhere, carrying something." Angelou remembered "a furniture store offering gaudy fake leopard-skin chairs" and "sportily dressed fops ... on 125th and Seventh Avenue saying, 'Got horse for the course and

[23] Author's interview with Elombe Brath, New York City, May 16, 1994; Dean E. Robinson, *Black Nationalism in American Politics and Thought* (New York: Cambridge University Press, 2001); Abiola Sinclair, ed. *The Harlem Cultural/Political Movements* (New York: Gumbs & Thomas, 1995). See also Gerald Horne, *Mau Mau in Harlem? The U.S. and the Liberation of Kenya* (New York: Palgrave Macmillan, 2009).

[24] Author's interview with Ernest Kaiser, New York City, May 13, 1994; Nashville *Globe*, August 16, 1957, Tuskegee Clipping File, hereafter TCF, reel 160. On Suez see Salim Yaqub, "Imperious Doctrines: U.S.-Arab Relations from Dwight D. Eisenhower to George W. Bush," *Diplomatic History* 26 (Fall 2002): 2–6, 15.

coke for your hope.' People wore multicolored African prints ... [and] moved through the streets like bright sails on a dark sea." The new esteem for Africa meant "that fewer people giggled or poked the sides of their neighbors when they noticed" Angelou's "natural hair style."[25]

Late fifties groups like the UANM are largely forgotten today outside New York. The UANM was nevertheless an important organization. True to its Garveyite roots, it maintained a steady interest in international affairs and courted anticolonialist leaders from other countries as early as 1952, when it held a press conference at Harlem's Hotel Theresa for Bahi Lagdam, secretary-general of revolutionary Tunisia's delegation to the United Nations. With Tunisia's nationalist leader Habib Bourguiba then under arrest, Lagdam appealed to African Americans for moral support. "We need the help of the American Negroes in our struggle," he told reporters. "We need their help in influencing other African nations to go on record for a UN hearing in our fight for freedom." Tunisia required thirty-one signatures from member states to induce the UN to investigate its grievances against a France that was unwilling to cede control (see Figure 1). Lagdam made a racial appeal, using Tunisia's African identity as a bridge to black Americans. He claimed that there was no discrimination in Tunisia because Islam forbids it and warned that if the Tunisian case was not addressed, it might escalate into another Korean War.[26]

The UANM in February 1957 hosted a dinner for the Sudanese, Moroccan, and Tunisian ambassadors and a lesser Libyan envoy and planned to send a representative to the ceremonies for Ghanaian independence. Lawson embarked on a fund-raising mission to attend the All-African Peoples' Conference in Accra in October 1958. He sought support from the Masons, Shriners, Elks, Oddfellows, and the National Medical Association, black America's answer to the American Medical Association. Lincoln University president Horace Mann Bond praised the UANM for its activism and knowledge of global issues.[27]

Sékou Touré, the president of Guinea, and his wife visited the United States officially in 1959 and wanted to see Harlem. An *Amsterdam News* columnist wryly noted that "during the days that the Tourés were in town, it was difficult picking out the Africans from the 125th Street Africans, what with all the drapes, rags, skull caps, bargain basement cloths and what not. Of course it was difficult to distinguish Mrs. Touré, too, since she wore chic French clothes most of the time."[28] Lawson achieved notoriety at a Harlem luncheon for Mrs. Sékou Touré when he barred an interpreter from the head table on racial grounds. He had instead acquired the services of Philippa Schuyler, a

[25] Maya Angelou, *The Heart of a Woman*, in *The Collected Autobiographies of Maya Angelou* (New York: Norton, 2004), 664.

[26] "Tunisian Diplomat Asks Negroes for Help," *Amsterdam News*, April 26, 1952, p. 3, 10.

[27] "UANM Entertains Ambassadors in New York City," *Pittsburgh Courier*, March 2, 1957, p. 17; and "Lawson Hurls 'Red' Cry," in ibid., January 24, 1959, p. 2; Atlanta *World*, August 21, 1958, p. 7, TCF, reel 168.

[28] Thomasina Norford, "On the Tour with Thomasina Norford," *Amsterdam News*, November 14, 1959, p. 12.

FIGURE 1. Tunisian leader Habib Bourguiba rejects De Gaulle's gradualist approach to decolonization. (Courtesy Bill Mauldin Estate)

well-known Harlem personality and the daughter of conservative journalist George Schuyler, as translator. Lawson's gaffe involved him in an angry exchange with State Department officials. Lawson was not the only one committing faux pas. The city of New York mistakenly hung out Ghanaian flags

for the Tourés' motorcade arrival. What is most important here is the nationalists' ability to command the attendance not only of the Guinean delegation, but
also of a former president of Liberia, Liberian and Haitian UN delegates, the
president of the New York NAACP chapter, and Manhattan borough president
Hulan Jack. Members of the Muslim Brotherhood, and the NOI, then led in
New York by Malcolm X, also attended. Black nationalists mounted diverse
challenges to the status quo that ranged from disputing conventional beauty
standards to trying to make Harlem, often viewed as a forlorn ghetto, the
hub of Pan-African international activity. They sought the power to redefine
African-Americans' identity within the United States as well as their relationship to the larger world.[29]

At a second festive event featuring the Guineans at the Harlem YWCA, tensions between black nationalists and integrationists were evident in the room as
the audience booed Hulan Jack and NAACP branch president Joseph Overton,
integrationists who extensively networked with whites. According to Malcolm
X, the nationalist leaders present were not responsible for the insults to guests.
"In my opinion the booing was spontaneous and unorganized," he told the
Amsterdam News. It was "the audience in general ... an audience made up of
the 'Negro masses'" whose disaffection with integrationists was "on a larger
scale than is publicly admitted."[30]

The Guinean visit evoked strong feelings in African Americans outside
Harlem. Chicago-based *Ebony* published a series of photographs that included
Sékou Touré's trip to North Carolina. The Tarheel State had shown Touré
a Potemkin village of smiling black and white faces that belied the conflicts
occurring there. Freda V. Love, writing to the editor of *Ebony* from Portland,
Oregon, compared Touré's royal reception in the South to the everyday plight
of African Americans. Love noted that "Touré, a foreigner with basically the
same racial (an important consideration in the United States) background as
ours, was *publicly* welcomed in areas where we do not venture and welcomed
by the same forces that oppose us." She called for change. "*Ebony*'s picture
story makes me wonder when ... all of us will cease standing passively and
being occasionally mollified with political crumbs."[31]

Some black nationalists of the period did not wonder when change would
occur; they called for exit. The nationalist strain was not merely rhetorical. It
was predicated on the belief that African Americans did not share the same
interests as whites and consequently required a separate political community.
The UANM, for example, had not abandoned an earlier dream of establishing communities of return in Africa. Since the late 1940s, it had worked on a
repatriation bill and found a senator to support it, William "Wild Bill" Langer

---

[29] Plummer, *Rising Wind*, 275–6.
[30] James Booker and Wilmer, Lucas, Jr., "U.S. State Department May Make Harlem 'Off Limits,'"
    Amsterdam News, November 14, 1959, p. 1, 25; "Who Booed NAACP? Here Are Both Sides,"
    Amsterdam News, November 14, 1959, p. 1. 3.
[31] Claude Sitton, "Touré Impressed by Carolina Visit," *New York Times*, October 30, 1959, p. 5;
    Freda V. Love to the editor of *Ebony*, vol. 15, May 1960, p. 22.

of North Dakota. The organization approached Langer after securing written approval from the Liberian government to recruit African-American immigrants. Monrovia, miffed at Washington's solicitous attention to fledging states and liberation movements and its disregard of an old friend, was dissatisfied with the amount of U.S. assistance it received. Liberia consequently turned to an old standby, the nationalist remnant that still had affinities for what had once been the only sub-Saharan republic. UANM activists perceived Langer, described by one scholar as an "isolationist on foreign policy and to the left of the New Deal on domestic issues," as a good choice to present the bill because, unlike the southern bigots most closely associated with past repatriation legislation, he had no other connection to the race question. North Dakota had scant black population. The *Pittsburgh Courier*, however, suspected Langer of playing another kind of politics with the repatriation bill and with certain civil rights amendments he proposed to tack on to unrelated legislation. He was attaching these riders, the newspaper speculated, to ensure that bills he opposed would not pass.[32]

The legislation had a rough ride in the Senate. Tom Connally of Texas, chair of the Foreign Relations Committee, let Langer know that the State Department disliked the bill and thought Liberia too poor to sustain mass migration. The Foreign Relations Committee tabled it. After Connally resigned the chair, Langer reintroduced it. This time a subcommittee heard the bill, but NAACP opposition kept it locked up there. In the interim, the *Brown* decision and the mobilization of white "massive resistance" heightened racial tension nationally and led likely lawmakers to distance themselves from what had become a hot potato. In the nineteenth century, those wishing to remove blacks from North America in order to ensure the purity of a white republic raised the subject of black expatriation, then referred to as colonization, in Congress. The issue reappeared in the 1930s and 1940s only when unequivocal racists like Senator Theodore G. Bilbo of Mississippi broached it. Even if blacks endorsed it, the proposal was now perceived as too inflammatory to pursue.[33]

In 1959, with a sympathetic J. William Fulbright chairing the Foreign Relations Committee, the Langer bill was revived. Fulbright thought "the proposal ... a reasonable one. With the emergence of such countries as Ghana, Guinea, and in the future, Nigeria, it seems to me that the scope of the legislation should be broadened." Langer died late in 1959, however, and so, finally, did his bill, after Senator Russell Long of Georgia refused to take it up, saying that as a southerner, he could not afford to do so.[34]

---

[32] Edith W. Hedlin, "Earnest Sevier Cox and Colonization: A White Racist's Response to Black Repatriation, 1923–1966" (PhD diss., Duke University, 1974), p. 178; "What's Senator Langer's Story?" *Pittsburgh Courier*, January 21, 1950, p. 16.

[33] Hedlin, "Earnest Sevier Cox and Colonization," 183, 194, 200–6.

[34] Ibid., 172, 178, 183, 188–9, 192–230. See also Charles Pope Smith, "Theodore G. Bilbo's Senatorial Career. The Final Years, 1941–1947" (PhD diss., University of Southern Mississippi), p. 1983.

The Langer bill and the back-to-Africa movements of the 1950s have been treated as embarrassments, throwbacks to a past supposedly made obsolete by the growing desire of many African Americans for inclusion in, rather than separation from, the mainstream. Francis N. Nesbitt writes that black nationalist initiatives "lived 'below the radar screen' of the black and white press and have thus been erased from the recent historiography of black internationalism."[35] At the same time that pressure for desegregation welled up from groups previously uninvolved in race relations brokerage, African-American communities increased their interest in African developments. Nor were Harlem activists the only protagonists. Black nationalists in Chicago worked on reviving Garveyism, no longer perceived as a fantasy. "Many American Negroes who laughed at a late Marcus Garvey for his passionate interest in Africa are now trying desperately to get recognition as 'friends' of Ghana," publicist Louis Martin slyly noted.[36] African independence meant that black nationalism could no longer be dismissed. The task now was to determine what relationships diaspora communities would have with these new nations.

African reluctance to assume responsibility for social conflicts made in the USA rendered mass emigration unfeasible. The new countries needed skilled workers. Ghana made it clear it wanted no paupers. Finance minister Komla A. Gbedemah asserted that his country "cannot have people coming ... who will be destitute and charges at Government expense." Ghana accepted immigrants who could support themselves and contribute their talents to the nation. Yet, the old dream of expatriating the entire black population of the United States hung on. The American Colonization Society, which had been founded in 1816, continued to exist; it supported a school in Monrovia. In 1961 the directors of the society "became convinced that there was no longer the possibility" of carrying on its work and decided to dissolve it. They chose trustees of an educational foundation, the Phelps Stokes Fund, to manage the society's assets, viewing that foundation's mission in Africa as closest to their own. The colonization society completed this process of devolution in 1965 when a Maryland circuit court handed over some $168,500 in negotiable securities and real estate in Monrovia and Grand Bassa County, Liberia.[37]

Black nationalists' activities and far-reaching goals have escaped the attention of historians who have focused chiefly on the integrationist – and outward looking – black protest politics of the time. Peace activist Homer A. Jack

35 Francis Njubi Nesbitt, *Race for Sanctions: African Americans against Apartheid, 1946–1964* (Bloomington: Indiana University Press, 2004), 13.
36 F. H. Hammurabi, "The Pen – Mightier than the Sword," *Chicago Daily Defender*, February 6, 1957, p. 4; "Plan Revival Of UNIA Here," May 21, 1957; p. 5; Lee Blackwell, "Off the Record," ibid., May 22, 1957, p. 10; Louis Martin, "Off the Cuff," ibid., July 17, 1958, p. A8.
37 Gbedemah quoted in "Unwanted Negroes," editorial, *Pittsburgh Courier* October 4, 1958, p. A8; brochure, *The Phelps-Stokes Fund and Its Work, July 1, 1963–June 30, 1965*, p. 23, 21, Rockefeller Fund. Phelps Stokes Fund-American Negro Studies, RG 1.2, Ser 200, Box 77, folder RAC; Joshua Evans, Jr. to Edward Robinson, August 24, 1953, folder ACS, Phelps Stokes Fund Records, Box 50, SC.

dismissed the UANM as a relic, but the organization had links to the future, when Black Power advocates would recover its legacies. While black nationalism was being discredited by those who believed that there was light at the end of a centuries-old racist tunnel, nationalism as a motor force of organization and development abroad received due respect from U.S. officialdom and policy elites. Roosevelt University and the University of Chicago hosted the Scottish Africanist George Shepperson, in town to do research and give lectures. In New York, international law expert Philip C. Jessup chaired a Council on Foreign Relations panel to explore issues arising in the increasingly vocal UN General Assembly. It was more and more understood that the United States needed to combat anti-Americanism and communist exploitation of the colonial issue in order to keep its global leadership position while continuing to maintain a proindependence stance.[38] Within the two major political parties, moreover, opinions on which public policies to pursue varied considerably.

The NSC reflected on the growing importance of nationalism, calling it "the great issue in Africa today. At the moment, all others, no matter how important, are subordinate to it. Our policies in any field will be of little or no value if we ignore this issue." The NSC's report, "U.S. Policy toward Africa South of the Sahara Prior to Calendar Year 1960," admitted the enormous political diversity on the continent and acknowledged that "sentiment and pressures for self-government are everywhere increasing at an accelerated rate." Experts thought "premature independence would be as harmful to our interests in Africa as would be a continuation of nineteenth century colonialism, and we must tailor our policies to the capabilities and needs of each particular area as well as to our over-all relations with the metropolitan power concerned. It should be noted," the report cautioned, "that all of the metropolitan powers are associated with us in the NATO alliance or in military base agreements."[39]

Washington walked the measured tightrope between honoring the respective nationalisms of metropoles and aspiring colonies while remaining unresponsive to nationalist stirrings from subalterns at home. Symbolic linkages had cemented the conventional political relationships that lent minority support to Democratic Party candidates and to a liberal line associated with the New

---

[38] Homer Jack, "America's Growing Concern for Africa," Papers of the NAACP (Frederick, Md.: University Publications of America, 1982–96), Part 14, Race relations in the international arena, 1940–55, reel 10; Ernestine Cofield, "English Scholar Shepperson Says," Chicago Defender, April 25, 1959, p. 11; Philip C. Jessup to Ralph Bunche, October 17, 1956, Ralph J. Bunche Papers, Box 107, Council on Foreign Relations Study Group on Colonial Problems, UCLA; Mason Sears, Years of High Purpose (Washington, D.C., University Press of America, 1980), 71–85.

[39] National Security Council, (hereafter NSC) 5818, U. S. Policy toward Africa South of the Sahara Prior to Calendar Year 1960, August 26, 1958, in Foreign Relations of the United States (hereafter FRUS), XXVI 1958–1960, Africa (Washington, D.C.: Government Printing Office 1992), p. 28. An earlier version of the text appears in the DDRS as NSC 5719/2 with the date of August 23, 1957.

Deal alliance of labor, urban professionals, and immigrants. Symbols proved less attractive to constituents who benefited little from that coalition. Malcolm X began articulating their growing dissatisfaction. As he attacked U.S. foreign policy liberalism, the FBI followed his ideas closely, sending verbatim transcripts of his speeches to its Washington headquarters. "The earth is becoming filled with fast-awakening DARK nations, who are tossing off the yoke of white imperialism," Malcolm told a Detroit audience in 1957.

Here in the strongest white country on earth are 17 MILLION Black people in a most unique and strategic position, wherein even in our down-trodden condition as second-class citizens we can greatly influence the selection and election of the individual who will sit in the strongest seat of white authority today. We have become like the "third man", Daniel, in the land of Babylon (Dan 5:29) and even as Joseph was in the land of bondage. (Holy Quran 12:56)

We affect both foreign and domestic policy. The majority of earth's people are non-white (Africans and Asians). Today they are beginning to realize that this white man can not love or treat them and better [*sic*] than he (in sincerity) can love or treat us. Thus we become the YARDSTICK by which all Dark Nations of the earth can measure the real attitude of the white public here in America, as well as the attitude of her president.[40]

Malcolm typically enlarged his appeal to his listeners by mixing acerbic political insights with biblical authority. His success owed as much to his ability to shatter cold war truisms and present his arguments in lay terms as to his skills as an orator. The explanatory power of race as well as religion fortified his project. As targets of repression in a society where race is foundational, African Americans often viewed world affairs through a racial lens. Malcolm X enhanced the linkage, speaking of the Mau Mau revolt in Kenya as "pushing the English devil" out of Africa, and of the Vietnamese driving the "French devils" out of Asia. China, portrayed by Malcolm as a "black" country, had defied the imperialists through its capture of eleven U.S. pilots. Indonesians were similarly engaged in hastening the demise of white supremacy in their conflict with the Dutch.[41]

The logic of anticommunist vigilance was susceptible to the same line of attack. Malcolm, first identified by the FBI as a subversive in 1953, challenged the customary definition of subversion. "You hear us talking about the white man and you want to go away and tell him we have been subversive," the FBI reported him as telling New York listeners. The black experience, he suggested, led to a different approach to the issue. "Here is a man who has raped your mother and hung your father from his tree, is he subversive?" With the trope

---

[40] Report of the New York Office, April 23, 1957, Malcolm X FBI File 100–399321, Sections 10–16, (Wilmington, Del.: Scholarly Resources, 1995), Reel 2.

[41] Malcolm X quoted in Special Agent in Charge (SAC) Philadelphia, to the Director, April 30, 1954; Report of the New York Office, January 31, 1956, ibid. On symbols and imagery in black nationalist oratory see Mark B. White, "The Rhetoric of Edification: African American Didactic Literature and the Ethical Function of Epideictic," *Howard Journal of Communications* 9 (April 1998): 125–36.

of subversion dismissed, Malcolm brushed aside cold war limits on civil rights and anticolonial activism.[42]

Malcolm X also popularized a discourse of patriarchal control of women, which, cloaked in benign claims of chivalry, guided many future approaches to gender relations among black dissidents. Under white domination, he preached in 1957, women have "reached a position of importance never before achieved in history" in "a society dominated by sex." Eve, created by God to serve Man, was the original temptress, "and the one she was created to serve has become her slave." In contemporary America, she accomplished this enslavement through seductive behavior, expressed by immodest dress and makeup. "When a man marries a woman, he gives her his name. She gives up her own. Same as when [the] white man brought [the] black man to this country and gave him his name. The name shows ownership. When a woman is through with a man, she divorces him and takes back her maiden name." Black Muslims performed a similar renunciation. "In Islam, the black man denounces his slave name and takes the unknown X." Malcolm told the women in his audience that they should not try to dominate their husbands. Men should not let their wives work for whites but should keep them at home. "In this hell of North America the devil advertises everything with pictures of naked women and she follows it up by copying these styles." Malcolm took direction here from NOI head Elijah Muhammad, who had spoken weeks before on "How to Unite, Control and Protect the So-called American Woman." Black women were too susceptible to the lures of big cities and towns, the Prophet complained. They "are allowed too much freedom."[43] Black Power in this formulation included power over women.

Malcolm X arrived in New York City as a Muslim minister in 1954. Elombe Brath recalled that "it was the preponderance of Black nationalist street corner speakers that changed Malcolm's modus operandi of promoting the Nation of Islam's tenets." He began to take meetings out to the street, engaging non-Muslims, and linking the NOI's beliefs more closely to Garveyite traditions of interest in Africa. He coordinated a conference with the Ethiopian Orthodox Church and with street corner speaker Carlos Cooks in 1957, an event planned to coincide with the September opening of the UN General Assembly. Various African leaders and black organizations sent greetings to this meeting, which passed resolutions to abolish the word "Negro" and substitute "African" or "black," to mobilize black material resources globally, to revive Garvey's African Community Leagues, and to synchronize efforts across groups.[44]

[42] Report of the New York Office, January 31, 1956; SAC, Boston to the Director, May 4, 1953, Malcolm X FBI File.

[43] Report of the New York Office, April 23, 1957; FBI Report, May 17, 1960, ibid.; Ted Watson, "Messenger Muhammad Stresses Closer Protection for So-Called Negro Women," *Pittsburgh Courier*, March 9, 1957, p. 20.

[44] Interview with Elombe Brath; Peniel E. Joseph, *Waiting 'Til the Midnight Hour: A Narrative History of Black Power in America* (New York: Henry Holt, 2006), 13; Nashville *Globe*, August 16, 1957, TCF, reel 160.

Under Malcolm X's leadership, the NOI became more involved in world affairs. In December 1957, it hosted a lengthy Harlem meeting on colonial and neocolonial issues. The assemblage sent greetings from Elijah Muhammad to the Afro-Asian conference then taking place in Cairo. Representatives from the governments of Egypt, Ghana, Iraq, Morocco, and the Sudan attended the proceedings. Malcolm X had carefully cultivated these contacts. "We knew that Malcolm has always maintained excellent relations with top Arabs at the UN," journalist Louis Lomax wrote in 1963. "Few, if any, of these meetings were ever public. But they did occur and there is every indication that they are still going on."[45]

Malcolm skillfully negotiated the Muslim world's varied character. When King Saud of Saudi Arabia visited New York, he was feted by oil magnates and financiers but cold-shouldered by municipal authorities in a city where supporters of Israel were numerous. Saud also received bad press from the black media because of the continuing practice of slavery in his country. While Malcolm knew this, he nevertheless sought Saudi support to bolster the NOI's claim to religious legitimacy. At the same time, he did not neglect Egypt's secular Pan-Arabism. Lomax noted, "Black Muslim bazaars open with the reading of cabled greetings from 'Our Beloved Brother Gamal Abdel Nasser.'"[46]

Malcolm X also worked out a fruitful relationship between the NOI and the *Pittsburgh Courier*, then still the most widely circulated black weekly with a readership and editorial agenda that reached far beyond the Iron City's precincts. With the help of longtime journalist George Schuyler, the *Courier* devised a scheme to satisfy its readers' curiosity about the new nations by publishing features about them that those governments would subsidize themselves. The *Courier* thus accomplished two goals simultaneously: it attracted readership in a sagging market and acquired subsidies for it. The paper planned a special feature series on Muslim countries with background provided by popular historian J. A. Rogers. The *Courier* should ensure that officials in Muslim states see it, Schuyler advised, to lead them to support a larger project. U.S. Muslims, he thought, "would simply eat it up," further enhancing sales.[47]

By the end of 1960, radio stations in seventy-three major cities carried Elijah Muhammad's program. His growing influence likely contributed to Nasser's decision to meet Fidel Castro in Harlem during the UN General Assembly meeting in September of that year. Popular historiography still locates the black nationalist thrust of the mid-twentieth century in the latter part of the 1960s,

---

[45] Louis E. Lomax, *When the Word Is Given* (Cleveland and New York: World Publishing, 1963), 72.

[46] "Oil, Bank Leaders at Banquet to Saud," *New York Times*, January 31, 1957, p. 5; Dana Adams Schmidt, "U.S. Aides Upset by Outcry against King Saud and Tito," ibid., January 30, 1957, p. 1; Lomax, *When the Word Is Given*, 131. See also Manning Marable, *Malcolm X: A Life of Reinvention* (New York: Viking, 2011), 166; Robert Vitalis, *America's Kingdom: Mythmaking on the Saudi Oil Frontier* (Palo Alto, Calif.: Stanford University Press, 2007).

[47] George Schuyler to Percival Prattis, April 10, September 29, and November 8, 1957, Prattis Papers.

succeeding the nonviolent direct action campaigns in the South. Setbacks experienced by the Christian-based movement, it is often argued, embittered participants and created openings for Islam and revolutionary nationalism, expressed as Black Power. It is now clear, however, that black nationalism accompanied rather than followed that phase of civil rights insurgency, serving as a counterpoint to its universalist claims.[48]

The NOI disturbed those who were committed to racial integration. CBS television reporter Mike Wallace in 1959 produced a broadcast on it entitled "The Hate That Hate Produced." The documentary exploited the shock many people felt at discovering that not all blacks eagerly embraced the ideal of inclusion in U.S. society and that some had radical critiques of its shortcomings. The camera probed the unusual dress of Muslim women at a time when Islam was a mystery to most Americans. It then suggested, by selectively quoting Malcolm X, that Muslims were an aberration, born of their own distorted interpretation of American life.[49]

The "hate group" label troubled the Nation during a vital period of its expansion. White hostility made foreign Muslims reluctant to establish contact with it. The Nation hired a black public relations firm to help repair an image that was equally tarnished in most black media. Decolonization aided the Nation's cause by making the idea of black sovereignty less alien to the public. Yet, the Nation found Malcolm X, its most powerful orator, banned from speaking at City University of New York campuses, a distinction he shared with communists.[50]

Other American Muslim organizations, many of them predominantly black, attacked the NOI at this time, questioning its fidelity to orthodox theology. Critics ranged from the Ahmadiyya movement to the Karachi-based World Federation of Islamic Missions, to the Muslim Brotherhood, U.S.A. The Nation addressed the problem by seeking the stamp of legitimacy from religious authorities in Arabia. Elijah Muhammad planned a 1959 pilgrimage to Mecca to establish his bona fides, as only legitimate Muslims can make the Hajj. He sent Malcolm X ahead to arrange it, but since Malcolm was not dispatched until July, after the main pilgrimage season was over, tongues continued to wag.[51]

---

[48] FBI report, Racial Tension and Civil Rights, March 1, 1956 encl. with J. Edgar Hoover to Maxwell Rabb, March 9, 1956, Eisenhower Papers, Ann Whitman File, DDRS; *New Jersey Herald News*, December 31, 1960 and December 17, 1960 in *Freedom of Information Act Materials on the Civil Rights Movement, 1958–1969*, ed. David Garrow, microfilm, SC; Benjamin Karim with Peter Skutches and David Gallen, *Remembering Malcolm* (New York: Carroll & Graf, 1992), 138, 139; Marable, *Malcolm X*, 136.

[49] L. Masco Young to Claude Barnett, December 14, 1959, CBP, part 2, reel 10.

[50] "Black Muslims or the Nation of Islam," November 28, 1962, USIA Reports, U.S. National Archives and Records Administration, hereafter NARA, Record Group (RG) 165; Robert H. Terte, "City Colleges Bar Communists from Speaking on Campuses," *New York Times*, October 27, 1961, p. 13.

[51] *Amsterdam News*, October 22, 1960, pp. 1, 25; Malcolm X to Alex Haley, April 25, 1964, Alex Haley Papers, SC.

Saudi religious authorities did admit Elijah Muhammad to Mecca, in spite of his espousal of beliefs that ran counter to conventional Islam. Why did they admit a man who asserted that white people were devils? Louis Lomax suggests that they excused the NOI for several reasons. First, the lack of a firm bureaucratic hierarchy and official line in Islam meant that judges might entertain a range of opinions about the sect. Second, the Nation's anti-Zionist posture was rare among U.S. organizations and provided a counterpoint to the preponderance of pro-Israeli sentiment among "moderate" African-American leaders. Third, if the NOI could help enlarge the Muslim community in America, so much the better. Its eccentricities could perhaps be fixed later. To that end, Mahmoud Yusef Shawarbi, chief representative in America of the Federation of Islamic Missions, began to mentor Malcolm X.[52]

Not long after Elijah Muhammad's pilgrimage, Shawarbi soft-pedaled criticisms he had once made of the NOI. He spoke at an Afro-Asian Bazaar sponsored by Malcolm's Temple No. 7 and attended by twenty-five hundred persons in November 1960. "We Africans gave civilization to the world thousands of years ago," said the Egyptian, photographed with Malcolm X for a *Courier* article. "We must see to it that civilization endures." Shawarbi linked the NOI desire to honor the black past with contemporary anxiety about the future of Muslim societies in an encroaching secular world. Race served as a metaphor to effect this union. "Elijah Muhammad described the connections between African Americans and colonized peoples through a language of naturalized race," Melani Mcallister writes. Shawarbi could appropriate discourse that stressed Egypt's ties to Africa, a gambit in line with Nasser's efforts to expand his continental influence.[53]

Before the NOI founded *Muhammad Speaks* on Malcolm X's initiative in 1961, the *Courier* was the leading source of news about African-American Muslims, and Malcolm provided most of its stories. The NOI also arranged with the Los Angeles *Herald-Dispatch* to publish a weekly column by Malcolm called "God's Angry Men."[54] These agreements helped the black press during an era of straitened circumstances. The Muslim connection gave the *Courier* entrée to Middle Eastern circles. A year after the U.S. Marines landed in Lebanon to restore order in its 1958 civil war, editor Percival L. Prattis received correspondence from a Lebanese, who fulminated against U.S. racism and invited him to visit Beirut. This networking broadened the scope of the *Courier's* reportorial capacities, but the relationship with Muslims remained an uneasy one. Editorial and ideological differences led to conflicts. The usually

---

[52] Marable, *Malcolm X*, 168–9, 301; Lomax, *When the Word Is Given*, 72–3; Bruce Perry, *Malcolm: The Life of a Man Who Changed Black America* (New York: Station Hill Press, 1991), 261.

[53] "All Muslims Are Brothers," *Pittsburgh Courier*, November 12, 1960, p. 2; Melani McAlister, "One Black Allah: The Middle East in the Cultural Politics of African American Liberation, 1955–1970," *American Quarterly* 51 (3) (1999): 627.

[54] Gerald Horne, *The Fire This Time: The Watts Uprising and the 1960s* (New York: Da Capo Press, 1997), 123.

bubbly Prattis worried greatly about the public impact of Wallace's documentary. Unfavorable articles about the NOI also appeared in *Time* and *U.S. News and World Report*. To make matters worse, Prattis found himself being accused of anti-Semitism.[55]

Prattis had traveled to Israel in 1954 and had written several favorable articles about the country. He antagonized many of his Jewish acquaintances, however, because he denied the scope of the Holocaust. The American Jewish Committee informed him of its worries about black anti-Semitism. The reproach stung. "You just don't criticize Jews and walk the streets of America," colleagues and Los Angeles *Herald-Dispatch* publishers Sanford and Pat Alexander asserted. The belief that powerful Jewish interests could harm the *Courier* led Prattis to attempt a tricky balancing act to woo and appease Muslims and Jews simultaneously.[56]

In correspondence with a Jewish woman, Prattis said Islam in the United States distressed him. He endorsed the popular view of the NOI as an anti-Semitic "hate group." Prattis then embarked on a second Middle Eastern tour, apparently paid for by the American Christian Palestine Committee. That group and others financed visits to Israel by a number of prominent African Americans in the late 1950s. After the Suez crisis, Israel and its U.S. allies wanted to alter the image of Israel as an imperialist power and counteract the admiration that many black Americans felt for Nasser. They sought to accomplish this by exposing visitors to Israel's nation-building successes and stressing its ties to Christianity and sites of Bible history.[57]

Prattis nevertheless maintained contact with the NOI. "African American investments in the Arab-Israeli conflict have a significant history aside from the tensions of black-Jewish relations," Melani McAllister proposes. They emerged from "a history that developed within the black community as part of a search for religious and cultural alternatives to Christianity." Reformulations of identity derived from the process. "The struggle to define a black culture was never separable from the process of constructing transnational definitions of blackness – definitions that connected African Americans to people of color and anticolonialism all over the world, including, quite centrally, the Middle East."[58] Prattis's deeds can also be understood as the pragmatic actions of an editor trying to keep his newspaper afloat during a time when black institutions were becoming victims of their own integrationist success. Hard times required juggling the interests vying for favorable press in black journals and extracting whatever benefits they could provide. Jewish or Muslim animosity could bring the *Courier* down.

[55] Gebran Majdalany to Percival Prattis, June 10, 1959; Prattis to George Schuyler, August 20, 1959; Paul Orentlicher to Prattis, May 14, 1957; Prattis to Miriam Jackson, February 2, 1960, Prattis Papers.

[56] Prattis to Hugh Y. Orgel, March 5, 1959, Prattis Papers; Sanford Alexander and Pat Alexander to Benjamin Davis, May 31, 1957, Benjamin Davis Papers, SC.

[57] Prattis to Miriam Jackson, February 2, 1960, Prattis Papers.

[58] Melani McAlister, "One Black Allah," 647.

Prattis's dilemma illustrates the impact that black nationalism was having on African-American life. It mirrors to some extent the tightrope Malcolm X walked between the orthodox conservatism of the Saudi kingdom and Egypt's secularism. Rifts between the religious and secular elements of Malcolm's program later manifested themselves in conflicts between his two rival groups, Muslim Mosque, Inc., and the Organization of African American Unity. Islam, when practiced by African Americans within a political context, was important, but not because of the number of worshippers or the mass appeal it exercised. By all accounts, these were relatively modest. Some of the most interesting recent students of American Islam have stressed its discursive potency and its ability to oppose the negative social, political, and psychological constructions that enmeshed black Americans. Ronald Judy's study of Muslim slave narratives revealed how antebellum whites privileged or emancipated literate African Muslim slaves whom they failed to reduce to the anomalous status of "Negroes." Unlike "Negroes," those shadowy artifacts of the Atlantic trade lacking humanity, personality, or origins, black Muslims appear in antebellum literature as distinct persons with genuine histories, character, and abilities, thus making them unsuitable for chattel slavery. Contemporary scholars have seen Islam as inoculating black people against assaults on their identity. For the modern psyche in the diaspora, ravaged by slavery, rejecting the badge of inferiority conveyed by the "Negro" persona and adopting instead a new religion and self could be liberating.[59]

Developments on the world stage soon corroborated this perspective. NOI member Booker Johnson recalled 1960, the year that seventeen African states became independent, as the peak era of the street speakers in Harlem. "You had Lawson, [Edward] Davis, Malcolm X and Carlos Cooks – they were the pioneers, they were the cornerstone up there on that corner at 125th and Seventh Avenue, and Chock Full O'Nuts Restaurant was their United Nations. These leaders had studied. Many of them had been incarcerated by the power structure. They knew what they wanted to do."[60] It was in this spirit that Malcolm X and others took on conventional integrationist leaders (see Figure 2).

Why did nationalists choose separatism at the very moment when it appeared that Jim Crow barriers would collapse? They had defined an agenda based on the determination that minority status in the United States is fixed and permanent, and racism indissoluble. Separatist organizations saw segregation as a reality that drew black people together, while integration dispersed them. Segregation meant organizing an independent group life "in the belly of the beast," creating rules for living and defining social and cultural practices that promote physical and mental health, and mounting an oppositional political culture. It meant reaffirming both personal and collective histories and identities. Only from

59 Ronald A. T. Judy, *(Dis)Forming the American Canon: African-Arabic Slave Narratives and the Vernacular* (Minneapolis: University of Minnesota Press, 1993).
60 Rosemari Mealy, *Fidel and Malcolm X, Memories of a Meeting* (Melbourne: Ocean Press, 1993), 29.

HUGE 6-HOUR OUTDOOR

HARLEM FREEDOM RALLY

SEVENTH AVENUE and 125th STREET
"HARLEM SQUARE"

Saturday, May 13th, 1961

1 P.M. to 7 P.M.

MIN. MALCOLM X.

To: RALPH BUNCHE, THURGOOD MARSHALL, ROY WILKINS, MARTIN LUTHER KING and GARDNER C. TAYLOR:

"You parrot the white man's false charges against Mr. Muhammad!! You are invited to this Harlem Freedom Rally as our guests so you can prove Mr. Muhammad is wrong and that you, not he, speak for the Black Masses!!!"

Principal Speaker:

MUSLIM MINISTER MALCOLM X

All Harlem Leaders Invited

Surprise Guests - Free Entertainment - Surprise Program

FOR INFORMATION:

TEMPLE No. 7 RESTAURANT -- MO 3-9772

(Meals will be served at: Temple No. 7 — 102 W. 116th St., 4th Floor)

FIGURE 2. Harlem was a major arena for black nationalist challenges to integrationist leadership. (Handbill in the NAACP Papers)

such a position of strength, they argued, could blacks restore their autonomy in their necessary negotiations with the majority society.

Integrationist leadership, white and black, did not appear to be acting on behalf of this imperative. Instead, prominent liberals seemed to work at cross-purposes from the mission of establishing black political and cultural integrity and empowerment. They made vigorous efforts to keep nationalist discourse outside the frame of debate. Kennedy-era pundit Arthur Schlesinger Jr., for example, declared in an altercation with Malcolm X that beliefs like Malcolm's were an evolutionary dead end. When Nkrumah traveled to Harlem as the prime minister of Ghana, the interracial American Committee on Africa (ACOA) tried to exclude black nationalist orator Carlos Cooks from a rally in front of the Theresa Hotel where the Ghanaian was speaking. Nkrumah crossed the street where Cooks's African National Pioneer Movement was holding a counterrally and personally invited Cooks to address the ACOA-sponsored event. Cooks arrived with his red, black, and green flag and sat on the podium with Nkrumah, Malcolm X, Adam Clayton Powell, and others. The approving crowd insisted on hearing his views.[61]

To cold war liberals, black nationalism charted a course that drifted away from the normative civil rights movement agenda, but in some respects, the drift was more apparent than real. The focus on community building engaged nationalists early on along with issues outside those usually defined as salient to black Americans. Southern-based civil rights insurgency was not far behind. It arrived independently at the concerns that black nationalists focused on directly through its own engagements with urban issues and with peace and African decolonization. In the context of white domination, however, nationalist conflicts with liberal integrationists had the overall effect of strengthening the hand of civil rights moderates, who could then promote themselves as sane alternatives to black extremism. Martin Luther King numbered among these, accepting the conventional media's antagonistic depictions of nationalist organizations. In an address to the National Bar Association, King distanced the nonviolent movement from activists whom he termed racial supremacists.[62]

It was left to ordinary black politicians in the late 1950s such as Robert Nix, Adam Clayton Powell Jr., and Charles Diggs Jr. to negotiate these seemingly disparate strands of black political thought as both separatism and acculturation, respectively, drew inspiration from such current events as the *Brown* decision, Ghanaian independence, and the Civil Rights Act of 1957. Powell, attuned to the views of his constituents, often joined Malcolm X and other nationalists in attacks on civil rights moderates. In so doing, they preceded by years similar assaults by Black Power militants.[63] Yet he and other black

[61] Michael Curtin, *Redeeming the Wasteland: Television Documentary and Cold War Politics* (New Brunswick, N.J.: Rutgers University Press, 1995), 233; "Malcolm X Rips JFK Advisor," *Pittsburgh Courier* February 4, 1961, p. 10; Robert Harris, Nyota Harris, and Grandassa Harris, eds. *Carlos Cooks and Black Nationalism from Garvey to Malcolm* (Dover, Mass: Majority Press, 1992), xx–xxi.

[62] "Address at the Thirty-fourth Annual Convention of the National Bar Association," *The Papers of Martin Luther King*, Jr., vol. 5: *Threshold of a New Decade, Jan. 1959–Dec. 1960* ed. Clayborne Carson et al., (Berkeley: University of California Press, 1992–2005), 269.

[63] Jackie Robinson's press release, Vital Information Press, December 1, 1963, folder Malcolm X and Adam Clayton Powell attack, Box 127, Bunche Papers, UCLA.

elected officials tried to link black voters' growing interest in Africa to integration and cold war foreign policy.

Black Democrats saw Eisenhower's inaction on both racial reform and developing countries as indicative of a regime out of step with current realities. Charles C. Diggs Jr., of Detroit, a member of the House Committee on Foreign Affairs, represented the United States at the All-African People's Congress in Ghana in December 1958. Americans, he declared, had failed to grasp "the tremendous import of the accelerated nationalism movement in modern Africa," and the conference itself, attended by members of women's, youth, cooperative, and trade union organizations from African and Arab states, was a "historic" first. Yet, neither the White House nor the State Department had sent greetings, reflecting their indifference. Diggs pointed out the paltry 1.5 percent of the total U.S. foreign aid package that Africa received between 1944 and 1955 and called for less reliance by policy makers on the colonial powers' views and desires. Diggs went on to chair the House Committee on Foreign Affairs subcommittee on Africa in the 1970s and proved vital in keeping African issues before Congress.[64]

Powell joined Diggs in understanding what decolonization meant for U.S. foreign policy. Powell had opposed colonialism since his political career began in the 1940s. Nationalists and Caribbean immigrants in his district had sensitized him to the question, and he remained in contact with leftists to whom he owed electoral debts. He believed his ownership of the issue could leverage him politically, so he attended the Afro-Asian Conference in Bandung, Indonesia, in 1955. Powell attempted two simultaneous feats there: muting anti-Americanism and providing the Eisenhower administration with bipartisan advice on the new states. The record hints that Powell might also have tried his hand at informal and secret negotiation with Chinese premier Chou En-lai over the release of captured U.S. airmen.

Returning home, Powell met with State Department officials and tried to convince them that Bandung had not been motivated by racism. The United States could prevent reactive hostility from non-Europeans, he suggested, by making some changes. The U.S. Foreign Service, for example, should better reflect the country's racial composition. An integrated U.S. delegation at the UN would also be helpful, as General Assembly votes on human rights tended to break down along the color line.[65] Powell endorsed antiapartheid activism

[64] Charles C. Diggs, Jr., "U.S. Policy on Africa, Indifferent – or Irresponsible?" *Africa Today* 6 (January/February 1959): 20; Paul Delaney, "Africans and Black Americans Open Conference in Washington," *New York Times*, May 26, 1972, p. 3; Randall Robinson, *Defending the Spirit: A Black Life in America* (New York: Dutton, 1998), 94–5; Donald R. Culverson, *Contesting Apartheid: U.S. Activism, 1960–1987* (Boulder, Colo.: Westview Press, 1999), 92.

[65] Cary Fraser, *Ambivalent Anti-Colonialism: The United States and the Genesis of West Indian Independence, 1940–1964* (Westport, Conn.: Greenwood Press, 1994), 72, 71; Annette T. Rubinstein et al., eds., *Vito Marcantonio: Debates, Speeches, and Writings, 1935–1960* (Clifton, N.J.: August M. Kelley, 1973), 128, 151; Plummer, *Rising Wind*, 249–53; Adam Clayton Powell in the *Congressional Record*, April 18, 1956, 6596–98. For a positive appraisal of Powell, see Roger Wilkins, *A Man's Life* (New York: Simon & Schuster, 1982), 324–5.

and attended Ghana's independence celebration. The Powell photograph archive at the Schomburg Center for the Study of Black Culture in New York attests to his ubiquitous presence at 1950s Harlem events graced by foreign notables.[66]

Such politicians were not alone in efforts to effect solidarity with African countries while coaxing U.S. officialdom to be more helpful to developing countries. African leaders themselves skillfully played on black American sensibilities. No one did so as adroitly as Nkrumah, who knew American racial politics well. He had lived in the United States for years and studied at historically black Lincoln University. Nkrumah closed the 1958 All-African People's Conference in Accra by declaring that he was "delighted to see so many people of African descent from abroad attending the conference. We take their presence here as a manifestation of their keen interest in our struggles for a free Africa. We must never forget that they are part of us. These sons and daughters of Africa were taken away from our shores and despite all the centuries which have separated us they have never forgotten their ancestral links."[67] African-American conference participants, however, like Africans living in Europe who represented cultural organizations, were "fraternal" delegates only, with no voting power. "A last-minute ruling by the Steering Committee," Mercer Cook reported, "reduced fraternal delegates to the status of mere observers."[68] Only contingents from African trade unions and political parties had decision-making roles. A delegation representing all U.S. blacks would have been problematic in any case, given ideological differences among African Americans ranging from Republican conservatism to Communism and various forms of nationalism. Diggs described himself as "an observer for the U.S. government."[69]

All, however, were collectively welcome to join a celebration in Accra called Africa Freedom Day. This April 15 holiday enjoyed worldwide commemoration in 1959, with festivities held in a number of African countries and in New York, Paris, London, and Chicago. At New York City's first celebration, Kenyan politician Tom Mboya addressed an appreciative crowd of three thousand at Carnegie Hall. Nigerian musician Olatunji and African-American trade unionist A. Philip Randolph also took the stage. Audience members included civil rights leader Daisy Bates, baseball star Jackie Robinson, and former First Lady Eleanor Roosevelt.[70]

[66] James H. Meriwether, *Proudly We Can Be Africans: Black America and Africa, 1935–1961* (Chapel Hill: University of North Carolina Press, 2002), 160; the Adam Clayton Powell, Jr. Portrait Collection, SC, and his appearance in the portrait collections of many of his contemporaries.

[67] Nkrumah's closing remarks at the All-Africa People's Conference, December 1, 1958, quoted in Nesbitt, *Race for Sanctions*, 35.

[68] Mercer Cook, "The New Africa Charts Its Course…but the 'Strategy' of the Africans Remains Unclear," *AMSAC Newsletter* 2 supplement #2 n.d., 1959, p. 6, 2.

[69] Diggs, "U.S. Policy on Africa, Indifferent – or Irresponsible?" 20; *Washington Herald*, November 30, 1958, p. A20, TCF.

[70] "Africa Speaks at Carnegie Hall," *Africa Today* 6 (May–June 1959): 17, 19.

While Africa Freedom Day was a joyous occasion, it illustrated some of the limitations of Pan-African politics, which was becoming an affair of nation-states. Those in the diaspora could affirm and celebrate African independence, but their own political status in relation to it was ambiguous. African governments often perceived diaspora constituents as cheerleaders whose bond with the continent was based on a shared history of exploitation that was more racial than cultural. Yet implicit in the African agenda of African Americans was the hope that a renewed and strengthened Africa could help ameliorate the condition of black people in the United States.

The possibility that the diaspora and African states might have divergent interests seemed a faint cloud on the horizon in 1959 when both nationalist and integrationist dreams seemed on the verge of fulfillment. The year 1959 was one of great expectancy, according to writer Thulani Davis in her novel of the same name. The world was changing. The Baltimore *Afro-American* in January polled black luminaries on their predictions for the year. NAACP leader Roy Wilkins looked forward to a limit on anti–civil rights filibustering in the Senate. Horace Mann Bond, then dean of Atlanta University's School of Education, and Baptist lay leader Nannie Burroughs gloomily forecasted more racial tension and little progress, but others were more upbeat. NAACP board chair Channing Tobias anticipated breakthroughs in employment, and Morehouse College president Benjamin Mays predicted that "the South will run out of tricks."[71] Formal segregation did grow steadily untenable, as did a foreign policy that ignored the global majority outside Europe and weakened U.S. influence in much of the world. America's once-isolated subcultures began to enter the mainstream. Racism, under attack in its remaining foreign and domestic redoubts, seemed doomed as the determinant of Americans' life chances.

In the midst of this optimism, Martin Luther King Jr. corresponded with an Angolan student, Deolinda Rodrigues Francisco de Almeida. Fearful that a new extradition treaty between Brazil and Portugal would lead to her deportation from Sao Paulo, Brazil, where she had been living, Rodrigues briefly attended Drew University and then departed in 1962 to serve as the director of the Volunteer Corps for Refugee Assistance in Leopoldville, Congo. King advised Rodrigues that Angolans should create a leader or leaders to "stand as a symbol for your independence movement. As soon as your symbol is set up," King counseled, "it is not difficult to get people to follow, and the more the oppressor seeks to stop and defeat the symbol, the more it solidifies the movement." He sent her a copy of his book, *Stride toward Freedom*. King's recommendation reflects the model of insurgency prevalent at the time: he suggested a leader-centered movement based on the recouping of rights, a strategy that had partial success in the U.S. South and would, he hoped, produce results

---

[71] Thulani Davis, *1959* (New York: Grove Press, 2001); "'South Will Run Out of Tricks,' – Benjamin Mays," Baltimore *Afro-American*, January 3, 1959, p. 5.

against apartheid and colonialism. Rodrigues, back in Angola, was murdered by counterrevolutionaries in 1967.[72]

The Democratic presidential campaign in 1960 exploited the restlessness that pervaded the country as the 1950s neared their end. Deep structural forces were undermining the era's cultural conservatism, and in retrospect, the political certainties of the time seem more apparent than real. Current events added to the disquiet – restlessness among minorities and economic recession at home, the resurgence of anti-Americanism in Latin America, renewed Pan-Arabism, and the USSR's successful launching of the *Sputnik* satellite all diminished any sense of complacency lingering from earlier years.[73]

There were also stirrings on the Right. The most conservative Republicans had never wholly approved of the grandfatherly Dwight D. Eisenhower. They perceived Ike as insufficiently confrontational with the Soviets, while his secretary of state, John Foster Dulles, could not comfortably separate Communism, nationalism, and neutralism in his own thinking. The administration failed to support the Europeans when they confronted Nasser over control of the Suez Canal and remained ambivalent on Algeria until it became clear that French policy meant trouble for the United States. Eisenhower refused to go along with conservative legislators on right-to-work laws, and his decision to send federal troops to Little Rock had not endeared him to segregationists. The president served two terms and retained his personal popularity, but some eight million voters abandoned the Republican Party between 1954 and 1958. Between 1958 and 1968, the party prevailed in congressional contests only in the Midwest.[74]

Many blacks numbered among GOP defectors. Only twenty years separated the 1936 presidential election that marked the African-American turn toward the Democratic Party and Eisenhower's reelection in 1956. Much black support for the Democrats during that twenty-year period had focused on Franklin D. Roosevelt rather than the party as a whole. There was no reason to expect the realignment to be permanent, especially as Dixiecrats still dominated the South, held senior positions on major congressional committees, and blocked legislative change on civil rights. That the Republicans could woo black voters back to the party of Lincoln remained a possibility. In order to do so, however, they would have to solve the same problem that Democrats did: reconcile racial reform with conservative demands to hold the line on integration.[75]

[72] Martin Luther King to Deolinda Rodrigues, July 21, 1959, December 21, 1959, pp. 345–6; Rodrigues to King, November 28, 1959, p. 346 n, 250–1, 250 n.1 in *King Papers*.

[73] Brennan, *Turning Right in the Sixties*, 25–7.

[74] Egya N. Sangmuah, "Eisenhower and Containment in North Africa, 1956–1960," *The Middle East Journal* 44 (1) (Winter 1990): 80–1; Brennan, *Turning Right in the Sixties*, 21–4.

[75] On the political history of this period, see Nancy Weiss, *Farewell to the Party of Lincoln: Black Politics in the Age of FDR* (Princeton, N.J.: Princeton University Press, 1983); Ralph J. Bunche, *The Political Status of the Negro in the Age of FDR*, ed. Dewey Grantham (Chicago: University of Chicago Press, 1973).

The Eisenhower administration halfheartedly reached out to the black electorate by supporting minor civil rights laws and appointing a handful of African-American officeholders, who were kept on the margins of decision making. The disappointed E. Frederick Morrow, hired as a race relations aide, later claimed that the White House had lost its opportunity to influence the direction of the black freedom struggle. Its dereliction resulted, he believed, in the discrediting of traditional black leadership and the strengthening of radical voices. A 1958 meeting of prominent black citizens with Eisenhower organized by A. Philip Randolph came to naught because of official indifference. A white race relations adviser on Eisenhower's staff later recalled that Morrow had had trouble because he was not qualified to do anything most White House staffers needed.[76] This, of course, raises the question why they chose him in the first place. Since the collapse of Reconstruction, the GOP kept some blacks in the fold as window dressing and through the distribution of petty patronage, but few party leaders had ideas for creating a more productive relationship.

Ike's stalwartly anticommunist vice president, Richard M. Nixon, proved more resilient. Nixon briefly enrolled in the Los Angeles chapter of the NAACP. He endorsed moderate civil rights reform and anticipated the independence of the sub-Saharan states by lobbying for a more visible U.S. presence in Africa.[77] Although often perceived as tense and rigid during his presidential years, Nixon in the late 1950s strove for a different image. Ethel Payne, Washington Bureau chief for the *Chicago Defender*, once casually invited him to a party. She was stunned when he actually showed up with Pat Nixon and a bottle of 119-proof whiskey in his coat pocket.[78] The vice president journeyed to Ghana's independence celebration and linked support for its aspirations to the quest for cold war allies (see Figure 3) "We cannot talk equality to the peoples of Africa and Asia and practice inequality in the United States," Nixon declared. He pressed for the creation of a Bureau of African Affairs in the State Department. After the Sharpeville massacre, the Eisenhower administration issued a condemnation of South Africa. If, as one historian has suggested, Nixon designed these stances to target black voters in 1960, he did not return to these positions in subsequent years as president of the United States. Adlai Stevenson described Nixon's interest in Africa as shallow. During the Ghana independence celebration, he told journalist C. L. Sulzberger, "All Nixon seemed to do was rush

[76] E. Frederick Morrow interviewed by Ed Edwin, New York City, January 31, 1968, p. 36, 46, 48, Columbia University Center for Oral History. See also Morrow's brother's account of his own ambassadorship to Guinea during the Eisenhower years, John H. Morrow, *First American Ambassador to Guinea* (New Brunswick, N.J.: Rutgers University Press, 1968); Maxwell Rabb interviewed by Steven Lawson, New York City, October 6, 1970, pp. 17–18, Columbia University Center for Oral History.

[77] Rabb interview, pp. 33, 34–7; A. M. Rivera, Jr., "Nixon Reiterates His Concern for Africans," *Pittsburgh Courier*, March 9, 1957, p. 2.

[78] Ethel L. Payne interviewed by Kathleen Currie, October 13, 1987, Washington, D.C., Washington Press Club Foundation interviews, online at http://npc.press.org/wpforal/payn6.htm, accessed February 15, 2005.

around shaking hands and kissing babies. Nixon saw one African official who was educated in America at Lincoln College. Nixon did not know this and was deceived by the fact that the man was wearing native costume, a very scanty affair." When the African informed Nixon that Stevenson had visited a few years ago, "Nixon replied in fine pidgin: 'Him Democrat, me Republican.'"[79]

Democrats, meanwhile, positioned themselves to benefit from Republican lethargy on race and colonialism. Algeria was a test case. The U.S. consul in Algiers answered to the Bureau of European Affairs. The Africa Bureau, created in 1958, handled other North African matters, including those involving Algeria's near neighbors, Tunisia, Morocco, and Libya. The bureaus differed in their support for Algerian independence, with European Affairs taking a procolonial position. The United States did not recognize the provisional revolutionary Algerian government and, because of French pressure, declined, after a brief overture, to receive its delegates formally.

The government nevertheless continued unofficial contacts with the National Liberation Front (FLN). through the CIA so as to dissuade the rebels from moving into the Moscow camp. While it kept a suspicious France abreast of communications with the Algerians, the Quai d'Orsay continued to believe that the Americans simply awaited a chance at hegemony in North Africa. When the Fourth Republic collapsed in May 1958 and Charles De Gaulle returned to power, Eisenhower and Secretary of State John Foster Dulles deferred to him, hoping that he could end the Algerian crisis. By spring 1959 U.S. officials had stopped talking to the FLN. The UN delegation, ordered to shore up De Gaulle, sat out votes critical of France, whose cooperation the United States wanted in European security matters.[80]

The Algerian problem became an American one because it tied the United States to an outmoded imperial concept and forced it to increase its NATO defense burden, as France had committed most of its troops to Africa. Anti-French sentiment in North Africa could easily become anti-Americanism, but if Washington played its cards right, it could open the region to enhanced U.S. influence. A tentative effort was made when the AFL-CIO sent operative Irving Brown to Algeria. Brown had helped build centrist unions in France during the early years of the cold war with the support of the CIA. His International Free Trade Unions Conference (IFTUC) made little headway in organizing North African workers before his expulsion. Robert Lacoste, the French minister resident in Algeria, dryly observed "that the

---

[79] Ethel L. Payne, "'Bias Perils U.S.,' Nixon Warns," *Chicago Defender*, April 13, 1957, p. 1; Thomas J. Noer, "New Frontiers and Old Priorities in Africa," in *Kennedy's Quest for Victory: American Foreign Policy, 1961–1963* ed. Thomas. G. Paterson (New York: Oxford University Press, 1989): 255, 256; Cyrus L. Sulzberger, The *Last of the Giants* (New York: Macmillan, 1970), 409.

[80] Jeffrey A. Lefebvre, "Kennedy's Algerian Dilemma: Containment, Alliance Politics and the 'Rebel Dialogue,'" *Middle Eastern Studies* 35 (2) (1999): 62–4; Lacoste quoted in Irwin M. Wall, *France, the United States, and the Algerian War* (Berkeley: University of California Press, 2001), 186.

FIGURE 3. Pat and Richard Nixon, shown with Ghanaian Finance Minister Komla A. Gbedemah (right) at Ghana's independence celebration. (National Archives)

IFTUC would do better to concern itself with the plight of blacks in the American South."[81]

But French repression in North Africa also depended on a racialist discourse, one that discounted the nation-building capacities of Algerians. De Gaulle did not think that the rebel colony would ever become genuinely independent, regardless of formal political sovereignty. He denied that any great Arab civilization had ever existed. What Arabs knew, he declared, they had learned from Christian slaves. As a group, they were "anarchic," headstrong, and emotional. Former secretary of state Dean Acheson, then advising Kennedy, agreed. "If France and all Frenchmen were pulled out [of Algeria] tomorrow," he remarked, "[their] departure would reveal all the more starkly to the Arabs their two implacable enemies,... their own incredible fecundity and the desert."[82]

Students of imperialism have noted the frequency with which Western leaders attributed sexualized traits to dominated peoples in Africa, Asia, and Latin

---

[81] Sangmuah, "Eisenhower and Containment in North Africa," 80–1; Wall, *France, the United States, and the Algerian War*, 4, 5, 16, 32, 81, 125, 135, 147–8.

[82] Matthew Connelly, "Taking Off the Cold War Lens: Visions of North-South Conflict during the Algerian War for Independence," *American Historical Review* 105 (3) (2000): 744, 769; Sulzberger, *The Last of the Giants*, 72, 73; Dean Acheson, *Power and Diplomacy* (New York: Atheneum, 1962), 126.

America. Policy makers might speak of subject and dependent territories as female.[83] Opinions about the putative sexual habits and fertility of colonial populations also formed part of this discourse. President Franklin D. Roosevelt, for example, had joked about the high birth rate in Puerto Rico. "I guess the only solution is to use the methods which Hitler used effectively," FDR remarked. "It is all very simple and painless – you have people pass through a narrow passage and then there is the brrrrr of an electrical apparatus. They are there for twenty seconds and from then on they are sterile." In discussing the "race problem" in Panama with Charles Taussig, chair of the wartime Anglo-American Caribbean Commission, the president ascribed great virility to the country's West Indian immigrants. "Each Jamaican man slept with three women every week," he quipped. Taussig told Roosevelt that "he did the Jamaicans an injustice; that sleeping with only three women in a week was a sign of impotence."[84] The suggestion of unbridled sexuality joined a fascination with nonwhite breeders whose fertility could overrun the West. Acheson's reference to the Arab birth rate resonates in the context of the era's growing preoccupation with the "population explosion" and the view that the "safety valve" of emigration could channel discontent.

Algeria's French governor-general thought that remittances from Algerians working in France would raise the colonial standard of living, Westernize the immigrants' value systems, and neutralize both conflict and the desire for independence. U.S. officials entertained similar ideas about Puerto Ricans, and the Colonial Office about British West Indians. The immigration of hundreds of thousands of colonial subjects to their "mother countries" during the 1950s underscored the belief that such movement would relieve political unrest. This, combined with the economic benefits of the money immigrants sent home, and the need for labor during a period of rising affluence and growth in the metropoles, would thus kill multiple birds with one stone.[85] Racism nevertheless threatened to subvert this project for France. "To the extent that the French succeeded in representing their struggle as a race war or jihad," Irwin Wall has commented, "they hurt themselves more than the Algerians. The image of an

---

[83] V. Spike Peterson, "Feminist Theories within, Invisible to, and beyond IR," *Brown Journal of World Affairs* 10 (2) (Winter/Spring 2004): 35–46; Charlotte Hooper, "Masculinist Practices and Gender Politics: The Operation of Multiple Masculinities in International Relations," in *The "Man" Question in International Relations*, eds. Marysia Zalewski and Jane Parpart (Boulder, Colo: Westview Press, 1998), 14–27; Ann Laura Stoler, *Race and the Education of Desire: Foucault's History of Sexuality and the Colonial Order of Things* (Durham, N.C.: Duke University Press, 1995).

[84] Roosevelt and Taussig quoted in William Roger Louis, *Imperialism at Bay, 1941–1945: The United States and the Decolonization of the British Empire* (Oxford: Clarendon Press, 1977), 486–7, n. 26.

[85] Thomas H. Lockett to the Department of State, February 27, 1952, *FRUS, 1951*, X, *The Near East and Africa* (Washington, D.C.: Government Printing Office, 1982), 385, 387, General Lewis Clark to the Department of State, May 19, 1964, ibid., 39; Connelly, "Taking Off the Cold War Lens," 748; Howard Winant, *The World Is a Ghetto* (New York: Basic Books, 2001), 261–3.

anarchic and implacably anti-Western Algeria – ever present in Western perceptions – only undermined their argument that it could be pacified, prosperous and remain an integral part of France."[86]

Excluded from diplomatic recognition by the Western powers, representatives of the Algerian provisional revolutionary government pressed their case before the United Nations. They mounted a major public relations campaign to win the approval of UN delegates. The revolutionists held quiet talks with oil company executives and cultivated a variety of opinion makers. French intelligence agents early in December 1958 covered a meeting on Algeria sponsored by ACOA and the Carnegie Endowment for International Peace at the New School for Social Research in New York City. The Algerians received good press in U.S. newspapers and engaged in successful fund-raising. They addressed academic audiences and NGOs, including black nationalist groups that tied the Algerian struggle to the broader colonial issue.[87]

Democrats made Algeria a central concern. Chester Bowles, in 1959 a freshman representative from Connecticut, was appointed to the House Foreign Affairs Committee. Bowles was formerly ambassador to India, where he made his opposition to racial discrimination and colonialism known. He published *The Coming Political Breakthrough* (1959), in which he called for "a broader, less doctrinaire approach to foreign policy than was actually in effect." He scheduled a successful two-day Washington conference for media on international relations, followed by regional meetings in Chicago, Denver, Cleveland, and Louisville, to which the press and opinion leaders were invited.[88]

Liberal Democrats coupled their stance on racial and colonial questions with a more visibly aggressive posture toward the Soviets. Presidential contender Senator John F. Kennedy articulated it forcefully in extended comments on premier Nikita S. Khrushchev's U.S. visit. Kennedy warned citizens against relaxing their anticommunist vigilance, in spite of their desire for peace. His own talk with Khrushchev persuaded him of how tough an adversary he was. Talk is cheap, he noted, and Khrushchev had not made any concessions on Berlin or other outstanding issues. No one should be deceived: the differences between the Soviet and American systems were fundamental and ineradicable, and "the real roots of the Soviet-American conflict cannot be easily settled by negotiations." Kennedy nevertheless maintained that the two states had some common interests, including a mutual fear of nuclear war and consequent environmental catastrophe, a recognition that the arms race limited what nations could achieve outside the military sphere, joint opposition to nuclear proliferation, and a desire to benefit from the useful economic and cultural exchanges

---

[86] Wall, *France, the United States, and the Algerian War*, 258.

[87] Marvin Evans, *Algeria: France's Undeclared War* (New York: Oxford University Press, 2012), 139–40; Nashville *Globe*, August 16, 1957, TCF, reel 160.

[88] Chester Bowles, *Promises to Keep: My Years in Public Life, 1941–1969* (New York: Harper & Row, 1971), 286–7, 350.

that peace would make possible. Entente on these concerns would not end the
cold war but would keep the temperature low.[89]

Kennedy repeated his cautionary counsel at a New York dinner in memory
of 1928's Democratic candidate, the Roman Catholic Al Smith. Smith became
the foil for Kennedy to advance his candidacy as a Catholic and as a putative
invigorator of a nation grown effete. Kennedy described Al Smith as a stal-
wart populist who made good without losing sight of his roots. His leadership,
Kennedy suggested, was just the kind that present circumstances required. A
nation gone soft and corrupt needed conscientious, disciplined leadership.

Kennedy delivered a jeremiad, noting "the slow corrosion of luxury, the
slow erosion of our courage." He cited growing drug use, criminality, and problematic youth. The Selective Service System currently rejected almost half of
potential conscripts. Reviving old fears about U.S. military readiness, Kennedy
asserted that troop quality had declined since World War II, and that almost a
third of the U.S. POWs during the Korean War collaborated with the enemy.
The truth of this statement took a back seat to Kennedy's desire to toughen up
the body politic. The United States had to prove to the world that the American
way was the true revolutionary path. Citizens must accept the "discipline, sacrifice, and vitality" needed to do so.[90]

As the youngest presidential candidate, Kennedy made an advantage out of
what some considered a liability. In a speech defending his campaign against
former President Harry S. Truman's accusation that his backers were pressuring
delegates, Kennedy insinuated that Truman was an elderly relic. "This is still a
young country, founded by young men 184 years ago today and it is still young
in heart, youthful in spirit and blessed with new young leaders in both parties,
in both houses of Congress and governors' chairs throughout the country."[91] In
one sentence, Kennedy managed to repeat the word "young" and its cognates
no fewer than five times. The activism of young people, later deplored as rifts
in U.S. society became more visible, lay rooted in the call to arms of one of the
most prominent members of the political establishment.

Following Kennedy's victory, the black scholar L. D. Reddick hailed what he
saw as a new era of accessibility. Intellectuals and creative people were no longer persona non grata in government circles, he enthused. Playwright Arthur
Miller, for example, was expressly invited to Kennedy's inauguration. Miller
had not been summoned to a Washington function since being subpoenaed
as a possible subversive by a congressional committee years before. Reddick
attributed the Democratic triumph to "the votes of the cities, labor, the liberals

---

[89] Remarks of Senator John F. Kennedy on Nikita Khrushchev's visit to the United States. National
Kennedy for President Clubs press release, n.d., John F. Kennedy Pre-presidential Papers, 1946–
1960; Senate Files; Speeches and the Press, John F. Kennedy Presidential Library, Boston.

[90] Kennedy quoted in Robert D. Dean, *Imperial Brotherhood: Gender and the Making of Cold
War Foreign Policy* (Amherst: University of Massachusetts Press, 2001), 169, 170.

[91] "Transcript of Senator Kennedy's News Conference Replying to Truman Attack," *New York
Times*, July 5, 1960, p. 20.

and the minorities" and looked forward to "a progressive redirection of both foreign and domestic policy" by a government he viewed as a "coalition."[92]

Washington's African policy had already begun changing, Reddick noted, with Eisenhower somewhat more hospitable toward African visitors and a more upbeat set of administrators in African Affairs at the State Department. In a speech at historically black Coppin State Teachers College in Baltimore, Reddick made a pitch for more minority representation in the Foreign Service and on the staffs of major newspapers and magazines. Africans had assured him that black Americans would make effective liaisons between the newly independent countries and the United States. He also called for government to allot historically black colleges and universities their fair share of federal contracts related to foreign aid and African education. The "Negro colleges," he reminded his audience, "trained both Nkrumah and [Nigerian leader Nnamdi] Azikiwe," but African studies at such institutions received just 2 percent of all moneys disbursed for the purpose.[93]

Whatever the promise of improved relations with Africa, Kennedy faced the task of uniting two disparate wings of his party. The standard approach, the "southern strategy," had been to court the South, where most black voters were disenfranchised, by avoiding the issue of racial justice and implying sympathy for the white supremacist goals of Dixiecrats. The size of northern African-American electorates and their position as swing voters made this tactic harder to pull off. Democrat Adam Clayton Powell Jr. had endorsed Eisenhower in 1956 in reaction to Adlai Stevenson's use of the "southern strategy." In 1960, he had refused to support Kennedy until late in the campaign, and only after Kennedy made certain promises.

The candidate found that he could appeal to black voters in ways that recalled Franklin D. Roosevelt's use of symbolic gestures, such as the "Black Cabinet" of informal advisers. Kennedy made Powell, newly appointed to the House Education and Labor Committee, his personal adviser on urban affairs, and the Democratic National Committee now boasted an Urban Affairs Subcommittee. He also agreed to support the *Brown* decision and undertake vaguely delineated civil rights initiatives if elected.[94] These pledges did not affect events in those states where racial disparities and racial violence remained starkest. They did, however, give greater visibility to northern cities, with their aging infrastructure and progressively indigent populations.

Symbolic gestures continued with an African policy that matched the Democrats' determination proactively to oppose communist penetration of the Third World with their desire to retain black voter loyalty, as Democrats in 1960 could not consider the black electorate "a cat in the bag." The historic

[92] Reddick, "Africa, the Confederate Myth and the New Frontier," 2.
[93] Ibid., 4–8.
[94] Geoffrey Pond, "Powell May Back Johnson in Race," June 26, 1960, p. 45; "Harlem Leader Talks to Kennedy," July 7, 1960, p. 18, Raymond Robinson, "Powell to Back Kennedy Ticket," September 20, 1960, p. 42, *New York Times*; Lee A. Daniels, "The Political Career of Adam Clayton Powell, Paradigm and Paradox," *Journal of Black Studies* 4 (December 1973): 124–5.

African-American realignment with the Democratic Party in 1936 held constant only in presidential elections. After Roosevelt's death, it correlated with the closeness of electoral outcomes. A Democratic president could avoid antagonizing the Dixiecrats by attending to areas of race relations less threatening than civil rights law enforcement. Kennedy's wooing of African leaders thus provided opportunities to achieve two simultaneous goals: he could show an interest in emerging states that would help secure their allegiance to the West and appease African-American voters without directly challenging entrenched white supremacists.[95]

In the mid-twentieth century the U.S. interpretation of black grievances as entirely domestic stymied activist efforts to develop a holistic approach to racial justice. The official perspective reduced the available vocabulary with which minority communities could contest brutality and insist on accountability from public authorities. A breakthrough occurred when decolonization and the "cold war imperative" opened a window of opportunity that eventually closed, but not before important advances in rethinking African-American potential were made.

Sputnik signaled the desire for transformation during this period, even when particular constituencies had not decided what their specific objectives were. Elites both black and white were still not wholly committed to civic equality. Large segments of the clergy remained conflicted about a civil rights movement that claimed black Christianity as foundational even as they jockeyed for position in its ranks. Varying liberal and conservative prescriptions for modernization left racial hierarchies intact, and to the extent that national security took priority, reformers hardly altered the system. The integration of the armed forces, a legacy of the Truman period; the *Brown* decision; and the sending of troops to Little Rock, Arkansas, in 1957 constituted the major cold war–driven efforts in the 1950s to align U.S. social practice with its democratic rhetoric. Yet for the most part, the superpower conflict provided an excuse to leave Jim Crow intact. Symbolic politics, such as practiced by Kennedy as the new decade began, was intended to bridge the gap between talk and action. Speeches, formal dinners for African presidents, encouragement of politically minded youths, and highly touted appointments of blacks as envoys disguised the superficiality of the changes. The great powers faced a mighty dilemma in accommodating the democratic aspirations of minorities in the developed nation-states and majorities in emerging countries, while keeping customary structures of domination intact.

African-American enthusiasm for nationalist projects had historically waxed and waned in response to events in the United States. In the late 1950s, civil

---

[95] Ronald W. Walters, *Black Presidential Politics in America: A Strategic Approach* (Albany: State University of New York Press, 1988), 37. Yet overall Walters discounts the independence of the black "swing vote." Richard D. Mahoney, *JFK: Ordeal in Africa* (New York: Oxford University Press, 1983), 30, 31; Cary Fraser, "Understanding American Policy toward the Decolonization of European Empires, 1945–64," *Diplomacy & Statecraft* 3 (1) (1992): 112.

rights insurgency, especially in the South, and elite and institutional endorsement of integration led to the temporary eclipse of nationalism. According to a venerable African-American proverb, however, "Every shut eye ain't sleep and every goodbye ain't gone." Nationalism expressed itself beneath the surface of liberal complacency among those for whom integration had little tangible worth. It remained vital in Harlem, where a profound cynicism about the pretensions of liberalism thrived. It did not emerge at the end of the civil rights era but instead accompanied it, mounting insistent critiques of movement pieties. Ideas earlier proposed by Garveyites took on new life as African independence advanced from the abstract and utopian to the actual. These did not spring full-blown from dissatisfaction with liberalism but existed in embryo all during the period of the freedom movement's successes.

Black nationalism helped construct the cultural and political relationships that diaspora peoples enjoyed with Africa, but ambivalence shadowed the diaspora in a world community dominated by the sovereign states in which they lived. As "creolized" minorities in the West, diaspora populations had often played missionary to Africa, but notions of stewardship grew obsolete in an age of independence and advances in education. The mind-set of Baptist ministers serving as brokers and evangelists at home would be equally displaced abroad. Socially and culturally, African Americans shared with other Americans a fitful if inchoate desire for change in the late 1950s. The country was on the cusp of a new era, but if its aspirations presented new opportunities, they also posed problems that many did not anticipate and were at a loss to resolve.

2

Peace or a Sword?

If many Capahosic participants had ties to an older, traditional GOP and retained a quid pro quo approach to politics, more internationally minded Republicans began to rival Democrats in looking outward at a global environment in transition. They looked for counsel to such figures as Harvard professor Henry Kissinger, for whom Urban League director Lester Granger wrote a policy paper during the Eisenhower years. Kissinger had directed a seminar focused on the status of the United States in the world. Granger's contribution, "The Racial Factor in International Relations," advocated decolonization and racial reform. Granger used conventional cold war arguments to suggest approaches for improving the United States' image. He called for a coherent State Department program for foreign visitors of color and recommended removing materials in United States Information Agency (USIA) libraries that denigrated African Americans. Granger placed considerable emphasis on propaganda work, including "good will missions," foreign aid, and the integration of the Foreign Service.[1]

In line with the Urban League's focus on placing minority candidates in jobs, his recommendations leaned heavily on the appointment of "American Negroes of high qualification" for overseas posts. He expressed skepticism, however, about sending popular black entertainers on foreign tours. Granger "seriously questioned," for instance, whether having jazz trumpeter Louis Armstrong play before a "shouting, swaying, rocking and rolling Gold Coast audience," advanced the best interests of the United States. Instead of Satchmo's sweaty vulgarity, the punctilious Granger believed, "skillful, well-trained and highly intelligent" blacks would be far more appropriate representatives. The Urban League director's disdain for such authentic expressions of African-American culture as jazz was not rare at the time.[2]

---

[1] Lester B. Granger, "The Racial Factor in Our International Relations" and J. I. Coffey to Henry Kissinger, August 1957, Special Studies Project Collection, Rockefeller Brothers Fund, RAC.
[2] Granger, "The Racial Factor in Our International Relations," 8–18, 21–4, 28, 14.

In spite of this conservatism, one of Kissinger's aides objected to what he considered Granger's strong language, suggesting that reference to "neo-fascists" in South Africa be omitted from the paper and that language critical of the State Department be revised. The man worried that Granger's proposal to have the Foreign Service reflect the actual U.S. population would "result in a serious drain upon the relative small pool of trained Negro manpower in this country."[3]

Kissinger himself praised Granger's analysis. He wondered whether Granger's conclusions simply called for "making the best of a bad situation." "If so," Kissinger mused, "I would think that we would gain from having a paragraph or two in your paper to the effect that while the U.S. has much of which to be proud in its handling of racial problems, it equally has much still to do. It would then follow that the suggestions which you make are addressed to the manner and method of presenting our case rather than to the substance of the issue itself, which in the long run is the only sure way of improving attitudes abroad."[4] The White House and the State Department thereafter followed this advice. They did not have to solve the U.S. racial crisis; they only had to manage the way the world perceived it. The permanence of racism was implied.

There were alternatives to this formula, although Kissinger might disapprove of efforts actually to solve the American dilemma. Recruiting African Americans into the Foreign Service would help the world see the United States as a diverse society, but by the time that Granger wrote his paper, Americans of African descent were already involved in an array of international activities and were often seen as representative of their country. The talent that Granger sought was already in the field.

The activist William Sutherland provides an example. Sutherland met some of Granger's criteria but not others. A Bates College graduate, he had a "direct connection" with Africa. "On my father's side, there was an old patriarch named Scipio Vaughan. And he had been a slave," Sutherland told an interviewer. As Vaughn lay dying, he instructed his sons "to go back to Africa, to where he came from. And he told them where he came from.... And these two sons went back to Nigeria, but they always kept up a correspondence with the family." As a result, Sutherland numbered among the few African Americans able to trace their genealogy and attend family reunions in Africa. His extended family spanned three continents and included Nigerian jurists, Scots and Britons, and such prominent black American figures as Jewel Lafontant and Mabel Smythe both of whom became U.S. ambassadors.[5]

[3] J. I. Coffey to Henry Kissinger, August 2, 1957; Coffey to Lester B. Granger, February 11, 1957, Rockefeller Brothers Fund Special Studies Project Collection, RAC.

[4] Henry A. Kissinger to Lester B. Granger, August 3, 1957, ibid.

[5] Sutherland interviewed by Prexy Nesbitt and Mimi Edmunds, New York City, July 19, 2003, *No Easy Victories* interviews, online at http://www.noeasyvictories.org/interviews/into1_sutherland.php, accessed June 2, 2011; Era Bell Thompson, "The Vaughn Family: A Tale of Two Continents," *Ebony*, February 1975, pp. 53–9, 62–3. For Mabel Smythe, see below.

Sutherland had turned out to be another kind of ambassador. Drawn to pacifism from an early age, he refused induction during World War II and spent four years at Lewisburg Federal Prison, where he established lasting friendships with fellow pacifist inmates Dave Dellinger and Ralph diGia. Sutherland led a sit-down strike at Lewisburg over its segregated eating facilities. After the war ended, he began working in the antiapartheid movement and planned a trip to Nigeria to see African family members and work with Nigerian nationalist leader Nnamdi Azikiwe on the *West African Pilot* newspaper. Pegged as a subversive during the early cold war, when colonialism and McCarthyism hampered both civil rights insurgency and African nationalism, Sutherland was denied entry to the still-colonized Nigeria by British authorities. In 1953 he went instead to the Gold Coast, a colony that had achieved a measure of self-rule although it had not yet debuted as sovereign Ghana.[6] While in Africa, Sutherland would play a major role in efforts to make nonviolent direct action the way to effect colonial independence.

As for Granger and Kissinger, American planners for the 1958 Brussels World's Fair went to work implementing their prescription for U.S. race relations, treating reform as a work in progress. As Michael Krenn has shown, the U.S. pavilion featured an exhibit called "Unfinished Business," meant to cast an optimistic spotlight on black and white conflict and seeking to undo the damage caused by the Little Rock crisis of the previous year. "Coping with domestic racial problems and promoting the international prestige of the United States became … increasingly related activities during the Eisenhower years," Krenn notes, "as it became painfully obvious that America's problematic race relations were having a negative impact on U.S. diplomacy."[7]

Foreigners clearly observed the tension between U.S. practice and U.S. pretensions. Germans, for example, had noted military segregation during the occupation years and the contradiction between Americans as debunkers of Nazi ideology and their almost reflexive racism. By the mid-1950s, however, U.S. officials were expected to pay lip service to antiracist ideals. Occupation authorities then issued propaganda that foreshadowed Kissinger's recommendation. The United States would now acknowledge the imperfections of its democracy in the present in the interests of promoting democracy in the future. A few years later, however, the State Department was removing books by black authors deemed controversial from the shelves of its information libraries in Europe, and when Supreme Court Justice Earl Warren

---

[6] Sutherland interview; transcript of "The Good War and Those Who Refused to Fight It," (Paradigm Productions, 2000), online at www.pbs.org/itvs/thegoodwar/GW_transcript.pdf, accessed June 6, 2011.

[7] Michael L. Krenn, "'Unfinished Business': Segregation and U.S. Diplomacy at the 1958 World's Fair," *Diplomatic History* 20 (Fall 1996): 591. See also Kenneth W. Heger, "Race Relations in the United States and American Cultural and Informational Programs in Ghana, 1957–1966," *Prologue* 31 (Winter 1999), online at www.archives.gov/publications/prologue/1999/winter/us-and-ghana-1957–1966–1.html, accessed June 6, 2011.

visited Germany in 1959 he refused to talk about the *Brown* decision or other contested issues.[8]

At the same time, opinion makers in and out of government began to accept the idea that colonialism and racism were outmoded. Even the Belgians had to present themselves as facilitators of a future independent Congo. Members of the black Congolese Force Publique shepherded visitors around the World's Fair pavilions as organizers purveyed the notion that Congolese freedom was a gift, the product of benevolent Belgian tutelage. These troops were meant to show how a white command structure could produce disciplined black soldiers.[9] Dependent territories had to become modern states ruled by indigenous people, but decolonization could not be achieved through revolution. Nonviolence must characterize the freedom struggle in Africa, as Africans absorbed Western political traditions through education and religious training. An NSC internal document commented on "the long record of humanitarian work in Africa through missionary and similar organizations." Indeed, "much of the good reputation we enjoy results from this type of activity." State Department planners put trusted black educators on guest lists for receptions hosted for visiting Africans it wished to court.[10] Cultural, educational, and religious activities still played an important role in orienting African peoples toward the U.S. and European democracies. The earlier missionary goal of spreading "civilization" slowly gave way to a more sophisticated objective, that of instilling secular ideas that would lead to a popular embrace of Western political values.

African independence clearly suggested future opportunities for U.S. enterprise, but at a cost. Most colonies needed help educating their populations and updating their infrastructures. The Eisenhower administration did not want to shoulder this burden. Ike shared with De Gaulle an irritation with African desires to move forward rapidly. The former metropoles, Ike believed, should rework their relationships with these emerging polities and take responsibility for their modernization and financial stability. The French plan for a Francophone African community fit well with these prescriptions. Yet it was also "vital," the president thought, "that the Western nations operate together without competing with one another."[11]

---

[8] Brenda Gayle Plummer, "Brown Babies: Race, Gender, and Policy in the Postwar Era," in *Window on Freedom: Race, Civil Rights, and Foreign Affairs, 1945–1988*, ed. Brenda G. Plummer (Chapel Hill: University of North Carolina Press 2003), 67–91; David Braden Posner, "Afro-America in West German Perspective, 1945–1966" (PhD diss., Yale University, 1997), pp. 143, 248–9.

[9] Kevin C. Dunn, *Imagining the Congo: The International Relations of Identity* (New York: Palgrave Macmillan, 2003), 61–2.

[10] NSC 5818, U. S. Policy toward Africa South of the Sahara Prior to Calendar Year 1960, August 28, 1958, in *FRUS, XXVI, 1958–1960, Africa*, p 26; Claude Barnett to David N. Howell and Dalton F. McClelland, June 25, 1960, Channing H. Tobias Papers, YMCA Collection, University of Minnesota; Barnett to Luther H. Foster, June 23, 1954, CBP-Pt 3 – Subject Files on Black Americans, 1918–67, Series 3, Philanthropic and Social Organizations, 1925–66, reel 2.

[11] Memorandum of conversation, French President de Gaulle and Eisenhower discuss the independence of the African nations and how to prevent them from going Communist, September 3, 1959, White House, DDRS.

The desire of black leaders in the United States to align themselves with decolonization underlay much African-American interest in Africa at midcentury. Implicit ideas about U.S. blacks as a modernizing vanguard also influenced the social sciences. In 1960, two African-American scholars, Hugh Smythe and Mabel Smythe, published a sociological study called *The New Nigerian Elite*. Hugh Smythe had done research in Nigeria in 1957–8 on a Ford Foundation fellowship and two years later codirected the volunteer program Crossroads Africa with the Reverend James Robinson.[12] Like many who studied Africa during this period, the Smythes were greatly interested in modernization and national independence. How would colonies make the transition to sovereignty? How would they constitute their nationalities? Who would lead and how? What would be the leadership group's sources of legitimacy?

The Smythes intensively interviewed 156 educated Nigerians, understood to be a representative sampling of a larger grouping. All were male except four, and occupations ranged from secondary school teachers to politicians and members of the professions. Two-thirds were civil servants. These "elite" men, mostly in their thirties and forties, were depicted as torn between self-interest and nationalist idealism, and as having inherited the hierarchical traditions of the British colonial period.

The authors, both of whom subsequently became ambassadors, Hugh Smythe to Malta and then to Syria, and Mabel Smythe to Cameroon, recognized that many characteristics of this elite were "predetermined" at the onset – as were the plans for securing the safety of foreign interests. They nevertheless wrote as if the groups they studied had developed spontaneously, from the nexus of urbanization, Westernization, and decolonization. They shared the modernizationist belief that the processes of development, including industrialization and the expansion of democratic institutions, followed behavioral rules and were subject to standardization.[13] In this respect, liberal theory yielded nothing to Marxism's laws of social development. Both mainstream Western and Marxist appraisals of developing countries at the time implied the existence of significant binaries: tribalism versus civic society, tradition versus modernity, and so on.

Washington's policy of courting indigenous elites mirrored the task that Africa-interested middle-class elements in black America wished to assume, a role that officials thought could absorb some black demands for full participation in government. The use of blackness to help the United States represent itself in Africa tacitly marshaled race as the point of connection between Africans and African Americans. At the same time, facilitated by the expansive

12 Hugh Smythe and Mabel Smythe, *The New Nigerian Elite* (Stanford, Calif.: Stanford University Press, 1960). See biographical data in the Preface to the Hugh Smythe Papers, reel 1, SC.

13 See for example, Mabel M. Smythe and Hugh H. Smythe, "Economics and Business Administration Offerings in Negro Colleges," *Journal of Education Research* (December 1944): 298–312; Lester D. Crow, Walter I. Murray, and Hugh H. Smythe, *Educating the Culturally Disadvantaged Child* (New York: David McKay, 1966).

reach of U.S. power, it threatened to erase Africa itself, reducing it to a backdrop for consolidating African-American gains at home and a bargaining chip in negotiations between white and black American power brokers.

The New Nigerian Elite is important as a historical marker not only because it faithfully reproduced certain modernizationist assumptions, but also because it usefully traces the beginnings of where some African Americans stumbled in their appraisals of African societies. Many assumed that decolonization and desegregation shared the same dynamic and, in the most exaggerated renditions, were interchangeable. Certainly, struggles against colonialism and racism share a history. Many scholars have detailed their relationship and their link to other global issues such as the cold war. But they are not identical; nor can they be understood without reference to the specific contexts in which they unfolded.

The experience of dancers Katherine Dunham and Pearl Primus provide an example. These artists sought to adapt traditional African choreography to their respective conceptions of modern dance but met resistance from dance communities in Liberia, Ghana, and Nigeria. Dunham in particular could hardly be called a shill for U.S. interests: her sharp denunciations of Jim Crow made her persona non grata to the State Department, which never called on her to tour. West African critics nevertheless rejected what they considered the bowdlerization of indigenous art forms and did not feel they needed modernizing or distilling to reflect a consciousness that was not their own. They derived little benefit from the professional success of these women from the States and did not recognize their own art in the dancers' hybrid creations.[14]

Hugh and Mabel Smythe's interests and backgrounds had placed them among a new kind of expert ready to benefit from the opportunities that top-down token integration made possible. Hugh Smythe had been W. E. B. Du Bois's research assistant in the late 1940s when Du Bois was crafting "An Appeal to the World," a petition to be presented to the United Nations on behalf of African-American human rights. It is perhaps not surprising, then, that the Smythes would have envisioned in Nigeria a "Talented Tenth" leadership cadre of precisely the type that Du Bois imagined but, ironically, situated it in Africa at the same time that the concept of elite stewardship began showing its age in the United States. By 1960, the year the Smythes published their book, new individuals and organizations had overtaken the U.S. civil rights establishment and were choosing new methods to pursue racial justice. In Nigeria, the groups the authors considered elite had a different connection to their country than did the black middle class that came of age in post–World War II America.

As a national bourgeoisie rather than a minority middle class, the Nigerians had a range of options unavailable to African Americans. They could, for

---

[14] Julia L. Foulkes, "Ambassadors with Hips: Katherine Dunham, Pearl Primus, and the Allure of Africa in the Black Arts Movement," *in Impossible to Hold*, eds. Avital Bloch and Laura Umansky (New York: New York University Press, 2004), 81–97; *Nigerian Daily Telegraph*, June 5, 1962, article reprinted in *Liberator* 2 (July 1962): 11.

example, focus on education and consumerism as the motor for development or, alternatively, construct a society where abundant cheapened labor and low local production costs would fuel the industrial takeoff that Walt Rostow and other specialists of the time argued was essential for progress.[15] Opinions in Nigeria differed over this question. Before the massive exploitation of petroleum, for example, Nigeria's economy depended heavily upon peasant production, but traditional agriculturists could not get start-up capital from national banks. No counterpart to this situation existed in black America; nor were African Americans as a collectivity able to prescribe development policies for the United States as a whole. The class distinctions and potential for class conflict manifest in the Nigerian situation were occluded in the United States, where race had always trumped class, and where repression encouraged racial solidarity and the suppression of intraethnic differences. The invention of Nigeria based on the geographic assumptions and predilections of British administrators resulted in a nation of more than one hundred ethnic groups and languages. No parallel existed in the United States. Such fundamental variations in the history and political status of African Americans as a national minority, and Nigerians, respectively, were often overlooked in racially essentialist discourses.

It is important to note, however, that the Pan-African tendency to dissolve critical differences in the African world was sometimes a strategic deployment. This deployment became problematic once the original conditions for its use transmuted. Conducting wars of national liberation called for a skill set different from that needed to run a nation-state. Similarly, the requirements for organizing a reform movement, such as the U.S. civil rights movement, were not necessarily the same ones needed to sustain the popular momentum the movement created. The beginning of independence in Africa and the partial successes of U.S civil rights insurgency would pose new challenges for Pan-Africanist strategies in the years to come.

The U.S. freedom struggle in the 1950s and early 1960s was firmly based on nonviolent direct action and formed part of a larger community of social movements, including the peace movement, with which it shared adherents. Conversations among activists took place across a spectrum from center to Left, and across oceans. As Doug McAdam has noted, "established organizations/networks are themselves embedded in long-standing activist subcultures" that "function as repositories of cultural materials." Over time, participants learn from past struggles and choose, discard, or revise what history has to offer. Movements created out of specific conditions in particular countries can also resonate with the national experience of people in other places. "If it was once sufficient to interpret or predict social movements around the

---

[15] Nick Cullather, "Miracles of Modernization: The Green Revolution and the Apotheosis of Technology," *Diplomatic History* 28 (April 2004): 246, 254; Donal Cruise O'Brien, "Modernisation, Order and the Erosion of a Democratic Ideal: American Political Science, 1960–1970," *Journal of Development Studies* 8 (4) (1972): 351–78.

shape of the nation state, it is less and less possible to do so today," Sidney Tarrow observes.[16]

Shared ideology and personnel effected close connections between civil rights and peace advocates. These actors also influenced, and were influenced by, foreign groups and individuals engaged in anticolonial activity. Before the rise of armed resistance, key African leaders Kwame Nkrumah of Ghana and Kenneth Kaunda of Zambia endorsed nonviolent civil disobedience as a way to liberate the remaining African colonies. In the United States, a distinct internationalist peace movement emerged after World War II, but the Korean War and McCarthyism nearly killed it during the cold war's bitterest years. African-American musical artists Charlie Parker, Marian Anderson, and Pearl Primus numbered among early supporters of the antinuclear movement, as did W. E. B. Du Bois, sociologist E. Franklin Frazier, and educators Charlotte Hawkins Brown and Benjamin Mays. Peace activists were widely discredited as Communist dupes until Stalin's death sufficiently eased East-West tensions that U.S. peace campaigns could be resumed without risk of lethal punishment. In 1955, Quakers issued a statement, "Speak Truth to Power," that reclaimed religious and ethical ground for a movement besmirched by cold war politics. The Montgomery bus boycott and subsequent nonviolent campaigns lent new credence to the pursuit of peace.[17]

The terrifying power of nuclear weapons aroused widespread fear, especially as post-*Sputnik* anxieties led to more armament and the growth of the defense establishment. In response, one of the more conventional organizations, the National Committee for a Sane Nuclear Policy (SANE), launched a series of civil disobedience demonstrations in 1957. SANE was part of an emerging middle-class movement in the United States and Britain, but affluent Western citizens were not the only ones concerned about the issue. The threat of atomic warfare also troubled African nations. The Conference of Independent African States, held in Ghana in April 1958, resolved that nuclear testing should be suspended and means taken to reduce the arms race. It called for African representation in international arms control agencies.[18]

Peace surfaced as an issue in the U.S. debate over civil rights in a way that related it to global concerns. Dissident NAACP leader Robert F. Williams wrote

[16] Doug McAdam, "Culture and Social Movements," in *New Social Movements*, eds. Enrique Laraña, Hank Johnston, and Joseph R. Gusfield (Philadelphia: Temple University Press, 1994): 43; Sidney Tarrow, "States and Opportunities: The Political Structuring of Social Movements," in *Comparative Perspective on Social Movements*, eds. Doug McAdam, John D. McCarthy, and Mayer N. Zald (Cambridge: Cambridge University Press, 1996), 53.

[17] Gerald Horne, *Black and Red: W. E. B. Du Bois and the Afro-American Response to the Cold War* (Albany, N.Y.: SUNY Press, 1986), 127; Mid-Century Conference for Peace conference call, April 28, 1950, Mary Church Terrell Papers, LC, reel 10; Carey McWilliams, *The Education of Carey McWilliams* (New York: Simon & Schuster, 1979), 222.

[18] Lawrence S. Wittner, *Rebels against War: The American Peace Movement, 1933–1983* (Philadelphia: Temple University Press, 1984); Richard Taylor, *Against the Bomb: The British Peace Movement, 1958–1965* (Oxford: Clarendon Press, 1988); "Unanimity and Moderation: The Accra Conference," *Africa Today* 5 (May–June 1958): 11.

an article for the September 1959 issue of the journal *Liberation* entitled "Can Negroes Afford to Be Pacifists?" The NAACP had suspended Williams as chair of the Monroe, North Carolina, chapter for advocating armed self-defense. Williams did not believe in the efficacy of any single response to the provocations and injustices that black people experience in the United States. He claimed that many who expressed commitment to nonviolence at home "were too weak-kneed to protest the warmongering of the atom-crazed politicians of Washington."[19] Ever since the American Revolution, it had been commonplace to support black civil rights by referring to African-American participation in the country's wars – where they had borne arms – and thus their entitlement to citizenship. Defending oneself at home, however, was another story. Williams's remarks challenged tacit assumptions about the civil rights movement's aims. Was the purpose of full citizenship only to allow blacks to participate in U.S. imperialist ventures?

Martin Luther King Jr. replied to Williams in the next issue of *Liberation*. He reasserted his consistent opposition to war, regardless of the "rank and nationality" of its perpetrators. He reminded readers that he had "signed numerous statements with other Americans condemning nuclear testing" and in the past had allowed his name to be used in antiwar campaigns "without concern that it was then 'unpopular' to so speak out."[20] The Williams and King debate suggests that the issues evoked by black insurgency could not be confined to the domestic arena. African Americans based the struggle against racial oppression and discrimination on Western society's highest moral principles. Was the price of citizenship their abandonment?

In Ghana, Nkrumah understood such discontents and employed them to add authority to his drive for leadership on the African continent and beyond. Delegates appointed by their governments who attended the Conference of Independent African States condemned nuclear armament, racism, and colonialism. Nkrumah and his adviser, the noted Pan-Africanist George Padmore, intended the second conference, convened in December, to rally liberation organizations, trade unions, and oppositional political parties across Africa. This All-African People's Conference also featured the invited attendance of representatives from the diaspora who could participate only in the plenary proceedings. As in Manchester at the Pan African Congress of 1945, trade unionists, politicians, and future independence leaders dominated the meeting, and those without nationality in African states and territories were relegated to auxiliary roles. The three hundred delegates from sixty-five organizations and political parties worldwide included Tom Mboya, a young labor leader

[19] Robert F. Williams, "Can Negroes Afford to Be Pacifists?" *Liberation* 4 (September 1959): 4–7.

[20] Martin Luther King, Jr., "The Social Organization of Nonviolence," *Liberation* 4 (October 1959): 5–6. For King's peace advocacy, see Jason Berger, *A New Deal for the World: Eleanor Roosevelt and American Foreign Policy* (New York: Columbia University Press, 1981), 126; King's address at the 36th annual dinner of the War Resisters League, February 2, 1959, in *The Papers of Martin Luther King, Jr.*, vol. 5: *Threshold of a New Decade, January 1959–December 1960*, ed. Clayborne Carson (Berkeley: University of California Press, 2005), 125.

from Kenya, and Congo politician Patrice Lumumba, whose attendance had been facilitated through Bill Sutherland's pacifist connections in Belgium. Representative Charles Diggs from Detroit and delegates from the NAACP, ACOA, and the Council on African Affairs were present. The USSR and China "sent sizable contingents." Nkrumah's hosting of these meetings pointed to the scope of his ambitions.[21]

Conferees debated the Algerian question intensely with Egyptian and Algerian participants who pressed the conference to recognize the necessity of violent revolution. As many African trade unionists and politicians remained committed to Gandhian approaches to liberation, the meeting ended with a compromise on the issue of armed force. Delegations hammered out a statement that privileged both nonviolent civil disobedience and revolutionary action. "Recognizing that national independence can be gained by peaceful means in territories where democratic means are available," the draft read, the conference "guarantees its support to all forms of peaceful action. This support is pledged equally to those who, in order to meet the violent means by which they are subjected and exploited are obliged to retaliate." This statement did not rule out violence and provided an opening for an idea originally floated at the conference, which became more popular in later years: an All-African People's Revolutionary Army might engage imperialists if moral suasion did not work.[22]

Nkrumah's innovation, perhaps partly inadvertent, was to challenge the fictitiousness of African states, whose frontiers, everyone acknowledged, were wholly artificial. Because they were artificial, they allowed room for political organization that transcended states and presaged a federated Africa. "Nkrumah's vision thus created spaces for diaspora minorities that could not be assimilated into a nationalist framework." In mounting such a challenge, Nkrumah courted opposition, not the least of which emanated from other African leaders who perceived him as an empire builder. Julius Nyerere of Tanzania, for example, saw the Ghanaian's call for African unity as a subterfuge for undermining other governments. "Some people are willing to use their great talent to wreck any chance of unity on our continent," Nyerere snapped at an Organization of African Unity (OAU) meeting in Nkrumah's presence,

[21] W. Scott Thompson, *Ghana's Foreign Policy, 1957–1966* (Princeton, N.J.: Princeton University Press, 1969), 111; Brenda Gayle Plummer, *Rising Wind: Black Americans and U.S. Foreign Affairs, 1935–1960* (Chapel Hill: University of North Carolina Press, 1996), 279; Russell Howe, "Independence Strategy to Be Discussed," *Washington Post and Times Herald*, November 30, 1958 p. A20; Sutherland and Meyer, 34, 35; Evan White, "Kwame Nkrumah: Cold War Modernity, Pan-African Ideology and the Geopolitics of Development," *Geopolitics* 8 (2) (2003): 99–124. Vernon McKay, *Africa in World Politics* (New York: Harper & Row, 1963), 109–11.

[22] Homer A. Jack, "Russia and the West, Cairo vs. Accra: Ideological Conflicts," *Africa Today* 6 (January–February 1959): 11–17; McKay, *Africa in World Politics*, 109–11; Patrick Duncan, "Non-Violence at Accra," *Africa Today* 6 (January–February 1959): 32; Robert J. C. Young, "Fanon and the Turn to Armed Struggle in Africa," *Wasafiri* 20 (Spring 2005): 38.

"as long as some stupid historian can record that they wanted unity at a time when nobody else did."[23]

Nkrumah rooted his outreach programs in a traditional Pan-Africanism dating to the conferences held in Europe between 1900 and 1945. The advent of independence, however, created governments in Africa and the Caribbean whose geopolitical relationships were qualitatively different from those of diaspora populations that remained permanent minorities in their homelands. The older Pan-Africanism became progressively tenuous, with metropolitan minorities increasingly relegated to the role of cheerleaders and volunteer lobbyists for African causes.

The OAU provided an overlay of Pan-African sentiment, but was ultimately a council of states that did not utilize the energies of those who lacked standing in governmental bodies. As Opoku Agyeman remarks:

Is it not the case that the pan-Africanism of the O.A.U. is the kind which postulates no direct threat to national sovereignty, since all the O.A.U. does is to provide for continental co-operation as between sovereign independent states? Will pan-Africanism be able to maintain its thrust once the nation-states have had a chance to become stronger, when nationalism begins to freeze into nationality, when frontiers have become permanent, and sovereignty has become sovereignly important?[24]

Once national liberation movements evolved into ruling parties and state bureaucracies, the disparities between national majorities in their home countries and those who remained racial-ethnic minorities in theirs became evident.

One of the most critical Pan-African moments in the late 1950s remarkably engaged the multiple issues of nonviolent direct action, diaspora cooperation, peace, and colonial resistance. The revitalized peace movement tended to focus on Northern Hemisphere conflicts inherent in the standoff between the Western and Eastern blocs. The Hungarian revolt, the Berlin crisis, and the Cuban missile crisis captured the most attention. Few heeded other regions where peace became a vital issue for reasons other than bloc politics. One of these was Africa. Peace entered the debate in Africa as a by-product of the quest to end colonialism and racism. The Defiance Campaign of 1952, launched by Africans and Asians against apartheid in South Africa, and the Mau Mau revolt of the Kikuyu in Kenya had led to deliberation in sub-Saharan countries about the best strategies and tactics to use in the fight. Strong voices supported nonviolence. Indeed, the South African Defiance Campaign preceded similar religiously influenced protest activity in the U.S. South.[25] Throughout the decade, many Africans continued to believe that nonviolent decolonization of the entire continent was both possible and desirable.

[23] White, "Kwame Nkrumah," 119; clipping, *Washington Post*, July 21, 1964, TCF, reel 207.
[24] Opoku Agyeman, "The Osagyefo, the Mwalimu, and Pan-Africanism: A Study in the Growth of a Dynamic Concept," *The Journal of Modern African Studies* 13 (December 1975): 666 n. 3.
[25] Plummer, *Rising Wind*, 232, 233; Thomas J. Noer, "Martin Luther King, Jr. and the Cold War," *Peace & Change* 22 (April 1997): 116.

The Algerian revolutionary war drew a shadow over this sunny presumption. France's zealous pursuit of maintaining its rule in Algeria heightened political tensions on the continent. In October 1956, French pilots intercepted a Moroccan plane and arrested passenger Ahmed Ben Bella and other Algerian rebel leaders. Morocco subsequently broke off relations with France. In February 1958, the French military used U.S.-built planes to bomb a rebel village inside Tunisia. French border incursions in search of Algerian insurgents seeking shelter in neighboring countries invited regional warfare and threatened to introduce East-West hostilities into Africa.[26]

France's program of nuclear weapons testing in the Sahara affronted African states and territories. De Gaulle's government created a crisis by imperiously dismissing the apprehensive demarches of African nations. News that French and American firms had formed a consortium to explore for Saharan oil and build a pipeline through Algeria indicated that France would give no quarter to Algerian nationalists. Plans also entailed the construction of a modern military-industrial complex.[27]

The character of France's nuclear program itself raised further anxieties. The French objective, a London *Times* correspondent later explained, was to develop "a nuclear device small and compact enough to be used either as a tactical weapon by troops in the field, or as the warhead of a short-range rocket." Such a device could detonate a hydrogen bomb that France would develop in the future, but its small size would be of little use in a confrontation with powers like the USSR or the United States. What other foes could it be used against effectively? French scientists were also conducting experiments to study the effects of radiation on Saharan rodents.[28]

This was the context of the broad African opposition to the French atomic project. Elements in the British peace movement and the Ghanaian government hastily mobilized against French objectives. They coordinated demonstrations at the French embassy in London in late August 1959 and in Trafalgar Square. The focus was antiimperialist as well as antinuclear. An atomic stronghold in the Sahara, anticolonialists understood, facilitated French domination not only in Algeria but on the African continent as a whole. Peace advocates had widespread Afro-Asian support at a time when the "Bandung spirit" still prevailed in chancelleries.[29] At the UN, twenty-two countries proposed that the General Assembly vote a measure of "grave concern" about French nuclear testing in

[26] Irwin M. Wall, *France, the United States, and the Algerian War* (Berkeley: University of California Press, 2001), 50–4, 109–12, 69–72, 93, 148; Charles P. Howard, Sr., "Deadline Nears for France in Algeria," Baltimore *Afro-American*, September 12, 1959, p. 12

[27] "Prospecting in the Sahara U.S. Share in Concession," *Times* (London), January 22, 1959, p. 8:C.

[28] "French Explode Third Atomic Bomb: Detonator for Hydrogen Type?" *Times* (London), December 28, 1960, p. 8:A.

[29] The Asia-Africa Conference in Bandung, Indonesia in 1955 identified commonalities of interest and areas of potential cooperation among newly independent states. See George McTurnan Kahin, *The Asian-African Conference* (Ithaca, N.y.: Cornell University Press, 1956).

Africa. The resolution, also supported by Warsaw Pact signatories, passed by a vote of fifty-one to sixteen. The United States and Britain sided with a defiant France on the "grave concern" vote. "Nonaligned states," W. Scott Thompson observed, "could play a balancing act that gave them a voice in world affairs such as they were seldom to have again in the ensuing half-decade."[30]

William Sutherland, who had gone to live in Ghana in 1953, now worked as a secretary for Ghanaian finance minister Komla A. Gbedemah. Gbedemah held pacifist views and had once presided over the global organization World Federalists. Sutherland received permission from Nkrumah to mount a protest against French nuclear testing. Planning for the Sahara protest began in the autumn of 1959.[31]

France's bomb project aroused a cross section of the Ghanaian population to demonstrate in protest, evoking the unity that had characterized the proin-dependence movement years earlier (see Figure 4). Traditional rulers, such as the powerful Asantahene of Kumasi, gave the campaign their blessing as nationalists, rather than as leaders of specific ethnic groups. Ghana sponsored Sutherland's visits to antiwar events in the United States and Britain to coordi-nate action among such organizations as the Committee for Nonviolent Action (CNVA) and the British Direct Action Committee.[32]

Twenty persons, fourteen of them Africans and six from the United States and Europe, made up the Sahara Protest Team. The demonstrators planned to confront French authorities at Reggan, the nuclear facility in the Algerian desert two thousand miles from Accra. Citizens from Ghana, Nigeria, Britain, France, and the United States participated, and so did Jonathan Leabua, who, thirty-three years later, became president of Lesotho. The noted pacifist A. J. Muste from the Fellowship of Reconciliation flew in to meet the group in northern Ghana. He endorsed a proposition of Gbedemah's: if nuclear testing was safe, then let the French test their bombs in France. Bayard Rustin, a career African-American peace and civil rights activist, raised a substantial sum for the team. He and others made it clear that the demonstrators opposed French policy, not the French people, a point underscored by the participation of two French peace activists.[33]

---

[30] Taylor, *Against the Bomb*, 157; "Big U.N. Vote Calls On France to Drop Bomb Plan," *Times* (London) November 21, 1959, p. 6; Thompson, *Ghana's Foreign Policy*, 111.

[31] Jean Allman, "Nuclear Imperialism and the Pan-African Struggle for Peace and Freedom," *Souls* 10 (2) (2008): 87, 89; Lindesay Parrott, "U. N. Vote Calls on France to Omit Sahara on France Bomb Test," *New York Times*, November 21, 1959; p. 1.

[32] William Sutherland and Matt Meyer, *Guns and Gandhi in Africa* (Trenton, N.J.: Africa World Press, 2000), 36; Wall, *France, the United States, and the Algerian War*, 138, 161–2; Taylor, *Against the Bomb*, 157–8; A. J. Muste, "Africa against the Bomb," in *The Essays of A. J. Muste*, ed. Nat Hentoff (New York: Bobbs Merrill, 1967), 399.

[33] Sahara Protest Team Fact Sheet, December 4, 1959, Bayard Rustin Papers, reel 1 (Bethesda, Md: University Press of America, 1988); Daniel Levine, *Bayard Rustin and the Civil Rights Movement* (New Brunswick, N.J.: Rutgers University Press, 2000), 116–88; John D'Emilio, *Lost Prophet: The Life and Times of Bayard Rustin* (New York: Free Press, 2000), 281, 286, 312; Sutherland and Meyer, *Guns and Gandhi*, 37–9; Muste, "Africa against the Bomb," 397,

FIGURE 4. Ghanaians protest French atomic testing in the Sahara, September 2, 1960. (Corbis)

While Ghana facilitated the protest and served as a central mobilizing point, Accra required all volunteers to sign statements specifying that they were not representing Ghana. This was prudence rather than backtracking on Nkrumah's part. The angry mood in Paris, French aggression in Indochina and Algeria, and France's fractured relations with neighboring Guinea made the Ghanaian wary of risking armed confrontation with this pugnacious power.[34]

The Sahara team left Accra on December 5, 1959. They traveled through northern Ghana, pausing to hold rallies. "The plan was to get as close to the test site as possible," Sutherland recalled, "letting folks know about the French plans and preventing the testing through our physical presence." The French stopped the group at the frontier post of Bittou but did not arrest them. The team handed out leaflets written in local languages and found a positive reception among the population. French police, recognizing this, then forbade them access to the villages. Some friendly African border patrols allowed them to

398, 403–4; "Protest Team Drive towards Sahara Attempt to Reach Atom Test Site," *Times* (London), December 7, 1959, p. 8:F.

[34] "Protest Team Drive towards Sahara Attempt to Reach Atom Test Site," S.C. Saxena, "Disarmament: The African Perspective," *Strategic Analysis* 22 (7) (1998) online; Muste, "Africa against the Bomb," 402–3.

cross into Upper Volta (now Burkina Faso), but there they were jailed. The next day French authorities had them taken back to Ghana. Bayard Rustin and Sutherland sang "Negro spirituals" at the Upper Volta checkpoint. The Sahara protest took place outside Europe but drew together unique energies in support of a nuclear-free and decolonized Africa.[35]

Rustin proved invaluable in the campaign, helping to join disarmament with African desires for neutrality, environmental safety, and peaceful development. Sutherland later reminisced: "It was so exciting because we felt that this joining up of the European anti-nuclear forces, the African liberation forces, and the U.S. civil rights movements could help each group feed and reinforce the other."[36] These ties had already been forged. "By the time of the Sahara protest," historian Richard Taylor has written, "there were firm ideological and personal links between American pacifists (and civil rights activists such as Bayard Rustin) and their pacifist counterparts in Britain."[37] American activists followed up the campaign in Africa with support demonstrations. The CNVA picketed the French Government Tourist Office in New York on a daily basis. It planned a major demonstration in Philadelphia for the January opening of the French National Exposition.[38]

In spite of the links between U.S. and European peace groups, doubts persisted in some quarters about the strength and depth of African sentiment. Yale University Africanist Leonard W. Doob traveled in northern Nigeria, "whose radio and press were filled at the time with blasts against the French plan to drop atomic bombs in the Sahara." Doob believed that only the elites were worried. "I asked people in villages the question, 'Do you know what the French Government plans to do in the Sahara Desert?'" Doob reported. "The modal answer was, 'What is the French Government?'" The provincialism of rural Africa had long served as an excuse to dismiss African opinion as a whole, but even Doob had to acknowledge, "This will change fast." Certainly, if farmers in the U.S. heartland were not expected to be foreign policy sophisticates, there was no reason to require the same of their African counterparts.[39]

As the Sahara protesters' activities received international attention and were approved in other African countries, Gbedemah sent them back for another try at the border. This time they crossed into French colonial territory at night

---

[35] Jervis Anderson, *Bayard Rustin: Troubles I've Seen* (Berkeley: University of California Press, 1998), 219–21; Brenda Gayle Plummer, "Peace Was the Glue: Europe and African American Freedom," *Souls* 10 (2) (2008): 111–13; Scott H. Bennett, *Radical Pacifism: The War Resisters League and Gandhian Nonviolence in America, 1915–1963* (Syracuse, N.Y.: Syracuse University Press, 2003), 231–5.

[36] Sutherland and Meyer, *Guns and Gandhi*, 36–7.

[37] Taylor, *Against the Bomb*, 167. See also Frances M. Beal and Ty dePass, "The Historical Black Presence in the Struggle for Peace," *The Black Scholar* (January/February 1986): 2–7.

[38] James Peck to A. J. Muste, December 16, 1959, Rustin Papers, reel 1.

[39] Leonard W. Doob to Pendleton Herring, September 17, 1959, SSRC (access 2) 1, Committee Projects subseries 3, box 17 folder 127, RAC. Robert C. Ruark, "Africa Isn't Marshall's Business," news clipping, n.d. in *FBI Documents Regarding Thurgood Marshall* (computer file) (Washington, D.C.: U.S. Dept. of Justice, Federal Bureau of Investigation, c. 1998).

with the aid of "a local guide along a path usually used by smugglers." "We hid in the bush," Sutherland remembered. The next day they took the road to Ouagadougou, hitching a ride in a truck. The driver betrayed them, however, delivering them to a police station, where they were arrested. The Reverend Michael Scott, best known to history for his antiapartheid courage, was with the group, which French authorities again sent back to Ghana.[40]

The arbitrary character of territorial borders in Africa formed a subtheme of the protest, and one that Nkrumah made clear. That the French test would be conducted in airspace that France claimed as its own linked newer technology with the boundary problem on the ground. The colonial powers had erected barriers to the free flow of people, trade, and communications across frontiers. French officials' actions had underscored this point, not only by keeping protesters out, but by claiming that geographically noncontiguous Algeria was in reality a part of France. To Nkrumah, the success or failure of the effort actually to reach Reggan was unimportant. Making these political realities visible was what counted.[41]

The final attempt was made on January 17, 1960. The team succeeded in advancing sixty-six miles inside Upper Volta before being turned back. On February 13, France carried out the planned nuclear test despite outrage all over Africa. Ghana froze all French assets in the country. President Habib Bourguiba of Tunisia, addressing an angry Tunis audience of 100,000, alerted them that his government would eject the French from their military base in Bizerte and urged them to march on the French embassy. Anti-French demonstrations took place in Syria, and in Egypt Nasser claimed that France intended the bomb for "our beloved sister Algeria" and deplored "the carrying out of atomic experiments in the Arab world."[42]

France ignored the objections of the Arab League and those of independent African states. Nigeria, a colony approaching a population of 60 million and expecting independence in 1961, also expressed anxiety about French testing. British Prime Minister Harold Macmillan journeyed to Lagos in January 1960 as part of a tour of several African colonies soon to be free. Macmillan had conferred in London with Nigerian Prime Minister Alhaji Abubakar Tafewa Balewa about Nigerian trepidations. Fears worsened when Mac was evasive about the extent of his support or disapproval of France's Sahara initiative. Student protesters met him in Lagos and Ibadan, carrying placards with such messages as "Hail MacNATO, We who are about to be bombed salute thee," and "Hands Off Africa." The students knew nothing of Britain's secret determination to be noncommittal about France's problems and the undisclosed

[40] Sutherland and Meyer, 39–40.
[41] "Warning to Air Lines on Sahara Atomic Tests," *Times* (London) January 9, 1960, p. 6:E; Kwame Nkrumah, *I Speak of Freedom: A Statement of African Ideology* (London: Heinemann, 1962), 212–15.
[42] "France Asked to Leave Bizerte Base February 8...," *Times* (London), January 26, 1960, p. 10; "President Nasser Joins In," ibid., February 15, 1960; p. 8.

FIGURE 5. Bill Sutherland. (Courtesy of the Sutherland family)

protocol Macmillan had signed with the Americans that committed the two powers to avoid assisting a French atomic effort they both disapproved. Pressed by members of Parliament on such issues as nuclear proliferation, the prime minister had obliquely referred to the desirability of a test ban treaty among the United States, Britain, and the USSR. As a combined force, he insinuated, these powers could more readily bring France to heel.[43]

Macmillan's African tour took place in the aftermath of racial unrest in Britain itself. Immigrants from the British West Indies began arriving in the

[43] Gabrielle Hecht, *The Radiance of France: Nuclear Power and National Identity after World War II* (Cambridge, Mass.: MIT Presses, 1998), 209; "Nigerian Nuclear Fears – PM Balewa has called on Mac to Give Him Nigerian Views," *The Times* (London), September 19, 1959, p. 5; "Students' Reception For Mr. Macmillan: Banners and Humour," ibid., January 15, 1960, p. 1; Cabinet Conclusions, May 21, 1958; U.K. Bermuda Conference delegation to the Foreign Office, March 25, 1957, House of Commons proceedings, November 11, 1959, p. 4, in *Macmillan Cabinet Papers, 1957–1963*, CD-ROM (London: Adam Matthew Publications, 1999).

United Kingdom after World War II to satisfy a labor shortage. As their numbers grew, so did conflicts with white Britons, which culminated in the Notting Hill riots of 1958. These shocked Britain and the world, and their occurrence on the eve of African independence sensitized Her Majesty's government to the perilous path ahead. Britain could no longer point a finger at America, North Carolina governor Luther H. Hodges snidely remarked to the canon of St. Paul's Cathedral, London. The canon, John Collins, a leader of the British organization Campaign for Nuclear Disarmament, had condemned the absurdity of North Carolina's "Kissing Case," where authorities had imprisoned two black primary school boys for kissing a little white girl. The Notting Hill riots "far surpassed, in violence," Hodges retorted, "anything that has ever occurred in North Carolina."[44] Like the United States, Britain found itself with an internal racial minority and a simultaneous need to establish good relations with new states made up of non-European peoples while placating Australians and New Zealanders worried about "the risk" that "coloured members of the Commonwealth … might ultimately outnumber the older members." As in the United States, racial conflict in Britain unleashed a veritable cottage industry of specialists, publications, and committees devoted to the solution of racial problems. The Committee for African Organizations, a group composed of Caribbeans and West Africans in London, readily linked British race relations to foreign policy issues and, most specifically, to colonialism and the cold war.[45]

The nexus of France, its sub-Saharan empire, the Algerian revolution, and nuclear proliferation shaped American preparations for De Gaulle's spring 1960 visit to the United States. "As long as the Algerian conflict continues, France will be a liability in U.S. relations with the Afro-Asian bloc, as well as in the Middle East," an NSC memorandum suggested. The observation indicates that Democratic Party pundits were not the only ones urging a revised position on colonialism. Eisenhower himself subsequently "brought up the subject of atmospheric testing and expressed his conviction that it must be brought to an end."[46]

Observing the French atomic testing issue from afar, a U.S. State Department Bureau of Intelligence report perceived the "extreme dismay" that "newly independent nations of Africa have expressed at the prospect of atomic fallout in

---

[44] Luther H. Hodges to Canon L. John Collins, January 2, 1959, Committee to Combat Racial Injustice Papers, Box 2, folder, 4, Wisconsin Historical Society.

[45] Cabinet Conclusions, May 22, 1957; July 1, 1958; September 8, 1958, in *Macmillan Cabinet Papers*; "Race Tension Increased by Murder," and "Coloured People Have Lost Confidence," *The Times* (London), Tuesday, May 19, 1959, p. 6. See also Paul Gilroy, *"There Ain't No Black in the Union Jack:" The Cultural Politics of Race and Nation* (Chicago: University of Chicago Press, 1991), 156–60; Kennetta Hammond Perry, "'Little Rock' in Britain: Jim Crow's Transatlantic Topographies," *Journal of British Studies* 51 (January 2012): 155–77.

[46] Paper Regarding U.S. Policy toward France, NSC, April 9, 1960; Preparatory discussions for President Eisenhower's meeting with De Gaulle, April 27, 1960, DDE Diaries, Folder: Staff Notes, April 1960 (1), Box 32, Eisenhower Papers, Ann Whitman File, DDRS.

'their' continent." The report's insertion of quotation marks around "their" implied that these states had no legitimate proprietary claims on African soil. It discounted the importance of French nuclear efforts and noted that Africans' "sometimes violent emotional reaction" to the atomic program might prevent France from shouldering the foreign aid responsibilities that the United States did not want to assume itself in the former French colonies.[47] The Bureau of Intelligence thus dismissed African apprehension about atomic testing as emotionalism and showed greater anxiety that the United States might be asked to help the emerging countries than with the prospect of nuclear war.

Four years later, this attitude had barely changed. Noting that the OAU was considering a resolution to make Africa a nuclear-free zone at its upcoming meeting in Cairo in 1964, the assistant secretary of defense for international security affairs worried that the measure, if successfully passed, would prevent the United States from transporting nuclear weapons across the continent or along its coastal waters. Cold war secrecy was involved. "Approval of the resolution could adversely affect our transit rights since our policy is neither to confirm nor deny the presence of nuclear weapons aboard our ships or aircraft. We would have to answer, or fail to transit." The Joint Chiefs of Staff opposed the nuclear-free zone, and the secretary of state instructed U.S. embassies in Africa to lobby host governments to reject or modify it.[48]

The predisposition of the great powers to do as they wished in Africa was reflected in France's decision to detonate another device at ground level on April 1, 1960, whereupon Nigeria broke off diplomatic relations and called for international sanctions against France. In Ghana, Nkrumah continued to prefer Gandhian methods over revolutionary violence in the struggle against imperialism. What he called "positive action" included moral suasion, education, strikes, boycotts, and civil disobedience: all forms of "legitimate political agitation." In light of French intransigence, Nkrumah and Michael Scott decided to call a continentwide conference to address France's nuclear policy and enact the Ghanaian leader's ideas on nonviolence. Ghana's ruling Convention Peoples Party (CPP) thus hosted an April 19 conference attended by representatives of several African states where the mood, as described by a historian of the British peace movement, was "militant and angry."[49] Organizers invited U.S. civil rights leader Ralph Abernathy, A. J. Muste, and activists from four continents to this Positive Action Conference for Peace and Security in Africa. Advocates of nonviolent direct action debated such partisans of armed struggle as Frantz

---

[47] Muste, "Africa against the Bomb," 407; "Students' Reception For Mr. Macmillan: Banners And Humour;" U.S. State Department, Bureau of Intelligence and Research, Report No. 8374. December 6, 1960, p. 24.

[48] Memorandum from the Assistant Secretary of Defense for International Security Affairs (McNaughton) to Secretary of Defense McNamara, July 10, 1964; memorandum from the Department of State's Executive Secretary (Read) to the President's Special Assistant for National Security Affairs (Bundy), *FRUS 1964–1968*, XXIV, *Africa* (Washington, D.C. 1999) online edition.

[49] Taylor, *Against the Bomb*, 163.

Fanon. The crises posed by bomb testing in the Sahara and the Sharpeville massacre provided the convocation's larger context.[50]

Nkrumah pledged £30,000 to build a Positive Action Centre for cadre training. When the center was established as promised, however, it was called the Kwame Nkrumah Institute and had as part of its mission the development of CPP and Ghanaian trade union cadres. Sutherland did not think that many Ghanaians were really committed to nonviolence. The Sahara campaign failed to convert Africans to the techniques that had worked in India and that appeared to be making an impact in the United States. The Mozambican revolutionary Eduardo Mondlane thought that pacifists were "too good and nice" to be effective combatants against a vicious Portuguese colonial regime. Bloke Modisane, a representative of the Pan-African Congress of South Africa, told a Briton that nonviolence was just "a prelude to the revolution." Whites in alliance with blacks must be prepared to shoot other whites. The African peace movement nevertheless enjoyed more mass support in Ghana than the peace movement did in Britain or the United States.[51]

Still defiant, Paris authorized the detonation of a bomb two days after Christmas 1960. The harmattan season when cool Saharan winds blow dust south into the countries of the Sahel and the forest belt, had begun, this time carrying unknown quantities of radioactive motes. Africans were livid. While international pressure eventually led France to relocate its nuclear program to Polynesia, far away from large empowered populations and vociferous criticism, its contempt for African life did little to affirm Africans' flagging faith in nonviolence at the turn of the decade.[52]

Ghana in 1961 hosted the World without the Bomb Assembly in Accra, but by then, African states, while still concerned with nuclear destruction and the intrusion of cold war politics in regional affairs, were focusing more on eradicating colonialism. "There was little space or time for the radical experimentation of the previous years," Sutherland recalled. "It is the tragedy of our century," Nkrumah told the Ghanaian legislature, "that the scientific ability developed by the nations of the world has completely out-run their collective political responsibility." The Ghanaian wondered whether it was "possible that the small and uncommitted nations may be able to bridge this gap by

[50] "Second Sahara Atomic Test Weapon of Usable Size Exploded," *Times* (London), April 2, 1960, p. 6; G. Saxena, "Disarmament: The African Perspective;" Taylor, 159, 161, 164–6; B. Marie Perinbaum, *Holy Violence: The Revolutionary Thought of Frantz Fanon* (Washington, D.C.: Three Continents Press, 1982), 73.

[51] William Sutherland to A. J. Muste, August 25, 1962, World Peace Brigade Papers, Wisconsin Historical Society, Box 1 folder 3; Sutherland and Meyer, *Guns and Gandhi in Africa*, 164.

[52] "French Explode Third Atomic Bomb Detonator For Hydrogen Type"; "African Outcry over Sahara Test," *Times* (London), December 30, 1960, p. 6; Jean-Marc Regnault, "France's Search for Nuclear Test Sites, 1957–1963;" *The Journal of Military History* 67 (4) (2003): 1240–1; Jeffrey T. Richelson, *Spying on the Bomb: American Nuclear Intelligence from Nazi Germany to Iran and North Korea* (New York: W. W. Norton, 2006), 200–6.

constructive suggestions and proposals." Time, however, was running out for forbearance as pacifism lost favor.[53]

Sutherland left Ghana in 1961. A failing marriage, difficulty reconciling his beliefs with Nkrumah's evolving espousal of armed revolution, and the growing suppression of dissidents led him, in search of power for nonviolent transformation in Africa, to head for Tanzania (see Figure 5). As advocacy of armed struggle increased in Africa, Nkrumah suggested to the National Assembly of Ghana the creation of "an African High Command" for the military defense of the continent as a whole. In ensuing years, the idea of international brigades organized to fight reactionary regimes and colonialism in southern Africa was floated variously by diaspora activists and heads of state and became a feature of Cuba's foreign policy in Africa.[54]

Soon after Sutherland left Ghana, his former boss, Komla A. Gbedemah, denounced Nkrumah's policies and went into exile. In the wake of Ghanaian defection from the nonviolent direct action camp, politicians Kenneth Kaunda and Julius Nyerere became the most prominent proponents of peaceful political change in Africa. After the independence of most West African states, attention turned to southern Africa and the exiled liberation organizations based in Dar es Salaam, Nairobi, and Lusaka. In Tanzania, Sutherland collaborated with Bayard Rustin to organize a march into still-colonized Northern Rhodesia, today Zambia.[55] He hoped to recoup the Sahara protest's historic moment, when African leaders still believed it possible to secure freedom and racial justice peacefully. The great powers, however, responded only to force.

Sutherland found himself drawn to the World Peace Brigade, headquartered in Dar es Salaam and premised on "a Gandhian approach at the international level." Michael Scott, Muste, and Indian socialist J. P. Narayan chaired the brigade, with Nyerere and Kaunda serving as patrons. Sutherland attended the brigade's founding conference and remained in Tanzania, serving as a liaison between the national liberation groups and U.S. civil rights activists. The threat of a World Peace Brigade march to still-colonized Zambia, accompanied by a simultaneous Zambian general strike, worried colonial authorities. With Rustin's help, Sutherland worked with Kaunda, then head of the Zambian

---

[53] Sutherland and Meyer, *Guns and Gandhi in Africa*, 42; Osagyefo Dr. Kwame Nkrumah, An Address to the National Assembly, April 18, 1961, pamphlet, n.p., at the Dr. Kwame Nkrumah Digital Collection Lincoln University, Pennsylvania, http://www.lincoln.edu/history/nkrumah/gp/gp-a212–61–62a/ra-01.htm, accessed October 24, 2010.

[54] Kwame Nkrumah, "Tragedy in Angola," Address to the National Assembly of Ghana, May 30, 1971, pamphlet, n.p., Nkrumah Digital Collection, http://www.lincoln.edu/history/nkrumah/gp/gp-a1948–60–61/01.htm, accessed October 24, 2010. Lebert Bethune, "Malcolm X in Europe," in *Malcolm X, the Man and His Times*, ed. John Henrik Clark, (New York: Macmillan, 1969), 231; Piero Gleijeses, *Conflicting Missions: Havana, Washington, and Africa, 1959–1976* (Chapel Hill: University of North Carolina Press, 2002), 193; Young, "Fanon and the Turn to Armed Struggle in Africa;" Che Guevara, *The African Dream* (New York: Grove Press, 1999).

[55] Bayard Rustin to A. J. Muste, February 22, 1962, World Peace Brigade Papers, Box 1, folder, 3; Sutherland and Meyer, *Guns and Gandhi*, 42; "2 Yanks Map March into N. Rhodesia," *New York Post*, March 26, 1962, p. 22.

United National Independence Party, to organize a march from Dar es Salaam to Lusaka. Demonstrators in East Africa set out in March 1962, some of them stationed on the Zambian-Tanzanian border awaiting Kaunda's instructions to enter Zambia. But similarly to the way that African-American labor leader A. Philip Randolph abandoned his threatened March on Washington in 1941, Zambian nationalist leader Kenneth Kaunda called off the peace march in exchange for guarantees that Britain would expedite his country's independence.[56] British authorities later protested to President Julius Nyerere for letting the marchers encamp on Tanzanian soil. Rustin, for his part, found himself sharply reprimanded by the U.S. State Department and the U.S. embassy in Dar es Salaam. In hindsight, it appeared that Kaunda used the peace movement to further nationalist rather than internationalist ends.[57] His action nevertheless highlighted the unease that the great powers felt when faced with initiatives that crossed the artificial territorial boundaries set in place by colonial history.

The Sahara antinuclear protest in 1959 remains little known, but it marked not only a confluence of interests among international social movements, but also the arrival of Africans as conscious stakeholders in global politics. A notorious catastrophe with more immediate ramifications was the Sharpeville massacre of 1960. On March 21, 1960, South African police turned submachine guns on a massive demonstration in the black township of Sharpeville in the Transvaal. African protests focused on a central feature of apartheid. In order to rationalize racial discrimination, economic inequality, and the denial of civil rights to "Bantus," the Pretoria government maintained the fiction that they were foreigners. The state created "native reserves" based on ethnicity and pretended that these were protonational entities. Black Africans were supposed to live there unless they had permission to leave and seek employment in the white areas. In order to police the movements and work histories of the indigenous people, the South African government forced them to carry internal passports, called passbooks.

The peaceful protest against the passbook laws, sponsored by the Pan African Congress of South Africa, drew twenty thousand unarmed participants. It ended with the deaths of at least sixty-nine persons, most of them women and children. Pretoria showed its iron hand, making seventeen hundred arrests arrests and declaring martial law throughout the country. Sharpeville became a milestone in the struggle against apartheid and minority rule and a symbol of the racism and imperialism that still prevailed on the continent. For William

---

[56] Smith Hempstone, "2 Yanks Map March into N. Rhodesia;" compendium of memoranda from Bayard Rustin to A. J. Muste, Arlo Tatum, S. Dhadda, and Hugh Brock, March 8, 1962 and Muste to William Sutherland, May 21 and May 24 1963; World Peace Brigade Papers, Box 1, folder 3; Anderson, *Bayard Rustin*, 235.

[57] "Peace Brigade Urged," *New York Times*, January 3, 1962, p. 23; "Call for Strike," *Times* (London), February 26, 1962, p. 10; ibid., March 8, 1962, p. 11 column 3; Anderson, *Bayard Rustin*, 234, 235.

Sutherland, "the Sharpville Massacre was a key turning point for a decision to engage in armed struggle rather than carry on the nonviolent approach."[58]

Soon after Sharpeville CORE and ACOA mounted a joint demonstration in New York City in support of black South Africans. Protesters marched from a local Woolworth's store (that chain then under fire for segregated lunch counters in the South) to the South African consulate, making apparent the similarity between Jim Crow and apartheid. In the San Francisco Bay Area, the International Longshoreman's Association (ILA) refused to handle cargo entering from or destined for South Africa. Dockworkers called for solidarity from other unions and for United Nations action. In the course of the 1960s other maritime workers joined the condemnation of apartheid.[59]

The antiapartheid campaigns began to unfold in the United States as a peaceful movement, but challenges to nonviolent protest began to resonate ever more loudly abroad. The Martinique-born psychiatrist Frantz Fanon, who had hovered at the margins of the Society of African Culture (SAC), rejected its political silence in the midst of the powerful conflicts swirling across Africa. Fanon's first book, *Peau noire, masques blancs* (*Black Skin, White Masks*), published in 1952, psychoanalytically dissected the pathologies that colonial society inflicted on the psyche, viewing these ills from the standpoint of the French West Indian subject.[60] Fanon had attended SAC's first Congress of Black Writers and Artists in Paris in 1956 and the second in Rome in 1959. At both meetings, his speeches questioned nonviolent direct action.[61] Fanon used *Présence Africaine* and other journals as vehicles to acquaint Africa-interested publics with the Algerian revolution.[62] Subsequent books, *Les damnés de la terre* (1962) [*The Wretched of the Earth* (1963)]; *Pour la révolution africaine; écrits politiques* (1964) [*Toward the African Revolution: Political Writings* (1967)]; *L'an v de la Révolution algérienne* (1966) [*A Dying Colonialism* (1966)]; focused more directly on Algerian themes and on the advocacy of violence as a legitimate weapon against colonial rule.[63]

Several circumstances delayed the global impact of these writings and their influence in the English-speaking world. Fanon remained on the fringes of

---

[58] Sutherland interview.

[59] "Dockmen Ask Boycott," *New York Times*, April 11, 1960, p. 6; Donald R. Culverson, *Contesting Apartheid: U.S. Activism, 1960–1987* (Boulder, Colo.: Westview Press, 1999), 44–5; "Danes Bar South Africa Cargo," *New York Times*, July 6, 1963, p. 4.

[60] Frantz Fanon, *Peau noire, masques blancs* (Paris: Éditions du Seuil, 1952); *Black Skin, White Masks*, trans. Charles L. Markmann, (New York: Grove Press, 1967).

[61] Perinbaum, *Holy Violence*, 73, 74.

[62] "Fondements réciproques de la culture nationale et des luttes de libération," *Présence Africaine* 24–5 (February–May 1959).

[63] *L'an v de la Révolution algérienne* (Paris: F. Maspero, 1966), published in English as *A Dying Colonialism*, trans. Haakon Chevalier (New York: Grove Press, 1966); *Les damnés de la terre* (Paris: F. Maspero, 1962), published in English as *The Wretched of the Earth*, trans. Constance Farrington (New York: Grove Press, 1963); *Pour la révolution africaine; écrits politiques* (Paris: F. Maspero, 1964), published in English as *Toward the African Revolution*, trans. Haakon Chevalier (New York: Grove Press, 1967).

international black literary networks. Annoyed by *négritude* writers' enchant-
ment with an idealized African past and with the "African personality," he was
attracted to the brutal realism in the works of black American writer Richard
Wright, then a Paris resident. Wright did not respond, however, to Fanon's early
efforts to establish a correspondence. Wright and Fanon knew many of the
same figures, such as Jean-Paul Sartre and Simone de Beauvoir, but they apparently failed to connect with one another. As the Algerian revolution intensified,
Fanon became more involved with it and less concerned with a metropolitan
literary scene he had come to despise as effete and reactionary.[64]

Just as the luster of nonviolent direct action began fading in Africa, it reached
the zenith of its power in the United States. Early in October 1960, Indian Prime
Minister Jawaharlal Nehru, in New York to attend the UN General Assembly
meeting, participated in a CORE ceremony to mark Mahatma Gandhi's birth-
day. There he expressed his approval of the sit-in movement then spreading
across the United States.[65] Nehru spoke however, against the backdrop of the
international shock of Sharpeville. "After Sharpville, people's confidence in
nonviolence was shaken," Sutherland remembered. Pretoria's brutal actions
"and the militant uprising which followed was a calamity that almost brought
down the South African government." Sutherland recalled how "international
bankers were frightened, the money was flying out of there, and the economy
was significantly destabilized. If it hadn't been for Chase Manhattan Bank's
assistance, the [South African] government might really have fallen." In any
case, the longtime activist counseled, nonviolent direct action as a tactic was
no guarantee of nonviolent results. "A militant nonviolent movement must be
ready to face casualties, just as those engaging in armed struggle face the possibility of casualties." It was clear that "the events surrounding Sharpville led to
the official banning of the ANC and the PAC, and their subsequent launching
of the armed struggle."[66]

Sharpeville also drove home the fact that in 1960 no black organization that
existed on either side of the Atlantic could systematically address African realities as a whole. In the United States, the old Council on African Affairs had fallen
victim to cold war anticommunism. What relationship would people of African
descent in the diaspora have to independent nations? Some institutional linkages
did exist. The African-American Institute produced a plethora of Africa-related
programs but was a paragovernmental body with little actual black American
representation. Its name referred to communication among states and state
agencies, not to a hyphenated ethnicity. Other organs were AMSAC, which
concentrated on cultural, rather than political matters, and ACOA, which represented an interracial professional elite. As one author has noted, "ACOA was
constrained by its roots in liberal, anticommunist organizations while trying

[64] Michel Fabre, "Frantz Fanon et Richard Wright," in *L'Actualité de Frantz Fanon*, ed. Elo Dacy (Paris: Kartha, 1986), 169–80.
[65] "Nehru 'Pleased' by Sit-in Movement," *Amsterdam News*, October 15, 1960, p. 8.
[66] Sutherland interview; Sutherland and Meyer, *Guns and Gandhi in Africa*, 150–1.

to support an African liberation movement that was becoming increasingly radical."[67] The NAACP, which continued to monitor African events and took policy stands on African questions, avoided a Pan-Africanist identification per se. In any event, its mission remained chiefly domestic.

African freedom, of course, did not depend on NAACP endorsements, and the tide of sovereignty in 1960 made African nations more difficult for Western governments – and diaspora populations – to dismiss. As NCNW member Vivian Beamon put it, "Our interest in Africa started with anthropology and the creative arts, and has gradually become political. Independence in Africa jolted the American Negro and helped stimulate our civil rights movement, which in turn has helped stimulate civil-rights movements in Southern Rhodesia, Mozambique, and South Africa. Everything ties together."[68]

While Beamon may have not clearly separated national liberation struggles from civil rights reform, many Africans drew this distinction. Well into the 1960s, pacifists and civil rights proponents believed that transplanting techniques from the freedom movement in the American South to Africa, though difficult, was possible. "If, for example, a tried and able group of AfroAmericans [*sic*] from the Birmingham scene (meaning the whole movement in the South) could be brought over here," Sutherland wrote from Dar es Salaam, "with strategists like Bayard [Rustin] ... and we could work out a realistic driving project with snowball potential, I'm sure the SW Africans[,] Eduardo Mondlane of Mozambique – even [Joshua] Nkomo would listen."[69]

Sutherland and others clearly understood that Africans had to be in the forefront of any sustained strategy of nonviolence on the continent, but a suggestion of the old missionary-related stewardship inflected their discussion of how black Americans would assist nonviolent direct action projects. This is apparent in the belief that veterans of Dixie campaigns could arrive in Africa and put the strategy together in spite of a lack of knowledge of local conditions. They would create a model of liberation in the likeness of the sit-ins, boycotts, and Freedom Rides in America, suggesting that the U.S. experience had universal applicability. Muste recognized the problematic situation of peace advocates in Africa. He understood that their "real contacts" had "traditionally" been with white elites. They had fooled themselves into thinking that they could broker differences between African dissidents and the colonial status quo. In reality, however, "no such middle ground" as they sought to occupy existed. Workers like George Houser of ACOA and Bayard Rustin would have to embed themselves in African communities.[70]

Certain State Department officials believed that an NGO devoted to African affairs could assist U.S. objectives in Africa if it could be corralled into a

---

[67] Francis Njubi Nesbitt, *Race for Sanctions: African Americans against Apartheid, 1946–1994* (Bloomington: Indiana University Press, 2004), 25–6.

[68] Special Interest," *New Yorker*, October 17, 1964, p. 44.

[69] Sutherland to A. J. Muste, May 31, 1963, World Peace Brigade Papers, Box 1, folder 4.

[70] A. J. Muste to Lyle Tatum, August 15, 1962, ibid., Box 1, folder 3.

serviceable arm of American foreign policy. The State Department wanted to know how citizens felt about African questions but persisted in seeing Africa through the rivalry with the Soviets. Anticolonialism and antiracism took second place to suppressing left-wing insurgencies. "Our primary strategic military aim" in sub-Saharan Africa "is to deny it to Communist control," the NSC acknowledged in 1960. "Our thinking was that, so far as any major effort was concerned, black Africa should have a relatively low priority. This did not mean that we should not make an effort but rather that our efforts should be limited to technical assistance and some individual projects like Volta Dams." The result of this indifference was waffling on decolonization at the UN and in relations with European allies even when the USSR was not directly at issue. For most of the 1950s, policy makers concerned themselves with the dangers posed for Africa by radical trade unionism originating in Western Europe, while tacitly recognizing the Soviet sphere of influence in Eastern Europe.[71] The State Department, White House, and other government entities failed to benefit from the energies that civil rights and national liberation struggles were unleashing because they underestimated their range and intensity, their ability to share strategies, tactics, and discourses, and their fundamental opposition to many U.S. policy aims.

Apart from cold war competition, the United States and newly emerging countries did not always share the same assumptions about what constituted democracy and human rights. Tension over these issues increased as new nations populated the Commission on Human Rights and other UN bodies. According to political scientist Howard Tolley, "the Western members and their ideological allies in Asia and Latin America who controlled the Commission through the 1950's promoted a classical liberal conception of human rights."[72] Their emphasis was on individual freedom from state repression rather than the rights of minorities, a cause seen as more attractive when it focused on the failings of Communist governments.

Yet domestic and international pressures forced U.S. officials to admit a relationship between injustice to African Americans and colonialism and racism in Africa. This implied a broad critique of U.S. society that was inherently risky. Unmanaged, it could form a matrix of dissent sufficiently commanding

[71] "Theme of First ACOA Conference-'Is Colonialism Dying in Africa?'" *Africa Today* 1 (June-July 1954): 1; Secretary of State Acheson to Certain Diplomatic and Consular Offices, January 16, 1951, *FRUS, 1951* X, *The Near East and Africa* (Washington, D.C.: Government Printing Office, 1982), 1210–11; NSC 6005/1, April 9, 1960, *Documents of the National Security Council, 1947–1977* (Washington, D.C.: University Publications of America, 1980); NSC 456, August 8, 1960, DDRS. (The version of NSC 456 published as NSC 6005 in *FRUS*, XXVI, *1958–1960, Africa*, omits much of the dismissive appraisal of Africa that is in the DDRS edition.) George Houser, "Meeting Africa's Challenges: The Story of the American Committee on Africa," *Issue* 3 (Summer/Fall 1976): 18. On Cold War labor politics in Africa, see Yevette Richards, *Maida Springer, Pan-Africanist and International Labor Leader* (Pittsburgh: University of Pittsburgh Press, 2000).

[72] Howard Tolley, Jr., *The UN Commission on Human Rights* (Boulder, Colo. and London: Westview Press, 1987), 37.

to challenge the state's legitimacy, expand popular participation, and disrupt existing patterns of authority. Channeled, it could be presented as a moral campaign that society would undertake, thus supporting and enhancing state claims to perfectibility while undercutting radical assertions that fundamental change was necessary. While some black activists seemed content to have a seat at the table where these issues were debated, others perceived that "sponsorship" meant that their voices would be marginalized. The latter sometimes developed a deeper appraisal of U.S. policy, while the former often became board members and consultants on "the Negro problem."

The uphill struggle for rights in the United States thus continued to lag. Violence still rocked the U.S. South, and observers noted that Congress had yet to pass strong civil rights legislation. African envoys encountered bias in housing and public accommodations in New York and Washington. These experiences held up a mirror to the lives of black people in the United States. Many remembered how Gbedemah's 1958 decision to test the Jim Crow laws on the well-traveled Route 40 corridor between New York City and Maryland verified the reality of discrimination. The refusal of a Howard Johnson's restaurant to serve him a glass of orange juice made international headlines and prompted, by way of contrition, a hasty invitation to the White House. Also recalled was how in 1960 Secretary of State Christian Herter encouraged the Ghanaian embassy counselor to observe elections in rural Georgia as a showcase of democracy. R. M. Akwei accordingly traveled to Mableton, Georgia, where local whites roughed him up. The State Department fumbled its apology, leading to a formal protest by Ghana.[73]

While the stark polarities of white versus black, colonialism versus freedom, and racism versus tolerance had early impact, they became ambiguous in the era of African self-rule. One of the most discouraging examples of these complexities unfolded in the Congo. After Ghanaian independence in 1957 and plans for the incipient independence of other African states, Belgium hastily set up a timetable for Congolese sovereignty. Few Western governments showed enthusiasm for the prospect, fearing radical Pan-Africanism and Communist infiltration. Rapid decolonization sacrificed the extended education, modernization, and acculturation that many believed the Congo required. Belgium had not trained many African technicians, and Congolese university graduates were few. There was no large educated indigenous bourgeoisie in the manner

---

[73] K. A. Gbedemah to Bunche, November 21, 1957, Ralph Bunche additions, Box 3 folder "Correspondence – 1957–1960 Africa," Ralph Bunche Papers, SC; Sutherland and Meyer, *Guns and Gandhi in Africa*, 42–3; Pittsburgh *Courier*, November 19, 1960, p. 1. For the race issue as it affected foreign diplomats of color in the United States, see Thomas J. Schoenbaum, *Waging Peace and War* (New York: Simon & Schuster, 1988), 381–3; Renée Romano, "No Diplomatic Immunity: African Diplomats, the State Department, and Civil Rights, 1961–1964," *Journal of American History* 87 (September 2000): 546–79; Michael Krenn, "The Unwelcome Mat: African Diplomats in Washington, D.C. during the Kennedy Years," in *Window on Freedom*, 163–80.

of "the new Nigerian elite." Belgium had even barred black Americans from the colony, fearing they would "whet the appetite for Independence."[74]

Attorney Adlai Stevenson, the putative liberal and erstwhile Democratic presidential candidate, represented diamond and bauxite interests in West and Central Africa. He enthused about Belgian initiatives in the Congo to a skeptical Cyrus L. Sulzberger.[75] The State Department shared Sulzberger's doubts about how adequately the Belgians had prepared the Congolese for nationhood. Director of the Budget Maurice Stans, of subsequent Watergate fame, went to Africa to scout out conditions. Stans, who would help establish the African Wildlife Foundation, had traveled and hunted in the continent since 1948. He reported to the NSC about his Congo experiences a few months after Congolese independence: "Mr. Stans, while disclaiming any expertise, said he had formed the impression that many Africans still belonged in the trees."[76]

Trouble began at the rite to hand over power to the new Democratic Republic of the Congo on June 30, 1960. Congolese premier Patrice Lumumba found himself written out of the scripted ceremony, a harbinger of things to come. King Baudouin of Belgium made a paternalistic speech, and, near the end of the proceedings, Lumumba seized the microphone. The U.S. ambassador to Guinea, William Morrow, recalled the new Congolese leader, "lashing out in some of the most bitter French I have ever heard" against Belgian wrongdoing in his country. The actual text of Lumumba's speech, however, reveals no factual inaccuracies.[77]

Within days of the transition, the Congolese army mutinied against its Belgian officers and attacked white civilians, who began fleeing the country in panic. The assaults on whites prompted Belgium to land troops. In the interim, the fragile coalition politics that had brought Lumumba and President Joseph Kasavubu together broke down. The imminent collapse of the central government emboldened secessionists in wealthy Katanga Province, which produced most of the world's cobalt and diamonds, as well as copper, tin, and uranium. Interested Europeans encouraged Katanga separatists to declare their independence on July 11, under the leadership of Moïse Tshombe. Financiers and industrialists hoped for a pliable Katanga regime where business would continue as usual. At the Congolese government's request, the UN Security Council took up the crisis on July 14, 1960, and organized an emergency military task

---

[74] Stephen R. Weissman, *American Foreign Policy in the Congo, 1960–1964* (Ithaca, N.Y.: Cornell University Press, 1974), 44.

[75] Cyrus L. Sulzberger, *The Last of the Giants* (New York: Macmillan, 1970), 409–10. On Stevenson's work in Africa, see *The Papers of Adlai Stevenson*, vol. 7, ed. Walter Johnson (Boston: Little, Brown, 1977), passim.

[76] Memorandum of discussion at the 432d meeting of the National Security Council, 14 January 1960, FRUS XXVI, 1958–1960, Africa, 77.

[77] John H. Morrow, *First American Ambassador to Guinea* (New Brunswick, N.J.: Rutgers University Press, 1968), 153; Dunn, *Imagining the Congo*, 76–7. The full text of the speech can be found in *Lumumba Speaks: The Speeches and Writings of Patrice Lumumba, 1958–1961*, ed. Jean Van Lierde (Boston: Little, Brown, 1972), 220–4.

force ostensibly to preempt the Belgians and restore order until the legitimate government could rally. The expedition consisted of soldiers from states not permanently represented on the Security Council, a ploy designed to forestall both Soviet and U.S. direct intervention and reassure Belgian nationals and other Europeans with a stake in the former colony.[78]

It soon became clear that Lumumba had a different understanding of the UN mission. He expected it to end the secession and put the Belgians in their place, that is, back in Belgium. The UN's emphasis on police functions and its failure to be firm with Brussels angered Lumumba and led him to request Soviet assistance. The United States then swung into action. The Congo was now a cold war concern. A consensus developed in the White House and the NSC that Lumumba should be removed. A campaign of vilification accompanied staff discussions, as if top security officials had to rev themselves up to justify liquidating the Congolese leader. Lest racism be thought a motive, they sought and received corroboration for Lumumba's alleged maniacal character from Ralph Bunche, whose vituperative reactions to the Congolese leader were surprising in such a normally cool-headed diplomat.[79] CIA director Allen Dulles told President Eisenhower that Lumumba was a drug addict. He had a penchant for blondes, a predilection historians would later learn he shared with certain U.S. presidents. Subsequent intelligence reports described him as mentally ill. "Lumumba was not yet disposed of and remained a grave danger as long as he was not disposed of," Dulles warned Ike. A CIA forensic expert was instructed to poison an anonymous "African leader."[80]

[78] Studies of the Congo crisis include Lise A. Namikas, "Battleground Africa: The Cold War and the Congo Crisis, 1960–1965" (PhD diss., University of Southern California, Los Angeles, 2002); Nzongola-Ntalaja, "United States Policy toward Zaire," in *African Crisis Areas and U.S. Foreign Policy*, eds. Gerald J. Bender, James S. Coleman, and Richard L. Sklar, (Berkeley: University of California Press, 1985): 225–38; David N. Gibbs, *The Political Economy of Third World Intervention: Mines, Money, and U. S. Policy in the Congo Crisis* (Chicago: University of Chicago Press, 1991); Michael G. Schatzberg, *Mobutu or Chaos? The United States and Zaire, 1960–1990* (Lanham, Md.: University Press of America, 1991); Madeleine G. Kalb, *The Congo Cables: The Cold War in Africa from Eisenhower to Kennedy* (New York: Macmillan, 1982); Henry F. Jackson, *From the Congo to Soweto: U.S. Foreign Policy toward Africa since 1960* (New York: W. Morrow, 1982); Stephen R. Weissman, *American Foreign Policy in the Congo, 1960–1964* (Ithaca, N.Y.: Cornell University Press, 1974).

[79] Nzongola-Ntalaja, "United States Policy toward Zaire," 225–38; Ralph Bunche to Andrew D. Cordier, August 9, 1960, Correspondence, unnumbered boxes, Andrew D. Cordier Papers, Columbia University. Mrs. Henry E. Gumbel to Bunche c. August 30, 1960; Bunche to Gumbel, September 3, 1960, Congo mission June '60, correspondence A-F; Georges Dennler de la Tour to Bunche, February 10, 1962, correspondence re Congo 1962, Ralph J. Bunche Papers, UCLA, Box 125.

[80] Dunn, *Imagining the Congo*, 91–2; Stephen R. Weissman, "An Extraordinary Rendition," *Intelligence and National Security* 25 (April 2010): 198–222; Ludo de Witte, *The assassination of Lumumba* (London and New York: Verso, 2001); Christopher Andrew, *For the President's Eyes Only: Secret Intelligence and the American Presidency from Washington to Bush* (New York: HarperCollins, 1995), 253.

U.S. officials also disapproved of Lumumba's ideas on modernization. While in New York in 1960, Lumumba contacted the Phelps Stokes Fund with an eye to recruiting African-American talent for technical projects in the Congo. U.S. officials also disliked his having signed a contract with a venture capitalist they did not trust. "It was evidence of Lumumba's desire to receive bilateral technical and other assistance from all quarters in addition to UN assistance." Throwing the Congo open to foreign investment was not an idea to which U.S. policy makers objected on principle; the problem was that the emporium that Lumumba seemed to be inaugurating would not be controlled by people they knew.[81]

An emergency session on the Congo convened in the General Assembly on September 17, 1960, with thirty-two heads of state attending. While the presence of new members called for celebration, the Congo crisis lent gravity to the occasion. The assembly rejected Guinea's request that it seat Lumumba's delegation as the official one but proposed creating an advisory group that comprised African states that would monitor UN Congo operations.

Army elements under the command of Joseph Mobutu broke away from the dissolving Congolese central government in mid-September. President Kasavubu, ostensibly to save what was left of the crumbling state, agreed to have Lumumba arrested and handed over to secessionists in Leopoldville. Lumumba escaped and was en route to his home base in Stanleyville when he was again captured. This time he would not break free. U.S. embassy second secretary Frank Carlucci recalled that "in December 1960, a US Senate Study Mission to Africa arrived in the Congo." Carlucci was drinking beer with Senator Gale McGee from Wyoming "at an outdoor café" when, presumably unbeknownst to McGee, "a truck passed by with the bound Lumumba in the back." In December 1961, Lumumba, beaten and tortured, was executed by agents of the secessionist, Moïse Tshombe. He "was cut off before he could show what he could do," Bill Sutherland regretfully recalled.[82] Lumumba's murder infuriated the African world but seemed temporarily to appease Western powers and interested corporations. If Lumumba had been the real problem in the Congo, that problem should have been solved. It was not.

Chester Bowles's report for the president in mid-December 1962 recommended continued U.S. support for the weak Lumumbist regime of Cyrille Adoula if Adoula agreed to keep the Soviets out and protect Tshombe's "legitimate interests as a province leader during the unification process." If Tshombe refused an ultimatum to sign a peace agreement, Bowles proposed, the UN should forcibly prevent Katanga from moving copper. The Joint Chiefs and the European Bureau opposed this plan, with the generals claiming that Tshombe's mercenaries were too strong for UN troops to overcome. Bowles's viewpoint

---

[81] "Reticent about Financing," *New York Times*, July 24, 1960, p. 2.
[82] Weissman, "An Extraordinary Rendition," 221. Sutherland interview.

briefly prevailed, but 1962 witnessed a gradual lessening of the already dubious American commitment to the Congo's political integrity.[83]

Katanga had become a cause célèbre for right-wing elements in Europe and the United States, its unpopularity with the Baluba-speaking majority in Katanga Province notwithstanding. Katanga's short-lived autonomy led to a Baluba uprising and thousands of deaths. The overt Belgian presence in the rebel province's militia appalled defenders of Congo unity. The province had put out a call for white soldiers of fortune, who poured into the country from South Africa and Rhodesia. A handful of former Nazis and Italian fascists, helped to deploy by the Belgian mining company Union Minière, arrived from Europe. In the United States, conservatives founded the American Committee for Aid to Katanga Freedom Fighters. The committee had the support of such worthies as Roman Catholic fundamentalist L. Brent Bozell; his brother-in-law, *National Review* founder William F. Buckley; William Miller, chair of the Republican National Committee; Senator James O. Eastland of Mississippi; and Arizona senator Barry Goldwater.[84]

A Belgian publicist hired by Tshombe bought airtime on black radio stations and placed ads in the *New York Times* and the *Washington Post*. The American Committee for Aid to Katanga Freedom Fighters reached out to black conservatives, naming professional anticommunist Max Yergan chair of the committee and recruiting the journalist George Schuyler and his daughter, Philippa Schuyler. If, as is still generally assumed, African-Americans' opinion on foreign issues meant little, why did supporters of neocolonialism pay publicists to solicit their support? The inclusion of figures like the Schuylers and Yergan on the committee aimed at offsetting accusations of racism. Katanga also attracted such opportunists as the notorious Caribbean-born aviator "Colonel" Herbert Julian. As the erstwhile "Black Eagle," Julian had graced the Harlem Renaissance with his piloting exploits. He thereafter gave up flying for gunrunning, an offense for which UN authorities deported him from the Congo. The committee made little headway in black communities, however. Its advocacy of Portuguese colonialism, its support for apartheid, and its implicit disregard for African freedom did not sit well with U.S. blacks during a time of transition in race relations. The organization had better luck with Katanga as fodder for right-wing agitation and as a problem it hoped to fling in Kennedy's face when he sought reelection.[85]

Katanga's best advocates nevertheless comprised more than a crackpot fringe. Former president Herbert Hoover and former vice president Richard

[83] Chester Bowles, *Promises to Keep: My Years in Public Life, 1941–1969* (New York: Harper & Row, 1971), 428.

[84] Gibbs, *The Political Economy of Third World Intervention*, 86, 87.

[85] "Friends of Katanga 'Freedom Fighters' Scrape Bottom of the Barrel to Form Birchite Front Group," *Liberation* 1 (October 1961): 1, 4; Baltimore *Afro-American*, August 15, 1974, p. 20; Houser, "Meeting Africa's Challenges," 21; advertisement, *Washington Post*, January 9, 1963, p. A11; Roger Hilsman, *To Move a Nation* (New York: Doubleday, 1967), 253, 255, 262 n. 1, 262 n. 2.

Nixon numbered among those who made their secessionist sympathies known. Familiars of the *National Review* were prominent voices on an issue subsequently adopted by the John Birch Society and the Committee of One Million, originally part of the old China Lobby. Just as conservatives had castigated Harry Truman in 1950 for the "loss" of China, they now denounced the UN and the Kennedy administration for opening the door to Communist incursions into black Africa. Katanga provided new grounds for staging the cold war and rebuffing the principle of international organization. Additionally, certain foreign policy veterans had private financial interests in the Congo. Some, like George McGhee, a Texas oilman and former assistant secretary of state, argued that the United States should recognize Katanga. State Department Africanists did not agree. Europeanists, while not favoring secession, discounted the overall significance of African affairs.[86]

The Congo episode upended the hope of an Africa united against racism and imperialism and able to render moral assistance to beleaguered African descendants in the diaspora. It also helped define the contours of U.S. policy in Africa for much of the twentieth century. As of this writing, neither the State Department nor the CIA has released fifty-year-old documents that affirm what both scholars and historical actors themselves have determined was the vigorously proactive role the CIA played in the Congo.[87] The assassination plan generally understood to have been authorized by Eisenhower was the stick used to discipline the Congolese and, by extension, all newly independent Africans. The carrot was foreign aid and missionary and philanthropic help in creating African middle classes, the presumed vanguard of stable democracies. Washington officials discussed a proposal for a "U.S. commission to aid in the training and education of African people to take over leadership and administration of new African nations." Americans in the past were "inhibited by our relationships with the colonial offices, which are now passing from influence. We have had no coordination of public and private efforts." While the United States lacked the history that could help it make imperialist "sense" of a fractured African country like the Congo, some saw in African Americans a possible link to Congolese realities. The U.S. government had "an asset few other nations can match – our own large negro [*sic*] population and the efforts they are so anxious to make in this regard," read a State Department memorandum. "Compared to what the Africans have available, the poorest U.S. school is Harvard itself." For the proposed commission to function on the presidential level, it "should take advantage of our main asset at the very outset and be bi-racial in character."[88]

---

[86] Gibbs, *The Political Economy of Third World Intervention*, 122–3, 120.

[87] Weissman, "An Extraordinary Rendition," 209; Larry Devlin, *Chief of Station, Congo: A Memoir of 1960–67* (New York: Public Affars, 2007).

[88] Department of State, Congo crisis and establishment of a U.S. commission to aid in the training and education of African people to take over leadership and administration of new African nations, Miscellaneous, n.d., pp. 1–3; see also PCIAA – 31/2, The President's Committee on Information Activities Abroad, Africa, July 18, 1960, p. 29, DDRS.

In the summer of 1960, the Phelps Stokes Fund, a conduit for aid to African-American scholars and to historically black colleges and universities, inaugurated a major policy shift. It stopped making individual grants and instead put its resources into improving African schools and black schools in the American South.[89] The foundation anticipated a tenfold increase in the number of Africans studying in the United States, with Howard University projected as a major center of activity. African education, the new approach mandated, was now an immediate priority and coincided with the State Department's new commitment. Foggy Bottom believed that the Congo crisis "warrants the appointment of a Presidential Commission empowered to coordinate the public and private opportunities to step up our effort by many times."[90] Potential black candidates for commission membership included the familiar "moderate" figures: Ralph Bunche; psychologist Kenneth Clark; Lester Granger; James Nabritt, president of Howard University; Jackie Robinson; and Phelps Stokes president and former Tuskegee Institute head Frederick Patterson.

Just as Americans were busily reassessing Africa, the Soviets were doing likewise. After failed post-Stalin efforts to control the direction of the Chinese revolution, Moscow turned its attention to other rural countries. Stalin had been wrong, Khrushchev asserted, to place so little credence in African and Asian ability to sustain Communist revolutions. The USSR began founding institutes for the academic study of Africa at the same time that similar initiatives materialized in the United States. Improved intelligence gathering and additional funding for African students accompanied Soviet efforts.[91]

The Americans and Soviets alike sought to create partisans among the new countries' educated leadership. African-American elites wished to inject themselves into this process. What better advisers on monitoring this transition, they reasoned, than expert people of color? "Black social scientists and historians have been in greatest demand," John H. Stanfield has written, "when white elites perceive a crisis in their racial authority. This was particularly apparent between the world wars and during the 1960s." Openings for black academics and policy wonks generally prove temporary, however. "When elites resolve their racial crisis of authority or are distracted by other pressing issues, as in the 1950s and post-1960s," Stanfield commented, "the market for scholarship on blacks decreases along with the elite sponsorship of black entry into the social sciences."[92]

[89] Phelps Stokes Fund press release, July 5, 1960, SSRC Records, Series 1, subseries 3, Box 17, folder 127, RAC.

[90] Department of State, Congo crisis and establishment of a U.S. commission to aid in the training and education of African people ...., 2.

[91] Odd Arne Westad, *The Global Cold War* (Cambridge: Cambridge University Press, 2006), 68; Laurence H. Shoup and William Minter, *Imperial Brain Trust* (New York: Monthly Review Press, 1977), 215, 216.

[92] John H. Stanfield, *Philanthropy and Jim Crow in American Social Science* (Westport, Conn.: Greenwood Press, 1985), 6.

For the moment, however, black voices were part of the punditry, and influential institutions developed Africa-focused programs with the input of African-American professionals. Establishment figures showed willingness to communicate with black foreign policy audiences. Assistant secretary of state for African affairs Joseph C. Satterwaite in 1960 addressed the Howard University Division of Social Science annual conference. The subject was "Problems of Emerging African States." Attendees included Baron Leopold Dhanis, counselor of the Belgian embassy, and Douglas Williams, colonial attaché at the British embassy. The same year, the Rockefeller Brothers Fund began to finance Operations Crossroads Africa, a volunteer program originated in Harlem by the Reverend James Robinson. Crossroads expanded from its original summer work camp model to a broader program that provided teachers for Africa. The program soon started a Caribbean branch operation. "A Crossroads experience in Africa has been a key factor in getting a number of young American black leaders involved in African affairs," a Rockefeller Brothers Fund committee reported. State Department support of Crossroads, to bring "bright young African leaders" to the United States, began in 1964.[93]

Quickening activities among both governmental groups and NGOs and projections about the increased salience of decolonization led the Eisenhower White House to try an eleventh-hour reversal of its long-standing lethargy re Africa in 1959 and 1960. The effort bowed to the changing world picture and to the desire to garner black votes for Richard Nixon's presidential run. The NSC recommended that the government "seek to correct distorted African views of U.S. race relations, emphasizing, where appropriate, progress made by the United States in the race relations field." The administration continued to slip up, however, neglecting, for example, to include any black people in its official delegation to Nigeria's independence celebration. An African-American contingent, including Martin Luther King, Thurgood Marshall, A. Philip Randolph, and W.E.B. Du Bois, did attend the ceremony as private guests of the Nigerian government.[94]

Ike's successor, John F. Kennedy, only appeared to open a new chapter in U.S. relations with Africa. Handling the race problem, as Henry Kissinger advised Lester Granger, involved managing perceptions rather than substance. For a decolonizing Africa, improving America's reputation accompanied the creation and expansion of indigenous bourgeoisies that appreciated and absorbed the

[93] Rayford W. Logan to Mordecai Johnson. March 23, 1960, Rayford W. Logan Papers, MSRC; William S. Moody memorandum, June 1, 1972; Rockefeller Brothers Fund, executive committee, docket memo, July 14, 1971, Rockefeller Brothers Fund, Operation Crossroads Africa, series 4, box 205, RAC.

[94] Dwight D. Eisenhower, *Waging Peace, 1956–1961* (New York: Doubleday, 1965) 578; NSC Report #6005/1: U.S. Policy toward West Africa, April 9, 1960, *Documents of the National Security Council, 1947–1977*, reel 4; S; James H. Meriwether, "'Worth a Lot of Negro Votes': Black Voters, Africa, and the 1960 Presidential Campaign," *Journal of American History* 95 (December 2008): 737–63; Chicago *Defender*, October 15–21, 1960; Baltimore *Afro-American*, November 19, 1960, TCF.

values of an advanced capitalist society. Myriad methods lent themselves to achieving this end, including student airlifts and foundation support.

As civil rights insurgency developed, it drew on historical links and on new conversations with other social movements with which it shared an ideological orientation and personnel, including the peace and disarmament movements. At the same time great power resistance to change and entrenched white settler rule in southern Africa led to growing acceptance of armed struggle as the most effective means of liberation. Nonviolent civil disobedience now became the conservative option, repudiated more and more in both Africa and the diaspora. A "one size fits all" approach to global racism and exploitation could not be sustained.

3

"Freedom's Struggle Crosses Oceans and Mountains"

Pope John XXIII, the fourth of thirteen children born to a family of tenant farmers in rural Italy, on May 15, 1961, issued an encyclical titled *Mater et Magistra*. Here the pontiff defined the Roman Catholic Church's position on "Christianity and social progress." The pastoral benevolence in the document's tone might seem paternalistic to the contemporary secularist, but the encyclical constituted a critical departure from the church's decades-long inertia on social and political issues. The Vatican was now responding to the tenor of the times. "There is a ... keener interest in world affairs shown by people of average education," the pope observed. "We are witnessing the break-away from colonialism and the attainment of political independence by the peoples of Asia and Africa." Changing times required a reaffirmation of Christian values. "The solidarity which binds all men together as members of a common family makes it impossible for wealthy nations to look with indifference upon the hunger, misery and poverty of other nations whose citizens are unable to enjoy even elementary human rights," *Mater et Magistra* noted. "Glaring economic and social imbalances" undermine global security.[1]

Pope John XXIII criticized self-interested forms of foreign assistance designed to create dependency and enhance wealthy states' pursuit of "their own plans for world domination." Exploitative aid practices "would in fact be introducing a new form of colonialism – cleverly disguised, no doubt, but actually reflecting that older, outdated type from which many nations have recently emerged." They would "have harmful impact on international relations, and constitute a menace to world peace." For the Vatican, the "whole raison d'être" of the state was "the realization of the common good in the temporal order." It identified this goal with a free market and embraced capitalism but rejected materialism of the socialist kind.[2]

---

[1] *Mater et Magistra Encyclical of Pope John XXIII on Christianity and Social Progress*, May 15, 1961, viewed online at http://www.vatican.va/holy_father/john_xxiii/encyclicals/documents/hf_j-xxiiI_enc_15051961_mater_En.html
[2] Ibid.

A year later the church canonized a seventeenth-century Peruvian mulatto. St. Martin de Porres, a Dominican friar, had long symbolized the Afro-Latin faithful in the New World. The canonization of this "black" saint occurred in the midst of decolonization, the expansion of the antiapartheid movement in South Africa, the U.S. civil rights movement, and increased awareness of Latin America's impoverished peoples of color. The church had turned its attention to justice, and only months before St. Martin's ascent, it convened the Vatican Ecumenical Council, or Vatican II.[3]

The council's purpose was to update the church in view of the unprecedented historical developments of the twentieth century. The pontiff sought a more democratic ecclesiastical body whose incorporation of the vernacular would strengthen it as a universal community and ensure its survival into the infinite future. The church's new objectives were consonant with the public policy pronouncements of John F. Kennedy, the United States' first Catholic president, whose election signified the "arrival" of American Catholics in the mainstream of the world's most powerful nation. The popular U.S. goals of outreach to Latin America and other developing areas, anticolonialism, anticommunism, and the quest for an end to poverty thus received both sacred and secular affirmation. A second encyclical, *Pacem in Terris*, issued in 1963,[4] gave further backing to proponents of racial equality, decolonization, and peace.

Eisenhower's poor health and lackluster responses to calls for change had helped Kennedy in the 1960 presidential election. Those interested in Africa hoped for a fresh approach from the new administration. Kennedy, inaugurated in January 1961, delivered a speech to Congress on foreign policy that invited a different perspective on international issues. But the president-elect wanted to name Arkansas senator J. William Fulbright, an avowed segregationist, as secretary of state. If FDR in 1937 did not let black pressure prevent him from appointing Alabama senator Hugo Black to the Supreme Court, and eight years later, if strenuous black objections did not hinder Truman from recommending governor James Byrnes of South Carolina for secretary of state, by 1960 times had changed. Disapproval made Kennedy reconsider. He named another southerner, Rockefeller Foundation president Dean Rusk, a racial liberal.[5]

3 "Pope Proclaims Mulatto Saint," *Chicago Daily Tribune*, May 7, 1962, p. 13; "Negro Saint's Day Held Blow to Racism," *New York Times*, November 4, 1962, p. 48; Patrick Allitt, *Catholic Intellectuals and Conservative Politics in America, 1950–1975* (Ithaca, N.Y.: Cornell University Press, 1993), 10, 84; Gayle Murchison, "Mary Lou Williams's Hymn Black Christ of the Andes (St. Martin de Porres): Vatican II, Civil Rights, and Jazz as Sacred Music," *The Musical Quarterly* 86 (4) (2002): 592.

4 *Pacem in Terris*, Encyclical of Pope John XXIII on Establishing Universal Peace in Truth, Justice, Charity, and Liberty, April 11, 1963, online at http://www.vatican.va/holy_father/john_xxiii/encyclicals/documents/hf_j-xxiii_enc_11041963_pacem_En.html; Allitt, *Catholic Intellectuals and Conservative Politics in America*, 61.

5 Enoc P. Waters, "JFK Couldn't Act on Fulbright as FDR Did on Black in 1937," *Amsterdam News*, December 24, 1960, p. 2.

In spite of high hopes, Kennedy was never fully attuned to either Africa or African Americans. George Ball recalled "the mood ... at the beginning of 1961" as so complacent that "even though Montgomery and Little Rock were place names with epic connotations, those at the top reaches of the Administration showed only a shadowy appreciation of the civil rights movement and the turbulence it would create. The new President spoke of that 'goddamn civil rights mess,'" Ball remembered, "considering it more an embarrassing problem than a serious cause that had gained many proponents."[6] During the May 1961 Freedom Rides, a journalist asked activists whether they agreed that the demonstrations humiliated the country on the eve of the Kennedy-Khrushchev summit, as both the secretary of state and the attorney-general had suggested. The Reverend Ralph Abernathy chose to respond. "Doesn't the Attorney General know we've been embarrassed all our lives?"[7] Formal Jim Crow was simply no longer acceptable, and Freedom Riders ignored White House pleas to cancel their southern campaigns.

Kennedy as a senator had proposed open U.S. support for the Algerian revolution but during the presidential campaign changed his tune, defending arms sales to France for use in North Africa. He deferred to De Gaulle on North African matters and rebuffed efforts by the FLN to secure a public endorsement. As voting time approached, the Democratic Party remained silent on Algeria. Worldwide pressure on France to surrender the colony nevertheless peaked after the General Assembly meeting of September 1960.[8] Once in office, Kennedy delegated his anticolonialism to appointees G. Mennen "Soapy" Williams, Wayne Fredericks, Adlai Stevenson, and Chester Bowles. This group of administrators held a nuanced view of the nationalism that had so troubled John Foster Dulles. They saw Afro-Asian reluctance to participate in the cold war as a potential source of strength for the West.[9] Kennedy's Africanists argued that genuine nationalism would work in the United States' favor. Cold war commitments were less important than new countries' dedication to their own freedom, which, if successfully realized, would render communist doctrines unattractive. Soapy Williams rebelled against the ban on meeting with Algerian rebels and held talks with FLN officials in October 1961. Pro-European, hard-line cold warriors in the State Department and the

---

[6] George Ball, *The Past Has Another Pattern* (New York: W. W. Norton, 1982), 165; Chester Bowles, *Promises to Keep: My Years in Public Life, 1941–1969* (New York: Harper & Row, 1971), 446.

[7] "Tension and Justice," *Newsweek*, June 12, 1961, p. 37; Abernathy quoted in Taylor Branch, *Parting the Waters: America in the King Years, 1954–1963* (New York: Simon & Schuster, 1988), 474.

[8] Jeffrey A. Lefebvre, "Kennedy's Algerian Dilemma: Containment, Alliance Politics and the 'Rebel Dialogue,'" *Middle Eastern Studies* 35 (2) (1999): 65–6; Irwin M. Wall, *France, the United States, and the Algerian War* (Berkeley: University of California Press, 2001); author's interview with Elombe Brath, May 16, 1994, New York City.

[9] St. Clair Drake to Melville and Frances Herskovits, September 13, 1960, Melville and Frances Herskovits Papers, Box 67, folder 681, SC. For an elaboration of the Africa Bureau's viewpoint, see Bowles, *Promises to Keep*, 614–15; Lefebvre, "Kennedy's Algerian Dilemma," 66–7, 71, 72.

Pentagon favored deferring to the former empires on colonial questions. Not to do so, they argued, might push De Gaulle, who had taken France out of NATO, into even greater military independence.

In bygone days, race would not have registered as a measure of the United States' international performance. Now it was significant. Kennedy needed to retain the black voters who had supported his candidacy, win the propaganda battle with the Soviets, and establish favorable relations with the new states. "The great battleground for the defense and expansion of freedom today is the whole southern half of the globe – Asia, Latin America, Africa and the Middle East – the lands of the rising peoples," he told Congress. These countries "are sites of a revolution which we would support, regardless of the 'cold war,' and regardless of which political or economic route they should choose to freedom." Communists nevertheless sought to exploit the righteous discontents of emerging peoples, and the president framed them as terrorists. "Their aggression is more often concealed than open. They have fired no missiles; and their troops are seldom seen. They send arms, agitators, aid, technicians and propaganda to every troubled area. But where fighting is required, it is usually done by others." They were "guerrillas striking at night," "assassins," "subversives and saboteurs and insurrectionists."[10]

In spite of Kennedy's suggestion that Third World nationalism should be separated from the cold war, the red adversary was portrayed as not only an enemy of the United States but also as a foe of the newly decolonized. Kennedy created a sense of urgency in making a case for shielding infant states from subversion. Vigorous initiatives for Africa by bold New Frontier activists should therefore be expected. Under Secretary of State Chester Bowles made a strong pitch for such departures. He called for more "Kennedy men" in the Foreign Service. Arthur M. Schlesinger, Jr., special assistant to the president, seconded these views. The problem in the Foreign Service went even deeper, Schlesinger added. "It receives a group of spirited young Americans at the age of 25 and transforms them in the next twenty years into a collection of eunuchs."[11] Schlesinger mentioned the "emasculation" of competence, initiative, and idealism several times, recapitulating the gendered discourse often characteristic of Kennedy-era official rhetoric. It was incumbent on White House loyalists to transform U.S. diplomacy.

In doing so, they would face an uphill battle with a staunchly Eurocentric State Department, whose European Affairs division enjoyed primacy. This branch did not take Africa seriously and did not want to antagonize NATO allies over African issues. The Africa Bureau's relative weakness, and defense analysts' warnings about jeopardizing access to strategic minerals, contributed

---

[10] Transcript of Kennedy Address to Congress on U.S. Role in Struggle for Freedom. *New York Times*, May 26, 1961, p. 12.

[11] Under Secretary of State Chester Bowles to President Kennedy, July 28, 1961, pp. 66–71; and Arthur M. Schlesinger, Jr. to McGeorge Bundy, August 11, 1961, pp. 72–5, in *FRUS, 1961–63*, XXV *Organization of Foreign Policy; Information Policy; United Nations; Scientific Matters*.

to a lukewarm attitude toward decolonization, and especially toward the Congo crisis, where emboldened secessionists in Katanga soon learned they had little to fear from the United States.[12]

The Africa Bureau targeted the Portuguese colony of Angola and apartheid in South Africa as critical concerns. While Soapy Williams and others never succeeded in curtailing the influence of European Affairs, they maintained the back door channel to Algeria. This included clandestine CIA-sponsored arms shipments to the FLN and a secret "education voucher program" for Algerian students who had been expelled from French universities. This initiative resembled the airlifts of African students from Kenya and Angola designed to create pro-American sentiment among future African leaders. The CIA even conveyed a dying Frantz Fanon to the United States for cancer treatment.[13]

Fanon's death in 1961 and the banning of his works in France meant that several years passed before the texts became widely available in both the original French and English translation. The Algerian revolution was thus nearly accomplished and Fanon dead before his admirers in North America and elsewhere had the opportunity to interpret his work.[14] Diaspora readers were enthralled by Fanon's blunt and brilliant language and trenchant insights about the colonial condition. During an era when hundreds of thousands of people intensely studied theoretical scholarship from a variety of disciplines in order to find ways to effect the collective liberation of colonized peoples and racial-ethnic minorities, the discerning psychiatrist seemed to offer good counsel on oppressive political, cultural, and social conditions.

His own intentions, however, were more modest. While the civil rights movement put African Americans in the headlines, "by contrast what Fanon found so debilitating about the colonial situation was the invisibility of blacks," Richard King has noted. Fanon insisted on the particularity of all national cultures and remained skeptical of Pan-Africanism. These aspects of his work tended "to undermine rather than to support the colonial analogy and use of violent struggle by black Americans."[15]

The youthful Ahmed Ben Bella was another face of the Algerian revolution. Ben Bella conferred with Martin Luther King Jr. when he visited the United States in October 1962. He had been imprisoned for the previous five years but "displayed a surprisingly intimate knowledge of the struggle and problems of the Afro-American," the radical black journal *Liberator* observed.

[12] Roger Hilsman, *To Move a Nation* (New York: Doubleday, 1967), 247, 256–7; Bowles, *Promises to Keep*, 427; Thomas Noer, *Soapy: A Biography of G. Mennen Williams* (Ann Arbor: University of Michigan Press, 2005).

[13] Ibid., 73–5; Wall, *France, the United States, and the Algerian War*, 240; James H. Meriwether, *Proudly We Can Be Africans: Black America and Africa, 1935–1961* (Chapel Hill: University of North Carolina Press, 2002), 146–8. On Angola, see Richard D Mahoney, *JFK: Ordeal in Africa* (New York: Oxford University Press, 1983), 188–222.

[14] David Macey, *Frantz Fanon* (New York: St. Martin's Press, 2000), 26.

[15] Richard H. King, *Civil Rights and the Idea of Freedom* (New York: Oxford University Press, 1992), 183.

Ben Bella condemned racism, warning that the United States would become a second-rate power unless the problem was successfully addressed. In the interim, Washington remained cautious about the Algerian insurgency and during its course never publicly admitted its expectation that the Algerians would break free. The United States ultimately recognized the Algerian government only after France did so. While acknowledging Ben Bella's personal integrity, U.S. policy makers, as a result of cold war–driven fears, were uncomfortable with his popularity in sub-Saharan Africa and his country's close relations with the Cuban revolutionary regime.[16]

Similar circumspection characterized U.S. relations with Guinea, a former French colony at loggerheads with France. Guinea's president, Sékou Touré, supported Lumumba and doubted the sincerity of the United States' anticolonialism. Kennedy let Touré know that his administration endorsed Eisenhower's position on the Congo. If Touré expected Kennedy to hold different views, he was disappointed. When a deputation of Democratic senators – Frank Church, Robert F. Kennedy, Gale McGee, and Frank B. Moss – arrived in Guinea in December 1960 they received less than a fervent reception. Touré was in Sierra Leone when they landed in Conakry. When he finally appeared, the delegation was made to wait to see him. The White House in retaliation decided not to implement a bilateral agreement signed during the last months of Ike's presidency. For their part, the senators recommended that the United States do just enough in Guinea to keep the door open.[17]

To the extent that South Africa was a litmus test for genuine policy revision, continuity rather than change remained the hallmark there also. The United States rhetorically condemned apartheid and endorsed nonviolent change, but its opposition to expelling South Africa from the UN or applying any mandatory sanctions neutralized these cautious steps. Washington rejected any action by UN members in concert against apartheid and acquiesced to the regime's harassment of dissidents. American authorities provided Pretoria with a supply of uranium 235 and took a purely legalistic approach to Southwest Africa, now Namibia, a trust territory that South Africa controlled in a manner contrary to the UN charter.

U.S. agricultural requirements also benefited South Africa. The "loss" of Cuba sent traders on a search for sugar. When South Africa left the British Commonwealth and forfeited its sugar subsidy, Congress came to the rescue. The American Negro Leadership Council on Africa (ANLCA), formed in 1961, protested the quota in a letter to Soapy Williams. With the support of the International Longshore and Warehouse Union, activist opposition to

---

[16] Lefebvre, "Kennedy's Algerian Dilemma;" "Ben Bella on Afro-American Liberation," *Liberator* 2 (December 1961): 14; Dr Martin Luther King, Jr., "My Talk with Ben Bella," *Amsterdam News*, October 27, 1962, p. 13. Piero Gleijeses, "Cuba's First Venture in Africa: Algeria, 1961–1965," *Journal of Latin American Studies* 28 (1) (1996): 159–95.

[17] Adrian Pelt to the Secretary General, October 15, 1959, Andrew W. Cordier Papers, Box 136, Columbia University; John H. Morrow interviewed by Celestine Tutt, May 11, 1981, Phelps Stokes Fund Oral History Project on Black Chiefs of Mission, SC, pp. 86–91.

U.S.–South African trade included a dockside demonstration by the NAACP, CORE, and the Women's International League for Peace and Freedom in the Bay Area against the unloading of the Dutch ship *Raki*. Yet nothing shook the Kennedy administration's claim that importing South African sugar did not constitute endorsement of apartheid.[18]

In spite of rhetorical celebration of African independence, the Kennedy White House proved ungenerous when faced with the opportunity to promote substantial change in Africa. Relations between the United States and Ghana had begun to sour while Eisenhower was still president. His successor did not improve them. Elite observers of Nkrumah – government officials, foundation executives, Western expatriates, corporate heads – considered his leadership autocratic and worried about his ideological proclivities. Washington decision makers used Nkrumah's desire to complete a major hydroelectric dam project as leverage against him. They wanted unambiguous loyalty from the Ghanaian leader and held out like a carrot promises of assistance for the ambitious Volta River hydroelectric dam. The project, begun during the late colonial period, was thought to have the potential to electrify the entire country and supply energy to neighboring states. Four years after independence, the United States was still hedging on its commitment to help build the dam, and Nkrumah began talks with an Italian firm. When the White House learned that he would visit the USSR, it suspended action on the dam until his return. The Soviets wined and dined Nkrumah in Moscow, where he praised Soviet support of national liberation movements and condemned colonialism at a diplomatic function in terms so harsh that the British contingent walked out.[19]

Angered by the Moscow visit, Kennedy consulted Prime Minister Harold Macmillan. Macmillan did not share Kennedy's vindictive perspective. He argued that the West could not chance losing the Volta project to Khrushchev. Funding it risked a great deal of money on an unstable country, Kennedy replied. (He did not explain how Ghana had suddenly become "unstable" in spite of Nkrumah's supposed ironclad dictatorship.) Bowing to Macmillan's advice, Kennedy sent an envoy to Accra to exact promises in exchange for U.S. support of the dam. Nkrumah had to accept a permanent representative of the World Bank, agree never to nationalize the smelter Kaiser Aluminum would build, and agree to a free press and civil liberties.[20]

In spite of actions that had become conventional in U.S. policy circles, the White House managed to preserve the illusion that it was making fundamental

[18] Tom Price, "Local 10 Commemorates Anti-Apartheid Boycott," *The Dispatcher* 62 (10) (November 2004): 2; Donald R. Culverson, *Contesting Apartheid: U.S. Activism, 1960–1987* (Boulder, Colo.: Westview Press, 1999), 60–2.

[19] William A. Hance, "The Volta River Project in the Gold Coast," Working Paper #1, Council on Foreign Relations file, Ralph Bunche Papers, UCLA; Mary E. Montgomery, "The Eyes of the World Were Watching: Ghana, Great Britain, and the United States, 1957–1966" (PhD diss., University of Maryland, 2004), p. 73.

[20] Ibid., 165; Dean Rusk, *As I Saw It* (New York: W. W. Norton, 1990). Harris Wofford, *Of Kennedys and Kings* (New York: Farrar, Straus, Giroux, 1980), 306.

changes. Nkrumah encouraged this, letting Britain know that it was in the Anglo-American interest to use Ghanaian progress as a symbol of what Africa as a whole could achieve with Western support. The dam was ultimately built and completed in January 1966 but did not have the critical impact on regional development originally hoped.[21]

For Americans, linking Africa to a bigger slate of ideas was intended to exhibit the vitality, idealism, and generosity of U.S. society. The Peace Corps, whose volunteers went mostly to Africa, was the organization in which the most publicly visible Africa policy would be played out. The enthusiasm that initially greeted the Peace Corps can be attributed to the multiple origins of the voluntary service idea. Its roots ranged from Mahatma Gandhi's vision of a "peace army" to conventional missionary practice, to social work–oriented settlement house projects, to the federal programs enacted during the New Deal. Secretary of State Dean Rusk wanted fresh faces in his department. Lack of advanced qualifications was not necessarily a fault, but in his eyes, a possible advantage. Graduate degrees, he held, were "a dime a dozen" and talent can emerge from "often unlikely places." The new breed of Foreign Service officer should enter the field uncorrupted by either pedantry or punditry. "I would not want to be quoted on this," he wrote to Under Secretary of State for Administration William H. Orrick Jr., "but ... my impression is that the graduate school experience tends to snuff out the 'gleam in the eye' of many young people."[22]

The opportunity to channel the energies of restless youth was undoubtedly important, but New Frontiersmen saw idealism as an instrument of policy rather than as an objective. "What President Kennedy wanted was not a true generational mobilization, which might have threatened loss of control," Thomas Engelhardt has written, "but the look of mobilization to shore up American power."[23] The president viewed the corps as a cold war weapon that neatly joined his call for national revitalization at home to dominance abroad. Others could make of it what they wanted.

The idea of a domestic equivalent to the Peace Corps percolated through Kennedy administration circles. Black New York politicians Adam Clayton Powell Jr. and J. Raymond Jones had pressured Kennedy to attend to urban affairs in exchange for their support. Social service professionals, with the help of Powell and others, initiated ambitious pilot social welfare programs in New York City to serve as national models. Egged on by elements of its urban electoral base, the administration presented a feasibility report to Congress on what would later become Volunteers in Service to America (VISTA). The

[21] Montgomery, "The Eyes of the World Were Watching," 175; Evan White, "Kwame Nkrumah: Cold War Modernity, Pan-African Ideology and the Geopolitics of Development," *Geopolitics* 8 (2) (2003): 107.

[22] Rusk to Orrick, August 27, 1962, *FRUS XXV, 1961–63, Organization of Foreign Policy*, 107.

[23] Thomas Engelhardt, *The End of Victory Culture* (Amherst: University of Massachusetts Press, 1995), 166.

idea aroused the hostility of southern legislators fearful that what civil rights workers were doing privately would now be done with the stamp of federal approval and with public money. They forced Kennedy officials to disavow any intent that the volunteers would pursue a civil rights agenda or engage the race question. Dixiecrats and conservative Republicans ultimately remained suspicious of the program, which stagnated in committee for the duration of Kennedy's presidency.[24]

During the New Deal in the 1930s and 1940s, white southern leaders had accepted activist federal programs to the extent that they could retain local control over the disbursement of funds and decide who the beneficiaries would be. This time around, Dixiecrats found themselves fighting a rearguard action against outside efforts to alter politics and culture in their region. CORE and SNCC had begun grassroots organizing in the rural South, in remote areas where long-standing poverty and illiteracy had assured local satraps of perpetual domination. Their rule was now challenged.

The Peace Corps and civil rights volunteers shared a tendency to operate against the current of bureaucratic centralism and more readily accept innovation and improvisation. While Peace Corps projects and those of SNCC, for example, certainly differed in the degree of hostility that their foes unleashed against them, a comparable implicit set of values underlay their respective missions. Considerable emphasis was placed on the simplicity in which volunteers, whether in the American South or abroad, were expected to live, and on their dedication to the populations they pledged to serve. Their missions contained the germ of an antimaterialism that defied conventional wisdom and soon folded into a set of attitudes and practices that came to be labeled as countercultural. Both the Peace Corps and SNCC had tried to dodge the political fate of being appended to conventional organizations, thus augmenting their aura of independence and originality. Many volunteers were in their thirties, and even forties, but youth became the prevailing metaphor for the idealism that these programs supposedly represented.[25]

Kennedy administration liberals tried to rewrite idealism into foreign affairs activism and argued that the United States could not afford to acquiesce to neocolonialism, risking permanent damage to its reputation in Africa. While the Africanists in the State Department argued against the balkanization of the Congo, others showed little concern for African unity. In this view, African sovereignty was dispensable and the division of the continent into microstates

---

[24] On Powell, Lee A. Daniels, "The Political Career of Adam Clayton Powell, Paradigm and Paradox," *Journal of Black Studies* 4 (December 1973): 115–38; Ben Keppel, *The Work of Democracy: Ralph Bunche, Kenneth B. Clark, Lorraine Hansberry, and the Cultural Politics of Race* (Cambridge, Mass.: Harvard University Press, 1995), 150. Christopher T. Fisher, "'The Hopes of Man': The Cold War, Modernization Theory, and the Issue of Race in the 1960s" (PhD diss., Rutgers University, 2002), pp. 139–46.

[25] Gary May, "Passing the Torch and Lighting Fires: The Peace Corps," in *Kennedy's Quest for Victory: American Foreign Policy, 1961–1963*, ed. Thomas. G. Paterson (New York: Oxford University Press, 1989), 286–8; Wofford, *Of Kennedys and Kings*, 306.

posed few difficulties. In South Africa, cold war concerns joined with profit making to undermine African freedom and in the Congo, deferred national unity and stability indefinitely.[26]

Superpower dominance in the Security Council ensured that the status quo would change little, but a diversifying General Assembly membership began disputing the hitherto uncontested might of the great powers. The General Assembly in 1962 directed the Commission on Human Rights to draft declarations and conventions that prohibited member states from engaging in racially discriminatory acts. The documents outlined ways to end such practices and make offending governments institute reforms as the commission launched more investigations and accepted testimony from nongovernmental sources.[27]

In the course of the succeeding decade, delegations from Africa and Asia focused relentlessly on race, colonialism, and independence from the dictates of the most powerful nations. Yugoslavia, which viewed itself as a communist state unbeholding to the Soviets, took the lead in organizing a conference of nonaligned leaders. The Belgrade Conference of 1961 invited governments and national liberation movements perceived to be open to relations with both Eastern and Western blocs. Cuba, though tied to the USSR, was included as it continued to have diplomatic relations with some Western states. Yugoslav president Josip Tito spearheaded the conference's focus on economic development. Participants called on the wealthy nations to tithe themselves 1 percent to generate funds for aid programs to be administered through the UN, to avoid the strings often attached to bilateral arrangements.[28]

The momentum generated by these nations led to the establishment of the United Nations Conference on Trade and Development (UNCTAD) in 1964 but was not ultimately sustained. Assistant Secretary of State for International Organization Affairs Harlan Cleveland noted with satisfaction that in spite of "swirling majorities" and a rising "emotional temperature" in UN councils caused, he believed, by the Afro-Asian penchant for oratory rather than action, the United States continued to prevail in matters of substance. "It is essential to make a distinction between what is symbolic and what is real in the UN," Cleveland observed. *Liberator* editor Daniel Watts sardonically attested to this view. "I personally witnessed many scenes in the North Delegate Lounge of the United Nations in which African delegates were openly bought and paid for by neocolonialist spokesmen," Watts claimed. "In fact, it became a rule that if an African Ambassador delivered

[26] Namikas, "Battleground Africa," 150;

[27] Howard Tolley, Jr., *The UN Commission on Human Rights* (Boulder, Colo., and London: Westview Press, 1987), 89.

[28] Mark T. Berger, "After the Third World? History, Destiny and the Fate of Third Worldism," *Third World Quarterly* 25 (1) (2004): 12–13; Helen E. S. Nesadurai, "Bandung and the Political Economy of North-South Relations: Sowing the Seeds for Re-Visioning International Society," in *Bandung Revisited: The Legacy of the 1955 Asian-African Conference for International Order*, eds. Amitav Acharya and See Seng Tan (Singapore: NUS Press, 2008), 79, 80.

a particularly strong anti-colonialist speech in the General Assembly he was merely upping his price for the sell-out."[29]

The term "swirling majorities" referred to the instability of the new states' bloc vote. "The Asians and Africans do not consistently vote together," *Time* magazine reported. "Since 1960, Africans have voted with the U.S. about 30% of the time, with Russia on 25% of the roll calls. By contrast, the Asians sided with Washington on only about 20% of the votes, with Moscow more than 30% of the time. Yet on nearly one roll call in three, the Africans and Asians voted differently from both Russia and the U.S."[30]

Cleveland did not take into account the varying political ideologies in play at the UN. Most Western countries saw the organization through the lens of a liberal capitalist tradition that focused on individual rights and civil liberties and sought to restrain the power of government to impede these. Even so, the West showed considerable tolerance for temporizing over rights when issues of colonialism and racial discrimination were on the table. The Afro-Asian and Warsaw Pact states were more likely to emphasize the rights of groups, including colonized majorities, and consequently the right of self-determination. The United States firmly declared its commitment to ending colonialism but argued that independence for states that were unready compromised their futures. UN ambassador Stevenson thought African countries were rushing the process. In spite of these concerns, the United States and its European allies did not have real plans for orderly transitions. Fast was too fast, but slow, apparently, not slow enough.[31]

Governments commonly identified and condemned actions by others of which they themselves were guilty. The United States countered critics of Jim Crow with attacks on the Soviet treatment of Jews. The USSR responded with a resolution condemning all forms of fascism and endorsed a provision that identified Zionism as racist. Algeria, Cameroon, and Tanzania joined the Soviets in encouraging the Human Rights Commission to focus primarily on colonial problems. Such an emphasis would divert attention from less than ideal internal conditions in these and other countries. After passage of the Civil Rights Act of 1964 gave the United States cover, American delegates could propose that no country be exempt from external scrutiny.[32]

[29] Harlan Cleveland to Dean Rusk, May 2, 1961, FRUS XXV, *Organization of Foreign Policy, 1961–63*, p. 333; Daniel Watts, "The Carmichael/Cleaver Debate," *Liberator* 9 (September 1969): 5.

[30] Cleveland to Rusk, May 2, 1961; Cleveland to Adlai Stevenson, June 22, 1962, p. 449, in *FRUS, XXV 1961–63, Organization of Foreign Policy; Information Policy; United Nations; Scientific Matters*; "The UN: Prospects Beyond Paralysis," *Time* April 2, 1965, online at http://www.time.com/time/magazine/article/0,9171,941002,00.html, accessed June 7, 2011.

[31] Tolley, *The UN Commission on Human Rights*, 37, 191; Lord Home to Dean Rusk, July 29, 1963, pp. 574–5 and Rusk to the Mission to the United Nations, August 13, 1963, pp. 576–7; Department of State, Bureau of International Organization Affairs, "United States Strategy at the 18th General Assembly," n.d., pp. 580–3, all *FRUS*, XXV, *1961–63*.

[32] John David Skrentny, "The Effect of the Cold War on African-American Civil Rights: America and the World Audience, 1964–1968," *Theory and Society* 27 (1998): 273.

In spite of hopes that the new UN majority would take the world into an era of multilateral, diffused power, the seemingly intractable difficulties facing poor nations constrained their options. Their domestic problems, including economic development, the status of minorities, and human rights, provided an opportunity for Western powers to fend off the attacks they made on racism and colonialism. Washington had already plotted its circumvention of the new majoritarianism. "We tend to forget how near we are to the postcolonial period," Cleveland observed. "We must plan how to lead the Afro-Asians in matters of their next major attention so that trends will be more in accordance with United States interests and traditional beliefs."[33]

State Department officials viewed the Belgrade Conference through the same lens that had colored their perspective on the Afro-Asian Conference in Bandung six years before. George Kennan, then U.S. ambassador to Yugoslavia, questioned the authenticity of participants' claims to nonalignment and criticized the "demonstrations of anti-colonial and anti-western emotionalism" he believed would ensue. White House adviser Arthur Schlesinger suggested two choices for President Kennedy to consider. The United States could either dissuade "moderate states" from participating or coax them to do so and thereby mute leftist thunder. Neither course, except in the case of Latin American allies, would be productive. The best course, Schlesinger advised, was to do nothing "and trust [the natural] forces of disintegration." Foreign Service veteran Loy W. Henderson shared Harlan Cleveland's belief that the new states lacked both vision and political maturity. Henderson was not positive about international staff from weak countries. "Whenever we set up a committee composed of small powers who have no worldwide feelings of responsibility," he commented in off-the-record remarks, "they commence to horsetrade for points rather than looking at it from the worldwide point of view."[34]

Oddly, State Department officials had difficulty applying such broadmindedness to their own optic. Cleveland deplored what he considered a radical turn in the civil rights movement, making known his distaste for "agitators" who used "the UN system to expose grievances." He saw such figures of note as James Baldwin, Bayard Rustin, and James Farmer as dangerous black militants. To focus on southern outrages, the assistant secretary believed, detracted from the attention that human rights violations by other nations should rightly receive. Cleveland tried to spin the race issue positively, placing it in the context of the "expansion" of rights universally. By "defusing certain human rights

33 Kennan's July 14, 1961 cable, cited in James G. Hershberg, "'High-Spirited Confusion': Brazil, the 1961 Belgrade Non-Aligned Conference, and the Limits of an 'Independent' Foreign Policy during the Cold War," *Cold War History* 7 (August 2007): 378; Schlesinger quoted in ibid., 384. Cleveland's remarks as transcribed in Jenkins, to the Assistant Secretary of State for Far Eastern Affairs, Walter P. McConaughy, June 1, 1961, *FRUS, 1961–63*, XXV, 347.
34 Transcript of Background Press and Radio News briefing, November 30, 1960, Loy W. Henderson Papers, LC.

questions through quiet fact-finding," other countries' abuses could "be handled in a less political way."[35]

In spite of Cleveland's reservations, the General Assembly adopted the Convention on the Elimination of All Forms of Racial Discrimination on December 21, 1965. Arthur Goldberg, appointed U.S. ambassador to the UN that year, signed the treaty, but the State Department did not forward it to either the Senate or the White House. The treaty permitted designated UN personnel to act as ombudsmen in internal matters pertaining to race in member states. The United States delayed ratification until 1994, decades after similarly advanced countries had done so.[36]

The UN was not the only venue available to air concerns about colonialism and discrimination. Emperor Haile Selassie of Ethiopia hosted the first meeting of the OAU in May 1963. Thirty-two heads of state convened in Addis Ababa for the historic occasion. One scholar, seeking to understand this unprecedented display of African potential, wondered whether these countries could conduct truly autonomous foreign policies. Some signs were bright. It was becoming clear that "small powers have had a way of thwarting some of the best designs of big powers on both sides of the fence."[37]

African and Asian states' circumscribed power contrasted with the hopes they inspired among diaspora communities wishing to increase their own political capital where they resided. The spotlight beaming on former colonies allowed activists as different from one another as Martin Luther King Jr. and Malcolm X to begin disengaging from the U.S. exceptionalist framework that limited the repertory of struggle. Political leaders, whether popular or elected, could craft their images with the international stage in mind. Black nationalism could serve as a stepping-stone to a global sensibility. As Representative Adam Clayton Powell had earlier discovered in Harlem, black nationalists in large urban communities could be an important constituency. Philadelphia congressman Robert Nix understood this also. The FBI reported his attendance at a Muslim rally in his home district, where Nix sat between Malcolm X and Elijah Muhammad. Redefinition was an important part of this process. CBS News might paint Muslims as crazed and isolated fanatics, but black politicians knew better. The newspaper *Muhammad Speaks* created a new way to challenge mainstream media news reportage. The paper, founded by Malcolm X and edited by the skilled non-Muslim Richard Durham, recuperated the wide-ranging coverage characteristic of the black press in decades past. In its early years, *Muhammad*

[35] Thomas W. Wilson to Harlan Cleveland, September 27, 1963, p. 663; Cleveland to Dean Rusk, November 27, 1963, p. 625, in *FRUS,* XXV, *1961–63.*

[36] Frank Newman, "The New International Tribunal in Racial Discrimination," *California Law Review* 56 (November 1968): 1560–7.

[37] Bernard B. Fall to Kenneth W. Thompson, January 20, 1961, Rockefeller Foundation, Howard University-Merze Tate-Australian expansion) RG 2, series 200S, box 522, folder 4458, RAC.

Speaks revived a standard by which other African-American weeklies could measure themselves.[38]

For the United States, the use of Islam as a trope of resistance by African Americans, the growing frequency with which the Middle East figured in global politics, and the enfranchisement of African states in the world community played major roles in dissolving the boundaries between the foreign and the domestic in areas where race helped shape consciousness. At the same time, African-American Islam and, more broadly, African-American protest and resistance, has borne the stamp of being made in the USA, which is why black insurgency is not always understood. In some respects, African Americans did not meet the usual criteria of an oppressed national minority. As an ethnic group affluent compared to many of the world's people, and not set apart from the majority by impenetrable language or social differences, it largely shared the Christian beliefs of the majority and was exposed through schooling and the media to common cultural influences.

Spatial separation, however, has been extensive and underwrites many of the inequalities of contemporary U.S. life. The boundary marked by the inner city was one that many liberals, black and white, wished to transgress. Public policy makers, social workers, and civil rights activists in the 1960s often understood communities like Harlem as ghettos to be demolished, their residents dispersed to better neighborhoods. A Capahosic conference of "moderate" black leaders in 1965 reached precisely that conclusion.[39] Despair, social disorganization, and poverty, in this view, explained black attraction to oppositional sects and beliefs. The conviction that blacks' problems were environmental cast doubt on the idea that they had any real affinity for foreign places and peoples. But the view of the ghetto as unchanging and unchangeable except through demolition did not endure. By the end of the 1960s "the other side of the tracks" had become the borders of an internal colony, perceived by residents and reformers alike as analogous to embattled national liberation zones overseas, famously portrayed in a noted film of the time, *The Battle of Algiers* (1966). This analogy, too, proved ephemeral.

The United States Information Agency (USIA) stepped up its outreach to Africa and Asia, using African-American culture to advertise the good life. Publicists apparently saw little irony in touting the virtues of democracy while removing books by such writers as Richard Wright and Roi Ottley from U.S.

---

[38] *New Crusader*, August 20, 1960, p. 1, quoted in Supplemental Correlation Summary, September 25, 1963, *FBI File on Malcolm X*, microfilm, 2nd ed. (Wilmington, Del.: Scholarly Resources, 1996). For Richard Durham, see Barbara Dianne Savage, *Broadcasting Freedom: Radio, War, and the Politics of Race* (Chapel Hill: University of North Carolina Press, 1999), 260–9; William Barlow, "Commercial and Noncommercial Radio," in *Split Image: African Americans in the Mass Media*, 2nd ed., eds. Jannette L. Dates and William Barlow (Washington, D.C.: Howard University Press, 1993), 215–19.

[39] James Farmer, *Lay Bare the Heart* (New York: Arbor House, 1985), 197; the National Committee against Discrimination in Housing, (NCDH) report, "The 1965 Capahosic Fair Housing Conference," May 26–8, 1965 (New York: NCDH, 1965).

libraries in Europe. Music fared differently. The feel-good performances of Louis Armstrong and other artists the State Department and the USIA sent abroad helped to mute foreigners' perceptions of the conflicts occurring in the United States.[40]

Protest, however, began inflecting American music in the early 1960s, including the attitude of Satchmo himself. Increasingly savvy foreign audiences recognized this and began rejecting bland, officially sponsored talent. For defenders of the American status quo, the solution to that problem was to use black disaffection as proof not only that dissidence was tolerated, but that permitting foreign audiences to hear it under official auspices demonstrated the tolerance and stability of the United States. This also mediated the various depictions of African Americans as undesirable or reputable, respectively, by attributing their power and vitality to their Americanness and their deficiencies to their blackness. The national problem of race thus became a problem of representation. Efforts to nail down a consensus on racial equality met ongoing challenges from defiant white citizens and ambivalence in policy circles. The pushback from blacks and the cycle of counterviolence meant that the USIA had to continue broadcasting its official story long after the dirty bird Jim Crow had supposedly been shot down.

Not all succumbed to the narrative's lure. Malcolm X cautioned African leaders to greet U.S. claims of racial transformation with skepticism. "Many of you have been led to believe that the much publicized, recently passed Civil Rights Bill is a sign that America is making a sincere effort to correct the injustices we have suffered there," he told African heads of state. "This propaganda maneuver is part of her deceit and trickery to keep the African Nations from condemning her racist practices before the United Nations, as you are now doing as regards the same practices of South Africa." Laws already on the books were not implemented. The

United States Supreme Court passed a law ten years ago making America's segregated school system illegal. But, the Federal Government has yet to enforce this law even in the North. If the Federal Government cannot enforce the law of the highest court in the land, when it comes to nothing but equal rights to education for African-Americans, how can anyone be so naive as to think all the additional laws brought into being by the Civil Rights Bill will be enforced?[41]

Malcolm was not the only one who felt that legislation alone was inadequate, and that the rhetoric of democracy had to be matched with concrete results. Continued activism at home found its counterpart abroad. Since the early twentieth century, minorities had used international councils of state to

[40] Frances Stonor Saunders, The *Cultural Cold War: The CIA and the World of Arts and Letters* (New York: New Press, 1999), 292; David Braden Posner, "Afro-America in West German Perspective, 1945–1966" (PhD diss., Yale University, 1997), p. 147 n. 41; Penny Von Eschen, *Satchmo Blows Up the World* (Cambridge, Mass.: Harvard University Press, 2004).

[41] Malcolm X's address to the Organization of African Unity, Cairo, Egypt, in Cairo, Egypt, July 17, 1964, in *FBI File on Malcolm X*, Sections 65–79, Reel 9.

bypass the authorities to which they were subject and make appeals for justice, territorial integrity, language rights, and the like. At times, particular balances of global power strengthened their positions. African Americans joined others in petitioning, in turn, the League of Nations, the United Nations, and the Organization of African Unity. By the early 1960s, the promise of full integration into U.S. life led some civil rights activists to interpret freedom as the unimpeded right to share as citizens in all national projects, including war. Joseph McNeil, one of the famed Greensboro Four lunch counter demonstrators, later became an airman and participated in the bombing of North Vietnam. McNeil's quarrel was with Jim Crow, not with U.S. foreign policy. He "publicly criticized the anti-war position taken by Stokely Carmichael as chairman of SNCC." Charlotte, North Carolina, sit-in demonstrator Charles Jones testified before the House Un-American Activities Committee (HUAC) in 1960 about a trip to Vienna he made the year before as a delegate to the Seventh World Youth Festival. HUAC considered the festival Soviet-sponsored. Jones explained his presence there by citing his desire to let Europeans know that U.S. race relations were not as bad as commonly depicted. Nashville sit-in leader Diane Nash "explicitly connected the student movement with the struggle against communism. If blacks had an equal chance for educational opportunities in the South," she suggested, "maybe some day a Negro will invent one of our missiles."[42] Yet as the struggle for basic rights continued in the United States, it became more evident that the anticommunist obsession served very well to shore up white supremacy. Those committed to social change increasingly questioned how conflating racial justice with subversion could be in the national interest.

The impetus given to such questioning by government and private elites who encouraged voluntarism and civic engagement cannot be overestimated. The word "relevance" resonated throughout the epoch as many sought to remake their education to fit their perception of what society needed. In this sense, student activism belonged simultaneously to utilitarianism and a utopianism deeply entrenched in American culture. Youth rejection of the status quo, then, was neither total nor immediate. Mike Thelwell, a student at Howard University early in the decade, recalled a campus debate between Bayard Rustin and Malcolm X that he attended with fellow students Courtland Cox, Charles Cobb, and Stokely Carmichael, among others.

Bayard presented his position: the urgency of a nonviolent struggle against segregation and discrimination, the necessity for black inclusion in all the political, economic, and educational institutions of American life; the importance of organized mass pressure upon the federal government. Malcolm then took the floor, launched into his black nationalist message, and, astonishingly, turned the audience around. In an electrifying performance, he articulated many of the things that weren't being openly said by the black middle class; and he did so in such a biting and uncompromising style that he had

---

[42] Clayborne Carson, *In Struggle: SNCC and the Black Awakening of the 1960s* (Cambridge, Mass.: Harvard University Press, 1981), 13, 14, 17.

the audience literally shouting. It was Malcolm's occasion. We felt that if he hadn't won the debate in analytical terms he had certainly won the audience in visceral terms. Only when we cooled off the next day did we recognize that we had not been converted after all. The black nationalist position still wasn't a viable one. Malcolm had mesmerized us, but he hadn't shaken most of us out of our pro-Rustin position.[43]

Howard students were still wedded at the time to a vision of reform most closely associated with the NAACP, which remained a major force opposing separatism as well as segregation. As delegates resolved at the association's 1961 convention, black nationalism was "inconsistent with the aims and philosophy" of the group. It supported national liberation in Africa but saw the black struggle in the United States as a minority issue subject to national laws. Those drawn to militant organizations were frustrated with the slow rate of change, delegates believed. Persons concerned about the baneful influence of hate groups could counter them by supporting the NAACP and similar bodies that offer alternatives to black nationalism.[44]

As centuries-long U.S. residents, African Americans imbibed much of the American Creed even though they did not have full citizens' rights. Continued discrimination, however, created ambivalence and hampered complete endorsement of the ideology. Black opinion historically had swung between identification as Americans during periods of relative calm when change seemed possible, and alienation and disaffection during epochs of intensified repression. The colonization and emigration movements of the 1850s, for example, marked an era when Congress and the Supreme Court had fastened the noose of slavery more tightly around the neck of the republic. The temporary abandonment of expatriation during Reconstruction signaled renewed hopes for citizenship. By 1960, many took a pragmatic view of race in both the American and African contexts. "I am ... inclined to believe," journalist Percival Prattis wrote, "that the man-in-the-street may have less knowledge about what is taking place in Africa than the intellectual, but what he does know has more significance for him than for the intellectual."[45]

Prattis pegged black nationalism to current political conditions. "The less discrimination there is against the Negro in the United States," he believed, "the less he is interested in establishing any other loyalty than his loyalty to the United States. He will feel proud of the success of African countries, but he will basically recognize that he is an American and that these Africans could merely indicate his potential. He doesn't feel that these countries belong to him in the same sense that many Jews feel that Israel belongs to them."[46] Protesters Nash and McNeil's comments suggest that many civil rights protesters retained

[43] Thelwell quoted in Jervis Anderson, *Bayard Rustin: Troubles I've Seen* (Berkeley: University of California Press, 1998), 238.
[44] Author's telephone interview with Courtland Cox, June 21, 2012; NAACP 52nd annual convention resolutions, July 15, 1961, Philadelphia, in Ralph J. Bunche Papers, UCLA, Box 113, NAACP Board.
[45] Prattis to James B. Herzog, July 21, 1960, Percival L. Prattis Papers Box 144–6, MSRC.
[46] Ibid.

a view of the United States as an eminently redeemable country where a sense of belonging could be acquired through the hard work of eliminating racism. Once they had eradicated that cancer, Americans could unite as a people in the pursuit of common national objectives without regard to the impact on people in other countries. Progress, then, meant the suppression or eradication of the differences among citizens that led to conflict. The United States had the unique power, through its perfectible political institutions, to realize universal freedom and equality.

These respected movement veterans also implied that access to the opportunity structure of American life trumped other concerns. Bayard Rustin, whose career united civil rights with peace work, joined them in this perspective. Rustin believed that individual activists could appropriately belong to peace groups. "Negro students, who only a year ago were exclusively concerned with civil rights, are today engaging in peace action," the War Resisters League member noted, but civil rights organizations should not adopt peace as part of their agenda. This, he asserted, "would be distinctly unprofitable and perhaps even suicidal." Wars have traditionally provided opportunities for black men they otherwise would not have had, he observed. Rustin, himself a conscientious objector during World War II and imprisoned for the stance, did not fault young men who otherwise would be unemployed for enlisting in military service.[47]

Not all integrationists held such a bifocal viewpoint. The NAACP, like other liberal organizations, was put on the defensive during the McCarthy period but never wholly abandoned its practice of weighing in on international matters. In 1961, for example, it castigated the U.S government for failing to guarantee fair housing to diplomatic representatives from nonwhite countries and deplored incidents in which envoys encountered bias while trying to rent or buy property in the United States. It favored the establishment of a federal fair housing policy for the District of Columbia. The NAACP endorsed the UN Congo operations and took on the McCarran-Walter Immigration Act, criticizing its racially discriminatory features and urging its revision. Turning its attention abroad, the association deplored the continued existence of slavery in the Persian Gulf. The shameful human rights records of Saudi Arabia and Yemen did not qualify them for U.S. military assistance. The group condemned apartheid in South Africa and the "white Australia" policy of barring immigrants of color. It advocated an America where the achievement of racial justice would further the nation's other domestic and foreign objectives. The end of racism logically implies the end of the struggle against it. Nationalists, in contrast, continued to define a particular interest grounded in history, culture, and ancestry that would carry on past the successful conclusion of the civil rights fight.[48]

---

[47] War Resisters League form letter, February 1962, Box 7, folder "Correspondence 1962," Students for a Democratic Society (SDS) Records, Tamiment Library, New York University; Bayard Rustin, *Down the Line: The Collected Writings of Bayard Rustin* (Chicago: Quadrangle Books, 1971), 170, 168.

[48] NAACP 52nd annual convention resolutions, Philadelphia, July 15, 1961.

The CNVA offered an alternative approach to the link between domestic change and foreign affairs. In the spring of 1963, it conceived and carried out a "Cuba Walk." Marchers set out from Quebec and made their way south to Key West. They planned to defy all Jim Crow laws along the way. The ultimate target was Cuba, which they hoped to reach by mid-December. As the racially integrated band of participants marched through Georgia, they carried signs advocating an end to the arms race, the abolition of segregation, and normalization of relations with Havana. They utilized the networks that southern activists had established, getting aid and shelter from black churches. For most liberals, CNVA had muddied the waters in mingling civil rights with the issue of recognizing Cuba. In troubled Albany, Georgia, where inmates had just been murdered in jail, some of the demonstrators were arrested.[49] They did not succeed in reaching Cuba, but they initiated a discussion of peace and justice issues seldom allowed to cross national borders or pierce Jim Crow's cotton curtain.

New York City with its long-standing black communities and big foreign population played a large part in effecting a fusion between foreign and domestic issues. A broad-based black intelligentsia included a cadre of outspoken nationalists who put their stamp on African-American culture and politics in the coming decade through the Black Arts movement and other initiatives. Dissatisfied with the moderation and summitry of organizations like the ANLCA, they harshly criticized European colonialism and U.S. foreign policy. Daniels Watts, editor of the *Liberator*, founded the Liberation Committee for Africa (LCA) with Richard Gibson, who also chaired the pro-Castro Fair Play for Cuba Committee. The *Liberator* did not separate nationalists into "revolutionary" and "cultural" camps; nor did it categorically oppose networking with white organizations. "We at LCA," Daniel H. Watts wrote, endorse "the uniting of all forces engaged in the CIVIL RIGHTS struggle. To the liberal white community we say join us, not lead us, work with us, support us." Watts's enterprise quickly grew. The *Liberator*'s board of directors would soon feature actor Ossie Davis, writer Len Holt, Harlem book dealer Louis Michaux, Baltimore *Afro-American* publisher George B. Murphy Jr., former Garveyites Richard B. Moore and Hugh Mulzac, and civil rights attorney Paul Zuber, among others.[50]

The venerable Harlem Writers Guild was another progenitor of the cultural activity that developed side by side with organized support for African

[49] "Quebec to Guantanamo March," *Liberation* 8 (March 1964): 4–5; SNCC Papers, Series IV Executive Secretary Files, 1959–7a reel 5; Dave Dellinger, "Ten Days with the Cuba Walk," *Liberation* 8 (January 1964): 5–9, 30–1; Ralph DiGia, "Cuba Walkers Win Major Concession from Georgia Officials," *Liberation* 8 (March 1964): 6–7; Marty Jezer, *The Power of the People* (Philadelphia, 1987), 148–9. On Gibson, see Lawrence P. Jackson, *The Indignant Generation: A Narrative History of African American Writers and Critics, 1934–1960* (Princeton, N.J.: Princeton University Press, 2011), 349–51, 470, 501; and James Campbell, *Paris Interzone: Richard Wright, Lolita, Boris Vian, and Others on the Left Bank, 1946–60* (London: Secker & Warburg, 1994), 224–31.

[50] *Liberator* 2 (June 1962): 5; masthead, ibid. 2 (August 1962): 1.

decolonization and the southern movement. Current events provided these authors with an opportunity to join literary production with political action. The guild began in Harlem living rooms in the late 1940s. Its members included at various times novelists John O. Killens, Chester Himes, Maya Angelou, and Paule Marshall and the historian John Henrik Clarke. Politically active guild members contributed more to the emerging black nationalist ethos of the 1960s than is generally appreciated. Women artists and writers played a major role in the organization, and the extent of their involvement has been neglected. In addition to Angelou and Marshall, their numbers included the writer Rosa Guy and jazz singer Abbey Lincoln. The latter formed another group, called the Cultural Association for Women of African Heritage. Their networks, with the Harlem Writers Guild at the core, spun off the nationalist collective On Guard, headed by Rosa Guy.[51]

On Guard and the Liberation Committee for Africa are best known historically for the fierce protest of Lumumba's assassination that they mounted in the visitors gallery at the UN Security Council in 1961 in cooperation with the UANM. According to the *New York Times*, more than twenty-four persons were injured when sixty people, mostly black, burst into the Security Council in "the most violent demonstration ... in the world organization's history." The protest interrupted Adlai Stevenson's first formal speech as U.S. ambassador to the UN. After guards ejected them, the demonstrators maintained a picket line across the street from the Secretariat. Another line formed in front of the Belgian consulate, where Paul Robeson Jr. joined the black nationalists. That night, two hundred marchers strode through Midtown Manhattan, shouting, "Congo, yes! Yankee, no!" until charged by mounted police near Times Square. Harlem groups refused to let whites and black communists join their lines.[52]

This action underscored the growing rift between white and black dissidents while revealing the common ground on which leftists and liberals of all hues stood. Both groups, in spite of their mutual antagonisms, cherished a vision of a color-blind society and opposed black separatism. The War Resisters League even included as one of its organizational goals "combating the growth of black nationalism in the U. S."[53] As stated, the league's goals seemed oddly old-fashioned and paternalistic. It shared with citizens Nash and McNeil of sit-in fame the view that full inclusion in national life was imperative for blacks,

---

[51] James Smethurst, "Poetry and Sympathy: New York, the Left, and the Rise of Black Arts," in *Left of the Color Line: Race, Radicalism, and Twentieth-Century Literature*, eds. Bill V. Mullen and James Smethurst (Chapel Hill: University of North Carolina Press, 2003); author's interview with Ernest Kaiser, New York City, May 13, 1994; Abiola Sinclair and Klytus Smith, eds., *The Harlem Cultural Political Movements 1960–1970: From Malcolm X to Black Is Beautiful* (New York: Gumbs & Thomas, 1994); Maya Angelou, *The Heart of a Woman* (New York: Random House, 1981), 143–53.

[52] "Riot in Gallery Halts U.N. Debate," *New York Times*, February 16, 1961, p. 1; Brenda Gayle Plummer, *Rising Wind: Black Americans and U.S. Foreign Affairs, 1935–1960* (Chapel Hill: University of North Carolina Press, 1996), 303–4.

[53] War Resisters League form letter.

although it might disagree with them about the types of activities deemed appropriate. Once the task of suppressing difference was achieved, it would remain for Americans of every ideological persuasion to make moral choices about their role in the world.

Schisms among putative progressive forces were reflected in the growing estrangement of African Americans from the United Nations. If a wide spectrum of black organizations from the moderate NAACP through the communist Civil Rights Congress to the UANM had once perceived the UN as the best forum for presenting their grievances to the world, in 1961 that body stood condemned as a collaborator and facilitator of imperialist crimes. Daniel Watts subsequently complained that the Secretariat had become unfriendly to black reporters and visitors. After the incident at the Security Council, African Americans were questioned, shadowed, and harassed by UN security personnel when they visited the facility.[54]

Even as the liberal political coalition began splintering around irreconcilable demands, the conviction that Americans as a whole should participate energetically in world affairs and convert others to their ideals of liberty and prosperity enjoyed wide acceptance. The popular press helped disseminate the new voluntarism. *Life* magazine prepared the public for sweeping expenditures in Latin America in 1961 when it sent veteran photographer Gordon Parks, an African American, to Brazil. Parks recorded the "Catacombs," a hillside slum overlooking Rio de Janeiro. He documented the impoverished life of Flavio da Silva, a sickly malnourished boy. Parks's stark photography graphically illustrated Latin America's problems for *Life*'s millions of readers. Lives such as Flavio's primed the pump for Cuban-style revolutions, *Life* implied. The story preceded the announcement of a new hemispheric initiative, the Alliance for Progress, intended to address and alleviate the presumed causes of communist insurgency. The United States would underwrite a multibillion-dollar aid project aimed at technical improvements in agriculture, land reform, incentives to industrialization, and personal income growth.[55]

The Cuban revolution had forced Washington's attention southward during the previous administration. Cuba had begun moving rapidly into the Soviet camp by the time of Kennedy's election. Observers suggested that other Cubas might be in the offing unless something was done: poverty and social inequality in the American republics made them susceptible to red blandishments during a period of deteriorating Soviet-American relations. Like Eisenhower, Kennedy

[54] Carole Collins, "Fatally Flawed Mediation: Cordier and the Congo Crisis of 1960," *Africa Today* 39 (3) (1992): 5–22; "Racism in the U.N.," editorial, *Liberator* 3 (April 1963), p. 1; Lowell P. Beveridge, Jr., *Domestic Diversity and Other Subversive Activities* (Minneapolis: Mill City Press, 2010), 268, 269.

[55] "Freedom's Fearful Foe," *Life*, June 16, 1961, pp. 86–96, 98; "Letters to the editor," ibid., July 7, 1961, pp. 15–16; "The Compassion of Americans Brings a New Life for Flavio," ibid., July 21, 1961, pp. 24–35; William O. Walker, III, "Mixing the Sweet with the Sour: Kennedy, Johnson, and Latin America," in *The Diplomacy of the Crucial Decade: American Foreign Relations during the 1960s*, ed. Diane B. Kunz (New York: Columbia University Press: 1994): 51–2.

had both a carrot and a stick in mind. The stick manifested itself through efforts to unseat Castro and Rafael Trujillo of the Dominican Republic, one of the region's most egregious figures on the Right. The carrot consisted of money for modernization. Kennedy's maiden address to Congress on foreign policy emphasized that nations receiving U.S. aid should already "share" the American perspective on freedom because "no amount of arms and armies can help stabilize those governments which are unable or unwilling to achieve social and economic reform and development."[56]

This proviso put brakes on the pace of change in Latin America but implied that there could be no such restraints on the eradication of poverty at home, which reformist discourse tended to encourage. The "rediscovery" of home-grown hardship, heralded by the 1962 publication of Michael Harrington's *The Other America: Poverty in the United States*, stimulated efforts to neutralize the conditions that could lead to domestic unrest and cold war vulnerability. Photographer Parks, for example, had not finished with the subject of destitution and desperation. He later published a photo essay about the Fontenelles, a black American family of ten with an unemployed father, struggling to survive a New York winter. The Brazilians and the Americans "lived across the world from one another," Parks wrote, "but they shared the same tragedy."[57] Both stories coincided with the unfolding of important moments in U.S. history. Public policy had to provide hope, if not substantive change, for the poor everywhere. How this would be accomplished served as the centerpiece for many of the coming decades' conflicts.

The White House initially thought that massive transnational assistance programs like the Marshall Plan were as applicable to agricultural countries as to industrialized ones that had been ravaged by war. The Foreign Assistance Act of 1961 created the Agency for International Development (AID), which combined earlier programs. The new agency was organized on geographic rather than functional lines, with a chief administrator answering to the secretary of state and holding the rank of undersecretary. Four regional deputies would be assistant secretaries. The White House drew heavily on Harvard and MIT specialists who ascribed to a countrywide approach to aid. Rather than organize assistance by project, they endorsed the idea of a total integrated package that would transform "entire social structures and ways of thought and life."[58]

The comprehensive Kennedy administration plans threatened to marginalize conservatives, who in 1961 made another attempt to impose their own

---

[56] Stephen G. Rabe, "Latin America and Anticommunism," in *John Foster Dulles and the Diplomacy of the Cold War*, ed. Richard H. Immerman (Princeton, N.J.: Princeton University Press, 1990), 187; Walker, "Mixing the Sweet with the Sour," 58; "Transcript of Kennedy Address to Congress on U.S. Role in Struggle for Freedom," *New York Times*, May 26, 1961, p. 12.

[57] Michael Harrington: *The Other America; Poverty in the United States* (New York: Macmillan, 1962); clipping, *Business Week*, June 27, 1964, Schomburg Clipping File, SC; "Harlem Family: The Fontenelles," *Life*, March 8, 1968, pp. 48–63.

[58] Robert A. Packenham, *Liberal America and the Third World* (Princeton, N.J.: Princeton University Press, 1973), 61–2.

agenda on change for Africa and, by extension, other developing states. African leaders were invited to make presentations and be questioned at a Capahosic conference scheduled for June. Taking a page from the White House book, the Capahosic organizers wanted to centralize development projects and ensure African cooperation but emphasized corporate input rather than government spending. Invited participants included the counselor of the Ivorian embassy, Simeon Ake; Nathan Barnes, the Liberian ambassador; the Nigerian consul in New York; and a representative from the Ghanaian embassy. The educators and philanthropists would be from Columbia University, Teachers College, the Old Dominion Foundation, the African Research Foundation, the New World Foundation, the Ford Foundation, the Phelps Stokes Foundation, the African-American Institute, and the United Negro College Fund. The African Service Institute, the International Cooperation Administration (ICA), and the State Department represented the interests of missionaries and government officials. AMSAC was the only African-American group invited.[59]

Capahosic organizers solicited contributions from industry, advertising, and finance. Their guest list included the Pepsi Cola Company; E. R. Squibb and Sons; Olin Mathieson; the advertising firm of Batten, Barton and Osborn; and Robert W. Hudgens, president of International Development Services.[60] The ground had begun to shift, however, from under the feet of the old-style racial moderates and their allies in the business community. It became difficult to distance an interest in black people – on any side of the Atlantic – from an overtly liberal civil rights and anticolonial agenda. The case of Wilton S. Dillon is instructive. Dillon, a white southerner, was executive secretary of the Phelps Stokes Fund until he quit in 1962 to become a professor at Atlanta's newly desegregated Emory University. His goal was "to teach medical students, residents in psychiatry and advanced students in the social sciences something about the social revolution now going on in the South, and then make comparisons with the changes in Africa and Asia." He would network with historically black Atlanta University and eventually establish links with African universities and recruit African students.[61] Dillon had traveled from paternalistic stewardship to educational innovation.

Traditionally white colleges and universities, as well as foundations, began heavily recruiting black American students in the early 1960s. Just as it underwrote African education ventures, the Rockefeller Foundation funded recruitment drives and high school prep classes through selected institutions. Dartmouth College and Yale, Brown, and Harvard Universities planned similar initiatives. Princeton tried hard to shed its image as the nineteenth-century redoubt of southern planters' sons who sometimes moved to campus with their

[59] List enclosed with F. D. Patterson to Claude Barnett, May 10, 1961, CBP, Series G, reel 3.
[60] Ibid.
[61] Wilton S. Dillon, "The World Role of African Universities," excerpt from Dillon's speech at the University of Ghana, January 11, 1962, pamphlet, in National Council of Negro Women Records (NCNW), Series 10, Box 1, folder 4; Dillon to Claude Barnett, February 6, 1963, CBP, Part 3 Series 3-Philanthropic and Social Organizations, 1925–66. Reel 2.

enslaved servants in tow.[62] The institution that former Princeton resident and football star Paul Robeson could not have attended in the 1920s because of his race now shared the hope that educational inclusion would break down Jim Crow barriers and that acculturation would mute black dissidence, whether nationalist, liberal, or Marxist.

The burgeoning interest in Africa and in civil rights at home, registering with great impact in diverse social and political circles, cannot be separated from a need to redesign racial thought and practice. The prospect of sovereign Africans and African Americans with full civil rights posed challenges of adjustment for global society. What would replace the old hierarchies? The aestheticization of Africa as begun by AMSAC was no longer sufficient. "There are times," AMSAC organizer John A. Davis commented after the Sharpeville massacre, "when men of culture can no longer confine their interests to things cultural." By the time of AMSAC's April 1963 conference, titled "Southern Africa in Transition," participants were no longer limited to artists and writers but included national liberation leaders Oliver Tambo of South Africa and Ndabaningi Sithole of Zimbabwe. AMSAC and Davis also had second thoughts about the Congo. "Whether we agree or not as to Nkrumah's support of Lumumba," John A. Davis wrote to historian Rayford Logan, "we can certainly all agree now that he was right in his support of a unified Congo and the legitimacy of the Parliament."[63]

Yet armed struggle did not fit in AMSAC's vocabulary. Its culturalism, no less than the "race work" done by turn-of-the-century missionaries, yielded to a government- and corporate-sponsored paternalism. But even committed liberals tended to discount the potential of mass publics. As CORE director James Farmer recalled, "The perception of my staff was not of a mass movement, but of a small, tightly disciplined cadre of well-trained individuals. Nor was their thinking at this point in terms of something that would galvanize the entire black community and drive it into action." When someone recommended that CORE publicize its impending Freedom Ride with "a kick-off rally at Harlem's Abyssinian Baptist Church," so as to "get the black community in on the ground floor of this burgeoning new nonviolent movement," not every staffer agreed. Astonishingly, Marvin Rich, the director of community relations, was among them. "We are not interested in the black community," Rich declared. "We are interested only in the ACTIVISTS in the black community." This perspective

[62] Leland C. DeVinney's memorandum of interview with John Merrill Knapp, November 8, 1963; "A Step toward Enlarging the Pool of Qualified Negro Candidates for Higher Education," report, November 15, 1963; DeVinney's memorandum of interview with John Merrill Knapp, Jeremiah S. Finch, and Parker Coddingon, November 11, 1963, Rockefeller Foundation Records, Princeton University-Remedial Education, 1963, ser 200, boxes 80–81, folder 688, RAC.

[63] Milfred C. Fierce, "Selected Black American Leaders and Organizations and South Africa, 1900–1977, Some Notes," *Journal of Black Studies* 17 (March 1987): 317; Daniel H. Watts, "American Negro Leadership Conference on Africa." *Liberator* 3 (January 1963): 14; John A. Davis to Rayford W. Logan, January 24, 1962, Rayford W. Logan Papers, series 166, Box 166–7, folder AMSAC, MSC.

contributed to subsequent conflicts in CORE and to the expulsion of white members later in the decade.[64]

Historians frequently depict the 1960s as an era in which rebellious and undisciplined masses confronted venerable authorities and traditions. In some renderings of the history, both individual and collective quests for social justice, peace, and other improvements stem from defiance of orthodoxy and refusal to validate customary authority. Such an angle loses sight of the encouragement given to dissenters and reformers by conventional institutions and leaders. Support for change came from conservative churches as well as from the president of the United States and other members of his administration. By giving voice to idealistic impulses as the pope did, and by providing blueprints for action, as the New Frontier did, elites inspired a considerable amount of the activism that they would subsequently deplore.

It was not in the interests of the federal government and establishment figures flatly to resist groundswell advocacy. They hoped at best to manage it. The Kennedy administration's effort to control southern black insurgency exemplifies one approach to the dilemma. Wealthy New Yorker Stephen Currier, a Kennedy family friend, began civil rights fund-raising in 1963. Working through his Taconic Foundation, he focused on supporting voter registration campaigns. The plan was to distribute money proportionally among civil rights groups according to the size of each one's 1961 budget.[65]

CORE leader James Farmer, who earlier had disagreed with the Kennedys over civil rights policy, opposed the Taconic program. Taconic's funding proposal was biased against the smaller – and more militant – organizations, he claimed. Farmer asserted that Attorney General Robert F. Kennedy had offered CORE and SNCC tax-exempt status if they would stop the demonstrations that were making the news on a daily basis, generating a backlash from southern whites, and embarrassing the nation overseas. In short, the White House and its allies wanted the most active groups to get out of the mass mobilization business and into offices where they could help channel black votes into the Democratic Party.[66] As a Democratic president straddling the uneasy coalition of Dixiecrats and national liberals, Kennedy sought to skirt dramatic flare-ups and, above all, avoid Eisenhower's position in Little Rock in 1957. So as not to send federal troops to the South and reopen an ancient wound, black demands would have to be mediated.

Pollsters had discovered that outside the South, endorsement of civil rights registered highest with the affluent and well educated.[67] Elite support for change left those opposed to civil rights with nowhere to go in the short run.

[64] Farmer, *Lay Bare the Heart*, 197.
[65] Ibid., 215, 219, 220.
[66] Ibid.
[67] Hazel Erskine, "The Polls: Demonstrations and Race Riots," *Public Opinion Quarterly* 31 (4) (1967): 655–67; Richard Aviles, "Racial Threat Revisited: Race, Home Ownership, and White Working Class Politics in the U.S., 1964–1976," University of Wisconsin-Madison, Department of Sociology, unpublished paper, 2010.

Blatant racism no longer belonged in polite circles, and no strong conservative movement crystallized before 1964. Sociobiological arguments remained at the foundation of segregationist discourse, and these rapidly lost both popularity and coherence when viewed in national and international contexts. Psychologist Kenneth B. Clark, famous for the "doll studies" that influenced the Supreme Court's *Brown* decision, exposed the ironies of America's double standards in an interview granted in 1963. "Africans in America are treated with more respect than black men who are American citizens," he told *Pageant* magazine. "If a Negro with a turban and a flowing robe can be shown respect once the State Department or some other government official says, 'Look, you can't do this,' well, then it is absurd if somebody with the same skin color dressed in American clothes is not given the same respect."[68]

Clark's point drew on the connection between progress on African issues and domestic racial reform. The heads of organizations involved in civil rights activity in the United States joined with AMSAC and ACOA to form a new organization in 1962. James Farmer of CORE, Dorothy Height from the NCNW, Martin Luther King Jr. representing SCLC, A Philip Randolph of the Negro American Labor Council, the Urban League's Whitney Young, and Roy Wilkins from the NAACP issued a conference call in August. The decision to establish the American Negro Leadership Conference on Africa (ANLCA) with labor economist Theodore Brown as its director reflected the reality of new players on the world scene.

What distinguished the committee that drafted the call to create an Africa-oriented group from past efforts is the conscious linkage it made between decolonization and antiracism on the continent and civil rights in the United States while deftly separating interest in Africa from black nationalism per se. "We believe the nineteen million American Negro citizens must assume a greater responsibility for the formation of U.S. policy in sub-Sahara Africa," the committee wrote. Activism on behalf of Africa would thus shift from the missionary-inflected custodial imperative that had characterized many past African-American efforts to demands on Washington. Members would address Foggy Bottom as hyphenated Americans claiming a policy voice, rather than as uprooted Africans. The committee claimed that the civil rights movement and African liberation drew on the same moral foundation, and that achieving freedom abroad could facilitate justice at home. The ANLCA saw itself chiefly as a pressure group that would employ "the normal channels of diplomacy." It did not contemplate mass membership. Not everyone was satisfied, however, with so conservative an approach. The radical black San Francisco physician Carlton Goodlett, publisher of the *Sun Reporter* and a longtime peace activist, reproached the East Coast orientation of the conference and the silence on linked questions of peace and disarmament.[69]

---

[68] Interview with Kenneth Clark, "Probing the Negro Revolt," *Pageant*, October 1963, p. 149.

[69] James H. Meriwether, "The American Negro Leadership Conference on Africa and Its Arden House Conference: Politicizing and Internationalizing the Relationship with Africa,"

The first ANLCA meeting convened in the select environs of Arden House, the Upstate New York mansion that railroad heir and politician W. Averell Harriman bestowed on Columbia University, a venue chosen to reflect the high seriousness of the meeting. Ninety individuals from an assortment of civic, professional, labor, fraternal, and civil rights groups assembled to discuss foreign affairs. State Department representatives were excluded. The ANLCA drew on the growing expertise of academic Africanists to prepare briefing papers. It located itself at the center of a new establishment of church activists, peace proponents, and intellectuals who would weigh in on African issues for the rest of the twentieth century.

ANLCA organizers perceived their task as a "new phase in the civil rights struggle." While they hoped to make relations with African states a central feature of black American protest by harnessing minority voting potential to a revised set of policies, they carefully differentiated their goals from what they termed "separatism." What they instead intended was standard ethnic lobbying. They cited the American Jewish Congress as an example of a model organization that brought a powerful electoral group to bear on U.S. postures in the Middle East, and whose modus operandi merited study. In the meanwhile, the *New York Times* reported, "in the final plenary session at which the committee resolutions were amended and adopted, all phraseology that might have involved the United States Government in any unpleasantness with its European allies was rejected as politically unsound and of no practical value to the conference."[70] In a sponsored entrance into the policy arena, the ANLCA would try to influence U.S. foreign policy without naming Washington's collusion with colonialism and racist powers.

In mid-December selected ANLCA delegates met for three hours with President Kennedy to report the resolutions voted at Arden House. Although Soapy Williams thought the ANLCA was more interested in federal jobs for blacks than in international issues per se,[71] the delegates extensively criticized the U.S. course of action in Africa. ANLCA director Theodore E. Brown, James Farmer, Dorothy Height, Martin Luther King Jr., A. Philip Randolph, Roy Wilkins, and Whitney Young insisted that Washington provide much more aid to African countries and take steps to ensure that the diplomatic corps more accurately reflected America's multiracial composition. The U.S. UN delegation, moreover, should better respond to African-American opinion. Kennedy's acceptance of such a lengthy meeting with domestic constituents offering feedback on foreign affairs affirms the view that he saw those

Afro-Americans in New York Life and History 21 (2) (1997), online; Carleton Goodlett to Theodore E. Brown, September 10, 1962, Goodlett Papers.

[70] M.S. Handler, "Leading Negroes Agree on Goals: Arden House Session Asks South Africa Sanctions Committee Membership," *New York Times*, November 26, 1962, p. 17.

[71] Memorandum from the President's Deputy Special Assistant for National Security Affairs (Carl Kaysen) to the President's Assistant Special Counsel (White), December 17, 1962, *FRUS, Africa, 1961–1963*, online.

aspects of African policy not governed by cold war considerations as serving electoral aims.[72]

As for African Americans, Francis N. Nesbitt has correctly suggested that the desire for an organization devoted to managing relations with African countries and weighing in on government policy owed much to the rise of black nationalist organizations in the 1950s and the vitality that African independence lent them. It should be noted, however, that most proactive nationalist groups, such as the UANM, the Cultural Association for Women of African Heritage, and the African Nationalist Pioneer Movement, were New York–based – and even more narrowly, often Harlem-based. The cultural primacy of Harlem notwithstanding, they did not necessarily reflect nationwide African-American sentiment. It should also be remembered that a progressive orientation toward decolonization and racial transformation was not the exclusive property of either black nationalists or the Left. Martin Luther King Jr., for example, had worked with Chief Alfred Luthuli of South Africa in mobilizing international opinion against apartheid.[73]

Explosive events rocked the United States in 1963 and diverted world attention to violence in Birmingham, Alabama; the March on Washington; and the assassination of President Kennedy. These critical moments put Africa out of the headlines and on the back burner for a time. The ANLCA nevertheless persisted in defining a mission broad enough to link Africa to the civil rights movement. It abandoned its provisional character, voting itself into permanence at an April meeting in New York City. ANLCA representatives confronted Ambassador Stevenson, who was quite chummy with the white South African elite, meeting socially and professionally with diamond tycoon Harry Oppenheimer and Oppenheimer's proxy, Maurice Tempelsman, a Stevenson client. The ANLCA rebuked the UN delegation's voting record on southern Africa and its racially unrepresentative makeup.[74]

The ANLCA remained on shaky ground in spite of such departures. It struggled to follow up on its initiatives and constitute itself as a continuous African-American policy voice. Plagued by lack of money, it competed for the same funding sources that constituent organizations did. Perennial institutional problems, such as the small numbers of black Americans trained as Africanists or in skilled capacities and available for African service, further diminished the

---

[72] ANLC, Resolutions; *Washington Post*, December 18, 1962, TCF; George M. Houser, "Freedom's Struggle Crosses Oceans and Mountains: Martin Luther King, Jr. and the Liberation Struggles in Africa and America" in *We Shall Overcome: Martin Luther King, Jr. and the Black Freedom Struggle*, eds. Peter J. Albert and Ronald Hoffman (New York: Pantheon Books and the United States Capitol Historical Society, 1990), 186: Plummer, *Rising Wind*, 307–8.

[73] Nesbitt, *Race for Sanctions*, 44–6; Lewis V. Baldwin, *Toward the Beloved Community: Martin Luther King, Jr., and South Africa* (Cleveland: Pilgrim Press, 1995), 35–8.

[74] Houser, "Freedom's Struggle Crosses Oceans and Mountains," 187. See also Michael L. Krenn, *Black Diplomacy: African Americans and the State Department, 1945–1969* (Armonk, N.Y.: M. E. Sharpe, 1999), 126, 134; Adlai Stevenson to Alicia Patterson, March 25, 1958, Walter Johnson, ed., *The Papers of Adlai Stevenson*, vol. 7 (Boston: Little, Brown, 1977), 181 n. 218.

ANLCA's effectiveness. Clout ultimately rested on the combined strength of the membership base rather than on the ANLCA itself. Some member groups had their own separate history of activism on African issues.[75]

Certain partisans of a new Africa policy thought the ANLCA's approach risky. Africanist historian John Marcum, teaching at historically black Lincoln University in the early 1960s, worried about civil rights leaders running the organization. Marcum had observed Kennedy's using Africa as a proxy issue to soothe black constituents. His successor might easily do the same thing: "accept policy suggestions on African areas from this organization to compensate for the fact that he found it difficult to make concessions to other Negro organizations on domestic issues." Carlton Goodlett agreed. Civil rights leaders should eventually leave ANLCA. Rights for African Americans and liberation for Africans "mustn't be traded off against each other."[76]

Yet others believed these issues were related and should be pursued in tandem rather than as competitors for the same resources and constituents. The United States had long acquiesced in South African racial policies, but the question of shore leave for U.S. naval personnel suggested that black civil rights were indeed linked to international issues. The U.S. embassy in Pretoria informed naval officials of the local racial customs visiting sailors were expected to observe. Interracial sex was illegal in South Africa, and seamen on shore leave should not be deceived by the light complexions of mixed-race women – "Cape coloreds" – they might encounter in Capetown. The embassy also worried about possible conflict between African Americans and South African whites as black sailors traversed the city (see Figure 6). "Segregation definitely raises problems for the consulates," wrote ambassador J. C. Satterthwaite, "and for any negro [*sic*] officers." It would be best to limit the number and duration of U.S. fleet visits to South African ports.[77]

Pretoria's resistance to race mixing, rather than U.S. protests, ultimately reduced the number of visits. Prime Minister Verwoerd subsequently prohibited mixed crews from the aircraft carrier U.S.S. *Independence* from going ashore and publicly condemned U.S. embassy social functions to which black Africans were invited. The United States had to perform a balancing act that poised it between white South African intransigence, on one hand, and world opinion, on the other hand. Global viewpoints had electoral consequences not only at home but also in the United Nations, where the United States sought the support of other countries.[78]

---

[75] Meriwether, "The American Negro Leadership Conference;" text of telegram in Theodore Brown to conference participants, January 8, 1963; Theodore Brown to Goodlett, January 17, 1963; Goodlett to Brown, March 18, 1963, Goodlett Papers; *New York Times*, November 25, 1962; George W. Shepherd, Jr., *Anti-Apartheid* (Westport, Conn.: Greenwood Press, 1977), 97–8.

[76] "Special Interest," 45.

[77] U.S. Embassy, Pretoria, telegram No. 741, December 18, 1963, Johnson Library, NSF, Countries, India, IOTF, Vol. 1, sanitized, DDRS.

[78] Memorandum from Charles E. Johnson and Ulric Haynes of the National Security Council Staff to President Johnson, July 13, 1965, *FRUS* XXVI, *Africa*, 1031.

FIGURE 6. African-American sailors encounter local children in Cape Town. (Bailey's African History Archive)

The ANLCA seized on the shore leave problem, as well as on the exclusion of black personnel from U.S. scientific stations in South Africa.[79] Military and defense considerations again preserved the racism that Washington was being pressured to abandon in other sectors of administration. The White House, the State Department, and the NSC, sensitized by restiveness at home and aware of the heightened repression in South Africa that led to the imprisonment of Nelson Mandela and other black leaders, began developing contingency plans for an exit from the troubled nation.

Not every branch of government wanted a phaseout. Opposition to disengagement arose from the Joint Chiefs of Staff (JCS) and the U.S. ambassador. These personages argued that failure to support the South African regime would lead to communism. They cited China and Cuba as examples of the consequences of U.S. neglect of dictatorial but anticommunist governments. "As long as communist penetration and racial discord in Africa remain an active threat to Free World interests," JCS chair General Maxwell Taylor argued, "stability in South Africa is desirable and the United States should do everything that its political and moral position permits to contribute to this." Better race relations could not materialize, Taylor held, if the "highly developed South African economy" was disrupted.[80]

---

[79] Shepherd, Jr., *Anti-Apartheid*, 97–8; Fierce, "Selected Black American Leaders and Organizations and South Africa," 318.

[80] Memorandum from the Joint Chiefs of Staff to Secretary of Defense McNamara, JCSM-439-64, Washington, May 22, 1964, *FRUS*, XXIV *Africa, 1964–1968*. For Cold War considerations in

The Kennedy administration had begun moving away from an earlier enthusiastic – if symbolic – embrace of Africa, and the president was considering approving the sale of two submarines to South Africa in exchange for missile and satellite tracking facilities. Both Secretary of State Dean Rusk and Secretary of Defense Robert McNamara favored the deal as a foreign exchange moneymaker, although it would incense Africans. This was less important to them than the chance that deferring the transaction would not only prevent the use of South African facilities but also give Pretoria an opportunity to buy ships from France or Britain. Unbeknownst to the 250,000 persons massed on the Capitol Mall in freedom's name on August 28, 1963, for the March on Washington for Jobs and Freedom, Kennedy quietly okayed the sale of C-130 parts to the apartheid state on that very day.[81]

Decision makers had similar sentiments about the Congo. As early as 1952 a Council on Foreign Relations (CFR) study group had stressed the critical role of the Congo's store of strategic minerals, its salience to future Central African developments, and the need to keep its resources in Western hands. Once formal colonialism was no longer feasible, a likely African had to be found who would serve as a custodian of Western interests there. The popular premier of the first Congolese government, Patrice Lumumba, was deemed unreliable. In the chaos that followed the destruction of his regime, the politician Moïse Tshombe emerged with a secessionist plan to safeguard the wealth of Katanga, the Congo's most resource-rich province.

Under the circumstances, the ANLCA's demand that the United States denounce Tshombe was ignored, and its attacks on South Africa simply pushed the Katanga question into the shadows. USIA director Carl Rowan, an African American, was "deeply concerned" that the navy planned to send an atomic-powered task force on a friendly visit to Cape Town. In light of African anxiety about nuclear weapons, it hardly seemed fitting to tie coziness with Pretoria to the atom. The navy and the State Department found exceptions to such circumspection, however, and periodic, low-key naval visits to South Africa continued.[82]

The ANLCA's failure to influence U.S. policy toward Africa owes as much to a confluence of interests as to its own inability to develop a sustained and forceful program. Its leaders headed their own organizations and had prior commitments. Other problems, however, can be attributed to Washington's inability to turn the ANLCA into an effective instrument of its own. Career Foreign Service officer Ulrich Haynes, an African American, put it succinctly. "The fact

U.S. policy toward Africa, see Thomas Borstelman, *Cold War and the Color Line: American Race Relations in the Global Arena* (Cambridge, Mass.: Harvard University Press, 2001).

[81] Memorandum of conversation between President Kennedy, Secretary of State Rusk, et al., September 9, 1963, in *FRUS XXV*, 1961–3, pp. 588–90; Rusk and McNamara, memo for the President, September 16, 1963, pp. 64–9; National Security Assistant McGeorge Bundy's memo for Rusk and McNamara, September 23, 1963, p. 70, in *South Africa and the United States: The Declassified History*, ed. Kenneth Mokoena (New York: New Press, 1993).

[82] *Birmingham World*, December 9, 1964, p. 3, TCF, reel 207; Carl Rowan to the President, July 17, 1964, DDRS; Houser, "Freedom's Struggle Crosses Oceans and Mountains," 187.

is that this particular group has proven itself to be a loose conglomeration of disparate organizations which lacks the expertise and background to be of any real help to us in formulating African policy." Haynes, who, like his supervisor Robert Komer, saw no need for an independent African-American voice in foreign policy, thus made it clear that the State Department's aims and those of the liberal African-American policy audience did not match. White House staffer Lee C. White suggested that insofar as the ANLCA was "not going to evaporate; it would therefore make sense to do what we can to make it an asset rather than an extra burden in this already difficult area."[83] His pragmatism did not prevail. The CIA also failed to benefit from organized black interest in Africa. While ANLCA leaders may have wished to serve as brokers and interpreters between African and U.S. national politicians and intelligentsias and their own constituencies, there was little consensus on African questions.

The ANLCA's structure was formal and its membership restricted, but it was not the only point of contact between African Americans and African states. Expatriates in Ghana, for example, hoped to use their skills to contribute to nation building in their host country. Kenya enlisted civil rights attorney Thurgood Marshall to help draft its first constitution. Black American émigrés kept in touch with events in the United States that bore on racial justice. In Accra and other capitals, they arranged parallel protests in front of U.S. embassies to mark the occasion of the 1963 March on Washington (MOW). In Paris, James Baldwin and the actor William Marshall organized a demonstration at the U.S. embassy. They collected "hundreds of signatures" of support, which film star Burt Lancaster conveyed a week later to MOW participants in Washington.[84]

In 1964, Georgia-born Morris Abram, serving in the UN Subcommission for the Prevention of Discrimination and the Protection of Minorities, decided to tackle adverse foreign opinion about U.S. race relations. He arranged a visit to Atlanta for his UN colleagues. The tour, privately funded, took subcommission members past "wonderful black homes, acres and acres and acres, some with tennis courts and swimming pools." Visitors also planned to attend a Klan rally. As Abram recalled it, "Mr. Boris Ivanov, the Russian, comes up to me, and he says – we were at the home of a black woman who was entertaining us for coffee – 'Are all these homes we've been seeing black?' I said, 'Every one of them, and I want to tell you something, Mr. Ivanov.'" Abrams went in for the kill. "'This will sort of break up your rather unified image of what capitalism is and what socialism is. These are all black capitalists. The Mayor is a capitalist,

[83] Haynes quoted in Krenn, *Black Diplomacy*, 135. See also Lee C. White to President Johnson, December 28, 1964 in *FRUS*, XXIV, 1964–1968, *Africa*, online.

[84] Kevin K. Gaines, *American Africans in Ghana: Black Expatriates and the Civil Rights Era* (Chapel Hill: University of North Carolina Press, 2006); Mary L. Dudziak, *Exporting American Dreams: Thurgood Marshall's African Journey* (New York: Oxford University Press, 2008). William Marshall to Bayard Rustin, September 14, 1963, Bayard Rustin Papers (Bethesda, Md.: University Publications of America, 1988), reel 5, folder MOW 1963, General Correspondence September 1–14.

and all of these people who have been so good to you and who are interested in improving race relations are capitalists, and they are for equal rights. This afternoon we're going to see the Ku Klux Klan demonstrating downtown, and I want you to know that under every one of those sheets beats a proletarian heart.' He turned and walked away."[85]

Abram's junket gave his Soviet guest a privileged look at black Atlanta's upper crust, a world being made to substitute for the decidedly less privileged lives of African Americans generally. Had the tourists ventured into Georgia's heartland, the material success story would have had to be substantially revised. But it was not possible for Abram to stray from the script. The truth still had to play second fiddle to managing cold war rivalries.

Reform efforts during the Kennedy era ultimately clashed with continued racism and anticommunist priorities. The attempt to take a principled stand on human rights ran into difficulty when officials vetoed staffing a rapporteur in the UN Human Rights Commission who would have to report on violations in the United States. While that official would have no power to investigate or sanction, and the commission could not act on individuals' complaints, U.S. authorities still thought the political risks too high. By the time of Kennedy's death, the government had largely reverted to convention: placing containment of communism above other considerations. The period is thus marked by both the persistence and culmination of older foreign policies. The "Camelot" romance masked a conservative turn in world affairs. Whether the encouragement given to idealism was a Pandora's box or a window of opportunity depends on the observer's point of view. Elites and opinion makers responded to crises by exploring ways to effect a peaceful transition to racial equality and maintain political stability. In addition to top-down changes, they wanted an approving constituency for their projected adjustments. They encouraged voluntarism but did not want popular enthusiasm to turn radical. For them, a regime liberal at home and conservative abroad promised an even balance between justice and order.

---

[85] Morris Abram interviewed by Michael L. Gillette, May 3, 1984, Johnson Presidential Library, internet copy; H. Timothy Lovelace, Jr. "Making the World in Atlanta's Image: SNCC, Morris Abram, and the Development of the UN Race Convention," paper presented at the 95th meeting of the Association for the Study of Afro-American Life and History, Raleigh, N.C., October 2, 2010.

4

Meeting Odinga

Shortly before Christmas in 1963, a group of SNCC volunteers arrived at a downtown Atlanta hotel to meet a foreign visitor. The guest was Oginga Odinga, the Kenyan minister for home affairs and a leading figure in the country's struggle for national independence. The hotel, the Peachtree Manor, was one of only a few desegregated hostelries in the city. Odinga was much admired for his forthrightness among SNCC workers. He had criticized the United States for its failures on the racial front and had defended Kenya's decision to seek amicable relations with the Eastern bloc as well as with Western states. Georgia's only black state legislator arranged Odinga's State Department–initiated visit.[1]

The SNCC workers entertained Odinga and Joseph Murumbi, minister of state, with freedom songs. After the meeting, accompanied by Odinga, they adjourned to a restaurant near the hotel, where they were refused service. A spontaneous sit-in ensued. Once Odinga left, the Atlanta police swooped in and arrested the group, dragging some physically to jail, where they vowed to remain over the Christmas holiday. SNCC then sent telegrams to President Johnson and Soapy Williams, telling them that Atlanta should be removed from the list of venues for visiting African envoys.[2]

Sitting in jail, SNCC member Matthew Jones wrote a catchy song later recorded by the SNCC Freedom Singers called "Oginga Odinga." The song chronicled the group's visit, joining the refrain "Freedom Now" to the Swahili word for freedom, "Uhuru," and evoking association with Kenya's Mau Mau movement, so dreaded by whites. "If you white folks don't straighten up," the lyrics threatened, "I'm going to call Jomo Kenyatta," the most powerful man in Kenya. Jones's linkage effectively exposed the hollowness of Atlanta's – and

---

[1] "Welcome to Our African Brothers," editorial, *Atlanta Daily World*, December 22, 1963, p. 6; "Kenya Leaders Blast U. S.," *Chicago Daily Defender*, December 26, 1963, p. 11.
[2] "Jail 17 in Atlanta Sit-In," *Chicago Daily Defender*, December 24, 1963, p. 4; "17 Seized in Atlanta in Restaurant Sit-In," *New York Times*, December 22, 1963, p. 25. The sources differ as to whether Odinga participated in the sit-in. The *Times* claimed that he did not.

by extension, America's – desegregation efforts. It revealed U.S. hypocrisy to Africans who were fighting to free the continent from colonialism and apartheid while experiencing American-style Jim Crow firsthand.[3]

SNCC volunteers risked their lives running schools and registering voters in the most violent and repressive areas of the South. They set out to break through to rural backwaters where time seemed to stand still for black residents. A hardly sympathetic FBI agent described the typical worker, whose pay averaged ten dollars a week. "A field secretary spurns all comforts and luxuries. Straw hat, blue jeans, denim jumper, and sandals became the SNCC uniform in the Mississippi countryside and the southern ghetto."[4] Those dodging bullets on isolated country roads and persuading frightened tenants to claim their rights could no more rely on generous material and moral support from the liberal establishment than they could count on the FBI's protection. SNCC, a novelty in its origins and its operations, nevertheless received considerable attention from its earliest years.

The group aroused much interest among foreigners, whose exposure to African Americans was limited, and generated sympathy among those critical of the United States. Early in its work, SNCC received expressions of solidarity from abroad. The Nederlandse Studenten Raad (Netherlands Student Council) followed the progress of the sit-ins. The Federation of Canadian University Students sent messages of protest to the governors of Virginia and South Carolina condemning the incarceration of sit-in demonstrators in their states. A white South African woman physician, active in the South African Liberal Party, had been moved by a speech Martin Luther King gave in Britain. She had "followed with keen interest the achievements of the sitin movement" and planned to visit Atlanta. John M. Cabot, the U.S. ambassador to Poland, had faced insistent interrogation about U.S. race relations. He was impressed by what he read of SNCC's work in Greenwood, Mississippi, and sent the organization two hundred dollars.[5]

Such encouragement prompted SNCC to look beyond the confines of conventional domestic support for civil rights. Its internationalism preceded the Vietnam War and had varied origins. Irving Davis, who later headed SNCC's International Affairs desk, had met Algerian nationalists while serving in the U.S. Army in France in the late 1950s. Frances Beal lived in Paris during the Algerian revolution and, with Richard Wright's daughter, Julia Wright Hervé,

[3] Matthew Jones, "Oginga Odinga," on *Voices of the Civil Rights Movement: Black American Freedom Songs, 1960–1966* (Smithsonian Folkways Recordings, 1997).

[4] Typescript report, "SNCC," enclosed with R. W. Smith to W. C. Sullivan, August 8, 1967, FBI File on the Student Nonviolent Coordinating Committee, reel 1.

[5] W. H. de Beaufort to SNCC, March 10, 1961, SNCC Papers, Series IV, Executive Secretary Files, 1959–72 reel 5; copy of telegram from Federation of Canadian University Students to Governors Almond and (illegible) and Virginia attorney-general [Albertis Sydney Harrison?], date illegible, 1961, ibid., reel 5; Margaret A. Nash to SNCC Secretary, December 15, 1961, ibid., reel 9; John M. Cabot to *Harper's Magazine*, November 19, 1963, clipping in ibid., reel 5. "Envoy Instructs 400 Poles on U.S.," *New York Times*, October 19, 1962, pp. 1–2.

networked with black American and French colonial expatriates. Donald Harris went to Zambia as an Operation Crossroads volunteer when that country was a colony and, with John Lewis, secured money from ACOA to attend its 1964 independence celebrations. SNCC employed some of its international expertise closer to home when in 1963 it encouraged the establishment of Friends of SNCC support committees at the Canadian Universities of Western Ontario and Toronto, respectively.[6] As Fanon Che Wilkins has observed, "SNCC's internationalism was far more organically rooted in the organization and the experiences of its members than has heretofore been acknowledged, and it operated in tension and in tandem with the organization's domestic agenda." While racial violence was most acute in Dixie, SNCC members understood "as previous generations of black freedom activists had – that the problems that black folk faced in the United States extended far beyond the borders of Mississippi and Alabama." This awareness helps explain the growing power in SNCC of a black nationalism that remained attentive to, and took counsel from, events and personalities overseas.[7]

SNCC also had early contacts with student peace organizations, including the Washington Project Turn toward Peace Student Council and the Student Peace Union. Although Bayard Rustin would later claim that civil rights and peace work should remain separate activities, in 1961 he was encouraging young people in SNCC to invite a War Resisters League speaker to address such topics as Gandhism, the Berlin crisis, and colonialism. SNCC had other mentors among older adult activists. Fanon Che Wilkins has described sociologist St. Clair Drake's friendship with James Forman, who became SNCC executive secretary in 1961. Drake worked at Roosevelt University, an early institutional pioneer in African studies. Personally acquainted with Nkrumah, Drake encouraged his protégé to develop a Pan-African perspective. Forman subsequently forged "extensive contacts with African student organizations in the United States interested in developing formal working relationships with civil rights groups." SNCC, highly regarded in its early years, joined the ANLCA.[8]

[6] Fanon Che Wilkins, "'In the Belly of the Beast': Black Power, Anti-imperialism, and the African Solidarity Movement, 1968–1975" (PhD diss., New York University, 2001), p. 77; Stephen Michael Ward, "'Ours Too Was a Struggle for a Better World': Activist Intellectuals and the Radical Promise of the Black Power Movement, 1962–1972" (PhD diss., University of Texas, Austin, 2002), p. 192, 244; John Lewis, with Michael D'Orso, *Walking with the Wind: A Memoir of the Movement* (New York: Harcourt, Brace, 1998), 294; Tom Wakayama to Ruby D. Robinson, November 18, 1963, SNCC Papers, Executive Secretary Files, reel 10.

[7] Fanon Che Wilkins. "SNCC and Africa Before the Launching of Black Power, 1960–1965," *Journal of African American History* 92 (Winter 2007): 469; Crusaders for Freedom press release, May 17, 1961, in SNCC Papers, Executive Secretary Files, reel 5; Robin D. G. Kelley and Betsy Esch, "Black like Mao: Red China and Black Revolution," *Souls* 1 (Fall 1999): 14.

[8] Peter Allen to SNCC, January 25, 1962 and various communications from the Student Peace Union, SNCC Papers, Series I, Chair Files, 1960–9, reel 10; Rustin to Chuck McDew, October 17, 1961, ibid., reel 2; Wilkins, "SNCC and Africa before the Launching of Black Power," 473–5.

Strong impressions from members' travels further fortified SNCC's global outreach. John Lewis, recently returned from Africa, presented a paper at the February 1965 staff meeting that declared that the struggle for liberation in Africa and the United States "is one of the same." "It is a struggle against a vicious and evil system that is controlled and kept in order for and by a few white men throughout the world." Lewis raised questions about the U.S. role in the Congo and Washington's position on apartheid. If "one man, one vote" is acceptable in the United States, what is wrong with it in South Africa? "We are caught up with a sense of destiny," he wrote, "with the vast majority of colored people all over the world who are becoming conscious of their power and the role they must play in the world." The organization's southern work nevertheless took priority over international activities. By mid-1962 SNCC was ceasing to be a student group. "Most of the SNCC staff members have taken one or two years out of school or career to work in the South full time," Forman told United Auto Workers (UAW) president Walter Reuther.[9]

SNCC volunteers were not the only ones confronting Dixie's laws and customs. There were many different reasons for challenging the entrenched Jim Crow system. For some, bigotry had to yield ground to the profit motive if the South was to join an advanced national economy. Yet local firms and individuals often could not make the necessary adjustments without external pressure. When the utility company Houston Power and Light refused electricity to a naval base to protest the U.S. Navy's support of integration, Vice President Lyndon B. Johnson swung into action. He told the utility company, whose CEO was Mississippi senator James Eastland's cousin, that Houston could lose millions in federal contracts for the NASA satellite tracking station if it persisted in bias. The corporation came around. While JFK worried that strong-arming might unduly antagonize segregationists, the southerner LBJ declared that threats were the best way to deal with them.[10]

Johnson reconciled segregationists to the loss of the old economy by proposing substitutes. This was a critical task. Between 1940 and 1960, Mississippi alone lost two congressional seats because of the out-migration of both whites and blacks, many pushed out of agriculture. Between 1960 and 1965, sixty thousand African Americans between the ages of fifteen and forty-four left the state. Young black people in particular had long been perceived as a threat to the status quo. "Back in those days when I was of draft age," veteran activist Aaron Henry reminisced about the World War II years, "all of the smart blacks or smart colored or smart dark, whatever it may have been then, the one way to get rid of them was to put them in the Army, other than hanging them or shooting them." Mississippi was moving on to less labor-intensive

---

[9] John Lewis's paper for February 1965 staff meeting, SNCC Papers, Chair Files, reel 2; Forman to Reuther, June 29, 1962, ibid., Series IV, Executive Secretary Files, reel 10.

[10] "Reject Anti-Bias Clause," *Chicago Daily Defender*, August 16, 1961, p. 11; Taylor Branch, *Parting the Waters: America in the King Years, 1954–63* (New York: Simon & Schuster, 1988), 863–4.

farming, but industrial growth still lagged. The state could not fully employ its graduates. A five-year survey conducted in the late 1950s and early 1960s indicated that local firms hired only 21 to 35 percent of the graduating engineers at Mississippi State University, at the time all white. Only 57.8 percent of prospective teachers found jobs at home. The state's per capita income was the lowest in the country in 1963, and the number living in poverty the highest.[11]

Other southern states made a faster transition to a mixed economy though most found that, like Mississippi, they first had to rid themselves of the tenants and sharecroppers that SNCC was trying to organize. Florida launched a campaign to purge the welfare rolls of unmarried mothers on moral grounds. Social workers filed negative reports about almost fifteen thousand families, 91 percent of whom were black. Half of these families and some thirty thousand children had their fifteen-dollar-a-month relief allocation stripped away. Louisiana followed similar policies, with the removal in 1960 of twenty thousand children from welfare. While a ruling by the federal Department of Health, Education, and Welfare forced Louisiana to rescind its decision, such practices continued through the decade, enhanced by overt bias. The surplus food freely given to poor white women in Polk County, Florida, for example, was unavailable to black mothers unless they could prove they had jobs. Growers and canneries paying low wages were the major industries in the county. Tacit understandings between employers and welfare officials kept local labor cowed and dependent. By the mid-1960s, many of the more ambitious workers had deserted the countryside. The southern black population would level off in coming decades, but the rural areas never recovered their former numbers.[12]

Federal policies helped to create the Newer South and its technocratic, professional white middle class that would soon deny to others the entitlements they themselves benefited from. Sun Belt affluence did not alleviate the plight of those displaced from agriculture but unabsorbed by the new economy. Growth did not dispel discrimination. Mississippi in 1962 received $650 million in federal funds, including $2 million from the Federal Aviation Administration to build a jetport in Jackson with segregated terminal facilities. At the time of Kennedy's assassination, the Dallas aircraft industry, with a payroll of 15,000, employed only 250 African Americans. Improved conditions for southern

[11] Walter Rugaber, "In the Delta, Poverty Is a Way of Life," *New York Times*, July 31, 1967, Sec. 1 pp. 1:1–3, 16:3–8; Dale Carter, *The Final Frontier: The Rise and Fall of the American Rocket State* (London: Verso, 1988), 204–6; Charles Evers interviewed by Joe B. Frantz, April 3, 1974, Johnson Presidential Library, internet copy; James W. Silver, *Mississippi: The Closed Society* (Harcourt, Brace, & World, 1966), 81, 277.

[12] Lisa Levenstein, "From Innocent Children to Unwanted Migrants and Unwed Moms: Two Chapters in the Public Discourse on Welfare in the United States, 1960–1961," *Journal of Women's History* 11 (4) (2000): 10–33; Frances Fox Piven and Richard Cloward, *Regulating the Poor: The Functions of Public Welfare* (New York: Vintage, 1974), 140–1, 141 n. 27, 138; Frank Hobbs, and Nicole Stoops, Demographic Trends in the 20th Century, U.S. Census Bureau, Census 2000 Special Reports, Series CENSR-4 (Washington, D.C.: U.S. Government Printing Office, 2002), 73, 82, 98.

whites, however, enlarged their stake in cold war militarism and strengthened the appeal of a racial politics revised for modern times. Regional conservatives abandoned the formal rituals of Jim Crow but continued to oppose the social investment that would raise the status of the least privileged part of the population.[13]

By the time John F. Kennedy was shot down in Dallas, all but the most obdurate white supremacists were beginning to realize that the era of "white" and "colored" signs in public places was ending. In a process that began two generations earlier, the regime that necessitated rigid control of black people yielded to a set of complex changes. Mechanization overtook the plantation just as corporate capitalism conquered the family farm. Some aspects of the Old South, however, proved hard to kill. Dixiecrat opposition and a growing Republican right wing would soon pose problems for Democratic Party rule in the region.[14]

New federal spending alleviated uneven development in some places. Most defense dollars dispensed in the former Confederacy went to Georgia, home of Lyndon B. Johnson's good friend Richard Russell, and Texas, Johnson's home state. During Johnson's presidency, Sun Belt defense contractors increased their share of national security largesse from $9.5 billion to $16 billion. The biggest prizes went to C-5A aircraft construction at Lockheed's Marietta, Georgia, plant, and to Fort Worth, where General Dynamics built the TFX fighter plane. Beneficiaries of these programs, including the disingenuous NASA administrator James Webb, stoutly denied that they were intended to favor certain states. In areas where out-migration diminished the threat of black electoral power, many segregationists found they could live with both civil rights and the welfare/warfare benefits that stemmed from Johnson's distributionism.[15]

Federal money, heavily oriented toward defense and military applications of aerospace and other technologies, reinforced local conservatism and militarism. It provided an important springboard for the foreign policy revisions that Johnson would make as president. With such stalwarts as Russell; John Stennis (D. Miss.), Senate Committee on Armed Services; John L. McClellan (D. Ark.), Senate Committee on Government Operations; Russell Long (D. La.), Senate Finance Committee; Representative Edward Hébert (D. La.), House Committee on Armed Services; Representative Mendel Rivers (D. S.C.); and Representative Carl Vinson (D. Ga.), serving on or heading key congressional

[13] Arthur Schlesinger, Jr., *A Thousand Days: John F. Kennedy in the White House*, rep. ed. (New York: Fawcett Crest, 1967), 868; Jack H. O'Dell, "How Powerful Is the Southern Power Structure?" *Freedomways* 4 (Winter 1964): 89; Carey McWilliams, *The Education of Carey McWilliams* (New York: Simon & Schuster, 1979), 254;

[14] Branch, *Parting the Waters*, 863–4.

[15] Kirkpatrick Sale, *Power Shift: The Rise of the Southern Rim and Its Challenge to the Eastern Establishment* (New York: Random House, 1975), 137, 136; Bayard Rustin, *Down the Line: The Collected Writings of Bayard Rustin* (Chicago: Quadrangle Books, 1971), 123; James E. Webb interviewed by T. H. Baker, April 29, 1969, Johnson Presidential Library, internet copy.

committees, southern transitions promised continuity as well as change. Public policies increasingly reliant on armor reflected this.[16]

The Sun Belt exemplifies the role of the state in helping to rehabilitate a region that, thirty years before, Roosevelt had called the nation's number one economic problem. The transformation was not total, but it represented a federal effort that far surpassed in capital outlay the resources that were put into racial reform. As Americans cast off the cultural relics of segregation, they generated the structural means for its reproduction. National defense, the lion's share of the state's reason for being, provided a critical ingredient for the latest iteration of racial difference.

Public policy makers had yet to address another problem whose reach extended beyond the South. If the outward signs of discrimination were vanishing, then how should the enduring poverty and social disfranchisement of the black population be explained? New York provided an example of growth coupled with the continued exclusion of minorities from opportunity. The state promoted the 1964 World's Fair as part of a major foreign trade initiative under the aegis of Governor Nelson A. Rockefeller. Countries as different from one another as Denmark and Sierra Leone sought commercial opportunities at the fair. Organizers used its theme, "Peace through Understanding," to highlight the "300 pretty guides and hostesses at the 35 foreign pavilions," who "in their colorful native costumes – delicate saris and form-fitting Chinese cheongsams – or stylish Western uniforms" created a festive atmosphere. The American exhibits reprised the U.S. triumph in Moscow when, during the famous "Kitchen Debate," Vice President Nixon trumped Soviet Premier Nikita S. Khrushchev in extolling the virtues of America's consumer economy. Perhaps to avoid a repeat of that scenario, the Soviets were no-shows in New York. Whatever the fair's attractions, another facet of life in New York City soon revealed itself.[17]

CORE organized protests at the exposition "to point up the contrast of the glittering fantasy world of technical abundance and the real world of discrimination, poverty, and brutality faced by the Negroes of America, North and South," director James Farmer explained. "For every new car that is shown at the World's Fair we will submit a cattle prod. For every piece of bright chrome that is on display, we will show the charred remains of an Alabama church. And for the grand and great steel Unisphere, we'll submit our bodies from all over the country as witnesses against the Northern ghetto and Southern

---

[16] Joseph A. Fry, *Dixie Looks Abroad: The South and U.S. Foreign Relations, 1789–1973* (Baton Rouge: Louisiana State University Press, 2002), 238–40; Daniel Welsh, "Building Lyndon Johnson," *Ramparts* 6 (December 1967): 59–60.

[17] Douglas Dales, "State Seeks to Spur Exports and Lure Industry," January 6, 1964, p. 85; "Sierra Leone Hopes to Gain by '64 Fair," January 20, 1964, p. 77; William M. Freeman, "Danes Establish a Design Center," February 9, 1964, p. F13; Henry Raymont, "Fair Guides Play Diplomatic Role," April 26, 1964, p. 84; Tania Long, "Soviet Spurns Bid to Exhibit at Fair," September 19, 1964, p. 25, all *New York Times*. On the "kitchen debate," see Elaine Tyler May, *Homeward Bound: American Families in the Cold War Era* (New York: Basic Books, 1988), 18–19.

brutality."[18] The Brooklyn CORE chapter planned an April automobile stall-in in which drivers would deliberately run out of gas on the highways leading to the venue. The stall-in had little popular support and failed to materialize; however, CORE mounted sit-ins and picket lines at the fairgrounds.[19]

James Farmer's vehemence expressed black New Yorkers' experience of Jim Crow in the heart of what many people took to be America's most liberal city. New York in reality suffered serious decline in its traditional industries during the era. The advent of containerization made its docks less critical as shipping points for factories that could now move freight more cheaply and be located elsewhere. Increases in clerical employment did not sufficiently offset the loss of unskilled jobs. High rates of black unemployment and job discrimination were a major cause of discontent. That the president of the World's Fair Corporation was the developer Robert Moses, a man with a long-standing and open hostility toward African Americans, furthered the event's link to bias. Massive public school student boycotts in 1964 protesting de facto segregation and inferior schooling roiled New York City. The largest pulled 464,000 students out of classes. Similar strikes occurred in Philadelphia, Chicago, and other cities. While world attention focused on southern abuses, a northern civil rights movement loomed in Dixie's shadow.[20]

White backlash began coalescing over opposition to black demands. In an insightful *Liberator* article written decades before historians uncovered the seeds of contemporary right-wing politics, C. E. Wilson noted how repudiation of GOP presidential candidate Barry Goldwater had not lessened the popularity of his ideas in many localities or tempered the unease many whites felt about race. Once African Americans began protesting northern injustices and demanding change, the simple moral equations that had worked well in Dixie began to trouble the waters of tolerance. *Liberator* writer Ossie Sykes found it ominous that fair housing initiatives had failed in three important states carried by Lyndon Johnson: New York, Ohio, and California.[21] Civil rights struggles in the North, Midwest, and West occurred against bastions of privilege

[18] Fred Powledge, "Demonstrations Atop Unisphere and Giant Orange Considered," *New York Times*, April 21, 1964, p. 30.

[19] Craig Turnbull, "'Please Make No Demonstrations Tomorrow': The Brooklyn Congress of Racial Equality and Symbolic Protest at the 1964–65 World's Fair," *Australasian Journal of American Studies* 17 (1) (1998): 22–42.

[20] *Robert Moses and the Modern City: The Transformation of New York*, eds. Kenneth Jackson and Hilary Ballon (New York: W. W. Norton, 2007), 121, 177; Jeanne Theoharis, "Introduction", x, 2 and Jeanne Theoharis, "'I'd Rather Go to School in the South': How Boston's School Desegregation Complicates the Civil Rights Paradigm," 125, in *Freedom North*, eds. Jeanne Theoharis and Komozi Woodard (New York: Palgrave Macmillan, 2003). See also Martha Biondi, *To Stand and Fight: The Struggle for Civil Rights in Postwar New York City* (London and New York: Cambridge University Press, 2003).

[21] C. E. Wilson, "The Backlash Myth," *Liberator* 4 (October 1964): 9–10; Ossie Sykes "Who Won the Election?" ibid., 4 (December 1964): 5. *Washington Post*, editorial, January 29, 1978, in Joint Center for Political Studies Vertical File, Washington, D. C.

where white ethnics fought to preserve group strongholds, union seniority, and exclusive political entitlements.

These factors help explain the responses to demonstrations that CORE mounted at the Florida, Louisiana, and Maryland pavilions. Security agents deemed the latter a "sensitive area" because President Johnson was scheduled to open the fair officially there. Planners expected sixteen thousand invited guests at the April 22 event, including diplomats, celebrities, politicians, and important business figures. Robert Moses and others claimed that CORE's campaign had no relevance to this international trade show. CORE's message, however, was that unless the United States addressed the problem of racial injustice, there would be no business as usual. Police set up a zone where up to three thousand detentions could take place without fair goers' knowledge. One thousand Pinkerton guards, assisted by the Secret Service, the FBI, and the New York Police Department, oversaw tightened security. The Queensborough district attorney's office assigned detectives and an assistant D.A. to expedite investigations and arrests on site.[22]

Faulty microphones that allowed the voices of demonstrators chanting, "Freedom Now!" to drown out his televised voice marred Johnson's opening address. To *New York Times* reporter Jack Gould, CORE's "bad manners and disrespect" were unprecedented. "Apparently disquieting history was made in five minutes yesterday," he grumbled. Ironically, LBJ "had been trying to tell his audience ... that democracy did not hide its problems in censorship." By day's end, police had arrested James Farmer, Bayard Rustin, and Michael Harrington. Gould's "disquieting history" portended trouble to come as the United States maintained its split personality as beacon of freedom *and* enforcer of repression.[23]

That trouble soon arrived. On July 1, an off-duty police officer shot and killed a black teenager in Harlem, triggering disturbances that led to five hundred arrests. Incidents of fighting and looting spread throughout the New York metropolitan area during July and August. A reporter queried Africans working at the fair about their reaction to the violence. Responses were mixed, ranging from shock and fear, to criticism of black American militancy or identification with it. U.S.-style racial conflict was alien to most, who had never experienced anything similar in their homelands. As journalists fanned out over the fairgrounds, recording their general impressions, one of them saw two workers stitching the neck of a fiberglass brontosaurus at the Sinclair Oil exhibit.[24] In ways unintended, this sighting symbolized the dilemma in which American society found itself. Makeshift repairs on a dinosaur would no longer suffice to move the country in the direction of genuine progress.

[22] Robert Alden, "Core Maps Tie-up on Roads to Fair," *New York Times*, April 10, 1964, p. 1, 21; Richard J. H. Johnston, "Fair Sets Up Areas to Hold Agitators," ibid., April 21, 1964, p. 1, 30.

[23] Jack Gould, "Pickets' Chants Fail to Break Voice," ibid., April 23, 1964, p. 79; Fred Powledge, "CORE Chief Among Scores Arrested on Grounds," ibid., April 23, 1964, p. 28.

[24] Philip H. Dougherty, "Africans at Fair Shocked by Riots," *New York Times*, July 27, 1964, p. 18; McCandlish Phillips, "About the Fair," ibid., May 6, 1964, p. 28.

To LBJ, the ability of civil rights demonstrators to shout him down at the fair demonstrated to foreign visitors the strength and resilience of U.S. democracy. African Americans were Americans, and for him, their grievances would be settled within the constitutional framework. Johnson did not maintain the rhetorical idealism of Camelot regarding anticolonialism and emerging nations; nor did he embrace African-American internationalism. White House officials joined him in discouraging the formation of a black foreign policy lobby. Instead, they tried to persuade civil rights organizations to join a "raceless" consensus on policy but stumbled on southern Africa in their refusal to challenge apartheid and minority rule.

After the Kennedy administration's rhetoric, its advocacy of voluntarism, and its symbolic gestures toward Africa, Johnson's approach deflated the hopes of the African-American policy audience. If JFK's Peace Corps emphasized the optimism and public spiritedness engendered by service work abroad, LBJ's restored more of the bureaucratic centralism typical of conventional government.[25] The truth was that no president had evinced much enthusiasm for black activism in the American South or elsewhere. Ike sympathized with segregationists. Kennedy opposed the sit-ins and freedom rides and encouraged black voting (for Democrats) instead. Johnson's influence squelched the Mississippi Freedom Democratic Party's (MFDP) bid for representation at the 1964 Democratic Party convention.

Justice was central to the lukewarm fashion in which many African Americans began responding to cold war tensions and the growing Vietnam conflict. The widely respected basketball star Bill Russell mirrored their views when he commented, "I can't get excited over Germany or Vietnam. I will always remember the summer of 1962 when, with my two sons, and over $1,400 in my pocket, plus an $8,000 car, I traveled to Louisiana to visit my grandfather. My sons and I weren't going to rape nobody, yet, we couldn't stop to eat or sleep. What do you tell a boy of 5 when he is hungry. Nobody can justify this to me."[26]

Unlike Bill Russell, certain civil rights leaders felt tied to White House policies and to prowar donors who formed part of Johnson's camp. Just as the Dixiecrats that Johnson supported through aerospace and defense development agitated for aggression against the North Vietnamese communists, so did the Republican Party's growing right wing. After Barry Goldwater raised the possibility of a nuclear strike in Vietnam, the normally reticent UN Secretary General U Thant broke his customary silence to condemn the notion as lunacy. Speaking at a summer press conference in Ottawa, he declared, "Lastly, and this in my view is a very important element, if I may say so, there is a racial factor in such a projected operation." U Thant cast doubt on whether the United States would have used against Germany the bombs it rained down on Japan at the end of World War II.[27]

---

[25] Harris Wofford, *Of Kennedys and Kings* (New York: Farrar, Straus, Giroux, 1980), 325.
[26] Russell quoted in *Liberator* 4 (February 1964): 10.
[27] Daniel H. Watts, "Secretary-General Speaks Out against Racists," *Liberator* 4 (July 1964): 16.

After alleged unprovoked attacks on U.S. vessels by the North Vietnamese navy in Vietnamese waters, Johnson on August 5, 1964, asked Congress for war powers. The Tonkin Gulf Resolution authorized him to take defensive action and identified Southeast Asia as a region vital to U.S. national security interests and global order. This ramping up of militarization did not sit well with all civil rights advocates. The issue was not at first the correctness of the U.S. position in Vietnam. Like Bill Russell, critics instead linked the war to the injustice of segregation. This included drafting black men who could not vote. Combined with the use of the Selective Service as an instrument to quell dissent and remove parts of the black population deemed troublesome, the Vietnam conflict, whatever its own merits or demerits, did not serve the interests of the fundamental domestic change the nation required.[28]

Not surprisingly, the groups and individuals with the fewest links to liberal elites were among those most forcefully protesting inequities and numbered among the earliest vocal anti–Vietnam War critics. Malcolm X played a part in the heightened consciousness of the link between the war and racial oppression by substituting a discourse of human rights for one of civil rights. "Civil rights actually keeps the struggle within the domestic confines of America," he explained on a WBAI-FM radio program. African Americans would thus have to seek remedy at the hands of the very people oppressing them. "Human rights," however, "goes beyond the jurisdiction of this Government," and framing the black condition as such would make it possible to attract outside help. "Our problem is not a Negro problem or an American problem, but rather it has become a human problem, a world problem, and it has to be attacked at the world level."[29] In the face of what was at best American ambivalence about the civil rights movement, and the approving responses of world audiences to black revolt, the search for foreign support was a rational reaction. The tactics of moral suasion and invidious comparison could also be applied usefully within the larger framework of human rights.

Another black perspective on the war came from economist Robert S. Browne, who brought personal experience to bear on the Southeast Asian conflict. Browne, employed in the U.S. foreign aid missions to Vietnam and Cambodia from 1955 to 1961, married a Vietnamese woman and learned to speak Vietnamese. In an essay written for *Freedomways*, Browne proposed that the civil rights and antiwar movements shared a common moral foundation. Also shared, Browne believed, was "the common heritage of subjugation and exploitation which has been [the] lot" of the global "community of colored peoples." This, he argued, "has created a vague sense of community" fed by "the problems of underdevelopment which all share and in their common revulsion

[28] James Dickerson, *Dixie's Dirty Secret: The True Story of How the Government, the Media, and the Mob Conspired to Combat Integration and the Vietnam Antiwar Movement* (Armonk, N.Y.: M. E. Sharpe, 1998), 101.

[29] "Malcolm X Speaks the Prospects for Freedom," transcript, January 7, 1965, WBAI-FM, Pacifica Radio Archive, North Hollywood, California.

to any expression of white racial superiority and colonialism, of which they have all been victims." The economist deplored "America's obsessive fear of the American Negro's intimacy with other colored nationals" and characterized press accounts that depicted the Vietnamese as antiblack as at variance with his own personal experience. Browne perceived African-Americans' relation to the war as offering both danger and opportunity. They should "steer a careful course between the Scylla of American racism and the Charybdis of foreign intrigue." Yet black Americans could "use their unique position" to be international peacemakers.[30]

During the summer of 1964, Guinean president Sékou Touré invited SNCC activists to Guinea through entertainer Harry Belafonte, a major contributor to civil rights groups. Touré wanted SNCC people to "share ideas with young Guineans." SNCC workers, stressed by the violence of Freedom Summer and the setback at the Democratic National Convention, needed a break. A group of eleven, including Bob and Dona Moses, Mrs. Fannie Lou Hamer, Julian Bond, James Forman, Donald Harris, and John Lewis, made the three-week trip to Africa. As Lewis related in his autobiography, fellow PanAm passengers included Peace Corps volunteers en route to assignments who shared a spirit of camaraderie with the SNCC people.[31]

John Lewis's second African trip impressed him with the visual manifestations of black liberty. "With all the flying I'd done in the United States, this was the first time I'd ever seen black pilots. And that was just the beginning. In every city I visited, I was struck by the sight of black police officers, black men behind the desks in banks, black people not just on bicycles but also behind the wheels of Mercedes. Black people in *charge*. Black people doing for *themselves*."[32] James Forman recalled that in Guinea, "our group spent its time resting, reading socialist literature (for the first time in most cases)," attending cultural events, talking to Guinean officials, and several times meeting with the president, Sékou Touré. The U.S. Defense Intelligence Agency subsequently described these meetings as "lessons in revolution" received at Touré's feet, but Fannie Lou Hamer marveled at her access. Touré personally visited the SNCC delegation in their guest quarters. "Imagine the president coming to see us," Hamer commented, "when in the United States we couldn't even go to see the president."[33] Lewis and Hamer's responses to Guinea show how African Americans have often reacted to life and travel abroad. Residence overseas made possible an escape from what many experienced as a psychically draining and narrowly repressive society at home. The comparative freedom from

[30] Robert S. Browne, "The Freedom Movement and the War in Vietnam," *Freedomways* 5 (Fall 1965): 467, 472–3, 476–8, 480.

[31] Lewis, *Walking with the Wind*, 293–5. See also the account of the trip in James Forman, *The Making of Black Revolutionaries* (Washington, D.C., Open Hand Publishing, 1985), 407–11.

[32] Lewis, *Walking with the Wind*, 295, emphasis in original.

[33] Forman, *Making of Black Revolutionaries*, 409–10, Hamer quoted on p. 408; Department of Defense, Counterintelligence Research Project, CI Special Project, 10 October 1967, Student Non-Violent Coordinating Committee (SNCC), "World Travel," p. 8, DDRS.

discrimination they found contrasted significantly with the barriers they faced in the United States.

The sight of black people in autonomous communities and employed in capacities conventionally denied them in the United States deeply impressed these travelers. Clearly, options other than brutality, discrimination, and degradation were possible for blacks. For those who had trudged down the unpaved byways of the Deep South and witnessed the deprivation of populations without fundamental rights, the freedom struggle in the United States resembled the national liberation movements of African and Asian peoples. That many developing countries and their nationals received SNCC representatives with the honors appropriate for dignitaries encouraged a latent statist vision, with the black community perceived as an *imperium in imperio*, an embryonic and captive power in the toils of empire.

If some considered SNCC radical, John Lewis recalled that the Africans he encountered on the continent were more radical still: "That was eye-opening." Africa was new to the comparatively young activists but not to black nationalists who had kept up a counterpoint to integrationist dicta throughout the 1950s and 1960s. Some of the older ones who had belonged to such organizations as the Ethiopian Peace Movement and the UANM faded away, but their discursive traditions and grassroots appeal had not. Malcolm X's gift was to absorb these and add to them a familiarity with African politics and contacts with various African and Middle Eastern diplomats stationed at the United Nations.

Malcolm had received funds from Egypt, the CIA learned, and his fortunes had improved since he left the Nation of Islam, according to the State Department. The FBI added his international activities to its close surveillance, noting his friendship with the Ghanaian UN General Assembly president Alex Quaison-Sackey and recording the numbers of diplomatic license plates on cars parked outside venues where he spoke. Five hundred persons had attended a meeting of his Organization of African American Unity (OAAU) in December 1964, when he introduced A. M. Babu, a leader of the Zanzibar revolution. Che Guevara, in New York for the General Assembly proceedings as Cuba's official delegate, was invited to that meeting but could not attend and instead sent greetings.[34]

Malcolm X traveled in Africa in 1964 and early 1965. In Ghana he organized an OAAU branch among African-American expatriates.[35] SNCC members John Lewis and Donald Harris were in the cafe of the New Stanley Hotel in Nairobi one day when he walked up and greeted them. He had just arrived

---

[34] FBI Director to Special Agent in Charge (SAC) (New York), December 2, 1964; LHM, "Malcolm K. Little," December 8, 1964; SAC (New York) to LHM, February 8, 1965, *FBI File on Malcolm X* 100–399321 Sections 1–9 reel 1 (Wilmington, Del.: Scholarly Resources, 1995). See also Manning Marable, *Malcolm X: A Life of Reinvention* (New York: Viking, 2011), 361.

[35] Peter Goldman, *The Death and Life of Malcolm X* (Urbana: University of Illinois Press, 1979), 215, 181.

from Cairo where, helped by recently appointed OAU secretary general Diallo Telli, he introduced the OAAU to the OAU. He had known Telli in New York when Telli was Guinea's permanent representative to the United Nations. "As Malcolm talked," Lewis remembered, "it was clear Africa was doing for him the same thing it was doing for us – providing a frame of reference that was both broadening and refreshing. He told us how happy he was to see SNCC reaching out like this to Africa.... He talked about the need to shift our focus, both among one another and between us and the white community, from race to class."[36]

U.S. authorities did not worry so much about what Malcolm might say as they did about what he might do. The world already knew about the contradictions between America's democratic professions and its actual practice. More dangerous was the possibility that Malcolm would collaborate with revolutionary elements abroad to foment trouble by organizing as-yet inchoate urban rebels in American ghettos or recruit volunteers to Africa's wars of liberation. U.S. officials in Africa were accordingly instructed to avoid him. Mel McCaw, the black director of the Nairobi branch of the Institute of International Education, threw a party for the Muslim leader to meet the African-American residents in Nairobi and planned a second fete that would include Kenyan guests. The U.S. embassy pressured its staff to skip the event. McCaw later told author Peter Goldman that Ambassador William Attwood had strongly berated him. "He said, 'What are you trying to do, set up some kind of cleavage in the U.S community here?' I said no. He said: 'Well, what is the point of raising these issues by having special black parties?'" Attwood issued a veiled threat to have McCaw fired.[37]

Attwood objected less to African Americans' practicing social exclusion than to the chance that Malcolm's message of radical Pan-African solidarity would influence Africans in a city where revolutionary ideas were already percolating. There were reasons to fear such an outcome. Cuba launched its mission to aid the Lumumbist guerrillas in the Congo at the same time that Malcolm was planning his trips to Accra, Dar es Salaam, and Cairo, leading sites of support and asylum for the liberation groups. U.S. intelligence had discovered the Cuban plan to train African insurgents by February 1964. The NSC Special Group on Counter Insurgency stepped up its quest for information and increased its support for the Congolese Army, with the CIA enlisting Cuban exile pilots to strike rebel targets. That Congolese civilians were caught in the crossfire did not seem to bother anyone in Washington.[38]

The CIA discovered a training center for black cadres near the city of Santiago, Cuba. Its report to Walt Rostow, special assistant to the president,

[36] Author's telephone interview with James Turner, April 2, 2012; Lewis, *Walking with the Wind*, 296, 297.

[37] Goldman, *The Death and Life of Malcolm X*, 215.

[38] Lise A. Namikas, "Battleground Africa: The Cold War and the Congo Crisis, 1960–1965" (PhD diss., University of Southern California, Los Angeles, 2002), 407, 408.

titled "Training of Negroes in Cuba," alleged that the trainees included African Americans who would return to the United States and, schooled in the arts of subversion, fan the flames of violence and rioting "to bring about a Negro revolution in the United States."[39] As it turned out, the revolutionists in training were Africans, Asians, and Latin Americans intending to return to their home countries. The alarmism about a black invasion of the United States was calculated to create momentum for a reactive strike against Cuba. Fears that African Americans would join paramilitaries and that groups like SNCC could become avatars for global radicalism pushed domestic discontent into the international sphere. The prospective worldwide movement against colonialism and racial discrimination, Washington worried, played squarely into the hands of Moscow, Peking, and Havana. Malcolm X was abroad when the Harlem "riot" of 1964 took place. The FBI and local New York authorities wanted to attribute the unrest to him but were never able to find a smoking gun.

The spirit of protest could not be attributed to one person. Selma, Alabama, was ground zero as global audiences watched footage of Bloody Sunday, March 7, 1965, when Dallas County sheriffs' deputies, state troopers, and the civilian posses they organized mowed down some six hundred civil rights demonstrators like corn stalks in a field. The protesters, intending to march to the state capital, Montgomery, were stopped by the police and vigilantes on the Edmund Pettis Bridge. A child participant, Sheyann Webb, later remembered "hundreds of policemen, state troopers, billy clubs, dogs, and horses." She recalled "outbursts of tear gas," which had rendered local activist Amelia Boynton Robinson unconscious. Among those attacked was John Lewis of SNCC, who suffered a broken skull. "I began to just try to run home as fast as I could,... And I ran and I ran and I ran. It was like I was running for my life."[40] Indeed, the Selma campaign claimed three lives. The first fatality was Jimmie Lee Jackson, a Baptist Church deacon in the nearby town of Marion, where African Americans were also protesting. On March 11, James Reeb, a Unitarian minister from Boston, was beaten to death by a group of whites. Two weeks later, Klansmen shot Detroit resident Viola Liuzzo to death on a local highway.[41]

---

[39] Central Intelligence Agency, "Training of Negroes in Cuba," sanitized, n.d., no. 1266, DDRS.

[40] Sheyann Webb oral history, *Voices of Freedom: An Oral History of the Civil Rights Movement from the 1950s through the 1980s*, eds. Henry Hampton and Steve Fayer (New York: Bantam Books, 1990), 228–9.

[41] Studies of the Selma movement include Richie Jean Sherrod Jackson, *The House by the Side of the Road: The Selma Civil Rights Movement* (Montgomery: University of Alabama Press, 2011); J. Mills Thornton III, *Dividing Lines: Municipal Politics and the Struggle for Civil Rights in Montgomery, Birmingham, and Selma* (Montgomery: University of Alabama Press, 2006); Mary Stanton, *From Selma to Sorrow: The Life and Death of Viola Liuzzo* (Athens: University of Georgia Press, 1998); Sheyann Webb-Christburg, Rachel West Nelson and Frank Sikora, *Selma, Lord, Selma: Girlhood Memories of the Civil Rights Days* (Montgomery: University of Alabama Press, 1997); Amelia Platts Boynton, *Bridge across Jordan: the Story of the Struggle for Civil Rights in Selma, Alabama* (New York: Carlton Press, 1979); David J. Garrow, *Protest at Selma: Martin Luther King, Jr., and the Voting Rights Act of 1965* (New Haven, Conn.: Yale University Press, 1978).

In addition to condoning the savage brutality that prevented black citizens from exercising their constitutional rights, Selma elites had other plans. The Industrial Development Board of Selma was in the midst of luring the giant Erie, Pennsylvania–based Hammermill Paper Company to town. The board proposed that Hammermill retrofit an old plantation and convert it into a pulp mill. Its timing was problematic: a month before the proposal became public in early February, Martin Luther King Jr. traveled to Selma and was arrested there.[42] Yet even after Bloody Sunday, Hammermill accepted the local offer and resisted pleas to reconsider. The chairman of its board liked the climate in Selma. He professed he was drawn to "the character of the community and its people" and claimed he could use moral suasion on the likes of Sheriff Jim Clark and Alabama Highway Patrol Director Al Lingo to ensure peace. Protests ensued at Hammermill's Pennsylvania headquarters, but the company was undeterred.

While civil rights historiography has focused on white Selma's intransigence and the internal divisions among SCLC, SNCC, and the Dallas County Voters League over tactics, there is more to the story. Hammermill was an early example of the direction that the latest incarnation of the New South would take. Governor George Wallace promised the company exemption from state and local taxes, and new infrastructure at public expense. Hammermill in turn promised civil rights leaders that its plant facilities would not be segregated.[43]

SNCC, however, was not buying it. The organization had been active in the area since 1963 and understood the stake that local black people had in the outcome of the conflict. In a letter to Hammermill's president, John Lewis noted "that the moneys which would build your plant were in part collected from people who have no say in their disposition. And the funds which the agreement allows you to keep from the tax reserves could be better used for community improvement."[44] SNCC's commitment to the empowerment of the poor opposed it to the ambitions of segregationists who hoped to remake the region through economic restructuring and lip service to federal demands for less open repression.

Sections of the South could now be redefined as the "Sun Belt" as southern elites exchanged formal Jim Crow for development. Federal dollars poured into new facilities and industries, but the location of African Americans in the economy meant that many would remain on the margins of prosperity.

[42] Jane Ingold, "The Best Known Name in Paper: Hammermill," Spring 2010. The Pennsylvania Center for the Book, Pennsylvania State University, http://www.pabook.libraries.psu.edu/palitmap/Hammermill.html, accessed June 22, 2011; *Titusville* (Pa.) *Herald*, May 12, 1965, p. 1; "Hammermill Paper Urged to Confer," *Pittsburgh Courier*, May 22, 1965. p. 5; Special Agent, Cleveland, report, SNCC, October 25, 1965, FBI File on the Student Nonviolent Coordinating Committee, reel 1.

[43] Randolph Hohle, "The Rise of the New South Governmentality: Competing Southern Revitalization Projects and Police Responses to the Black Civil Rights Movement 1961–1965," *Journal of Historical Sociology* 22 (December 2009): 516, 517.

[44] Lewis quoted in ibid., 517.

Job bias did not end but became harder to detect in an environment that now emphasized technical expertise. National security arguments lent urgency to modernization and simultaneously sidelined demands for racial justice, as the focus on defense enhanced and furthered southern conservatism.

President Johnson had helped move the Civil Rights Act of 1964 through Congress and signed it with relish. At the same time, he vigorously promoted the latest New South manifestation, which muted the "massive resistance" of a decade before. The civil rights act provided for a Community Relations Service whose purpose was to help put out fires in local conflicts and induce opposing sides to negotiate mutually acceptable agreements. In Selma, the service, caught between an unyielding white elite and a civil rights community intent on righting wrongs, proved ineffective. The broader context of its difficulties lay in the impossibility of blending such disparate aims. The New South and the "beloved community" could not be merged. Johnson himself tried to change the terms by refusing to meet with Martin Luther King to discuss Selma. This played badly with those who were already disillusioned by the refusal at the Democratic National Convention in 1964 to seat the Mississippi Freedom Democratic Party. That the deaths of the Reverend James Reeb and Viola Liuzzo, both white and from northern cities, received more federal attention than the continuous violence suffered by southern black people was also noted and resented. "Despite Johnson's rhetoric of support for the civil rights movement's goals," Randolph Hohle comments, "the federal government's response was contradictory and uneven." The Community Relations Service "advise[d] local authorities on how to stop the movement while simultaneously pushing for expanding protective legislation." Hohle concludes that all parties got something out of "the paradox of federal intervention" although for different reasons.[45] Many of the most committed activists, however, perceived that the share allotted to the oppressed was unjustly small. That understanding would have important consequences for the freedom struggle in the coming years.

African Americans had historically been isolated by the racist practices of the U.S. government and civil society, although never completely cut off from global currents. For figures like Fannie Lou Hamer, travel was an awakening. While many of the experiences that newly minted travelers had were eye-opening and fruitful, not every international experience was always positive. The encounters that a group of black reporters had in the Dominican Republic illustrate how such travel could be manipulated.

Trujillo, a U.S. ally and "*our* sonofabitch" in Washington parlance, had ruled his country for three decades. He and family members controlled most of the lucrative enterprises and owned a substantial proportion of the land. Trujillo forcefully suppressed all serious political opposition, hunting down exiled foes in other countries. The generalissimo's agents meddled in the affairs

[45] David J. Garrow, *Bearing the Cross: Martin Luther King, Jr. and the Southern Christian Leadership Conference* (New York: HarperCollins, 2004), 378, 380, 387; Hohle, "The Rise of the New South Governmentality," 522.

of neighbor governments, supporting right-wing coup attempts and harboring filibusterers.[46] In spite of Trujillo's brutality and long-standing compliance with U.S. demands for order and "stability" in the Caribbean, his power began waning in the late 1950s. Cuban insurgency created a "radical flank effect,"[47] causing centrists, including U.S. analysts, to cast about for a middle ground between revolutionary communism and reactionary authoritarianism as a political solution for Caribbean and Central American unrest. After the Cuban revolution, the ban on Cuban sugar led U.S. importers to search elsewhere for supplies. Trujillo's personal control of the Dominican crop left few opportunities for U.S. investors and a disgruntled local bourgeoisie.

The generalissimo had maintained his power in part through skillful manipulation of the governing class in Washington, the press, and public sentiment. He complemented his blackmail of misbehaving U.S. congressmen – whom he lured into compromising situations – with well-honed attention to the fine points of U.S. culture and politics. Those on his payroll included the arch-segregationist senators James Eastland of Mississippi and Allen Ellender of Louisiana respectively. Long before U.S. Major League Baseball began recruiting Dominican players, Trujillo was luring African Americans to island teams. Dominican politicians cagily exploited U.S. race problems. As suspect as Dominican elections were, color did not prevent anyone from voting. The absence of overt segregation allowed the country to present itself as a racial utopia to certain black American reporters who were both gullible and cynical.[48]

Dominican professionals established an organization called the Dominican-African Cultural Association that responded to reports of racial violence and anti-Semitism in the United States and to anti–West Indian rioting in the United Kingdom. Trujillo was the honorary president. The association did not limit itself to racial concerns; it claimed to oppose intolerance everywhere. Over the years, Trujillo had made the country a refuge for "all displaced Spaniards," Jews, and Japanese, its spokesman asserted. Trujillo did accept Spanish Loyalist refugees in the 1930s but more recently had given asylum to the Cuban dictator Fulgencio Batista and to the former Argentine president Juan Peron. The refugee policy had coherent goals. In addition to controversial political figures, Trujillo favored immigrants without African ancestry. In spite

---

[46] Michael R. Hall, *Sugar and Power in the Dominican Republic: Eisenhower, Kennedy and the Trujillos* (Westport, Conn.: Greenwood Press, 2000); Charles D. Ameringer, *The Caribbean Legion: Patriots, Politicians, Soldiers of Fortune, 1946–1950* (University Park: Pennsylvania State University, 1996), 137.

[47] On "radical flank effects," see Herbert H. Haines, *Black Radicals and the Civil Rights Mainstream, 1964–1970* (Knoxville: University of Tennessee Press, 1988).

[48] Tim Weiner, *Enemies: A History of the FBI* (New York: Random House, 2012), 218–9; Marion E. Jackson. "Sports of the World," *Atlanta Daily World*, June 19, 1958, p. 7; "Don Clendenon Returns Home from Dominican Ball League," ibid., December 14, 1961, p. 7; "May Take Steps to Halt Raids," *Pittsburgh Courier*, August 4, 1951, p. 16; Bernard Diederich, "Baseball in Their Blood: the San Pedro Syndrome," *Caribbean Review* 14 (Fall 1985): 15; Charles J. Smith, III, "Many Afro-Dominicans Elected: Color Was No Barrier at Polls in Dominican Voting," *Norfolk Journal and Guide*, December 31, 1960, p. 8.

of his own background and the killing of a nephew by a racist Florida deputy in 1946, he shared with Dominican elites a desire to "improve" the country through whitening. Europeans and Asians would counteract the effects of the large numbers of Haitian residents as well as Dominicans' own mixed heritage. Contempt for Haitians ran especially deep, culminating in a 1937 massacre when thousands of Haitian immigrant workers were brutally murdered.[49]

The Dominican-African Cultural Association invited Baltimore-based black documentary filmmaker and publicist Bill Alexander to address its meeting at the University of Santo Domingo, where he received an honorary doctorate. Alexander praised Dominican health and educational facilities and the lack of open racial bias. The Baltimore *Afro-American* learned that Trujillo would admit any African-American high school or college student who wished to enroll in an educational institution. Why did Trujillo defer in this way to African Americans? By early 1959 the Eisenhower administration was searching for ways to eliminate Trujillo, increasingly seen as an embarrassment in spite of his staunch anticommunism. Sensing the chill in the Washington air, Trujillo now presented himself as a champion of racial justice. On the heels of the Little Rock school desegregation crisis, the invitation to black students subjected the United States to invidious comparison. The absence of legal segregation in the Dominican Republic made it seem racially progressive, in contrast. The ploy also sent a signal to disgruntled Dominicans as well as foreigners inclined to criticize the dictatorship.[50]

Trujillo also boasted the support of black conservative George Schuyler, whose Pittsburgh *Courier* columns, "Views and Reviews," described the Dominican Republic as idyllic. In visits dating from 1949, he incredibly found no slums, prostitution, or mendicancy. Dark-skinned people could work in the hotels and banks and on newspaper staffs. Schuyler remained impressed by the "modernity, cleanliness, orderliness and discipline" he saw. The regime was an autocracy that should be described only as "authoritarian" because Schuyler had observed no "fear and terror." He blamed "fellow travelers" and "liberals" in the media for the bad press Trujillo received and communists for the various plots to overthrow him.[51]

Dominican officials went out to their way to court black American journalists believed influential, but not every reporter was snowed. A discussion of a

[49] *Pittsburgh Courier*, November 1, 1958, p. 6; *People's Voice*, November 9, 1946, p. 16, 32; Robert D. Crassweller, *Trujillo: The Life and Times of a Caribbean Dictator* (New York: Macmillan, 1966), 84; Juan Manuel Garcia, *La matanza de los haitianos* (Santo Domingo: Ed. Alfa & Omega, 1983).

[50] "Bill Alexander Is Overseas Speaker," *Baltimore Afro-American*, December 6, 1968, p. 7; Weiner, *Enemies*, 219–222. For other Trujillo propaganda activities in the United States see Stephen Rabe, *Eisenhower and Latin America* (Chapel Hill: University of North Carolina, 1988), 157.

[51] George Schuyler, *Pittsburgh Courier* "Views and Reviews," December 20, 1958, p. 12; December 27, 1958, p. 12; "George Schuyler Looks at Latin America," ibid., May 5, 1965, p. 10. See also "New Troubles Brewing in the Caribbean," mss., February 1, 1959, in George Schuyler Papers, SC.

1959 junket revealed mixed sentiments. *Ebony's* Simeon Booker thought black Americans "should be wary of lending support" to such as Trujillo. Others disagreed. Writer Roy Garvin hoped that "honest dictatorship" of the Dominican variety could improve conditions in neighboring Haiti. "If dictatorship can do what it can there in comparison to Haiti," he declared, "then I'm for dictatorship for colored people." A belief in the salutary effects of "authoritarianism" was not the only reason that some black journalists endorsed Trujillo. Photographer Clifton Cabell claimed that most of the criticism was from envious persons who had not been invited on the trip. The opinions of some who had traveled were swayed by the favorable treatment they received, handling they merited at home but did not receive because of their color. *Afro-American* columnist Pearlie Cox, for example, "had a ball" in the Dominican Republic, and Trujillo had kissed her hand. By contrast, in the United States, she could "hardly get inside the fence around the White House," much less approach the frosty Eisenhower.[52]

Junkets of the sort that Cox enjoyed have a long history. That increasing numbers of African Americans embarked on such trips to such places as Israel and the Soviet Union does not mean that the African-American foreign policy interest is based on naiveté, as certain scholars have snidely implied. In the search for power, all parties have their interests at heart, although the resources at their disposal to realize their goals may vary.

The NAACP exemplifies a continued, principled foreign policy voice. The association took some of the most comprehensive positions on international issues of any African-American organization. It condemned Portuguese colonialism and South African apartheid, which it felt should be opposed nonviolently. It called on U.S. investors to pressure Pretoria through divestment and urged its branches to participate in antiapartheid demonstrations. The association sought U.S. government support for the General Assembly initiative to impose sanctions. "Having passed the Civil Rights Bill in our own country," the 55th Convention resolutions read, "our nation is in a good moral position to advocate justice and equality for the oppressed nonwhites in that country."[53]

Help for developing nations remained a constant in NAACP deliberations, and the group criticized Johnson's $200 million cut from the aid budget. The association praised the Peace Corps program and backed the United Nations, mentioning in particular the genocide and human rights covenants. It identified as an important goal aligning U.S. African policies with its own anticolonial

[52] Alice Dunnigan, "Woman Governor of Dominican Republic: 'There Is No Segregation of Color, Religion, or Sex in Our Country,'" *Pittsburgh Courier*, February 7, 1959, p. 16. "Dominican Republic Stirs Press Debate," Baltimore *Afro-American*, March 7, 1959, p. 17. On black White House correspondents' problem with Eisenhower, see Alice Dunnigan, *A Black Woman's Experience – from Schoolhouse to White House* (Philadelphia: Dorrance, 1974), 366–83.

[53] NAACP 55th annual convention, Washington, D. C., resolutions, June 22–27, 1964, pp. 26, 27, 28, in Ralph J. Bunche Papers, UCLA, Box 113, NAACP Board.

and antiracist objectives and joined ANLCA in order to strengthen the link between its foreign and domestic interests.[54]

In spite of this history, the NAACP had no better luck than the ANLCA in changing opinions at either Foggy Bottom or Pennsylvania Avenue. Its stance did not jibe with how President Lyndon Johnson framed African issues. The White House did not take a proactive stand against apartheid or make major increases in aid to African countries. Johnson's domestic style was reflected in his approach to emerging nations. For him, the twilight of colonialism should preclude resentments. Accustomed to dickering with colleagues at home, LBJ anticipated a quid pro quo and expected the same from aid recipients. This meant support for anticommunism and the growing U.S. commitment in Southeast Asia.

The recurrence of heavy fighting in the Congo opened another stage from which the United States' international commitments were questioned. "By the middle of 1964," Richard Gott notes, "the old Lumumbist left – backed by China and the Soviet Union – controlled much of the Congo."[55] A UN peace-keeping force arrived to prop up the weak central government, but UN member states' failure to agree on how to bear the expense led to its quick withdrawal. Rather than commit ground troops that might draw the Soviets directly into the area or ask for soldiers from Europe and rekindle the flame of colonialism, Prime Minister Möise Tshombe, on U.S. advice, recruited white mercenaries from Belgium, Rhodesia, and South Africa. This move put the Congo on the agenda at the Cairo meeting of the OAU in July and prompted Algeria, Egypt, Ghana, Guinea, Mali, and Tanzania to recognize the Lumumbist rebels.[56]

By October, a thousand white soldiers of fortune had arrived in the Congo. They seized Albertville and marched on Stanleyville, where the rebel government took European civilian hostages as insurance against the invaders. The U.S. Air Force then dropped Belgian paratroopers into Stanleyville from U.S. transport planes. The Belgians, Britons, Americans, and mercenaries planned a pincer movement to capture Stanleyville and dispose of the Lumumbists for good.[57]

These heavy-handed operations owed a considerable debt to Johnson's interpretation of cold war threats and electoral challenges. The president did not want to be outdone by Barry Goldwater in anticommunist militancy during an election year, and Chinese and Soviet assistance promised to Congolese insurgents genuinely alarmed the administration. Calculations about how much the

[54] Donald R. Culverson, *From Sharpeville to Soweto to Sanctions: The Rise of American Anti-Apartheid Activism, 1960–1987* (Boulder, Colo.: Westview Press, 1999), 44–5; NAACP 55th annual convention resolutions, June 22–27, 1964, pp. 26, 27, 28, NAACP Papers.

[55] Richard Gott, "Introduction," in Che Guevara, *The African Dream* (New York: Grove Press, 1999), xvi.

[56] Thomas Noer, *Soapy: A Biography of G. Mennen Williams* (Ann Arbor: University of Michigan Press, 2005), 281–3; Amrit Wilson, *U.S. Foreign Policy and Revolution* (London: Pluto Press, 1989), 99; Che Guevara, *The African Dream* (New York: Grove Press, 1999), xviii–xix.

[57] Namikas, "Battleground Africa," 481–2; Wilson, *U.S. Foreign Policy and Revolution*, 99.

Congolese could profit from communist help, or whether a military solution best fit the country's circumstances, did not enter into the picture. Hindsight, based on revolutionist Che Guevara's writings, suggests that the Congolese lacked the ability to utilize bloc aid effectively. Guevara had tried to train and unite disparate rebel factions and deploy them against the mercenaries but had had to acknowledge defeat and withdraw his small, secret force.[58] The ultimate result of American and European collective action, however, was to permanently damage U.S. relations with many African leaders, including Nkrumah.

The White House worried that Nkrumah, an early Lumumba ally, could wreck the status quo in Africa, by aiding Congo rebels and turning friendly regimes against the United States. He might allow the Soviets to use air facilities under construction in northern Ghana. In the course of the 1960s, Nkrumah's government listed to the Left. It opposed the U.S. invasion of the Dominican Republic and the bombing of North Vietnam. That Soviets and East Germans staffed the Ghanaian Bureau of African Affairs, which was helping national liberation movements in various parts of the continent, also troubled U.S. officials.[59]

Internally, the once-popular Nkrumah grew distant from the populace. Genuine assassination plots explained some of his suspiciousness, but growing Western animosity convinced him that the threats were emanating from North America. Ultimately, as Mary E. Montgomery argues, the U.S. "inability to understand the aspirations of independence; and refusal to accept alternative ideological choices ... led to the demise of Ghana's first government."[60] In spite of Nkrumah's worsening reputation, African Americans continued to view him positively. Optimism about Ghana's prospects even reached into the elite black circles sometimes tapped for diplomatic talent. At the end of 1965, President Johnson appointed Peace Corps official Franklin Williams ambassador to Ghana. The ambassadorship had remained vacant for nearly six months. Williams, an attorney and the nephew of James E. Amos, one of the first black FBI agents, was, in the words of one scholar, "possessed of a curious confidence ... that Nkrumah could be redeemed. For that reason alone many of the diplomatic corps in Accra thought that Williams was being used as a smokescreen to cover American hostility."[61] A Ghanaian newspaper, the *Spark,* shared this view. It noted the continuing disfranchisement of African Americans in parts of the U.S. South and the persistence of racism. A black ambassador who defends U.S. policy in Vietnam and South Africa, the *Spark* editorialized, might as well not be black. Why does Washington refuse to name black ambassadors to such

[58] Guevara, *The African Dream,* 125–9, 218, 223.

[59] Scott Thompson, *Ghana's Foreign Policy, 1957–1966* (Princeton, N.J.: Princeton University Press, 1969), 394, 396.

[60] Evan White, "Kwame Nkrumah: Cold War Modernity, Pan-African Ideology and the Geopolitics of Development," *Geopolitics* 8 (2) (2003): 99–124; Montgomery, "The Eyes of the World Were Watching," 210–15, 221, 238.

[61] J. Edgar Hoover to P. Kenneth O'Donnell, May 17, 1963, Franklin Williams Papers, SC; Montgomery, "The Eyes of the World Were Watching," 397.

posts as London or Paris? it demanded. Williams also found himself distrusted by expatriates. Soon after Nkrumah was deposed in 1966, the ambassador revealed his adherence to cold war orthodoxy. In a speech to the Council on Foreign Relations in October, he denounced Nkrumah as a dictator and saluted the new Ghanaian government for its anticommunism. In Accra, "radicalism has given way to realism." Williams then found himself apologizing to African Americans in his own social circle who were appalled that the Ghanaian coup took place during his residency.[62]

Poor relations with Ghana reflected a major transition in U.S. foreign policy in the Johnson years as Southeast Asia bogged down LBJ. His administration reprised the venerable notion that Europeans should be the ones most active in African affairs. Only if there was a danger of a victory for communists, as in the Congo, did he wish to take action. He reversed Kennedy's attempts at detente, expanded involvement in Vietnam, stopped the secret overtures to Havana, and resumed support for Cuban exile filibustering operations.

Johnson expected loyalty on these issues from African Americans, whose long-standing struggle for civil rights legislation he had endorsed and promoted. Johnson assumed that racial minorities, once having attained full citizenship, had no need to define themselves as separate constituencies in international matters. According to NSC staffer Robert Komer, Johnson "doesn't think it at all a good idea to encourage a separate Negro view of foreign policy. We don't want an integrated domestic policy and a segregated foreign policy." LBJ did not want another ethnic lobby, "(a la the Zionists) which might limit his freedom of maneuver."[63] The irony was that Johnson did indeed create separate policies by abandoning in the international arena the principles he had gamely supported at home.

"We receive Negro and liberal deputations all the time which ask us to apply 'sanctions' against South Africa and Rhodesia," McGeorge Bundy and Ulrich Haynes informed Johnson. "We tell them that such measures would only make things worse, but what is there that would make things better?"[64] Bundy and Haynes understood that U.S. policy in southern Africa was blocked. They were unwilling, however, to suggest breaking the impasse. While the Johnson administration insisted that U.S. investments in the apartheid regime did not determine its policy, and that it did not depend on South Africa's strategic minerals, it was unwilling to disengage from those investments and resources, arguing that sanctions would further limit U.S. influence and provoke possible

---

[62] *The Spark*, January 28, 1966, clipping; Franklin Williams to Jesse E. Gloster, February, 1966; boiler plate letters, of which Williams to Charles Delgado, March 4, 1966, is representative; speech to the Council on Foreign Relations, New York City, October 1967, all in Williams Papers.

[63] Robert A. Packenham, *Liberal America and the Third World* (Princeton, N.J.: Princeton University Press, 1973), 91. Komer quoted in Michael L. Krenn, *Black Diplomacy: African Americans and the State Department, 1945–1969* (Armonk, N.Y.: M. E. Sharpe, 1999), 134.

[64] McGeorge Bundy and Ulrich Haynes (NSC staff) to President Johnson, June 10, 1965, *FRUS*, XXIV, *1964–1968, Africa*, 1029.

retaliation. Any release from business as usual in South Africa would have to be voluntary.[65]

Haynes and Bundy registered their uncertainty as to how to address the South African problem in a memorandum to President Johnson. "We are … deeply concerned about the accelerating trend toward Government-sanctioned racial discrimination ('apartheid') and extreme political repression in South Africa," they wrote. "'Apartheid' in particular is a major handicap to the Free World in its efforts to stabilize the political situation in Africa and keep the Chicoms [Chinese Communists] and Soviets out."[66]

White House staffer Lee C. White did not welcome black advice on foreign policy but expected pressure to continue. "I am confident that the organization is not going to evaporate," he wrote to Johnson about the ANLCA; "it would therefore make sense to do what we can to make it an asset rather than an extra burden in this already difficult area." Komer and NSC colleague Haynes understood that such groups were "just what [Johnson] doesn't want." They recommended that the White House deter Roy Wilkins, Martin Luther King Jr., A. Philip Randolph, and Dorothy Height from pursuing lobbying. If they kept on nevertheless, "we should guide [it] toward a non-racial outcome, i.e., it should include whites as well as Negroes."[67]

Foreign relations professionals generally persisted in their conviction that public opinion, in their view naïve, uninformed, and idealistic, meant little. Henry S. Villard, who held ambassadorial posts in Africa during Eisenhower's two terms, criticized black leaders who advocated U.S. support for OAU efforts to end the redeveloping Congo conflict. These people did not know, Villard asserted, that Senegalese president Léopold Senghor thought it best to let African chancelleries handle the crisis. Villard did not indicate why he thought African-American leaders necessarily had to agree with Senghor; nor did he elaborate on Senghor's differences with many other African heads of state.[68]

Secretary of State Dean Rusk met in early March 1965 with Roy Wilkins; John Davis, president of AMSAC; and Theodore Brown, to discuss aid for Africa. Rusk, noncommittal on upping the aid budget and realizing what had animated his African-American visitors in the past, asked them to recommend likely black candidates for the Foreign Service. The tenor of Haynes's memorandum of the meeting suggests that Rusk happily agreed with what Wilkins et al. were saying about integrating the State Department in order to put them

---

[65] John Walton Cotman, "South African Strategic Minerals and U.S. Foreign Policy, 1961–68," *Review of Black Political Economy* 8 (Spring 1978): 284; McGeorge Bundy and Ulrich to President Johnson, June 10, 1965, *FRUS, 1964–1968, Africa*; Memorandum from Gordon Chase of the NSC Staff to the President's Special Assistant for National Security Affairs (Bundy) September 13, 1965, ibid., 1040.

[66] Bundy and Haynes to Johnson, June 10, 1965.

[67] White to Johnson, December 28, 1964; memorandum from Robert W. Komer and Ulrich Haynes of the National Security Council Staff to the President's Special Assistant for National Security Affairs (Bundy), March 3, 1965; *FRUS, 1964–1968, Africa.*

[68] Henry Serrano Villard, *Affairs at State* (New York: Thomas Y. Crowell, 1965), 90.

off. For their part, the delegation did not press him on anything. They wanted Rusk to travel to Africa but accepted his excuse that he did not have time. They requested no meeting with Johnson. From the NSC point of view, the discussion was a success. It "was given minimal press coverage and is not likely to give rise to any undesirable repercussions," Haynes commented.[69]

But differences on international issues based on diverse understandings of race and its impact could not be papered over so easily. If Americans were to face the outside world united, as Johnson believed they should, then the diplomatic community itself should reflect the nation's diversity. If race did not matter, as the White House and NSC insisted, black ambassadors should find assignments anywhere. Instead, they were sent to countries mostly hostile to the United States and less important in the greater calculus: Hugh Smythe to Syria, Nathaniel Davis to Bulgaria, and Franklin Williams to Ghana. Perhaps officials thought that ambassadors of color could deflect the animosity of their hosts or, alternatively, that they did not merit choice appointments. Former Foreign Service officer Terrence Lyons endorsed the second explanation. LBJ only responded to Africa when crises occurred, according to Lyons, and thought it a good place for punishment assignments.

Johnson believed that his general support of African-American leaders' domestic agendas should guarantee black conformity to his foreign policy designs. In 1964 and early 1965, before the Vietnam War strained the budget – and before the impact of war casualties was felt in minority communities – much loyalty could be readily presumed. The administration accepted the conventional liberal view of the causes and remedies for discrimination and poverty. LBJ himself offered environmental explanations for the nation's racial afflictions.[70]

In contrast, U.S. social science retained a catastrophist strain that sited current problems in past trauma. The assistant secretary of labor, economist Daniel P. Moynihan, saw matrifocal family structure, rather than chronic unemployment, lack of education, and racism, as the cause of black community distress. In a March 1965 report for the Labor Department Office of Policy Planning and Research titled "The Negro Family: The Case for National Action," Moynihan criticized the political demand for "equality of results." Whether or not intended, he provided a way for society to dodge the consequences of generations of injustice by rooting the origins of disadvantage in personal morality, "an ethically plausible way," Nikhil Pal Singh writes, "of explicitly recasting black people outside the circuits of symbolic kinship comprising the national community."[71]

[69] Memorandum from Ulrich Haynes to the President's Special Assistant for National Security Affairs (Bundy), March 4, 1965, *FRUS, 1964–1968, Africa*, 295.

[70] Jennifer Frost, *"An Interracial Movement of the Poor": Community Organizing and the New Left in the 1960s* (New York: New York University Press, 2001), 159.

[71] United States Department of Labor, Office of Policy Planning and Research, The Negro Family: The Case For National Action, [Moynihan Report], March 1965; Nikhil Pal Singh, "Culture/Wars: Recoding Empire in an Age of Democracy," *American Quarterly* 50 (3) (1998): 495.

"Northern cities have created a second-class status which has resulted in 'cultural castration' of the lower-class Negro male," a Chicago Urban League official, echoing Moynihan, declared. Poor blacks "are locked into a pattern of poverty and ... unstable family life."[72] Poverty and instability suggested that the remasculinization of African-American men required not only economic adjustments, but also a shift in how they expressed their manliness. The ideal, also hard for whites to realize by the late 1960s, was the family wage, the breadwinner salary generous enough to allow a wife to stay home. Black men could not really be men until they were economically superior to their wives. Plays and films about black people such as *Raisin in the Sun* and *Nothing But a Man* reflected this theme. While these dramas ranged widely in their concerns, popular interpretations tended to pounce on the need for black male self-assertion.[73]

There were already indications that more than a few African Americans shared the idea that black manhood per se had been a major casualty of racial oppression. The retort to racism's bleakest past, of which castration was both a literal as well as a symbolic aspect, was a strong rejection of accommodationism, often construed as feminine. In 1964, insurgents in the Harlem chapter of CORE forced the resignation of the chair, Gladys Harrington, a social worker. Certain black men vociferously called for "black male leadership" to promote Harlem's interests more forcefully than would the demure Harrington. As suggested by their stance in meetings, masculinist proponents had a particular type of black man in mind: rough, aggressive, and "street." No less a reasoned thinker than radical organizer Jack O'Dell premised the acquisition of real political power by blacks on the reaffirmation of masculine authority. "History has confronted us with a moral imperative to secure governmental power," he wrote in *Freedomways*. "There is no other viable course of action if we are to be free, and it is increasingly a matter of *manhood* maturity to face up to that reality" (Emphasis his).[74]

Paternalism played a role in this masculinism. Abuses of women and children were rife under slavery and Jim Crow when white supremacy denied the patriarchal control to black men that would have allowed them to shield dependents. When James Meredith planned a 1967 march based in Hernando, Mississippi, where he had previously been shot, he refused to let women and children participate, ostensibly for their protection.[75] James Farmer, running as a Republican against Shirley Chisholm for Brooklyn's 12th District congressional seat, characterized her as "bossy," "a would-be

[72] Chicago Urban League press release, n.d., 1960s, CBP, Part 3 – Subject Files on Black Americans, 1918–1967, Series I-Race Relations, 1923–1965, reel 8.
[73] Nancy McLean, *Freedom Is Not Enough: The Opening of the American Workplace* (Cambridge, Mass.: Harvard University Press, 2006), 60.
[74] Karin L. Stanford, *Black Political Organizations in the Post-civil Rights Era* (New Brunswick, N.J.: Rutgers University Press, 2002), 86–7; Jack O'Dell, "The Threshold of a New Reconstruction," *Freedomways* 5 (Fall 1965): 500.
[75] Dickerson, *Dixie's Dirty Secret*, 141, 143.

matriarch," who had shed the reticence deemed appropriate for women.[76] Highly placed civil rights activists thus espoused viewpoints that affirmed normative U.S. ideas about gender and tended to exclude women from visible leadership.

Southern blacks and whites alike often coupled dismissiveness of women with an exaggerated deference toward them. This etiquette, based on the antebellum idealization of white women, suggested that chivalry should also extend to black women. If this meant guarding them from racist insult, then black men should be willing to incur the risks of challenging white authority. Montgomery, Alabama, civil rights leader E. D. Nixon accused black men of cowardice and passivity in the face of racism during the renowned bus boycott. Women were "bearing the brunt of the arrests," he asserted, and men were "backing down like 'little boys.'" Nixon called for stronger-willed behavior: "If we're gonna be mens, now's the time to be mens."[77] For women, however, protection was a double-edged sword. It required a reciprocal obligation to conform to particular male expectations about power.

The ideal woman understood the stresses that black men experienced and thus modified her demands on them. The requirement to protect the male ego rehearsed the narratives of female subordination and male empowerment that supposedly drove traditional white middle-class life. The irony was that in most matters, dissidents condemned white bourgeois conventions. Yet the idea that African Americans had been historically incorrect regarding the proper relations between men and women lay at the heart of many conflicts about correct politics.[78]

Some rejected the drive to conform black male behavior to white bourgeois standards and shift responsibility for the ravages of discrimination and deprivation onto the poor, and specifically on poor black women. Moynihan's assertion that American society had "broke[n] the will of the Negro people" was widely rejected. African-American society "lack[s] neither spirit nor strength nor vigor," two black women offered in rebuttal. African Americans "have given to this nation the only culture it has, the only humanity it has." Addressing the report's gender assumptions in *Liberator*, they noted that continued efforts to castrate black men meant that the job had not been finished. "Just who is the emasculated person in this society? Surely it is the white man whose dazzling symbols of power – his goods, his technology – have all but consumed his human essence. Yes, he is effective because his power enables him

---

[76] Shirley Chisholm, *Unbought and Unbossed*, rep. ed. (Boston: Houghton Mifflin, 1970; repr. Washington, D.C., Take Root Media, 2010), 91.

[77] Branch, *Parting the Waters*, 136. See also Philip Brian Harper, *Are We Not Men? Masculine Anxiety and the Problem of African-American Identity* (New York: Oxford University Press, 1996), 39–51.

[78] Edith Hambrick, "Black Woman to Black Woman" [sic] *Liberator* 9 (February 1968): 8. See also Douglas Edward Taylor's discussion of the gender debate in *Liberator* in "Hustlers, Nationalists, and Revolutionaries: African American Prison Narratives of the 1960s and 1970s" (PhD diss., University of North Carolina, Chapel Hill, 2002), pp. 115–16.

to rule; but he is emasculated in that he has become a mere extension of the things he produces."[79]

Moynihan had prescribed some remedies for the "tangle of pathology" he believed was the result of mother-headed black families. One was military service. "There is another special quality about military service for Negro men," he wrote.

It is an utterly masculine world. Given the strains of the disorganized and matrifocal family life in which so many Negro youth come of age, the Armed Forces are a dramatic and desperately needed change: a world away from women, a world run by strong men of unquestioned authority, where discipline, if harsh, is nonetheless orderly and predictable, and where rewards, if limited, are granted on the basis of performance. The theme of a current Army recruiting message states it as clearly as can be: "In the U.S. Army you get to know what it means to feel like a man."[80]

Moynihan promoted militarism at the historical moment of the United States' growing involvement in Vietnam. War, then, was not only the solution to communist expansion; it was also the cure for a pathological subculture that had denatured its males.

When Moynihan's report was published, black soldiers accounted for 23.5 percent of combat fatalities in Vietnam. Secretary of Defense McNamara nevertheless expressed concern about the 35 percent of American youth who did not qualify for military service because of poor performance on mental tests and subsequently signed on to Moynihan's message. Some 40 percent of the unqualified were black. Two years later – and at the height of U.S. engagement in Vietnam – he pushed to fruition a policy of lowering the test requirements for induction. Called Project 100,000, the plan aimed to add 40,000 formerly rejected troops in 1966 and 100,000 the following year. The White House and the Pentagon were optimistic: as a military program, the project satisfied the military's endless hunger for new bodies when "20 percent of Army deaths in Vietnam last year were Negroes."[81]

As a social program, Project 100,000 provided an escape hatch from the assumed ills of the matriarchal ghetto. This was a way to resolve the guns or butter controversy. Some 300,000 men joined as so-called New Standards recruits, half of whom were black. Many of them lacked the basic skills to qualify for specialized training, and half were shipped to Vietnam as combat soldiers. Less than 8 percent received any advanced instruction. In 1971 the Pentagon terminated the program because of its cost and the de-escalation of the war. A number of the New Standards men who survived combat suffered from posttraumatic stress syndrome and other injuries that impeded

---

[79] Jean C. Bond and Pat Peery, "Has the Black Man Been Castrated?" *Liberator* 9 (May 1969): 6–7.

[80] "The Negro Family: The Case for National Action."

[81] Remarks by Secretary McNamara to the National Association of Educational Broadcasters, Denver, Colorado, November 7, 1967, *Vital Speeches* 34 (4) (1967): 98, 101–2.

their employability and reintegration into society. Whatever benefits the black family was supposed to reap from the experiment proved elusive.[82]

The Pentagon's contribution to the War on Poverty aimed to inculcate in young blacks the proper idea of manhood. It signaled that the United States had officially rejected racism and was helping civil society catch up to the new modernity. Concurring pundits argued that opinion polls revealed a sea change in racial attitudes since World War II. As African Americans and other racial groups were absorbed into the nation, there should be no grounds for their holding a distinct worldview or pursuing an international agenda at odds with that of the United States.

This logic made conformity the norm and left little room for dissent. Mainstream rights organizations confronted a dilemma. They could retain influence if they avoided opposing a powerful president known to be unforgiving toward detractors. Johnson's collaborators stepped up to the plate to shore up the vacillating and combat a developing antiwar movement. They worked to assemble proadministration voices among civil rights leaders, with UN ambassador Arthur J. Goldberg dispatched to contact SCLC, and Special Assistant for National Security Affairs McGeorge Bundy soliciting the support of others deemed moderate.[83]

Those who had become determined in their dissent met vindictive responses. The president asked the CIA to investigate black entertainer Eartha Kitt. Kitt had criticized the Vietnam War at a White House dinner and subsequently found her gigs mysteriously cancelled. She was thus forced to take more work overseas, neutralizing her as a well-known antiwar presence at home. As Mary L. Dudziak has noted, dancer Josephine Baker suffered a similar fate during an earlier phase of the cold war. Syndicated columnist Jack Anderson observed the zeal with which the FBI and Attorney General Robert F. Kennedy investigated a variety of prominent African Americans. Only the most notorious white supremacists had FBI files, but almost every black of renown had a dossier, including black Republicans. The Internal Revenue Service became a tool of punishment, collecting political intelligence as well as financial data on individuals and groups, including nonprofits, deemed subversive by other branches of government. More than 40 percent of the material gathered by the IRS "special services" staff pertained to racial and ethnic groups.[84] In most cases, these open-ended investigations did not end in, and were not intended to end in, prosecutions.

---

[82] Neil Sheehan, "Military Ready to Absorb Influx of Former 'Rejects,'" *New York Times*, October 16, 1966, I:9; Lisa Hsiao, "Project 100,000: The Great Society's Answer to Manpower Needs in Vietnam." *Vietnam Generation* 1 (2) (1989): 14–37; Gregory A. Daddis, *No Sure Victory: Measuring U.S. Army Effectiveness and Progress in the Vietnam War* (New York: Oxford University Press, 2011), 185–7, 194, 199.

[83] Stewart Burns, *To the Mountaintop: Martin Luther King, Jr.'s Mission to Save America, 1955–1968* (New York: HarperCollins, 2004), 302.

[84] Louie Robinson, "Eartha Kitt Talks about White House Dispute," *Jet*, February 8, 1978, pp. 18–25; Mary Dudziak, "Josephine Baker, Racial Protest and the Cold War," *Journal of American History* 81 (September 1994): 543–70; Jack Anderson, "Black Activists Are FBI Targets,"

If a focus on Africa and censure from the government meant that some African Americans felt they could venture onto foreign policy terrain only if racial discrimination against Africans or people of African descent was involved, others took a broader view. At the CORE convention in 1965 a majority voted a resolution calling for U.S. troop withdrawal from Vietnam, but director James Farmer secured its tabling.[85] The schism in CORE reflects how the White House made support of the Vietnam War a test of loyalty to the president. Did America's liberal crusade for racial justice stop at the water's edge? With full citizenship once attained, at least on paper, should African Americans and their allies ignore U.S. policies and practices abroad that did not reflect the highest national ideals? The Reverend Andrew Young, an assistant to Martin Luther King, thought not. Activists had not fought, he declared, to create "a generation of black reactionaries who now vote, but who vote against foreign aid because of the editorials they read in their hometown newspapers in Shreveport and Natchez."[86]

If, as SCLC activist Reverend James Bevel argued, "civil rights" per se were no longer at issue, the poverty and disadvantage resulting from centuries of domination remained. What did the new freedoms mean, without the resources required to enjoy them? Labor leader A. Philip Randolph founded the A. Philip Randolph Institute to study ways to make the economic component of social justice central to change. The institute in 1966 sponsored the "Freedom Budget," a plan for full employment. The Freedom Budget was not racially specific and reflected a growing concern with economic issues. In New Deal fashion, it sought to use federal resources to address the needs of working people as such. Martin Luther King Jr.'s Poor People's Campaign and the National Welfare Rights Organization (NWRO), led by former CORE official George Wiley, subsequently developed as programs in which class shared prominence with race as a fulcrum of identity and hub of protest. In spite of this, certain functionaries associated with past welfare programs deemed the Freedom Budget unrealistic and refused to support it. The difference seemed to be that, unlike the New Deal, this time around, people of color would directly, rather than in piecemeal fashion, benefit from genuine efforts to eliminate poverty.[87]

The same problem confronted the Mississippi Freedom Democratic Party's challenge at the 1964 Democratic Convention. The Democratic Party's refusal

Washington Post, May 17, 1972, p. B13; Morton H. Halperin, Jerry J. Berman, Robert L. Borosage, and Christine M. Marwick, *The Lawless State: The Crimes of the U. S. Intelligence Agencies* (New York: Penguin Books, 1976), 202–3.

[85] Herbert Shapiro, "Impact of the Vietnam War on the Civil Rights Movement in the Midsixties," in *The Vietnam Antiwar Movement*, ed. Walter L. Hixson (New York: Garland, 2000), 75; Taylor Branch *At Canaan's Edge: America in the King Years, 1965–68* (New York: Simon & Schuster, 2006), 251.

[86] Young quoted in Fred Powledge, "Vietnam Issue Divides Leaders of Rights Groups," E 4.

[87] Dona Cooper Hamilton and Charles V. Hamilton, "The Dual Agenda of African American Organizations since the New Deal: Social Welfare Policies and Civil Rights," *Political Science Quarterly* 107 (Autumn 1992): 450.

to seat the MFDP as the official Mississippi delegation confirmed the growing cynicism among SNCC's grassroots organizers and other radicals about
the depth of the administration's commitment to real change. They knew that
FBI agents relayed information about voter registration campaigns to southern
segregationists. They had witnessed federal reluctance to protect black voters. After the betrayal at Atlantic City, SNCC essentially abandoned its commitment to the liberal agenda. Its approach to Africa, as well as its views on
Vietnam, differed fundamentally from those of the White House and its allies.
It was discovering the continent at a time when Johnson and his advisers were
turning away from it.

SNCC officially condemned military conscription in 1965. Diane Nash, no
longer desirous of seeing a black person invent missiles for war, was one of
four American women who traveled to North Vietnam to express solidarity in
December 1966.[88] SNCC opposed the war early but not without substantial
debate. Some black antiwar critics worried about the repercussions of bucking
the conformist trend. Others, like Robert Browne, were provoked into taking
a stand by the analogy they perceived between African-American suffering and
that of the Vietnamese. Courtland Cox compared dictator Nguyen Cao Ky to
Mississippi's Senator Eastland and saw southern tenants and Southeast Asian
peasants as similarly exploited. The death of navy veteran Sammy Younge in
Tuskegee at a racist's hands shattered the notion that African Americans could
earn respect and citizenship through loyal military service and catalyzed antiwar opinion in the organization.[89]

South Carolina–born Cleveland Sellers based his own decision to refuse
induction partly on the lily-white composition of draft boards in his native
state. In South Carolina and Georgia, only 6 of 670 board members were black.
Black Mississippians, denied voting rights in the Magnolia State and subject
to the draft, did not serve on Mississippi draft boards, where some Klansmen
were members. Sellers issued a press statement asserting that he refused military service and endorsed the Vietnamese struggle against the United States.
When the Iranians were ready to overthrow the shah, he vowed, he would
help them. Sellers also promised to support any Congolese and Latin American
revolts against U.S. thefts of natural resources.[90]

The MFDP began voicing antiwar sentiments. The link between the Vietnam
War and the freedom struggle was more than philosophical for the party.
Vietnam gave racists a cover. They could investigate "subversives," thus dis-
guising their real agenda. SNCC members and students from Tougaloo College

---

[88] "4 U.S. Women Get Visas from Hanoi," *New York Times*, December 17, 1966, p. 5.

[89] Cleveland Sellers, *The River of No Return* (New York: William Morrow, 1973), 148–9, 151;
James Forman, *Sammy Younge: The First Black College Student to Die in the Black Liberation
Movement* (New York: Grove Press, 1968); Nancy Weiss, *Whitney M. Young, Jr., and the
Struggle for Civil Rights* (Princeton, N.J.: Princeton University Press, 1989), 159.

[90] Sellers, *The River of No Return*, 189–91; Dickerson, *Dixie's Dirty Secret*, 101, 135, 137, 128;
Jeff Woods, *Black Struggle, Red Scare: Segregation and Anti-Communism in the South, 1948–
1968* (Baton Rouge: Louisiana State University Press, 2004), 199–202, 203, 209.

staged an antiwar protest at the Jackson, Mississippi, post office, one of several events that led to the forced resignation of Tougaloo's president for allowing students to engage in dissident activities.[91]

Martin Luther King Jr. also opposed the Vietnam War but initially expressed his views only within the confines of his organization and in private correspondence. His address to the August 1965 SCLC convention revealed his sharp disagreement with U.S. policy in Vietnam. Invited to the University of Newcastle upon Tyne in England to receive an honorary degree, King identified "the problem of racism, the problem of poverty and the problem of war" as critical worldwide concerns. He drew parallels between the ghettoization of Caribbean and Asian peoples in British cities and the plight of black Americans in U.S. urban centers.[92]

King spoke of a plan to correspond with all belligerents in Vietnam and coax them to the bargaining table.[93] SCLC's four hundred voting delegates accepted King's position but gave themselves two escape hatches on each side of the Vietnam question. SCLC activism, they resolved, must "be confined to the question of racial brotherhood." It was race, then, in the delegates' eyes, that gave SCLC its fundamental coherence. Nevertheless, King and the SCLC executive committee, "in the event of perilous escalation of the Vietnam conflict," could "alter this course and turn the full resources of our organization to the cessation of bloodshed and war." The resolution allowed the executive committee to check King's pacifist activities if necessary, while leaving open the possibility of greater commitment and cooperation with peace groups that shared SCLC's nonviolent philosophy and commitment to justice.[94]

King represented one instance of the civil rights leadership overflowing the bounds that originally contained it. SNCC represents another case in which the historical moment enlarged the role that black insurgency played. The U.S. intelligence community closely scrutinized its programs. FBI accounts of SNCC purported not to be concerned with its civil rights activity, which the bureau deemed legitimate, but rather the perceived danger of communist infiltration into the group. For the FBI, this could result from networking with organizations already on the attorney general's list. Other agencies investigated SNCC's growing foreign interests and the mounting discussion international brigades to combat the colonial regimes in southern Africa.

Federal authorities had an instrument to prevent citizen involvement in foreign wars. The Logan Act subjects to fines or imprisonment any citizen who communicates with agents of a foreign government to influence their actions "in relation to any disputes or controversies with the United States, or to

---

[91] Woods, *Black Struggle, Red Scare*, 199–202, 203, 209.

[92] Brian Ward, "A King in Newcastle: Martin Luther King, Jr. and British Race Relations, 1967–1968," *Georgia Historical Quarterly* 79 (3) (1995): 615, 633, 626–8.

[93] Adam Fairclough, "Martin Luther King, Jr. and the War in Vietnam," *Phylon* 45 (1) (1984): 19–39; Homer Bigart, "Dr. King to Send Appeal to Hanoi," *New York Times*, August 13, 1965, p. 1; "Dr. King May Make a Wider Peace Bid," ibid., August 14, 1965, p. 3.

[94] "Dr. King May Make a Wider Peace Bid."

defeat the measures of the United States." Assistant Attorney General J. Walter Yeagley asked the FBI to share any information it had that suggested Malcolm X had violated the law. He considered Malcolm's appeals to international bodies "inimical to the best interests of our country, [and] prejudicial to our foreign policy." The Justice Department also solicited information from U.S. missions in countries that he had visited. State Department Executive Secretary Benjamin H. Read thought that Malcolm had "for all practical purposes, renounced his U.S. citizenship."[95]

Read's opinion was portentous. The State Department was examining the possibility of deporting foreign-born black militants and revoking others' passports. As Stokely Carmichael sat in a hotel veranda with Shirley Graham Du Bois, the widow of W. E. B. Du Bois, one morning in Conakry two years later, a U.S. embassy employee approached him with a letter requesting that he yield his passport. Graham became nearly hysterical, warning Carmichael not to comply.[96] This is what they did to Du Bois, she told him. Passport denial and revocation were weapons that had been used against African-American activists since World War I when those wishing to attend the 1919 Pan African Conference in Paris, or to approach dignitaries at the synchronous 1919 Versailles Peace Conference, were forbidden to travel. Later, federal authorities stripped Paul Robeson of his passport, and Du Bois himself had been unable for that reason to attend Ghana's independence festivities in 1957.[97]

The manipulation of passports raised deeper questions about freedom that meshed with the fight against second-class citizenship in the domestic arena. Jim Crow and the practice of obedience associated with cold war loyalty legislation suggested to some African Americans that they needed viable alternatives to the constricted civic framework in which they were confined. White society continued, as it had in Woodrow Wilson's era, to expect racial minorities to defer to the prerogatives of white supremacy: national inclusion for blacks required sacrifice to the "greater good" of the polity as a whole. Demands for black rights could not take priority over the perceived international aims.

Intelligence agents learned in 1965 that certain unnamed nationalist organizations had received money from the Ghanaian, Algerian, Cameroonian, and United Arab Republic missions. "The matter is obviously one of great political sensitivity, both internationally and domestically," noted an unsigned State Department memorandum addressed to CIA director Richard J. Helms. "The Department considered the matter one of sufficient importance to discuss with President Johnson, who in turn asked Mr. J. Edgar Hoover to secure any further information which he might be able to develop." The FBI did not find

95 U.S. Code Title 18, Part I, Chapter 45, § 953; cited in Director to SAC (New York City) September 11, 1964; J. Walter Yeagley to J. Edgar Hoover, September 3, 1964, *FBI File on Malcolm X*.
96 Stokely Carmichael with Ekwueme Michael Thelwell, *Ready for Revolution: The Life and Struggles of Stokely Carmichael (Kwame Ture)* (New York: Scribner, 2003), 621.
97 Rayford W. Logan to John Hope Franklin, May 22, 1953, series 181-B, Box 181-4, Correspondence, John Hope Franklin, 1938–56 file, Rayford W. Logan Papers, MSRC; Jonathan D. Casper, *The Politics of Civil Liberties* (New York: Harper & Row, 1972).

anything, "a result which had been predicted by [name deleted] who said that no blonde Anglo-Saxon investigator would be able to penetrate the situation." The memorandum was written two days after Malcolm X was assassinated. Malcolm was dead but had created an example that others might follow.[98]

Once black radicals laid the groundwork for international cooperation, the linkages they made became more commonplace. Early in 1965 journalist Bill Worthy published an interview with Cambodian king Norodom Sihanouk in the *Baltimore Afro-American* magazine. The king complained of U.S. attempts to overthrow his regime as early as 1959. In a nod to black readers, Sihanouk told Worthy that his government would offer "political and moral support" to beleaguered African Americans in world councils if asked to do so. In July 1966 Floyd McKissick, then national director of CORE, planned a trip to Cambodia with the peace organization Americans Want to Know, to assess Cambodia's relationship to the war in Vietnam. Other members of the travel team included author Kay Boyle, antiwar Vietnam veteran Donald Duncan, and civil rights attorney William Kunstler. The program exemplifies another iteration of peace and civil rights linkages, observable earlier in the Sahara project and the Quebec to Guantanamo March. It drew together activists previously specializing in separate issues and placed them in conversation with non-Western states that had serious grievances against the great powers.[99]

Increased U.S. commitments in Southeast Asia put that region on the public radar screen. China was the shadow adversary. How extensive was its influence? How deeply did it penetrate the American Left? Defense Secretary Robert S. McNamara, in his memoir, *In Retrospect*, mulled over the era's obsession with the "Chicom" bogeyman and the failure to perceive China's weakness and growing isolation as it entered the throes of the Great Cultural Revolution. Officials therefore could not clearly evaluate the relationship between Chinese influence in Asia and Africa and the pursuit of the Vietnam War. Domestic events also shaped U.S. responses. CIA director John McCone told Johnson that the USSR and China wanted to "intensify the campus antiwar movement." J. Edgar Hoover described to the president in late April 1965 a forthcoming Students for a Democratic Society (SDS) mobilization in eighty-five cities, portrayed by the FBI director as "largely infiltrated by communists." The peace movement, he observed, was "woven into the civil rights situation which we know has large communist influence." Policy makers studied with concern General Lin Biao's September 2, 1965, speech that called for "people's war": the revolt of the rural masses against the cities and the underdeveloped world against the metropoles.[100]

[98] Richard Helms to J. Edgar Hoover, February 23, 1965, 1982; memorandum for Richard Helms, n.d., DDRC.

[99] *Afro-American Magazine*, January 23, 1965, p. 4, TCF; "McKissick Planning to See If Cambodia Is a Vietcong Haven," *New York Times*, July 11, 1966, p. 5.

[100] Robert S. McNamara, *In Retrospect* (New York: Random House, 1995), 214–15; Christopher Andrew, *For the President's Eyes Only: Secret Intelligence and the American Presidency from Washington to Bush* (New York: HarperCollins, 1995), 322.

Preoccupation with China was not confined to high councils of government. For some black nationalists, China served the same symbolic purpose that Japan had in the 1930s. As a nonwhite nation, independent of imperialist control, China could flout the West. Shortly after China exploded its first atomic bomb, the newspaper *Muhammad Speaks* published an article by a "roving reporter" who asked various black Americans whether the detonation disturbed them. The responses printed indicated that the employment counselor, the teachers, the homemaker, the insurance executive, and the student – solid members of the middle class all – believed that whites had met their comeuppance in the Chinese achievement. *Muhammad Speaks* accompanied the story with poll results indicating that 40 percent of interviewees relished China's implicit challenge to the West.[101]

African-American full citizenship meant participation in all aspects of U.S. national life, but identification with dominated subjects elsewhere exerted a centrifugal force. The goals of economic self-sufficiency, the right of armed self-defense, freedom from political domination, and freedom from mainstream cultural values that marginalized and deprecated black people tended to move aspirants away from fealty to the nation. Such aims did not move them away, however, from the nation form. Black Americans thus came to occupy symbolic – and ambiguous – space in the intersection where new and revolutionary states challenged the construction of power delineated by the cold war blocs.

---

[101] "China's Bomb Does Not Dismay Most Negroes," *Muhammad Speaks*, May 28, 1965, p. 4.

5

When Race Doesn't Matter

In the late autumn of 1946, José Adriano Trujillo, a World War II veteran and an adopted son of the Dominican Republic's strong-arm leader, set out on a road trip from New York with a Jamaican friend. With Miami as their destination, the two reached Bunnell, Florida, around midnight and stopped for food at the Green Tile Café. Denied service on color grounds, Trujillo protested loudly in English and Spanish and, according to later reports, went to his car to retrieve a pistol. The proprietor called the police and the arriving sheriff's deputy, after delivering a warning, shot and killed Trujillo.[1]

This incident did not travel far in the media, and the State Department's representative in Miami did not see fit to return from vacation to investigate it. José Adriano had clashed with the postwar South's understanding of status and entitlement, one very different from his own. Yet the tragedy did not alter Generalissimo Trujillo's clientelistic relationship with the United States or lessen his grip on the Dominican population. Years later, race continued to be a matter that Dominicans and Americans would sidestep in regard to one another, and as always, "law and order" prevailed over social justice in the rank order of U.S. priorities as far as Latin Americans were concerned.

Relations with the "sister republics" deteriorated rapidly after Kennedy's grandiose Alliance for Progress initiative. U.S. officials lacked real sympathy with the social democratic goals of hemisphere nationalists and actively sought to undermine most of them. UN Secretary General Dag Hammarskjöld's successor, U Thant, believed Johnson "incapable of comprehending the international currents and crosscurrents that the head of the most powerful country in the world should comprehend."[2]

---

[1] "Florida Deputy Sheriff Kills Adopted Relative of Dominican President," *St. Petersburg Times*, November 3, 1946, p. 9; "Florida Cop Kills Trujillo Nephew," *Palm Beach Post*, November 3, 1946, p, 1.

[2] William O. Walker, III, "Mixing the Sweet with the Sour: Kennedy, Johnson, and Latin America," in *The Diplomacy of the Crucial Decade: American Foreign Relations during the 1960s*, ed. Diane B. Kunz, (New York, Columbia University Press: 1994): 59, 60–3; U Thant, *View from the UN* (New York: Doubleday, 1978), 376.

With legal white supremacy under fire by the mid-twentieth century, defining national security as naturally opposed to the political will of nonwhite
majorities in foreign countries placed Washington officials in an untenable
position. They needed to eliminate race from conflicts with such powers. At
home, it was a preoccupation; abroad, it was made illegible. In the Dominican
Republic, a country that the United States invaded in 1965, national origin
stories that denied African ancestry abetted the project of racial conceal-
ment. This factor, and the doctrine of sovereign equality, helped U.S. authorities limit Jim Crow to the domestic sphere and place aliens of color beyond
its reach (even when they, like José Adriano Trujillo, experienced injustice
on Stateside visits or encountered U.S. racism in their home countries). By
consensus, racial awareness and racial discord had to stop at the proverbial
water's edge.[3] In terms of a carefully constructed logic, foreign "blacks" could
not be "black" at all.

Legal scholar Lani Guinier developed a concept of "political race" that helps
to explain some of the dynamics of the Dominican intervention. According to
Guinier,

political race is not defined exclusively by constructing a series of oppositions based on
color or genealogy. It may be transformed into a site of oppositional organizing, but
that does not mean organizing in opposition to white people. Black is not the opposite
of white; it is not a color at all in any essential sense.... There is no essential morpho-
logical or biological basis to the construction of racial groups, but the existence of such
groupings continues to have roots in both the empirical history of white supremacy and
in the discursive structure that supports it.[4]

For Dominicans, the fragile post-Trujillo democracy risked too great a rupture with the metanarratives of race and nation on which they had long relied.[5]
Both Dominicans and their neighbors, the Haitians, had assumed, in Guinier's
terms, respective political racial identities. Whether Amerindian and Castilian,
or black and Creole, the residents of Hispaniola shared beliefs that ultimately
enhanced Washington's power to make or break their governments. Given
Dominican racial realities and the backdrop of racial crisis in the United States
in 1965, one may well question the invisibility of race in contemporaneous
accounts of the affair. The intervention generated ample subsequent historical
scholarship but produced low-key press coverage and little public excitement:
odd, given the U.S. public's growing politicization at the time.

---

[3] Joseph A. Fry, *Dixie Looks Abroad: The South and U.S. Foreign Relations, 1789–1973* (Baton
Rouge: Louisiana State University Press, 2002), 233; Robert Vitalis, "The Graceful and Generous
Liberal Gesture: Making Racism Invisible in American International Relations," *Millennium:
Journal of International Studies* 29 (2) (2000): 331–56.

[4] Lani Guinier and Gerald Torres, *The Miner's Canary: Enlisting Race, Resisting Power,
Transforming Democracy* (Cambridge, Mass., and London: Harvard University Press, 2002),
107.

[5] Frank Moya Pons, *The Dominican Republic: A National History* (Princeton, N.J.: Markus
Wiener, 1998); David Howard, *Coloring the Nation: Race and Ethnicity in the Dominican
Republic* (Boulder, Colo.: Lynne Rienner, 2001).

Matters came to a head in the Dominican Republic in 1965, four years after compatriots gunned down the vicious autocrat Trujillo. After his assassination, Joaquín Balaguer, approved by Washington, became president. In spite of Trujillo's demise, the country seemed no further along on the democratic path. Juan Bosch's Dominican Revolutionary Party constituted the chief internal challenge to Balaguer. Bosch espoused social democratic principles opposed, respectively, by the leftists, who viewed Cuba as the best model for the country, and the business and military elites that had profited during the Trujillo regime. When Balaguer proved unable to curb the growing unrest, Bosch succeeded him.

Bosch spiked Washington's anticommunist radar through his advocacy of agrarian reform, his refusal to oppose Castro, and his desire to keep the United States out of Dominican affairs. Like Balaguer, Bosch wrestled with indifferent success against rising unemployment and general dissatisfaction. His overthrow on September 25, 1963, in a coup staged by General Elias Wessin y Wessin was widely condemned internationally, but the United States and nine European countries recognized the new government by the end of the year. The junta named Donald Reid Cabral to the presidency in an atmosphere of growing conflict as Bosch in Puerto Rican exile called for the restoration of the constitution. Civil war erupted on April 24, 1965, and featured early victories by Constitutionalist contingents who armed citizens in the capital and seized the national palace, the radio station, and an army barracks. Thousands of casualties ensued as air force units commanded by right-wing officers strafed the palace and other sites.

Late in April, a Vatican-negotiated ceasefire ceded control of certain vital areas to both Right and Left forces, ending the worst fighting. The United States, however, changed the equation by landing troops on April 28 in traditional gunboat diplomacy style. The ostensible purpose was to safeguard American lives and property.[6] Fear that the Dominican Republic would become another Cuba, however, led Johnson to boost troop strength, which ultimately

---

[6] Histories of the Dominican intervention include Russell Crandall, *Gunboat Democracy: U.S. Interventions in the Dominican Republic, Grenada, and Panama* (Lanham, Md.: Rowman & Littlefield Publishers, 2006); Fidelio Despradel, *Abril 1965: historia gráfica de la Guerra de Abril* (Santo Domingo, República Dominicana: Secretaria de Estado de Cultura, 2005); Franklin Franco Pichardo, comp., *La revolución constitucionalista de 1965: vista por actores y testigos* (Ciudad Universitaria, Distrito Nacional, República Dominicana: Editora Universitaria, 2005); Lawrence M. Greenberg, *United States Army Unilateral and Coalition Operations in the 1965 Dominican Republic Intervention* (Washington, D.C.: Analysis Branch, U.S. Army Center of Military History, 2004); Alan McPherson, "Misled by Himself: What the Johnson Tapes Reveal about the Dominican Intervention of 1965," *Latin American Research Review* 38 (2) (2003): 127–46; Eric Thomas Chester, *Rag-tags, Scum, Riff-Raff, and Commies: The U.S. Intervention in the Dominican Republic, 1965–1966* (New York: Monthly Review Press, 2001); G. Pope Atkins and Larman Curtis Wilson, *The Dominican Republic and the United States: From Imperialism to Transnationalism* (Athens: University of Georgia Press, 1998); Piero Gleijeses, *The Dominican Crisis: The 1965 Constitutionalist Revolt and American Intervention* (Baltimore: The Johns Hopkins University Press, 1978).

reached twenty-three thousand. He sent in the 82nd Airborne Division, already veterans of the riots accompanying the 1963 integration of the University of Mississippi. The unit would serve again in 1967 to restore "law and order" in rebel Detroit. At home, race was everything; overseas, it was not to be mentioned. Dominican adherents to the national constitution meanwhile chose Colonel Francisco Caamaño Deno, an officer known as a critic of U.S. policy in the region, as president. Rightists countered with a junta headed by General Imbert Barreras to serve as a check on Caamaño. The country then had two governments. That of Imbert drew censure for its brutality toward captured foes and its accusations of communism against a wide array of political activists. The radio station operated by the junta, anxious to prove international conspiracy as the source of the nation's problems, claimed that Argentine revolutionary Ernesto "Che" Guevara had been present and had died in the fighting.[7]

In spite of an official stance of neutrality, Johnson officials decided that the Imbert Barreras government was the legitimate one and now based U.S. intervention on supporting it and thwarting a communist takeover. The United States, in sending an occupation force to the Dominican Republic, violated articles 15 and 17 of the Organization of American States (OAS) charter and angered most Latin American governments. Adlai Stevenson, the embarrassed U.S. ambassador to the UN, was "obvious[ly] discomfort[ed] at having to defend the intervention."[8]

Half of the American Methodist missionaries assigned to Latin America rejected the action as harmful to their work. "We are distressed about the tendency of our Government, as illustrated in the Dominican crisis, to weaken or annihilate socially concerned moderate groups by identifying itself with right-wing, often military regimes," they declared in a message to home churches. The intervention also stirred up a hornet's nest beyond the Caribbean. Nelson Rockefeller, formerly Franklin D. Roosevelt's assistant secretary of state for Latin American affairs and then governor of New York, a figure with major interests in the hemisphere, expressed concern about the unilateral nature of Johnson's decision.[9] The foreign ministries of France and Norway, the USSR, and the UN Security Council also made their disapproval known.[10]

William Fulbright, chair of the Senate Foreign Relations Committee, declared that U.S. diplomats stationed in Santo Domingo misled LBJ about the communist threat. Any Latin American reform movement will attract reds, the senator advised, but change should not be opposed for that reason. Fulbright faulted

[7] Juan de Onis, "Junta Police Stir Dominican Anger," *New York Times*, June 7, 1965 p. 19; "Guevara Termed Slain in Dominican Rebellion," ibid., August 21, 1965; p. 6.

[8] Gleijeses, *The Dominican Crisis*, 261; U Thant, *View from the UN*, 371.

[9] "U.S. Dominican Action Hit by Methodist Missionaries," *New York Times*, June 21, 1965 p. 2; "Rockefeller Voices Doubt on Dominican Role of U.S," ibid., May 5, 1965 p. 3.

[10] Douglas Robinson, "Betancourt, in City, Scores U.S. for Its Dominican Intervention," *New York Times*, June 4, 1965, p. 9; U Thant, *View from the UN*, 370–4; Brian Urquhart, *Ralph Bunche – An American Life* (New York: W. W. Norton, 1993), 379, 383–4.

FIGURE 7. U.S. Army troops patrol the streets of Santo Domingo on May 6, 1965. (Getty Images)

the White House for unclear policy aims in the Americas. Change will occur whether or not the United States supports or resists it. The degree of communist influence, he stated, partly depends on how the U.S. government reacts.[11]

Policy had reverted to that of earlier times, and officials sought to salvage a shred of respectability by pressuring the OAS to accept a multilateral Inter-American Peace Force; it did so with a slim majority of votes. The subsequent "coalition of the willing" consisted of some fifteen hundred soldiers from Costa Rica, Nicaragua, and Honduras, none of which at the time enjoyed democratic governance. This military solution to Dominican problems exposed an interesting fault line along the path to good intentions. The United States had already sent more than one hundred Peace Corps volunteers to the island republic, where they engaged in such tasks as assisting fishermen and training teachers. Volunteers who spoke to *New York Times* reporter Matthew Arnold

[11] "Excerpts from Fulbright's Attack on U.S. Policy in Dominican Crisis," *New York Times*, September 16, 1965, p. 16. See also Thomas Borstelmann, *The Cold War and the Color Line: American Race Relations in the Global Arena* (Cambridge, Mass., Harvard University Press, 2001), 177.

expressed their desire to remain neutral in the Dominican conflict and consequently incurred the ire of the U.S. military. "Many of the soldiers don't understand that for the Peace Corps to be effective after the revolution it cannot take sides now," said one. "We are giving whatever help we can to anybody who needs it – without asking their politics – and some of us have been accused of being Communists by the G.I.'s." The impoverished barrios in revolt in the city of Santo Domingo had their own Peace Corps resident contingents. Volunteers identified with the communities they served. "There are people in my barrio who love me, who would die for me," asserted a reluctantly evacuated Minnesotan. "I want to get back as soon as I can."[12]

The Peace Corps ideal of service clashed with the other instrument of U.S. policy: armed force. The two approaches collided in the Dominican Republic and exacerbated differences among Americans. When rebels captured and held two U.S. Marines, Peace Corps country director Robert Satin successfully negotiated for their release, an initiative made possible by the relatively high regard the Peace Corps enjoyed locally. When the Army Special Forces wanted to fly helicopter missions into areas beyond the capital to gather intelligence, the State Department suggested using Peace Corps volunteers for this purpose. Peace Corps director Sargent Shriver, refusing to squander the Corps' accumulated goodwill, emphatically vetoed the idea.[13]

The Dominican interlude met with a curious silence on the part of the mainstream African-American press. The conflict occurred as national attention focused on strife in Selma, Alabama, and especially the ferocious police attack on civil rights protesters attempting to cross the Edmund Pettus Bridge to demonstrate in Montgomery. Few papers took note of civil war in Santo Domingo or published editorial comment about it. The New York *Amsterdam News* treated the Dominican intervention as an unwelcome distraction from the national task Americans faced at hand. Its editorial of May 22, 1965, characterized the Dominican civil war as fratricidal and "senseless" but reminded readers that the United States also has "very serious problems to solve right in our own backyard." Foreign affairs remained under the radar, Baltimore *Afro-American* editor and manager James D. Williams believed, "because so much attention has been focused on civil rights, that little energy is left for anything else." These weekly newspapers could not keep up a daily account of events on Hispaniola in any case, and Lyndon Johnson's current popularity with African Americans led to widespread acceptance of standard cold war arguments to explain the U.S. action. An April 1965 Gallup Poll recorded Americans in general approving of the intervention by a margin of 76 to 17 percent.[14]

---

[12] Martin Arnold, "Peace Corps Plea Frees Marines," *New York Times*, May 7, 1965, p. 15; Lawrence Yates, *Power Pack: U.S. Intervention in the Dominican Republic, 1965–1966* (Fort Leavenworth, Kans.: Combat Studies Institute, 1989), 102, 103, 173.

[13] Arnold, "Peace Corps Plea Frees Marines;" Tad Szulc, *Dominican Diary*, 302–3.

[14] *Amsterdam News*, May 22, 1965, p. 14; James D. Williams, "The Color Question in Foreign Policy," *Baltimore Afro-American*, June 5, 1965, p. 14; John M. Benson, "The Polls: U.S. Military Intervention," *The Public Opinion Quarterly* 46 (Winter 1982): 594.

The reaction of the United States' largest Spanish language daily, *El Diario/La Prensa*, was far less subdued but equally acquiescent to Johnson's goals. Puerto Ricans formed the preponderance of this tabloid's readership during the era. As U.S. citizens and people of color, Puerto Ricans were interested in the civil rights movement, and the paper covered both southern and northern events extensively. Its 1965 issues featured a serial on Malcolm X, profiles of African-American politicians, and large photo-spreads about protests and demonstrations. *El Diario* also wanted to go beyond covering strictly ethnic news and did features on such events as New York City's reception for astronauts.[15]

The paper began sporadically reporting unrest in the Dominican Republic in April 1965, but the death of Puerto Rican nationalist leader Dr. Pedro Albizu Campos overshadowed the early coverage. Like African-American papers, *El Diario* found domestic news competing with the Dominican story. Authorities in Puerto Rico, recalling nationalists' past attempts to assassinate President Harry Truman and other U.S. politicians, placed government buildings and the headquarters of important U.S. corporations under guard to prevent violent outbreaks in the wake of Albizu Campos's demise. Dominican events did not make front-page news until late in April.[16]

The landing of the 82nd Airborne in the capital, Santo Domingo, drew banner headlines for weeks. *El Diario* took a firm anticommunist line in editorializing on Latin America generally and readily interpreted leftist Dominican politics as an invitation to Castroism. Unlike the black press, the paper viewed Third World nationalism dimly, calling Nkrumah, Nasser, and Sukarno dictators and likening them to Hitler and Mussolini. In spite of their attention to the civil rights movement and to Malcolm X, the editors deplored the racialist consciousness typical of the United States. Puerto Ricans, they noted, ranged across phenotypes and had European, African, and Amerindian ancestry. Efforts to classify people racially, it believed, were a likely cause of both African-American "extremism" and Afro-Asian racial hypersensitivity.[17]

By the summer of 1965, greater attention turned to Dominican events as some onlookers began to experience what commentator James D. Williams called "a growing uneasiness about the correctness of the American stance in Vietnam and the Dominican [Republic.]"[18] Open condemnation of the intervention from an African-American organization arose first from an unexpected source: the McComb County, Mississippi, chapter of the Mississippi Freedom

[15] See such articles as Luisa A. Quintero's columns: "Hispanos con Constance Motley," March 1, 1965, p. 14; "King Dirige Negros a Inscripción en Alabama," March 2, 1965, p. 5; "Grisson [sic], Young Reciben Tributo NY," March 1, 1965, p. 14.

[16] "Incendios Destruyen Bosques en El Centro de Santo Domingo," April 21, 1965, p. 19; "Estado de Alerta en Puerto Rico," April 23, 1965, p. 3; "Derrocan Junta Dominicana," April 26, 1965, p. 1.

[17] "We Have Full Confidence in President Johnson," May 2, 1965, p. 2; "Back to the Middle Ages," March 4, 1965, p. 21; "An Odious Classification," ibid. (editorials in English and Spanish).

[18] Williams, "The Color Question in Foreign Policy," 14.

Democratic Party (MFDP). After a black county resident died while in the military, McComb party members memorialized him in a July 28, 1965, newsletter. The text, distributed as a pamphlet, sharply criticized U.S. foreign policy. "No one has a right to ask us to risk our lives and kill other Colored People in Santo Domingo and Vietnam, so that the White American can get richer," the pamphlet asserted.[19] The state organization, pressured by the Mississippi NAACP and Representative Charles Diggs of Detroit, quickly distanced itself from the McComb statement, but the cat was out of the bag. The landing of U.S. troops in Santo Domingo seemed to rehearse all-too-familiar tropes of racial and imperial domination.[20]

Silence about race clearly noticeable in most textual records of the Dominican conflict must be interrogated. Photographic evidence[21] suggests that the Constitutionalist street fighters were disproportionately dark-skinned, many of them poor and clearly of African descent. Veteran Latin Americanist James Petras recorded his impressions in an article for *Liberation* in September 1966. "Santo Domingo, with its bullet scarred buildings, its run-down commercial area, and its daylight streets full of unemployed men" he wrote, "appears like a southern Negro shantytown juxtaposed on Harlem." His account is one of the few penned by North Americans that do not occlude Dominican racial identity. During an era when civil rights insurgency revealed the centrality of race in U.S. life, and when revolts of the black and poor began to dot headlines, Dominican colorlessness in the media and official accounts is remarkable.[22]

This colorlessness is a multifaceted convention. Its first aspect centers on the assignment by international law of sovereign equality to all nations in spite of wide disparities in wealth and power. The Dominicans' island neighbor, Haiti, provides an example. In the nineteenth century, the great powers could reconcile the Haitian revolution neither with the concept of sovereign equality nor with their need for slave labor and black subordination. Their quarantine of Haiti, undertaken to secure the remaining colonies, entailed excluding Haiti from the community of nations. Quarantine ended when slavery did, but racism did not. The failure of sovereign equality continued in the incompatibility between a stereotypical view of people of color and their actual diversity. This conundrum faced Secretary of State William Jennings Bryan when in 1912 he received a briefing on Haiti. He famously remarked: "Dear me, think of it!

---

[19] Full text is in *Black Protest: History, Documents, and Analyses; 1619 to the Present*, ed. Joanne Grant (New York: Fawcett, 1968).

[20] Gerald R. Gill, "Afro-American Opposition to the United States' Wars of the Twentieth Century: Dissent, Discontent and Disinterest" (PhD diss., Howard University, 1985); Williams, "The Color Question in Foreign Policy," 14; Moreno, *Barrios in Arms*, 86.

[21] See, for example, the staff photography of the 82nd Airborne Division, published in Robert F. Barry, comp., *Power Pack: Dominican Republic, 1965–1966* (Portsmouth, Va.: Messenger, 1965); Yates, *Power Pack*; and Rafael Taveras, *Abril, la liberación efímera: (testimonio y análisis)* (Santo Domingo, D.R.: Ediciones Bloque Socialista, 1990). See also Vitalis, "The Graceful and Generous Liberal Gesture," 331–56.

[22] James Petras, "Revolution and Restoration," *Liberation* 11 (September 1966): 5.

Niggers speaking French."[23] Bryan evidently knew little about cultural het-
erogeneity among blacks and remained narrowly fixed on what he thought he
knew about African Americans. In terms of the logic suggested by difference,
foreign blacks could not be "black" at all.

The traditional Dominican masking of race abetted the colorlessness
attached to sovereign equality. As race did not rise to the level of political consciousness, it remained inert as a way to identify inequality and struggle against
it. A negative perception of blackness as situated in the personas of Haitians
furthermore led Dominicans with African ancestry to attribute their deviations
from a Caucasian phenotype to Amerindian heritage. More ironically, denial of
blackness created additional space for a Marxist-derived discourse of class that
minimized racial inequality as an explanation of social inequality and drove
race further into invisibility.

Yet race filtered indirectly into consciousness about the Dominican revolt
although it was rarely named as such. The Cuban Jesuit José Moreno, involved
with the distribution of food from relief agencies, discovered that some of the
boys from poor neighborhoods who were helping him were stealing. Moreno
pared down the number of his assistants but then became uncomfortable
with the preponderance of white middle-class teens working with him, "a
group of white middle-class people distributing food to a crowd of dark poor
Dominicans." The priest then actively recruited "some colored boys and girls
of the barrio."[24]

Moreno, a keen observer of the community he worked in, noted that

integration of lower-class commandos with middle-class communities became more
difficult when ideological or racial prejudices existed between the two groups. Middle-
class housewives complained that the commando members were all *tigres*, [gang mem-
bers] or that they drank and fought among themselves, or that they were communists.
However, the same housewives would not mind having a white middle-class student
member of the same commando in their homes.

Moreno's reminiscences belie the claim of color blindness associated with
conventional Latin American discourse. "When the revolution broke out
on April 24," he recalled, "radio commentator Peña Gomez appealed to the
masses to support the revolution. The masses trusted him because, although
well-educated and a leader in Bosch's party, he was a Negro from a poor
family."[25] Race for Dominicans did not have the fixed boundaries associated
with racial classification in the United States, but it remained salient as a social
marker.

Similarly, race, if understood in the bipolar terms characteristic of North
America, lacked resonance and urgency for the readers and editors of the
Puerto Rico–oriented *El Diario*. For this reason, the newspaper saw the racial

[23] John H. Allen, "An Inside View of the Revolution in Haiti," *Current History* 32 (May 1930): 325–9.
[24] Moreno, *Barrios in Arms*, 77.
[25] Ibid., 177, 90.

nationalism it observed in Harlem and elsewhere as demagogic and the abolition of color distinctions as part of the promise of U.S. life. Latin somatic ambiguity meant that many Puerto Ricans defied rigid racial classification, but as in the Dominican Republic, it did not erase a subtle joint hierarchy of color and class.

The U.S. military understood this indirectly as it paired its gunning down of rebels with social work. As GIs from the 82nd Airborne fought their way into the city of Santo Domingo during the initial days of the intervention, they stood on the Duarte Bridge looking across the Ozama River to "a complex of old wooden shacks and hundreds of poverty stricken Dominicans. We knew it was sniper infested and it had to be cleaned out," a soldier remembered.[26] The poorest areas with the darkest people took the most hits.

U.S. troops had invaded the Dominican Republic under the initial assumption that they were to evacuate U.S. citizens endangered by the fighting. President Johnson subsequently changed their mission to staving off a communist coup. Outside the White House, most policy officials doubted the extent of communist infiltration and control of the Constitutionalist movement. Some soldiers on the ground shared that assessment, including the Puerto Ricans hastily marshaled into service as translators at interrogations. According to military historian Lawrence Yates, "The fact that most rebels were not Communists but men fighting for a return to constitutional government convinced several of the newly arrived Puerto Ricans that the United States was backing the wrong side in the civil war." Interpreters holding this opinion found themselves transferred out.[27]

The provision of aid and efforts at ameliorative public relations that accompanied U.S. military actions also invoked North American understandings of race. General Bruce Palmer, commander of all the U.S. armed forces in the Dominican Republic, wrote that by May 3, troops were providing food and water to beleaguered Dominicans, who "showed friendliness and gratitude right from the start. It was evident," Palmer believed, "that the presence of many black American soldiers (about 30 percent in the average battalion of the 82nd Airborne Division), as well as some who spoke Spanish, helped establish friendly relations between our troops and the people of Santo Domingo" (see Figure 7).[28]

Latin Americanist James Petras disputed Palmer's interpretation. In his account, African-American GIs saw only their own comparative affluence. "U.S. white and Negro soldiers were equally brutal and equally condemned," he wrote. "Black Dominican workers told me that when they told North American Negroes to go back to the United States to fight for their own rights the Negroes responded, 'Will you pay me $400 a month?'" Petras denounced

[26] Barry, *Power Pack*, 21.
[27] Yates, *Power Pack*, 105.
[28] General Bruce Palmer, *Intervention in the Caribbean: The Dominican Crisis of 1965* (Lexington: University Press of Kentucky, 1989), 48.

mainstream civil rights leaders for their acquiescence to Johnson's policies. The circumstances under which black soldiers arrived in Santo Domingo discouraged solidarity with the locals. Troops recounting their battle experiences to the Baltimore *Afro-American* spoke of unnerving sniper attacks as bullets sidelined the question of color.[29]

At home, African Americans not on the front lines made race more central in their perceptions of Dominicans and the meaning of the U.S. intervention. Socialist Workers Party member Clifton DeBerry, in a letter to the Baltimore *Afro-American,* wondered how President Johnson could efficiently plan and execute an invasion of the Dominican Republic but could not protect black civil rights at home. GIs "are being used against the poor sections of Santo Domingo," DeBerry observed, "whose dark-skinned residents are being rocket bombed, and slaughtered for demanding restoration of their constitution."[30]

Opposition to U.S actions in the Dominican Republic was not confined to the Left. By November 1965, almost a third of a representative sample of Americans believed that sending troops to the Dominican Republic had damaged U.S. relations with other Latin American states.[31] More specifically, civil rights activists began opposing the incursion. "Lyndon [Johnson] in my opinion was wrong on the Vietnam War and the Dominican Republic," Alabama civil rights supporter Virginia Durr asserted. While members of social movement organizations worked on different issues, they often shared beliefs about democracy and racial equality. These had already put them in mutual contact and led them to more expansive definitions of justice than were conventional at the time.[32]

Although dramatic events at home neutralized the domestic impact of the Dominican occupation, it too eventually joined a broad-based critique of U.S. public policies generally. Those making the critique included members of the clergy, missionaries, and other lay religious who became prominent endorsers of peace and civil rights work.[33] Richard Shaull, a former Presbyterian missionary and theologian at Princeton Seminary, believed by the late 1960s that "the Christian faith can provide resources for being authentically revolutionary. It can produce the type of person whose own inward experience of death and resurrection equip him to let the old die when its time has come

---

[29] Petras, "Revolution and Restoration," 39 n; *Baltimore Afro-American*, May 15, 1965, p. 13.

[30] Clifton DeBerry to the editor, *Baltimore Afro-American*, May 15, 1965, p. 4.

[31] Gallup Poll (AIPO), November 18–23, 1965.

[32] Virginia Foster Durr, *Outside the Magic Circle: The Autobiography of Virginia Durr* (Montgomery: University of Alabama Press, 1985), 327; Fred Rosen, "Introduction: A Personal Note," in "NACLA: A 35 Year Retrospective," *NACLA Report on the Americas* 36 (Nov/Dec 2002): 12–13; McWilliams, *The Education of Carey McWilliams,* 222, 223. For participation in the U.S. civil rights movement by foreign affairs activists, see Joseph A. Sinsheimer, "The Freedom Vote of 1963: New Strategies of Racial Protest in Mississippi," *Journal of Southern History* 55 (May 1989): 217–44; Virginia Foster Durr, *Freedom Writer: Letters from the Civil Rights Years,* ed. Patricia Sullivan (New York: Routledge, 2003), 234, 301, 308–9, 312, 220–1.

[33] Patrick Allitt, *Catholic Intellectuals and Conservative Politics in America, 1950–1975* (Ithaca, N.Y.: Cornell University Press, 1993), 40, 41, 123–30; Moreno, *Barrios in Arms,* 128.

and frees him to give form to the new possibilities open before him."[34] Shaull and the missionary Fred Goff were in 1966 among the founders of the North American Conference on Latin America (NACLA). NACLA emerged in direct response to the Dominican crisis, and one of its primary roles was to "focus on systematic analyses of wealth and power in the Americas rather than on scandals or policy 'mistakes.'" The organization provided information about the hemisphere, intended to prevent an uninformed public from acquiescing to Washington's imperial adventures. With support from the Presbyterian and Lutheran Churches and the National Council of Churches, NACLA tapped into the reservoir of resources that growing numbers of activists shared. These now included scholarship, and the 1960s witnessed major efforts on the part of change agents to employ academia to advance their agendas.[35]

Church people were not alone in their response to the Dominican intervention. SNCC in January 1966 issued a statement declaring it had "a right and a responsibility to dissent with the U.S. foreign policy on any issue when it sees fit." SNCC charged the federal government with insincerity: it pretended to be concerned with Vietnamese welfare, just as it had falsely claimed sympathy for Dominicans and others. Newly elected chair Stokely Carmichael and other members of the group attended the Latin American Solidarity Conference in Havana. Johnson supporters rebuked SNCC for its assertions and its temerity in attempting to weigh in on foreign policy matters. Its radicalism became anathema to the conventional liberals who had supported its past work. When member Julian Bond, elected to the Georgia state legislature, endorsed SNCC's statement on foreign policy, he was denied his seat. Fifteen African ambassadors held a lunch for Bond to express their sympathy.[36]

Criticism of the intervention never reached the volume of anti–Vietnam War protest, in part because local armed resistance collapsed quickly. The Dominican interlude nevertheless helped convince many that U.S. involvement in shoring up questionable regimes was a troubling pattern. When the 82nd Airborne staged a parade through the streets of Santo Domingo City, complete with a marching band, one Dominican slyly inquired whether the selected tune was "Marching through Georgia" or "We Shall Overcome."[37] The confusion was not his: it lay rooted in U.S. ambivalence. Had the Yankees entered as conquerors or liberators?

[34] Edward B. Fiske, "The Mission Is Sometimes Revolution," *New York Times*, January 28, 1968, p. E7.

[35] Fred Rosen and Brady Tyson, "NACLA: A 35 Year Retrospective – 'The Movement' Gives Birth to NACLA," *NACLA Report on the Americas* 36 (November/December 2002): 13–17; Steven Volk, "The North American Congress on Latin America: The First Fifteen Years," *Radical History Review* 27 (1983): 195–200.

[36] Central Intelligence Agency report, n.d., 1971, DDRS; Cleveland Sellers, *The River of No Return* (New York: William Morrow, 1973), 150–1; clipping from *Spark*, January 28, 1966 in Franklin Williams Papers, Box 25, SC.

[37] Tad Szulc, *Dominican Diary* (New York: Dell Publishing, 1966), 173.

The United States siphoned off discontent by allowing more immigration. Remittances would help those left in poverty at home. Johnson conveniently signed the Immigration and Nationality Act of 1965 in October. The law, plainly a product of revised thinking about race, provided an outlet for both interloper and victim. Jesse Hoffnung-Garskof, in his study "'Yankee Go Home ... and Take Me with You!'" points to the irony of Dominicans' participating in anti-American demonstrations while applying to enter the United States. Hoffnung-Garskof provides a Gramscian reading: "The evidence suggests," he posits, that "United States hegemony in the Caribbean, usually taken to mean unchecked domination, actually shared some attributes with ... negotiated consent." He observes that "just as oppressed citizens of the United States have often used the idea of citizenship to demand redress, oppressed *subjects* of the United States used the theories of United States global leadership to demand other forms of redress. Ironically, the United States, no historic friend of social advancement or political power for the Dominican poor, became a place for unprecedented social mobility and for a measure of democracy."[38]

Hoffnung-Garskof's implied immigrant success story provides post facto justification for the intervention that seems to belie his insights. As subjects rather than citizens, Dominican immigrants encountered a society far less tolerant of racial ambiguity. They claimed a new position in the imperial order with their choice to relocate, including a path to success that reinscribed whiteness and reaffirmed the color hierarchy. As a U.S. ethnic minority, it was harder to fudge the color question. Lani Guinier comments: "Political race is not something you are; it's something you do. It's a decision you make" and can include the decision to not see race.[39]

As for Washington, top officials knew from the beginning that Dominican communists posed little threat. Aside from meeting potential challenges in forthcoming midterm elections, the intervention aimed mostly to assert control. The dismissal of accurate intelligence suggests a fabricated urgency that Johnson himself would later acknowledge. In the process, Dominicans bent increasingly toward the metropole, becoming more Caribbean and less Latin American – and thus politically blacker? – as more began perceiving their homeland as a waiting room for their final U.S. destination. Once in the States, they would simultaneously rehearse the narratives of cold war triumph, immigrant aspiration, and nonwhite subordination.

Short-term, low-intensity warfare, little experienced by Americans before the Korean conflict, would characterize U.S. military engagements in the second half of the twentieth century. In the Dominican Republic as well as in Vietnam, Panama, and Grenada, the legitimacy of intervention in foreign civil

---

[38] Jesse Hoffnung-Garskof, "'Yankee Go Home ... and Take Me with You!' Imperialism and International Migration in Santo Domingo, Dominican Republic, 1961–1966," *Canadian Journal of Latin American and Caribbean Studies* 29 (57–58) (2004): 61, 60. Emphasis in original.

[39] Guinier and Torres, *The Miner's Canary*, 107.

conflicts became inseparable from overall U.S. strategy. American inability or unwillingness to distinguish between communism and nationalism foreclosed the possibility of dialogue and engendered precisely what cold war policies meant to prevent. UN Secretary General U Thant attributed the United States' unchecked freedom of maneuver in the Caribbean to its tacit agreement with the USSR to honor their respective "spheres of influence." That understanding, he noted, "is the principal cause of the impotence of the United Nations in the performance of its primary function – to preserve peace." The Dominican intervention, he asserted, was a prime example of the problem.[40]

The specter of racism also haunted U.S. military forays into developing countries. SCLC activist the Reverend Andrew Young considered the intervention racist and attributed its peremptory character to Assistant Secretary for Latin American Affairs Thomas Mann. Young said Mann had grown up in Texas with stereotypical ideas about Mexicans, which colored his thoughts about Latin Americans generally and motivated his advocacy of intervention. According to George Ball, "Tom's basic philosophy with regard to Latin America was that the only group you could count on, who had any continuity, and the only stable element of the society was the military. So that you always found the right military and put them in control."[41] Martin Luther King Jr. opposed the Dominican intervention on principle, and some less famous than he shared his view. In early May 1965 the *Chicago Defender* sent its "inquiring photographer" to assess public opinion on the issue. While most of the people interviewed gave conventional cold war justifications for the intervention, one was different. Arlene Saunders, a beautician, was asked, "Do you think the Communists are behind the Dominican revolt?" "I can't really say if the Communists are to blame," Saunders replied. "We seem too quick to lay everything on the Reds if trouble breaks out anywhere in the world. The people of the Dominican Republic are trying to increase their economical status and if over-throwing the parties who hamper this causes civil war – civil war is the only answer." Skepticism from citizens like Saunders and politicians like J. William Fulbright cast doubt on whether the reasons for sending troops to Santo Domingo were legitimate. In that sense, the origin of the Vietnam era "credibility gap" lay in the Dominican crisis.[42]

Dissatisfaction with U.S. actions in the Dominican Republic and Vietnam, especially among liberal and Left organizations, abetted these groups' growing tendency to engage in citizen diplomacy. SNCC's pronounced movement in this direction was aided by the flurry of invitations to visit it received from such countries as Norway and Cuba. SNCC began its own outreach, creating support groups in Conakry, Guinea; Casablanca, Paris and Versailles, Toulouse,

[40] U Thant, *View from the UN*, 362.

[41] Stewart Burns, *To The Mountaintop: Martin Luther King Jr.'s Mission to Save America: 1955–1968* (New York: HarperCollins, 2004), 288; Andrew J. DeRoche, *Andrew Young, Civil Rights Ambassador* (Wilmington, Del.: Scholarly Resources Books, 2003), 29; George Ball interviewed by Paige E. Mulhollan, July 9, 1971, Johnson Presidential Library, internet copy.

[42] Inquiring Photographer, *Chicago Daily Defender*, May 5, 1965, p. 15; Yates, *Power Pack*, 173.

Brussels, and Amsterdam. Foreign sympathizers began setting up Friends of SNCC groups on their own initiative.[43] French volunteers printed materials to send to Francophone Africa and distribute at home. They also reached out to the black expatriate community. Famed restaurateur Leroy Haynes might let Friends of SNCC use his Paris facility for occasional meetings, they hoped, and musicians living in Paris might be persuaded to give benefit concerts.[44]

Not all SNCC workers endorsed internationalism. Alabama staff believed that "the black community in the rural South cannot at this stage relate in realistic terms with African unity." SNCC's focus, they argued, needed to remain where it had begun. "Black people must see concrete results" from local programming "before the total link can be made with our African brothers." A man "who does not have enough food to feed his ten children and who has seldom traveled beyond the limits of Sumter County, Alabama" would not resonate with Pan-Africanist aspirations.[45] Others took a similarly dim view of global solidarity. A black sailor from Georgia wrote to Stokely Carmichael, admonishing him for sidetracking his mission by supporting foreigners who were just as hostile as U.S. whites to the African-American struggle. "In Asia, negroes are discriminated against, even in whore houses." Henry Williams advised Carmichael to keep his eyes on the domestic prize.[46]

The Peace Corps was beckoning SNCC to consider working in tandem with it as a mainstream organization and summoned it in late winter 1966 to a meeting to "discuss the future of the Corps." "We hope to hear from you about the movements among student groups which are relevant to our efforts," the letter stated, "and how we might effectively relate the two. The Peace Corps is concerned that it remain and grow as a vehicle for social change in the developing Nations.... We are anxious to have your voice." SNCC staffer Mike Miller observed that since the Corps apparently saw something of itself in SNCC, perhaps there was a case for SNCC's becoming a legal alternative to the draft.[47]

The idea did not take off. SNCC would oppose any conscription as long as racial injustice prevailed. The camaraderie that Peace Corps and SNCC volunteers had shared on the 1964 flight to Guinea was a distant memory. SNCC leaders now portrayed the Corps as an intelligence arm of the federal government. Opposition to the Vietnam War proved a powerful catalyst in keeping radicals' attention focused on the world stage. John Lewis, speaking at a New York banquet, explained why SNCC became involved in foreign policy issues. The United States is sending troops abroad in the name of democracy,

[43] Julian Bond to Terri Shaw, October 19, 1964, Executive Secretary Files, reel 9; Vincent Ragsdale to Stokely Carmichael, July 14, 1966, Chair Files, 1960–1969, reel 2; Tom Wakayama to Ruby D. Robinson, November 18, 1963, Series IV Executive Secretary Files, reel 10, SNCC Papers.

[44] Kathi Simms to SNCC office, New York City, December 16, 1967, ibid., SNCC Papers, Chair Files, 1960–1969, reel 2.

[45] Proposal by the Alabama staff for the May 1967 SNCC staff meeting, ibid., reel 3.

[46] Henry B. Williams to Stokely Carmichael, n.d., ibid., reel 2.

[47] Mike Miller to Peter Franck, March 5, 1966, ibid., reel 2. See also Michael B. Standard to Betty Garman, February 24, 1965, Executive Secretary Files, reel 9.

he declared, "and we have yet to see one federal agent protect us or any of the Negroes with whom we work." He attacked the notion that activists, by addressing global concerns, undermined the civil rights movement and muddied the political waters. "What these people were really saying (even those with good intentions) was that Negroes are only allowed to speak about Negroes. But we are Americans too, and our government's role in Vietnam horrifies and shames us." Lewis also realized that draft boards sent induction notices to black men named as troublemakers by local authorities, a practice that hampered SNCC's goals in the South.[48] He alluded to the importance that Washington accords to the international climate and how it modulates its policies accordingly. SNCC, Lewis argued, should do the same.

Cuba became one focus of SNCC's foreign policy autonomy. African Americans had been attuned since 1960 to the Cuban revolution. Havana was increasing support for insurgencies outside its borders. As Cuban-Soviet relations cooled in the wake of the October 1962 missile crisis, the Castro regime resolved to forge alliances independent of Moscow. It hosted the first Tricontinental Congress in January 1966, from which stemmed two new formations, the Organization of Solidarity with the Peoples of Africa, Asia, and Latin America (OSPAAL) and the Latin American Solidarity Organization (OLAS). The messages promoting armed struggle appealed to U.S. militants and drew them to attend convocations of radicals from all over the world. Stokely Carmichael attended the OLAS meeting in Havana the following year.[49]

SNCC had already begun considering the potential of invited travel. At an October 1966 Central Committee meeting, members opined that junkets should not be confined to the leadership. They considered how a trip to Africa "can be used to give people in the ghetto an identification with" the continent "and enable them to see the struggle in its entirety." The committee expressed concern about the randomness of some of the travel, wanted more information about areas being visited, and sought a more coherent policy on how international contacts fit into the group's program. It indicated interest in organizing an International Affairs Commission.[50]

The commission was established in 1967 and through it SNCC applied for NGO status at the United Nations. James Forman, appointed to direct the commission, addressed the General Assembly on November 17 in a speech devoted largely to southern Africa. Forman's remarks are significant here because he described African Americans as a colonized people who were appealing to the world on that basis and because SNCC had followed Malcolm X's lead in

48 SNCC press release, January 26, 1966, ibid., Chair Files, reel 2.
49 Santiago Colás, "Silence and Dialectics: Speculations on C. L. R. James and Latin America," 134, in *Rethinking C. L. R. James*, ed. Grant Farred (London: Blackwell, 1996); Mark T. Berger, "After the Third World? History, Destiny and the Fate of Third Worldism," *Third World Quarterly* 25 (1) (2004): 20, 21; Frank, Rafalko, *MH/Chaos: The CIA's Campaign against the Radical New Left and the Black Panthers* (Annapolis, Md.: Naval Institute Press, 2011), 183.
50 "Suggestions for Direction of SNCC," SNCC Papers, Chair Files, reel 3; minutes of the Central Committee meeting, October 1966, reel 3.

internationalizing the terms of debate.[51] SNCC has been criticized for the attention it devoted to foreign contacts at the expense of intensifying its southern work. By the late 1960s, however, continued white defiance inside and outside Dixie, and a growing conviction that allies must be sought abroad, encouraged the internationalist approach.

Clayborne Carson suggests that these global outreach efforts accompanied mounting failures at home. While internationalism served as a unifying ideological theme, it left practical domestic politics at sea. "Just as SNCC's ties with the white New Left were based on common positions on foreign issues," he writes, "the tenuous threads that held together SNCC's factions were more often support for Third World Alliances than common positions about strategies for achieving black power."[52]

While Carson's point is well taken, SNCC – and the freedom movement generally – needed some triumphs. Faced with entrenched and dogged resistance, not only from hidebound racists but also from putatively liberal supporters elsewhere, the organization understandably began to focus on projects that offered some hope of success. Too often, the history of the sixties focuses on disruption and fails to stress concrete achievements and alternatives to the status quo that insurgents offered. Many had ideas about what should replace the old order they wanted to destroy. "We were coming out of the civil rights movement and there was a kind of sentiment that the struggle had gone as far as it could go here," former civil rights worker Sylvia Hill told an interviewer. Poverty offset the advantages of desegregation and voting legislation, she felt, "because it was really an economic issue and we were very disappointed when the civil rights movement would not allow John Lewis to raise the issue of economic inequities in this society after '63. So out of that, there began to be some international travel."[53]

In May 1967, SNCC declared itself a human rights organization rather than a civil rights group. It held that the problems facing African Americans were only partially resolvable through the medium of electoral politics. Opposition to specific U.S foreign policies did not constitute the whole of SNCC's international agenda. Its goals with respect to the world community, and particularly African countries and other developing nations, were to aid national liberation movements and to seek affiliation with the United Nations Educational, Scientific, and Cultural Organization (UNESCO) as an NGO with worldwide interests. As it had done domestically, SNCC took no anticommunist stand. It began to identify even more closely with newly independent states and socialist countries. Stokely Carmichael's travels took him to Vietnam, Algeria, Syria,

[51] The text of Forman's remarks is in "James Forman of SNCC Addresses the United Nations," *Liberator* (December 1967): 8–10.

[52] Clayborne Carson, Jr., "Blacks and Jews in the Civil Rights Movement," 581, in *Strangers and Neighbors: Relations between Blacks and Jews in the United States*, eds. Maurianne Adams and John Bracey (Amherst: University of Massachusetts Press, 1999).

[53] Sylvia Hill interviewed by Connie Fields, n.d., transcript courtesy of Clarity Film Productions.

Egypt, Guinea, Tanzania, the Scandinavian countries, Britain, and France. He met with a number of heads of state and major political leaders: Fidel Castro in Cuba; Ho Chi Minh in Vietnam; Sékou Touré in Guinea, with former Ghanaian president Kwame Nkrumah, who had been overthrown in 1966; and Julius Nyerere in Tanzania. In France, he rallied African and Caribbean students. His journeys in the summer of 1967 coincided with the Detroit insurrection, which had gained worldwide attention.

Carmichael arrived in England on a July speaking tour. "His visit was looked upon with trepidation by the British government and with eagerness by politically conscious blacks." Carmichael's words in a speech delivered in London ignited a fire: "Nobody had spoken like that in England in modern times." "My solution is an eye for an eye and a tooth for a tooth," Stokely told his audience at the Dialectics of Liberation conference, organized by psychiatrist R. D. Laing and others. "We are the majority, the colored people of the world!" Carmichael proclaimed. "We will confront imperialism in its heartland, and if we do not gain the freedom to be humans, we will burn America down from one coast to the other!"[54] Carmichael's passionate defense of vengeance so disturbed British authorities that the Special Branch national intelligence and security unit advised him to leave Britain before he could address a Caribbean group in Reading. He was banned permanently.[55]

British alarm should be seen in the context of the United Kingdom's post–World War II experience with race. Caribbean immigrants began arriving after the war to satisfy a labor shortage. Immigrants suffered especially from housing discrimination, and as their numbers grew, so did conflicts with white Britons, which culminated in the Notting Hill riots of 1958. These disturbances embarrassed Britain and shocked the world, and their occurrence on the eve of African independence sensitized Her Majesty's government to the issue of how new Commonwealth members would perceive British society.[56] The Conservative government passed the 1962 Commonwealth Immigrants Act,

[54] Carmichael quoted in Maria Höhn and Martin Klimke, *A Breath of Freedom: The Civil Rights Struggle, African American GIs, and Germany* (New York: Palgrave Macmillan, 2010), 113.

[55] SNCC members' travels are extensively documented in SNCC Papers, Series I, Chair Files, 1960–1969, reel 3. Frances Beal and Julia Wright to the Central Committee, July 26, 1968, series 24, box 3, folder 28; Papers of the National Council of Negro Women, Washington, D.C.; "Paris Officials Intervene, Allow Carmichael Entry," Chicago *Daily Defender*, December 7, 1967, p. 19. For Stokely Carmichael specifically, see Foreign Broadcast Information Service (FBIS), "Reportage and Comment on Stokely Carmichael's Activities and Statements Abroad from 6 October to 12 December 1967," Central Intelligence Agency, December 15, 1967. Stephen Jessel, "Black Power Prophet," *The Times* (London), July 19, 1967, p. 10; "British Ban on Stokely Carmichael," ibid., July 28, 1967, p. 1. Angela Davis, who was present at the Dialectics of Liberation Conference, described Carmichael's talk in *An Autobiography* (New York: Random House, 1974), 149.

[56] Chris Waters, "'Dark Strangers' in Our Midst: Discourses of Race and Nation in Britain, 1947–1963," *The Journal of British Studies* 36 (April 1997): 207–38; D. W. Dean, "Coping with Colonial Immigration, the Cold War and Colonial Policy: The Labour Government and Black Communities in Great Britain 1945–51," *Immigrants & Minorities* 6 (3) (1987): 328.

limiting the number of aliens granted work permits. When the Labour Party returned to power in 1965 it upheld the restrictions. In the meantime, the press was full of news about urban race riots in America. By the mid-1960s, Britain's economy was slowing and second-generation black Britons were having trouble finding jobs. The population continued to grow faster than available housing. Racism worsened as more citizens of color from the Commonwealth arrived, and Parliament in 1968 restricted the entry of British subjects of Indian origin. The neofascist and antiimmigrant politician Enoch Powell enjoyed significant support from resentful white workers.

An earlier cadre of black immigrants had founded civil rights organizations in Britain. One of the most notable, Campaign against Racial Discrimination (CARD), was thought moderate and often likened to the NAACP. The years 1965 through 1967 witnessed growing assertiveness among Britain's black minority. Malcolm X's 1965 visit to Smethwick, a town where embattled immigrants of color faced a hostile political climate, received considerable public attention. Participants in militant organizations, such as the Racial Adjustment Action Society (RAAS) and the Universal Coloured Peoples Association (UCPA) challenged CARD leadership. On one occasion, UCPA members went to a CARD meeting wearing pins that carried the slogan "Black Power" and the picture of a black panther. Expressions of solidarity with American radicals and publication of writing by W. E. B. Du Bois marked UCPA's program, as did the adoption of study groups, day care centers for children, and manifestos similar to the Black Panther Party's Ten Point Program.[57] Visitors ranging the spectrum from Martin Luther King to Black Panthers not only kept U.S. issues before the public but invited thinking about how American ideas could be altered to fit British circumstances.

Language and cultural affinities explain some of the black American impact on Britain, but the civil rights movement also influenced continental Europe. West Germany found itself in a ticklish position vis-à-vis the United States and the race question. The Federal Republic lay at the center of a divided Europe and depended heavily on the U.S. Army to underwrite its security. Germans winked at separate entertainment facilities for black and white GIs in their country even though segregation was against their own law. The ironies of defeat in a war fought largely in defense of a white supremacy that flourished among the victors were not lost on German sensibilities. German diplomats in the United States were nervous about racial conflicts among their hosts. The consul in Atlanta sent home a pamphlet published by a Georgia segregationist that recalled Nazi arguments. Envoys tried to dodge the American extremists who wanted to frequent German consulates. When the American Nazi

---

[57] Joe Street, "Malcolm X, Smethwick, and the Influence of the African American Freedom Struggle on British Race Relations in the 1960s," *Journal of Black Studies* 38 (6) (2008): 932–95; Robert G. Weisbord, "Black Power with a British Accent," *Negro Digest* 19 (May 1969): 31–2; Derek Humphry and David Tindall, *False Messiah: The Story of Michael X* (London: Hart-Davis, MacGibbon, 1977), 44–6.

Party demonstrated against black entertainer Sammy Davis Jr.'s marriage to Swedish actress May Britt, the German consul in Los Angeles felt compelled to make a public statement distancing the Federal Republic from American storm troopers.[58] To Germans, the term "racism" recalled the crimes of the Third Reich, although more than a trace of race hatred persisted into the postwar era. The existence of strong prejudice on the part of Americans, West Germany's protectors, only enhanced the ambivalence Germans experienced as they balanced between moral principle and a discredited past.

Attacks on immigrants of color, such as occurred during the British riot and the assaults on Algerians in Paris in 1961; colonialist arrogance; and racial discrimination formed part of the motif of a Europe that had to adjust rapidly to change. If reactionary tendencies pulled in one direction, a desire to defuse racial, ethnic, and international tensions counterbalanced them. The peace movement served as the common ground from which collaboration and understanding between European and African-American change agents sprang. In summer 1966, the Swedish public raised $100,000 for King, funds that he applied to voter registration projects in Mississippi and to SCLC's Chicago campaign, an effort to tackle discrimination in the urban North. The Nobel laureate's steadfastness in his pursuit of "justice without ever resorting to violence or letting loose the forces of hate" motivated the Swedish gift.[59] Some Scandinavian sentiment reacted to the sensationalist publicity attendant on U.S. media coverage of Black Power, which King had denounced. But most of it mirrored their own stake in the politics of peace, exemplified in their control of the Nobel Prize itself. This connection to peace became more significant as the Vietnam era proceeded.

King's foreign policy dissidence was a problem for the White House and the more conservative civil rights organizations. The administration countered an emerging antiwar movement by assembling supportive voices to pressure the wavering. Warnings had already rung out during the Dominican intervention. The Johnson administration awaited a report from newly appointed UN ambassador Arthur Goldberg, dispatched to bring King and other liberal leaders in line and prevent SCLC from officially adopting King's professed views. Goldberg, who questioned the wisdom of increasing U.S. commitments in Southeast Asia himself, had no trouble subordinating his beliefs to official policy and urging others to do the same.[60] George Weaver, an African American and head of the Department of Labor's Bureau of International Affairs, took King on in a speech before a New Jersey Masonic organization. Public disagreement with U.S. foreign policy, Weaver asserted – without mentioning King by name – endangered national security.[61]

[58] David Braden Posner, "Afro-America in West German Perspective, 1945–1966" (PhD diss., Yale University, 1997), p. 340–3, 342 n. 65, 64, 248–9.

[59] "Dr. King Receives $100,000 Donation," *New York Times*, July 6, 1966, p. 15.

[60] "Goldberg Invites Dr. King to U.N.," *New York Times*, August 25, 1965, p. 3; *Norfolk Journal and Guide*, September 1, 1965, p. 1.

[61] "Rights Movement Rapped for US Policy Criticism," Baltimore *Afro-American*, May 29, 1965; David L. Stebenne, *Arthur J. Goldberg: New Deal Liberal* (New York: Oxford University

Aside from sporadic rebellions, such as that by the Flint, Michigan, chapter, NAACP branches did not take antiwar positions between the summer of 1966 and spring 1967, allowing leadership to sidestep the issue. The Boston NAACP chapter's 1967 conference resolution implied that it would not condemn the U.S. role in Vietnam as long as the War on Poverty remained intact. NAACP members were forced to ponder how broadly they should construe their agenda. Secretary Roy Wilkins, responding to a query about the association's silence on Vietnam, replied that the NAACP was a civil rights organization and antiwar activity formed no part of its function. A resolution voted at the association's 1967 annual meeting urged the United States to make every effort to achieve "a just and honorable peace" in Vietnam. Most participants thought it "a serious tactical mistake ... to attempt to merge the civil rights movement with the peace movement or to assume that one is dependent upon the other." It was nevertheless a slippery slope: any NAACP use of the guns *and* butter argument would imply a prowar stance rather than the comfortable position that the war and civil rights were separate issues. Bayard Rustin, a veteran pacifist as well as civil rights activist, believed that those advocating black rights should make their commitment to peace as individuals only. "Negro people who are worried about foreign policy should join in organizations committed to an examination of foreign policy," he declared. Groups, however, should stick to their original mission. "If you've got a cancer society, it sticks to cancer. That's the nature of the American setup."[62]

Yet the "American setup" itself was changing, and the drive for black rights proved to be a mighty catalyst. Some thought the movement a victim of its own successes. According to King's assistant, the Reverend James Bevel, Johnson signed the "civil rights movement out of existence" when in 1965 he affixed his signature to the voting rights act. Yet, shrewd observers understood that legislative victories did not ensure implementation or lasting results. Once it overcame Jim Crow legal hurdles, the movement would need new focus and direction. Should it address itself to social justice in other parts of the world where the United States exerted a major influence on events? Urban League director Whitney Young saw a decisive link between specific foreign issues and race. He held that Southeast Asia, not populated by blacks, was an inappropriate field in which to concentrate activism on behalf of justice. South Africa, however, lay within the legitimate purview of an organization concerned with civil rights.[63]

Press, 1996), 356–7, 361; "U.S. Aide Warns Vietnam Critics," *New York Times*, August 20, 1965, p. 2.

[62] Manfred Berg, "Guns, Butter, and Civil Rights: The National Association for the Advancement of Colored People and the Vietnam War, 1964–1968," in *Aspects of War in American History*, eds. David K. Adams and Cornelis A. van Minnen (Keele, UK: University of Keele, 1997), 221, 222, 226. Roy Wilkins to Joseph Stern, March 17, 1966, Ralph J. Bunche Papers, NAACP Board, Box 113, UCLA; NAACP, *Annual Report, 1967*, 112; Fred Powledge, "Vietnam Issue Divides Leaders of Rights Groups," *New York Times*, August 29, 1965, p. E4.

[63] Whitney Young, "The High Cost of Discrimination," *Ebony* 20 (August 1965): 52; press release, National Conference of the Urban League, Miami, August 1, 1965, CBP, Part 3, Subject Files on Black Americans, 1918–1967, Series I, Race Relations, 1923–1965, reel 8.

By this reasoning, African-American assertiveness in foreign affairs only had legitimacy if it focused on racial issues affecting black people. Majority rule was thus a rightful concern and the prerequisite for any solution to the southern Africa problem. Rhodesia, politically and economically dominated by a white settler minority, had declared its independence of the British Commonwealth on November 11, 1965. White Rhodesians, under Ian Smith's leadership, determined to resist the tide of black sovereignty that had swept the African continent. "Smith has quite a nice little police state in embryo there," British Prime Minister Harold Wilson commented. Could the United States carve out a position on the settlers – and their control of strategic minerals – that would not undermine its official antiracist position and antagonize black Africa? "Rhodesia itself isn't very important to us," presidential adviser Robert Komer counseled, "but the point is that it's critical to all the other Africans. They see it as a straight anti-colonial issue, and all their anti-white instincts are aroused. So our stance on this issue will greatly affect our influence throughout Africa – it will be a test of whether we mean what we say about self-determination and racialism. It will be far more significant than the Congo in this sense."[64]

Komer also understood that Rhodesia as an embattled white redoubt appealed to the atavistic instincts of white supremacists and other homegrown right-wing elements. Smith's government appeared ready to exploit such Americans, and the attempt would assure a negative response from the "US Civil Rights groups [that] are beginning to focus on the problem," Foreign Service officer Ulrich Haynes predicted. Haynes's mid-April 1966 situation report noted that an enduring Rhodesian crisis would undermine Anglo-American objectives in Africa.[65]

ACOA and the National Student Christian Federation joined to form the Committee of Conscience against Apartheid in the summer of 1966. The group, led by A. Philip Randolph, targeted a cluster of banks participating in a revolving loan fund for South Africa by asking that organizations with accounts in those banks withdraw their deposits. Randolph led demonstrations against these institutions and began negotiations with some of them.[66] As for Bayard Rustin, the connection of apartheid to racial domination enabled him eventually to moderate his reservations about challenging U.S. foreign policy.

He and other reformers began losing patience with gradualist approaches to southern Africa. All else failing, the ANLCA held, Washington should entertain a military solution to ending white minority rule. In a departure from the nonviolence it advocated in domestic conflicts, the group endorsed armed struggle in South Africa, and political and material assistance for its national liberation

---

64 Message from Prime Minister Wilson to President Johnson, November 1, 1965, p. 834; Komer's memorandum for the President, December 6, 1965, attached to Komer to McGeorge Bundy, December 6, 1965, *FRUS* XXIV, *1964–1968, Africa*, 854.

65 Komer to Johnson, February 17, 1966, p. 897; memorandum from Ulrich Haynes to President's Special Assistant Walt Rostow, April 18, 1966, *FRUS 1964–1968, Africa*, p. 902.

66 Robert Kinloch Massie, *Loosing the Bonds: The United States and South Africa in the Apartheid Years* (New York: Doubleday, 1997), 218.

organizations. Initiatives included help for black South African students and refugees, boycotts and divestment programs, support for dockworkers' refusals to unload South African imports, and plans to aid political prisoners and their families. As an umbrella organization favoring increased opportunities for the African-American middle class, the ANLCA also pressed, characteristically, for more involvement of historically black colleges and universities in federal training and development programs.[67] The ANLCA's interests after 1966 reflected pressures by domestic nationalist organizations and civil rights activists committed to the immediatism of "Freedom Now." The group called for more contact between Africa and the African diaspora, including outreach to the foreign diplomatic community in Washington, D.C. It proposed a candidate roster to match black American technicians and professionals with sub-Saharan governments seeking expatriate expertise.

ANLCA leaders were less proactive about the Vietnam War. As early as mid-1966 the black public as a whole had begun to express strong disagreement with the course being pursued in Washington. Later that year, Gerald Gill records, "pollsters and social scientists alike noticed that blacks as a group ranked among the most dovish of Americans." Harris Polls conducted in 1967 suggested that "blacks, along with women and the poor, were far more supportive of the de-escalation of the war and the nation's withdrawal from Southeast Asia than were white males.... Moreover, black voters across the country were more inclined than were many white voters to support local referenda on the war."[68]

CORE's James Farmer attempted to quiet the war issue amid growing concerns within his organization. Participants at the June 1966 White House Conference on Civil Rights tried to introduce a resolution for withdrawal from Vietnam that Whitney Young blocked. Young asserted that the United States could prosecute the war and ensure full rights for all Americans simultaneously. Implied in the claim was the presumption that there was no reason to pursue social justice outside national borders. The polity, according to this argument, had ample capacity to accommodate change, as progress made on civil rights to date suggested. The Urban League director traveled to Vietnam in July 1966 to investigate the status of African-American soldiers. In spite of GI complaints about the small number of black commissioned officers, scarce promotion opportunities for enlistees, and callous white officers, Young's report appeared to whitewash military bias. The overrepresentation of blacks in combat, he concluded, owed less to prejudice than to reenlistments. His tour had the effect of fanning the flames rather than diminishing antiwar dissidence.[69]

[67] Resolutions of the ANLCA third biennial assembly, May 26, 1967, Washington, D.C., in Papers of the American Society of African Culture (AMSAC), folder 10, SC.
[68] *New York Post*, March 25, 1968, in Schomburg Clipping File, SC; Gill, "Afro-American Opposition to the United States' Wars." 328.
[69] Nancy Weiss, *Whitney M. Young, Jr., and the Struggle for Civil Rights* (Princeton, N.J.: Princeton University Press, 1989): 159, 161; Simon Hall, "The Response of the Moderate Wing of the Civil Rights Movement to the War in Vietnam," *Historical Journal* 46 (3) (2003): 669–701.

The ideal of creating an egalitarian America required the wherewithal that many concerned persons felt was wasted in a destructive and racist foreign war. Efforts by "moderates" in and out of government to suppress such views merely made their proponents angrier and more determined. Young's report led to open conflict between him and King. The men clashed at a February 1967 fund-raiser in Long Island. "As the evening drew to a close," Young's biographer Nancy Weiss narrates, they "exchanged angry words."[70] Bayard Rustin, like Young, had worried that antiwar concerns would dilute the civil rights mission. He nonetheless respected King's views and his freedom to utter them. Rustin made this clear in a March 1967 *Amsterdam News* column. Press criticism of King's antiwar stance, he wrote,

> may well reveal that America does not really believe that Negroes; as citizens, have yet come of age. Like children, we should be seen but not heard. I say this because the criticism of Dr. King was not limited to an evaluation of his proposals and his strategy for ending the war. It was, by and large, an attack on his right to debate, or even to discuss, Vietnam. In substance, many editorials seemed to be asking, "What is Dr. King doing discussing Vietnam?" or "Who gave him the right to make proposals about our [meaning white America's] foreign policy?"
>
> In a democracy all citizens have not only a right but also a solemn duty to vote, to advise on domestic affairs, and to address themselves to all aspects of foreign policy. As Americans, Dr. King and all other Negroes have such a duty. First, it is their duty as citizens. Second, it is their duty as black citizens, considering that twice as many Negroes proportionately are fighting and dying in Vietnam.
>
> Equally compelling for Dr. King, is the fact that he is a Nobel Peace Prize winner. As such he has a moral obligation to speak out for peace according to his insight as a man of God and in keeping with his conscience as a free man.[71]

Rustin later suggested that his disagreement with King was tactical rather than strategic. He himself opposed a war that he viewed as not in the national interest. But "Negroes should not try to express their position on peace through the Boy Scout organization, the Red Feather campaign, or civil rights organizations. They should do this through established peace organizations, and not place civil rights organizations in double jeopardy." Participation in antiwar campaigns was "distinctly unprofitable and perhaps even suicidal."[72]

Rustin based his opinions on his reading of Lyndon Johnson. LBJ's dislike for King preceded the latter's April 1967 Riverside Church sermon, the best known of his antiwar statements. To Johnson, King was "vain, preachy, communist-influenced" and failed to give the president the deference he thought he was due, asking for private meetings and canceling appointments. Johnson's aide Louis Martin speculated that King wanted to ingratiate himself with

---

[70] Weiss, *Whitney Young, Jr.,* 159.
[71] *Amsterdam News* column, March 3, 1967 in Bayard Rustin, *Down the Line: The Collected Writings of Bayard Rustin* (Chicago: Quadrangle Books, 1971), 169.
[72] Jervis Anderson, *Bayard Rustin: Troubles I've Seen* (Berkeley: University of California Press, 1998), 301.

militants by distancing himself from the president. Johnson, Martin thought, had similar anxieties about credibility. While he distrusted King, the president thought that Roy Wilkins identified too closely with the White House. Wilkins's loss of African-Americans' trust would thus diminish his value to Johnson. It was a curious situation: Johnson could not benefit from either his black friends or his black enemies. Oddly, the NAACP profited from this quandary. Its membership grew from 440,000 in 1965 to 462,000 in 1969.[73]

In the midst of the furor over the war, King tried to steer a course that preserved his position as the single most recognized figure in the freedom movement while avoiding the pitfalls of radicalism. U.S. peace groups organized a mid-May meeting with North Vietnamese officials in Paris. The FBI learned that King had planned to attend but then chose not to go. He did not want to encourage the Vietnamese to think that the peace movement had more influence than it actually did and worried about losing his hold on a progressively slippery centrist constituency (see Figure 8). King also feared that his passport would be seized if he went to Paris. He then decided that his primary antiwar task was to mobilize black opinion. He would travel abroad only when and if the public supported the cessation of bombing.[74] King agreed to speak at the massive April 1967 antiwar rally if Socialist Party leader Norman Thomas introduced him, and if liberals, rather than radicals, appeared on the podium. He resisted appeals to run for vice president in pediatrician and peace activist Dr. Benjamin Spock's presidential campaign but in August announced that he would not support Johnson's reelection unless the president revised his Vietnam policies.[75]

Whitney Young did not have King's problems. Like Roy Wilkins's, his link to Johnson tainted him in the minds of those dissatisfied with gradualism and the war. Johnson sent Young back to South Vietnam in the summer of 1967 with a group of business, labor, and civic leaders to observe elections. Young's

---

[73] Alex Poinsett, *Walking with Presidents: Louis Martin and the Rise of Black Political Power* (Lanham, Md.: Rowman & Littlefield, 2000), 163; Berg, "Guns, Butter, and Civil Rights," 238 n. 56.

[74] FBI Director to the President, Secretary of State, and CIA Director, May 13, 1967, Johnson Library, DDRS, 1986:000866. On passport problems, see *MANUSCRIPT*, May 7, 1945, p. 5 in Bunche Papers, Box 100, folder UNCIO memorabilia, UCLA; Darlene Clark Hine, "Paul Robeson's Impact on History," in *Paul Robeson: The Great Forerunner*, eds. editors of *Freedomways* (New York: International Publishers, 1985), 147–9; Rayford Logan to John Hope Franklin, May 22, 1953, Rayford W. Logan Papers, Box 181–4, Correspondence folder, f John Hope Franklin, 1938–56, MSC; W. E. B. Du Bois to Mohammed Awad, February 21, 1957, Bunche Papers, Box 127, folder Bunche on Du Bois, UCLA; United States Department of Defense, Counterintelligence Research Project, CI Special Project 10, October 1967, Student Non-Violent Coordinating Committee (SNCC), "World Travel," p. 11, Declassified Documents Reference Collection Online.

[75] Paul Hofmann, "Dr. King Is Backed for Peace Ticket," *New York Times*, April 22, 196, p. 32; William H. Chafe, *Never Stop Running: Allard Lowenstein and the Struggle to Save American Liberalism* (New York: Basic Books, 1993), 263, 264; Gene Roberts, "Dr. King to Back Peace Candidate," *New York Times*, August 18, 1967, p. 14.

FIGURE 8. King's precarious position captured in an editorial cartoon. (*Philadelphia Inquirer*)

conclusion that the elections had been fair drew the wrath of peace activists.[76] In the end, all three civil rights leaders lost out. King's estrangement from Johnson ended his leverage with the White House, and the cozy relations that Wilkins and Young had with the president made them his unappreciated creatures.[77]

Nearly a year later, a reporter at a King press conference in Newark, New Jersey, asked him whether he was "disenchanted" with Johnson. "Very much so," King replied. He could still support a Johnson candidacy if the president went to the peace table and escalated the War on Poverty. Tensions over Vietnam registered clearly at other leadership levels. New York Congressman Adam Clayton Powell Jr. called for troop withdrawal in March 1968, an action that signified that he would not be supporting Johnson's reelection. By October 1969, Whitney Young had changed his mind about the war and now

[76] Poinsett, *Walking with Presidents*, 163; Weiss, 162, 163.
[77] Bruce Miroff, "Presidential Leverage over Social Movements: The Johnson White House and Civil Rights," *Journal of Politics* 43 (February 1981): 20; Weiss, 159–60.

concluded King had been right. But by this time, LBJ was out of power and King was dead.[78]

The U.S. Left ascribed the Vietnam War to a larger imperialism, a view of the conflict increasingly shared by the progressive wings of the civil rights movement. Opinions differed about Vietnam to the end of the decade and beyond. Unanimity over African issues, however, remained fairly constant. Support for decolonization and opposition to white settler dominion in Africa were nearly universal features of African-American public opinion, but this did not always entail an exclusive embrace of Africa's most radical regimes and personalities. An earlier conservatism, albeit somewhat tempered by the times, continued to assert itself.

This conservatism, unlike that of Whitney Young, did not rest primarily on ties to white elites. It was instead linked to older Pan-Africanist notions of stewardship in Africa and to the thought of Booker T. Washington. Black nationalists like Marcus Garvey had shared with conservatives like Washington an interest in business development as a pathway to achieving economic and political power in both Africa and the diaspora.[79] Networks originally created to develop black American business enterprise could be expanded to embrace Africa. Associated Negro Press publisher Claude Barnett, an exemplar of this outlook, kept a sharp eye open for opportunities. A product of Tuskegee training himself, Barnett shared Washington's belief that Tuskegee methods could be adapted for African use. British colonial authorities had not adequately prepared their colonies for the technical expertise they would need, he reasoned. Africans, like African Americans, Barnett thought, seemed more interested in high-status professions than in practical business.[80]

Entrepreneurs like him who were interested in Africa nevertheless confronted a host of infrastructural and other issues. Stateside media companies began pushing their way farther into foreign markets as U.S. overseas business expanded after World War II. In most instances, black Americans' modest initiatives were buried in the well-financed onslaught unleashed by mainstream corporations. The colonial legacy often limited contact between neighboring countries. Telecommunications, for example, continued to be routed through metropolitan capitals. African Americans often lacked access to influential Africans, who, journalist Enoch Waters was convinced, were deliberately kept away from them by the State Department.[81]

[78] *New York Times*, March 28, 1968, p. 40.

[79] Willard B. Gatewood, Jr. *Black Americans and the White Man's Burden* (Urbana: University of Illinois Press, 1975); *Smoked Yankees and the Struggle for Empire: Letters from Negro Soldiers, 1898–1902*, ed. Willard B. Gatewood, Jr. (Urbana: University of Illinois Press, 1971).

[80] Barnett to Luther H. Foster, June 23, 1954, Reel 2; Claude Barnett to F. D. Patterson, July 18, 1955, reel 3, CBP, Part 3 – Subject Files on Black Americans, 1918–1967, Series 3 – Philanthropic and Social Organizations, 1925–1966.

[81] Michael Curtin, *Redeeming the Wasteland: Television Documentary and Cold War Politics* (New Brunswick, N.J.: Rutgers University Press, 1995), 61–5, 72–8, 82–3, 90; Prince Eket Inyang-Udoh III to Prattis, December 19, 1958 and February 4, 1959; Prattis to Prince Eket,

The publisher nevertheless soldiered on. Barnett wanted to create an African news service that blacks would privately own and control. His sale of the Associated Negro Press and his death in 1967 ended this ambition. Barnett's projected international agency did not continue, but an analogous organization, funded by the Central Intelligence Agency, did. The International Features Service ostensibly provided a conduit for a cold war liberal take on news features to be disseminated in Africa. Murray Baron, vice president of New York's Liberal Party, a reform Democrat organization, was the chief organizer. Baron brought in Roy Wilkins and UAW president Walter Reuther. "The CIA," write authors of a noted work on the agency, "came up with the cash to bring the combined forces of American civil rights and liberalism to Africa."[82]

Civil rights stripped of radicalism found favor in Nigeria, a target of efforts to build a pro-Western national bourgeoisie. The face that Nigeria showed to the world differed from that associated with Ghana, the West African nation to which Nigeria was sometimes compared. Unlike Ghana, Nigeria had no Nkrumah, a single leader with the charismatic ability to move audiences outside his own country. Ghana began strongly to symbolize, rightly or wrongly, African antiimperialist and antiracist militancy. Nkrumah's practice of utilizing diaspora expatriates as long-term consultants and aid workers strengthened this association. In Nigeria, such employees tended to be hired on short-term contracts.[83]

If Ghana stood in for radical Pan-Africanism, Nigeria meant business-oriented pragmatism, and many Americans of a conservative bent encouraged this orientation. The other face of Nigeria emanated from its northern states, ruled by Muslim aristocrats, whose sense of privilege the British had groomed from an early date.[84] While a mercantile community of southern and western immigrants

January 8, 1959, Box 144–7, Percival L. Prattis Papers, MSC; Enoch Waters to Claude Barnett, November 11, 1961, and Etta M. Barnett to the editors of the Associated Negro Press, April 4, 1963, CBP, Part 2, reel 7.

[82] Barnett to Roy Wilkins, November 30, 1960, CBP, Partt 3 – Subject Files on Black Americans, 1918–1967, Series I-Race Relations, 1923–1965, Reel 5; "Louis Martin to Set Up Newspapers in W. Africa," Pittsburgh *Courier*, February 14, 1959, p. 5; Alex Poinsett, *Walking with Presidents: Louis Martin and the Rise of Black Political Power* (Lanham, Md.: Rowman & Littlefield, 2000), 54–5; Enoch Waters to Claude Barnett, April, n.d., 1961, CBP, Part 2, reel 7. See also the perceptive portrait of the complex Barnett in Adam Green, *Selling the Race: Culture, Community, and Black Chicago, 1940–1955* (Chicago: University of Chicago Press, 2007), 94–7; Armistead S. Pride and Clinton C. Wilson II, *A History of the Black Press* (Washington, D.C.: Howard University Press, 1997), 166–7; Dan Schechter, Michael Ansara, and David Kolodney, "The CIA as an Equal Opportunity Employer," 61, in *Dirty Works 2: The CIA in Africa*, eds. Ellen Ray, et al., (Secaucus, N.J.: Lyle Stuart, 1969).

[83] Jackson Davis to Claude Barnett, May 8, 1946; and idem to idem, May 16, 1946; "Claude Barnett, 1941–1947," General Education Board, Phelps Stokes Fund – Educational Survey of Africa, July–December 1944, Series 1.2, subseries. 637.1 folder 2991, RAC. William B. P. Gray to Emmer Lancaster, December 21, 1949, Emmer Lancaster Papers, Records of the Department of Commerce RG 40, NARA; Claude Barnett to B. F. Few, February 18, 1956, CBP, Series A, part 2, reel 2; Anderson, *Bayard Rustin*, 145–9; Poinsett, *Walking with Presidents*, 54–5.

[84] Frederick Lugard, *The Dual Mandate in British Tropical Africa*, 4th ed. (Edinburgh and London: W. Blackwood, 1929).

resided in the predominantly Hausa states, northern Nigeria did not boast the commercial development characteristic of the South. Its strength instead lay in large landholdings and agricultural production that supported an elite stratum that was quite comfortable with class inequality.

Investors had little fear of expropriation in Nigeria, a country unlikely to establish a command economy. By 1961, a year after independence, U.S. firms had formed the Nigerian-American Chamber of Commerce. No Nigerians served on its board. The president, Harold Christensen, was from IBM. Other board members included representatives from the Chase Manhattan Bank, the Israel Commodity Company, Mobil Oil Company, Chase International Investment Corporation, Westinghouse, RCA, the Bank of America, PepsiCo, Texaco, Farrell Lines, and Citibank. This lineup reflected Nigeria's status as the most populous and potentially wealthy West African state.[85]

African and Asian decolonization, whether gained through bloody revolution or achieved through "orderly" transition with help from former colonizers, shared an important characteristic with racial movements in the United States. All called on powerful discourses that appealed to widely acknowledged understandings of justice. Reformers and revolutionaries on both sides of the Atlantic spoke in ways that veiled moral ambiguity and promoted binary perceptions of their struggles. Black freedom fighters resisting white racists, integration versus segregation, colonialism against national liberation – these were readily absorbed oppositional categories. They facilitated the networking done, for example, between the early antiapartheid movement and civil rights nonviolent direct action campaigns. They abetted later collaborations between more radical African states and African-American exponents of revolution and Black Power. The seeming clarity evoked in the struggle against racism and colonial oppression affirmed political idealism and moral certainty. If African conflicts were interethnic or involved political struggles against the state, however, it became more difficult to envision and articulate Pan-African politics. By the mid-1960s, coups deposed leaders in Algeria, Congo (Kinshasa), Dahomey (now Benin), the Central African Republic, Upper Volta (Burkina Faso), Ghana, and Nigeria, confounding anyone who relied on simple racial polarities to explain African unrest.

The Nigerian poet Christopher Okigbo provides an example of Africa's emerging complexities. Young, charismatic, a playboy, he was born in the eastern region that would later be known as Biafra. His shimmering verse began appearing in print as a national literature sprang forth in Nigeria. Okigbo, a scion of the Smythes' new Nigerian elite, attended secondary school at Kings College, Lagos, in the 1950s, where "students ... generally thought of themselves as epitomizing civilization and cosmopolitanism." Later, at the University College of Ibadan, he fit comfortably into literary circles populated by such poets, novelists, and playwrights as John Pepper Clark, Wole Soyinka, and Chinua Achebe.[86]

---

[85] "Nigeria: A Future U.S. Colony?" *Liberator* 2 (January 1962): 1, 4.
[86] Biographical information on Okigbo is from Obi Nwakanma, *Christopher Okigbo, 1932–67: Thirsting for Sunlight* (Woodbridge, UK: James Currey: 2010).

The early 1960s were years of promise for Nigeria and Africa as a whole, especially on the cultural front. Okigbo went on to become a founder of the influential Mbari Club of African artists and writers and served briefly an editor of the journal *Black Orpheus*. He later edited *Transition*, a periodical that originated in Uganda and featured in its pages such figures as Achebe, James Baldwin, Ali Mazrui, and Paul Theroux. Offered the Langston Hughes Prize for poetry at the 1966 Negro Festival of the Arts in Dakar, Okigbo rejected it. "I found the whole idea of a Negro arts festival based on color quite absurd," he said. "There is no such thing as African writing. There is only good or bad writing!"[87] For him, in art, imagination and skill trumped political and racial identity. These sunny presumptions, however, would be challenged as politics and ethnicity collided with Okigbo's life.

Accused of involvement in a coup attempt in January 1966, Okigbo and other Ibo academics on the Ibadan faculty began to worry about their personal safety as news of widespread killings of Ibos in northern Nigeria spread. Okigbo survived a failed assassination and fled to the Ibo redoubt in the East, where he took up arms in defense of the newly declared state of Biafra. "So, what would lead Okigbo then to abandon his place as a chronicler to accepting a death fighting for his 'beleaguered people'?" his biographer asks. "What would force Okigbo, the nationalist and universalist, to throw his weight solidly behind the secessionist East?"[88] The fragmentation of Nigeria as a nation undermined his desire to put aside issues tangential to art, even as these issues lay the groundwork for outsiders' ambivalent responses to the Nigerian tragedy. Okigbo argued when rejecting the Langston Hughes Prize that "race" did not matter, and it did not, except when it did.

The black diaspora response to the Nigerian civil war of 1967–70 was subdued. The conflict introduced indistinctness into the truths that freedom movements, both foreign and domestic, had laid down. The war was not a cold war issue since both the United States and the USSR supported the Nigerian federal government. Nor was it a racial issue as understood in the West.[89] The combination of these two absences cast it as a humanitarian crisis and hid from view the deeper relevance of the conflict for the rapidly shifting realities of the 1960s. The war marked in some respects the end of innocence for the champions of liberation because it could not be understood either literally or figuratively in black and white terms. These opposites do not only apply to skin color; they also pertain to the oppositional thinking that the cold war frame abetted. Tension between cold war enemies relied heavily upon creation of dichotomies. Policy makers and nongovernmental actors alike found themselves unable to address the new circumstances in the old language.

[87] Ibid., 223, 264.
[88] Ibid., 264.
[89] Piero Gleijeses, *Conflicting Missions: Havana, Washington, and Africa, 1959–1976* (Chapel Hill: University of North Carolina Press, 2002), 384.

A lack of vital U.S. commitments in Nigeria, a tradition of deferring to Britain over matters involving its former colonies, an inability to intervene in Africa as a result of Vietnam burdens, and concern not to alienate Biafra in case it miraculously prevailed, tempered official U.S. views of the war.[90] Washington supported the federal republic but, unlike Moscow, did not sell it arms. Nor were U.S. officials particularly perturbed about Soviet arms shipments. American support for Biafra was limited to humanitarian relief.[91] Yet, by 1967 Nigeria had replaced Ghana as the centerpiece of U.S. policy in sub-Saharan Africa. As one State Department official described it, "the stake the U.S. had in Nigeria [was] the biggest in Africa." Nkrumah's radicalism and ultimate overthrow had removed Ghana as the entry point into West African affairs that the United States would employ if needed. Nigeria, with a population approaching 60 million, with conservative, Anglophile rulers, and a market economy that predated colonialism, had seemed an apt replacement. Now it appeared to be unraveling. While the U.S. embassy urged the warring sides to come together, the lack of a clear ideological framework that Americans could apply to the hostilities, or any compelling interest, made the war hard to get a handle on. Even though the politics of Nigeria's recently discovered oil began bubbling to the surface during this time, Washington believed that Britain could best deal with Shell–British Petroleum's "exposed position."[92]

The Nigerian belligerents also defied what had become the comfortable logic of liberation politics. Biafra did not represent a Katanga-style secession, because it never intended to operate as a shill for outside interests. It did receive aid and recognition from such conservative states as Ivory Coast, Haiti, and Portugal, however. Lagos accused it of employing Portuguese mercenaries, yet federal Nigeria also used European pilots to fly bombing sorties against the rebel area. Lagos condemned the Biafrans for courting France, a target of recrimination by those who resented its treatment of Guinea and the masked neocolonialism of its Communauté Française. "The French are actively pro-Biafran," a member of the U.S. National Security Council reported. While the OAU endorsed Nigerian unity, four of its members recognized Biafra. UN Secretary General U Thant saw the Nigerian civil war as "strictly an internal matter and, therefore, outside the jurisdiction of the United Nations." The UN was unjustly criticized for not doing more, U Thant recalled, but the confines of international law prohibited intervention.[93]

---

[90] Information Memorandum from the Western Africa Country Director, Bureau of African Affairs (Melbourne) to Assistant Secretary of State for African Affairs (Palmer) April 18, 1968, *FRUS, 1964–68, Africa.*

[91] George A. Obiozor, *The United States and the Nigerian Civil War: An American Dilemma in Africa, 1966–1970* (Lagos: Nigerian Institute of International Affairs, 1993), 20–1.

[92] State Department to Embassy Nigeria, telegram, February 14, 1967, *FRUS, 1964–68, Africa.*

[93] Edward Hamilton, NSC Staff, to Walt Rostow, August 18, 1968, ibid. See also Anthony Lewis, "British Contend Biafrans Obstruct Peace Efforts," *New York Times*, June 10, 1968, p. 3; U Thant, *View from the UN*, 53.

Matters were further complicated. While Ibos predominated in the infant state, Biafra was also home to other ethnic groups. The "loyalties and movements" of "the non-Ibos" "were always suspected," N. U. Akpan recalled, in spite of their initial support for secession. Rebel leaders tried to build consensus by initiating "kitchen parliaments" designed to expand constituent access to government. This was a critical need, given Biafra's plan to collectivize land in non-Ibo areas, the most fertile soil in the region. While it is not the intention to analyze the civil war here, alienation over the land issue in non-Ibo minority areas clearly aided federal strategies to reclaim the rebel territory.[94] None of this was obvious to outsiders, whose view of the civil war was colored by press photography documenting famine as the conflict progressed.

Just as African countries divided on whether or not they would recognize Biafra, the issue confused diaspora communities. The initial reaction among African Americans was to affirm support for the federal government. In the midst of the war, Nigerian and African-American arts professionals devised a plan that promised to bind important elements of Nigeria and the diaspora together. Not atypically, it entailed a business adventure. After the incorporation of Nigerian Film Associates, Inc., in June 1967, founder Francis Oladele arranged to have playwright Wole Soyinka work with black American actor Ossie Davis to make motion pictures that would counter stereotypes about Africa. They planned to gear the films to a black American audience. Oladele recruited Henry Hampton, later known for his *Eyes on the Prize* civil rights series, to head the company. Foreshadowing the escalating interest in black filmmaking in the next decade, the firm prepared to film Soyinka's play *Kongi's Harvest* with mostly Nigerian actors and crew and some African-American players thrown in "for box-office appeal."[95]

The civil war dragged on and conditions deteriorated in Biafra. Christopher Okigbo was killed in action in September 1967, facing down federal tanks. In the conflict's third year, Charles Diggs (D. Mich.), chair of the House Foreign Affairs Subcommittee on Africa, led a delegation to Nigeria and Biafra in mid-February 1969. Diggs, the first African-American chair of the subcommittee, forcefully employed it as a progressive wedge into U.S. foreign policy on Africa. He gave visibility to such questions as apartheid and sanctions against Rhodesia by making them the subjects of congressional hearings. An important and understudied figure, Diggs drew a variety of nongovernmental actors into policy advisement, including Africanist scholars, civil rights and human rights organizations, and antiapartheid activists.[96]

The Detroit representative gave to his task a perspective informed by both standard Pan-African discourse and contemporary U.S. foreign policy.

94 Ntieyong U. Akpan, *The Struggle for Secession, 1966–1970: A Personal Account of the Nigerian Civil War* (London: Frank Cass, 1972), 93, 20, 126.

95 Edwin Bolwell, "Tarzan's Africa May Be up a Tree," *New York Times*, July 15, 1967, p. 13.

96 Donald R. Culverson, *Contesting Apartheid: U.S. Activism, 1960–1987* (Boulder, Colo.: Westview Press, 1999).

Secretary of State Dean Rusk regretted the fragmentation of Nigeria but believed Americans could do nothing but coax the belligerents to preserve national integrity. Twentieth-century nationalism necessitated the suppression of particularism, the abandonment of local communal forms of identification in favor of a universalist citizenship. Modernization required that new nations be economic entities large enough to function efficiently in world markets. The balkanization of Africa into microstates, a threat that had loomed over the Congo, was to be avoided at all costs.[97]

Biafrans consequently found Diggs's junket deflating. According to John Stremlau, author of an authoritative study of the war, Diggs's "team spent only two days in the enclave and the majority of its two-week mission traveling around Nigeria. Biafran officials had been briefed to appeal to Diggs's African heritage and to argue that Biafra represented 'the true awakening of the African man,' but it appeared that the black Congressman had made up his mind before coming." According to a Biafran commander, "Diggs and his Negroes talked only about pride in big units and the modernization of Africa.... Diggs was the worst of them all ... he only wanted to confirm his predisposition.'"[98]

Diggs, however, did not represent the totality of African-American opinion. CORE's Floyd McKissick firmly supported Biafra. In New York, two former teachers who had served in northern Nigeria collected food for Biafra and organized a candlelight vigil of twenty-four hundred in front of the UN Secretariat. The East Harlem Protestant Parish Children's Choir performed at the vigil, where, according to the *New York Times*, the racially integrated marchers were mostly young. Their plan was to have UNICEF take collected relief items to Biafra. The American Committee to Keep Biafra Alive claimed to take no stand in the civil war but wished to provide food and medicine. They deplored the "silence" of world leadership. The Reverend Dr. Eugene Carson Blake, general secretary of the World Council of Churches, criticized the inertia of governments and "call[ed] on churches to bring pressure on them." The black radical publication *Liberator* took a similar position, accusing the United States of genocide for not facilitating food shipments into rebel territory.[99] Interestingly, these entities shied away from the political choice that presented itself and ironically adopted the same perspective as most states did – that the Nigerian crisis was not a political but a humanitarian one, remediable by charity.

An international Catholic network backed by Irish American politicians and Ivory Coast president Houphouët-Boigny aided Biafra, but Biafra did not yield the same benefits to rightist aims that the Congo had in 1960, and no coherent

---

[97] John J. Stremlau, *The International Politics of the Nigerian Civil War, 1967–1970* (Princeton, N.J.: Princeton University Press, 1977), 375–6. For an alternative view of the lukewarm support for Biafra, see Ikenna Nzimiro, *The Nigerian Civil War: A Study in Class Conflict* (Enugu, Nigeria: Frontline Publishing, 1984), 79, 80.

[98] Stremlau, *The International Politics of the Nigerian Civil War*, 291.

[99] Obiozor, *The United States and the Nigerian Civil War*, 89. Will Lissner, "Marchers at the U.N. Urge Action to Save Starving Biafrans," *New York Times*, August 9, 1968, p. 2; Morris Kramer, "Biafra: While America Sleeps," *Liberator* 9 (March 1969): 6–11.

conservative agenda proved capable of coalescing around its statehood. French support was linked to De Gaulle's rivalry with the English-speaking world. The general wanted to detach disaffected areas from Anglophone control and so encouraged Quebecois separatism in Canada. Perhaps Biafra could be pulled into the French orbit. De Gaulle's 1969 resignation, however, foreclosed that possibility and made continued direct French support uncertain. Biafra thus proved inassimilable to the usual ways of parsing African experience. It was also Biafra's unlucky fate that most of the countries that recognized it were having their own problems.[100]

The Nigerian civil war erupted in a world distracted by other emergencies and dotted with other highlighted events. The preoccupation with Vietnam and the 1967 war between Israel and its Arab neighbors, both crises with greater cold war significance, sidelined the Nigerian struggle, which aligned both superpowers on the same side. East and West alike endorsed the efficiencies and possibilities of the Nigerian macrostate, and neither had vital interests in sub-Saharan Africa. Moral support for Biafra arose chiefly from nongovernmental Western publics.

Stremlau argued that the failure of pro-Biafran groups to change the policies of their governments demonstrates the limits of NGO influence on foreign policy. It demonstrates more than that. Public opinion was itself divided on the issue, and Biafra was not the unified state its propagandists displayed to the world. Marked by ethnic dissensus like the state from which it wished to secede, Biafra exposed the roots of today's conflict about the rightful ownership and use of wealth and resources in the Niger Delta. It forced acknowledgment of two larger questions: In whose interests was colonial independence initiated? Do postcolonial states exist for, or side by side with, the mass of their constituents? Biafra also problematized, in its own time and in the present, the presumption of solidarity among African peoples. It foreshadowed the end of the cold war by more than twenty years in exposing an analytical vacuum. Historians must reexamine how the Nigerian civil war is studied to assess its global, as well as Pan-African, implications. Must the countercitizenship that Pan-Africanists erected against the oppressions of imperialism now be turned against the military regimes and personal fiefdoms in present-day Africa and the diaspora?

The question confronting the world of what to do about Biafra was addressed in terms that almost everywhere privileged the unitary nation-state. Some of this was self-serving. U.S. Ambassador to Nigeria Elbert G. Mathews in 1967 asked Nigerian head of state General Yakubu Gowon not to undertake any actions in prosecuting the war against the rebels "that would do lasting damage to [the] Nigerian economy." Gowon consented, alluding to the non-Ibo minorities in Biafra whose allegiance to the secession was questionable. He contemplated letting Ibos form a "landlocked" "little Switzerland" away from the coast and

---

[100] CIA Directorate of Intelligence, "Biafra Two Years after Secession," May 29, 1969, p. 7, sanitized, incomplete, DDRS.

the petroleum in the ethnic "minority areas." The State Department, evidently concerned about the oil fields and refineries, instructed U.S. corporations to pay no royalties or fees to the rebel government. With oil off the table, the Nigerian civil war was, in Walt Rostow's words, merely a "family quarrel."[101]

The great powers' chancelleries preferred a unitary Nigeria, even if disguised under the cosmetic of federalism. "One Nigeria," paralleled the centrist rhetoric of universalism in the United States and the dismissal of subnational politics. Lyndon Johnson famously decried the rise of an African-American foreign policy audience. Other ethnic lobbies suggested to him the pitfalls of diplomacy defined by and deferring to such interests. When Richard Nixon later traveled to Britain as president, Prime Minister Harold Wilson persuaded him similarly to reject any African microstate based on the fiction of an uncomplicated nationality.

As a humanitarian crisis, Biafra signaled what was to come, as the cold war, displaced onto nonwhite peoples, lost the ethical threads that purported to connect it to a higher, moralistic enterprise. If African states in 1960 needed help and protection to keep them aligned to their respective senior partners in the global North, thirty years later their vulnerability was assured. The end of superpower competition drove the nail in the coffin. Mass publics soon became accustomed to – and hardened by – the sight of starving children and corpses by the roadside.

The Nigerian civil war erupted as the task of including people of color in definitions of citizenship opened up strains in the social fabric not unlike the challenges that sovereign equality posed for the international community. Pan-Africanist discourse and practice lacked forceful language to address the problem of the late twentieth century, no longer necessarily, as in W. E. B. Du Bois's words, one of the color line alone. Du Bois's genius was in shifting color from the margins to the mainstream of global conflict. While liberation movements might frame struggle in clear and narrow terms to gain mass support, such frameworks can now suppress rather than validate the legitimate claims of the publics they were originally intended to serve.

---

[101] State Department to Embassy Nigeria, telegram, July 20, 1967, *FRUS 1964–1968, Africa.*

6

Embracing the Globe

Just as the Congo crisis cast a pall over earlier optimism about independent Africa, the Nigerian civil war heightened the pessimism in official circles. Only five years after the exhilaration of 1960, the CIA's National Intelligence Estimate took a dim view of the African states. Lagging growth "in most areas will be very slow; indeed, setbacks are probable in a number of countries," the report noted. "There is a desperate shortage of virtually all kinds of technical and managerial skills; indeed, the basic institutions and staff for economic development are often inadequate or absent. Moreover, it is highly unlikely that most African countries will obtain external assistance or investment on anything approaching the scale required for sustained economic development." Loy Henderson, retired but still prominent, regarded many African nations as "mini-states," "so insignificant" that they hardly merited a consulate. It was cheaper, however, to name ambassadors to them and spare the cost to the departmental budget that appointing a regional ambassador, traveling frequently and required to entertain lavishly, would entail.[1]

Fourteen months later, a State Department task force charged with reviewing Africa policy remained dismissive. It declared that Washington's "primary concern with Africa has been, and will continue to be for some time, to prevent events in the continent from complicating a search, largely conducted elsewhere, for solutions to the problems of war and peace, or from interfering with our central strategic and political preoccupations in other regions."[2] The ethnic tensions then overtaking Nigeria would be of no great concern unless they had the potential to affect matters in areas of greater interest to policy makers.

Analysts pronounced the outlook dim, but officials continued to dangle the prospect of help on major infrastructural projects before needy nations. The

---

[1] Central Intelligence Agency, National Intelligence Estimate/1/NIE 60/70–65, Problems and prospects in Sub-Saharan Africa, April 22, 1965, in *FRUS, 1964–1968*, XXIV, *Africa* (Washington, D.C. 1999) online edition; Loy W. Henderson to George W. Renchard, November 7, 1967, Loy W. Henderson Papers, Container 7, "Foreign Service Correspondence," LC.

[2] Report of the Task Force on the Review of African Development Policies and Programs, July 22, 1966, *FRUS 1964–1968*, *Africa*, online.

North Vietnamese would win a Mekong Delta project rivaling the Tennessee Valley Authority if they would drop their objections to negotiations while U.S. jets bombed their country. Nkrumah of Ghana could have had his Volta River hydroelectric dam if he had submitted to inconsistent and often capricious American demands. U.S. authorities strongly condemned the acceptance of aid from Warsaw Pact countries even as they thought it unlikely that most African states would ever remain genuinely Marxist. "The policies of the Western powers," Bill Minter notes, "though often strikingly varied to the casual glance, were all rooted in a consensus that ruled out African efforts for liberation. United States policy seemed to offer new support for African self-determination, but in case after case, the promise evaporated."[3] Denial of the most critical assistance postponed the hope of an African "Great Leap Forward" and contributed to the continent's dismal social, economic, and political situation in the twenty-first century. U.S. officials castigated Africans' own efforts to break through economic stagnation, requiring dependence and stasis of them in order to maintain an idiosyncratic view of peace and stability. Some heads of state, like Tanzania's Julius Nyerere, sought to cultivate the limited space in which they could evade cold war pressures: working with minor European states or attempting self-finance.

African desires for progress found a complement in the generations-old preoccupation of black Americans with racial uplift. From its beginnings in the eighteenth century, racial uplift had always had both a domestic and a foreign component. The goal of evangelizing Africa and founding modern states and economies there accompanied and sometimes galvanized domestic efforts at teaching and learning trades, improving literacy, and creating a professional class. Thus Booker T. Washington, associated with the aims of a black southern petty bourgeoisie, sponsored an early agricultural experiment in Togo, where German colonialists employed Tuskegee-trained African Americans to instruct Togolese in cotton production.[4]

Projects begun over the years by African Americans or Caribbean colonial subjects were premised on some form of ideological commitment to advancing the race. These included Garveyite plans for cooperatives in Liberia in the 1920s and development schemes in Ethiopia in the early 1930s. Self-help constituted an integral part of racial uplift thought. While it could encourage political quiescence, it could also, especially in later iterations, promote activism. When uplift entered the stream of ideas that are grouped together as Black Power, it strongly reasserted the need to disavow white leadership, accommodationism, gradualism, and compromise. The intransigence of U.S. segregationists and white imperialists in southern Africa alike had demonstrated the limitations of moral suasion and nonviolence as means to achieve black liberation.

[3] William Minter, *King Solomon's Mines Revisited* (New York: Basic Books, 1986), 138.

[4] Andrew Zimmerman, *Alabama in Africa: Booker T. Washington, the German Empire, and the Globalization of the New South* (Princeton, N.J.: Princeton University Press, 2012); Michael O. West, "The Tuskegee Model of Development in Africa: Another Dimension of the African/ African-American Connection," *Diplomatic History* 16 (July 1992): 371–87.

The U.S. civil rights movement, in the glory days of sit-ins and freedom rides, did not fully address the need for economic opportunity. Martin Luther King Jr. planned to expand rights claims to encompass issues of wealth distribution. His Poor People's Campaign sent thousands to Washington, D.C., to erect a squatters' camp called Resurrection City and draw global attention to the existence of poverty in the world's richest nation. After his assassination, efforts by SCLC and other groups to keep the issue before the government and the public washed away in the capital's spring rains, and police ultimately forced the evacuation of the camp.

Years before that debacle, however, Malcolm X's prescription to achieve freedom "by any means necessary" entailed economic initiatives. In a similar spirit, H. Rap Brown, SNCC chair in 1967, wrote to Oliver Tambo, deputy president of the African National Congress (ANC) of South Africa. Brown informed Tambo that SNCC was calling for a black boycott of General Motors cars because of GM's South African investments. He followed this with an open letter to African Americans requesting that medical supplies and money be sent to Tambo, then in Tanzanian exile. Black youth should stay in school, Brown exhorted, so they could learn the skills needed to help Africa. They should form an international army to fight liberation wars on the continent. He called on U.S. blacks to attend UN debates on African questions. SNCC's recently formed International Affairs Commission proposed "an African-American skills bank" to Julius Nyerere. Black Americans with specific vocations would help with nation building in Tanzania. They would construct roads and teach school, operate clinics, and train Tanzanians to replace them. These programs were to remain apart from and uninfluenced by U.S. government initiatives. While the proposed plan resembled the Peace Corps, SNCC likened it to Mississippi's 1964 Freedom Summer.[5]

To promote this internationalism abroad, James Forman and other SNCC representatives traveled in July to Kitwe, Zambia, where they and other NGO delegates were invited to observe the United Nations International Seminar on Apartheid, Racism, and Colonialism in Southern Africa. According to Forman, CORE and SCLC had also been invited, but the NAACP was originally excluded. After protests by U.S. ambassador to the UN Arthur Goldberg, the NAACP received a belated invitation but did not attend. SCLC was also absent. Ultimately, SNCC was the only organization that actually arrived to address the seminar.[6] The UN Special Committee against Apartheid planned the meeting, which reflected the body's growing frustration with South African

[5] "SNCC Joining Anti-Apartheid Fight in Africa," Chicago *Daily Defender*, August 30, 1967, p. 5. See also "Afro-American Support for the Liberation Movements," *Southern Africa* 1 (December 1967): 15–16.

[6] Howard Tolley, *The International Commission of Jurists: Global Advocates for Human Rights* (Philadelpia: University of Pennsylvania Press, 1994). James Forman, *The Making of Black Revolutionaries* (Washington, D.C.: Open Hand Publishing, 1985), 483. A list of invitees is in UN Special Committee against Apartheid, Informational note on the International Seminar on Apartheid, in SNCC Papers, reel 52, frame 371.

obduracy. "We can no more speak in the United Nations, as was done before, of persuading the South African régime to abandon apartheid or dissuading it from racialism," the Guinean Achkar Marof, chair of the Special Committee, wrote. "That has proved to be impossible. We need to encourage world opinion to support democratic changes in South Africa and a reconstruction of its society by a revolutionary process."[7]

The growing understanding among Africans that South Africa was not susceptible to suasion or amenable to negotiation complemented the Pan-African strategy SNCC wished to follow. Forman noted in his account of the Kitwe meeting that SNCC had few illusions about the UN's power to effect real transformation. It nevertheless understood that the UN provided a useful arena to network and communicate SNCC's aims. "There were delegates and liberation fighters around the very large rectangular table who were going to hear and to transmit to their sisters and brothers some of the ideas we would present." As Forman delivered a paper that sociologist St. Clair Drake had helped him prepare, Newark and Detroit were engulfed in fiery insurrections from which they ultimately did not recover.[8] Incidents of civil unrest in the United States were not "riots," Forman told attendees. They were "rebellions against the enforced enslavement" of uprooted Africans. "SNCC has never visualized the struggle for human rights in America in isolation from the worldwide struggle for human rights," he asserted. Forman greeted "the Freedom Fighters who languish in prisons and detention camps of southern Africa," observing that "the cells of Robin Island and the Birmingham jail look the same on the inside." Forman judged Kitwe a success. SNCC had overcome the barriers erected to UN access by going abroad and approaching foreign leaders directly. It found a friend in Kenneth Kaunda, now president of Zambia, who proved a sympathetic ally of U.S. civil rights activists and an advocate of African-American voluntarism in Africa.[9]

SNCC, however, had Tanzania in its sights. Tanzania, though geographically distant from the West African origins of African Americans, crested in popularity among black nationalists and radicals in the mid-1960s. Its president, Julius Nyerere, was both Pan-Africanist and Christian. An ardent foe of colonialism, he hosted southern African liberation organizations. Tanzania's comparative lack of ethnic discord and a judiciously balanced position toward cold war conflicts had earlier recommended it to Washington policy makers,

[7] Enuga S. Reddy, "United Nations and the Struggle for Liberation in South Africa," at http://www.anc.org.za/docs/misc/1992/roadtodemocracyl.pdf, accessed May 25, 2011.

[8] Forman quoted in Vanessa Murphree, *The Selling of Civil Rights: The Student Nonviolent Coordinating Committee and the Use of Public Relations* (New York: Routledge, 2006), 139. Fanon Che Wilkins, "'In the Belly of the Beast': Black Power, Anti-imperialism, and the African Solidarity Movement, 1968–1975" (PhD diss., New York University, New York, 2001), pp. 58, 75, 76; Campus program meeting, February 16, 1967, in SNCC Papers, Series I, Chair Files, 1960–1969, reel 3.

[9] Forman, *The Making of Black Revolutionaries*, 483–92; Simeon Booker, "Don't Send 'Us Your Uncle Toms,'" *Jet*, February 8, 1968, pp. 14–17

FIGURE 9. Malcolm X, left, with Abdulrahman Mohamed Babu (1924–1996), a leader
of the Zanzibar revolution. (Getty Images)

who sent it one of the first Peace Corps delegations. Nyerere's desire to create a
non-Marxist African socialism attracted black diaspora nation builders.

Rebels on the island of Zanzibar off the Tanganyikan coast in 1964 over-
threw the ruling sultanate and accepted a union with independent Tanganyika,
thus creating the nation-state of Tanzania. Washington analysts interpreted the
Zanzibar revolution through a cold war lens, failing to understand the racial
and ethnic antagonisms that had long brewed on this "spice island" where
black Africans labored on clove plantations under the political and cultural
domination of Arabs originally from Oman. Centuries of racial mixture had
blurred sharp distinctions between the two groups somatically, but disparities
of power and the backward-looking character of the sultanate had sparked
revolt.[10]

Zanzibari revolutionists made the rounds of the socialist capitals, thus
tainting them in U.S. eyes. One Zanzibar radical in particular was popular
with African-American dissidents. At a New York City meeting of Malcolm
X's Organization of African American Unity in 1964, Malcolm introduced the
attendance to Abdul Rahman Babu. "Babu was like a street brother in terms
of his demeanor and comfort level," journalist Charles Simmons, who met

[10] Jonathon Glassman, *War of Words, War of Stone: Racial Thought and Violence in Colonial
Zanzibar* (Bloomington: Indiana University Press, 2011), 289–93.

him in Tanzania, recalled. "He was earthy"[11] (see Figure 9). After the fall of Nkrumah when Pan-Africanist energy shifted to Tanzania and its welcoming stance toward the black diaspora, Tanzania seemed poised to replace Ghana as a place of exile for North American expatriates.

SNCC's skills bank idea coincided with a policy shift in Tanzania. By 1966, the euphoria of independence had given way to individual countries' pursuing bureaucratic self-interest and competing with each other for foreign aid. The November 1966 summit meeting of African states failed to agree about a sum earmarked to support the liberation movements quartered in Dar es Salaam. Disgusted, "Tanzania walked out of the conference in protest," thereafter devoting more attention to internal matters than to Pan-African ventures.[12] Thwarted in his aim of pursuing development through Western and Eastern Bloc aid programs that had strings attached, President Julius Nyerere authored a statement in early February 1967 known as the Arusha Declaration. Issued at a meeting of the Tanzania National Union (TANU), his ruling political party, Nyerere used the pleasant highland city of Arusha to reaffirm the importance of farming and village life to Tanzania's development.

Tanzania must lift itself up by its bootstraps, Nyerere mandated. "It is stupid to rely on money as the major instrument of development when we know only too well that our country is poor," he asserted. "It is equally stupid, indeed it is even more stupid, for us to imagine that we shall rid ourselves of our poverty through foreign financial assistance rather than our own financial resources." Nyerere envisioned an agrarian socialist society partly based on collectivization. Under TANU's direction, citizens were to work harder, longer hours and make willing sacrifices so that the Ujamaa program, roughly "family togetherness" in Swahili, could succeed.[13]

Tanzania presented Ujamaa as the Africanization of socialism, predicating it on cultural patterns that privileged, rather than undermined, families and small communities. Citizens could help achieve national prosperity by viewing the nation as an extension of their own families, clans, and ethnic groups. "The development of a country is brought about by people, not by money," Nyerere argued.[14] He realized that, as much as the family would be a model of the nation, the role of women in traditional Tanzanian society did not fit them for the modernization efforts he had in mind. Nyerere accordingly founded a women's organization, Umoja wa Wanawake wa Tanzania (United Women of

[11] Author's interview with Charles Simmons, Detroit, August 15, 1998.

[12] E. J. Kisanga, "Tanzania and the Organisation of African Unity (O.A.U.)," in *The Making of Foreign Policy in Tanzania*, eds. K. Mathews and S. S. Mushi (Dar es Salaam: Tanzania Publishing House, 1981), 103. On the deficiencies of *Ujamaa*, see James Scott, *Seeing Like a State: How Certain Schemes to Improve the Human Condition Have Failed* (New Haven, Conn.: Yale University Press, 1998), chapter 7.

[13] Arusha Declaration. reprinted in *Africa Report*, March 1967, pp. 11–13.

[14] Ibid.; Republic of Tanzania. Study of the Rural Development Programme: Ujamaa Villages and Rural Development Staff of Tanga, Kilimanjaro, Arusha (Dar-es-Salaam: Ministry of Regional Administration and Rural Development 1970).

Tanzania), as a branch of TANU. UWT activists encouraged rural women in Ujamaa villages to participate in planning and decision making.[15]

Both Tanzanian leaders and radical diaspora nationalists situated their respective struggles in the context of anticolonial resistance, neocolonial domination, and racism. Citizenship framed Tanzanian efforts, but black nationalists in the United States did not envision black communities as junior partners in the framework of a white American national belonging. Black citizenship was differently imagined. In both cases, as Wahneema Lubiano observes, nationhood "reinscribes the state in particular places within its own narratives of resistance. That re-inscription most often coheres within black nationalist narratives of the black family."[16]

The Tanzanian model for enfranchising women while preserving the family metaphor and conflating it with political and economic transformation resonated with U.S. blacks who were skeptical of the emerging women's movement at home and believed it a potentially divisive factor in the battle for freedom. Joyce Ladner argued that Dar es Salaam's approach to the status of women precluded Western patterns of feminism. Instead, it prescribed gender complementarity. The creation of a gender-neutral modern citizenry based on equal rights, she believed, made it "not necessary to take up the 'Women's Lib' banner."[17] Tanzanian ideology found favor with many young African Americans. The country's aspirations in the face of Western repression dovetailed with similar disillusionment with the liberalism of U.S. elites. Black youth expressed a growing determination to redefine civil rights activity as Black Power initiative, based on a more thoroughgoing political, cultural, and psychological liberation of the folk.

Historical scholarship generally portrays such Pan-African initiatives as SNCC's as adventurist and ill conceived, but the record suggests that members thought deeply about what they proposed to undertake. They worried about duplicating the Peace Corps' mistakes and sending people to Tanzania whose mind-set reflected modernizationist dogma and other U.S. biases. Forman asserted the need to recruit the most qualified people. "He pointed out that any kind of international affairs program that SNCC has will be relevant only to the degree that SNCC is effective in the U.S."[18]

As SNCC's ventures in Africa began to undermine conventional assumptions about what kind of actors can make public policy and carry out activities

[15] Joyce Ladner, "Tanzanian Women and Nation Building," *The Black Scholar* 3 (4) (1971): 22–4.

[16] Wahneema Lubiano. "Standing in for the State: Black Nationalism and 'Writing' the Black Subject," in *Is It Nation Time? Contemporary Essays on Black Power and Black Nationalism*, ed. Eddie S. Glaude Jr. (Chicago: University of Chicago Press, 2002), 158; Celina Romany, "Women as Aliens: A Feminist Critique of the Public/Private Distinction in International Human Rights Law," *Harvard Human Rights Journal* 6 (1993): 101.

[17] Ladner, "Tanzanian Women and Nation Building," 28.

[18] Campus program meeting, February 16, 1967, in *SNCC Papers*, Chair Files, 1960–1969, reel 3.

traditionally assumed by a state, the sedate National Council of Negro Women (NCNW) began questioning its own genteel identity and mannerly modus operandi. In a draft working paper on international relations in 1960–1, the NCNW focused on the globalization of world culture, the growing number of UN member states, and the rise to sovereignty of people of color.[19]

At a meeting to assess NCNW's mission and future direction, one participant wanted the group to become more proactive in international affairs. The times called for global cooperation and a U.S foreign service that more closely reflected the nation's demography. "Many women who come from other countries say that they just get tired of sitting on platforms, eating lunches and sitting on daises; they want to meet people, be part of the problems and learn things," she asserted.[20] NCNW's prim president, Dorothy Height, echoed the sentiment. Height soon acknowledged that her outspoken opposition to the phrase "Black Power" meant little. "It didn't take long to realize that simply talking about bettering race relations – without fundamentally changing the power relationships – would not get us very far," she recalled. "We had been treating symptoms rather than causes. There were still major roadblocks to full equality, and a more direct approach was urgently needed."[21] The NCNW subsequently published a pamphlet called "Two Minutes to Midnight" that expressed its sense of alarm about the civil unrest sweeping U.S. cities in 1967. A copy of a telegram bound into the pamphlet called for an emergency meeting of all major black women's groups in late September to discuss the crisis that blacks were facing.[22] An official unemployment rate for nonwhites of 7.3 percent during an era of prosperity suggested that a nation obsessed with war and lunar exploration, and ignoring the most fundamental needs of its citizens, would have no peace.

The NCNW's alienation was not an unprecedented development. Every Western country has conventional organizations that unusual circumstances bring into dialogue with radicalism, even in epochs of ascendant conservatism and comparative prosperity. The United States has plural traditions, with African-American forms serving as transnational catalysts. In the sixties and later, "the political militancy of people of color and its centrality within the left and progressive imaginary," in Nikhil Pal Singh's words, suffused a growing sense of both crisis and identification. This was global and could express itself in cultural form. Film critic Manthia Diawara, recalling his boyhood in Mali, observed how youth in the capital city of Bamako cultivated African-American styles. "Deracinated from nation and tribe," they "were also showing their

[19] Working Paper on International Relations 1960–1961, NCNW Papers, Series 10, folder "International relations, 1960, 1965–66," Bethune Museum and Archives, Washington D.C.
[20] Notes from the July 1966 meeting of the National Council of Negro Women at Capahosic, NCNW Papers, Series 10, Box 9, Folder 6.
[21] Dorothy Height, *Open Wide the Freedom Gates: A Memoir* (New York: Public Affairs, 2003), 151.
[22] "Two Minutes to Midnight," Series 10, Box 9, NCNW Papers; "Women Meet on Crises in Black Community," *Chicago Daily Defender*, October 30, 1967, p. 17.

belonging to Pan-Africanism and the African Diaspora." Whatever the frivolity and decadence of a commodified "Afropop" international culture, Bamako youth found that the dour nation-state, overlaid with both Muslim and Marxist austerity, failed to produce joy.[23]

Links to the world community reflected the increasing view that black people's needs were distinct from what passed as the U.S. "national interest." Following the logic of Malcolm X's emphasis on human rather than civil rights, a Black Panther Party delegation, presenting African Americans as colonial subjects, appeared at the UN to petition as the Civil Rights Congress and the NAACP had years before. Delegates claimed that racial oppression in the United States constituted a human rights violation that should evoke international concern. The Panthers' "Ten-Point Platform" called for a UN-sponsored referendum in which black Americans would determine whether they wished to remain U.S. citizens or have a homeland set aside for them. The party had toyed with the idea of offering this choice to whites, allowing them to remain Americans or accept nationality in a state controlled by blacks.[24] Embedded in what seemed to many an outlandish idea is the fact that after emancipation, the freed people were never given a choice as to their citizenship; nor was the white electorate consulted on the matter. If the idea of whites' agreeing to be a minority in a black-controlled state was ludicrous, no less unfounded was the notion of blacks' agreeing to minority status in one run by whites. The Panthers' logic exposed the shaky grounds upon which U.S. citizenship had been predicated. Such ideas advanced a growing sense among many African Americans – and not only leftists – that U.S. priorities at home and abroad were strangling black communities.

The Vietnam War furthered the approach of seeking foreign support for black goals. Western Europeans had long harbored anxieties about being the battleground upon which Soviet-American hostilities would be fought out. Former British prime minister Clement Attlee as early as 1948 advocated that Britain position itself as an alternative to Stalinism and the United States' seemingly unbridled capitalism.[25] The abiding concern of Europeans with peace and the existence in Western Europe of a mature infrastructure of linked organizations provided aid for an array of black liberation support and war resisters groups. Swedish activists consolidated their efforts in 1967 with the creation

---

[23] Manthia Diawara. "The 1960s in Bamako: Malick Sidibé and James Brown," in *Everything but the Burden: What White People Are Taking from Black Culture*, ed. Greg Tate (New York: Broadway Books, Random House, 2003), 189–90.

[24] Bobby Seale, *Seize the Time: The Story of the Black Panther Party and Huey P. Newton* (Baltimore: Black Classic Press, 1991), 66; Eldridge Cleaver interviewed by Henry Louis Gates in *Target Zero: A Life in Writing*, ed. Kathleen Cleaver (New York: Palgrave Macmillan, 2006), 257; Jennifer B. Smith, *An International History of the Black Panther Party* (New York: Garland, 1999), 68, 63.

[25] Marc J. Selverstone, *Constructing the Monolith: The United States, Great Britain, and International Communism, 1945–1950* (Cambridge, Mass.: Harvard University Press, 2009), 79.

of the United National Liberation Front Groups of Sweden (UNLF). This umbrella organization derived from antinuclear activism. The Swedish government had misgivings about the peace movement, but future prime minister Olof Palme, in early 1968 minister of education, participated in it, much to the consternation of conservatives in Stockholm and Washington, D.C. GIs who defected to Sweden were accorded residence on "humanitarian grounds" and provided with housing and a living allowance.[26] U.S. antiwar groups operated from Scandinavian countries. The American Deserters Committee published a broadside that instructed those contemplating going AWOL how to avoid getting caught and informing them how to find its field offices and liaisons in Denmark, Sweden, and elsewhere. Black soldiers formed their own Afro-American Deserters Committee, which combined resistance to racism in civil society and in the military with antiwar work.

European receptivity to African-American activism owes a debt to how Western Europeans parsed their own situation. Interest in African-American political agendas derived in part from an ongoing conversation among social movements across a spectrum from center to Left, and across oceans. As Doug McAdam has noted, "established organizations/networks are themselves embedded in long-standing activist subcultures" that "function as repositories of cultural materials." "Succeeding generations of activists" thus learn from past struggles and choose, discard, or revise what history has to offer. Movements created out of specific conditions in particular countries can also resonate with the national experience of people in other places. "If it was once sufficient to interpret or predict social movements around the shape of the nation state, it is less and less possible to do so today," Sidney Tarrow observes.[27]

After the Allied victory in World War II, the United States installed a Pax Americana in Western Europe and entered into an uneasy truce with the Soviets in which both powers grudgingly tolerated the existence of their respective spheres of influence but never acknowledged the legitimacy of each other's claims to domination. Neither was above searching for opportunities to undermine the troubled modus vivendi that prevailed for the next forty-four years. Nations under U.S. protection thus recovered from the war under the shadow of juggernauts and faced the real possibility that war could resume. The existence of nuclear arms enhanced feelings of insecurity among states caught in the middle. Secrecy accompanying the development of atomic weaponry and the exclusion of mass publics from debate about security issues also raised questions about the extent and strength of democracy. The exigencies of postwar reconstruction and sentiments of gratitude toward the United States for such programs as the Marshall Plan initially muted some of the fears.

---

[26] Carl-Gustaf Scott "Swedish Sanctuary of American Deserters during the Vietnam War: A Facet of Social Democratic Domestic Politics," *Scandinavian Journal of History* 26 (2) (2001): 123–42.

[27] Sidney Tarrow, "States and Opportunities: The Political Structuring of Social Movements," in *Comparative Perspective on Social Movements*, eds. Doug McAdam, John D. McCarthy, and Mayer N. Zald (Cambridge University Press, 1996): 53.

The restoration of prosperity, beginning in the 1950s, revived the desires of many Europeans for a more coherent and independent sense of national identity. Some questioned whether the interminable cold war standoff was having a deleterious effect on the future of their countries and began to suggest that security did not always mean compliance with U.S. and Soviet agendas. Roosevelt and Stalin had carved up Europe at the Yalta Conference in 1945, some reasoned, and neither had European interests at heart. The remedy, then, was to create a foreign policy for the continent that restrained its American and Soviet overlords and reaffirmed the identity and integrity of each country. A European "third way" would evaluate cold war policies on the merits of their overall impact, not solely in terms of their benefit to the superpowers.

The peace issue forged a harmony of interests among European and African-American activists and underlay the protest campaigns of the late 1960s. Europe had twice come close to self-annihilation during the twentieth century as global wars toppled governments and caused the deaths of millions. The problem of war and a sense of the helplessness of being wedged between two superpowers capable of mass destruction heightened sensitivities. Scholars frequently depict the antiwar movement as a campaign of youth, but many Europeans old enough to have lived through World War II endorsed its goals. When black dissidents arrived in Europe with a message that linked racial justice to peace, they often found receptive audiences. Governments inadvertently aided this process when they failed to resolve critical social and political problems within the scope of what they themselves considered legitimate. In the United States, in spite of the nonviolent movement's achievement of civil rights legislation, many black communities remained impoverished and racists learned clever ways to skirt the law.

Yet Europeans did not have to rely on the witness of American expatriates and visitors. Exchange students observed U.S. conditions firsthand. In 1948 Olof Palme, then a student, spent a summer hitchhiking in thirty-four states, encountering local racial customs in his sojourn through the South.[28] British students in America with travel money from the Harkness Foundation in the early sixties went to Montgomery, Alabama, where they visited Clifford and Virginia Durr, a white couple active in civil rights work there. Federal agents followed foreign students who visited the Durrs, but that did not prevent networking. Through the agency of one, Anthony Lester, Clifford Durr received an invitation to speak in London. Lester had joined a fledgling organization that investigated human rights abuses: Amnesty International, for which he journeyed to Mississippi in the summer of 1964 to draft a report. Jonathan

---

[28] Anthony Lewis, "Obedience or Candor between Friends?" *New York Times*, October 5, 1969, p. E12; *American Students Organize: Founding the National Student Association after World War II*, ed. Eugene G. Schwartz (Westport, Conn.: American Council on Education/Praeger Publishers, 2006), 532. See also the account of German student experience in Maria Höhn and Martin Klimke, *A Breath of Freedom: The Civil Rights Struggle, African American GIs, and Germany* (New York: Palgrave Macmillan, 2010), 108, 111.

Steele, another Briton who had stayed with the Durrs, participated in a voter registration campaign in Mississippi.[29] British students were not alone in assessing the American situation and taking an active part in social and political change away from their homes. Three Germans who played significant roles in the era's radical politics had traveled to the United States as exchange students. One, Karl-Dietrich Wolff, returned to Germany and helped raise funds to defend Black Panther Bobby Seale, who was accused of inciting a riot at the 1968 Chicago Democratic Party convention.[30]

European student contact with Americans during the height of the Vietnam War demonstrates the salience of peace as a motivating issue. Vietnam did not only impress European critics as a moral issue; it also revived the possibility of Soviet intervention and thus a conflagration that could bring down the stable order in Europe. Antiwar activity followed that reasoning. Support for soldiers who began deserting the U.S. military in significant numbers by 1967, being clandestine, often eludes the record. Organizations operating in Europe with a network of local collaborators spirited deserters to locations in Scandinavia, France, and elsewhere. Participants in this underground railroad included persons across the center-to-Left political spectrum, from Protestant clergy to erstwhile apolitical youth social clubs. Sometimes antiwar efforts reached fantastic extremes, as when a faction of the German student group Sozialistische Deutsche Studentenbund (SDS) planned to march to a U.S. military base near Berlin where they would "storm the barracks" in coordination with a group of Panther-affiliated soldiers who would stage a simultaneous mutiny. The plot was discovered and called off, however, when U.S. authorities announced that military police would shoot anyone invading the premises. More often resistance took the form of steady and determined opposition to the war, reflected in proliferating disobedience among U.S. troops.[31]

The transatlantic activism of the period contrasts significantly with earlier European engagements with the black diaspora. Europeans learned from the freedom struggles waged by African Americans in the second half of the twentieth century in political as well as cultural ways. What they absorbed from their knowledge of African-American insurgencies and their exposure to specific individuals, organizations, and movements was often indirect, filtered through discourses about politics and ethics, decolonization, and especially through local traditions of peace and antinuclear organizing. At the same time, Europeans retained significant ambivalence about race, especially in the context

[29] Virginia Foster Durr, *Freedom Writer: Letters from the Civil Rights Years*, ed. Patricia Sullivan (New York: Routledge, 2003), 234, 301, 308–9, 312, 220–1; 63. Doug McAdam and Dieter Rucht, "The Cross-National Diffusion of Movement Ideas," *Annals of the American Academy of Political and Social Science* 528 (July 1993): 70, 71.

[30] Höhn and Klimke, *A Breath of Freedom*, 108, 111, 114, 116.

[31] Nick Thomas, *Protest Movements in 1960s West Germany* (Oxford and New York: Berg, 2003), 159; "Max," "Problems of the GI Resistance in Europe," Michele Gibault Papers, Wisconsin Historical Society, folder 12.

of increased immigration of people of color after World War II, and specifically about African Americans, often seen simultaneously as victims of oppression and as examples of a debased American popular culture. A combination of doubt and expectation attends the contours and limits of African-American and European shared perspectives. Mixed feelings complicate discussions of connections that emphasize the therapeutic effects that freedom from Jim Crow had on black Americans fortunate enough to cross the Atlantic and live life in countries where race was not all-consuming.

It is important to emphasize that the civil rights and Black Power movements also provoked debate and action that European protagonists used to interpret and alter conditions in their own countries. Emphasis on culture has all too often suggested a one-way exchange, with blacks the net beneficiaries of European benevolence. As Yohuru Williams has observed, one common conception of black movements renders them "the product of foreign influences that extended from Marcus Garvey and Frantz Fanon to Che Guevara and Mao Tse-tung. Such images create the impression that African–Americans were greatly influenced by foreign contacts with little impact or contribution of their own."[32] A closer look at the connection between African Americans and Europeans reveals a richer and more nuanced set of relationships.

One such link relates to black protesters' efforts to get their message across. Popular pressure from European dissidents was sometimes successful in countering ministries' efforts to appease the United States by refusing entry to American dissenters. Stokely Carmichael, for example, was detained at Orly Airport. He had gone to France to attend an antiwar demonstration in Paris in December 1967. He spent the night on an airport bench, debating whether to return home, where he faced passport revocation because of his travel to Cuba and North Vietnam. In a sudden reversal, the French government cleared Carmichael for entry after a formal protest by the demonstration sponsor. The Vietnam National Committee reminded French officials of how Malcolm X had been barred under similar circumstances.[33]

France deported foreign dissidents known to have taken part in its own domestic turmoil in May 1968, and those remaining had to sign agreements that they would refrain from political activity. At Washington's request, the Ministry of the Interior banned the Paris American Committee to Stop the War, which found lodgings and work for resisters and deserters. Paris, shaken by the rebellion of French workers and students, and roiled by a run on the franc, yielded to U.S. pressure. France and Sweden barred the militant Robert F. Williams from entry. Germany kept Black Panther Eldridge Cleaver out because of his indictment for an extraditable crime in the United States. German, French, and

---

[32] Yohuru R. Williams, "American Exported Black Nationalism: The Student Nonviolent Coordinating Committee, the Black Panther Party, and the Worldwide Freedom Struggle 1967–1972," *Negro History Bulletin* 60 (July–September 1997): 1–13.

[33] "Paris Officials Intervene, Allow Carmichael Entry," *Chicago Daily Defender*, December 7, 1967, p. 19.

Danish officials extended the ban to his wife, Kathleen, even though she had no charges pending against her.[34]

Individuals might freely accuse their home countries of violating citizens' human rights, but governments faced constraints. Canada sheltered as many as thirty thousand U.S. deserters and men refusing the draft but made no official acknowledgment of the fact. Yet Sweden's hosting of far fewer offended Washington. In addition to the growing deserter population, Swedish money supported an information center for the Vietnamese National Liberation Front. Stockholm's January 1969 recognition of Hanoi further heightened tensions with the United States, which recalled its ambassador. South Carolina Senator Strom Thurmond urged sanctions against Sweden for aiding the enemy.[35]

As the U.S. presence in Vietnam neared the end of its second decade, military base society showed signs of strain. The armed services officially desegregated during the Truman era, but racism lingered on as a reflection of both senior brass values and attitudes at large in civilian society. The long era in which African Americans viewed military service favorably seemed to be closing, in spite of high black reenlistment rates. West Germany, where the United States had its largest defense installations in Europe, had been a hotbed of prejudice since the end of the postwar occupation. In addition to a segregated social life, housing discrimination, and unfairness in military justice, black soldiers were likely to incur the sporadic hostility of assorted American Nazis and Klansmen. Racial violence among Americans escalated in Vietnam, including a major disturbance in the brig at Long Binh. Conflicts also occurred away from the major theater of war, with outbreaks in Hawaii and North Carolina.[36]

In fiscal 1971, 98,324 U.S soldiers deserted, averaging a rate of more than 14 percent of active duty troops. Those who did not go AWOL were increasingly exposed to antiwar activism within the armed forces. The army initially tried to stop GI organizing through heavy-handed repression, but when it allowed troops to hold meetings, publish papers, and join dissident organizations, hundreds of ephemeral newspapers, newsletters, and pamphlets urging opposition to war and racism flourished. A mutiny in the Seventh Army caused the cancellation of the trial of fifty-three black soldiers in Darmstadt, West Germany, in October 1971. Black troops saw the problems in the military as complementing those in civilian life. They protested unequal treatment and lack of opportunities for promotion. Shipboard mutinies took place in the Pacific during the early 1970s as black sailors flatly refused to follow orders

---

[34] "Les Exiles Américains," September 1973, folder 2, and anonymous report, folder 12, Gilbaud Papers.

[35] H. Bruce Franklin, "The Antiwar Movement We Are Supposed to Forget," *Chronicle of Higher Education*, October 20, 2000, B10; John M. Lee, "U. S. Unpopularity in Sweden Has Eased but Remains High," *New York Times*, October 20, 1968, p. 6; Scott, "Swedish Sanctuary of American Deserters during the Vietnam War," 139–40.

[36] Wilkins, "In the Belly of the Beast," 152–6.

and engaged in pitched battles with other sailors and marines. News of these encounters spread via ship radio and multiplied accordingly.[37]

While many Europeans viewed politicized American soldiers sympathetically, others were less friendly. France had never been wholly hospitable to the deserters and resisters, who after 1968 decamped to Sweden. French anti-Americanism limited contacts between rebellious students and the GI population in France. Many American soldiers were newcomers to the political sophistication that percolated among many Europeans in their age cohort. According to "Max," identified by his first name in the reports emanating from the Quaker Centre in Paris, "the [U.S.] Army ... now concentrates its fire on a weak but essential link: the link between the GI and civilian population." Class and the "cultural/language barrier" often separated an educated European anti-war population from the working-class Americans most likely to be drafted.[38]

In Germany, where well-organized antiwar efforts had begun in 1967, it took a while for students to switch their slogan from "'Down with GI Murderers' to one of cooperation with soldiers who were increasingly anti-war." Many of the soldiers themselves objected to the left-wing aggressiveness of German students. During the antiwar march where plans to storm the U.S. military base were foiled, German protesters attempted to seize scaffolding erected by construction workers to use as platforms for rally speakers. The workers resisted by burning the demonstrators' picket signs. The result was a free-for-all, pitching students against workers. This scenario echoed similar conflicts between antiwar progressives and "hard hats" in the United States. The inability of the antiwar movement to close the class gap constituted one of its most haunting failures.[39]

Swedish activists began to resent the seeming apathy of American military refugees. "Most deserters were not political enough to meet the demands of the Swedish left," one historian claims. "In fact, the majority showed little interest in politics. As a result, a substantial number of those who had originally embraced the deserters grew progressively disillusioned, eventually turning their backs on the exiles."[40] In this climate, the black U.S. ambassador, Jerome Holland, was booed when he presented his credentials to the Swedish king. Angered by Sweden's antiwar politics, the Nixon administration had left the ambassadorial post vacant for fourteen months. Holland, conservative by the standards of the era, had the task of reviving and lubricating Swedish-American relations. Incidents in which he was called a nigger led the

[37] "Les Exiles Américains," and clipping from anonymous broadside, "Sailors Show How to Fight Back," Gilbaud Papers; "American Sailors Seek Political Asylum in Sweden," *Atlanta Daily World*, January 2, 1968, p. 4.

[38] Robert G. Weisbord, "Scandinavia: A Racial Utopia?" *Journal of Black Studies* 2 (June 1972): 481; Werner Zwick, "Black G.I. Who Fled to Sweden Gets 4 Months," *Chicago Daily Defender* (weekend ed.), April 6, 1968, p. 3A.

[39] "Max," Report on the GI Movement in Europe; Thomas, *Protest Movements in 1960s West Germany*, 159.

[40] Scott, "Swedish Sanctuary of American Deserters," 136.

Swedish Foreign Ministry to issue an apology. It was never clear, however, who was doing the name calling; certain African Americans on the scene appeared to be involved.[41] In any case, Holland bore the brunt of opposition to U.S. foreign policy. In a move perhaps designed to counter Eldredge Cleaver's book *Soul on Ice*, which had been translated into Danish, Holland's book, *Black Opportunity*, an upbeat, business-oriented appraisal of black life in America, was translated into Swedish.[42]

Europeans and white Americans were often receptive to African and diaspora music, literature, and art, especially if no politics were interjected. They could enjoy arts festivals, painting exhibits, jazz concerts, and the like, without understanding that participants in these events and their audiences did not necessarily share benefactors' perspectives. State Department cultural attachés promoted the view, according to Penny Von Eschen, "that jazz embodied a race-neutral expression of American freedom." This "clashed with the musicians' belief that jazz was deeply embedded in African American history and culture." The disparity became especially evident later when gospel and R & B groups toured. In spite of official efforts, foreign audiences never received a culturally neutral, raceless view of the United States through musical genres that so plainly spoke of the sufferings, passions, and preoccupations of blacks.[43]

Some scholars express skepticism about the significance of contacts between black activists and their European counterparts, as well as doubts about the extent of African-American politicization generally. "Black radicals ... tried to make the international connection by linking their fight to the world-wide struggle being waged by the poor and oppressed against imperialism," Manfred Berg writes. "Beyond the exchange of solidarity addresses and the granting of exile," Berg found little to indicate that black insurgency was "influenced by international developments."[44] Berg and other writers have looked in the wrong places for evidence.

Marxist scholars began addressing the status of African Americans in the 1920s. Soviet statism, the defects of the American Communist Party, and anticommunist repression limited Marxist influence on African Americans outside radical circles. By the 1960s, efforts to grapple with the elusive goal of

---

[41] On this subject see Edward Burton, "Racism on the Palace Steps?" *Scandinavian Journal of History* 34 (June 2009): 121–34; Fredrik Logevall, "The Swedish American Conflict over Vietnam," *Diplomatic History* (June 1993): 438–9, 438 n. 52; Ruth Link, "Ambassador Holland and the Swedes," *The Crisis* 78 (March 1971): 43–7.

[42] Jerome H. Holland, *Black Opportunity* (New York: Weybright and Talley, 1969); Weisbord, "Scandinavia: A Racial Utopia?" 484–5.

[43] Penny Von Eschen. *Satchmo Blows Up the World* (Cambridge, Mass.: Harvard University Press, 2004), 160–1, 168.

[44] Manfred Berg, "1968: A Turning Point in American Race Relations?" in *1968: The World Transformed*, eds. Carole Fink, Philipp Gassert, and Detlef Junker (Washington, D.C.: The German Historical Institute and Cambridge University Press, 1998), 400. See also Piero Gleijeses, *Conflicting Missions: Havana, Washington, and Africa, 1959–1976* (Chapel Hill: University of North Carolina Press, 2002), 364, 365, 381–2. Gleijeses claims that African Americans were indifferent to African issues before the 1975 Angolan conflict.

freedom and prosperity for African peoples motivated some black intellectuals to address issues of political and economic power directly in the present.
Marxism had provided tools for such analyses, but the cold war binary and
distrust of "white" scholarship and the white Left made these suspect, particularly in nationalist quarters. Not until the next decade would Marxism make
substantial inroads among black activists.

Elites sought validation of prevailing paradigms, such as the liberal universalism that for half a century suppressed a consciousness of the foundational
role of race in U.S. society and inhibited the evolution of race theory. By the
late 1960s, however, many thinkers began to reject the restrictions imposed
by positivist and consensus models. Harold Cruse damned what he saw as the
African-American intelligentsia's blinkered vision in his 1967 bombshell, *The
Crisis of the Negro Intellectual*.[45] In this widely read – and maligned – screed,
Cruse castigated what he considered the ignorance and irresponsibility of black
leaders, artists, and writers, and their failure to understand the cultural roots
of power in America.

The failure to resolve the problems of racism and injustice revived an interest in Marxist prescriptions for the ills of capitalist society. This, Cruse insisted,
led to error. Marxism could not explain why the American system did not function the way Marx claimed it should. Racism gave the lie to proletarian solidarity. Indeed, he argued, blacks and communists were in a similar bind: reds
have a theory and no movement, and blacks have a movement and no theory.
Every revolution since 1917, Cruse emphasized, emerged from rural societies deemed backward while the Western proletariat has become progressively
"conservative" and "pro-imperialist." It is un-Marxian not to accept what is
clearly observable in society, and if we accept the dialectic "that everything in
society is subject to change," Cruse posited, then we must also accept that the
role attributed to the white working class as historic vanguard can also change.
It "has abandoned the Marxian 'historical role' assigned to it." Cruse also took
issue with the idea of a proletarian historical mission, perceiving it as not too
distant from the notion of the white man's burden. "They cannot let go of
the idée fixe of the white working class 'saving' the world's humanity." "They
talk 'revolution' but revolution is being made by others." The passing of the
torch to non-European peoples thus introduced race, which Marxists had not
theorized,[46] into the equation.

Cruse had gone to Cuba in 1960 and described his visit as "one of the most
inspiring experiences I have ever had." He "suggested that black activists in
America were in need of an indigenous political orientation, similar to what
was occurring in Cuba yet unique to black American history and culture."
In line with his view of Harlem as the central site of African-American cultural and political achievement, he identified the terrain of struggle with the

45 Harold Cruse, *The Crisis of the Negro Intellectual* (New York: Morrow, 1967).
46 Harold Cruse, "Marxism and the Negro," part 1, *Liberator* 4 (May 1964): 8–11; "Marxism and
    the Negro," part 2, ibid., 4 (June 1964): 18.

urban location of African Americans. Cruse would observe that as long ago as 1930, James Weldon Johnson, in his depression era account of Harlem, *Black Manhattan*, discussed whether blacks could hold on to their stake in the cities. The view that an urban geographic position was strategically valuable became central to emerging Black Power thought.[47]

This theme also emerges in the work of psychologist Kenneth Clark, who is not generally perceived as militant or as a nationalist. Most famous for the "doll studies" that influenced the 1954 Supreme Court decision in *Brown v. Board of Education*, Clark had other accomplishments. He founded the Northside Center, a facility for treating psychiatric and behavioral disorders and delinquency in Harlem children. Clark's work on the inferiority complex and on pathology in black communities assigned only structural blame to whites for the plight of African Americans. The U.S. State Department considered him so moderate a figure that it proposed him for membership on a presidential commission to study how African countries could accelerate education and technical advancement.[48]

When New York City gave the Jewish Board of Guardians a grant to do social work in Harlem, however, Clark expressed his resentment of the slighting of Northside in favor of a charity with no ties to the neighborhood. It was "social work colonialism," he maintained. Clark's books, *Youth in the Ghetto* (1964) and *Dark Ghetto* (1965), depicted Harlem as locked out of the richer aspects of urban life. *Youth in the Ghetto* called for millions of dollars in recuperative assistance to Harlem youth and "involvement of the poor at decision-making levels in any ameliorative effort on their behalf." The study became the basis for one of the most ambitious antipoverty programs of the 1960s, Harlem Youth Opportunities Unlimited (HARYOU). *Dark Ghetto* described Harlem as "a philanthropic, economic, business, and industrial colony of New York City." Harlemites did not appreciate charity, he asserted. Those interviewed during the "riot" of 1964 expressed the same "bitter" feelings that "natives often feel toward the functionaries of a colonial power who, in the very act of service, keep the hated structure of oppression intact."[49] In spite of his conservative reputation, Clark maintained cordial relations with another Harlem personality, Malcolm X, who sometimes visited Northside Center. The psychologist

---

[47] Cruse quoted in Peniel E. Joseph, *Waiting 'Til the Midnight Hour': A Narrative History of Black Power in America* (New York: Henry Holt, 2006), 31. Harold Cruse, "Black and White: Outlines of the Next Stage," *Black World* 20 (May 1971): 22–3. See also Locksley Edmondson, "Black America as a Mobilizing Diaspora: Some International Implications," in *Modern Diaspora in International Politics*, ed. Gabriel Sheffer (London & Sydney: Croom Helm, 1986), 164–211.

[48] Kenneth Clark interviewed by Ed Edwin, March 19, 1976, Columbia University Oral History Collection; Department of State, "Congo Crisis and Establishment of a U.S. Commission to Aid in the Training and Education of African People to Take Over Leadership and Administration of New African Nations," DDRS.

[49] Kenneth Clark, *Dark Ghetto* (New York: Harper & Row, 1965), 174, 28; Clark interview, March 19, 1976.

ultimately retained faith in the capacity of U.S. society to respond positively to the needs of the urban poor. In that sense, his invocation of the colonial analogy differed substantially from that of Cruse. His understanding of the black condition in the cities nevertheless encouraged other analysts to develop more radical critiques.

One such thinker was James Boggs, a Detroit autoworker and socialist. In a 1965 essay called "The City Is the Black Man's Land," Boggs located the urban plat as the site of struggle against discrimination and poverty. "Since blacks became a majority in the inner-city population," he claimed, "they are now in line to assume the political leadership of the cities in accordance with the historical tradition whereby the largest ethnic minorities have successively dominated politics and civil service jobs in municipalities. The city is now the black man's land, and the city is also the place where the nation's most critical problems are concentrated." Boggs noted the historic white opposition to black urban empowerment as manifested through slum clearance schemes, gerrymandering, and the appointment of African-American officials answerable to political machines rather than to their constituents. Just as those recovering from colonialism in emerging countries need help, he argued, so do inner-city residents. Yet top-down direction in the War on Poverty does not work, Boggs asserted, because it "is essentially a program to keep the poor out of the political arena ... and to train them" for work that is becoming outmoded. Consequently, displaced and unemployed "black youths are sent as cannon fodder to die in the counter-revolutionary wars which the United States is carrying on all over the world as it replaces the old European colonial powers. Today the sun never sets on an American Empire which maintains bases in at least fifty-five different worldwide locations."[50]

Boggs understood that there would be resistance to blacks' climbing the socioeconomic ladder as ethnic whites had done. They would therefore have to break with normal politics and seize the cities through revolutionary means. Urban power meant radical change in the distribution of goods and services and the expropriation of property holders in spite of the overwhelming potential of the state to inflict violence on insurgents.[51]

Those American radicals interested in the Chinese revolution and Mao Tse-tung thought they could avail themselves of a Chinese version of the colonial model. According to Steven F. Jackson, China's "strategic doctrine of 'People's War' ... held that the advanced industrial nations constituted the 'cities' of the world, and the poor nations of Asia, Africa and Latin America were the 'countryside.' By fomenting revolution in the various 'rural' areas of

[50] James Boggs, *Racism and the Class Struggle: Further Pages from a Black Worker's Notebook* (New York: Monthly Review Press, 1970), 57, 39–40, 42–3.

[51] Stephen Michael Ward, "'Ours Too Was a Struggle for a Better World': Activist Intellectuals and the Radical Promise of the Black Power Movement, 1962–1972," PhD diss., University of Texas, Austin, 2002.

the world, eventually the liberation movements would surround and overrun the urban areas, just as they had in China during its civil war."[52]

Interest in Maoism crested during the period of the Great Proletarian Cultural Revolution in China, whose brutal reality China's sympathizers never understood. Though associated with the Red Guard rebel youth of the 1960s, the purging of bourgeois elements had its ideological origins in the Yenan period of Chinese communist internal exile. The Yenan epoch colored the graphical imagination of Black Panther artist Emory Douglas. Later, Panthers sold the little books of Mao's aphorisms, emulated by the exiled Nkrumah in 1969. The Cultural Revolution's excesses, however, led to the discrediting of Maoism in China itself.[53]

Though arguably one of the more isolated of the revolutionary societies, China became a template for certain insurgents. Its attractiveness lay in its claim to empower the masses while modernization was occurring. Rather than passive recipients of change, the Chinese people were pictured as independent and in control of the development process. They would improve the economy and world standing of their country through their own efforts, without embracing decadent Western values. In milieus where examples of struggle were fervently studied, China stood as a model nation.[54]

By 1970, however, Black Panther theorist Huey Newton was having second thoughts about nation-states. He proposed recognizing an expanded set of groups to whom the colonial model applied. Newton now saw imperialism as so lethal as to have emptied nationalism of meaningful content. "Every nation of the world has been violated by the ruling circle of North America, and every nation has thus been transformed. They are no longer nations," he told a Boston College audience in November 1970. Liberation for the oppressed required a new axis of identification. What Newton called intercommunalism was a transnational diaspora of oppressed peoples. He had elaborated on this theme at the ambitious Revolutionary People's Constitutional Convention weeks earlier. That assembly aimed to promote the unification of the U.S. Left by bringing together Black Power, feminist, and gay and lesbian organizations.[55]

Even as analogies between African Americans and colonized subjects were debated, those parts of the federal government most concerned with foreign

[52] Randall B. Woods, "The Politics of Idealism: Lyndon Johnson, Civil Rights, and Vietnam," *Diplomatic History* 31 (January 2007): 1–18; Steven F. Jackson, "China's Third World Foreign Policy: The Case of Angola and Mozambique," *China Quarterly* 142 (1995): 396.

[53] Andrew Ross, "Mao Zedong's Impact on Cultural Politics in the West," *Cultural Politics* 1 (March 2005): 5–22. See also Robin D. G. Kelley and Betsy Esch, "Black like Mao: Red China and Black Revolution," *Souls* 1 (Fall 1999): 6–41.

[54] Arif Dirlik, "The Third World," in *1968: The World Transformed*, eds. Carole Fink, Philipp Gassert and Detlef Junker (Washington D.C. and Cambridge, UK: German Historical Institute and Cambridge University Press, 1998), 300, 301.

[55] Garrett Epps, "Huey Newton Speaks at Boston College, Presents Theory of 'Intercommunalism,'" *Harvard Crimson*, November 19, 1970, accessed on-line; Judson L. Jeffries, *Huey P. Newton: The Radical Theorist* (Jackson, Miss.: University of Mississippi Press, 2002), 78–82.

affairs distanced themselves from interpretations that made race legible as a factor in U.S. life and available as a way to infuse struggles over rights with global meaning. It is not likely that officials always understood how a transnational interpretation of race could alter customary thinking about power. They failed to recognize, for example, that the United States' racist culture was rather singular in the world community and served as a deterrent to the creation of sound urban policies, with profound consequences for both the civil society and the political economy.[56] They did have an inkling, however, that racial consciousness clashed with the national habit of suppressing knowledge about domination. They accordingly dissuaded emergent Caribbean labor politicians from networking with American radicals and tried to keep foreign diplomats of color unaware of racial dynamics in U.S. society. George Kennan recalled that when he "was in the State Department we used to have to maintain a special agency in Miami to keep Latin American diplomats from getting hotel rooms there and to urge them to get aboard the next plane to Washington." In the years preceding Congolese independence, African Americans found themselves barred from entering the Congo. While Brussels issued the ban, it was Washington that feared that black Americans could dangerously "whet the appetite for Independence."[57]

Government officials met efforts to desegregate the Foreign Service with the caveat that other countries, including Caribbean and African ones, did not wish to receive black ambassadors. Africans, especially, they cautioned, considered the posting of a black ambassador insulting, as it suggested that Washington was ghettoizing them by sending someone viewed as second rate. Historian Michael Krenn asked former ambassador Terence Todman, an African American, about this issue. Todman, a veteran of lengthy service in the diplomatic corps, told Krenn, "I am prepared to say that that business about not being able to send [African Americans] was purely concocted within the State Department. It was made out of whole cloth. It was a total lie.... The problem has been, and is, in the United States of America."[58] The desire to suppress any independent, ethnic black voice in foreign policy synchronized with the strategy of denying the salience of race as a factor in American life. Pressure to acknowledge that salience would nevertheless increase.

Federal authorities, while dismissing the colonial model, set out to quell urban unrest with military help. The army became more active in Stateside intelligence gathering, comprising a workforce larger than either the FBI or the

---

[56] On this subject, see Robert A. Beauregard, *Voices of Decline: The Postwar Fate of U.S. Cities* (New York: Routledge, 2003).

[57] Cary Fraser, *Ambivalent Anti-Colonialism: The United States and the Genesis of West Indian Independence, 1940–1964* (Westport, Conn.: Greenwood Press, 1994), 114–15; Kennan quoted in Cyrus L. Sulzberger, *The Last of the Giants* (New York: Macmillan, 1970), 313; Stephen R. Weissman, *American Foreign Policy in the Congo, 1960–1964* (Ithaca, N.Y.: Cornell University Press, 1974), 44.

[58] Michael L. Krenn, *Black Diplomacy: African Americans and the State Department, 1945–1969* (Armonk, N.Y.: M. E. Sharpe, 1998), 52, 126.

Secret Service. Its domestic surveillance activities, which date to World War I, were stepped up to meet the challenges that dissent posed for military recruiting and combat. It began collecting information about black communities at least by 1966 and accelerated this task after September 1967, when former deputy defense secretary Cyrus Vance called for data that could predict the onset of riots. As a result of the comparative ease of conducting intelligence operations at home the Counter Intelligence Analysis Branch (CIAB) created domestic dossiers thicker than its foreign military files.[59] Young soldiers could readily pass as students and report on dissident organizations. The lack of a student privacy law before 1974 gave the military access to academic records.[60]

Army officials tended to view racial unrest in martial terms and used counterinsurgency metaphors. "Looters were a kind of 'enemy' and marching protesters 'dissident forces.'" One critic commented that "the Army's domestic intelligence machine worked like a giant vacuum cleaner which indiscriminately pulled in any information remotely related to political activism." CIAB tried to estimate the likelihood of revolt on the basis of sociological and historical data and classified specific cities by the probability of erupting violence. None of its reports was brilliantly researched. CIAB established a "racial desk," but its all-white analysts lacked familiarity with the phenomena they were studying. Its "left-wing desk" was separate, sharing functions with the international section. After King's assassination, the Pentagon created a Joint Chiefs' Contingency Fund and planned a secure facility from which it could guide military operations against homegrown insurrectionists. Federal authorities coordinated their activities with police forces and private firms pioneering sophisticated technology. The Aerojet Corporation, best known for rocket engine design and contributions to the moon launch, debuted an urban tank for use in quelling ghetto revolts. The virtually impregnable vehicle, equipped with a night vision camera, was impervious to improvised explosive devices, and its interior boasted "the aesthetics and comfort features of a luxury passenger car."[61]

A crisis atmosphere promoted information sharing among agencies aimed at protecting national security, preventing violence, and maintaining the existing social and political order by "disrupting" and "neutralizing" groups and individuals perceived as threats. The Black Nationalist program began in 1967

[59] Federal Data Banks, Computers and the Bill of Rights, Hearings before the Subcommittee on Constitutional Rights of the Committee on the Judiciary, United States Senate, 92nd Congress, 1st Session, February 23–25; and March 2–4, 9–11, 15, 17, 1971 (Washington, D.C.: Government Printing Office, 1971), 11–14.

[60] Testimony of Christopher Pyle, ibid., 188–9; Joan M. Jensen, *Army Surveillance in America, 1775–1980* (New Haven, Conn.: Yale University Press, 1991), 240–3.

[61] Military Surveillance, Hearings Before the Subcommittee on Constitutional Rights of the Committee on the Judiciary. United States Senate 93rd Congress 2nd Session, 1974; Senate Report 94–755 of the Select Committee to Study Government Operations, with Respect to Intelligence Activities, United States Senate, April 23, 1976, 5, 79–184; "Aerojet History," http://www.aerojet.com/about/history.php, accessed July 4, 2011; "1984 Supercar for 1968 Superfuzz," *Los Angeles Free Press*, December 15–22, 1967, p. 1.

with an FBI directive to "expose, disrupt, misdirect, discredit or otherwise neutralize" the target group. A "Ghetto Informant Program" was designed to give advance warning of disturbances that could result in large-scale civil conflict. Worried about Martin Luther King Jr. as a "black messiah" who would "unify and electrify the movement," the bureau aimed its sights at SCLC.[62]

Keeping blacks on the margins of society denied their centrality to the nation, but repressive activities and discourses suggested that curbing black insurgency was fundamental to national security. The FBI, for example, in its efforts to track and contain dissidents from Marcus Garvey to Stokely Carmichael, inadvertently wrote its own fractious, if often inaccurate, history of African Americans long before publishers realized that something was lacking in textbook portrayals of U.S. life. Similarly, as the 1960s ended, the House Un-American Activities Committee (HUAC) published a report that constituted a virtual history of black radicalism from the 1930s to 1968. The preface to the document began with a study of the thought of various writers on war and revolution, including Mao Tse-tung, Che Guevara, and General Vo Nguyen Giap of Vietnam. The report detailed participation by American communists in the Spanish Civil War and the Philippines' Huk rebellion. HUAC could understand the global events it described only by attributing them to a shadowy Soviet empire deemed to be the mastermind of black discontent and subversion. It could not fathom how U.S. internal conditions could produce opposition. It also left unanswered the question of why African Americans, deemed so nonessential to any definition of Americanism, should require such vigilance when they went abroad.

America was under attack by "mixed Communist and black nationalist elements," the report declared. HUAC described the international networks and activities of Malcolm X, Robert Williams, and Harlem leader Bill Epton. Because many revolutionaries from southern Africa had been trained in communist countries, HUAC interpreted the national liberation organizations as communist fronts. The committee theorized about the causes of civil unrest and the nature of mob behavior. Its report blamed irresponsible politicians and evaluated but dismissed the likelihood that the dreaded race war of the era's imaginings would occur. HUAC did have some ideas about what to do if sustained trouble continued. Its plan suggested curfews, sieges, suspension of civil liberties, a passbook law for ghetto residents, informers, and the revival of detention centers in the event of insurrection.[63]

At later hearings before a subcommittee of the Senate Judiciary Committee, testimony suggested that the intelligence community was less attuned to the thinking of radical groups than to mechanically amassing data on participants

[62] FBI Headquarters to all field offices August 25, 1967, in Final Report of the U.S. Congress Senate Select Committee to Study Governmental Operations with Respect to Intelligence Activities, 94th Congress, 2nd Session, Senate Report 94–755, 1976, p. 20, 21, 252–3.

[63] United States Congress, House Committee on Un-American Activities, Guerrilla Warfare Advocates in the United States, 90th Congress, May 6, 1968.

and networks. One witness testified that his superiors "could not differentiate between the Weathermen faction and the American Friends Service Committee … that was the general atmosphere."[64] After King's assassination, the Pentagon created "a directorate for Civil Disturbance Planning and Operations." The June 1968 assassination of Robert Kennedy appeared to confirm the need for more of such preparations, which continued on a covert basis during the Nixon years. As most targets could not clearly distinguish among different branches of clandestine government agencies, military intelligence activity could proceed undetected.[65]

Black college enrollments doubled between 1964 and 1970 and prompted the intelligence community to scrutinize historically black schools more closely. Surveillance also focused on African-American bookstores as disseminators of subversion and as the haunts of troublemakers. According to a late October 1970 FBI memorandum, campus incidents involving black students increased by at least 23 percent from the academic year 1968–9 to 1969–70. Black student activism contributed to a 1970 FBI rule change that allowed it to begin surveillance of young people at age eighteen rather than twenty-one. The FBI "felt that every Black Student Union and similar group, regardless of their past or present involvement in disorders, should be the subject of a discrete preliminary inquiry through established sources and informants to determine background, aims and purposes, leaders and key activists." The "alarming" increase in black student "extremist" activity, if coupled with a coordinated program, "would present a grave potential for future violent activities at U.S. schools." The FBI rued the dearth of black student informants.[66]

The CIA also took an interest in the issue, lending equipment to domestic police departments and training their personnel in exchange for shared intelligence that "tended to circumvent" the FBI and Justice Department.[67] Like the FBI, the CIA had trouble identifying black student leaders. "Articulate, demanding, and radical, these students have been responsible for much of the current campus related unrest and disorder," read the agency's report "The Black Militant Threat." "Outrageous demands professed to be non-negotiable and supported by white sympathizers (faculty, students and non-students) and Third World Liberation Front (an amalgam of Blacks, Mexicans, Filipinos

---

[64] Testimony of Agent John M. O'Brien, Hearings before the Subcommittee on Constitutional Rights of the Committee on the Judiciary.... p 115.

[65] Jensen, *Army Surveillance in America*, 240–4, 246.

[66] Stephen Ward, "Scholarship in the Context of Struggle: Activist Intellectuals, the Institute of the Black World (IBW), and the Contours of Black Power Radicalism," *Black Scholar* 31 (Nos. 3–4:2001): 42–53. Testimony of Charles Brennan, former assistant director of the FBI Domestic Intelligence Division, September 25, 1975, and memorandum of executive conference, October 29, 1970. Special Report of the FBI Ad Hoc Committee on Intelligence, June 1970, pp. 102–3, 158, in U. S. Senate, Hearings Before the Select Committee to Study Governmental Operations with Respect to Intelligence Activities, 94th Cong, 1st session vol. 2,"Huston Plan."

[67] House Select Intelligence Committee report, *Village Voice*, February 16, 1976, p. 89.

Chinese, Japanese, and Indian students) have made it possible for this relatively small percentage of dissidents to disrupt large universities and colleges."[68]

The Royal Canadian Mounted Police (RCMP) also began scrutinizing the Black Power movement, coordinating with the FBI. Well before the era of the Underground Railroad and the Indian Wars, events in the United States had affected Canadian security. In 1967, the same year that residents of Windsor, Ontario, watched the southern sky redden with flames from Detroit's insurrection, the RCMP launched the Key Sectors program to improve its ability to investigate persons and groups deemed subversive. Those now included Caribbean and Canadian Indian radicals and student protesters. The RCMP feared synchronization between Canadian and American dissidents. Accordingly, its agents attended events at Canadian universities and monitored disaffected blacks, taking care to probe any ties they discovered among militant groups.[69]

Caribbean students and residents in Canada had become more vocal in their support of Black Power and criticisms of neocolonialism. Aside from the Africans and Caribbean citizens whose Canadian residence was in large part a function of Commonwealth ties, Canada had another black population in Nova Scotia that dated from the period of the American Revolution when the British army in retreat evacuated black loyalists from the Patriot areas. Canada proved an indifferent asylum as generations of black Nova Scotians had lived and died in penury and suffered severe discrimination.[70] But Canada's worries lay elsewhere. Historian Steve Hewitt explained that Canadian authorities feared being drawn into the maelstrom on their southern border. "The RCMP's interest in Red and Black Power movements reflected two realities: a growing concern with the possibility of violence and the belief that the growth in the likelihood of violence occurring was connected, directly and indirectly, to problems in the United States." In the mid-1960s, those problems were manifest. "Through watching television, Canadians knew well the chaos and violence in the streets of their southern neighbour: political assassinations and riots in cities such as the one in Los Angeles where thirty-four people died in August 1965."[71] How would Canada insulate itself?

Governments were not the only entities doing research on the "opposition." While police and military authorities were preparing for "war" in the streets, social movement organizations became more attuned to the political dynamics of the communities they were trying to transform. Even in the earlier days of voter registration campaigns and antisegregation protests, civil rights organizations preceded specific actions with astute assessments of wealth holding

---

[68] CIA Confidential Report, January 16, 1969, "The Black Militant Threat to CIA," DDRS.

[69] Records of the Canadian Security Intelligence Service (CSIS), African Liberation Support Committee-Canada (ALSC-C), Library and Archives, Canada, RG 146; Steve Hewitt, *Spying 101: The RCMP's Secret Activities at Canadian Universities, 1917–1997* (Toronto: University of Toronto Press, 2002), 138, 140, 152–5.

[70] A general history of Canadians of African descent is Robin Winks, *The Blacks in Canada*, 2nd ed. (Montreal: McGill-Queen's University Press, 1997).

[71] Hewitt, *Spying 101*, 159.

and power in particular localities. SNCC, for example, began new projects by analyzing the local elites: who the principal employers were, what the demographics were. For Birmingham, Alabama, it compiled a list of national corporations active in the city, the names of the directors, and the civic associations and charities with which they were associated. It produced similar reports on Orangeburg, South Carolina, and Lee County, Virginia.[72]

Internationally, similar research into the structure of authority included the World Peace Brigade's study of Northern Rhodesia. Investigators probed the mining companies, their links to politics, and the interlocking relationships among industrial and financial companies operating in southern Africa. Broadsides published in Paris provided information about the Portuguese colonies and the Palestinian crisis.[73] NACLA, discussed in a previous chapter, linked activist and academic communities involved with Latin America. Such research aimed to reveal and explain how elites maintained the status quo. Ironically, the emerging field of U.S. social history began with radical commitments that insisted on the primacy of the local and of nonelite voices and came to discount the kinds of studies of power that activists were doing.[74]

The research done to support mass mobilization and nonviolent direct action was necessarily compact and functional. Researchers drew on scholarship to undermine the intellectual foundations on which racism and imperialism were premised. Historians and anthropologists had excavated the "African past" earlier in the twentieth century and had debunked the notion that blacks were people without history or reason. Works such as C. L. R. James's *The Black Jacobins* (1938), Melville Herskovits's *The Myth of the Negro Past* (1941), Eric Williams's *Capitalism and Slavery* (1944), and W. E. B. Du Bois's *The World and Africa* (1947) were the products of earlier grappling with the consequences of oppression.

While those scholars and others had largely discredited sociobiological racism in the academy, modern thought continued to impute the ongoing problems of non-Western peoples to cultural deficits. Predominantly white universities, many of them effectively segregated, profited from cold war–driven payouts from foundations and the government as social scientists prognosticated on the requisites for Third World growth and prosperity. These almost always

---

[72] Notes c. 1963? SNCC Papers, Series IV Executive Secretary Files, 1959–1972, reel 6, passim. "Social Structure of Orangeburg, S.C.," in ibid., reel 9.

[73] Michael Scott, World Peace Brigade Submission to U.N. Committee on Colonialism, June 5, 1962, World Peace Brigade Papers, North American Regional Council, Box 2 folder 1. "Ou en sont les mouvements de libération des colonies portugaises?" Etudes anticolonialistes fiches d'information no. 2, December 1962, in ibid., Wisconsin Historical Society.

[74] Nancy McLean in *Freedom Is Not Enough: The Opening of the American Workplace* (Cambridge, Mass.: Harvard University Press, 2006), reproves social historians' neglect of corporate elites, 344. Similar insights derive from Bryan D. Palmer in "Rethinking the Historiography of United States Communism," *American Communist History* 22 (2) (2003): 151. See also Robert Vitalis, "The Graceful and Generous Liberal Gesture: Making Racism Invisible in American International Relations," *Millennium: Journal of International Studies* 29 (2) (2000), especially p. 336.

involved the abandonment of preindustrial habits, the embrace of technologies that had worked well in affluent Western countries, and a successful propulsion – through strength of will as much as through science – into the industrial age. The prescription for African Americans, although a racial-ethnic minority rather than a sovereign people, was somewhat similar. Such scholars as the sociologist E. Franklin Frazier, the historian Stanley Elkins, and the economist Patrick Moynihan reckoned that centuries of slavery and oppression had ill fitted American blacks for life in a competitive modern democracy. Most lived in the South, itself an island of underdevelopment in an advanced nation. In order to take their rightful place in U.S. society, African Americans would have to shed the regional atavisms of the past, including rural customs and female-headed families, and pattern their behavior on that of successful whites. The cultural deprivation model fed into long-standing missionary impulses in which the moral character, rather than the material condition of the downtrodden, had to be improved.[75]

Both in the United States and abroad, the basic premise began with a "native" traumatized by colonial rule and its putative modernizing effects. The native then adopts the desired behaviors or persists in dysfunctional conduct. This line of inquiry and its attendant assumptions about the deficiencies of the human subject met challenge as intellectuals from Latin America and the Caribbean began providing alternative interpretations of poor countries' problems and aspirations. Social scientists like Lloyd Best, Andre Gunder Frank, Norman Girvan, Robert Hill, Arthur Lewis, Trevor Munroe, Rex Nettleford, and Colin Palmer varied from one another on The Right-Left political spectrum. They nevertheless shared a common interest in explaining the origins, operations, and functions of the unfavorable political and economic circumstances in which fledgling states found themselves during the independence era. While African decolonization is often the standard reference point, Caribbean nations also numbered among the countries achieving sovereignty in the 1960s. Most had black majority populations, but many citizens in the island republics did not feel enfranchised at home. The perpetuation of colonial economies, class divisions, and skin color politics were sources of grievance. Popular resistance troubled heads of new states because demands for radical change shed doubt on the legitimacy of their administrations and threatened to complicate their relations with the major powers.[76]

Toleration for dissent thus had limits in the new Caribbean countries. Radical scholars proved dangerous for having strong intellectual credentials,

[75] Michael E. Latham, *Modernization as Ideology: American Social Science and "Nation Building" in the Kennedy Era* (Chapel Hill: University of North Carolina Press, 2000), 65–7; Charles W. Mills, *The Racial Contract* (Ithaca, N.Y.: Cornell University Press, 1997), 14.

[76] See Brian Meeks, "The Rise and Fall of Caribbean Black Power," in *From Toussaint to Tupac: The Black International since the Age of Revolution*, eds. Michael O. West, William G. Martin, and Fanon Che Wilkins (Chapel Hill: University of North Carolina Press, 2009); David Austin, "All Roads Led to Montreal: Black Power, the Caribbean, and the Black Radical Tradition in Canada," *Journal of African American History* 92 (Autumn 2007): 516–39.

many, ironically, obtained from metropolitan universities. One such individual was the Guyanese historian Walter Rodney. Rodney had been an undergraduate at the University of the West Indies (UWI). By 1966, he held a doctorate from the School of Oriental and African Studies, University of London. In London, mentored by the Trinidadian revolutionist and intellectual C. L. R. James, he networked with likeminded Caribbean and African expatriates. Rodney's career as a history professor coincided with new states' desire to use their own nationals' expertise to address problems of development and governance – as long as they could safely absorb these experts' critiques of the status quo.[77]

Rodney's distinguished study, *A History of the Upper Guinea Coast*, marked him as a major scholar and led to a teaching post at the University of Dar es Salaam in 1966. He found the atmosphere congenial, but when a job opened up at UWI in 1968, he returned to the Caribbean and established a reputation as a public intellectual. Growing interest in African affairs in the Caribbean provides the larger context in which Rodney united regional concerns with those on the African continent. As in the United States, African independence prompted anticolonial and antiracist activism in the islands. Students on the UWI campus were sensitized to world events, having protested the Sharpeville massacre in 1960 and the Rhodesian Universal Declaration of Independence in 1965. The Guild of Undergraduates donated money to SNCC in 1968. Rodney did not confine his lectures to the university community, however. He associated with Rastafarians, a group then belittled by the Jamaican bourgeoisie, and with working-class Kingston residents, a breach of local class etiquette at the time. Rodney called these contacts and conversations "groundings" and later published a small volume of them called *Groundings with My Brothers*. Because he linked African history to the Jamaican experience of colonialism, Jamaican authorities considered him a troublemaker. The home affairs minister had "never come across a man who offers a greater threat to the security of this land."[78] A subsequent work, *How Europe Underdeveloped Africa*, exposed European domination as an engine of African poverty and confirmed Rodney's reputation as a committed antiimperialist.

Upon the shock felt in Jamaica in the wake of Martin Luther King's assassination, Rodney's lectures focused on the implications of U.S.-style Black Power for the Caribbean. He discussed the history of slavery and East Indian indenture and criticized the Chinese and Syrian minorities for their role as intermediaries in bolstering a regime that exploited black laborers. Rodney's description of Black Power as the self-assertion of the majority disrupted the smug discourse of Jamaican multiculturalism, and his associations with working-class

---

[77] Rupert C. Lewis, *Walter Rodney's Intellectual and Political Thought* (Detroit: Wayne State University Press, 1999).

[78] Walter Rodney, *The Groundings with My Brothers* (London: Bogle-L'Ouverture Publications, 1969). Obika Gray, *Radicalism and Social Change in Jamaica, 1960–1972* (Knoxville: University of Tennessee Press, 1991), 151; Austin, "All Roads Led to Montreal," 527.

people and venues promoted a cross-class alliance that elites deemed subversive. When he left the country to attend the 1968 Congress of Black Writers in Montreal, where participants from many countries sought to define Black Power, Jamaican authorities seized the opportunity to bar his return. Rodney then returned to Tanzania and taught at the University of Dar es Salaam from 1969 to 1974.[79]

Because of patterns of migration and acculturation, lifeways among African Americans and peoples of Caribbean descent have historically been linked. The history of Caribbean radicalism remains distinct from its North American counterpart, but overlaps occur when the phenomenon of reciprocal influence is considered and when the impact of transatlantic slavery, racism, and population movements comes into play. As Winston James revealed, Caribbean radicalism became so firmly embedded among U.S. blacks that its island origins were often disguised.[80] When immigrants were naturalized and intermarried with U.S. blacks, their focus comprised a hemispheric – if not wholly Pan-African – perception of the nature of oppression. For the English-speaking Caribbean, especially, Britain's recessional pushed the United States and Canada into view as the succeeding hegemonic powers. Critics began to examine Caribbean governments' relations with these powers with a keener eye. The 1960s witnessed a growing confluence of views among black radicals living and working in the islands and on the mainland.

Diaspora groups merging in Canada marked an intriguing Black Power triangulation. Canada's rapidly growing black population included descendants of eighteenth-century Loyalists and fugitive slaves, Caribbean and African immigrants, and African Americans who in the twentieth century simply moved to a region they perceived as less fraught with racial tension and violence. The proximity to one another of cities such as New York and Montreal, Detroit and Windsor, and Toronto and Buffalo tended to erase national boundaries as ideas flowed across the Great Lakes and rivers (see Figure 10).

The 1968 Black Writers Conference in Montreal situated Black Power as an international phenomenon featuring diverse participants. The conference venue, McGill University, had previously hosted "West Indian Affairs." conferences. The meetings had attracted a wide array of scholars, many of them the senior architects of contemporary Anglo-Caribbean intellectual culture. Such individuals as the writer George Lamming and the political theorist and organizer C. L. R. James took proactive roles. Younger persons were also involved, including Robert Hill, who would later edit the monumental Marcus Garvey papers.[81]

---

[79] Maurice St. Pierre, "Diasporan Intellectuals in Post Independent Guyana, Jamaica, and Trinidad and Tobago: A Generational Analysis," *Souls* 10 (2) (2008): 148, 149; Gray, *Radicalism and Social Change in Jamaica*, 151–7; Max V. Krebs to U. S. Embassy, Dar-es-Salaam, September 23, 1974, U. S. Department of State Central Files, RG 59, NARA, hereafter SDCF.

[80] James, *Holding Aloft the Banner of Ethiopia Caribbean Radicalism in Early Twentieth-Century America* (New York: Verso, 1998).

[81] Sean William Mills, "The Empire Within: Montreal, the Sixties, and the Forging of a Radical Imagination" (PhD diss., Queen's University, Kingston, Ontario, 2007), pp. 184–91; Austin, "All Roads Led to Montreal," 82.

1951	18,000
1961	32,100
1971	34,400
1981	239,500

Source: Statistics Canada, censuses of population

FIGURE 10. Canada's black population, 1951–1981.

Speakers at the 1968 conference included the African-American psychiatrist Alvin Poussaint, veteran black nationalist Richard B. Moore, and Walter
Rodney. The program featured Harry Edwards, the black American athlete
and later sociologist who played a major role in inspiring the protest by black
athletes at the Mexico City Olympics. SNCC's James Forman and Stokely
Carmichael participated. Others speaking but not on the program included
poet Ted Joans, and the Trinidadian provocateur Michael X. Planners invited
Black Panthers Eldridge Cleaver and H. Rap Brown, and author Leroi Jones,
who did not attend. In spite of the literary conference call, the event was
more an activists' meeting than a writers' convocation. Participants recalled
an almost evangelical atmosphere, Wilkins reports. The international meaning
of Black Power thus developed not within a single national community but
across the diaspora. The contagious enthusiasm of the meeting disturbed the
Jamaican government and enhanced its fears of Rodney's influence. Jamaica
banned works by African-American radicals and publications from China, the
USSR, and Cuba. It suppressed demonstrations by students and other youth
after Rodney's expulsion as an "outside agitator."[82]

The treatment of Rodney coincided with a particularly critical moment in
the intellectual life of the African diaspora and on the African continent. The
flowering of scholarship attendant on decolonization was rife with cautious
optimism about the possibilities of both economic and cultural development
and the role of indigenous theorists and technicians in helping to realize it.[83]
Under normal circumstances, historically revolutionary Haiti would play a role
in these conversations, but at that time it was under the rule of a ruthless
dictatorship.

François Duvalier had withstood a number of plots and coup attempts in
the 1960s and was in no mood to tolerate unconventionality. The isolated
Black Republic nevertheless had a window on the world through the emigrants
who supported it through remittances and occasional home visits. Returnees to

---

[82] Austin, *All Roads*, 25; Alfie Roberts, *A View for Freedom* (Montreal: Alfie Roberts Institute,
2005), 73–8. The conference is described in joyful terms by Dennis Forsythe, "The Black Writers
Conference: Days to Remember," pp. 57–69; and L. R. Butcher, "The Congress of Black Writers,"
pp. 69–74, in *Let the Niggers Burn: The Sir George Williams University Affair and Its Caribbean
Aftermath*, ed. Dennis Forsythe (Montreal: Our Generation Press, 1971); Grace Livingston,
"Chronic Silencing and Struggling without Witness: Race, Education and the Production of
Political Knowledge" (PhD diss., University of Wisconsin, Madison, 2003), p. 198; Ambassador
Vincent De Roulet to the Secretary of State, June 22, 1973, SDCF.
[83] McLean, *Freedom Is Not Enough*, 61.

Haiti from the United States soon learned what was acceptable at home. A former U.S. military attaché described how the Tonton Macoute, Duvalier's secret police, dragooned returning teenagers with Afro haircuts. "After they had spent interminable hours in the Station de Police, barbers suddenly appeared, and each shaggy head or beard or high-style Afro was shorn." Duvalier personally issued a clear warning to the terrified youth and their families. "As you know, I do not like to have to say the same thing twice."[84] Papa Doc's regime maintained the fiction that it represented all the black power Haitians would ever need. In places where it was possible, however, a new international critique of power that pinpointed the structures of domination, whether white or black, colonial or independent, emerged.

Like the U.S. government, Caribbean governments perceived young alienated blacks as national security threats. The preponderance in the national period of the same commercial and political elites that had ruled the area during late colonial times continued to mar prospects for genuine majority participation in many countries. Enacting popular democracy in the region and creating economies that would break decisively with old plantation patterns generally confounded regional administrations. Dissenters took to heart Frantz Fanon's warning in his essay "The Pitfalls of National Consciousness" that many leaders of developing countries felt greater loyalty to corporate and political entities in the West than to their own publics.

For generations, the Caribbean had exported intellectual talent to metropolitan countries. It now faced the challenge of harnessing its brainpower to the task of revitalization at home. The 1960s and early 1970s witnessed an outpouring of social science scholarship in developing countries that specifically addressed modernization. As Simon Gikandi notes in a somewhat different context:

For most of the 1960s and 1970s, knowledge about postcolonial nations was mediated primarily by intellectuals and writers based in "Third World" countries. The most significant works by what were then known as "Third World" intellectuals such as Ashis Nandy in psychology, Walter Rodney in history, Rex Nettleford in culture, and Andre Gunder Frank in political economy, were published and primarily read in their nations and regions and within the "underdeveloped" world."[85]

This intellectual ferment would have occurred even in the absence of Black Power radicalism. What raised the stakes were the voices of many highly educated and ideologically attuned young people.

In the French Caribbean, integration with France put subjects in touch with transatlantic currents. Martinican poet and politician Aimé Césaire had joined such members of the metropolitan cultural elite as Louis Aragon, Simone de Beauvoir, André Breton, Pierre Boulez, Marguerite Duras, Michel Leiris, and

---

[84] Robert Debs Heinl and Nancy Gordon Heinl, *Written in Blood: The Story of the Haitian People, 1492–1971* (Boston: Houghton Mifflin, 1978), 660.

[85] Simon Gikandi, "Globalization and the Claims of Postcoloniality." *South Atlantic Quarterly* 100 (3) (2001): 646.

Jean-Paul Sartre in protesting Parisian police violence against Arabs during the Algerian war of independence.[86] Francophone convocations in Europe and North Africa brought intellectuals from the diaspora together. Scholar Bennetta Jules-Rosette compared the first International Congress of Black Writers and Artists (1956) at the Sorbonne with the second congress held in Rome in 1959, the first World Festival of Black Arts in Dakar (1966), and the 1969 Pan-African Cultural Festival in Algiers. She observed that Pan-African rhetoric had changed over the period from a stylized *négritude* to a highly politicized nationalist consciousness that stressed the liberation of the continent. Black Power fed into that stream... By the end of the 1960s, Francophone Caribbean intellectuals were focusing on decolonization and a recuperation of Caribbean history that relied more on empiricism than mystique.

The 1969 Pan-African Cultural Festival in Algiers "marked a strong rapprochement among Americans, North Africans, and sub-Saharan African delegates by virtue of their shared commitment to political activism," Jules-Rosette suggests. "By 1969, the black Americans were aware of the importance of the civil rights and black power movements as social movements with implications on a world-wide scale. Thus, they were able to share in the discourse of decolonization and nation building that constituted the foundation of Pan-Africanism." To Jules-Rosette, "the 1969 symposium communications were ideological rather than academic in tone," and "marked a political and generational break."[87]

Guests at the festival included politicos and cognoscenti from many countries, representatives of liberation movements, and an African-American delegation that boasted musicians Nina Simone and Archie Shepp, playwright Ed Bullins, and poet Don Lee (Haki Madhubuti). Other participants were Stokely Carmichael (Kwame Ture) and Julia Hervé, daughter of novelist Richard Wright. The Black Panther Party made a point of its solidarity with the Palestinians and held a press conference with Al Fatah, the political bureau of the Palestine Liberation Organization (PLO). Eldridge Cleaver, in 1969 head of the party's international section, headquartered in Algiers, denounced Zionists for seizing Palestinian lands and condemned the United States for supporting their actions. He counseled African nations not to accept Israeli aid, which merely cloaked U.S. neocolonial ambitions.[88]

Most chronicles of the Black Power period capture only part of the cultural explosion that marked the epoch and reflected its rapidly changing consciousness. In addition to the Black Arts movement's outpouring of creative work in the United States, the late 1960s and early 1970s witnessed a

---

[86] Jean-Luc Einaudi, *La bataille de Paris. 17 octobre 1961* (Paris: Éditions du Seuil, 1991), 225.

[87] Jules-Rosette, *Black Paris*, 70–1, 73. For more on the festival, see Anthony J. Ratcliff, "Liberation at the End of a Pen: Writing Pan-African Politics of Cultural Struggle" (PhD diss., University of Massachusetts, 2009), pp. 107–39.

[88] Hoyt Fuller, "Algiers Journal," *Negro Digest* 19 (October 1969): 84; Smith, *An International History of the Black Panther Party*, 77.

proliferation of historical scholarship and the republication of forgotten classic African-American texts. The hunger for knowledge about black people tapped an epistemic vein that W. E. B. Du Bois in his *Encyclopedia Africana* project had tried unsuccessfully to enlist foundations to fund. "Inadequate Black faculty, low enrolment of Black students, courses which were 'lily white' in content and bigoted college professors have been the hallmark of the American university since the founding of Harvard College in 1636," Addison Gayle Jr. observed.[89] Now institutions sought to let some unconventional people and subject matter trickle in while leaving the academy's central mission of mainstreaming white students untouched.

Emphasis on the college education of minority youth was new. It became an attractive option as elites began to prioritize the creation of a stable black middle class as a hedge against disorder. Princeton University began a summer outreach program for black male high school students in the early 1960s. Of the forty boys in the 1964 class, thirty-six applied for college admission. Princeton wanted its remedial education program to be "an experiment and ... a precedent in the search for and encouragement of ability and leadership among the Nation's underprivileged groups."[90]

School after school began following the trend leaders in the gradual desegregation of higher education and its curriculum. Liberal foundations and the administrators who transitioned between the worlds of philanthropy and public service came to believe that further opening the doors of opportunity could blunt the appeal of radical strategies to racial minorities. According to a report considered by the John D. Rockefeller III Fund, "black college students have been at the center of much of the unrest which has become a dangerous phenomenon threatening the very fibre of American society." The report proposed foundation funding for a national black student organization that would help young African Americans meet their educational goals while steering them away from revolutionary objectives. These efforts echo the airlift of African students earlier in the decade who were transported to the United States for similar purposes.[91]

With help from the Phelps Stokes Fund, Princeton's Human Relations Council responded to pressures for change when it sponsored a "convocation of scholars" at the fund office in February 1966. Princeton contemplated establishing a "center for American Negro Studies." An African-American book collection in its Firestone Library, for which the university received a Rockefeller Foundation grant, would serve as the anchor. Interest in data collection about blacks increased during this period as Phelps Stokes Fund records reveal a

[89] Addison Gayle, Jr., "White Don Quixotes, Black Sancho Panzas," *Liberator* 10 (October 1970): 8.

[90] Robert F. Goheen to George Harrar, January 20, 1966; "A semester's course in American History," (syllabus), summer 1966, RF, Princeton University-Remedial Education, 1967, series 200 boxes 80–81 folder 691, Rockefeller Foundation, RAC.

[91] "Black Students in Higher Education," n.d., John D. Rockefeller III Fund, Series 1, Box 18, folder 19, RAC.

preoccupation with basic statistical and bibliographic information gathering on African Americans that nearly trumped its primary interest in the consolidation of programs. The fund was so taken with the empirical recovery of black history and society that it undertook to do some of the research itself rather than delegate the task to universities and find money to support it.[92]

The philanthropic model of reform promoted by foundations emphasized development through individual acculturation. They responded to the challenge of Black Power initiatives that were taking a collective view of progress. Militants often perceived individual success stories as co-optive, because they did not necessarily advance the interests of black communities as a whole. When large numbers of whites began abandoning central cities, thus creating new space for the practice of ethnic politics, the stage was set for a collectivist urban politics appealing to nationalists.

Poet and playwright Amiri Baraka (Leroi Jones) found himself occupying that stage. He had grown up in New Jersey and returned there to establish a cultural center in Newark called Spirit House. His goal was the creation of a lively and emancipatory urban art and cultural space. Rebellion in Newark in the summer of 1967 changed the dynamic. The six-day cycle of midsummer violence cost twenty-three lives. Baraka himself was beaten and jailed. The first National Black Power conference, planned before the Newark uprising but deeply inflected by it, constituted a formal break with liberal integrationism.[93] In the aftermath, Newark voters toppled a corrupt city hall and elected a black mayor. With a community base in Spirit House, poet Baraka and his associates founded the Congress of Afrikan Peoples (CAP). From the very beginning, the FBI had Jones and his organization in its sights. Its contacts identified Jones "as the person who will probably emerge as the leader of the Pan-African movement in the United States." Ever on the lookout for black saviors who were therefore enemies, FBI director J. Edgar Hoover instructed the Newark office to report frequently. CAP warranted "aggressive, imaginative, attention."[94]

CAP rooted its program for transformation in a studied Pan-Africanism. Baraka invited mayor Kenneth Gibson to a dinner and reception to honor Nyerere, who was traveling to the United States to address the UN General Assembly. CAP urged Gibson to attend an "African Fashion Show" where Tanzania's ambassador to the UN would speak. CAP thus positioned itself as

[92] John P. Davis to F. D. Patterson, November 4, 1966, Rockefeller Foundation, Phelps Stokes Fund-American Negro Studies, RG 1.2, Ser 200, Box 77, folder 652; grant-in-aid application, July 18, 1966, Princeton University Library-American Negro, 1966–1967, ser 200, box 80–81, folder 68; A Presentation to the Rockefeller Foundation from the Phelps Stokes Fund, ibid., Box 77, folder 652, RAC.

[93] "LeRoi Jones Seized in Newark after Being Hurt," *New York Times*, July 15, 1967, p. 11. An account of Baraka's activities in Newark is in Komozi Woodard, *A Nation within a Nation: Amiri Baraka (Leroi Jones) and Black Power Politics* (Chapel Hill: University of North Carolina Press, 1999).

[94] Director, FBI to Special Agent in Charge (SAC), Newark, October 9, 1970, *The Black Power Movement*, Part 1, reel 1.

a Pan-African broker between Newark, a center of local black political power and culture, and an African state. This internationalist dimension recalled earlier initiatives by James Lawson and Malcolm X. It also meshed with time-honored ethnic politics as practiced by white immigrants and their descendants in the wards of U.S. cities. African Americans should give practical support to African countries, Baraka declared, in the same the way that Jews back Israel. He wanted Newark to create "an office of African Affairs" and pursue cultural exchanges with Africans to benefit the city and create black business opportunities. A nationalism that sought out venues for capitalist development was at odds with the Marxism that Baraka would later espouse, and these opposing methods would become a major source of contention within the Black Power movement.[95]

The contrast between liberal educators' plan for the embourgeoisement of black youths through individual achievement and nationalists' emphasis on community uplift demonstrates the contest for power as the rules of the game changed. Upward mobility, elites thought, would end ghetto violence. Community control, Black Power advocates believed, would give the inner city the access that white hyphenates had long enjoyed.

---

[95] Baraka to Gibson, October 7, 1970, ibid. For CAP generally, see Ratcliff, "Liberation at the End of a Pen," 195–208.

7

Race, Space, and Displacement

Proponents of more educational opportunity for minority youth saw schooling as the avenue to social peace. But the liberal response to youth unrest was not the only one. The FBI's approach was governed by its police orientation and a broadly punitive attitude that continues to suffuse U.S. society.[1] The Bureau helped to create and disseminate a popular view of outlaw culture in which young thugs engaged in violence for individual rather than collective ends. There was little room to consider political motivations and collective action outside the framework of criminal conspiracy. Revolutionists in this formulation were far from stolid Stalinist bureaucrats. Instead they acted, like other malefactors, more from narcissistic impulses than from moral conviction.

The thin line that had always separated revolutionaries from outlaws aided the FBI's work. A tension existed between the potential for politicizing delinquents and their centrifugal tendencies toward solipsism and vice. Radicals like Max Stanford believed that youth gangs had revolutionary promise and published this opinion in the *Liberator* in January 1965. The article hit the press around the same time that Malcolm X's autobiography appeared. *The Autobiography of Malcolm X* and Stanford's essay both focused on the salvation of the so-called lumpenproletariat, the term Karl Marx had applied to jobless workers at the lowest economic levels, criminals, and the rootless. Malcolm X claimed that the Nation of Islam had redeemed him from lumpen status. The Black Panther Party, formed in Oakland, California, began to proselytize street organizations. Black Panther Alprentice "Bunchy" Carter, a member of the five-thousand-strong Los Angeles Slausons, brought a branch of it into the party in 1967. Like Malcolm earlier, Carter converted to Islam while jailed and met Eldridge Cleaver when both were at Soledad Prison.[2]

[1] U. S. Senate, Hearings Before the Select Committee to Study Governmental Operations with Respect to Intelligence Activities, 94th Cong, 1st session, Apr. 1976, v. 2 "Huston Plan," pp. 102–103.

[2] Robin D. G. Kelley. "Stormy Weather: Reconstructing Black (Inter)Nationalism in the Cold War Era," in *Is It Nation Time? Contemporary Essays on Black Power and Black Nationalism*, ed. Eddie S. Glaude Jr. (Chicago: University of Chicago Press, 2002), 81–2; Laura Pulido, *Black,*

While such figures as Malcolm X and Eldridge Cleaver gave voice to alien-ated youths through their writing and speeches, an increasingly popular Frantz Fanon underscored the plight of the marginalized unemployed. Interestingly, nei-ther Malcolm nor Eldridge Cleaver, in spite of the way they talked, hailed from this class. Neither did Black Panther Huey Newton, the child of working-class immigrants from northeastern Louisiana.[3] Black radicals' rediscovery of class engaged the debate about its primacy – or not – over race. Activist organiza-tions of the period may have identified with specific classes: the rural poor, industrial workers, the petty bourgeoisie. In fact, many group memberships crosscut these divisions. Not all Panthers were from the streets and not all devotees of black capitalism had middle-class backgrounds.

As liberalism could not settle the issues of continuing racial discrimination, deprivation, and the domestic fallout from an enervating foreign war, Fanon's texts grew in appeal. Fanon and Mao Tse-tung wrote of peasantries, but the question of a black peasantry in the United States was settled long ago by the failure to enact agrarian reform during Reconstruction. Recognizing that African Americans were now tied to a late capitalist market economy, militants like Huey Newton and Cleaver seized upon that economy's ills to identify a class they believed could carry the burden and hope of transformation.

A contrasting perspective on the lumpenproletariat was that of economist Daniel Patrick Moynihan, whose 1965 brief on the "lower class Negro family" ignited lasting controversy. Five years later Moynihan repeated his insistence that "the Negro lower class must be dissolved" and turned into a stable work-ing class. Its existence exacerbated white working-class racial antagonism, Moynihan asserted. "Take the urban lower class out of the picture and the Negro cultural revolution becomes an exciting and constructive development." Moynihan, then entering the phase of his career in which he would be identi-fied with neoconservatism, reproached Johnson's War on Poverty because it "defined a large portion of the population as somehow living apart from the rest." Instead, the economist believed, it would be better to "seek programs that stress problems and circumstances that all share, especially problems which working people share with the poor."[4]

The working-class problems Moynihan alluded to were part of the profound changes rocking the industrial world. Blue-collar workers were as vulnerable to structural transformations in the labor market as those below them on the pecking order. Richard Nixon, elected in 1968, devised a winning strategy to

Brown, Yellow, and Left: Radical Activism in Los Angeles (Berkeley: University of California Press, 2006), 71, 103; Akinyele O. Umoja, "The Black Liberation Army and the Radical Legacy of the Black Panther Party," in *Black Power in the Belly of the Beast*, ed. Judson L. Jeffries, (Urbana and Chicago: University of Illinois Press, 2006), 227.

[3] See Wahneema Lubiano's comments on "the insistent focus on only the most economically and politically marginal" in "Standing In for the State: Black Nationalism and 'Writing' the Black Subject," in *Is It Nation Time?* 160.

[4] "Text of a Pre-Inauguration Memo from Moynihan on Problems Nixon Would Face," *New York Times*, March 11, 1970, p. 30.

head off the possibility that white labor would link up with radical insurgency. He framed white workers' discontent as the angst of patriots put upon by subversives, parasites, and criminals. The return of "law and order" in the face of challenges by rioting blacks and college students would restore agency to this suffering "moral majority" portrayed as selflessly fighting America's wars and paying taxes, but having little voice in the destructive liberal policies of the previous eight years. "Nixon was well aware of the right–left tensions within organized labor dating from his time in the Eisenhower administration," writes labor historian Jefferson Cowie. "He sought to exacerbate that split by simultaneously courting the right-wing unions and attacking the left within the labor movement."[5] The overarching goal was to break labor's alliance with the Democratic Party and, in so doing, recreate for Nixon's blue-collar supporters a preindustrial notion of the citizen-mechanic, always white and always male.

Turmoil in the house of labor was not limited to either shop-floor issues or animosities among fractions of the working class. Just as the understanding of what it meant to be a worker was undergoing transition, ethnic identity partially began to substitute for class as whites began appropriating African-American Black Power discourses and practices. Writer Alex Haley's best-selling book *Roots* purported to trace his lineage to Gambia and later, as a television series, drew one of the largest audiences in broadcast history. This phenomenon occurred just as the status of white workers was being eroded and evoked a parallel preoccupation with white immigrant "roots" that precipitated demands for Irish American and Italian American studies in the academy and travel abroad to seek out ancestral places.[6] Ethnic studies, restorationist for blacks, would be naturalizing for whites.

The white "mechanic" and loyal patriot, whose immigrant ancestry confirmed his essential Americanness, stood apart from minority workers. In Detroit and elsewhere, race created a labor elite and favored white communities as they protected their status from blacks under the pretext of guarding homes, neighborhoods, and seniority. Better-paid white workers often defended the most hawkish policies at home and abroad, and others sometimes found in the comforts of white supremacist doctrines emotional compensation for social and economic anxieties.

Nine black autoworkers from Detroit's Dodge Main plant, who included the editors of the Wayne State student paper *Inner City Voice*, started the Detroit Revolutionary Union Movement (DRUM) in the spring of 1968 after a wild-cat strike on May 2. Both white and black workers participated in the action, intended to protest speedup. Consequent disciplinary response, however, fell

[5] Jefferson Cowie, "Nixon's Class Struggle: Romancing the New-Right Worker, 1969–1973," *Labor History* 43 (3) (2002): 270.

[6] Matthew Frye Jacobson, *Roots Too: White Ethnic Revival in Post-civil Rights America* (Cambridge, Mass.: Harvard University Press, 2006); Stanley Aronowitz, "Between Nationality and Class," in *Race, Identity, and Citizenship: A Reader*, eds. Rodolfo D. Torres, Louis F. Mirón, and Jonathan Xavier Inda (Malden, Mass: Blackwell, 1999): 314.

disproportionately on blacks, with five being fired. DRUM seized the moment to launch an all-out attack on racism in the auto industry and in the city at large.[7] It protested the monopolization of supervisory positions by whites, the UAW's failure to combat racist company practices, and the union's support of the notoriously brutal Detroit police.

This oppositional stance toward the UAW derived from rapidly changing industrial conditions. The average age of the workforce dropped during the baby boom. Younger workers wanted democratic unionism and a greater voice in industrial management. Those who married young, as many Americans did in the 1960s, strove to match if not surpass the consumer-oriented lifestyle their parents had achieved earlier in the postwar era. But their social aspirations confronted increased living costs and real-wage decline. These setbacks were paired with a contrasting expansion of the middle class as more white Americans became college-educated and entered the professions. Many blue-collar workers felt left behind.[8]

Social movement discourse and practice had introduced a vocabulary of contestation, some of which originated in labor struggles of times past, and some of which derived from southern protest. SNCC organized Freedom Unions in Mississippi and Tennessee, but organized labor remained cool to its efforts. The United Farm Workers Organizing Committee, not AFL-CIO unions, encouraged California farm labor in 1966. African American, Mexican American, and white women members of an aviation local protested race and gender bias and picketed the 1966 UAW convention in Long Beach, California. Under George Meany's leadership, the AFL-CIO had become jingoist and authoritarian. It evinced little interest in organizing the growing ranks of women and nonwhite workers and adopted a gradualist approach to racial reform. Civil rights insurgency contributed to volatility in the plants and abetted organizing efforts outside the established unions, many of which remained indifferent to minority workers. Labor unrest even extended to the U.S. Postal Service, where employees went on nationwide strike in March 1970 for the first time in 102 years.[9]

Antiwar sentiment emerged early in minority-dominated locals and unaffiliated labor organizations. In July 1964, the president of New York City's heavily African-American and Latino Drug and Hospital Employees Local 1199

[7] Author's interview with Charles Simmons, Detroit, August 15, 1998; "Niggermation," *Liberator* 10 (December 1970): 5–6; James Geschwender and Judson L. Jeffries, "The League of Revolutionary Black Workers," in *Black Power in the Belly of the Beast*, 135–62; Kelley, "Stormy Weather," 75.

[8] "Niggermation," 8; Jefferson Cowie, "'No Time for Dreams': The Unmaking of the American Working Class in the 1970s," lecture, Havens Center, University of Wisconsin – Madison, March 31, 2009.

[9] Charles Denby, *Indignant Heart: A Black Worker's Journal* (Detroit: Wayne State University Press, 1989), 263–4; John P. Windmuller, "The Foreign Policy Conflict in American Labor," *Political Science Quarterly* 72 (June 1967): 210–11, 219–20; Jacob Potofsky interviewed by Neil Gold, New York City, 1964; Columbia University Oral History Collection; Aaron Brenner, "Rank-and-File Rebellion, 1966–1975" (PhD diss., Columbia University, 1996), 3, 93, 106.

spoke out against "the aggressive and dangerous foreign policy we are pursuing in South Vietnam." The Negro American Labor Council, founded by Philip Randolph as a caucus within the AFL-CIO to combat discrimination within labor's ranks, broke with U.S. policy in June 1967. The organization called for ending a war "where the black youth of this country are fighting and dying in ... high disproportionate numbers." In the face of widespread hunger and poverty, the United States should redirect its resources to the improvement of society at home (see Figure 11).[10]

The prospect of withdrawing from conventional unions appealed to many black workers. In New York City, young black women constituted 75 percent of the rank and file in the Telephone Traffic Union. These operators engaged in wildcat strikes because their white leadership failed to represent their interests. Black Bell system employees subsequently formed the short-lived Telephone Workers Revolutionary Union Movement (TELRUM) to address the blatant bias at New York Telephone. Like its Motor City counterparts, this "RUM" identified with worldwide antiimperialist struggles. The allegiance of these movements, Detroit autoworker and intellectual James Boggs asserted, was "to the black community, not to organized labor."[11]

DRUM members spoke to their grievances in a weekly eponymous newsletter. Through *Drum*, activists sought to redirect the thrust of black trade unionism. They proposed that African Americans stop paying union dues and instead channel their money toward initiatives in their neighborhoods. They militated for equal pay for black Chrysler employees in South Africa. A three-day strike organized by DRUM at Dodge Main on July 7, 1968, achieved 70 percent compliance from black workers. Management, nonplussed, fired no one. DRUM took the precaution of protecting jobs by staffing picket lines with people who did not work at the plant.[12]

Black labor insurgency continued as the Ford Revolutionary Union Movement (FRUM), the Eldon Avenue Revolutionary Movement (ELRUM), the General Motors Revolutionary Union Movement (GRUM), and the Harvester Revolutionary Union Movement (HRUM) emerged at their respective plants. A January 1969 wildcat strike at the Eldon Avenue Chrysler gear and axle plant, prompted by a punitive action by management, succeeded because blacks were a large segment of the Eldon Avenue workforce.[13]

---

[10] Philadelphia Workers' Organizing Committee, "Racism and the Workers Movement," Class Struggle Unionism Pamphlet No. 1, p. 288; "Twenty Years in the Hospitals: A Short History of 1199," *1199 News*, special ed., December 1979, p. 475; "NALC Head Asks Labor Aid March of Poor", *The Worker*, June 2, 1968, pp. 333–4, 319–20; all in *Black Workers: A Documentary History from Colonial Times to the Present*, eds. Philip S. Foner and Ronald L. Lewis (Philadelphia: Temple University Press, 1989).

[11] Venus Green, *Race on the Line* (Durham, N.C.: Duke University Press, 2001), 246; Brenner, "Rank-and-File Rebellion," 200; James Boggs, *Racism and the Class Struggle: Further Pages from a Black Worker's Notebook* (New York: Monthly Review Press, 1970), 95–9.

[12] David M. Lewis-Colman, *Race against Liberalism: Black Workers and the UAW in Detroit* (Urbana: University of Illinois Press, 2008), 98.

[13] Geschwender and Jeffries, "The League of Revolutionary Black Workers," 141–2.

DRUM occupied potentially critical space between the organization of African Americans in urban communities and the creation of a militant labor movement. Bias in the auto plants and the UAW hampered full black participation in conventional unionism, but work was part of the general demand for equity and justice. Participants who were not autoworkers supported many of DRUM's efforts but also complicated its struggle. The situation in Detroit was complex and unique: black workers could be students *and* workers, attending Wayne State University. No rigid class divide separated these groups, but the theoretical formulations and abstractions of the students and intellectuals who attached themselves to the movement did not suit everyone.[14]

White radical labor activists echoed some of these developments but focused more on the economy and shop-floor issues. An ephemeral white-edited journal, *Steel on the Move*, averred that Big Steel was in trouble from foreign competition. Newer facilities in Germany and Japan produced steel more efficiently. The U.S. industry could compete only by modernizing plant or cutting costs. New factories were prohibitively expensive, so cost cutting translated into more work and less pay for workers who complained about speedup and overtime.[15]

An intellectual cadre followed black labor into the League of Revolutionary Black Workers, founded in 1969, and dominated its executive board. The league wanted to maintain the momentum created in the plants without succumbing to the spontaneity that had characterized the initial wildcat strikes. It also needed to square a broad perspective on imperialism with the bread and butter issues that preoccupied most factory employees. Detroit radicals found themselves divided into two camps. All wanted to end racism, to gain more labor control of the workplace, and to foster egalitarian foreign and domestic policies on the national level, but pathways to achieving these aims diverged. Line workers tended to espouse black nationalism, whereas those supporting the struggle from the universities or white-collar occupations were more attracted to Marxism. Debates over the primacy of class or race never ended and did little to advance concrete goals.[16]

The Detroit-based Black Workers Congress (BWC), founded by remnants of various nationalist organizations in 1970, struggled over the "correct line." The congress quickly established itself in twenty cities but did not withstand an early power struggle that alienated allies. The Detroit experience was not readily duplicated elsewhere, although black labor militancy developed in other parts of the country. In Ford Motor's Mahwah, New Jersey, plant, a group that subsequently called itself United Black Brothers of Mahwah was formed. In

[14] Elizabeth Kai Hinton, "The Black Bolsheviks: Detroit Revolutionary Union Movements and Shop-Floor Organizing," in *The New Black History*, eds. Manning Marable and Elizabeth Kai Hinton (New York: Palgrave Macmillan, 2011), 211–28.

[15] *Steel on the Move*, July 1, 1971, in *The Black Power Movement, Part 1, Amiri Baraka from Black Arts to Black Radicalism* (Bethesda, Md.: University Publications of America, 2001) reel 6.

[16] Muhammad Ahmad (Maxwell Stanford, Jr.), *We Will Return in the Whirlwind: Black Radical Organizations, 1960–1975* (Chicago: Charles Kerr Publishing, 2007), 259, 260, 262, 267.

Chicago, bus drivers, nearly three-quarters of whom were African Americans, walked off the job in protest of racially discriminatory seniority rules.[17]

Marxists in the BWC believed that the Black Panthers, though sincere revolutionaries, were mistaken in perceiving lumpen elements as progressive. The Panthers had made that error, congress members believed, because they knew little about industrial workers. Only the working class, the congress contended, could lead, with a revolutionary communist party in the vanguard. BWC records were replete with millenarian rhetoric about the general crisis of imperialism, vilification of bourgeois politicians and cultural nationalists, and lengthy disquisitions on the Comintern's 1928 screed on the national question. According to BWC's analysis, SNCC, in spite of its genuine achievements in the South, was chiefly the vehicle of "the radical Black petty bourgeoisie." It was defunct by 1970. As for the BWC, its ultimate disintegration dispersed its members, "some to the Ford Foundation, others to Africa, others underground and still others, nowhere."[18]

The League of Revolutionary Black Workers shared BWC's views on the unreliability of all classes other than the working class. It also criticized the Panthers for adventurism. Déclassé elements could become revolutionary, the league conceded, but as a group they had no real power to effect change and demonstrated little class solidarity. They were disorderly and individualistic to an extreme. Workers, in contrast, had absorbed industrial discipline and, most important, could disrupt production.[19]

These black labor organizations have been faulted for their adherence to a traditional Marxist view of class.[20] It should be recognized, however, that just as they were attempting to define a principled class politics, popular culture, especially as filtered through the commercial lenses of the entertainment industry, was working on the public's perception of radicalism. The political scientist Cedric Robinson describes how Hollywood effected "the appropriation and re-presentation of Angela Davis's public image." Davis, a Marxist philosophy professor, became a fugitive in 1970 when a gun registered to her was used in an armed attempt to free a radical prisoner, George Jackson, from a California courtroom. Jackson was on trial for the murder of a guard. His brother Jonathan tried to rescue him, a failed attempt that resulted in Jonathan's death and that of the judge and two of the inmates on trial with George Jackson. The actress

[17] Geschwender and Jeffries, "The League of Revolutionary Black Workers," 136–7.

[18] "The Black Liberation Struggle: the Black Workers Congress, and Proletarian Revolution," in *The Black Power Movement. Part 1, reel 4.*

[19] Geschwender and Jeffries, "The League of Revolutionary Black Workers," 145; Ahmad, *We Will Return in the Whirlwind*, 266. For a defense of the lumpenproletariat as a revolutionary class, see Ahmad A. Rahman, "Marching Blind: The Rise and Fall of the Black Panther Party in Detroit," in *Liberated Territory: Untold Local Perspectives on the Black Panther Party*, eds. Yohuru Williams and Jama Lazerow (Durham, N.C.: Duke University Press, 2008), 181–231.

[20] A similar criticism of the Eldon Avenue Revolutionary Union Movement's (ELRUM) racial practices is found in Dan Georgiakias and Marvin Surkin. *Detroit: I Do Mind Dying* (New York: St. Martin's Press, 1975), 112, 116–77, 121–2.

Pam Grier portrayed a Davis-like figure in a series of films that depicted her in sexy attire dispatching various miscreants with gunfire. "Film ... transported Davis's form from a representation of a revolutionist to that of an erotic Black nationalist, largely devoid of historical consciousness," Robinson writes. "This was achieved by eviscerating the original's intellectual sophistication, political and organisational context, doctrinal commitments."[21]

Hollywood certainly bore responsibility for depicting nihilism and criminality as normative in African-American society and stripping dissent of its political origins and context, but scripts for understanding the caricatured heroes and villains of cinema were also written by those claiming solidarity with revolution. "White liberals and 'intellectual revolutionaries' did indeed provide the audiences [for black militants]," one of Bayard Rustin's correspondents reminisced. "Eldridge [Cleaver] was amused but sad as well early in that game. He learned that if he spoke in detail and with serious intent to an audience, they yawned. But if he said 'mother fucker' several times, they went into spasms of absurd joy."[22]

A world away from America's contentious race politics and Detroit's labor conflicts, scientists and engineers planted the Stars and Stripes on the moon in July 1969. Television sets everywhere locked onto the inky lunar night as an American touched gently down and bounded lightly across the eerie sands of a satellite that from earth appeared flawlessly white. The moonwalk concealed black discontent in the midst of national celebration. NASA would eventually diversify the astronaut corps, who numbered among the smartest, most intrepid citizens. Just as Nashville sit-in activist Diane Nash had hoped that a Negro would invent one of the United States' missiles, the idea of racially integrated space teams was already circulating. "I suppose its international implications are even more important than the domestic political one," an attorney wrote to President Kennedy's deputy special counsel. "The Russians don't have any Negroes to shoot into space."[23] But the Soviets included Afro-Cuban cosmonaut Arnaldo Tamayo Méndez in their aerospace research program before the United States launched any African Americans into the ether.

The initial dearth of black astronauts was one irony in the space program's contribution to U.S. international prestige. Another was the Kennedy Space Center's location in Brevard County, Florida, an area facing very earth-bound problems of hunger and malnutrition. As Dale Carter observes:

Even as a million converged on Cape Kennedy to witness the start of Apollo M's epic voyage, thousands of Brevard County inhabitants who qualified were being denied

[21] Cedric J. Robinson, "Blaxploitation and the Misrepresentation of Liberation," *Race & Class* 40 (July–September 1998): 1–12.

[22] Kay Hansen to Bayard Rustin, n.d., *Bayard Rustin Papers* (Bethesda, Md.: University Press of America, 1998), Reel 1.

[23] Edward Wynne to Meyer Feldman, Deputy Special Counsel to the President, October 10, 1962, John F. Kennedy Library, quoted in Lynn Spigel, *Welcome to the Dreamhouse: Popular Media and Postwar Suburbs* (Durham, N.C.: Duke University Press, 2001), p. 176 n. 21.

federal food aid because the local authorities had not set aside matching funds. The $2.5 million spent by Brevard County annually on road maintenance amounted to over twice its annual welfare expenditure. As the only Black doctor in the locality remarked, "I guess they're more concerned about promoting tourism in Brevard County than caring about hungry people."[24]

That physician reported treating "malnourished children with prominent ribs and potbellies." A reporter interviewed a black mother of six who had been a housekeeper at the Cape Kennedy Hilton but was laid off and received a pittance from welfare. Her family had almost nothing to eat by the end of the month. On the basis of per capita income, however, Brevard County, with its population of a quarter million, which had grown with the aerospace industry, was affluent. Richard Muldrew, chair of the county commission, acknowledged the disparities. "I know some people are hungry and we're going to do everything to end it here," he declared. "But sometimes these people are like little animals. They get into a cave and won't come out. You have to go in and feed them." County Commissioner Lori Wilsson agreed that the Brevard County poor were less than deserving. They were lazy. "If someone's hungry enough, there are honest ways of earning a dollar aren't there? I know of citrus growers looking for people. I've heard person after person looking for a domestic."[25]

In spite of plantation thinking in places like Brevard County, or perhaps because of it, the South became an important site of employment for the skilled whites who held technical and scientific jobs at NASA. They represented the New South's latest incarnation, a region that would finally be absorbed into the national marketplace of culture and consumption. Boosters looked forward to a new era of industrialization and urbanization, achievable without invoking the specter of race. NASA engineers lived psychic worlds apart from Dixie's inner cities and the remnants of a once-populous rural labor force. Economic restructuring could minimize intergroup friction – and contact – while leaving the black poor in place. Under the circumstances, civil rights struggles at polling stations, courthouses, and schools barely touched the charmed existences of those who could eliminate racial worries and blacks from their social and spatial reality.

SCLC nevertheless tried valiantly to demonstrate the incongruities in South Florida. It took low-income families from five southern states to Cape Kennedy in time for the moon launch to highlight the problems of hunger and unemployment throughout the country. Fewer blacks than whites enthused about the space program. SCLC's Ralph Abernathy announced that he represented "the people of the 51st state of hunger." Some of those accompanying him held signs with such messages as "Rockets or Rickets?" and "Billions

[24] Dale Carter, *The Final Frontier: The Rise and Fall of the American Rocket State* (London: Verso, 1988), 227.
[25] Bernard Weinraub, "Bustle at Cape Bypasses the Hungry," *New York Times*, July 14, 1969, 1:6–8, 23:2–4.

FIGURE 11. This *Pittsburgh Courier* cartoon dramatized the Vietnam era's guns or butter dilemma. (Courtesy of Kimberly Milai)

for Space and Pennies for Hunger." "To the nation's black poor," *Ebony* later editorialized, "watching on unpaid-for television sets in shacks and slums, the countdowns, the blastoffs, the orbitings and landings had other-worldly alienness – though not the drama – of a science fiction movie. From Harlem to Watts, the first moon landing in July of last year was viewed cynically as one small step for 'The Man,' and probably a giant step in the wrong direction for mankind.'"[26]

Florida was not the only state with a nutrition problem. Mississippi's LeFlore County used food as a means of control. In 1962, it distributed surplus to twenty-six thousand people, of whom 90 percent were African Americans. LeFlore did not participate in the food program the following year, a choice that coincided with a black voter registration drive in Greenwood, the county seat. In Mississippi, civil rights groups and a medical team that found widespread hunger "approaching starvation" among black children pressured federal authorities to order changes in food aid administration there. A tug of war ensued between southern conservatives and northern liberals in Congress. When the Senate Subcommittee on Manpower, Employment, and Poverty held hearings in July 1967 on Mississippi poverty, New York senator Jacob Javits and agriculture secretary Orville Freeman got into a shouting match over what Javits and others saw as Freeman's foot dragging on relief. Freeman asserted that every Mississippi county had a food program but not all New York counties could boast the same. "Nobody's starving in New York," Javits snapped. "Be careful. Be very careful," Freeman warned. "I'll find them for you."[27]

Representatives hostile to feeding needy Americans also numbered heavily among the opponents of overseas food assistance programs. Long-term Louisiana congressman Otto Passman had opposed the Marshall Plan and maintained a steady resistance to foreign aid as a government policy throughout his career. "I don't smoke and I don't drink," he declared. "My only pleasure in life is kicking the shit out of the foreign aid program of the United States."[28]

The amount of food aid Americans supplied abroad did not always correlate neatly with need. Instead, the largest nations benefited the most, receiving more assistance in proportional and absolute terms, and those hosting U.S. military bases received substantial help. Policy makers focused on countries that occupied strategic geopolitical positions, such as the Horn of Africa. Conditions in Ethiopia, for example, with its recurrent cycles of famine, could spark a revolt against the wobbly regime of Emperor Haile Selassie. The imperial government nonetheless resisted U.S. efforts to prioritize hunger relief over the arms it required to remain in power, often hiding evidence of famine in the countryside

---

[26] Ibid., Steve Huntley, "SCLC in Space Parley," *Chicago Daily Defender*, July 16, 1969, p. 4; "Giant Leap for Mankind?" *Ebony Magazine*, September 1969, p. 58.

[27] Rep. William F. Ryan to Orville Freeman, March 25 1963, SNCC Papers, Series IV Executive Secretary Files, reel 9; "Food Aid Program Revamped by U.S.," *New York Times*, June 27, 1967, 1:2; Nan Robertson, "Javits and Freeman Trade Shouts at Hunger Inquiry," ibid., July 13, 1967, Sec. 1 pp. 1:2–4, 24:1.

[28] Joseph A. Fry, *Dixie Looks Abroad: The South and U.S. Foreign Relations, 1789–1973* (Baton Rouge: Louisiana State University Press, 2002), 252. For Passman generally, see Randolph Jones, "Otto Passman and Foreign Aid: The Early Years," *Louisiana History* 26 (1) (1985): 53–62, and Dan Morgan, *Merchants of Grain* (New York: Penguin, 1984), 393.

and barring outsiders' travel to troubled areas.[29] It reprised on a deeper scale the grim miseries of Dixie's unreconstructed backwaters, hidden behind the glossy surface of the New South's latest show projects.

Given an American propensity to view the poor punitively, and the mixed motives and conflicted priorities of the foreign assistance program, it is not surprising that ambitious activists thought that they could do a better job than the U.S. government of helping Africans. Nyerere was "enthusiastic in principle" about the Pan African Skills Bank, a product of extensive networking by James Forman in Dar es Salaam in July 1967. Forman, Irving Davis, and other SNCC workers planned to publicize the group's activities in support of African liberation movements and nudge the bank forward. SNCC's big selling point was the bank's independence: it could not be suborned because it would have nothing to do with official U.S. projects. Tanzanians remained somewhat wary, however, especially since by 1967 SNCC was receiving bad press in the United States. Pan-African planning was also constrained by some Tanzanians' opposition to internationalism, a mirror of misgivings in the U.S. civil rights movement itself. Just as some felt that foreign affairs exhausted energies better spent defeating U.S. racism, Tanzanian critics thought Dar-es-Salaam was taking unnecessary risks and diverting scarce resources to utopian plans.[30] After considerable deliberation and with some trepidation, Tanzanian authorities accepted SNCC's proposal, but work did not begin until 1970. In the interim the SNCC Central Committee began pulling back from internationalism. "The revolution must happen here, not over there."[31]

The revolution's location was not an either-or choice. SNCC, which in 1969 changed its name to the Student National Coordinating Committee to reflect its distance from its origins, never entirely abandoned internationalism, Neither did the more conventional SCLC. The Poor People's Campaign, headed by the Reverend Ralph Abernathy after King's death, did not limit itself to a domestic agenda. Secretary of State Dean Rusk received Abernathy, the Reverends Andrew Young and Jesse Jackson, and other representatives of the campaign in early May 1968. The delegates challenged Rusk on almost every aspect of U.S. policy. They wanted changes in Washington's stand on southern Africa, immigration, foreign aid, support of dictatorships in Latin America, food policy, and southwestern land claims submitted by Mexican Americans. They criticized the denial of fishing rights to American Indians and the federal failure to provide jobs for Alaska natives. The Vietnam War was heatedly condemned. Rusk perceived the grievances as "intemperate" and refuted "allegations that

[29] Richard Vengroff and Tsai yung Mei, "Food, Hunger, and Dependency: PL480 Aid to the Third World," *Journal of Asian and African Studies* 17 (3–4: 1982): 250–65; Edward Kissi, "The Politics of Famine in U.S. Relations with Ethiopia, 1950–1970," *International Journal of African Historical Studies* 33 (1) (2000): 113–31.

[30] Fanon Che Wilkins, "'In the Belly of the Beast': Black Power, Anti-imperialism, and the African Solidarity Movement, 1968–1975" (PhD diss., New York University, 2001), pp. 74–7.

[31] Central Committee Notes for Publication, October 28–30, 1968, SNCC Papers, Series I, Chair Files, 1960–1969, reel 3.

the U.S. was a warfare, not a welfare, state. These accusations were either too general, specious, or propagandistic," he believed, "to be subject to individual response."[32]

In his formal reply to the Poor People's Campaign, Rusk reiterated the gist of the U.S. position on South Africa, Rhodesia, and Portugal. The Johnson administration supported sanctions against Rhodesia and rejected arms provision for South Africa. Moral suasion, officials held, was the way to induce Pretoria to abandon apartheid and permit self-determination for its Southwest Africa mandate. Rusk's response to domestic concerns was hazier, perhaps as befits the head of a department charged only with foreign affairs. In any event, his stock answers did not impress the group. "Besides reiterating time-worn policies which have guided our foreign policies for the past few years," Marian Wright commented, "Secretary Rusk gave to us no evidence that he is willing to seriously consider the demands of the poor people of this nation."[33]

Nixon's 1968 election victory did not cheer the mainstream civil rights organizations or Black Power advocates. Expecting little from the incoming Republicans, leaders debated poverty at a National Black Economic Development Conference in Detroit, sponsored by the Inter-religious Foundation for Community Development (IFCO). James Forman unveiled an ambitious project for African-American advancement at the springtime meeting. His "Black Manifesto" demanded reparations for slavery. The $500-million price tag would purchase a land bank for southern farm cooperatives, create publishing houses and metropolitan television networks, and maintain a $20 million strike fund. The plan also called for a Black Anti-Defamation League, training centers that would provide the basic skills needed to improve employability, and a fund-raising campaign to make the conference permanent and start cooperatives in African countries. Some of Forman's supporters aggressively interrupted church services as they tried to collect money from white congregations, eliciting angry responses from clergy and worshippers.[34]

Black Manifesto solicitors made their bids during a period of declining public support for black aspirations and a worsening economy. An alternative would have been to use grants from churches to supplement contributions from black communities themselves, inasmuch as any revolution in America depended on changing not only the allocation of resources but also their origin. In spite of its essentially supplicant posture, the Black Manifesto clashed with the philanthropic community. IFCO had been designated as the broker for funds that Manifesto promoters raised but proved reluctant to play this role.

[32] Secretary of State Dean Rusk to President Johnson, May 3, 1968, *FRUS*, XXXIV, *1964–1968, Energy, Diplomacy, and Global Issues*, online. See also Ralph David Abernathy, "Some International Dimensions of the Peace Movement," *Freedomways* 11 (3) (1971): 237–40.

[33] Secretary of State Rusk to Ralph Abernathy, May 23, 1968, and note citing Marian Wright, June 14, 1968 in *FRUS, 1964–1968, Energy, Diplomacy, and Global Issues*.

[34] "Unit Seeks $500-Million 'Assessment,'" *Chicago Daily Defender*, May 5, 1969, p. 3, 13; "White Pastor Hits Manifesto," ibid., June 3, 1969, p. 5; Wilkins, "In the Belly of the Beast," in *Black Power in the Belly of the Beast*, 54–6.

Forman accused it of blocking a large grant from the Methodist Church to the National Black Economic Development Conference.[35]

The Black Manifesto straddled a curious position in the spaces between begging, demanding, and taking. The ability of Forman and others to cow some churches and foundations temporarily did not amount to a genuine call for reparations, which required the acknowledgment and consent of many more segments of U.S. society. One of the manifesto's flaws was that it did not question the legitimacy of the agents from which it sought relief. Gifts from the powerful, even if extracted by threat or coaxed by moral suasion, would remain short-term or revocable until the donors lost the ability to make them.

To what extent did black publics endorse such initiatives? To what degree did radical philosophies influence the thinking of large numbers of people? Scholars have not been the only ones concerned with these questions. Government agencies and research firms addressed them at the time. Considerable attention focused on the Black Panther Party and how the public perceived it. Results of a 1969 Gallup Poll that included black respondents outside the big cities appeared less certain about what the Panthers stood for and less positive about their contribution to African-American advancement. A year later findings by the research firm Market Dynamics contradicted these results, contending that the Panthers enjoyed substantial support. The company polled African Americans in New York City, San Francisco, Detroit, Baltimore, and Birmingham, Alabama, and found that respondents thought the Panthers had been the third most effective civil rights group after the NAACP and SCLC in the previous two years. Sixty-two percent of those questioned approved of the party.[36]

Researchers also wanted to know whether the era's rebelliousness was the product of foreign subversion. The intelligence community took up the question, with the CIA contending that black unrest was homegrown. The Nixon administration, however, intent on discovering evidence of foreign intrigue, encouraged the FBI to expand its overseas operations. According to one of journalist Seymour Hersh's contacts, "the White House had a 'preoccupation' with the extent of foreign control over domestic radicals and blacks. 'Whenever kids went abroad,' the source said, 'there were those in the White House who were convinced that they were meeting with Communists and coming back with dope.'"[37]

[35] Ninety percent of respondents to a May 1969 Gallup Poll that surveyed a national sample opposed payment of "500 million dollars to Negroes because of past injustices," US Gallup 781.Q007. Stephen Michael Ward, "'Ours Too Was a Struggle for a Better World': Activist Intellectuals and the Radical Promise of the Black Power Movement, 1962–1972," PhD diss., University of Texas, Austin, 2002, p. 156; Louis Cassels, "Black Manifesto Called 'Flop,' but U.S. Churches Not Ignoring It," *Chicago Daily Defender*, July 14, 1969, p. 6.

[36] Gallup Poll's "Negro Survey," May 1969. For a view of black opinion as mirroring that of whites, see Manfred Berg, "Guns, Butter, and Civil Rights: The National Association for the Advancement of Colored People and the Vietnam War, 1964–1968," in *Aspects of War in American History*, eds. David K. Adams and Cornelius A. van Minnen (Keele, UK: University of Keele, 1970), 230–1. Yohuru R. Williams, "American Exported Black Nationalism: The Student Nonviolent Coordinating Committee, the Black Panther Party, and the Worldwide Freedom Struggle, 1967–1972," *Negro History Bulletin* 60 July–September (1997): 13.

[37] Seymour M. Hersh, "Alien-Radical Tie Disputed By C.I.A.," *New York Times*, May 25, 1973, p. 1.

FIGURE 12. Black Panther Party member Elbert "Big Man" Howard and Jean Genet at a New Haven, Connecticut rally, May 1, 1970, in support of Panther Bobby Seale, then imprisoned. (Getty Images)

The record suggests that black insurgents influenced, as much as they were influenced by, dissidents they met overseas. The French playwright Jean Genet was drawn to the Black Panther Party's deployment of style and described the organization in lyrical terms. Genet lived with party members for three months while visiting the States during late summer and fall 1968, writing about conditions for blacks as he observed the Democratic Party convention in Chicago. The adventurous French writer accompanied the Panthers on speaking tours to universities and opened doors for them in elite circles (see Figure 12). He aided French support groups for the Panthers and advocated the release of George Jackson and the subsequently apprehended Angela Davis. Genet employed the term "political prisoner," a category that U.S. authorities tended to dismiss, to describe them. In the States again in the spring and summer of 1970, Genet gave speeches, later anthologized, that appeared in the French and U.S. press. Gay and an ex-convict himself, Genet had written five books while in prison in France. He entered the United States illegally because American authorities refused him a visa. "I am meddling," he wrote, "in the affairs of America because it set an example for me by meddling in my own affairs and in the affairs pretty much everywhere, of the entire world."[38]

---

[38] Pascale Gaitet, *Queens and Revolutionaries: New Readings of Jean Genet* (Cranbury, N.J.: Associated Universities Press, 2003), 85, 86; Robert Sandarg, "Jean Genet and the Black Panther Party," *Journal of Black Studies* 16 (March 1986): 269–282; Jean Genet, *The Declared Enemy:*

French philosopher Michel Foucault shared aspects of Genet's outlaw sensibility and his attraction to black rebels. His interest in African-American insurgency would bear directly on his scholarship. He had learned about the Panthers from Tunisian students. Forced to leave Tunisia because of his active support for radicals, Foucault returned to France and subsequently traveled to the United States, where he worked at the University of Buffalo in 1970. He extended his knowledge of the United States in a trip to the Deep South.

While in the States, Foucault encountered California inmate George Jackson's writings. Foucault had learned from Genet about Jackson, who, like Genet, had developed his talents "in the carceral world."[39] Genet appealed to Foucault to assist him in Jackson's defense. Foucault then edited and introduced the French translation of excerpts from Jackson's *Soledad Brother: The Prison Letters of George Jackson*, for which Genet penned the preface.

Foucault taught in Upstate New York, an epicenter of the U.S. prison network. He was not there when the Attica Rebellion of 1971, an event that marked a period of major upheaval in American prisons, occurred but visited Attica the following year. The turmoil in the penal system formed part of the context in which his *Surveiller et punir: Naissance de la prison Discipline and Punish: The Birth of the Prison* appeared in 1975.[40] The prominence of outlaws and prisons in turn-of-the-decade narratives made it easier for federal officials to link political unrest to crime and justify the various programs of espionage, infiltration, and repression.

In this environment, President Nixon inveighed against lenient judges who supposedly coddled criminals and used the oft-repeated mantra "law and order" as a way of signaling his desire to suppress protests and revolt, and to curb the rebellious behavior of minorities and the young. Two contrasting ideas about race seemed at once to contradict and reinforce one another in the Nixon White House. On one hand, the president did not think much of blacks' abilities. "You have to face the fact that the whole problem is really the blacks," chief of staff H. R. Haldeman in his diary recalled the president's saying. Nixon "pointed out that there has never in history been an adequate black nation, and they are the only race of which this is true. P[resident] says Africa is hopeless, the worst there, is Liberia, which we built." Nixon, an abortion opponent,

Texts and Interviews (Stanford, Calif.: Stanford University Press, 2004), 39. See also Jean Genet, *Prisoner of Love* (New York: New York Review Book, 2003); Amy Bugo Ongiri, "Prisoner of Love: Affiliation, Sexuality, and the Black Panther Party," *Journal of African American History* 94 (Winter 2009): 69–86.

39 Gaitet, *Queens and Revolutionaries*, 20.

40 Institut Mémoires de l'édition contemporaine (IMEC), Michel Foucault Archive, online at http://www.michel-foucault-archives.org/spip.php?article182, accessed January 8, 2008. Foucault described Attica in *Telos* 19 (Spring1974): 154–61. See also David Macey, *The Lives of Michel Foucault* (New York: Knopf, 2005).

made one exception to its use: "There are times when an abortion is necessary. I know that. When you have a black and a white or a rape."[41]

On the other hand, no *public* acknowledgment of black inferiority and incompetence could be made. As Haldeman parsed Nixon's advice, "The key is to devise a system that recognizes this while not appearing to. Problem with overall welfare plan is that it forces poor whites into same position as blacks. Feels we have to get rid of the veil of hypocrisy and guilt and face reality." Part of the reality for Nixon was the stir created by sociobiological arguments, freshly articulated in the 1970s, that linked race to intelligence. "The P[resident] made the point that it was important for him to know these things and then do everything possible to deny them – that is, the genetic-racial problem." As the nation's leader, he had to submerge his own beliefs so as not to stir up "latent prejudice."[42]

This stance found a revealing echo in Nixon administration policy toward Africa and the United Nations during these years. As described by NSC staffer W. Marshall Wright:

In both Africa and in the UN our policy is essentially defensive. Neither is central in any way to US foreign policy operations or interests. We deal with them because they are there, not because we hope to get great things out of our participation. We aim at minimizing the attention and resources which must be addressed to them. What we really want from both is no trouble. Our policy is therefore directed at damage limiting, rather than at accomplishing anything in particular. That being true, there is (or at least, I can find) no broad and positive conceptual base which can credibly be put forward to explain why we do what we do in Africa and the UN. The real base we cannot mention. The task then is to put the best possible face upon essentially negative roles, and to try to make them sound more positive and more integrated than they actually are.[43]

Whatever had to remain unspoken, Nixon, an astute politician, found himself dealing with blacks at home on a firmer basis than the fact that "they are there." They had a role to play in his calculus. The "southern strategy" of courting segregationists in hopes of establishing a solid foundation for a new conservatism and party unity did not constitute the only tool in Nixon's chest. Just as he courted white ethnics and skilled white workers, early in his first

---

[41] Haldeman's diary entry, April 28, 1969, H. R. Haldeman, *The Haldeman Diaries: Inside the Nixon White House*, CD-ROM (New York: Sony Imagesoft, 1994); Charlie Savage, "On Nixon Tapes, Ambivalence over Abortion, Not Watergate," *New York Times*, June 23, 2009.

[42] Haldeman's diary entries, April 28, 1969; Thursday, October 7, 1970, *The Haldeman Diaries*. Sociobiology is traced in Alexander Alland, Jr., *Race in Mind* (New York: Palgrave Macmillan, 2004); Edwin Black, *War against the Weak: Eugenics and America's Campaign to Create a Master Race* (New York: Thunder's Mouth Press, 2004); Edward J. Larson, *Sex, Race, and Science: Eugenics in the Deep South* (Baltimore: Johns Hopkins University Press, 1995); William H. Tucker, *The Funding of Scientific Racism* (Urbana and Chicago: University of Illinois Press, 2002); Charles Lane, "The Tainted Sources of 'The Bell Curve,'" *New York Review of Books* 41 (December 1, 1994), 14–19.

[43] Wright to National Security Adviser Henry Kissinger, January 10, 1970, *FRUS, Foundations of Foreign Policy, 1969–1972* (Washington, D.C.: Government Printing Office, 2003), p. 163.

term Nixon hoped to identify a conventional black middle-class constituency that would vote Republican and oppose both the civil rights establishment and Black Power zeal. The gambit failed, and the president found himself side-stepping confrontations with such figures as Ralph Abernathy. "There's no use dealing honestly with these people," Haldeman recorded sourly.

They obviously want confrontation not solutions; despite the best of intentions, these efforts at establishing communications with the black leadership were rarely successful. They usually ended up, as this one did, with the black leaders using the White House forum as a platform to attack the P and his policies. The meetings themselves tended more to confrontation.... Pretty fed up with blacks and their hopeless attitude.

Nixon also concluded that no meeting of minds would occur with African-American spokespersons. "[The] Key is to limit all our support and communication to the blacks and totally ignore the militants, etc."[44]

In spite of Johnson administration efforts to prevent the development of a black foreign policy audience and the Nixon White House decision in effect to shut out black leadership altogether, issues of interest to African Americans found expression through other channels. The Congressional Black Caucus and the House Subcommittee on Africa played a vital role. In 1960 African-American representation in Congress consisted of only William Dawson, Charles Diggs, Robert Nix, and Adam Clayton Powell Jr. These men represented voters in Chicago, Detroit, Philadelphia, and New York City, respectively, where blacks had settled during the twentieth-century migrations. Minority representation in Congress grew with the expansion of voting rights and population shifts. In 1969, the black caucus in the House of Representatives began to flex its muscle. Members absented themselves from newly elected Nixon's State of the Union address because he refused to meet with them as a body. The subsequent fallout from that action led Nixon to relent and schedule a meeting. The caucus sent the White House a list of sixty recommendations, including more aid to Africa, a Family Assistance Program for the working poor, and other measures. Nixon pretended to endorse these proposals, but according to Haldeman's memoirs, he had no intention of acting on them. When the caucus asked for an answer to its wish-list memorandum by May 17, 1969, the response was sent a day late and did not address key points. Instead, it reiterated Nixon's own policies.[45]

The congressional caucus formalized itself in 1971, adopting the name Congressional Black Caucus (CBC) at the suggestion of New York representative Charles Rangel, who had defeated Adam Clayton Powell Jr. for Harlem's seat. The CBC now had thirteen members and provided a venue for public discussion of foreign and domestic policy. By 1971, congressional staffs as a whole were larger and professionalized. Legislators could now rely on informed opinion on Africa-related issues and on access to the relatively new

[44] Haldeman's diary entries, Tuesday, May 13, 1969; Saturday, February 7, 1970.
[45] Carolyn P. DuBose, *The Untold Story of Charles Diggs* (Arlington, Va.: Barton Publishing House, 1998), 95–106.

Congressional Research Service. The black think tank, the Joint Center for Political Studies, founded in 1970 by Howard University and the Metropolitan Applied Research Council, was also an important resource.[46]

Africa had become peripheral to White House concerns by the late 1960s, but Congress remained a place for debate on African affairs, as ably organized by Representative Charles Diggs of Detroit. Diggs, the first African American elected to Congress from Michigan, attended historically black Fisk University until he was drafted in April 1943 and became a second lieutenant in the Army Air Force. Upon transfer to the army base at Tuskegee, Alabama, Diggs met fighter pilot Chappie James and singer Lena Horne when she was performing at the officer's club. Glamour, however, was fleeting. There were few facilities on base for African-American soldiers, who had trouble finding such basic services as barbershops. White subordinates tried to avoid saluting Diggs, and his awareness of how German POWs received better treatment than black GIs bothered him.[47]

On returning to Detroit after his June 1945 discharge, Diggs studied at Wayne State University and was elected to Congress in 1954. He attended the farcical 1955 Mississippi trial of the men who murdered the young Emmett Till, acting informally in that capacity as black America's representative. The Detroiter combined civil rights activism and advocacy for Africa with cold war liberalism, remaining staunchly anticommunist. In the same year as the Till trial, he signed a petition to keep the People's Republic of China out of the UN. His cold war stance did not interfere with his anticolonialism, however. Like Powell, he arraigned the Eisenhower administration's lackadaisical Africa policy, and his criticisms of the State Department's racial practices continued into the Democratic succession. A decade later, Representatives John Conyers and Adam Clayton Powell raised objections to the Vietnam War, but Diggs used his influence to stop the Mississippi Freedom Democratic Party from organizing local draft resistance.[48]

In 1968, Diggs became chair of the House Subcommittee on Africa. Randall Robinson, the founder of the lobby TransAfrica, recalls that he "kindled, virtually alone, what little congressional interest there was in Africa" and opened hearings to academics and activists. Diggs probed conflicts between African

[46] Hanes Walton, *Invisible Politics: Black Political Behavior* (Albany, N.Y.: SUNY Press, 1985), 187; Joyce Jones, "The Silent Force," *Black Enterprise* 25 (April 1995): "Congress to Gain Black Members," *Focus* 1 (November 1972): 4–5.

[47] Biographical information from DuBose, *The Untold Story of Charles Diggs*.

[48] *Chicago Defender*, October 15–21, 1960; James Jackson to Benjamin Davis, April 15, 1955, Benjamin Davis Papers, Correspondence, Box 1, SC; Randall Robinson, *Defending the Spirit: A Black Life in America* (New York: Dutton, 1998), 94; Francis Njubi Nesbitt, *Race for Sanctions: African Americans against Apartheid, 1946–1994* (Bloomington: Indiana University Press, 2004), 35; Andrew J. DeRoche, *Andrew Young, Civil Rights Ambassador* (Wilmington, Del.: Scholarly Resources Books, 2003), 66; Donald R. Culverson, *From Sharpeville to Soweto to Sanctions: The Rise of American Anti-Apartheid Activism, 1960–1987* (Boulder, Colo.: Westview Press, 1999), 92.

governments and the West, including apartheid and divestment from South Africa and sanctions against Rhodesia and the remaining colonial regimes.[49]

Robinson fondly remembered Diggs's role in creating access for succeeding policy activists. "As tenaciously as he fought for new and constructive American policies, he saw himself also as something of a steward for young African-American policy professionals. I was newly hired and with him in meetings with Alex Haley and Secretaries of State Henry Kissinger and Cyrus Vance. More with a grunt than with ceremony, he opened doors to countless careers and shoved us through." Attorney Goler Butcher, TransAfrica founders Randall Robinson and Herschelle Challenor, political scientist Ron Walters, and Detroit Urban League director Francis Kornegay had all served at one time on Diggs's staff.[50]

After a trip to South Africa to assess conditions, Diggs issued a report that strongly endorsed sanctions against South Africa, including a ban on its sugar exports, and advocated educational and cultural outreach to black South Africans. He opposed the tacit anticommunist alliance between the United States and the apartheid regime that provided an excuse for Pretoria to receive military aid. Nuclear cooperation and arms trading should end, as should strong corporate ties between the two nations. "Our government," Diggs wrote, "decries violence as a means of liberation, without condemning the violence which the South African government uses to enforce the subjugation of the majority of the people"[51] (see Figure 13).

Diggs is remembered in association with the divestment campaigns. Divestment enjoyed its greatest popularity as a tactic in the mid-1980s, but its origins predate that decade. A. Philip Randolph chaired the Committee of Conscience against Apartheid in 1966, with sponsorship from labor, Congress, clergy, and celebrities. The committee urged Chase Manhattan Bank and Citibank customers to withdraw their accounts by Human Rights Day 1966. They ultimately withdrew $22 million, nearly equaling the amount these banks had extended to South Africa.[52]

Efforts to sideline the international work of figures like Diggs, or ignore the ferment in African-American communities and in the nation at large, never fully succeeded. While the intelligence agencies made dilatory attempts to understand doctrinal differences among dissidents, politicians mostly lumped

---

[49] Robinson, *Defending the Spirit*, 94.

[50] Ibid., 94–5; Du Bose, 232–4, 61, 62.

[51] Diggs quoted in Eric J. Morgan, "Our Own Interests: Nixon, South Africa, and Dissent at Home and Abroad," *Diplomacy and Statecraft*, 17 (3) (July 2006): 487.

[52] George M. Houser, "Freedom's Struggle Crosses Oceans and Mountains: Martin Luther King, Jr. and the Liberation Struggles in Africa and America" in *We Shall Overcome: Martin Luther King, Jr. and the Black Freedom Struggle*, eds. Peter J. Albert and Ronald Hoffman (New York: Pantheon Books and the United States Capitol Historical Society, 1990), 195–6. See also David Hauck, Meg Voorhees, and Glenn Goldberg, *Two Decades of Debate: The Controversy over U.S. Companies in South Africa* (Washington, D.C.: Investor Responsibility Center, 1983), 96, 127–30.

FIGURE 13. Earlier activists' work paved the way for the renewed antiapartheid campaigns of the 1980s. (Courtesy of Lincoln Cushing and the African Activist Archive)

them together, making no vital distinctions between the center and the Left. In spite of the White House's dismissive tone toward its critics, Nixon occasionally tried to defuse tension, including his famous midnight visit to antiwar students keeping vigil at the Lincoln Memorial. Cabinet officers had trouble maintaining a stolid front faced with large-scale public discontent. They had suffered a wide array of psychosomatic symptoms and stress disorders as the Vietnam War continued. During the Nixon years, the "kids" who the president snidely observed were gravely disturbing their parents included the offspring of his own staff.[53]

This angst was compounded by the common notion, shared even by communists, that rebel youth wanted only to confront authority rather than solve important problems. A Czech journalist, observing Stokely Carmichael at a Havana conference, described his radicalism as "primitive passion and enthusiasm, pathos, lack of ability to understand the realities of our world, underestimation of strategy, tactics, and experience of the international communist movement." Stokely had no answers: He "represents a program which is limited only to destruction, because even Carmichael could not answer the question 'how do you see it afterwards?'"[54]

It is reasonable to suppose that Carmichael did not necessarily see that as a valid question. He proposed that "political direction develops as we move," that is, that revolutionary practice would engender solutions to political problems. In this view, SNCC could very well be temporary, to be succeeded by a new formation appropriate for changing conditions. Carmichael used China as an example of unrehearsed policies in a country where original Marxist doctrines did not seem to apply. He agreed with colleagues like James Forman that black insurgency needed an ideology, but Forman believed that revolutionary struggle should be guided by antecedent principles. Carmichael, however, was open to improvisation in a changeable world that eluded mechanical laws.[55]

Given the diversity of African-American views in the early 1970s and the size of the black population, no unchanging group opinion could be assumed. Indeed, volatile and contentious domestic politics complicated efforts to articulate a black foreign policy. Those efforts nevertheless occurred. If scholars are content to focus only on the eccentric or sensational aspects of Black Power, they will miss the exertions that were made across the political spectrum to delineate a new politics.

The Black Panther Party issued a conference call for a Revolutionary People's Constitutional Convention, an invitation for radical groups to meet in Philadelphia, the historic birthplace of the U.S. Constitution. Attendees would rewrite that document to benefit those who were excluded from enjoying full civil rights. The Panther goal was to bring together a splintering American Left that was scattering into diverse separate movements, including the emerging

[53] Robert Dean, *Imperial Brotherhood: Gender and the Making of Cold War Foreign Policy* (Amherst: University of Massachusetts Press, 2001), 240; Haldeman's diary entry, December 24, 1970; Peter Haldeman, "Growing Up Haldeman," *New York Times Magazine*, April 3, 1994, 30–5, 48, 58, 64, 65.

[54] Translation of an article by Karel Jezdinsky entitled "Fifty More Vietnams?" in the Czech-language periodical, *Reporter*, No 19, Prague, 22 September 1967, pp. 24–5, reprinted in FBIS, "Reportage and Comment on Stokely Carmichael's Activities and Statements Abroad from 6 October to 12 December 1967."

[55] Stokely Carmichael with Ekwueme Michael Thelwell, *Ready for Revolution* (New York: Scribner, 2003), 670; James Forman, *The Making of Black Revolutionaries* (Washington, D.C., Open Hand Publishing, 1985), 431–2.

gay rights and women's liberation challenges to the status quo. The Panthers sought to surmount obstacles to the development of a united front against racism and imperialism. "The newly articulated politicization of gender and sexuality" needed attention.[56]

The convention took place over the Labor Day weekend, shortly after a series of police raids on Panther headquarters in Philadelphia aimed at preventing the event from taking place. Civil rights and civil liberties advocates foiled this plan, and six thousand people arrived in the City of Brotherly Love anticipating a keynote speech by Huey Newton, who had returned to civilian life after three years in prison. The convention failed to mend the splits among the various participants, and some left the meeting angry and disappointed. Yet it broke new ground in seeking acceptance of diversity, an imperative that would bear fruit in years to come.[57]

For the moment, the breakdown of the Revolutionary People's Constitutional Convention convinced many African-American activists that they should focus on identifying and consolidating a specifically black agenda. One consequence of this determination was the creation of the National Black Political Convention. This conference was historically significant because it tried to surmount factionalism, engage grassroots actors, and define issues outside the conventional electoral arena. Called by Diggs late in November 1971, the meeting would convene in economically troubled Gary, Indiana. Gary rapidly lost its white majority population and its corresponding revenue base in the course of a decade, making the election of the African-American Richard Hatcher as mayor somewhat of a pyrrhic victory for the financially strapped city.[58]

Although the historic prototype for the meeting was the Negro Convention movement of the early nineteenth century, more effective communication, if not better concord, had developed since the time of the abolitionists. Now black legislators, who had not existed in antebellum times, wanted to establish their control over Black Power momentum. In Diggs's view, the convention was about "unifying black political power under national direction." To that end, he, with other elected officials and leading activists, mapped out a strategy in a series of meetings, including one in the District of Columbia held in early March 1972 where the principals involved were Diggs, Richard Hatcher, and Leroi Jones (Amiri Baraka), the latter accompanied by unsmiling, sunglassed bodyguards.[59]

---

[56] The text of the conference call is in *The Black Panthers Speak*, 2nd ed., ed. Philip Foner (Cambridge, Mass: DaCapo Press, 2002), 267–278. See also Duchess Harris and Adam J. Waterman, "Babylon Is Burning," *Journal of Intergroup Relations* 27 (2) (2000): 18.

[57] Harris and Waterman, "Babylon Is Burning," 17–33; Father Paul M. Washington, with David M. Gracie, *"Other Sheep I Have": The Autobiography of Father Paul M. Washington* (Philadelphia: Temple University Press, 1994), 126, 128.

[58] Cedric Johnson, *Revolutionaries to Race Leaders: Black Power and the Making of African American Politics* (Minneapolis: University of Minnesota Press, 2007), 96.

[59] For the nineteenth century origin of national black political summits, see Howard Holman Bell, ed., *Minutes of the Proceedings of the National Negro Conventions, 1830–1864* (New

More people arrived in Gary the opening day of the convention than hotels could accommodate. Some participants stayed in private homes and others thirty-five miles away in Chicago. A press corps of five hundred kept the public informed of the agenda while, in a festival atmosphere, vendors sold African artifacts. The convention was a Who's Who of the black political elite. Attendees included aspiring politician Coleman Young, later mayor of Detroit; Representative Louis Stokes and his brother, Carl Stokes, mayor of Cleveland; Mississippi politico Charles Evers; Representative Ronald Dellums; and future California representative Mervyn Dymally. Georgia state senator Julian Bond appeared, as did National Urban League president Vernon Jordan and Frank Reeves, director of the Joint Center for Political Studies. Arthur Fletcher, director of the United Negro College Fund; Robert Brown, special assistant to President Nixon; and Andrew T. Hatcher, President Kennedy's former assistant press secretary, participated. Marion Barry, then president of the District of Columbia School Board, and Ronald Walters, director of the Political Science Department at Howard University, arrived from Washington, D.C. David Dinkins, Basil Paterson, and Percy Sutton, formidable New York City figures, attended, as did the nationalist Owusu Sadaukai (Howard Fuller) and CORE's Roy Innis. Louis Farrakhan of the Nation of Islam, the Black Panther Bobby Seale, and activist-performer Harry Belafonte took part. The list was overwhelmingly male. Malcolm X's widow, Betty Shabazz; LBJ protégée Barbara Jordan; NCNW president Dorothy Height; Coretta Scott King; California state legislator Yvonne Braithwaite; nationalist icon Audley (Queen Mother) Moore; and Beulah Sanders from the National Welfare Rights Organization (NWRO) numbered among the prominent and visible women, but none was invited to speak.[60]

Balmy temperatures and a celebratory mood suggested that black America was on the threshold of a new era. As Diggs's biographer described it:

The weather was like spring, as the temperature rose above sixty degrees. Some men were walking around in their shirtsleeves. There were also young women strolling around in hot pants.... Men and women in designer clothes joined forces with those who were resplendent in colorful robes and fancy headdresses. It was a lively crowd ranging from mothers carrying babies on their hips to whole families of men, women, and children....Red, black, and green liberation flags were seen all over the streets of Gary.... It seemed that anything was possible in that atmosphere.[61]

Outward euphoria masked internal struggles. Participants represented widely diverging viewpoints and jockeyed for their place within the leadership. The major questions at Gary were whether there should be an independent black

York: Arno Press, 1969) and Howard Holman Bell, *A Survey of the Negro Convention Movement, 1830–1861* (New York: Arno Press, 1969). Johnson, *Revolutionaries to Race Leaders*, 8–98; DuBose, *The Untold Story of Charles Diggs*, 164, 155, 158.

60 Ethel L. Payne, "Hatcher's Problem: What to Do with 8,000 Folks?" *Chicago Daily Defender*, March 9, 1972, p. 2; Johnson, *Revolutionaries to Race Leaders*, 91, 103, 104, 125, 266 n. 43.

61 DuBose, *The Untold Story*, 167.

political party and whether nationalism, rather than integrationist politics, was the best strategy for the freedom struggle. Lawmakers wanted to master the proceedings while remaining in the Democratic Party during an election year. For them, integrating African Americans into the larger system constituted the best politics.

The convention opened for business at a local high school at 1:15 p.m. on March 11, four hours behind schedule. After a few speeches and songs, plenary session attendees became unruly when media scaffolds blocked their view of the stage. They began chanting and would not stop until the scaffolds were dismantled. A voice vote was taken to make Diggs, Hatcher, and Baraka the convention's permanent chairs. The tally was very close, but Diggs called it for "ayes" anyway. Pandemonium then broke loose, with some people rushing the speakers' podium and being constrained by guards. After a recess to restore cool, a new vote was taken, but the results remained the same.[62]

A number of draft resolutions that passed that day exposed partisan rifts. The CBC later disavowed in writing a resolution passed by voice vote that Israel should retire to its pre-1967 borders. Diggs, not surprisingly, opposed the formation of a black independent political party, and the Michigan delegation walked out of the convention in protest of some of the resolutions. Diggs nevertheless expressed optimism at the convocation's outcome and thought it had successfully set up the machinery for nationwide political coordination. "'The unity is admittedly fragile,' he acknowledged, and 'there is a lot of work to be done,'" but he believed the meeting had effectively begun it.[63]

Convention resolutions included sweeping national reforms. Participants endorsed proportional representation of African Americans in Congress, better civil rights law enforcement, greater political independence for the District of Columbia, the end of the death penalty, and freedom from harassment by U.S. intelligence agencies. Nationalists sought an opportunity for a vote on whether there should be a black fifty-first state. In the end, Nixon's 1972 reelection and the defection of African-American elected officials unwilling to break Democratic Party discipline derailed convention goals and sparked new grassroots interest in creating an independent black party.[64]

Later that spring, the CBC sponsored a two-day Washington conference attended by two hundred persons to deliberate the best ways to influence U.S. policy on Africa. The confab was meant to follow up the Gary convention, but this time, the CBC controlled events. Kenyan and Somali representatives to the UN were present, as were C. L. R. James and Robert Browne of the Black Economic Research Center. The talks were planned to coordinate with a rally organized by the African Liberation Day Committee, an organization that

[62] Ibid., 167, 169.

[63] Warren N. Holmes, *The National Black Independent Party: Political Insurgency or Ideological Convergence?* (New York: Garland, 1999), 30. On the Michigan walkout, Ethel L. Payne, "That Moment of Truth in Gary and Beyond," *Chicago Daily Defender*, March 18, 1972, p. 8.

[64] Johnson, *Revolutionaries to Race Leaders*, 109; Holmes, *The National Black Independent Party*, 30.

would morph into the African Liberation Support Committee (ALSC), created in July 1972 to carry on solidarity work.[65]

Among the many well-known figures who attended the Gary convention, one was missing: Representative Shirley Chisholm from Brooklyn, New York declared her candidacy for president of the United States in January 1972. In March, the Gallop Organization asked a national sample of adults which of the candidates running for president they would refuse to vote for. George Wallace was the most unpopular, with 43 percent of those polled rejecting him. Chisholm was second at 21 percent.[66] Her unpopularity was not limited to whites. She emerged as a national figure during a fierce rejection of feminist politics by many African Americans who associated themselves with Black Power as an ideology, however poorly defined. The requirement that effective leaders be men persisted in many circles and helps explain Chisholm's absence at Gary.

Chisholm had surmounted such obstacles locally because she had won election in a district where the majority of voters were working-class women, defeating civil rights icon James Farmer in the process. As filmmaker Shola Lynch observed, "While Farmer's campaign rolled through neighborhoods on sound trucks with men in dashikis playing drums to share his message with the general community, Chisholm took her campaign to the ladies. She worked subway stops during their morning and evening commutes, parks, churches, shopping districts, housing projects, and had coffee klatches in homes all over the district." Chisholm did not consciously set out to be a feminist candidate, but interestingly, "won the Congressional seat by a 2.5 to 1 margin, the exact ratio of female to male voters" in her district.[67]

The Brooklyn politician represented a side of the African-American political debate for which Black Power rhetoric lacked a ready response: How should black leadership address the economic and political needs and goals of women? While more than half the eligible black electorate failed to cast ballots in 1972, the total picture was more complicated. Scholar Marjorie Lansing used data from the 1972 presidential election and Census Bureau reports from 1964 and 1968 to analyze black women's political behavior. This constituency, she asserted, "held the lowest levels of political efficacy and the lowest levels of trust in the federal government, and viewed sex discrimination as sharply affecting

[65] Paul Delaney, "Africans and Black Americans Open Conference in Washington," *New York Times*, May 26, 1972, p. 3: 4–5; Cedric Johnson, "From Popular Anti-Imperialism to Sectarianism: The African Liberation Support Committee and Black Power Radicals," *New Political Science* 25 (4) (2003): 490.

[66] Gallup Poll (AIPO), March 24–27, 1972.

[67] Shola Lynch, "Afterword," in Shirley Chisholm, *Unbought and Unbossed*, repr. ed. (Boston: Houghton Mifflin, 1970; repr. Washington, D.C., Take Root Media, 2010),. See also Joshua Guild, "To Make That Someday Come: Shirley Chisholm's Radical Politics of Possibility," in *Want to Start a Revolution? Radical Women in the Black Freedom Struggle*, eds. Dayo F. Gore, Jeanne Theoharis, and Komozi Woodard (New York: New York University Press, 2009), 257.

them." Nevertheless, since the mid-1960s, black women's rate of increase as voters had been greater than that of any other "sex/race group." Their behavior contradicted the common notion that low-income poorly educated people would not vote. Young black women's participation rates exceeded that of young black men, and middle-aged black women voted at the same rate as their male cohorts.[68]

These phenomena escaped Black Power leaders, who were lambasting conventional civil rights leaders as weak and feminized eunuchs. Some discourse took on openly homophobic and misogynist overtones, as when, for example, an author referred in the pages of *Liberator* to "the *effeminate* projections of the Rustins, the flabby orientation of the Farmers, and the shuffling act of the Kings." The new black manhood was confrontational and lean: it rejected "an ethic" that would make African Americans "freakish, fat, and fairly satisfied" with the status quo.[69]

Chisholm, a middle-aged black woman of Caribbean descent whose constituency included emerging groups such as the National Organization of Women, was not perceived as a Black Power candidate in spite of her outspokenness on questions of race and her professed independence from white political elites. The energetic posture she struck, "unbought and unbossed," placed her in the genealogical company of such female politicians as Frances Perkins and Eleanor Roosevelt, remnants of an earlier protofeminist and Progressive era strand in the Democratic Party. But none of these figures appealed much to angry young black men. Chisholm's drive and political skills did not help her with the new militants.

If parts of the black electorate rejected feminism and women's leadership and parted company with Democratic politicians over support for Israel, Africa was a matter on which most could agree. Just as it served as a symbolic issue that smoothed over discord between African Americans and the Kennedy administration in the early 1960s, a decade later it served the same purpose within black circles. The argument can be made that, absent concrete gains on the racial front after 1965, black elected officials used Africa to shore up their credibility with skeptical constituencies. It also suggests that the disorganization and resentments at Gary did not accurately reflect African-American political potential.

As black liberals found themselves cut off from White House access in the 1970s, they became more open to Black Power ideologies and more prone to rely on rallying their respective bases. The lack of fruitful communication with the Nixon administration, however, created problems for them in their pursuit of civil rights goals at home and African liberation abroad. Nixon's foreign policy, while ostensibly unrelated to domestic issues, contained linked

---

[68] Marjorie Lansing, "The Voting Behavior of Black American Women," in *A Portrait of Marginality: The Political Behavior of the American Woman*, eds. Marianne Githens and Jewel L. Prestage (New York: D. Mckay, 1977), 379–81.

[69] *Liberator* 5 (July 1965): 7. Emphasis in original.

assumptions that governed the public policy of his administration generally and conditioned the way he responded to challenges from African Americans.

While Nixon demonstrated less interest in domestic than in foreign affairs, his opinions about the international scene shed significant light on his ideas about internal governance. As concerns Vietnam, his belief that Asian prosperity and stability were the best bulwarks against communism echoes his remarks as vice president during the so-called kitchen debate with Soviet premier Nikita Khrushchev. At a Moscow trade fair where the latest U.S. kitchen appliances were displayed, Nixon told the Soviet leader that it was in the consumer economy, where life would be made easier for the average citizen, that the American way of life would trump the Soviet. Levittown tract home builder William Levitt famously said, "No man who owns his own house and lot can be a communist. He has too much to do."[70] Nixon's endorsement of "black capitalism" similarly made the argument that affluence was the best cure for black unrest.

When Nixon ran for president in 1968, he continued to adhere to GOP orthodoxy and went further to the Right in supporting the Katanga secession. But he also began promoting himself as a change agent. In an article published in *Foreign Affairs* in October 1969, Nixon laid out his foreign policy perspective. The Pacific Rim formed the centerpiece of his thinking. In Asia, anticolonial fervor was waning, he asserted. For young Asians, "the old nationalist slogans have less meaning ... than they had for their fathers." They now held their own leaders to account. Anxiety about China, furthermore, was replacing Asian antagonism toward the West.[71]

Moderates applauded Nixon's policy of simultaneously suppressing the antiwar movement, widening the Indochina war, and reaching an agreement with the North Vietnamese in January 1973. As Mary Brennan has speculated, if Nixon's term had ended in 1973 he might have provided an opening for the resurgence of liberal Republicanism. Watergate, however, and the president's other problems further undermined Americans' trust in government, a reaction that those on the hard Right could use to subvert the appeal of a strong federalism. While Jimmy Carter's election exemplified the national backlash to the Watergate scandal, politicians on Nixon's right "were the big long-term winners." The elimination of Nixon "undermined the centrist position in the party, thus clearing the way for conservatives."[72]

None of this was apparent, however, when Nixon shared his views with readers of *Foreign Affairs*. The United States, bogged down in Vietnam, could not do much to help noncommunist Asian states resist the Chinese bogey, he wrote. They would have to step up to the plate themselves to ensure their own security, creating regional agreements that the United States could support.

[70] Levitt quoted in Stephen J. Whitfield, *The Culture of the Cold War* (Baltimore: Johns Hopkins University Press, 1996), 73.

[71] Richard M. Nixon, "Asia after Vietnam," *Foreign Affairs* 46 (October 1969): 112.

[72] Mary C. Brennan, *Turning Right in the Sixties: The Conservative Capture of the GOP* (Chapel Hill: University of North Carolina Press, 1995), 136, 137.

Americans would remain silent partners except upon request and as a last resort. Unlike SEATO, which had been a Western initiative, the energy for Asian defense would have to be supplied by the governments themselves. Writing during an era that witnessed a proliferation of independent states in the global South and the spread of Marxist thought, Nixon addressed the apparent growing diversity among communists. He dismissed any claim that radicalism in a multilateral world threatened Western interests any less than the centralized Kremlin variety. "National Communism poses a different kind of threat than did the old-style international communism, but by being subtler it is in some ways more dangerous."[73]

Nixon asserted his Wilsonian commitment to gradualism. "From the standpoint of those dedicated to peace and an essential stability in world order," he declared, "the desideratum is to reach those ends by evolutionary rather than revolutionary means." The economic prosperity of such powers as Japan, Taiwan, and Hong Kong had been a product of such evolution, and, in the process, compromises were made. Not every noncommunist Asian state was a perfect democracy, and the democratic form, Nixon believed, might not be appropriate for all peoples. In any event, progress took time and expectations should not be too high. "Too wide a gap between reality and expectation always produces an explosive situation," he cautioned.[74]

The centerpiece of Nixon's foreign policy projections involved a revised approach to the People's Republic of China. As a nuclear power with a population exceeding 1 billion, China could not be left to its own devices. It had to be drawn into the international community. China, not a signatory to any nonproliferation treaty, could "scatter its weapons among 'liberation' forces anywhere in the world." It was thus important to prevent the "major nuclear powers" from being drawn into "'wars of national liberation' supported by Moscow or Peking but fought by proxy." The best way to handle China, Nixon believed, was to help noncommunist Asian countries withstand Maoist pressures by underwriting their economic prosperity and self-defense. To that end, Japan should shoulder more of the military burden and India should loosen state controls over private enterprise. No anti-Chinese alliances would be necessary, for China could be helped to redefine itself as a "great and progressing nation" rather than "as the epicenter of world revolution."

Breaking with a generation of U.S. hostility toward China, an antagonism to which Nixon had contributed, meant that the People's Republic would have to be defanged, at least rhetorically. The Chinese were now simply misguided hotheads. "Dealing with Red China is like trying to cope with some of the more explosive ghetto elements in our own country," Nixon wrote. "In each case a potentially destructive force has to be curbed; in each case an outlaw element has to be brought within the law; in each case dialogues have to be opened; in each case aggression has to be restrained while education proceeds;

---

[73] Nixon, "Asia after Vietnam," 113, 115.
[74] Ibid., 117, 188.

and not least, in neither case can we afford to let those now self-exiled from society stay exiled forever."

Nixon's *Foreign Affairs* article revealed more than the outlines of the future opening to China. By defining colonialism as a dead issue, the candidate made it possible for officialdom to ignore Africa, where colonial domination and white supremacy were still very much alive. The desire to insulate the great powers from the proxy wars for which they were and continue to be responsible abetted the process of eliminating Africa from consciousness and preventing it from emerging in policy beyond crisis events. Nixon's characterization of "national Communism" as equally menacing as the Kremlin variety made no distinction between nationalism and communism and thus tarred with the same brush independence movements in southern Africa and Soviet and Chinese national objectives. The president's opposition to revolutionary insurgency, coupled with a tolerance for lapses in democratic practice, meant that in spite of the innovative opening to China, his policies would remain solidly ensconced in an ongoing conservatism.

Quotation marks around the word "liberation" in Nixon's *Foreign Affairs* text suggest his skepticism about any radical enterprise, and his observations about Asia demonstrate his commitment to gradualism. In Stateside matters, the "explosive ghetto elements" demanding Freedom Now had to be talked down. A veiled threat accompanied Chinese ambitions as well as those of the inner city: the use of force is never precluded. Nixon's policies revealed a coherent worldview in which the U.S. tutelary mission abroad continues, as does its aversion to revolutionary insurgency and its willingness to trade democracy for stability. The common theme is repeated at home in the desire to educate (civilize) black militants, favor gradualism over radical change, and transform African-American life through *embourgeoisement*.

The White House created a Domestic Council consciously patterned after the National Security Council (NSC). According to Edwin L. Harper, who was special assistant to the president and assistant director of the Domestic Council from 1970 to 1973, its director, presidential adviser John Ehrlichman, had the council issue papers that were modeled on NSC memoranda. The council's main task was to provide analysis to guide initiatives that Nixon wished to undertake. With Ehrlichman its director, the Domestic Council became a staff-driven body independent of cabinet heads. The Office of Economic Opportunity (OEO), a Domestic Council member agency, also imitated the NSC in its staff development.[75]

Individuals who would subsequently be associated with foreign policy making applied their expertise to Nixon's efforts to refashion the home front.

---

[75] Caspar W. Weinberger with Gretchen Roberts, *In the Arena: A Memoir of the 20th Century* (Henry Regnery, 2001), 191–2; Walter Williams, *Honest Numbers and Democracy* (Washington, D.C.: Georgetown University Press, 1998), 57; Edwin L. Harper, "Domestic Policy Making in the Nixon Administration: An Evolving Process," *Presidential Studies Quarterly* 26 (Winter 1996): 49.

Caspar Weinberger was secretary of health, education and welfare from 1973 to 1975. Serving as undersecretary was Frank Carlucci, who first attracted world attention for his exploits in the Congo when the United States joined other Western powers in decapitating the Lumumba government. Nixon made Donald Rumsfeld, later a secretary of defense, OEO director. Daniel Patrick Moynihan, brought into the administration to direct the Urban Affairs Council, subsequently represented the United States as ambassador to India. Like the State Department, the Domestic Council was largely "pale and male." According to historian Joan Hoff, it boasted only one female staffer. This is not surprising when it is considered that Nixon consciously planned to exclude from domestic policy making the social workers, civil rights professionals, and community activists – many of them women and people of color – who were visible during the Johnson years.[76]

Nixon's domestic team expressed itself well in figurative rhetoric. The *New York Times* published "Text of a Pre-Inauguration Memo from Moynihan on Problems Nixon Would Face." Moynihan claimed that just as the United States was at war abroad, it was at war at home. The "cultural elite" was at war with society and had been so since the mid-nineteenth century. Lyndon Johnson was one of the casualties: "the first American President to be toppled by a mob." The enemy was not foreign. "It was a mob of college professors, millionaires, flower children, and Radcliffe girls. It was a mob that by early 1968 had effectively physically separated the Presidency from the people."

On the other side of the water, the economist noted, the war in Asia remained financially manageable through tax increases and deficit spending. The consumer economy continued to be robust. Insofar as there was no clear and immediate end in sight to American domestic problems, Moynihan insisted, it was now time to turn down the bombast. Much of that bombast, he thought, came from African Americans. Other racial-ethnic minorities deserved attention.[77]

Moynihan's depiction of African-American ferment as mostly cultural removed politics from the mix. His desire to obliterate the black poor in order to have them arise, phoenixlike, as prosperous blue collars echoed the ideology driving the war in Vietnam. Both U.S. foreign and domestic policy were linked by the belief that wayward populations – blacks and Vietnamese – could be remade. In both instances, the specific character of this remodeling required the abandonment of precapitalist behaviors and assimilation to habits of mind and customs that U.S. officials associated with Western rationalism, sobriety, and individualism. It was possible according to this logic to impose a rational framework on the problems of poverty, backwardness, and underdevelopment. Such experiments as strategic hamlets and urban renewal presented themselves as scientific trials and at the same time preserved the view of poverty as a

[76] Harper, "Domestic Policy Making in the Nixon Administration," 44, 42; Joan Hoff, *Nixon Reconsidered* (New York: Basic Books, 1994), 101; H. R. Haldemann, diary entries, May 13, 1969, February 7, 1970.

[77] "Text of a Pre-Inauguration Memo," *New York Times*, March 11, 1970, p. 30.

moral failing and cultural deficit. By the time Moynihan's advice to Nixon was published, however, fewer still believed in the possibility of reforming people with whom one was at war. What was left was the perception that these recalcitrants had character flaws, a belief on which Moynihan ultimately fell back.

Curing these faults – on both sides of the Pacific Ocean – thus became a task for government. Nixon embraced a form of Black Power that lent itself to the conservative thread that had woven through African-American communities for generations. Even Daniel Watts, the maverick editor of *Liberator*, was attracted to Nixon's emphasis on moneymaking and hard work. The journal published an essay entitled "Nixon and Black Power" by the white conservative Bruce Kesler, who argued that blacks lacked the capacity to "stand alone." Black Power, he asserted, could only be created through "economic strength and self-management" as successfully deployed by Jewish and Irish Americans. But ethnic politics as practiced by other hyphenated Americans was no panacea: until blacks learned to bargain, the Democratic Party would always take their votes for granted. Instead, African Americans should make tactical alliances with "slightly right-of-center" Republicans, Kesler prescribed. Nixon, in this interpretation, was the only national figure who genuinely supported black economic aspirations. The best way to determine Nixon's sincerity on the question of black capitalism, Kesler suggested, was to take him up on his word.[78]

Corporate leaders had earlier anticipated the Nixonian version of black capitalism. The Interracial Council for Business Opportunity, organized in 1963 by the Urban League and the American Jewish Council, had as cochairs Harvey C. Russell, a vice president of PepsiCo, and Rodman Rockefeller, vice president of International Basic Economy Corporation, respectively. The civil rights movement would fail, Russell warned, unless blacks achieved some measure of economic self-sufficiency and general improvement. The council attracted one hundred business leaders, including representatives of IBM, Chemical Bank, and Schenley Distillers, whom it asked to donate expertise. The Rockefeller Brothers Fund granted the project $25,000.[79]

These developments took place at the turn of the decade when it appeared possible to diversify the GOP's constituency. The Republican Party might attract those African Americans who remained unmoved by Stokely Carmichael or Huey Newton. Maurice Stans, commerce secretary during Nixon's first administration, later recalled that "minorities, based on business ownership, constituted the equivalent of a Third World nation of 50 million people within the boundaries of the United States." The meager minority entrepreneurial sector and the increasing welfare burden, Stans believed, indicted former administrations and pointed to "a growing national dilemma." This "wasted human capital" needed retrieval to help "the United States to maintain its position as the leading nation of the world with the most advanced quality of living." The

---

[78] Bruce Kesler, "Nixon and Black Power," *Liberator* 8 (September 1968): 11; editorial, "Richard Nixon," ibid., 8 (December 1968): 3.
[79] *Business Week*, June 27, 1964, clipping, TCF.

solution to black poverty and urban unrest, leading Republicans suggested, lay in making capitalist opportunities more readily available. People who owned property would not burn down buildings or loot stores. Rather than distribute funds to irresponsible community organizations, why not provide set-asides for minority contractors in the construction industry and promote black business development?[80] Republicans had not yet wholly dismissed a welfarist role for government. The movement of the mostly white electorate toward the anti-federalism of the early twenty-first century was a gradual process.

Republican senator Edward W. Brooke, an African American, enthusiastically endorsed efforts to encourage black entrepreneurship. He advocated equity investment by white capitalists underwritten by the Small Business Administration. "Minorities must be increasingly willing to share in joint ventures with businessmen of other races," he admonished. Now that a foundation of civil rights legislation was firmly established, attention must turn to economics. "Politics and economics are the civil rights movements of the seventies!"[81]

Accordingly, the administration targeted the Office of Minority Business Enterprise (OMBE) under the Commerce Department's direction. While minority firms received funds through the Small Business Administration during the Johnson years, the OMBE initiative was more focused. It revived the essence of a forgotten Commerce program from the 1940s, the Department of Negro Affairs,[82] but enlarged its scope to include other racial-ethnic groups and abandoned the segregation on which the earlier program had been premised. Stans and Nixon had no interest in perpetuating Jim Crow. Instead, they intended OMBE to acculturate aspiring black people to corporate America and integrate black consumers into the national market. The commerce secretary was particularly pleased with the franchising initiatives. Under the guidance of large corporations, minority franchise holders could profit while learning the best business practices. Franchise holding had the potential of transforming marginal "mom-and-pop" businesses that depended on a segregated clientele. Separatism had no place in this rendering of black capitalism. Neither Nixon nor Maurice Stans was naïve enough to think that he could create more than a modest increase in black enterprise. But beyond the agenda of mainstreaming black economic activity lay the ambition to inculcate in African Americans a cultural value system believed typical of middle-class whites and loosen the Democratic Party stranglehold on the black vote.[83]

[80] Maurice H. Stans, "Richard Nixon and His Bridges to Human Dignity," *Presidential Studies Quarterly* 26 (Winter 1996). 179, 180, 181; Dean Kotlowski, "Black Power Nixon Style: The Nixon Administration and Minority Business Enterprise," *Business History Review* 72 (1998): 409–45.

[81] Edward W. Brooke, "Black Business: Problems and Prospects," *Black Scholar* 6 (April 1975): 5, 2.

[82] For this program see Emmer Lancaster Papers, Division of Negro Affairs, Records of the Department of Commerce, RG 40, NARA.

[83] Stans, "Richard Nixon and His Bridges to Human Dignity," 180; remarks of Sallyanne Payton in *Richard M. Nixon: Politician, President, Administrator*, eds. Leon Friedman and William

Ironically, traditional Republican paternalism, as historically manifested by Booker T. Washington and wealthy conservatives' funding of the Urban League, made it easy for Nixon to endorse black capitalism. Minority set-asides in the construction industry incurred the resentment of blue-collar whites, but to such GOP supporters as the Chamber of Commerce and the National Association of Manufacturers, the unions had become too big and corrupt and should be taken down. Antiunionism was the motor of business acquiescence to affirmative action, because a less racially restrictive labor market would cut into union control of jobs.[84]

The Republican Party also became a home for certain blacks who resonated with the fading echoes of Garveyism. As has been documented elsewhere, Garvey's affinity for Booker T. Washington had much to do with the desire for enterprising self-sufficiency. The biography of Gloria Toote, assistant secretary of the Department of Housing and Urban Development during the Nixon and Ford administrations, is telling. Raised in Harlem, Toote was the daughter of Bishop Frederick Augustus Toote, a Bahamian immigrant, leader of the Garveyite African Orthodox Church, and a vice president of the Universal Negro Improvement Association. Gloria Toote joined the Republican Party after graduating from Howard University Law School in 1954. She would become assistant secretary of the Department of Housing and Urban Development during Nixon's second term.[85]

Former CORE director Floyd McKissick numbered among those who received the conservative message in a pragmatic spirit. African Americans, he believed, should subordinate partisanship to the effective achievement of specific goals. McKissick supported Nixon's presidential bid in 1968 and again in 1972. As one of the few African Americans that Nixon smiled on, his reward was federal support for building a new town in his native North Carolina, to be named Soul City. Part of McKissick's inspiration derived from current thinking about how to address the structural and social problems of America's troubled cities. At the time that he was envisioning Soul City, developer James W. Rouse had realized his project of creating the new town of Columbia, Maryland. Rouse's achievement suggested that McKissick's dream of a pleasant, thriving city untainted by racial discrimination and crime could be attained in rural Warren County. Unlike the embattled Algiers suggested by the colonial model and uprisings in northern cities, this burg would be the home of all races living in peaceful cooperation. McKissick enlisted the services of architect Harvey Gantt to design the city's industrial center. Gantt would later unsuccessfully

F. Levantrosser (New York: Hofstra University, 1991), 180; Jerome H. Holland, *Black Opportunity* (New York: Weybright and Talley, 1969), 113–14.

[84] See Nancy McLean, *Freedom Is Not Enough: The Opening of the American Workplace* (Cambridge, Mass.: Harvard University Press, 2006), 98–9.

[85] Clipping, *New York Magazine*, November 21, 1977, in Joint Center for Political Studies Vertical File. See also Angela D. Dillard, *Guess Who's Coming to Dinner Now? Multicultural Conservatism in America* (New York: New York University Press, 2001).

challenge right-winger Jesse Helms in the 1990 and 1996 senate races in North Carolina.[86]

Unlike Columbia, Maryland, which was near Washington, D.C., and government jobs, Soul City faced an uphill struggle for development. Warren County's small workforce was predominantly black and mostly uneducated, and the county could not make generous concessions on taxes and utilities. It had no industrial infrastructure in place. Corporations relocating to the "Sun Belt" rarely chose sites with those traits. General Motors, moreover, made clear its objection to the name "Soul City," which it found unappealingly racial. GM, burned by black labor militancy in Detroit, and facing a crisis in the auto industry, shied away from the hint of militancy. Soul City also incurred the hostility of soon-to-be senator Helms, who saw it as a liberal Trojan horse invading his turf. The subsequent failure of the project exposed basic problems in black conservative approaches. The site of what McKissick and his supporters hoped would attract energetic newcomers is today a prison where African-American inmates return as slaves of the state rather than as proud homeowners.[87]

As Booker T. Washington himself ultimately came to understand, no matter how docile African Americans made themselves, or how wedded to the tenets of the free market, white priorities would always trump black aspirations. Soul City, moreover, did not squarely address the question of how an enterprise that straddled the fence between integration and black nationalism could operate under the umbrella of a white dominated market system. McKissick, espousing a cultural pluralism not readily understood at the time, opened Soul City to white residents. Critics nevertheless perceived the decision to name its streets after black figures and otherwise present it as an African-American town as separatist. The view that black gains under capitalism could equal those of whites nevertheless continued to be debated[88] and constantly recurs in both apologetics and discourses of progress.

Entrepreneurialism could be best sustained among African Americans when separated from explicitly conservative ideology. The publication *Black Enterprise*, founded in 1970 by Earl G. Graves Sr., provides an example. It became profitable within two years and remained so through the early

[86] On Soul City, see Devin Fergus, "Black Power, Soft Power: Floyd McKissick, Soul City, and the Death of Moderate Black Republicanism," *Journal of Policy History* 22 (2) (2010): 148–92; Timothy J. Minchin, "'A Brand New Shining City': Floyd B. McKissick, Sr. and the Struggle to Build Soul City, North Carolina," *North Carolina Historical Review* 82 (April 2005): 125–55; Roger Biles, "The Rise and Fall of Soul City: Planning, Politics, and Race in Recent America," *Journal of Planning History* 4 (1) (2005): 52–72; Christopher Strain, "Soul City, North Carolina: Black Power, Utopia, and the African American Dream," *Journal of African American History* 89 (Winter 2004): 57–74. On Columbia, Maryland, Joseph R. Mitchell and David Stebenne, *New City upon a Hill: A History of Columbia, Maryland* (Charleston, S.C.: History Press, 2007).

[87] Minchin, "A Brand New Shining City," 142, 140; Fergus, "Black Power, Soft Power," 180.

[88] See, for example, Andrew F. Brimmer, "Economic Integration and the Progress of the Negro Community," *Ebony* 25 (August 1970): 118–21; and Dunbar S. McLaurin, "Short-Range Separatism," ibid., pp. 123–5.

twenty-first century.[89] While clearly promoting the gospel of wealth, the magazine's editorial position did not attack conventional liberal goals. Its ongoing success suggests that many of its readers share an ongoing interest in profit with their white compatriots. That Graves could have begun the magazine during the zenith of Marxist influence among the black reading public and kept it going implies that we cannot understand this period in African-American history solely through the lens of radical organizations. Like the radicals, many civil rights establishment leaders scorned the Nixon administration's program, but black capitalism continued to have broad appeal. To propose that all interest and activity around black capitalism was opportunistic or cynical is to misunderstand how many African Americans interpreted liberty. If poverty and dependency were cornerstones of white supremacist control, political freedom required sufficient material resources to secure economic independence.

Graves and the economist Andrew Brimmer advocated emancipation from the structural constraints of ghetto business. They wanted minority entrepreneurs to embrace the more profitable racially nonspecific world. Isolation, they held, could not be sustained when the nation was moving toward increasingly integrated markets. Gunnar Myrdal had earlier attacked the insular world of black business for different reasons, telling the Howard University class of 1962 that they could not "cry for the breaking down of walls of segregation and discrimination while, at the same time, hoping to retain petty monopoly preserves among Negro clientele."[90] Myrdal said nothing about breaking down white monopoly preserves. Unlike their white peers, black capitalists apparently were expected to be simultaneously altruistic and self-serving.

The growing political engagement of U.S. people of color provoked many responses. If the South in the early twenty-first century is closely associated with the GOP, its power in Dixie remained fledgling in the late 1960s. National Republican leaders were reluctant to embrace segregationists. They instead advocated attracting more newly enfranchised blacks to the party. Nixon, and figures like House Minority Leader Gerald Ford and Senator Thruston Morton, thought it mistaken to associate with the cantankerous and unreconstructed racist fringe. Yet as Nixon had learned, segregationists had retained power and their votes were important. Republicans at first finessed the issue, helping to elect such "moderates" as George H. W. Bush, Howard Baker, and Winthrop Rockefeller in southern states. The GOP remained a minority party for some time to come, blossoming only when tacit racism joined religious fundamentalism and right-wing populism in a potent mix.

[89] Columbus Salley, *The Black 100: A Ranking of the Most Influential African-Americans, Past and Present* (New York: Citadel Press, 1999), 313–15; Dan Moreau, "Change Agents," *Changing Times* (November 1990): 112.

[90] Earl G. Graves, Sr., *How to Succeed in Business without Being White* (New York: HarperCollins, 1997); Andrew Brimmer and Henry S. Terrell, "The Economic Potential of Black Capitalism," paper presented to the annual meeting of the American Economic Association, New York, December 29, 1969; "Negroes Are Asked to Face Integration," *New York Times*, June 9, 1962, p. 22.

8

Africa and Liberation

In September 1970, Howard Fuller (Owusu Sadauki) arrived in Dar es Salaam as a representative of both the southern-based Student Organization for Black Unity (SOBU) and Malcolm X University, which he had founded in Greensboro, North Carolina. Malcolm X University emphasized science and engineering, fields often weak at conventional black colleges and universities and much in demand in developing countries. SOBU had worked on labor and housing issues in North Carolina, earning local respect. It developed a Pan-African Medical Program that collected and donated equipment and supplies to African liberation organizations. SOBU appointed a liaison officer to connect it with the revolutionary Southwest African People's Organization (SWAPO) and with African student unions. The group established "fraternal relations" with the Palestine Liberation Organization (PLO) and some Iranian student associations. Fuller met with foreign revolutionists abroad and published an account of his travels in the *African World,* a SOBU newsletter that included news of student activism in United States and overseas reports provided by correspondents in Canada, Africa, and the Caribbean. In line with the African socialist agenda espoused by Nyerere, SOBU embraced a plan to have black students work as agricultural laborers in the U.S. South in preparation for serving rural African societies. This Pan African Community Work program, in the words of historian Fanon Che Wilkins, would help college students complete the "awesome responsibility of committing class suicide."[1]

In spite of its determination to set out on a socialist path unique to it, the Tanzanian government had reservations about black American activists as well as misgivings about the African liberation movements it hosted. The Lusaka Manifesto of 1969, signed by Tanzania and the leaders of the frontline states – those bordering on the white settler regimes and Portuguese colonies – resolved

---

[1] Cedric Johnson, "From Popular Anti-Imperialism to Sectarianism: The African Liberation Support Committee and Black Power Radicals," *New Political Science* 25 (4) (2003): 484–5; Fanon Che Wilkins, "'In the Belly of the Beast': Black Power, Anti-imperialism, and the African Solidarity Movement, 1968–1975" (PhD diss., New York University, New York, 2001), p. 202.

to discourage armed struggle in southern Africa if the Portuguese, Rhodesians, and South Africans came to the bargaining table. The OAU subsequently endorsed the signatories' position that outside countries could not determine the best way for inhabitants of southern Africa to pursue independence. The accord infuriated the freedom fighters, who had not been party to it. In 1971 Lusaka was superseded by the Mogadishu Declaration, which stated that since the imperialists had no intention of negotiating, there was no way to avoid warfare.[2] In the interim, the Nyerere regime worried about possible attacks from the white settler and colonial states, maneuvering by internal dissidents, and the chance that the actions of foreign fighters could open doors to subversion in Tanzania itself.

The wave of military coups in Africa in 1965 and 1966 had diminished prospects for peaceful transition to independence for the remaining colonies. The Sino-Indian border war and the Indo-Pakistani war further eroded hopes of harmony among developing countries and undermined India's stance as a disinterested moral authority in world affairs. The charismatic leaders associated with the early exhilarating phase of decolonization began to die or be deposed. Nehru died in 1964, and Sukarno, Ben Bella, and Nkrumah were overthrown between 1965 and 1966. The leftist Moroccan politician Ben Barka disappeared in Paris in 1965, as Cuba wrote off Congolese insurgents as hopeless.[3]

Guinean president Sékou Touré gave Nkrumah asylum and an honorary copresidency in exchange for the support the Ghanaian had rendered earlier when the French decamped with important resources after Guinea's independence. From the capital of Conakry, Nkrumah turned his talents to political theory, writing critiques of imperialism and urging on nascent revolutionary movements. He received guests from various parts of the globe, including Stokely Carmichael, whom he later mentored when the Black Power advocate, in self-imposed exile, decided to live and eventually died in Guinea.[4]

In late summer 1971 Howard Fuller, also known as Owusu Sadauki, accompanied attorney Robert Van Lierop and photographer Robert Fletcher to the liberated areas of Mozambique. Van Lierop and Fletcher's purpose was to make a film that would expose U.S. audiences to the anticolonial war being fought by the Frente de Libertação de Moçambique (FRELIMO). Neither man was a professional cinematographer; nor were the two the first to capture Mozambique's struggle on celluloid. They were, however, the first African Americans to enter the liberated zone, and the subsequent film, *A Luta Continua*, became a staple on the protest circuit. It was smuggled into Portugal and South Africa and

[2] Walter Bgoya, "From Tanzania to Kansas and Back Again," in *No Easy Victories*, eds. William Minter, Gail Hovey, and Charlie Cobb, Jr., (Trenton, N.J.: Africa World Press, 2007): 105.

[3] Richard Gott's introduction to Che Guevara, *The African Dream* (New York: Grove Press, 1999), xxxvii, xxxviii.

[4] See Stokely Carmichael with Ekwueme Michael Thelwell, *Ready for Revolution: The Life and Struggles of Stokely Carmichael* (New York: Scribner, 2003).

screened there. In New York, a memorable showing took place on a Harlem street with a bedsheet for a screen. The filmmakers made the Mozambican struggle known to a broader audience by supplying *Ebony* magazine with text and photographs for a feature article that ran in February 1973. Revolutionary leader Samora Machel and other FRELIMO cadre played prominent roles in determining how Mozambique would be depicted. In an era still not free of jungle stereotypes, Mozambicans understood how powerful their own representation of their national purpose could be in fixing their place in the world community.[5]

In a conversation with Sadauki, Machel rejected talk of sending a black volunteer army to Mozambique. "When [I] asked how the masses of our people in the United States could best support them," Sadauki related, "I was told the most useful thing we can do at this stage is to provide them with strong moral support by showing the world our concern through massive Black protest and demonstration against U.S. involvement in Southern Africa." Machel's response to the query about international assistance typified African revolutionaries' responses to an idea that continued to travel in militant circles. Frantz Fanon was an early advocate, having suggested the creation of "an All-African People's Revolutionary Army, or African Legion" at the All-Africa Peoples Conference in Ghana in 1958. When Stokely Carmichael visited Cuba seven years later, he told his hosts that he wanted to organize an African-American brigade to help the Partido Africano da Independência da Guiné e Cabo Verde (PAIGC) win its war against the Portuguese in Guinea-Bissau. A Cuban intelligence officer accompanied Carmichael to PAIGC headquarters in Guinea, where he laid this proposal before the guerrilla leader Amilcar Cabral. Cabral accepted a plan to bring in up to thirty fighters if they were trained outside Guinea-Bissau. He wanted revolution there to be unmistakably indigenous. Bissau and Cuba also worried about how the United States might react to a brigade, and as a result, Havana refused to offer training facilities in Cuba. Although Nyerere agreed to allow African-American volunteers to train in Tanzania, nothing came of the plan.[6]

SNCC chair H. Rap Brown proposed to UN Secretary General U Thant in 1967 that SNCC send an international brigade to Southwest Africa, now Namibia. Brown had few illusions that the UN would endorse the venture but elaborated it as a matter of principle. Eldridge Cleaver developed a similar idea. While in Cuban exile, he proposed founding a Cuban branch of the Black Panther Party that would host guerrilla training for U.S. militants. "Our

[5] Sadauki quoted in William Minter, "An Unfinished Journey," in *No Easy Victories*, 31; Joseph F. Jordan, "The 1970s: Expanding Networks," in ibid., 117, 118; "The Quiet War in Mozambique," *Ebony* 28 (February 1973): 92–6, 98–9; Mantha Diawara, *African Cinema: Politics and Culture* (Bloomington: Indiana University Press), 89, 90.

[6] Robert J. C. Young, "Fanon and the Turn to Armed Struggle in Africa," *Wasafiri* 20 (Spring 2005): 38; Wilkins, "In the Belly of the Beast," 231; Piero Gleijeses, *Conflicting Missions: Havana, Washington, and Africa, 1959–1976* (Chapel Hill: University of North Carolina Press, 2002), 193–4.

highest hope was to have a center in the Caribbean that would prepare revolutionary cadres to slink back into the United States, many to blend with the urban scene and function as guerrillas on the sidewalk level." Cleaver advocated low-intensity warfare. "No major confrontations with the army and police, no battle at Little Big Horn or Gettysburg, but much disruption and chipping away at a decaying power structure that was becoming increasingly anti-democratic and invariably more fascist." His scheme resembled the foiled plans of antislavery martyr John Brown, envisaging "trained and equipped forces [that] would be dropped into the mountain area of North America," and "small mobile units that could shift easily in and out of rural areas, living off the land, and tying up thousands of troops in fruitless pursuit."[7]

Such ideas galled Black Power's opponents. Mississippi senator James O. Eastland entered a statement in the *Congressional Record* to warn "our people to be aware of the direct chain which reaches from Cuba into our cities, our campuses, our conventions, our lives – and which threatens the life of this Republic." Eastland saw the brigades as the leading edge of a communist assault. Participants in the Venceremos Brigade, U.S. volunteers who went to Cuba to help harvest sugarcane, were targets of suspicion. "Venceremos means 'we shall win,'" the senator wrote. "Now, who, exactly, is 'we' – and what exactly, could canecutters be seeking to win?" Perhaps it never occurred to the senator that they might be seeking victories like the ones that Mississippi cotton pickers desired. To Eastland, the use of the word "brigade" summoned up memories of the "hardened revolutionaries" of the Abraham Lincoln Brigade in the Spanish Civil War. It was clear, he concluded, that the Left had no genuine interest in farming, which was not the real reason they were going to Cuba. His *Congressional Record* entry included a list of names and addresses of Americans who had traveled there.[8]

It is uncertain whether Eastland would have objected to the recruiting later planned by CORE director Roy Innis. In late summer 1971, Innis and five other CORE members went to Kenya and Tanzania, where they held audiences with Jomo Kenyatta and Julius Nyerere (see Figure 14). CORE had abandoned the integrationism that characterized it in the 1960s, becoming a conservative black organization. It at first followed a script laid out by more radical groups: the pursuit of a nationality status for African Americans that would be recognized by the United Nations. It subsequently moved far to the right, supporting segregation and filing an amicus brief in a Virginia case to support Nixon's opposition to busing. Innis promised Jonas Savimbi, leader of the Angolan national front União Nacional para a Independência Total de Angola (UNITA), that CORE would recruit black Vietnam veterans to assist his struggle against the Cuban-supported Movimento Popular de Libertação de Angola (MPLA).

---

[7] H. Rap Brown to U Thant, December 4, 1967, SNCC Papers, Series VIII, General Files, reel 52. Cleaver quoted in Jennifer B. Smith, *An International History of the Black Panther Party* (New York: Garland, 1999), 73.

[8] *Congressional Record*, March 16, 1970, 7462–7.

Such a gesture would align CORE with an organization aided by both South Africa and the CIA and would reserve a place for Innis among the era's arch-conservative stalwarts. Accusations of financial irregularities dogged him in connection with CORE junkets to Africa and Europe.[9]

African Americans were not the only diaspora group interested in military support for African revolutions. During a state visit to Tanzania in September 1973, Jamaican premier Michael Manley broached the subject to his hosts, offering soldiers, medical assistance, and cash to the liberation movements. According to a report filed by the U.S. deputy chief of mission, Manley asserted that Jamaica's "independence is inextricably bound up with freedom which is bound to come from wars of liberation now going on in South Africa." His offer of aid was somewhat rhetorical, for the actual arrangement concluded was only for educational exchange: selected Jamaicans would attend the TANU cadre school and Tanzanians would study agriculture in Jamaica.[10] Information services and conventional assistance relationships were more to the liking of liberation organizations because foreign fighters could shed doubt on the authenticity of local struggles. Independent countries often remained wary of alliances with radicals not in power who might further complicate their relations with Western nations. Freedom fighter proposals were not new. They dated to 1935, when Africans, African Americans, and Caribbean island-ers envisioned international brigades to defend Ethiopia from Italian aggression. The United States and other colonial governments had prevented any volunteers from departing from their home territories, but the dream of liberating Africa from imperialism through armed struggle survived.

Just as connection with homelands seemed to give coherence to hyphenated white Americans' stance of national belonging and political power at home, many African Americans sought more than a sentimental or nostalgic link to Africa. This meant a tangible affiliation with a particular nation-state and an agenda that would interest the leaders of a specific African country. Tanzania, in spite of its reservations, espoused African socialism and provided sanctuary to guerrillas. It was the state that most closely fit the bill.

Progress on concrete ties to Tanzania was not as rapid as many wished. Advocates' fondness for Zanzibari revolutionist Abdul-Rahman Muhammad Babu, distrusted by Dar es Salaam even as he held a cabinet post, did not help matters. It was three years before the skills bank initially proposed by SNCC in 1967 became operational. The plan, now called the Pan-African Skills Project (PASP), had an office in Dar es Salaam and another in New York City's Riverside

[9] Simon Anekwe, "Tanzanian Ambassador Collects 'Mystery' Parcel," July 10, 1971, *Amsterdam News*, p. A3; Solomon Goodrich, "CORE visits Africa," ibid., October 16, 1971, p. C12; idem, "CORE Leader reports on trip to Africa," October 23, 1971, p. B11; Karin L. Stanford, *Black Political Organizations in the Post-Civil Rights Era* (New Brunswick, N.J.: Rutgers University Press, 2002), 90–1; *Angola Weekly News Summary* (N.Y.), January 29, 1976, p. 3; Linda M. Heywood, "UNITA and Ethnic Nationalism in Angola," *Journal of Modern African Studies* 27 (1) (1989): 64.

[10] Gordon R. Beyer to the Secretary of State, September 15, 1973, SDCF.

FIGURE 14. President Julius Nyerere listens to Roy Innis of the Congress of Racial Equality, at Government House, Dar es Salaam, Tanzania, in 1971. (Granger Images)

Church. PASP recruited more people than it could place, since Tanzania made the placement decisions and proceeded cautiously. Organizers fought hard to prevent recruits from falling into conventional expatriate expert lifestyles, and PASP workers received their salaries on an African pay scale. The first class of participants consisted of sixteen persons with vocations viewed as best suiting the needs of the host country, including a veterinarian, printer, electrician, bio-chemist, and engineer. In addition to directing practical work, the PASP office in Dar es Salaam served as a gathering place for a diverse collection of radicals and dissidents and functioned as a point of orientation for African-American tourists. The Angela Davis Defense Committee used it as a headquarters, as did the African Liberation Support Committee (ALSC) and the ad hoc Committee in Defense of the Vietnamese People. By mid-1972, these organizations were joined by field offices for Drum and Spear Press, Malcolm X University, and the Center for Black Education.[11]

---

[11] James Forman to Abdul-Rahman Muhammad Babu, January 4, 1968, SNCC Papers, General Files, reel 51; Ernest J. Wilson, "Implementing Pan-African Programs–Now," *Black World* (August 1971): 34–41; author's telephone interview with Courtland Cox, June 21, 2012; Anthony J. Ratcliff, "Liberation at the End of a Pen: Writing Pan-African Politics of Cultural Struggle" (PhD diss., University of Massachusetts, 2009), p. 124; Charlie Cobb, "Africa Notebook: Views on Returning Home," *Black World* no. 21, May 7, 1972, pp. 22–37.

Support for African liberation movements became the new face of Pan-Africanism for diaspora groups unable to penetrate government-level decision making. Between thirty and fifty-five thousand people attended the African Liberation Day demonstration in Washington, D.C., in May 1972. Planning for the observance involved numerous well-known figures on what was becoming a nationalist Left. These included Nelson Johnson from the SOBU, Amiri Baraka, Gina Thornton from the Universal Negro Improvement Association, the black Mennonite historian Vincent Harding, Black Panther Erica Huggins, black studies pioneers James Turner and Nathan Hare, the poet Don L. Lee, Angela Davis, and others. Endorsement and participation came from such elected politicians as Diggs, Conyers, Louis Stokes, and Julian Bond.[12]

Antiapartheid and liberation support groups developed a variety of activities. A boycott aided by the National Council of Churches and other religious bodies targeted the Gulf Oil Corporation's support for Portuguese colonialism. Randall Robinson, who went on to found TransAfrica, organized the Pan African Liberation Committee while working for the Roxbury Multi-Service Center in Boston. That group of some one hundred members focused on Gulf Oil's Angola operations and Harvard University's more than $300 million of Gulf stock. Randall recalled that black students constructed a mock cemetery on the Harvard campus to "memorialize Africa's war dead and call Harvard's role in the carnage to public attention." They invited Diggs and Representatives Louis Stokes and William Clay to meet with them, and Diggs issued a public statement of support. Harvard, however, remained unmoved by demands that it divest its Gulf holdings. Early in the morning on April 21, 1972, Robinson and thirty-eight others took over Massachusetts Hall, "Harvard's oldest building and the office of the president," for what would become a six-day siege. Sympathizers mounted a vigil outside. The legal scholar Derrick Bell joined them on the second day and was deputized to parley with the administration. On the fifth day Harvard agreed to send a representative to Africa to investigate, report, and make recommendations regarding the university's investments. The investigator spent two weeks in Angola and reported that there was no need for divestment.[13] By this time, it had become more difficult to argue that U.S. enterprises in southern Africa were having a salutary impact on Africa. Anticolonial wars in the region belied the notion that stability could be achieved through favoring business elites, repressive police forces, the military, and privileged white minorities.

African Liberation Day as an annual event thus had a history of resistance. The CBC prepared for the commemoration by convening African-American protest leaders, African UN delegates, and representatives from the liberation

---

[12] Richard E. Prince, "12,000 Blacks March to Support Africa," *Washington Post*, May 28, 1972, p. A1:1, A4:1; Johnson, "From Popular Anti-Imperialism to Sectarianism," 485–90.

[13] Randall Robinson, *Defending the Spirit: A Black Life in America* (New York: Dutton, 1998), 89–93. See also Peter Shapiro, "Gulf Redux May Shed More Heat Than Light," *Harvard Crimson*, October 7, 1972, online.

organizations. The ALSC was subsequently formed to preserve and extend the momentum. The first African Liberation Day was dedicated to Nkrumah, who died in Romania of cancer on April 27, 1972. George Wiley from the National Welfare Rights Organization, Elaine Brown from the Oakland chapter of the Black Panther Party, Elombe Brath of the New York–based African Nationalist Pioneer Movement, poet Don Lee, Roy Innis from CORE, Sadauki, and comedian Dick Gregory gave rousing speeches at the foot of the Washington Monument. Organizers did not limit their program to the Washington demonstration. In San Francisco, supporters gathered in a Fillmore District park, where Nelson Johnson, Walter Rodney, California politician Willie Brown, Richard Hatcher, and others addressed them. Ten thousand people honored the day in Toronto. Other observances were held in Montreal, Halifax, and Winnipeg.[14]

African liberation support and antiapartheid activities took place in Caribbean cities, coordinated with the ALSC in the United States. The Canadian branch maintained contacts in Martinique, Surinam, St. Martin, French Guiana, Antigua, Jamaica, Belize, St. Lucia, Dominica, and Puerto Rico. The antiimperialist character of the demonstrations and marches and their international reach led U.S. authorities to monitor the African liberation support movement for connections to Castroism, and more distantly, to the USSR and what some officials still considered a monolithic global communist movement.[15] The metropoles all interpreted their national security imperatives differently, but even those not mesmerized by the specter of world communism were unhappy about the rapid proliferation of transnational links.

By 1973, ALSC had developed thirty-five U.S. chapters, centered on African Liberation Day organizing committees. Its leaders included former SNCC leader Courtland Cox, Randall Robinson, radical sociologist Gerald McWhorter (Abdul Alkhalimat), and future prime minister of Grenada Maurice Bishop, active in Canada.[16] After a strong beginning, the alliance between black elected officials and ALSC weakened as the latter moved to the Left, but even conventional politicians shared black publics' estrangement from U.S. foreign policy in the 1970s.[17]

An African focus could complement but not supplant local struggles. African leaders continued to remind diaspora subjects of their obligations in

[14] Francis Njubi Nesbitt, *Race for Sanctions: African Americans against Apartheid, 1946–1994* (Bloomington: Indiana University Press, 2004), 77–8; Signe Waller, *Love and Revolution: A Political Memoir* (Lanham, Md., Rowman & Littlefeld, 2002), 55.

[15] Memorandum re International Day of African Solidarity – '73, May 4, 1973, ALSC-C, CSIS Records; Waller, *Love and Revolution*, 56; Johnson, "From Popular Anti-Imperialism to Sectarianism," 489; Ruth Reitan, *The Rise and Decline of An Alliance: Cuba and African American Leaders in the 1960s* (East Lansing: Michigan State University Press, 1999), 30.

[16] Wilkins, "In the Belly of the Beast" [dissertation], 192; Memorandum on International Day of Solidarity-1973 (Black Power), June 18, 1973, ALSC-C, CSIS Records.

[17] Abdul Alkhalimat and Nelson Johnson, "Toward the Ideological Unity of the African Liberation Support Committee: A Response to Criticisms of the A.L.S.C.," statement of principles adopted at Frogmore, South Carolina, June-July, 1973, mimeographed report in author's possession.

their birthplaces and of the need to remain clearheaded about aims. Amilcar Cabral traveled to the United States in February 1970 to deliver the Eduardo Mondlane Memorial Lecture at Syracuse University. At this event in honor of the slain Mozambican revolutionary, Cabral made clear his belief that global structures of domination rather than white people as such were the enemies of Guinea-Bissau and the Cape Verde Islands. He went on to speak in New York City and then Washington, D.C., where he testified before the House Subcommittee on Africa. Cabral returned to the United States in 1972 to attend the fourth committee session of the UN General Assembly. He traveled to Lincoln University, long associated with African education, where he received an honorary doctorate. Diggs and Sadauki were on hand for the occasion. Diggs complimented the PAIGC for its successes in Guinea-Bissau and averred that African Americans had a responsibility to ensure changes in U.S. policies related to colonialism. The often-brash Sadauki's remarks were less anodyne. Lincoln University, he contended, should not honor Cabral while inviting representatives from Gulf Oil, Polaroid, and the Dow Chemical Company to its Career Day. He presented Cabral with a check for $2,200 raised by the Boston ALSC chapter.[18]

Cabral condemned the racism ingrained in U.S. life but encouraged African Americans to think more broadly about class and discouraged blind emulation of other societies. Just as China's revolutionary history did not follow the Soviet pattern, transformation in Guinea-Bissau failed to conform to any recipe for "peasant revolution." Cabral's approach to his own country emphasized grassroots organizing. He did not think that revolutions could be successfully mounted from exile, or sparked by dedicated professional revolutionaries who lacked local ties. As for U.S. blacks, they would have to understand American conditions.[19] Any answer to the question of whether race or class was primary would have to be made in the United States. This "two-line struggle" seems quaint in the present epoch, when the view that class and race must be viewed in their symbiotic and dialogic wholeness is generally assumed. At the time, however, the fact of African-American minority status, the preponderance of race in shaping national life, and a structured distance from many other U.S. radical communities meant that the debate possessed a vitality less imaginable today.[20]

Ultimately, ALSC paid a price for the failure to take Cabral's advice about understanding the local environment. Maoists in the organization found their effectiveness compromised when China placed its nation-state interests ahead

---

[18] Minter, Hovey, and Cobb, *No Easy Victories*, 27–8; Wilkins, 217–21.

[19] Amilcar Cabral, "Connecting the Struggles: An Informal Talk with Black Americans," in *Return to the Source: Selected Speeches* (New York: Monthly Review Press, 1974), 71–92; Patrick Chabal, *Amílcar Cabral: Revolutionary Leadership and People's War* (Cambridge: Cambridge University Press, 1983), 68.

[20] See Kalamu Ya Salaam, "Tell No Lies, Claim No Easy Victories," *Black World* (October 1974): 18–34; and Modibo M. Kadalie, *Internationalism, Pan-Africanism, and the Struggle of Social Classes* (Savannah, Ga., One Quest Press, 2000), 222–45.

of the goals of world revolution by supporting UNITA, which the United States and the Union of South Africa also endorsed. China at the same time took an accommodationist stance toward white minority rule in the latter country.[21]

A further split within the group between Marxists and others emerged at a Frogmore, South Carolina, conference in June and July 1973 when some nationalists left the organization. ALSC chapters in Atlanta and New Orleans were more interested in local work and later opted out of attending the Sixth Pan African Congress in Dar es Salaam. ALSC's first national conference (as opposed to demonstration or march) in 1974 drew eight hundred people with the theme "Black Workers Take the Lead," a focus on the black working class that in Cedric Johnson's words "became mired in esoteric debates which rarely had anything to do with issues of immediate concern to the broader black citizenry." Radical attendees' fixation on the "correct line" subsequently squandered the chance to reach a larger black public by excluding "incorrect" speakers from the 1974 National Black Political Convention.[22]

In the zenith of its success, ALSC extended the legacy of a long history of organizational work by African Americans with an interest in African freedom. ALSC was cut from the same variegated cloth as the Universal Negro Improvement Association and the Council on African Affairs. In its emphasis on popular participation and motivation, it differed substantially from AMSAC and the ANLCA. As an NGO, it was prepared to work with institutions and politicians but not willing to subordinate its agenda to the smooth operations of partisan politics.

The emphasis of many Black Power studies on the expressive and literary culture of poets and artists, and of university-trained academicians, often eclipses the part played by working people in defining the issues and shaping popular responses to racial injustice and economic inequality. While earlier U.S. campaigns against apartheid, for example, seemed dominated by such middle-class activists as Bayard Rustin or ACOA founder George M. Houser, African-American blue-collar workers addressed the issue in ways that affirmed work's centrality to power in the United States, and their perception that the inequities they experienced were part of a larger system. The question of class leadership moved again to the fore. In simultaneous acts of rediscovering, imagining, or embellishing an "authentic" black society, middle-class culture brokers interposed themselves as griots and interpreters for the masses. Cultural translation and exposition helped legitimate the political decisions the would-be vanguard made on behalf of "the people," who were often absent from the process.[23]

[21] Robin D. G. Kelley and Betsy Esch, "Black like Mao: Red China and Black Revolution," *Souls* 1 (Fall 1999): 30.

[22] Johnson, "From Popular Anti-Imperialism to Sectarianism," 496; Kelley and Esch, "Black Like Mao," 30; Alkhalimat and Johnson, "Toward the Ideological Unity of the African Liberation Support Committee."

[23] In this regard, see Wahneema Lubiano. "Standing In for the State: Black Nationalism and 'Writing the Black Subject,'" in *Is It Nation Time? Contemporary Essays on Black Power*

Black labor nevertheless had a perspective on racism that put South Africa in its sights. Generations of equivocation from Washington failed to disguise the American role in perpetuating the archaic and bizarre apartheid system. The Massachusetts-based Polaroid Corporation numbered among firms in business in South Africa. It supplied Pretoria with the photographic equipment needed to maintain the pass laws and identity system. Each "Bantu" adult was photographed and his or her movements checked against the legal residence to which Africans were assigned.

Three African-American Polaroid workers took exception to the company's activities. Constituting themselves as the Polaroid Revolutionary Workers Movement (PRWM), they demanded that Polaroid end South African sales and publicly oppose apartheid. All profits earned in South Africa should aid African liberation movements. The PWRM enjoyed initial support from the Boston NAACP and the Greater Boston Ministerial Alliance. When the PRWM called for a global boycott of Polaroid products, it asked for and received a hearing before the United Nations Apartheid Committee. Its ability to be heard in that forum owed a debt to the endorsements it received from groups long identified with the struggle for racial justice in southern Africa. These included the African National Congress, Episcopal Churchmen for South Africa, and ACOA.[24]

Polaroid and its founder, Edward Land, had liberal reputations. A highly regarded scientist, Land served on the President's Foreign Intelligence Advisory Board under John F. Kennedy. In spite of his distinguished credentials, the workers claimed that Land engaged in Jim Crow practices in Massachusetts, paying blacks and white employees differently. Polaroid's collusion with racism in Africa, PRWM asserted, found a counterpart in the firm's policies at home. After the King assassination, Polaroid began recruiting black staff, enrolling ninety-two white-collar employees between 1968 and 1971. The company's salary policy, however, proved problematic. Polaroid's rule that new hires could not earn more than 15 percent of what they made on their last job ignored the national problem of systemic pay discrimination against blacks. The firm's African-American workforce found itself making less money than whites doing comparable work. By early 1971, some 17 percent of the new black employees had departed.[25]

Polaroid felt it could plausibly deny collaboration with the white minority regime in South Africa because a subsidiary handled its operations there. It

and Black Nationalism, ed. Eddie S. Glaude Jr. (Chicago: University of Chicago Press, 2002), 156–64, 160.

[24] "Strike against Polaroid," *Sacramento Observer*, January 21, 1971, p. A-22; Eric J. Morgan, "The World Is Watching: Polaroid and South Africa," *Enterprise & Society* 7 (September 2006): 520–49; Reisman, "Polaroid Power," 103; "In the News: Ken Williams," *Bay State Banner*, February 11, 1971, p. 5. On the Boston NAACP chapter, see *The Crisis* 74 (May 1967): 224–5.

[25] Editorial note, *FRUS, 1961–63*, XXV, *Organization of Foreign Policy; Information Policy; United Nations; Scientific Matters* (Washington, D.C., U.S. Government Printing Office, 2001), 180; Africa Research Group and Polaroid Workers Revolutionary Movement, "Polaroid and South Africa," March 21, 1971, unpaginated. Accessed online at the African Activist Project, Michigan State University, http://africanactivist.msu.edu.

started a plan it called an "experiment," which included creating educational opportunities for "Bantus" and upgrading the pay and benefits of black African employees. In a statement published in the *Bay State Banner*, a Boston-area African-American newspaper, Polaroid explained that apartheid was a system in which it could not "participate passively" and which it could not "ignore." The solution, company executives felt, was to remain in South Africa, attempting to create openings for black success.[26]

The PRWM denounced the "experiment" as a publicity stunt and debunked the company's claims that it practiced equal opportunity in hiring and promotion in South Africa, which would have been illegal under the country's laws. PRWM leader Ken Williams, who had resigned from Polaroid in the fall of 1970, claimed the plan simply disguised how the company's activities facilitated South Africa's "system of genocide." Polaroid's insistence on remaining in South Africa "comes as no surprise," Williams remarked, "for it shows clearly how important the ID 2 and other forms of Polaroid instant photography are to the maintenance of apartheid"[27] (see Figure 15).

In February 1971, Polaroid sent a memorandum to all personnel threatening with termination any employee who began or supported a boycott against its products. It countered the bad publicity about its South Africa ties by suspending and then firing the remaining two PRWM members, Caroline Hunter, a chemist, and Clyde Walton, a sales representative. Scrambling to salvage its reputation among African Americans, Polaroid donated $20,000 to the United Front Foundation, Inc., an organization in the predominantly black community of Roxbury. Unco-opted by the company's largesse, the United Front Foundation shared the money with the PRWM with funds ultimately going to national liberation organizations in Africa and activists in Cairo, Illinois, then the site of bitter racial struggles.[28]

A widespread sense of grievance against Polaroid among Boston-area African Americans was reflected in the refusal by another local social service organization of a substantial grant from the company. "Organizations such as ours have by necessity received funds from a variety of sources in order to survive and maintain quality service to our community," the Roxbury Multi-Service Center noted. "Therefore turning back a $10,000 grant to Polaroid is a very serious matter for us. It was only with careful thought and deliberation about the survival of all black people and not just this organization that we were able

---

[26] "An Experiment in South Africa," statement from Polaroid Corporation, *Bay State Banner*, January 14, 1971, p. 16.

[27] Carl W. Sims, "Critics Attack Polaroid 'Experiment,'" *Bay State Banner*, January 21, 1971, p. 1; Stephen Curwood, "Polaroid Claims Success in South Africa 'Experiment,'" *Bay State Banner*, January 6, 1972, p. 1.

[28] "Polaroid and South Africa;" C. W. Skinner, "Polaroid Workers Vow to Continue," February 18, 1971, p, 1; Stephen Curwood, "Polaroid Claims Success in South Africa 'Experiment,'" January 6, 1972, p. 1; Carl W. Sims, "UBA Chairman Explains Polaroid Decision," January 7, 1971, p. 1; Carl W. Sims, "Polaroid Gift Will Go to S. Africa, Cairo, Ill.," December 24, 1970, p. 1, all *Bay State Banner*.

FIGURE 15. The Polaroid Campaign's button, with red lettering on a green and black field, linked the colors of African-American nationalism to the black South African struggle. (Courtesy of Caroline Hunter and the late Ken Williams, creators and founders of the Polaroid Revolutionary Workers Movement (PRWM) and the Polaroid Boycott Campaign)

to state clearly and unequivocally on moral grounds that we could not accept the money."[29]

The Polaroid controversy resonated with a broader public concern about government surveillance. Technological advances, including instant photographic processes, made it easier to monitor individuals. The South African use of passbooks suggested that Stateside authorities could similarly gather information and track U.S. citizens. Just when Polaroid critics were expressing fears about "technological fascism," government officials were indeed spying on Americans. Coordinated Intelligence Programs (COINTELPRO) provided local police authorities with federal resources and operated just at the edge of popular consciousness. Critics shot down proposals to issue ID cards to welfare recipients and institute ID systems in public schools across the country. Long before governmental and corporate intrusions into privacy so characteristic of today's world became omnipresent, popular anxieties linked such measures with workers' concerns about technological displacement and alienating work.[30]

[29] "RMSC Explains Polaroid Veto," *Bay State Banner*, March 16, 1972, p. 1.
[30] FBI Headquarters to all field offices, August 25, 1967, Senate Report 94–755 755 of the Select Committee to Study Government Operations, with Respect to Intelligence Activities,

After being fired from Polaroid, Caroline Hunter became involved in a related campaign. People against National Identity Cards (PANIC) demonstrated on April 23, 1973, in Technology Square, Cambridge, Massachusetts. The target was still Polaroid. "Polaroid would like everyone to think that profits are being made on the family cameras and film that they sell," Hunter declared, "but their real profits come from the Polaroid ID-systems that are used in America and throughout the world." Governments in Southeast Asia, where the United States was still at war, had bought the systems. Argentina, Brazil, the Dominican Republic, Greece, Haiti, Jordan, and Trinidad had also made purchases. Authorities in perennially tense Israel used an ID system in the Gaza Strip. PANIC linked Polaroid to worldwide repression and revealed at the Cambridge rally the presence of a CIA office in a Technology Square office building. According to the *Harvard Crimson,* " the CIA wanted to be kept informed of the activity of Cambridge radicals because it feared for the safety of its office."[31]

Although the Boston chapter of the NAACP criticized Polaroid's South Africa ties, it accepted thousands of dollars in Polaroid scholarship money for black students. NAACP branch president Jack E. Robinson thought PRWM militancy "obsolete." "It is very unfortunate that the strategy of the PRWM fails to adjust itself to changing times," Robinson commented. "The emphasis should be shifted ... because if the workers in the PRWM are going to boycott all American companies doing business with South Africa they must give up their Gillette razor blades, stop driving Ford and General Motors cars and not save at the First National Bank."[32]

International law expert Michael Reisman articulated further disapproval of boycotts and sanctions as a weapon against apartheid. Writing in the journal *Foreign Policy*, Reisman asserted that foreign corporations would simply replace U.S. firms that withdrew from South Africa. While offering no defense of a regime he considered "evil," he noted that certain African states, in spite of their leaders' rhetoric, traded with the pariah government and headed regimes in which human rights were often honored in the breach. Reisman dismissed armed struggle in southern Africa as a "military fantasy" haunting U.S. church groups as well as radical organizations. He sought to rescue global capitalism from the ill repute that its rapport with Pretoria had created. "In the context of South Africa," he wrote, "the gravamen is not that people are making money, but that they are making it in ways which sustain or reinforce a system of social order repugnant to international law and morality."[33]

United States Senate, April 23, 1976, p. 20; Shirley V. Quarmyne, "40 Million Blacks in Sixty Seconds," *Los Angeles Herald Dispatch*, October 21, 1971, in Polaroid Revolutionary Workers Movement, "No Bullshit Boycott Polaroid," 1971, unpaginated, The African Activist Project, http://africanactivist.msu.edu.

[31] Harvard Crimson quoted in "PANIC observes CIA activities in Cambridge," *Bay State Banner*, April 26, 1973. p. 1.

[32] "Robinson Defends Polaroid Grant," ibid., November 11, 1971, p. 1.

[33] Michael Reisman, "Polaroid Power: Taxing Business for Human Rights," *Foreign Policy* (4) (1971): 104, 106, 107.

Proposing a way out of the dilemma, Reisman called for an international code of business practice. "The international businessman is an international citizen," he affirmed, "and, as such, is obliged to conform to the minimum standards of the United Nations Universal Declaration of Human Rights." Rules for doing business in places like South Africa would mandate nondiscriminatory practices and reserve a portion of profit to raise human capital in the host country through education. Reisman's ideas synchronized with a State Department–endorsed South African Leader Exchange Program, in which prominent white South Africans, including corporate executives and directors, would network with U.S. foundation heads and government officials like the Ford Foundation's Wayne Fredericks and Foreign Service officer Ulrich Haynes. Six years later, the Reverend Leon Sullivan would echo these ideas in his "Sullivan Principles," a formula for doing guilt-free business with Pretoria. But plans to have corporate capitalists and other establishment figures act as change agents in South Africa clashed with the hard reality of white resistance to equal opportunity for black Africans. Reisman's solution entailed "a separate 'division' in which Bantu would be placed in supervisory capacities" or, alternatively, the creation of "a subsidiary in one of the 'homelands' in which all positions would be reserved to blacks." Ironically, in his formulation, a now-discredited American-style Jim Crow would be the answer to South African inequality.[34]

Reisman perceived the crisis in southern Africa as a chance to explore "novel civic initiatives," as Polaroid appeared to be doing, but U.S. corporate and political leaders began thinking innovatively about apartheid only after resistance to white supremacy had stiffened in both the United States and South Africa. Financiers and industrialists traded and invested without a thought to such lofty subjects as human rights. Now, however, "the momentary conjunction of global interdependence and the obsolescence of contemporary political boundaries," Reisman suggested, provided the opportunity to devise a way to enact reforms without disturbing fundamental market relationships.[35] Somehow, the South African problem would have to be reduced to one of civil rights rather than human rights. Within the framework of civil rights, dismantling apartheid would be a formal political process that would enfranchise black Africans without disturbing the existing socioeconomic hierarchy. Democratic assimilation, not self-determination, would prevail. Enlarging the opportunities for a black managerial bourgeoisie in Africa would lessen the attraction of revolutionary solutions to the continent's problems. Similarly, allowing more minority talent to blossom at home would dull the intensity of black rage.

Militant black labor organizations flatly rejected this approach. Unlike the Polaroid Revolutionary Workers Movement, which only three subsequently

---

[34] The South African Leader Exchange Program, c. 1970–1, Rayford W. Logan Papers, MSRC, series 166, Box 49; Reisman, "Polaroid Power," 107–8.
[35] Reisman, 110.

fired Polaroid employees managed, the Revolutionary Union Movements mounted in Detroit had deeper roots. The southern civil rights movement made working-class African Americans in areas outside Dixie painfully aware of the shortcomings of northern freedom. While activism took place all over the country during the "high tide" of civil rights insurgency, the uncompromising brutality of many southern segregationists, the press they received, and the professed desires of national leaders to eliminate bias elevated events with racial content to mass consciousness. Line workers in the auto industry, who were historically class conscious and intermittently militant, numbered among the first to respond to the political stimuli of the era. According to the United Black Workers (UBW) from the Ford "plantation" in Mahwah, New Jersey, their organization was not "born overnight. Our involvement in liberation and struggle didn't grow out of the Viet Nam War, impeachment of the president, or any theoretical analysis learned in a classroom." The UBW newsletter, the *Black Voice*, detailed its early 1960s activism and contained an array of information about shop floor issues, police brutality, housing, and other matters.[36]

Many, like Charles Simmons of Detroit, had a family history of trade union participation and political views that were left of the mainstream. Muhammad Ahmad (Max Stamford) has written, "The centrality of industry around the auto industry in Detroit with a large entry of young African-American workers from 1964 to 1967 was unique ... a worker could look down the assembly line and see someone he had grown up with or gone to school with as a youth." Simmons, rooted by class and family history in Detroit's industrial world, enhanced his critique of U.S. foreign and domestic policy through his air force experiences. After seeing Castro and Malcolm X together in New York, he decided and announced publicly that he was not going to participate in any military action against Cuba. He then lost a security clearance and left the air force late in 1962. Simmons returned to Detroit, enrolled in Wayne State University, and supported himself through auto work. Like Amiri Baraka (Leroi Jones), he was considered an odd duck in the military; in the eyes of the brass, his NAACP membership made him radical. He would become more so. Simmons's interest in Cuba was affirmed during a trip to the island in 1964 in the company of two other Detroit residents, Luke Tripp and General Baker; all of them were deeply impressed by the achievements of the Cuban revolution. All three belonged to a black student group, Uhuru, which imported the radical journal *Crusader* into the United States for its author, exiled NAACP leader Robert Williams.[37]

Labor militancy joined hands with anticolonialism when activists appealed to dockworkers to refuse to unload Rhodesian chrome in U.S. ports. Rhodesia, a British colony in southern Africa, boasted a ruling minority of white settlers

---

[36] The *Black Voice*, vol. 4, no. 20, February–March 1974, and no. 21, April–May 1974, are representative issues.

[37] Author's interview with Charles Simmons, Detroit, August 15, 1998.

who numbered less than 10 percent of the population. The African majority had few political rights. Rhodesia struck out for independence in November 1965, believing it could maintain white minority rule in the face of global opposition. Britain and the United States refused to recognize Rhodesia's new status. The "Africanists" in the State Department persuaded the Johnson administration to agree to economic sanctions, including barring Rhodesian imports and prohibiting commodity sales to the rogue state.

The Rhodesians skillfully eluded sanctions through indirect marketing and courting right-wing elements in the United States, including the John Birch Society and the Liberty Lobby. During the Nixon presidency, Congress lifted the ban on Rhodesian chrome imports. Senator Harry F. Byrd, Jr. of Virginia spearheaded the change through an amendment to the 1971 Military Procurement Bill. The African liberation support movement subsequently turned its attention to repealing the Byrd amendment and protesting the renewed shipments.[38]

In March 1972, 600 protesters joined black dockworkers in Burnside, Louisiana, in an action against chrome deliveries for the Foote Corporation and Union Carbide. African-American students from Southern University, at the center of the campaign, established a Committee of Blacks against Oppression. The following month, 250 Lincoln University students and others protested Foote's violation of the sanctions. They set up a picket line at Foote's Pennsylvania plant, where black students from Swarthmore College and Cheyney State College joined them. Representatives from the Congress of African People, the All African Peoples Party, SOBU, and other groups participated. In Baltimore and San Francisco, members of the International Longshoremen's Association protested chrome importation.[39]

The chrome protests illustrate a signal moment of cooperation between workers and students and suggest paths to expanded collaboration. Black labor militancy could have been even more expansive had it not been for a deliberate policy on the part of the League of Revolutionary Black Workers. League leaders opposed exporting the Detroit example of organization because they felt they had not yet consolidated their local position.[40] That position was destined to remain unconsolidated. The league was a dead letter by 1973. A decline in auto sales, worsened by the energy crises of the early decade, led to layoffs of workers with the least seniority, those most likely to be militant. With many of the troublemakers gone, the UAW changed its tactics regarding black labor activism. Abandoning some of the bias that had led to black insurgency in the first place, it began opening up more staff positions for African Americans.[41] This was a pyrrhic victory, however, as the latter part of the 1970s

[38] Andrew DeRoche, *Black, White, and Chrome: The United States and Zimbabwe, 1953–1998* (Trenton, N.J.: Africa World Press, Inc., 2001), 151–5.

[39] ACOA Fact Sheet, December 1972, in Social Action Vertical File, Box 3, folder 2, Wisconsin Historical Society; Johnson, "From Popular Anti-Imperialism to Sectarianism," 490.

[40] Muhammad Ahmad (Maxwell Stanford, Jr.) *We Will Return in the Whirlwind: Black Radical Organizations, 1960–1975* (Chicago: Charles Kerr Publishing, 2007), 262.

[41] Geschwender and Jeffries, 151; Ahmad, *We Will Return in the Whirlwind*, 261.

witnessed the decline of auto work and the rapid deterioration of U.S. heavy industry altogether.

Activists protesting imports from white settler regimes depended on the cooperation of dockworkers. If they refused to unload shipments, cargo companies would have to rely on scabs and incur extra costs when they were forced to divert cargoes to harbors less accessible to demonstrators. In the best of times, however, protest could not keep pace with the volume of trade from southern Africa.[42] Dockworkers often delayed, rather than refused, unloading as a solidarity gesture. The unloading would take place after the demonstration was over. As technological change advanced, the tactic of having targeted cargoes met in cities such as Baltimore and Philadelphia with their large black populations lost its effectiveness.

In 1974 the United Mine Workers (UMW) sought to prevent the Southern Company, a utility holding company, from importing South African coal through strike actions and protest. UMW president Arnold Miller objected to "subsidizing South African conscript labor at the expense of American miners who will lose jobs to Blacks in South Africa working under slave labor conditions." When leaders of the International Longshoremen's Association in Mobile, Alabama, refused the UMW request to leave the coal on the ships, a local antiapartheid organization, the Coalition to Stop South African Coal, brought in a representative from the Zimbabwe African National Union (ZANU) to discuss the issue with the rank and file. These workers, many of whom were black, broke with the union and refused to unload the coal. The Southern Company then secured court injunctions to force the dockers back to work and stop the UMW picket lines.[43]

In spite of the intensity of the Detroit-based workers' movement, recession, technological change, and foreign competition made inroads into labor insurgency as the decade advanced. Strikes ceased, and, as Aaron Brenner observes, "workers rejected fewer contracts and engaged in less collective disobedience. Most tellingly, virtually all rank-and-file organization disappeared."[44] As wildcatters were silenced, union leaders recaptured lost ground but could not secure favorable contracts. They increasingly fought a rearguard action against employer demands that workers sacrifice more to keep their jobs. The era of the "rust belt," when entire cities would be drained of resources and hope for the future, had begun. Subtle but unmistakable changes in both the national and global economy cut deeply into radical black internationalism.

Central to Black Power thinking in the 1960s through the 1980s was the assumption that the African-American geographic position in the cities was permanent and thus strategically valuable. Both conservative and radical Black Power approaches shared this perspective. It was important to recoup the earning power of the working poor. Urban League head Whitney Young noted that

---

[42] ACOA Fact Sheet, December 1972.

[43] "Coal from South Africa," *Finally Got the News* 1 (October 1974): 7.

[44] Aaron Brenner, "Rank-and-File Rebellion, 1966–1975" (PhD diss., Columbia University, 1996), 282.

black purchasing power equaled $20 billion per annum and would double if bias did not exist. "This $20 billion we are losing," he declared, "is the equivalent of all U.S. exports shared with all the 130 nations of the world.... Ending discrimination would have the effect of doubling exports and probably would put another three million men to work."[45]

This vision of black potential within the confines of the market was clouded by angry white panethnic responses in which racial solidarity trumped divisions among whites based on religion, class, or nationality, and in which the theme of the ghetto as space to be liberated was refuted. The fiscal famine caused by suburbanization, structural change, privatization, and the control of space by absentees deprived cities of the material resources they would need to effect the liberation that the colonial model sought.[46]

The result – the decayed and troubled city – had further implications beyond the failures of economic justice for African Americans. As hopes for the rebirth of the city faded, federal and local authorities channeled urban unrest in another direction. As unemployment grew and public schools deteriorated, more inner city inhabitants found themselves in jail. "As the walls of the ghetto shook and threatened to crumble," Loic Wacquant has written,

the walls of the prison were correspondingly extended, enlarged and fortified,... Soon the black ghetto, converted into an instrument of naked exclusion by the concurrent retrenchment of wage labour and social protection, and further destabilized by the increasing penetration of the penal arm of the state, became bound to the jail and prison system by a triple relationship of functional equivalency, structural homology and cultural syncretism, such that they now [by the mid-1990s] constitute a single carceral continuum.... In the wake of the "urban riots" of the sixties, which in truth were uprisings against intersecting caste and class subordination, "urban" and black became near-synonymous in policy making as well as everyday parlance.[47]

Harold Cruse, whose 1964 work, *The Crisis of the Negro Intellectual*, raised hackles among the black intelligentsia, weighed in on the urban crisis. Cruse noted the controversy raging in New York City over construction of the State Office Building in Harlem. He saw it as a first step toward white reconquest of black urban space. Harlem stood to lose its character as the cultural capital of black America if a government presence and enterprises run by whites

---

[45] Connie Seals, Chicago Urban League press release, n.d., 1960s, in CBP Part 3-Subject Files on Black Americans, 1918–1967 (Frederick, Md.: University Publications of America, 1985), Series I-Race Relations, 1923–1965, reel 8; Whitney M. Young, Jr., "The High Cost of Discrimination," *Ebony*, August 1965, p. 51.

[46] Thomas J. Sugrue, The *Origins of the Urban Crisis: Race and Inequality in Postwar Detroit* (Princeton, N.J.: Princeton University Press, 1996), 211–17, 229; Stanley Aronowitz, "Between Nationality and Class," in *Race, Identity, and Citizenship: A Reader*, eds. Rodolfo D. Torres, Louis F. Mirón, and Jonathan Xavier Inda (Malden, Mass: Blackwell, 1999), 310; Lizabeth Cohen, *A Consumers' Republic: The Politics of Mass Consumption in Postwar America* (New York: Knopf, 2003), 388; Robert A. Beauregard, *Voices of Decline: The Postwar Fate of U.S. Cities* (New York: Routledge, 2003), 176–8.

[47] Wacquant, Loic. "From Slavery to Mass Incarceration: Rethinking the 'Race Question' in the US," *New Left Review* 13 (2002): 52, 55.

developed unchecked. In his view, Harlem's failure to mount an effective rejoinder to encroaching white power, and not the demise of Representative Adam Clayton Powell Jr. or other charismatic leaders, was the pivotal moment that spelled defeat for all the radical and nationalist black movements of the sixties. Ghetto dwellers in other cities never understood the critical salience of the issue. If they had, he insisted, there would have been a national black response to the New York state government's incursion. Instead, black Americans across the country, like black New Yorkers themselves, were attuned primarily "to local or regional concerns."[48]

An escalating illicit narcotics trade further dimmed hopes for urban revival. As historians Alfred McCoy and William B. McAllister have noted, most of the drugs were from countries bound in anticommunist alliance with the United States, where profit from drug exports cemented political ties and muted unrest in impoverished rural areas. In efforts to phase out these arrangements, federal officials, with varying success, swapped technical assistance and crop-substitution programs for agreements to eradicate narcotics production. Yet the problem of addiction worsened in U.S. cities. In New York City, Powell accused police officers of colluding with Harlem traffickers. While his claim was widely interpreted as an effort to divert attention from his own political troubles, he was proven right when the "French connection" probe revealed widespread corruption in the city's police department. Nixon, facing reelection in 1972, declared a war on drugs that focused on the demand for heroin, rather than the supply. This set the stage for a further iteration of the law-and-order theme that had helped elect him earlier.[49]

The view that the inner city was an internal colony and, in James Boggs's words, "the black man's land," became a cruel irony. It underscored the abandonment of cities by industry, the collapse of tax bases, the erosion of essential services and maintenance, federal indifference, and the deepening poverty of those who remained. Even the poor could not be assured of continuous residence as "slum clearance" and "urban homesteading" by affluent whites began displacing them in older neighborhoods by middecade, wiping out the dream of a renaissance.[50]

Acts of displacement translated the black rebel and militant into the street criminal, facilitated by narcotics and the repression of dissent. That black publics were confused by this displacement made state repression easier. Popular media, for example, seized upon the celebration of pimps, but not prostitutes,

---

[48] Harold Cruse, "Black and White: Outlines of the Next Stage," *Black World* 20 (May 1971): 22–4, 34.

[49] Liberation News Service, "The Drug Culture," *Liberator* 10 (July 1970): 8–10; Alfred McCoy, The *Politics of Heroin in Southeast Asia*, 2nd rev. ed (Chicago: Lawrence Hill Books, 2003), 387–460; William B. McAllister, *Drug Diplomacy in the Twentieth Century: An International History* (London and New York: Routledge, 2000), 235–6.

[50] Beauregard, *Voices of Decline*; Edwin L. Harper, "Domestic Policy Making in the Nixon Administration: An Evolving Process," *Presidential Studies Quarterly* 26 (Winter 1996): 41–56.

who were subjected to blatant misogynous abuse. The seminal film that inaugurated the fascination with prostitution, *Sweet Sweetback's Badass Song*, centered on a pimp whose embryonic and inchoate political consciousness provides the film's raison d'être. Sweetback's pimping rather than his militancy, however, served as a template for a stream of books and films that marked one face of late twentieth-century popular culture.[51]

The celebration of sex work involved an aesthetic turnabout from Black Power's insistence on the natural. One male critique of black women condemned popular cosmetic practices, including wigs, makeup, miniskirts, and straightened or tinted hair. "Stop dying your minds," wrote Octavius Abou in a letter to the editor of *Liberator*. Nationalists like Abou linked artifice to deception, seduction, and harlotry. The natural African woman was unadorned. Popular culture reversed this imagery in its embrace of pimping. Soon enough university-educated critics got into the act, including some who found revealed truth in Iceberg Slim's (Robert Beck's) semiautobiographical accounts of the exploitation of females, including the underaged. One admirer, writing in *Black Scholar*, asserted that Beck was a better writer than Ralph Ellison.[52]

Cedric Robinson's useful corrective to this glorification suggests that the blaxploitation film genre emptied black militancy of real political content. "Film-makers trivialised the troubled activists of the movement into the now familiar male counterrevolutionary creatures: the male prostitute ('"Sweetback'), the vigilante cops ('Gravedigger Jones' and 'Coffin Ed Johnson'); the dope pusher ('Shaft'); and the gangster ('Black Caesar', etc)."[53] The commodification of subaltern cultures was well under way.

Recent critics have analyzed the appeal of black gangsterism to whites, and especially youth, but in the 1970s, whites rarely patronized blaxploitation films. The observer must then ask why they appealed to their African-American audiences and what they reflected about the rapidly changing nature of U.S. popular culture and politics. As Bill Yousman would write about rap more than thirty years after many such films debuted, "strong conservative impulses are disguised by the 'outlaw' imagery employed by artists and the recording industry. These artists often disguise ultraconservative messages about fearing and hating difference, worship of money and material possessions, masculine power, and individual aggrandizement beneath images and postures that seem to represent defiance and dissent."[54] In this sense, blaxploitation reaffirmed

---

[51] Beth Coleman, "Pimp Notes on Autonomy," in *Everything but the Burden: What White People Are Taking from Black Culture*, ed. Greg Tate (New York: Broadway Books, Random House, 2003), 68–73; Richard Milner and Christina Milner, *Black Players: The Secret World of Black Pimps* (Boston: Little, Brown, 1973).

[52] Octavius Abou to the editor, *Liberator* (January 1969): 22; Peter Muckley "Iceberg Slim," *Black Scholar* 26 (1) (1996): 20.

[53] Cedric J. Robinson, "Blaxploitation and the Misrepresentation of Liberation," *Race & Class* 40 (July–September 1998): 1–12 [viewed online].

[54] Bill Yousman, "Blackophilia and Blackophobia: White Youth, the Consumption of Rap Music, and White Supremacy," *Communication Theory* 13 (4) (November 2003): 383.

|rather than challenged the least lofty of American social values and provided a vocabulary for the growth of conservative politics both within and outside black communities. The celebration of criminality affirmed the correctness of repressive public policies while legitimating the behavior that justified the growing punitiveness of the next episode of the war on drugs.[55]|

With black rebellion increasingly criminalized and the "race problem" being solved only on the level of representation, how would Americans make real progress? By the end of the 1970s, every Western country had its racial-ethnic minorities,/most the product of migration from colony to metropole./Conflicts assumed to be characteristic only of the United States would play out in cities and towns across Europe. As the power with some of the largest and most politically assertive racial-ethnic minorities, however, the United States continued to be the icon of communal race violence. Its legislative and judicial reforms already complete by the mid-1960s, few major changes could acceptably be made in a conservative society increasingly suspicious of national government and profoundly hostile to black entitlement.

The ongoing resistance to eradicating the remaining structural effects of racism did not surprise black nationalists. It aided the resurgence of the Nation of Islam after a brief eclipse following the assassination of Malcolm X. Focused on the Middle East, the Nation was the most prominent of black nationalist organizations but showed little direct interest in Africa beyond Libya. Its northern origins did not prevent it from expanding into Dixie, challenging the premises of classic civil rights activism on home turf. When the Ku Klux Klan tried to prevent Muslim organizing in Atlanta, Benjamin Karim recalls,

we went down there nevertheless, thousands of us. Along with the police, the FOI [Fruit of Islam] in its impressive paramilitary form secured a four-block area surrounding the temple. Brothers and sisters poured through the city streets toward the temple. Its seating could not accommodate most of them. They stood outside, on steps, on sidewalks, in the street. Atlanta felt our presence, and a mile away from the temple the Klan did too.[56]

According to FBI documents, NOI activity in the South began as early as 1955 when members left Philadelphia to proselytize after Emmett Till's murder and the Montgomery bus boycott. Wallace D. Muhammad contributed fifty dollars to a fund to help Little Rock journalists L. C. Bates and Daisy Bates recover financially after they lost their newspaper because of retaliation during the school crisis. Malcolm X toured southern states during the winter of 1960. The NOI did not intend to compete with the civil rights movement but to replace it with a different plan. It would follow an agenda with Tuskegee antecedents, forswearing political involvement and challenges to segregation

---

55 In this connection, see Coleman, "Pimp Notes on Autonomy," 68–73.
56 Benjamin Karim with Peter Skutches and David Gallen, *Remembering Malcolm* (New York: Carroll & Graf, 1992), 138–9.

and disfranchisement. Instead, the focus would be on farming and landown-ership.[57] Quietism did not ensure peace, however, as local whites continued to oppose any black moves that would alter power relations. NOI members met violent resistance in Baton Rouge and Monroe, Louisiana, and in Pell City, Alabama.[58]

NOI conservatism and disavowal of civil rights protest did not help it in New York City either, as a 1972 incident reveals. On April 14, two New York police officers entered Temple No. 7 in Harlem, allegedly in response to a distress call within. Ten armed men confronted them and a shoot-out ensued that cost one officer's life. Neighborhood residents responded angrily, overturning a patrol car, throwing bottles and bricks, and assaulting a white reporter. When police backup arrived, officers clubbed and beat people near the mosque entrance. The mosque's leader, Minister Louis Farrakhan, said that the police "charg[ed] into our temple like criminals and were treated like criminals." The raid renewed calls in Harlem for an all-black police force to patrol local streets. Historian Matthias Gardell relates that "Libya was alone among the Muslim countries to officially express its concern" over the attack. "The Libyan consulate sent a letter of support and in Tripoli, the United States chargé d'affaires was called in to receive an official protest from the Libyan government." Tripoli's offer of a $3 million loan to the NOI reciprocated groundwork that they, and especially Malcolm X, had done over the years.[59] Two Emirati governments more quietly helped the NOI, conveying funds to Elijah Muhammad via the prime minister of Abu Dhabi and the Qatari minister of finance, respectively.[60]

Animosity toward Israel was part of the quid pro quo, made easier by that country's own flawed public policies. Israel, trying to overcome its iso-lation, courted Afro-Asian opinion by offering aid to African states, includ-ing short-term student bursaries. It arranged junkets to the "Holy Land" for African-American clergy and journalists. Israel publicly opposed apartheid during most of the 1960s and supported the General Assembly's 1962 call for sanctions but abstained from endorsing South Africa's expulsion from the

[57] FBI report, "Racial Tension and Civil Rights, March 1, 1956," enclosed with J. Edgar Hoover to Maxwell Rabb, March 9, 1956, Eisenhower Papers, Ann Whitman File, DDRS; Director's office report on "Racial Situation," March 3, 1566, David Garrow FOIA Collection, SC; New Jersey *Herald News*, December 31, 1960 in David Garrow FOIA Accession, SC. "Muslim Leader Helps Mrs. D. Bates," *Baltimore Afro-American*, January 9, 1960, p. 6; FBI, "Racial Tension and Civil Rights, March 1, 1956," 15. FOIA Collection.

[58] Claude A. Clegg, *An Original Man: The Life and Times of Elijah Muhammad* (New York: St. Martin's Press, 1997), 165, 270; *Chicago Tribune*, January 13, 1972, 1D:2, and ibid., January 15, 1972, p. 2; *Muhammad Speaks*, January 21, 1972, p. 2; Mattias Gardell, *In the Name of Elijah Muhammad: Louis Farrakhan and the Nation of Islam* (Durham, N.C.: Duke University Press, 1996), 274; "Muslims in Alabama," *Time Magazine* 95 (February 2, 1970): 12.

[59] Gardell, 206; *Muhammad Speaks*, May 1972, pp. 16–17; June 9, 1972, p. 4; October 20, 1972, p. 6; October 27, 1972, p. 4.

[60] *Muhammad Speaks*, May 19, 1972, pp. 16–17; June 9, p. 4; October 20, p. 6; October 27, p. 4; Gardell, 206. The CIA, however, wrote the Nation of Islam off as a radical threat in 1971. [CIA report, 1971, in DDRC.]

UN. It recalled its envoy from Pretoria in 1963 and in 1966 favored ending South Africa's mandate over Southwest Africa, now Namibia. Beginning in 1967, however, South Africa and Israel strengthened their commercial ties. South Africa profited when the '67 War, and chronic bottlenecks in the Suez Canal forced East African exports to travel via the more costly Cape of Good Hope route.[61]

African-American opinion as a whole remained divided on Israel. Various prominent figures signed an ad published in several issues of the *New York Times* in 1970. The A. Philip Randolph Institute's page-long "Appeal by Black Americans for United States Support of Israel" defended the country, casting it as a democracy worthy of the fullest American support. This opinion was not universally shared. The Committee of Black Americans for the Truth about the Middle East castigated Israel on November 1, 1970, pointing out the theft of Palestinian land and discrimination against Arabs, which recalled Jim Crow. Committee members included, among others, Frances Beal, James Boggs and his wife Grace Boggs, the Detroit leader the Reverend Albert Cleague, Charles Simmons, and Robert Van Lierop. The ties between Israel and the United States, the committee asserted, constituted an unholy alliance of imperialist conspirators.[62]

Journalist C. L. Sulzberger claimed that "race lies close to the heart of the Arab-Israeli conflict although both sides are anthropologically Semitic." He noted the underlying theme of race in world affairs during the era. Sulzberger wrote an opinion essay in the *New York Times* titled "Foreign Affairs: The Black and White of It." He focused on "today's nastiest issue," race, "a universal problem." Sulzberger viewed "the black-white problem inside the United States" as "directly related to the black-white problem faced by American foreign policy."[63] Internationally, the expulsion of Asians from sub-Saharan Africa countries and growing anti-Asian sentiment in Britain seemed to prove his point.

A fragile alliance between civil rights "moderates" and supporters of Israel tried to connect Israel with themes of domestic freedom. Although they argued that U.S. racial conflict was a "family quarrel" and should not involve such matters beyond "the water's edge" as Vietnam, since the late 1950s they chose more and more to identify with Tel Aviv. The roster of supporters was a veritable

---

[61] Zach Levey, "Israel's Entry to Africa, 1956–1961," *Diplomacy & Statecraft* 12 (3) (2001): 87–114; idem, "Israel's Strategy in Africa, 1961–1967," *International Journal of Middle East Studies* 36 (1) (2004): 71–87; Y. D. Newsome, "International Issues and Domestic Ethnic Relations: African Americans, American Jews, and the Israel-South Africa Debate," *International Journal of Politics, Culture, and Society* 5 (1) (1991): 32.

[62] "An Appeal by Black Americans for United States Support to Israel," display ad, *New York Times*, June 28, 1970, p. 133; "An Appeal by Black Americans against United States Support of the Zionist Government of Israel," display ad, ibid., November 1, 1970, p. 172; Newsome, "International Issues and Domestic Ethnic Relations," 37.

[63] C. L. Sulzberger, "Foreign Affairs: The Black and White of It," *New York Times*, March 11, 1970 p. 46.

Who's Who of "responsible" Negro leadership with a sprinkling of those who had been associated with grassroots local programs. They included A. Philip Randolph, Roy Wilkins, Shirley Chisholm, Whitney Young, Carl Stokes, Robert Weaver, Louis Stokes, Jackie Robinson, Wyatt T. Walker, Martin Luther King Sr., Charles Diggs, Vernon Jordan, John Conyers, Raymond Pace Alexander, Eleanor Holmes Norton, Aaron Henry, John Lewis, John H. Johnson, William Lucy, Louis Martin, and C. L. Dellums.[64]

A surprise attack on Israel by Egypt and Syria on the Yom Kippur holiday, October 6, 1973, led to renewed regional fighting. Israel took heavy casualties but managed to tie down Egyptian forces and invade Syria. Egypt claimed to have shot down an Israeli plane manufactured in South Africa, and as Israel had supported the Security Council's resolution to ban arms sales to that country, this was taken as bad faith. On December 14, 1973, the UN General Assembly passed resolution 3151 G (XXVIII) condemning "the unholy alliance between Portuguese colonialism, South African racism, Zionism [*sic*] and Israeli imperialism." Israel subsequently discontinued any condemnation of apartheid in the UN. It named an ambassador to Pretoria and by the end of 1974 maintained diplomatic relations with only four African states.[65]

These events occurred as Middle Eastern powers began flexing their muscle as petroleum producers. The Organization of Petroleum Exporting Countries (OPEC), established in 1960 by Iran, Iraq, Kuwait, Saudi Arabia, and Venezuela, started with the premise that oil wealth could spur the development of member states. While non–Middle Eastern nations also joined OPEC, oil-rich powers of the Persian Gulf, through the control of exports and therefore prices, could assist neighbors whose lack of petroleum retarded their progress. For some, Pan-Arabism and oil were the way out of poverty and backwardness, but Pan-Arabism lost much of its luster after the Arab defeat in the 1967 war and Nasser's premature death three years later. OPEC began more closely to reflect the thinking of the conservative Gulf leaders. Petroleum as a political weapon might also help eliminate Israel as a force in the area.[66] Accordingly, the oil embargo of 1973–5 punished states seen as supportive of Tel Aviv.

The embargo worsened economic conditions in Africa. The OPEC states created a small loan fund in the African Development Bank to ease the effects of fuel prices, but the amount was insufficient to alleviate the continent's problems. Arab efforts to situate conflicts with Israel within the frame of antiimperialism broke apart on the shoals of oil. Governments were forced to borrow heavily from European and North American banks, ironically flush with petrodollars. A drought that devastated large parts of the Sahel combined with the energy crisis and quickly became a debt crisis. In spite of the years spent

[64] *New York Times* ad in Bayard Rustin Papers (Bethesda, Md.: University Press of America), reel 1.

[65] Zach Levey, "Israel's Exit from Africa, 1973: The Road to Diplomatic Isolation," *British Journal of Middle Eastern Studies* 35 (2) (2008): 208–15; Newsome, "International Issues," 33, 34.

[66] Nathan J. Citino, *From Arab Nationalism to OPEC: Eisenhower, King Sa'ud, and the Making of U.S.-Saudi Relations* (Bloomington: Indiana University Press, 2002), 146.

grooming African elites to emulate the West, the World Bank now argued that African officials should have customized rather than imitated the Western path to development. As African governments lacked the requisite skills to operate state industries efficiently, the bank urged more focus on agricultural production. Typically, the structural adjustment plans it advocated emphasized trade liberalization, fiscal austerity, and promotion of private enterprise.[67]

Leading African-American figures meanwhile continued to enter the lists on Israel's side. Los Angeles mayor Thomas Bradley, Roy Wilkins, Bayard Rustin, and singer Leslie Uggams numbered among celebrities who backed Israel in the 1973 war. The Randolph Institute sponsored a full-page supportive *New York Times* ad signed by seventy black trade unionists and paid for by a group of affluent Jewish Americans.[68] Randolph and Rustin eventually chaired and directed, respectively, an organization called Black Americans to Support Israel Committee (BASIC). BASIC's November 23, 1975, ad in the *New York Times* noted the impact of the OPEC embargo and averred that "Arab oil policies have had disastrous effects upon blacks in America and Africa." Arabs were niggling in their aid to African states in contrast to Israel, "small and isolated" though it was, which had done much more. Those linking the energy crisis to a pro-Israel agenda and condemning Arab nations failed to mention that Nigeria, Venezuela, and Indonesia were equally self-interested OPEC members.[69]

BASIC was at pains to explain the Israeli–South African rapprochement, especially after South African premier Vorster's visit to Israel in 1976 and expanded trade between the two countries. Rustin wrote to American Jewish Congress president Rabbi Arthur Hertzberg to express the "shock" and "chagrin" that African Americans felt about the Vorster visit. Hertzberg replied that after his own visit to Israel over the summer of 1976 and talks with local officials he had learned that the Vorster visit was in response to Israel's "virtual isolation in the world and its vulnerability to political attack, economic warfare and military invasion." Israel had not turned against black Africa, he asserted, but rather, black Africa, "under intense Arab pressure," broke diplomatic and commercial relations with Israel. These states "succumb[ed] to blackmail and turn[ed] away from a good and helpful friend." Israel needed South African trade, as did black chiefs of state Houphouet-Boigny of the Ivory Coast and Leabua Jonathan of Lesotho. In both cases, small states were pursuing their "economic survival," just as Israel was. Besides, the rabbi added,

---

[67] Beverly Carter to the Secretary of State, June 19, 1974, SDCF. See also Ashley Dawson, "New Modes of Anti-Imperialism," in *Exceptional State: Contemporary U.S. Culture and the New Imperialism*, eds. Ashley Dawson and Malini Johar Schueller (Durham, N.C.: Duke University Press, 2007), 253–4; Mark T. Berger, "After the Third World? History, Destiny and the Fate of Third Worldism," *Third World Quarterly* 25 (1) (2004): 9–39; Susan Strange, *The Retreat of the State: The Diffusion of Power in the World Economy* (Cambridge: Cambridge University Press, 1996), 169.

[68] Rabbi A. James Rudin, "American Blacks Express Solidarity with Israel," November 11, 1973, Rustin Papers, Reel 2.

[69] *New York Times* ad in Rustin Papers, Reel 1.

some African states were just as repressive as South Africa.[70] A later report by Moshe Decter entitled "South Africa and Black Africa: A Report on Growing Trade Relations" underscored Hertzberg's points and detailed how certain black African countries compromised themselves in trading with South Africa in spite of rhetoric they spouted in the General Assembly.[71]

Rustin indicated to Hertzberg that he understood the problem and remained committed to Israel's survival and cooperation with it. He likened the issue to Soviet-American commercial relations, which remained unimpeded by U.S. opposition to Soviet persecution of Jews. After consultations among BASIC, Hertzberg, and the Israeli consul-general, Israel "restated its position against apartheid and revealed that its volume of trade with South Africa is less than that of nineteen Black African states." BASIC continued its pro-Israel activities.[72]

BASIC was not the only initiative intended to sway African-American opinion. A Black-Jewish Information Center with headquarters in New York City's silk stocking district featured a Media Information Project that channeled favorable reports about Israel to the black press. The center also circulated stories that purported to explain why a Black Hebrew sect of U.S. origin had been expelled from Israel and an account of black and Jewish human rights organizations that, respectively, "vowed to put aside differences on issues such as the *Bakke* [affirmative action] case to work together on shared goals."[73]

In spite of efforts to mollify black establishment figures, antagonism toward Israel expressed at the UN and the OAU by African officials affirmed the hostility already brewing toward that country in many African-American circles. This joined a sentiment that associated Jewish "middlemen" with the economic subordination of inner city black communities, a theme linked to the internal colonialism model. The contrasting Muslim concern with Middle East issues raised questions about the habitual acceptance in civil rights leadership circles of pro-Israeli interpretations of regional events. Israel came to signify for many blacks an egregious example of Western racism and aggression.

Throughout this period, African-American discourses were contributing to a common idiom of dissent in a world experiencing the fallout from war, structural reorganization, and the disappointments of neocolonialism. A sense of connection did not depend on commonality of language or the diaspora traumas of slavery, migration, and dispersion. Nationalities that lacked a link to these experiences nevertheless found metaphorical purpose in black freedom struggles' frames. The varied origins of the group identified in the census as Asian Americans, for example, did not allow them to structure themselves as a discrete nation, but they nevertheless found themselves racialized and perceived as aliens. Some chose specific insurgent national traditions with which

---

[70] Bayard Rustin to Rabbi Arthur Hertzberg, August 27, 1976; Hertzberg to Rustin, September 1, 1976, Rustin Papers, reel 1.

[71] Moshe Decter, "South Africa and Black Africa: A Report on Growing Trade Relations," Rustin Papers, reel 1.

[72] Rustin to Hertzberg, September 14, 1976, Rustin Papers, reel 1.

[73] Victoria Free, Media Project Quarterly Report, March 1978, Rustin Papers, reel 1.

to identify. Dissident Chinese Americans in the Bay Area sought direct counsel from the Black Panther Party in establishing an organization called the Red Guards. Because of the political domination of Kuomintang sympathizers in Chinatowns, these communities experienced little overt radicalism, which young Chinese Americans learned from others. "Socialist Asia, regarded as an idealized representative of the Third World Left," Judy Tzu-Chun Wu writes, "served as a beacon of hope for activists of color in the United States."[74]

The phenomenon was not limited to the United States. The Black Panther Party of Israel provides an unusual example. The North African and Middle Eastern Jews who composed its membership acknowledged that they had no relationship with the U.S. party of the same name. They did not see themselves as revolutionaries but as reformers interested in a better deal in Israel for persons like them and actively dissociated themselves from the Left. They chose the Panther name to shock and provoke. As young people who had immigrated to Israel with their parents in the 1950s and 1960s, they hailed from the slums of Jerusalem, which experienced high rates of delinquency, drug use, and school incompletion. These children of so-called Oriental Jews, provided with menial employment and considered backward, "traditional," and premodern, fiercely attacked class inequality. They also saw race as part of their experience of alienation. The lighter-skinned European persona was favored over the swarthy phenotype that characterized many of non-European origin in Israel. The terms "black" and "white" were already in popular use to describe these differences.[75]

The Israeli Panthers experienced some of the problems plaguing their U.S. namesakes: factionalism, police brutality, and divide-and-conquer tactics by the establishment. Prime Minister Golda Meier said they were not "nice" because they threw Molotov cocktails at other Jews. A sympathizer suggested that they send a delegation to the United States to acquaint American Jews with their plight. The Panthers agreed, claiming that up to that point, American Jewish money only supported Ashkenazim rather than Jews per se. After they made their intentions public, it became de rigueur for public officials to meet with them, and American students began inviting them to U.S. campuses. One backer offered help on condition that they avoid American Black Panthers and other leftists if they came to the United States, but ultimately the trip was canceled.[76]

These Panthers framed their cause in terms of ethnocultural alienation and economic marginalization while proclaiming loyalty to the Israeli state. They made no critique of colonialism; nor did they discuss Arabs or express solidarity

---

[74] Judy Tzu-Chun Wu, "Revolutionary Travelers: People's Diplomacy, Third World Internationalism and American Orientalism," unpublished mss, pp. 17–18, 34. See also Daryl J. Maeda, "Black Panthers, Red Guards, and Chinamen: Constructing Asian American Identity through Performing Blackness, 1969–1972," *American Quarterly* 57 (December 2005): 1079–103.

[75] Deborah Bernstein, "The Black Panthers of Israel 1971–1972: Contradictions and Protest in the Process of Nation-Building" (PhD diss., University of Sussex, 1976).

[76] Ibid., 188, 206–9.

with them. They did not address international issues. They are pertinent to this narrative only because they borrowed and adapted a highly extensible tactical repertory available to anyone to employ for a variety of means, including purposes not originally intended by its creators. If the Black Panthers of Israel forced ethnicity proactively into Israeli consciousness, they did so using an instrument made in the USA by African Americans.

While African-American experience lent shape to how various groups framed their respective struggles, U.S. blacks did not play a decisive role in every event during the era of decolonization. An independent history of Caribbean revolt paralleled and intersected aspects of North American history but had its own dynamic. Black Power coincided with the growing realization that national independence had not produced equal opportunity and economic improvement for the masses of black people in the Americas. Black Power advocates decried the continuation of neocolonial politics under black Caribbean governments.

In Trinidad, large-scale unemployment and trade imbalances created unrest in April 1970. Trinidad, though a net exporter of petroleum, was not self-sufficient in it and, as a producer of sugar, had to seek preferential tariff agreements with Britain, Canada, and the United States for its sale. Trinidad had become independent in 1962, but it seemed to many of its citizens, both black and East Asian, that colonial politics had continued under a black government. An exacerbating factor was the jailing in Canada of a group of Caribbean students, including Trinidadians, who were accused of destroying a million-dollar computer at Sir George Williams University. The growing Caribbean student population in Canadian cities increasingly perceived Canada as another imperialist power. Those striking and demonstrating in Trinidad against Prime Minister Eric Williams's administration viewed the arrest of the Sir George Williams students as unjustified. Oil and sugar workers, students, and the unemployed created an oppositional umbrella group, National Joint Action Committee (NJAC). Carnival became an outlet for protest, as revelers took to the streets carrying posters depicting Stokely Carmichael, who had been banned from the country of his birth; Mao Tse-tung; and Malcolm X.[77]

Police in downtown Port of Spain in February 1970 attacked an NJAC demonstration that marked the occasion of the Sir George Williams students' trial. Local students then occupied the Roman Catholic cathedral and the Royal Bank of Canada. After the arrest of the group's leaders, some eight thousand to ten thousand persons assembled downtown in protest. Another mass meeting of ten thousand ensued on March 4, when bombing and arson followed police assaults. Insurrection peaked in Trinidad with arson in the capital and

---

[77] Delisle Worrell, "Canadian Economic Involvement in the West Indies," in *Let the Niggers Burn: The Sir George Williams University Affair and Its Caribbean Aftermath*, ed. Dennis Forsythe (Montreal: Our Generation Press, 1971), 41–56; Selwyn Cudjoe, "Trinidad: The Troubled Island," *Liberator* 10 May 1970, pp. 4–9; Alfie Roberts, *A View for Freedom* (Montreal: Alfie Roberts Institute, 2005), 81–4; David Austin, "All Roads Led to Montreal: Black Power, the Caribbean, and the Black Radical Tradition in Canada," *Journal of African American History* 92 (Autumn 2007): 533.

the burning of a Barclays Bank branch in the nearby town of San Juan. The authorities painted the protests as black racialist attacks on East Indians. To refute this, NJAC plantation workers organized trips to the countryside, where urban blacks were to assist East Indian sugar workers. The minister of industry denounced this move as a Cuban plot. Violence spiked again in April after the shooting of a black youth by the police. Some thirty-five thousand persons attended the funeral, which was followed by a wave of strikes, including those of the sugar workers and the powerful oil field workers union.[78] After the announcement of a mass march scheduled for April 21, Prime Minister Williams declared a state of emergency and arrested Black Power radicals and trade unionists. Newspapers were subject to censorship and radical literature banned. The day of the march, units of the Trinidadian army refused to obey a mobilization order and seized an ammunitions dump. The government was on the brink of collapse. Acting swiftly, Williams ordered the Trinidadian Coast Guard to fire on the mutineers and retake the arms cache. He acquired weapons from Venezuela and the United States, whose navies were standing by. While Williams succeeded in regaining control, the depth of popular rage was unmistakable. In May, sectors of the army mutinied with the aim of joining guerrillas already operating in the capital. The government suppressed the mutiny and banned outdoor political meetings.[79]

Trinidad and other island powers coupled repression with efforts to co-opt insurgent energies. Governments argued that Black Power was redundant in nations boasting black majorities. At the same time, they removed the more obvious neocolonial symbols. In Guyana, for example, the judiciary ditched the wigs they had inherited from British courtrooms. Trinidad finally allowed the widely proscribed Stokely Carmichael to visit his birthplace. Williams, a historian and the author of the classic work *Capitalism and Slavery*, had brilliantly analyzed imperialism in the late 1940s. Years later, accused of neocolonial authoritarianism, he responded to mutiny and rioting in the army by levying a surtax on corporations and by nationalizing the Bank of London and the Bank of Montreal. In Jamaica, Prime Minister Hugh Shearer endorsed Black Power when University of the West Indies students rioted against the ban preventing Walter Rodney from returning to his lecturer's job. In many Caribbean countries, the public reclaimed traditions disdained by the upper classes: carnival, Rastafarianism, and the patois of the common people.[80] For

---

[78] Tony Thomas and John Riddell, *Black Power in the Caribbean* (New York: Pathfinder Press, 1972), 4–5; Derek Humphry and David Tindall, *False Messiah: The Story of Michael X* (London: Hart-Davis, MacGibbon, 1977), 101; Oilfield Workers Trade Union, Trinidad, "A Brief History of the OWTU," http://www.owtu.org/documents, accessed November 29, 2010.

[79] Thomas and Riddell, *Black Power in the Caribbean*, 6, 7; Cudjoe, "Trinidad: The Troubled Island," 8.

[80] Selwyn Ryan and Taimoon Stewart with Roy McCree, eds. *The Black Power Revolution of 1970: A Retrospective*, (St. Augustine, Trinidad: I.S.E.R., University of the West Indies, 1995); Brian Meeks, *Radical Caribbean: From Black Power to Abu Bakr* (Barbados: Press University of the West Indies, 1996); Locksley Edmondson, "The Internationalization of Black Power: Historical and Contemporary Perspectives," *Mawazo* 1 (December 1968): 16–30.

Trinidad, the government's gestures did little to lessen sullen alienation. Only one-third of the eligible voters turned out for the May 1971 general elections, and opposition parties boycotted them, with the result that the ruling party took all legislative seats.[81]

Appeasement, however, was not the only weapon in official arsenals. Barbados endorsed Black Power but denied entry to foreign militants. Other nations worked with neighboring states to undermine the plans of Black Power advocates. In Guyana, endorsing Black Power provided a way for Prime Minister Forbes Burnham, with U.S. help, to neutralize the Indo-Guyanese politician Cheddi Jagan and stave off both Marxist politics and, for a time, the possibility of Indo-Guyanese political domination. Trinidadian writer Selwyn Cudjoe expressed concern about how Black Power would work in a society as racially mixed as Trinidad. Most black Trinidadians were not interested in reclaiming a land, Cudjoe asserted, that mostly now belonged to Asians or whites. Rather than creating a united front against Williams's government and helping the masses, he complained, Black Power proponents were more interested in infighting.[82]

Cudjoe's homeland and other parts of the region harbored a smoldering disaffection that paralleled the alienation felt throughout Africa and the diaspora. Insurgents harbored similar distrust of their bourgeoisies, identified imperialism in the structural inequality of their respective political economies, and honored indigenous cultural forms and practices long disdained as uncouth and unworthy. They counted among their ranks intellectuals trained in Western traditions but prepared to recast them in the service of a newly projected emancipatory culture.

The search to generate a knowledge that did not reproduce structures of domination was as keenly felt in the United States as in the Caribbean. Among the first scholarly organizations to feel the heat generated by change agents was the African Studies Association (ASA), founded in New York City just as the momentum of decolonization accelerated. The ASA united social scientists and humanists who studied Africa. It grew impressively through the mid-1960s and by 1970, as the preeminent organization in the field, controlled much of the funding for African studies projects in the United States.

At the same time, universities and foundations were recruiting African-American students to institutions where Africanist research was best supported and where black students had been in short supply. The work of recovery of the African past and issues confronting contemporary Africa resonated with the goals of both civil rights and Black Power proponents, and the ingress of younger scholars into the African studies field created challenges for its most established figures. Anthropologist Elizabeth Colson recognized this in a memorandum to the SSRC. "The professional meetings are now dominated

---

[81] Basil Wilson, "The Caribbean: Rumbles Left and Right," *Black World* 20 (August 1970): 23–6; Humphry and Tindall, *False Messiah*, 103.

[82] Cudjoe, "Trinidad," 9.

by the masses of young people just emerging from graduate status," she wrote. "Given the attacks on the professional associations by radical caucuses, right wing reactions, ethnic blocs, etc., large scale professional meetings which would normally bring together scholars concerned with Africa might not work for the next few years." There was an obvious "danger," she warned, "of allowing African studies to be taken over by young scholars who are not disciplined by rigorous standards."[83] This youthful cohort, ironically, was a product of efforts by the SSRC and other bodies only a few years before to admit more minority students to colleges and to introduce area studies programs.

Colson's comments reflected the tensions that erupted in Montreal in 1969 at the ASA's twelfth annual meeting, where more than half the conference sessions were cancelled or disrupted. Dissidents, including some whites, formed the alternative African Heritage Studies Association (AHSA). The ASA subsequently liberalized its rules, creating one that called for a racially balanced directorate. Many of its problems derived from the bifurcation in African studies, described previously, that had led to a segregated practice in the white and black academy, respectively, and to a popular history of Africa appreciated in black communities but kept separate and largely dismissed in predominantly white universities.

Herschelle Challenor, who would go on to work as a staff member for the House Subcommittee on Africa and later helped found TransAfrica, identified this intellectual Jim Crow as part of the problem. The Black Caucus in the ASA had previously challenged the organization to engage more with issues of antiracism and anticolonialism and be more inclusive of a wider range of practitioners in African studies. Its governing bodies should be racially integrated, and more Africans should be involved in its operations. The ASA seemed to set these demands aside, however, in the name of professionalism and objectivity. "Those white 'Africanists' who had consistently treated us as black 'Africanists' in the past, thereby defining our primary loyalties in their own eyes, suddenly expected us to be 'Africanists' who happened to be black and to join them, the 'academics' against other blacks," Challenor declared.[84]

Challenor's protest and that of others who founded AHSA not only focused on a sense of diaspora connection, but also condemned what they saw as the academy's rejection of the subaltern knowledge embodied in African-American popular history. AHSA consequently named John Henrik Clarke, a public intellectual, as its first president. It did not perceive itself as limited to academic

---

[83] Elizabeth Colson's memorandum, n.d., enclosed in Rowland L. Mitchell, Jr. to the Joint Committee on African Studies, October 22, 1970, SSRC Records, access 2, Series 1, sub-series 3, Box 18, folder 132A, RAC.

[84] Herschelle Challenor, "No Longer at Ease: Confrontation at the 12th Annual African Studies Association Meeting in Montreal," *Africa Today* 16 (December 1969): 4; Jerry Gershenhorn, "'Not an Academic Affair': African American Scholars and the Development of African Studies Programs in the United States, 1942–1960," *Journal of African American History* 94 (Winter 2009): 44–68.

networking and instead actively sought to influence how public schools, governments, media, business, and civic organizations used information about Africa and the African diaspora. The failure of ASA to do such work, AHSA members believed, revealed its ideological failures and compromises with racism and imperialism.[85]

Those who seceded from the ASA were not alone in their complaints. Other critics arraigned the marginalization of African Americans in African studies. African scholars disparaged the western biases of U.S. Africanists, their arrogance and suspect ethics while doing fieldwork, their ties to government and especially to intelligence agencies, and their denigration of values Africans deemed important. ASA publications rarely reviewed works by African scholars, an omission that evidently persisted into the 1990s.[86]

In the end, AHSA members did infiltrate the African studies mainstream. Diaspora concerns have since inserted themselves at numerous levels in anthropology, area studies, culture studies, the history of foreign relations, and various national and subnational histories. It is one thing to say that "black studies" broadly speaking pervaded the ivy tower because of the activism of resolute marauders, however, and another to explain why it remains there. If normalcy returned after the early 1970s, why the academy did not regain formerly lost traditionalist power remains to be explained. While some fields succeeded more than others in muting challenges and cordoning off unacceptable knowledge, the price they paid for their purity entailed a general loss of credibility outside their own charmed circles. The more successful disciplines learned to frame matters differently. The key to recovering normative ground was to shift the ground.

Suppressed knowledge at the margins could now be recognized. A burst of independent publishing, some of it ephemeral, disseminated newly valued information. Scholarly publications on African-American subject matter were not new, however. Decades earlier, Carter G. Woodson and W. E. B. Du Bois founded journals to publish African-Americanist research, the *Journal of Negro History* (1916) and *Phylon* (1940), respectively. Financial problems plagued these creditable publications from their inception, and their small press runs often made them inaccessible beyond college libraries and a small subscriber base. Structural as well as ideological problems prevented the larger academy from embracing the African-American experience.

A new monthly journal, the *Black Scholar*, hit newsstands and bookstores in 1969 on the wave of the era's popular insurgency. It rapidly expanded its circulation among a younger cohort of academics and general readers by

[85] Cyprian Lamar Rowe, "The Birth of the African Heritage Studies Association," *Black Academy Review* (Fall 1970): 3–9.

[86] Elliott P. Skinner to Eleanor Bernert Sheldon, November 9, 1973, SSRC Records, access 2, Series 1, sub-series 3, Box 18, folder 133, RAC; Paul Tiyambe Zeleza, "The Perpetual Crises and Solitudes of African Studies in the United States," *Africa Today* 44 (2) (1997): 197–8.

linking the current problems with which black communities wrestled to Du Bois's and Woodson's scholarly legacy. The *Black Scholar* was the brainchild of two African Americans, sociologist Nathan Hare and poet Robert Chrisman. Both were teaching at San Francisco State College in 1968 when students went on strike to demand that the administration establish a black studies program. Hare and Chrisman, the vice president of the American Federation of Teachers local, supported the students' action. While the college ultimately yielded to students' demands, Hare was fired and Chrisman demoted by the determined college president, S. I. Hayakawa. The journal they began publishing in November 1969 successfully complemented the drive to institutionalize black studies in the academy. While predecessor publications were thoroughly committed to expanding scholarship, they were not as explicitly premised on the political engagement that characterized the *Black Scholar*.[87]

Academics with activist credentials led in addressing these questions. One was Vincent Harding, in 1967 chair of the Department of History and Sociology at Spelman College. As a graduate student at the University of Chicago in the 1950s, Harding became a pacifist and a Mennonite. He traveled with church groups to the South to join campaigns for racial justice and subsequently became involved in civil rights activities in Alabama, Georgia, and Mississippi. Harding, with Spelman College colleagues, began planning a center devoted to African-American scholarship in Atlanta, a major city where black institutional life was firmly implanted. The idea attracted other scholars, such as Gerald McWhorter (Abdul Alkalimat) at Fisk University and A. B. Spelman at Morehouse College. After the King assassination, Coretta King asked Harding to head a Martin Luther King Library Documentation Project, which would be an archival repository for civil rights history. Harding then proposed blending the two projects, ultimately called the Institute of the Black World, which became operational early in 1970. The national agony over King's death seemed at first to ensure the financial survival of the institute, as it became a unit of the Martin Luther King Memorial Center. Distinguished writers, including historian and *Ebony* senior editor Lerone Bennett, historian Sterling Stuckey, and sociologist Joyce Ladner, joined the staff as senior researchers or fellows.[88]

From its inception, the institute had wanted to shape the content of what by the turn of the decade were some two hundred black studies programs across the country. To this end, they provided demonstration lectures, seminars, and model courses that could be adapted to the needs of particular colleges and universities. Institute affiliates networked with students and faculty at such

[87] Fabio Rojas, *From Black Power to Black Studies: How a Radical Social Movement Became an Academic Discipline* (Baltimore: Johns Hopkins University Press, 2007); Max Elbaum, "What Legacy from the Radical Internationalism of 1968?" *Radical History Review*, no. 82 (2002): 37–64; William M. Banks, *Black Intellectuals: Race and Responsibility in American Life* (New York: W. W. Norton & Company, 1996); "Notes," *Negro Digest* 19:2, December 1969, p. 33.

[88] Ward, "Scholarship in the Context of Struggle," 44, 45.

schools as Brooklyn College, Dartmouth, and Cornell University, as well as historically black institutions Fisk University and Howard University. The goal was to assist in creating curriculum that was "unashamedly devoted to the building of African peoples."[89]

The Institute of the Black World, a black academic center unconnected to a university, was the first body of its kind. Its relationship to a broader diaspora was embedded in its name. It provided fellowships for and hosted lectures by several major Caribbean intellectuals, including the revolutionist C. L. R. James, author of the classic history of the Haitian revolution, *The Black Jacobins*. Millions of readers already had their appreciation of the black past whetted by institute fellow Lerone Bennett's compelling popular history, *Before the Mayflower* (1962). Walter Rodney and the Jamaican historian Robert Hill, subsequently editor of the Marcus Garvey and UNIA papers, were also based at the institute at various times during its early years.[90]

Funding arrived fortuitously from the Ford Foundation, which had been eager to associate itself with King's name in spite of its fears about radicalism. Ford maintained its support even after the institute seceded from the King Center because of differences over the path the black freedom struggle should take. Ford Foundation president McGeorge Bundy had been a committed integrationist as the special assistant for national security affairs during the Johnson administration. After the expiration of Ford money in the early 1970s, the institute subsisted on a patchwork of grants before having to close its doors in 1983.[91] Its experience illustrated the extent to which black insurgency in the 1960s and 1970s sought to replace the imperatives of the humanities and mainstream social science with an alternative set of goals. Equally important was the challenge to common perceptions of who could be a thinker.

By the time *The Black Scholar* appeared, the educational establishment, faced with a barrage of epistemological challenges to the status quo, was already pledging allegiance to diversity. "Negro students create no problem so far as Princeton and its student body are concerned," Rockefeller Foundation associate director Leland C. DeVinney declared.[92] It is hard to contradict him: at the time of his writing, Princeton had twenty black undergraduates and no more than three black graduate students, too few for sustained rabble-rousing. Less obvious was trouble that black studies itself might cause in the academy. The *Brown* decision's integrationist logic was the same that helped naturalize

[89] An account of the institutionalizing of black studies is found in Rojas, *From Black Power to Black Studies*. Ward, "Scholarship in the Context of Struggle," 288.

[90] Rojas, 152. See also Rachel E. Harding, "Biography, Democracy, and Spirit: An Interview with Vincent Harding," *Callaloo* 20 (Summer 1997): 682–98.

[91] Melvin J. Fox, "Some Comments on Future Ford Foundation Support for the Foreign Area Fellowship Program and the SSRC/ACLS Joint Committee on Africa," draft, January 24, 1972, in SSRC (access 2) 1 Committee Projects subseries 3, box 18 folder 132A, RAC; Rojas, 154.

[92] Leland C. DeVinney's memo of interview with John Merrill Knapp, Jeremiah S. Finch, Parker Coddingon, November 11, 1963, Princeton University-Remedial Education, 1963, Rockefeller Foundation, series 200 boxes 80–81 folder 688, RAC.

black studies to the ivy tower. It held that all cultures are worthy of study and that legitimacy is determined by the skill that scholars give to that study. Ideology would take a back seat as academia decoupled black studies from street politics. Welcomed into the big tent of universal world culture, black studies' critical bite would become less incisive.

9

Agenda Setting on Two Continents

One day in autumn 1967, Dr. Donald Gatch, a white physician practicing in rural Beaufort County, South Carolina, smuggled a nine-year-old black girl into an operating theater. It was against the rules of his facility to perform surgery on indigent patients, so the operation, an appendectomy, was done surreptitiously. Once the child was on the table, the surgical team discovered that she had rickets. When they opened her abdomen, they found her riddled with worms. "These colored children don't have much to eat," a colleague observed, and when they did receive some nourishment, worms got to it first. Gatch tried but failed to secure funds from the local health department to remedy the widespread sickness and malnutrition. He had no better luck with foundations. The Rockefeller Foundation, whose hookworm program during the 1940s had been highly successful, now only addressed nutrition overseas. The National Institutes of Health worked only through universities.[1]

The Nebraska-born Gatch faced reprisal from area whites for embarrassing the state when the real issues, they thought, were the dirtiness and improvidence of blacks. Other local physicians publicly denied his claims, and white patients deserted his uncharacteristically integrated waiting room. Gatch was brought up on drug abuse charges and faced the loss of his license. Mississippi representative Jamie Whitten, chair of the House Agriculture Appropriations Committee, asked the FBI to investigate him. South Carolina's governor, fearing the impact of the doctor's revelations on investment and tourism, condemned him. Gatch eventually left the state.[2]

During Gatch's ordeal, an ambitious politician took up the cause of hunger in South Carolina while cagily distancing himself from the embattled physician.

[1] David Nolan, "The Hunger Doctor," *New York Review of Books*, March 11, 1971, accessed online, July 12, 2011; "Physician Tells of Malnutrition among Carolina Negro Children," *New York Times*, November 10, 1067, p. 18.
[2] Nolan, "The Hunger Doctor;" "Medic Who Exposed Plight of Hungry Blacks Charged," *Jet*, December 11, 1969, p. 5; "Dr. Gatch's Trial Is Continued in Beaufort County," Aiken S.C. *Standard*, January 14, 1970, p. 3-A.

Senator Ernest F. ("Fritz") Hollings professed astonishment at the famine conditions in the Beaufort area and at the ill health he witnessed on a tour conveniently scheduled after his 1968 election. He visited shacks that lacked running water and saw ragged people subsisting on fatback and oysters. Nutritional diseases, including pellagra and scurvy, took their toll. Hollings vowed to press South Carolina's unwilling counties to participate in the federal food stamp program.[3]

Hollings's stature as a senator and native son saved him from most of the animosity directed toward Gatch, but not all. He earned the nickname "Hookworm Hollings" from fellow South Carolinian representative Mendel Rivers. His senatorial colleague Strom Thurmond did not support him. Local newspapers accused him of pandering to blacks. An angry tobacco farmer approached him to say that food stamp provision meant that blacks would refuse to work. It was ironic, Hollings reflected, that an agricultural parity program "was paying farmers forty thousand dollars a year not to work, but a forty-cent breakfast for a child … was going to ruin his ambition."[4]

South Carolina was not alone, as the U.S. Public Health Service subsequently investigated malnutrition in Kentucky, Louisiana, Texas, and some Upstate New York counties. Officials found anemia, poor dentition, rickets, goiter, and stunted growth, problems thought typical only of developing countries. They uncovered several cases of kwashiorkor, a protein deficiency disease seen most commonly in African famines. Public Health Service plans to extend the study to more states, including Mississippi, were foiled by Whitten, concerned, perhaps, about what the findings might reveal about his home state.[5]

Food at the turn of the decade was an inescapable preoccupation. Food controversially became a pawn in U.S. relations with poor countries, helped finance the Vietnam War, and was extended or withdrawn depending on recipients' conformity to U.S. desires. Rising oil and fertilizer prices drove up food prices worldwide. "Food aid," wrote Leslie Gelb and Anthony Lake, "was becoming a public – if little understood – issue, as headlines about the Sahel, India, and Bangladesh became more dramatic." The Nixon administration decided to sell a substantial portion of the 1972 U.S. wheat harvest to the Soviets, thus increasing the domestic price of bread and other wheat containing products,[6]

The global food crisis crested just a few years after the federal government acknowledged the problem of domestic hunger. Poverty awareness stoked civil rights activism when authorities made racial distinctions among poor people, and when food donation programs were used to shore up segregation, obstruct voting, or maintain economic exploitation.[7] Poverty had often been treated as a passive by-product of discrimination. It was clearer now that it could serve as

3 Ernest F. ("Fritz") Hollings with Kirk Victor, *Making Government Work* (Columbia: University of South Carolina Press, 2008), 135. Hollings does not mention Dr. Gatch in this autobiography.
4 Ibid., 136, 133.
5 "Nutrition: One-Sixth of a Nation," *Time*, January 31, 1969, viewed online July 12, 2011.
6 Leslie H. Gelb and Anthony Lake, "Washington Dateline: Less Food, More Politics," *Foreign Policy* No. 17 (Winter 1974–75): 178.
7 Vivek Bammi, "Nutrition, the Historian, and Public Policy: A Case Study of U.S. Nutrition Policy in the 20th Century," *Journal of Social History* (1980): 636–40.

FIGURE 16. Protesters at the Department of Agriculture during the Poor People's Campaign, 1968. (Getty Images)

an engine of oppression, a vital component in maintaining a system of domination (see Figure 16).

When the Poor People's Campaign challenged that system, food constituted an important part of the protest agenda. The Department of Agriculture was a key stop on demonstrators' itinerary when they marched on Washington in the spring of 1968. The Poor People's Campaign drew attention to the irrationality in U.S. agricultural policy and federal collusion in supporting and maintaining the grotesque inequities that reconciled great wealth and vast landholdings with stunted and emaciated children.

Other NGOs took the food issue in hand, including the radical Black Panther Party, which created a widely emulated breakfast program for children. NGO activism on food forced public authorities to address hunger as a central issue. In the worst year of the African famine, Congress passed the Agriculture and Consumer Protection Act of 1973, making food stamps available nationwide.[8]

---

[8] Marjorie L. Devault and James P. Pitts, "Surplus and Scarcity: Hunger and the Origins of the Food Stamp Program," *Social Problems* 31 (June 1984): 552–53, 555.

Food provided a service opportunity for Jesse Jackson's Operation Breadbasket. A Baptist minister and a lieutenant of Martin Luther King Jr., Jackson adopted key elements of SCLC's southern style in his northern effort to further the Poor People's Campaign's unrealized economic goals. Breadbasket, based in Chicago, aimed to increase black employment in the city. It was a product of the Chicago freedom movement and SCLC's 1966 Chicago campaign. Jackson and his associates used the moral authority of black church tradition to name and shame discriminatory corporate practices. The threat of unfavorable publicity, picket lines, and potential sabotage persuaded Chicago businesses to negotiate. Supermarkets quickly agreed to hire African-American workers and purchase goods for sale from black manufacturers. While critics considered Breadbasket, and its successor, Operation PUSH (People United to Save Humanity), a shakedown operation and a vehicle for Jackson's personalist politics, it proved effective in breaking down some barriers to black employment in Chicago.[9]

PUSH was instrumental in drawing national attention to Africa. The so-called Green Revolution reduced chronic hunger in Southeast Asia but bypassed Africa entirely. There, postindependence leaders made early decisions to jump-start development by focusing on building an industrial sector, beginning with import substitution. With no large entrepreneurial class, states played a major role in the market as well as in planning. While the growth rate in most sub-Saharan countries averaged between 3 and 3.4 percent between 1961 and 1980, this figure masked a serious decline in per capita food production, which fell throughout the period as the population grew. The emphasis on state-run industries and the comparative neglect of agriculture meant recurring malnutrition, especially in remote rural areas. People living in the distant reaches of the Sahel that bordered the Sahara Desert were the most afflicted by the catastrophic drought of 1973, when an estimated 100,000 died.[10]

Jackson did not believe that government efforts went far enough in providing famine relief for African nations. In seeking help for Chad, Mali, Mauritania, Niger, Senegal, and Upper Volta, PUSH utilized a method of resource acquisition and distribution it had employed domestically. Jackson and his associates solicited large quantities of food from food processors like General Mills and from such supermarket chains as Jewel. He met with ambassadors from the affected countries and secured pledges of assistance from the mayors of several large cities, including Chicago. Jackson also approached the Nation of Islam, which held a fund-raiser attended by boxer Muhammad Ali and entertainers Stevie Wonder and Lola Falana. The event raised $10,000 for Operation PUSH

[9] Frady, *Jesse*, 253–5; Robert McClory, "Rave Reviews Fade for Jackson," *Race Relations Reporter*, March 1974, pp. 3–5.

[10] Richard Kennedy and Charles Cooper, NSC staff, to Henry Kissinger, September 7, 1973, in *FRUS, Foreign Economic Policy, 1973–1976* (Washington, D.C.: Government Printing Office, 2009), 861; F. Heidhues, et al., "Development Strategies and Food and Nutrition Security in Africa: An Assessment," International Food Policy Research Institute, 2004 (paper), p. 7, 8.

and $100,000 for UNICEF's Sahel drought relief campaign. While PUSH gathered more than sixty-five tons of food and medicine as well as cash donations, logistics problems delayed delivery as federal officials proved initially unresponsive to appeals to expedite the shipment.[11]

The ensuing post–Vietnam War recession was a serious blow to a U.S. economy that for the previous twenty-eight years had assumed its own infallibility. Several factors burst the bubble: the costs of the war, the oil embargo and sharp increase in the price of energy, the collapse of the Bretton Woods agreement, and competition from more efficient foreign industries. Planners faced stagflation, inflation coupled with high rates of unemployment. The public found itself buying expensive food with devalued money. The official unemployment rate reached an unprecedented post–World War II rate of 8.5 percent as output in heavy industry, automobiles, and construction shrank precipitously. African Americans, historically at the end of the pecking order, suffered official unemployment rates of 14 percent. The actual rate, which includes persons no longer looking for work, was higher.[12]

The critical food situation led representatives attending the 1974 World Food Conference in Rome to place food security in the broader context of historic exploitation and the constraints on subsistence farmers. Reflecting the growing global influence of feminism, the conference report laid exceptional stress on the role of women as food providers and advocated an end to the inequality most societies imposed on them.[13] In the United States, the link between poor women and food found strongest expression in controversies over welfare provision. If the UN saw women, who produced half of the world's food supply, as a valuable and underutilized source of human capital, many American leaders demonized poor women, and especially women of color, as parasites who produced only more hungry mouths. While the World Food Conference defined freedom from hunger as a human right, in the United States, the battle over the right to eat raged on into the twenty-first century.

The decline of U.S. monetary hegemony was soon followed by important changes in the domestic credit industry that would later assist the transition of the economy from production to finance. Easier credit could mitigate the stress and unrest caused by widespread poverty and unemployment. For most of U.S. history, personal credit was a prerogative of the affluent except in the agricultural sector. Even though credit made planting possible, debt made small farmers unwilling to spend, and country stores were recreational sites as much

[11] "Jackson Begins Drive to Aid Drought-Stricken Africans," *Jet*, July 26, 1973, p. 10; Barbara Reynolds, "'Coming Out' Party Bash for Muslims," *Chicago Tribune*, September 1, 1975, p. 1, 143; Marshall Frady, *Jesse: The Life and Pilgrimage of Jesse Jackson* (New York: Simon & Schuster, 2006), 106; Karin L. Stanford, *Beyond the Boundaries: Reverend Jesse Jackson in International Affairs* (Albany, N.Y.: SUNY Press, 1997), 52–3; Martha F. Lee, *The Nation of Islam, an American Millenarian Movement* (Lewiston, N.Y.: Edwin Mellen, 1988), 91.

[12] Unemployment by race, 1948–1980, U.S. Dept. of Labor, Bureau of Labor Statistics.

[13] United Nations, *Report of the World Food Conference*, Rome, November 5–16, 1974 (New York: United Nations, 1975).

as places of commerce. Blacks shopped less than whites and often faced humiliation when they did. As several historians have demonstrated, store boycotts were an important part of civil rights activity, indicating the importance that activists placed on equal treatment of African Americans as consumers. Many of the "riots" of the 1960s featured looting of stores for desirable commodities such as televisions. To the extent that they were "commodity riots," these disturbances reflected the inaccessibility of normal consumer outlets for urban poor people, who were often forced to pay usurious rates of interest on credit extended by avaricious local merchants or do without the goods that had become commonplace among the middle class.

In a widely publicized campaign, the National Welfare Rights Organization (NWRO) in 1969 pressured public welfare agencies to let relief clients use credit cards to make purchases and to persuade chain stores to accept them. NWRO actions included sending welfare recipients to department stores to attempt to charge items. The program received hostile media attention and fed into the growing public antagonism toward the poor. It was, however, prescient if premature, because this effort to mainstream low-income people predated important changes in the laws affecting credit. Social peace could be achieved through greater equality in the distribution of goods without disturbing the principle of ownership. The Equal Consumer Credit Act of 1973 made discrimination against all protected classes, including women and unmarried couples, Illegal. Poverty could now no longer be defined simply as destitution. Newly acquired access stripped the raw edge off deprivation and helped to depoliticize disadvantaged communities. As Ted Ownby noted near the end of the twentieth century, "today's poor people have unstable job prospects but plenty of chances for credit with high interest rates."[14] Challenges caused by the global food shortage and food price increases in the United States were a principal motive for the reform of the credit system. The 1970s enhanced understanding of how food related to the politics, foreign relations, and social structures of the world's communities.

Domestic poverty was in the midst of transition in the 1970s. The gut-wrenching deprivation of southern backwaters was not its only face. The debt cycle now could involve more commodities than the simple purchases that sharecroppers made at the general store in times past. Poverty could also subsist alongside prosperity, as in the sleek Sunbelt communities where new roads did not meet the unpaved shantytowns. The aerospace industry provides an example. While the towns and cities that housed it began changing in the 1970s as a result of African-American insurgency in the previous decade, the

---

[14] Annelise Orleck, *Storming Caesar's Palace: How Black Mothers Fought Their Own War on Poverty* (Boston: Beacon Press, 2006), 123; David Frum, *How We Got Here: The 70's, the Decade That Brought You Modern Life ... (for Better or Worse)* (New York: Basic Books, 2000), 93, 185; The Equal Credit Opportunity Act [ECOA], 15 U.S.C. 1691; Ted Ownby, *American Dreams in Mississippi: Consumers, Poverty, and Culture, 1830–1998* (Chapel Hill: University of North Carolina Press, 1999), 165.

National Aeronautics and Space Administration (NASA) itself continued to reflect the values of a declining era. Its high-paying technical positions were still closed to blacks and women in 1973. As author Kim McQuaid notes, "the only three females NASA had so far sent into space were two spiders and a monkey."[15] The astronaut "band of brothers" was all white. The complex nature of space research and astronaut training provided the agency with an excuse to maintain exclusion policies, but not every NASA job required an advanced physics or engineering degree.

Ironically, the one high-ranking woman in the agency was black, Ruth Bates Harris. NASA hired Harris as equal opportunity director but demoted her to assistant deputy director before she had even begun the job. If NASA could claim with some justification that it found women and minority engineers and scientists hard to locate, it could not make this argument for the many other job classifications that it had managed to avoid integrating. Harris claimed that even rocket scientist Werner von Braun, exposed in the early 1960s as a former Nazi, had acted "with courage and conviction" in advocating desegregation at the Marshall Space Flight Center in Huntsville, Alabama, which he directed. NASA's poor performance, then, was made in the USA, not in Hitler's Germany. Harris blew the whistle on the agency's foot dragging on employment desegregation and was subsequently fired.[16]

The NAACP Legal Defense Fund took Harris's case, increasing the pressure on the agency being exerted by such organizations as the National Urban League and the National Organization of Women (NOW). NASA's deputy director of public affairs deduced that "it may be time for us to go out and get ourselves a black astronaut."[17] The director reached that timely conclusion just a few years after the Supreme Court in 1971 ruled in the case of *Griggs v. Duke Power & Light*, a case that had important implications for NASA.

In *Griggs,* thirteen black employees filed a class-action suit challenging Duke Power Company's recently developed job requirements. These included a high school diploma, a mechanical aptitude test, and a general intelligence test. The plaintiffs demonstrated that the new requirements screened out a much higher proportion of black applicants than white. Duke Power could not show that the requirements were related to job performance. The Supreme Court prohibited any employment practice that operates to exclude members of a minority group that is not demonstrably related to job performance. Whether Duke intentionally discriminated was irrelevant. What interested the Court

---

[15] Kim McQuaid, "Racism, Sexism, and Space Ventures: Civil Rights at NASA in the Nixon Era and Beyond," in *Societal Impact of Spaceflight*, eds. Steven J. Dick and Roger D. Launius (Washington, D.C.: NASA Office of External Relations, History Division, 2007), 157, 169.

[16] Harris quoted in McQuaid, "Racism, Sexism, and Space Ventures," 166; "Space Agency Fires Black Woman Who Attacked Bias," *Jet*, November 15, 1973, p. 6; Ruth Harris, *Harlem Princess: The Story of Harry Delaney's Daughter* (New York: Vantage Press, 1991), 270.

[17] Stephanie Nolen, *Promised the Moon: The Untold Story of the First Women in the Space Race* (New York: Thunder's Mouth Press, 2002), 276.

were the consequences of centuries of past discrimination.[18] After *Griggs,* it was no longer acceptable for NASA to have the worst record of minority and female employment of any federal agency.

The international implications of NASA's race problem centered on the tracking stations it maintained in South Africa. Pretoria had made it clear that it would not permit African Americans to work at them. Domestic opposition to this policy made Washington consider arrangements with other Southern Hemisphere powers as well as emergency evacuation procedures should tensions escalate. "In the past," NSC staffers Charles E. Johnson and Ulrich Haynes wrote to President Johnson, "the US has quietly complied with South African racial practices by not sending Negroes to represent us at our Embassy or other official establishments. However, we probably cannot continue to avoid the issue."[19]

At home, the NASA problem surfaced in the context of public indignation surrounding the Watergate scandal and growing feminist pressure. Harris's treatment unleashed a firestorm of protest by numerous organizations, a threat by a lawmaker to vote against appropriations for NASA, and remonstrations from the CBC. Defensive efforts by NASA to find communism in Harris's past came up empty. The agency ultimately settled with her. Part of the agreement entailed stepped-up minority hiring programs. The Harris case also coincided with abortive efforts by the Nixon administration to fire the administrator of the State Department Bureau of Security and Consular Affairs, also a black woman. In Barbara Watson's case, the administration claimed it wanted a Republican in her slot. Both Watson and Harris, one black onlooker claimed, had run into trouble "because they were too aggressive in pursuing their goals."[20] Neither NASA nor the State Department was prepared for forthright and energetic African-American women to take leadership roles.

Meanwhile, Senator William Proxmire of Wisconsin, chair of the appropriations committee, called NASA executives to appear before it in January 1974. "Dispensing with any pretense at political courtesy," Proxmire ordered immediate "congressional monitoring" of NASA's hiring programs, the managers of which would answer to the Senate. Race remained a sensitive issue as NASA director James Fletcher resisted the order to appear before the committee. His Mormon faith posed a problem for him, as the laws he was obligated to uphold conflicted with some of the tenets of his religion as the Church of Latter Day Saints then interpreted them. The refusal at the time to admit blacks to the Mormon priesthood and views that clashed with feminist thinking posed a dilemma for Fletcher.[21]

[18] *Griggs v. Duke Power Co.,* 401 U.S. 424 (1971).
[19] Memorandum from Charles E. Johnson and Ulric Haynes of the NSC Staff to President Johnson, July 13, 1965, United States Department of State, *FRUS,* XXVI, *1964–1968, Africa,* 1031.
[20] James C. Fletcher's memorandum to all NASA employees, August 16, 1974, in Harris, *Harlem Princess,* 273–4; McQuaid, "Racism, Sexism, and Space Ventures," 177, 178; Judith Cummings, "Black Women in Public Life," *Black Enterprise,* August 1974, 33.
[21] McQuaid, "Racism, Sexism, and Space Ventures," 173.

While NASA's difficulties mirrored an attachment to older race and gender patterns, some of them illustrated the New(est) South's latest traits. Educated white newcomers to southern communities encountered different patterns of racial division. As Paul Gaston writes:

The gated community symbolized the new suburban society, distanced both spatially and ideologically from the city. Well-guarded out-of-reach property values insured the perpetuation of a homogeneous society of middle- and upper-middle-class families, thus helping to insure a new form of segregation. As this separation was accelerating, class now joined or even supplanted race as the primary dividing line.[22]

Space and its management in a terrestrial as well as cosmic sense also played a part in the society NASA helped to create. The whitening and professionalization of the South indicated the emergence of a new class formation but served to complement rather than succeed or displace the racial order.

There was more than one way to respond to a solidifying conservatism in the 1970s. One might embrace it; thoroughly reject it, as did radical organizations; or seek ways to turn it to one's advantage. The citizen diplomacy engaged in by James Forman and other radicals was not the only example of the genre. Jesse Jackson showed that black citizen diplomacy was not necessarily provocative.

Operation PUSH focused on integrating the "system" rather than challenging its basic framework. At a time when most Black Power advocates saw blue-collar workers or "the brothers on the block" as the vanguard of revolutionary change, Jackson began talking about providing the black middle class with "things to do." Their tasks would include lobbying and participating in consumer boycotts. Although the African-American business community numbered among its beneficiaries, Jackson denied that he was simply pursuing a form of black capitalism. "What we want is white folks' technology with black folks' love," he claimed. Nevertheless, PUSH's preferred method of aid to Africa, aside from food relief, took the form of trade agreements between African-American firms and their African counterparts. The Nixon White House signaled its endorsement of this modus operandi, for Jackson, like Floyd McKissick, was becoming the kind of black leader that Nixon hoped to cultivate. Jackson refused to endorse Democratic candidate George McGovern in the presidential race of 1972, and PUSH received federal funding shortly thereafter.[23]

Jackson sought to revive the periodic involvement of African Americans with Liberia. Liberia's star had dimmed after World War II as more vigorous African states became independent and their leaders internationally visible.

---

[22] Paul Gaston, "New South Creed: Looking Backward, 2001–1970," *Southern Changes* 24 (3–4) (2002): 18.

[23] Joel Dreyfuss, "Where Is Jesse Jackson Going?" *Black Enterprise* (October 1974): 26; Marshall Frady, *Jesse: The Life And Pilgrimage of Jesse Jackson* (New York: Simon & Schuster, 1996), 256; Devin Fergus, "Black Power, Soft Power: Floyd McKissick, Soul City, and the Death of Moderate Black Republicanism," *Journal of Policy History* 22 (2) (2010): 148–57.

Monrovia's conservatism and dependence on Washington enticed few young nationalists in the 1960s and 1970s. Yet, in his first foray into popular diplomacy, Jackson traveled to Liberia as a guest of President William R. Tolbert in an effort to interest his government in dual citizenship for black Americans. In his rhyming style, Jackson asserted that African Americans must now "move from *romance* to *finance* in our relationships with Africa" and "from *lip* service to *ship* service."[24]

President Tolbert traveled to the United States in June 1973 and, after meeting with Nixon, arrived in Chicago, where black journalists interviewed him. Tolbert identified Liberian needs for skilled personnel just as Tanzania had but never explicitly called for African-American immigration. Any attempt to position Liberia as an alternative to Tanzania in the African-American imaginary was doomed by Monrovia's reluctance to play that role and by African-American skepticism. While dual citizenship and extensive commercial exchanges never materialized, Jackson's venture set the stage for future interventions he would make on the world scene. In 1974, he endorsed but did not attend the Sixth Pan-African Congress. He viewed it as an opportunity for future input in U.S. foreign policy and as a stepping-stone for lucrative interaction between continental and diaspora entrepreneurs.[25]

David Du Bois, W. E. B. Du Bois's stepson, who had returned to the United States and was working for the Black Panther newspaper, rejected Jackson's dual citizenship idea. While the PUSH founder saw Africans as people who overproduce and underconsume, and African Americans as people who underproduce and overconsume, Du Bois claimed that neither produced nor consumed to their capacity because of exploitation, not group idiosyncrasy. U.S. corporations controlled Liberian resources, he reminded readers, and the number of U.S. blacks who could freely consume was minuscule in a society where the entire working class was hurting.[26]

Jackson's approach was meant to utilize the foreign relations climate that prevailed during Nixon's presidency. The Eisenhower administration had sensed that its responses to change in Africa and Asia were inadequate, although it did not succeed in changing its methods. President Kennedy subsequently made sophisticated use of Africa to cement ties with the black electorate. LBJ also courted black voters but disapproved of their independent policy activism. Nixon's approach was a departure from all of the above. To the extent that it is possible to talk about an architect of Nixon's Africa policy, that person would be Henry Kissinger.

[24] Charles L. Sanders, "Rev. Jesse Jackson Visits Liberia to Discuss Dual Citizenship Plan," *Jet*, December 7, 1972, pp. 12–15.

[25] Lee Ivory, "Talbert [sic] Attacks Colonialism," *Chicago Defender*, June 11, 1973, p. 6; Terrele Schumake, "Set Pan African Meet," *Chicago Defender*, June 11, 1974, p. 4; "10 Here to Attend African Congress," *Chicago Tribune*, June 13, 1974, p. S5.

[26] David Du Bois, "Dual Citizenship – Toward What End?" *Black Panther*, January 20, 1973, p. 8.

Kissinger's views were formed well before his appointment as national security adviser in the Nixon White House. In a 1957 address, Kissinger bluntly asserted that diplomacy is not "a popularity contest" based on a search for consensus. Instead, "foreign policy is really the art of effecting the will of the sovereign state," which must "balanc[e] risks" in determining how to proceed. Kissinger distinguished sovereign states from "weak and irresponsible" powers "who like to play major roles internationally and find it dramatic to do so and who can do so without paying any price." For such countries, rhetoric provides a respite from the problems and tough decisions they face at home. Foreign policy audiences formerly believed that "diplomacy was the alternative to war" and "that in the future, global conflict could be settled through negotiations." "We now find," he suggested, "that diplomacy emerges as the complement of war and that the dream of generations for universal peace, if it were realized, would in fact lead to the perpetuation of all disputes, however trivial."[27]

This bleak assessment underlay Kissinger's "realism" in Africa. Any initiatives pursued there would stem from what he and Nixon believed were in the best interests of the United States. As they saw African struggles for human rights, decolonization, and racial equality through a cold war lens, these issues became subordinated to the superpower conflict and devoid of intrinsic value. TransAfrica founder Randall Robinson quipped that Kissinger "seemed to think that a human right was a punch landed by a prizefighter." Africa was a pawn to Kissinger, who began his White House career focused only on the major countries that he thought mattered. In Africa, only the white settler governments seemed to him sustainable. Even before Nixon was elected, U.S. policy in Africa was driven by reaction to crises, defined only as short-term responses to immediate disasters. Failures to take a longer view would haunt Kissinger later as Marxist regimes gained power in southern Africa.[28]

Pessimism regarding African capabilities, approval of the white minority regimes' anticommunism, and stakes in the strategic minerals they exported led to what might charitably be called ambivalence regarding decolonization and racial equality in the region. The United States made retaining its military base in the Azores a priority, which led to courting Portugal and offering it arms, even when officials knew they would be used against African freedom fighters.[29]

---

[27] Kissinger's talk to the executive members of the Research Institute of America, pp. 2–4, Papers of the NAACP, Part 24: Special Studies, 1954–1965, Series B: Foreign Affairs-Leagues and Organizations, reel 27.

[28] Randall Robinson, *Defending the Spirit: A Black Life in America* (New York: Dutton, 1998), 109; Marshall Wright to National Security Adviser Henry Kissinger, January 10, 1970; *FRUS, Foundations of Foreign Policy, 1969–1972* (Washington, D.C.: Government Printing Office, 2003), p. 163.

[29] The literature on this subject includes Thomas Borstelmann, *Apartheid's Reluctant Uncle* (New York: Oxford University Press, 1993;) Andrew DeRoche, *Black White and Chrome: The United States and Zimbabwe, 1953–1998* (Trenton: Africa World Press, 2001); Gerald Horne, *From the Barrel of a Gun: The U.S. and the War against Zimbabwe, 1965–1980* (Chapel Hill: University

While East-West antagonisms provided a rationalization for bare-boned African policies, Kissinger had an inkling that radicalism in the global South was more diffuse and varied than conventional cold war arguments could grasp. "Soviet influence" in fledgling states, he wrote in a note to Nixon, "is due to government-to-government relations (particularly through Soviet military assistance) rather than to the influence of communist parties." Local allegiances and indigenous loyalties "in some parts of the Third World (especially Latin America)," he claimed, "have restricted the influence of communist parties; while the Sino-Soviet split, Soviet troubles in maintaining the cohesion of its 'commonwealth' in Eastern Europe, and the effect of both of these developments in hastening the fragmentation of international communism have increased the independence of communist parties."[30] For Kissinger, the end of central direction in the communist world did not mean a weaker communist movement but a stronger one.

Nixon's program also featured attempts to reshape the State Department and intelligence operations. The president regarded the Foreign Service as inbred and inefficient. Worse, it included holdovers from previous administrations who opposed his directives and often dragged their feet executing them. This problem was particularly salient for the Africa Bureau because the well-known conflicts of Nixon and Kissinger with Secretary of State William Rogers and the State Department deeply impacted Africa policy in those years.[31]

The Nixon-Kissinger approach lessened pressure on the white regimes while modestly boosting aid to black African nations. Kissinger asked an interagency task force to prepare an analysis in which several options were laid out. The one he selected, to tolerate the white minority governments and buy off other African states, would be hard to alter and offered no alternative if it failed to work. Critics saw it as a trap. This was the infamous "tar baby option," a policy alternative derived from National Security Study Memorandum 39.[32] In the Uncle Remus stories, where the "tar baby" originated, Br'er Rabbit is fooled into caring for an infant made of tar. When he gets stuck to it and cannot extricate himself, Br'er Wolf eats him. For Africa, the tar baby option meant that there would be no discernible changes in the U.S. posture.

of North Carolina Press, 2001); William Minter, *Apartheid's Contras: An Inquiry into the Roots of War in Angola and Mozambique* (Atlantic Highlands, N.J.: Zed Books, 1994).

[30] Memorandum from NSA adviser Henry Kissinger to President Nixon, October 20, 1969, *FRUS, Foundations of Foreign Policy, 1969*, p. 135.

[31] This issue is examined in detail in *FRUS, Organization and Management of U.S. Foreign Policy, 1969–1972* (Washington: D.C., Government Printing Office, 2006), p. 117.

[32] For a general overview of Nixon aid policy toward developing countries, see Memorandum of Conversation, 9–2–69, meeting held at San Clemente between Nixon, Kissinger, C. Fred Bergsten, NSC senior staff member, and Rudolph Peterson, Chair of President's Task Force on International Development, *FRUS, 1969–1976*, IV, *Foreign Assistance, International Development, Trade Policies*, 1969–1972 (Washington, D.C.: United States Government Printing Office, 2002); Anthony Lake, *The "Tar Baby" Option: American Policy toward Southern Rhodesia* (New York: Columbia University Press, 1976); DeRoche, *Black White and Chrome.*

The national security adviser became a target of resentment by African dip-lomats, State Department Africa Bureau officials, NGOs, and the diverse clus-ters of individuals and institutions with an active interest in decolonization and racial equality. Kissinger went them one better. His complaints about the Africa desk led to the serial resignations of three assistant secretaries holding that portfolio. The Africanists, he and Nixon believed, represented a discred-ited liberal Democratic outlook and their views were too close to those deemed radical.[33]

Kissinger's relations with black African governments worsened when he became secretary of state in 1973. As former assistant secretary of state for African affairs Donald B. Easum recalled, African envoys resident in Washington "were very antipathetic to Kissinger because it was then public in the press that he had written the famous National Security memorandum No. 39 for Nixon." Its declaration that "white minority rule is here to stay" and its repudiation of revolution "stood out in a lot of the press commentary." Kissinger's views ran counter to the public's increasing acceptance of racial equality and colonial freedom. "Many Americans were turned off by this, and there were a lot of groups pushing for a far different kind of approach to the independence move-ments in Africa....There was a lot of sentiment against the way in which the Nixon administration had been handling its approach to those issues."[34]

Soured relations with African states were reflected in Ghana and Nigeria's repeated refusals of Kissinger's requests to visit. His insistence on meeting only with heads of state rather than ministers of his own rank suggested arro-gance and presumption. Finally, the decision to dismiss the popular Easum and replace him with an official who lacked African experience and who had served in Chile during the overthrow of Chilean president Salvador Allende further rankled African sensibilities.[35]

This unresponsiveness to southern Africa made it more likely that nongov-ernmental actors would devise their own approaches to apartheid and colonial-ism. They increasingly shared a common perspective with dissident Africanists in and out of power. While Charles Diggs's work and the handful of interested functionaries in the executive branch did not constitute a movement, indiffer-ence to Africa at the highest levels of government created an opening for activ-ism in the ensuing decade when antiapartheid campaigns became broad-based and global. The conflicts between the Nixon-Kissinger Africa policy and that of liberal Africanists continued and manifested themselves in various ways. An example is Kissinger's attempt to sack W. Beverly Carter, the U.S. ambas-sador to Tanzania from 1972 to 1976. Carter, an African American, angered

---

[33] Donald B. Easum interviewed by Arthur Day, January 17, 1990, The Foreign Affairs Oral History Collection of the Association for Diplomatic Studies and Training, LC; Nathaniel Davis, "The Angola Decision of 1975: A Personal Memoir," Foreign *Affairs* p. 7.

[34] Easum interview.

[35] Ibid.; Davis, "The Angola Decision of 1975," 110; Jake C. Miller, "Black Legislators and African-American Relations, 1970–1975," *Journal of Black Studies* 10 (December 1979): 252.

Kissinger when he broke the rule that U.S. ambassadors should never accede to ransom demands and entered negotiations during a hostage crisis. The episode ended successfully with the American victims freed but prompted anger from President Mobutu of Zaire, a U.S. client, because the hostage takers were Congolese rebels. Kissinger recalled Carter from his post, but public outcry would not allow him to oust Carter from the Foreign Service.[36]

What saved Carter was his close identification with the institutions and NGOs most concerned with Africa and with desegregating federal employment. He also represented entities that most closely interlocked with segments of the political establishment. Carter had attended Lincoln University, which had historically been interested in Africa and graduated such notable students as Kwame Nkrumah and Nnamdi Azikiwe.[37] Carter, sixty-one at the time of his death in 1982, began his career as a journalist. He wrote for the *Philadelphia Tribune*, the *Pittsburgh Courier*, and the Philadelphia edition of the *Afro-American* during the years when the black press enjoyed strong circulation and was most engaged in foreign affairs reportage. Nkrumah invited him to Ghana to set up an information agency in 1952, enabling Carter to travel through West Africa while serving as a stringer for some newspapers. He briefly worked in public relations and began employment in the U.S. Information Agency in 1965. The future ambassador became a deputy assistant secretary of state for Africa in 1969 and was subsequently posted to Dar es Salaam.[38]

Carter was thus well connected in both government and nongovernmental circles. Kissinger's efforts to fire him were opposed by the *New York Times* and by journalist and former USIA director Carl Rowan, who blasted Kissinger's "monumental ego" and "tough-guy complex." The hostages whom Carter helped to free planned a public protest. The CBC requested and received an assuaging meeting with Kissinger, who then backed down. Carter's subsequent appointment to Liberia was likely seen as punishment by Kissinger but perhaps not by Carter, given his background. His story illustrates an instance when a rupture in the statist frame was backed up by an array of actors with commitments outside the government playbook.[39]

Such networks complicated Kissinger's exercise of state power. The broader issue of power, however, was not confined to the U.S. domain. We see it

---

[36] Minutes of the Secretary of State's 8 a.m. staff meeting, July 25, 1975, SDCF; "Diplomacy: Beyond the Call of Duty," *Time Magazine*, September 1, 1975, p. 10.

[37] On Lincoln University see Jason C. Parker, "Made-in-America Revolutions? The 'Black University' and the American Role in the Decolonization of the Black Atlantic," *Journal of American History* 96 (December 2009): 727–50; Horace Mann Bond to Channing Tobias, February 21, 1949, Phelps Stokes Fund Records, folder, "Lincoln University, 1949–1950, Box 20, SC; Carter interviewed by Celestine Tutt, April 30, 1981, Phelps Stokes Fund, Oral History Project on Black Chiefs of Mission, SC.

[38] "Beverly Carter, 61; Held High Positions as a U.S. Diplomat," *New York Times*, May 11, 1982, p. B14.

[39] "Diplomacy: Beyond the Call of Duty," 10; "Humane Diplomat," *New York Times*, August 14, 1975, p. 30; Linda Charlton, "Kissinger Queried on Envoy's Future," ibid., August 20, 1975, p. 5.

articulated in a critical struggle for control that took place in East Africa in 1974. The Sixth Pan-African Congress held in Dar es Salaam in June featured multiple contestants: states, elites, and dissidents saw the Congress as a venue for defining the future contours of the African world.[40]

Historians tend to focus on the ideological divisions at the meeting but have not paid sufficient attention to the challenges that all participants faced as the relationships between states and NGOs, shorn of rhetoric, confronted political realities. This was a new problem: before World War II, Pan-African congresses had convened with only delegates from a tiny number of weak independent states in attendance and with the proceedings dominated by individuals from the diaspora, many of whom represented no organizations. The war changed everything.

The 1945 Pan-African Congress in Manchester, England, differed markedly from its predecessors. For the first time, delegates from Africa represented trade unions and nascent labor parties that would win national elections in the post-colonial period. While the elderly W. E. B. Du Bois, a founder of the movement, made a belated appearance, he was never entirely in the planning loop. The Manchester conference represented the direction that Pan-Africanism would take in the ensuing decade: a movement premised on the imminent independence of states rather than on the aspirations of diaspora intellectuals.

A statist Pan-Africanism would face challenges when planning for a full-scale sixth congress, the first to be held in Africa itself, began in 1969. There had been smaller convocations, but the Sixth Pan-African Congress, the successor to Manchester, would be the first plenary of African and Africa-descended peoples since 1945. In the United States, organizing for it began with the initial call drafted by members of Washington, D.C.'s, nongovernmental Center for Black Education. The center, founded in 1968 by SNCC veterans with ties to Federal City College (later the University of the District of Columbia), was intended to address the overwhelming need for higher education in the district that the brand new Federal City College could not fulfill. Importantly, the center, unlike the college, would not have the constraints imposed by federal support. During the 1969 Congress of Black Writers in Montreal, C. L. R. James met staffers from the center and began working with them as an adviser and liaison to the liberation organizations. Nyerere's acquaintance with and respect for James had secured Tanzania as the host site for the Pan-African Congress.[41]

Nyerere supported the event on condition that it would be a project of the Tanzanian African National Union (TANU), the ruling political party, rather than the Tanzanian government. This fine distinction helped Dar es Salaam

---

[40] An able overview of the conference and its origins is provided by Fanon Che Wilkins in "Line of Steel: The Organization of the Sixth Pan-African Congress and the Struggle for International Black Power, 1969–1974," in *The Hidden 1970s: Histories of Radicalism*, ed. Dan Berger (New Brunswick, N.J.: Rutgers University Press, 2010), 97–114.

[41] Author's telephone interview with Courtland Cox, June 21, 2012; Fanon Che Wilkins, "'In the Belly of the Beast': Black Power, Anti-Imperialism, and the African Solidarity Movement, 1968–1975" (PhD diss., New York University, 2001), pp. 50–2.

distance itself from any attacks dissidents made on other African and Caribbean governments that could adversely affect diplomatic relations. Correspondingly, these governments expressed concern about the implications and consequences of the type of congress that James and his young protégés wanted.[42] That certain U.S. blacks had had adventurist plans to fight the white settler regimes also gave Tanzanian officials pause.

Yet delegations would arrive from all over the world, including Europe and Oceania, for the meeting. The administrative structure included an international steering committee and a group of prestigious individuals to serve as sponsors. A secretariat would be appointed as the administrative arm of the steering committee, with Courtland Cox named as secretary general. In the United States, organizing began with a set of regional planning committees that appointed two representatives from each of ten geographic areas. The Tanzanian government would make the final decision on which delegates could attend 6PAC, as it came to be called.[43]

Coordinator and SNCC veteran Judy Claude recalled the motivations of those planning the congress from North America. Most of the principals had been SNCC workers. "The question was, did we in the diaspora have anything we could offer Africa? Did we bring skills that we could offer?" Claude wondered whether "by building these ties with Africa and strengthening them, would they be of assistance to those of us in the diaspora? Would they deal with our circumstances so that we could always say that we had support of African countries, whether at the UN or at other international forums? We would always raise questions about the conditions of descendants in other parts of the world. That was the idea."[44]

Apart from the liberation of the remaining colonial enclaves, the congress would focus on economic development. It endorsed the black skills bank idea of matching expertise with need and identifying those in each region who possessed "scientific and technological capacities" with an eye to the future establishment of a research center at an African university. Organizers also projected the creation of a permanent secretariat and an information center based in Africa with worldwide branches.[45]

---

[42] A detailed account of the origins and planning of the Congress in the Americas is found in James Garrett, "A Historical Sketch: The Sixth Pan African Congress," *Black World* 26 (March 1975): 4–20. See also William Sutherland and Matt Meyer, *Guns and Gandhi in Africa* (Trenton, N.J.: Africa World Press, 2000), 214–19; Records of the Federal Bureau of Investigation, Classification 157, Headquarters Case Files 1957–1978, Box 662, serials 366–391, NARA, RG 65. (Hereafter FBI-NARA).

[43] Sixth Pan African Congress regional newsletter, "From Here to Tanzania," March 15, 1974, p. 3, FBI-NARA; Hoyt Fuller, "Sixth Pan African Congress: A Briefing Paper," *Black World* 23 (March 1974): 5–10.

[44] Judy Claude, "Some Personal Reflections on the Sixth Pan-African Congress," *The Black Scholar* 37 (4) (2007): 48; L. T. Levy, "Remembering Sixth-PAC: Interviews with Sylvia Hill and Judy Claude, Organizers of the Sixth Pan-African Congress," ibid., 37 (4) (2007): 42.

[45] The Sixth Pan African Congress – a Briefing Paper, n.d. mimeographed, FBI-NARA.

The U.S. embassy in Georgetown, Guyana, reported the Guyanese government's displeasure with a late March meeting of the Pan-African Congress's Caribbean Steering Committee. The prime minister and the foreign secretary believed that Guyanese "militants were using Pan-Africanism as [a] cloak and were only interested in finding [a] platform for their own dissidence, not in relations with Africa." Prime Minister Forbes Burnham consulted Nyerere, who heeded Burnham's counsel with respect to "Caribbean militants." Perhaps as a way to smooth over relations with transatlantic contingents and distance Tanzania from criticisms that diaspora radicals were making of their own and other governments, Nyerere appointed Bill Sutherland to work out of Tanzania's foreign office and interpret its interests to others at the congress. Sutherland was ideal for the role. "We used to stay at Bill's house," Courtland Cox recalled. "He was helpful because he knew people [and] always had a spare bedroom." On the Tanzanian side, foreign minister John Malecela asked African ambassadors resident in Dar es Salaam to form a committee to coordinate congress activities that would counterbalance NGO planning activities.[46]

According to Sutherland, C. L. R. James, like the African Americans he mentored, was primarily interested in popular

self-reliance and the Pan-African technical transfer of skills. From James' viewpoint, the real emphasis should be on people's movements rather than on government initiatives. So many regimes in Africa, he suggested, had been the agents or the co-exploiters of their own people.... That was the basis upon which James wanted to make the Call; to revive the spirit that had been there at the time of the Fifth Pan-African Congress.[47]

As it turned out, James did not attend the congress himself, even though he had been its most distinguished advocate and organizer, because of his objection to its heavily statist agenda. "I would have resigned instantly from any Committee which would have aimed at excluding legitimate public opinion from a Pan-African Congress," he informed Malacela. "I am absolutely certain that if the International Steering Committee persists in this policy, it will not only castrate the Congress. It will be laying the basis for what is bound to be a mortifying controversy over the African realities, and place obstacles instead of clearing the road for the future."[48]

The rift in the Pan-African movement between statism and popular participation was further indicated when the Ghanaian ambassador to the United States let it be known that the OAU insisted on controlling the disbursement of funds earmarked for the national liberation groups and the framing of Pan-African policy. "The ambassador said," according to the FBI, that "black Americans could best serve the liberation struggle in Africa through financial

---

[46] U.S. embassy in Georgetown (Krebs) to the Secretary of State, April 2, 1974; Cox interview; Carter to the Secretary of State, May 21, 1974, SDCF.

[47] Sutherland and Meyer, *Guns and Gandhi in Africa*, 217, 219.

[48] C. L. R. James to J. S. Malacela, June 5, 1974, FB-NARA.

aid to the OAU."[49] In this view, African Americans would function as donors to African causes rather than as active participants in revolution.

This was clearly not what C. L. R. James, Courtland Cox, and others had in mind. At issue was authority over the forthcoming congress, including the question of how the U.S. delegation would be constituted. Tanzania resisted certain African-American planners' efforts to restrict participation to the Black Power adherents they approved of and to censure conservative black governments. "The Tanzanians are insistent that they will not stage a Congress for the sake of racialism or to prove that black is beautiful," the *Trinidad Guardian* commented. The goals of Amiri Baraka, Owusu Sadauki, and Don L. Lee were not limited to managing black access to 6PAC. They also hoped to ensure that when Julius Nyerere traveled to the United States on a future visit, he would spend most of his time in black communities rather than with people selected by the State Department.[50]

A group of African Americans who arrived to live in a collective in a village near Nyerere's birthplace had weapons with them, a move that gave opponents of Pan-African initiatives the ammunition to allege that U.S. blacks conspired with the CIA and were planning a coup. Others worried about a possible link between diaspora militants and Zanzibari leftists, or about African-Americans' putative criminality. Because of the scare, certain group members were detained without trial, including some associated with the Pan-African Skills Project. Yet Tanzania appeared to shield the detainees from US. consular officials who were denied permission to interview them. [51]

In March, foreign ministry official Bernard Muganda sent out feelers to David Chinn, the U.S. embassy political officer, about the forthcoming event. Chinn took the opportunity to tell Muganda that the congress, unlike the one in postwar Manchester, which was sincerely motivated, might not maintain the "honorable tradition" of Pan-Africanism. The expected transatlantic delegates, he suggested, did not represent the diaspora as a whole. Muganda assured Chinn that Tanzania was not perpetuating racism. It saw the meeting as a vehicle to generate an exchange of ideas, recruit diaspora talent for development purposes, and garner support for southern African liberation. He promised Chinn that his government could "control the situation." The U.S. embassy reported to Washington its belief that "Tanzania is beginning to have doubts as to the wisdom of hosting the conference."[52]

[49] Airtel to U.S. Legation (Ottawa), n.d., FBI-NARA.

[50] Cox interview; enclosure in FBI report on the 6th Pan African Congress, March 22, 1974; report on Sixth Pan-African Congress, December 18 1973; Acting Director to U.S. Legation (Ottawa), June 25, 1973; *Trinidad Guardian*, date illegible, filed by FBI, December 23, 1972, FBI-NARA. See also Francis Njubi Nesbitt, *Race for Sanctions: African Americans against Apartheid, 1946–1994* (Bloomington: Indiana University Press, 2004), 79–82.

[51] Sutherland and Meyer, 230; Hoyt W. Fuller, "Notes from a Sixth-Pan-African Journal," *Black World*, October 1974, p.81; Charles Diggs to Linwood Holton, July 23, 1974; U. S. embassy to the Department of State, Quarterly Assessment for Tanzania April-June 1974, SDCF

[52] Memorandum of conversation between David Chinn and Bernard Muganda, March 14, 1974, 3–14–74, SDCF.

Fear of violence was a major factor in both Tanzanian and U.S. government perceptions. On New Year's Eve in 1972, one Mark Essex, a young African-American navy veteran, shot and killed nine people in New Orleans, wounding others. Essex had expressed hatred of whites and U.S. society in general, but the loner belonged to no organization and had no coherent politics. He did provide, however, an example of the kind of gun rampage that became all too common in the United States. Because the Essex incident had at the time few precedents within recent memory, and because he targeted whites and police officers, the incident alarmed those already frightened by Black Power. Yet the FBI tacitly acknowledged that the case for a link between Pan-Africanism and such violence was weak. Its records more commonly exploited Stokely Carmichael's rhetoric as boilerplate to justify the extent of its penetration of the congress.[53]

The Tanzanian ambassador to the United States, Paul Bomani, divulged to his U.S. counterpart his "frustration" with African-American attempts to dominate the forthcoming meeting. Some U.S. militants had, moreover, criminal records, not all of which stemmed from political activity. Bomani asserted that "Tanzania could not let the American Delegation set the agenda for the Congress since people of African descent around the world would be participating." He told Ambassador Carter that Dar es Salaam "was embarrassed at having so many discredited blacks involved in the early stages of the planning of the Congress," a situation that deterred more "responsible" elements from participating. His anxieties would seem confirmed later by the decision of the venerated SNCC veteran Bob Moses to skip the Congress even though he was in Tanzania. In search of respectability, Bomani and other African ambassadors tried to coax Charles Diggs into attending. Unspoken were the cultural misgivings associated with the influx of foreigners with alien habits and customs. In preponderantly Muslim Zanzibar, Tanzania's island state, a reaction against Western styles had already set in. In 1973, local authorities banned short dresses, wigs, and makeup for women and long hair and bell-bottoms or tight trousers for men. Large Afros and Jackson Five caps were also prohibited. Offenders faced corporal punishment or jail.[54]

Washington responded to fears about black militants by promoting the OAU as a counterpoise to the nongovernmental actors. The State Department's Bureau of Intelligence and Research early in January 1974 published a laudatory report, "The OAU: Ten Years Old and Getting Stronger," which stressed

---

[53] Special Agent in Charge (SAC) (Washington Field Office) to FBI director, August 8, 1973; idem to idem, July 12, 1973, FB-NARA. On Mark Essex see, "Death in New Orleans," *Time Magazine*, January 22, 1973, online at time.com.

[54] Diggs ultimately bowed out. Memorandum of conversation between Ambassador H. E. Paul Bomani and Ambassador W. Beverly Carter, May 1, 1974; Carter to the Secretary of State, May 24, SDCF; author's telephone interview with James Turner, April 2, 2012; "Watch Your Wear and Your Hair," *Los Angeles Sentinel*, March 15, 1973, p. B7; Thomas Burgess, "Cinema, Bell Bottoms, and Miniskirts: Struggles over Youth and Citizenship in Revolutionary Zanzibar," *International Journal of African Historical Studies* 35 (2) (2002): 287–313.

the organization's permanence and efficacy. Its timing was interesting in light of tensions between the OAU and nongovernmental congress organizers. Reaffirming the legitimacy of statist authority lay within a broader U.S. political tradition and supported black states' desire to contain radicals, especially those outside the control of specific national authorities. An executive order from President Nixon designated the OAU as "a public international organization entitled to enjoy certain privileges, exemptions, and immunities."[55]

Black radicals interpreted the reluctance of newly minted governments to support them as reflective of their neocolonial character, but this problem originated in the framework of political organization. How can diasporas be effectively represented in a world governed by councils of state? "The OAU already exists to serve the governments of African nation-fragments," participant Bai Kisogie wrote. "What then is the rationale behind another gathering of government spokesmen?" It made no sense, he declared, to turn a people's congress into yet another intergovernmental confab and selectively dismiss only some opposition voices. "Where is the government of the black people of the United States of America who fielded the largest 'national' delegation of the Congress?... Was approval sought from Richard Nixon before the delegates from the U.S. were recognised?" The state form meant that the interests of millions in and outside Africa remained unrepresented. Groupings like the OAU, being regional, were also unequal to the task. Just as Pan-African activists have historically had little answer to the problem of internecine conflict among Africans when racial domination is not a key factor, aside from calls for an abstract unity, they have had few coherent responses to statism's challenges.[56]

U.S. government records suggest that of all the federal agencies interested in 6PAC, the FBI was the most anxious. The bureau associated Pan-Africanism with the homegrown radicalism that it was repressing. A concern with civil disorders and "extremism" provided the rationale for extensive information gathering about the event and individuals known to be planning to attend it. Special agents also spread their net overseas, seeking to identify and conduct surveillance on persons who participated in a preparatory meeting in Kingston, Jamaica.

Popular unrest in North America strengthened ongoing ties between the intelligence services in Canada and the United States. Cooperation among the RCMP, the FBI, and the CIA now involved the exchange of information about black dissidents. When in November 1969 Fred Hampton and two other members of the U.S. Black Panther Party gave talks at the universities of Alberta and Saskatchewan, respectively, RCMP agents recorded their speeches, traced their phone calls, and followed them. Canadian officials were anxious to prevent contact between the Panthers and Quebec separatists, and between the

---

[55] Bureau of Intelligence and Research, "The OAU: Ten Years Old and Getting Stronger," January 4, 1974; White House press release, February 19, 1974, SDCF.
[56] Bai Kisogie, "State Exhibitionists and Ideological Glamour," *Transition* (46) (1974): 7; Ron Walters, "The Future of Pan-Africanism," *Black World* (October 1975): 4–18.

American Indian Movement and increasingly militant Canadian aborigines.[57] Canada hosted a growing number of Caribbean students and immigrants, and official concerns about coordination between radical elements in these populations and African-American dissidents led the RCMP to provide intelligence on Pan-African activities in Commonwealth countries. The Canadians were also active in the United States, furnishing the only spy in attendance at the July 21, 1973, Pan-African steering committee meeting in Washington, D.C. While the FBI and RCMP collaborated extensively, they took pains to hide that cooperation, thus concealing a transnational effort.[58]

Opposition to Black Power across metropoles sharpened radical Caribbean perceptions that the new nations faced an imperialist juggernaut whose individual national differences masked a unitary neocolonial purpose. Independence had not produced relief from the stagnant economy of the colonial period. Black faces in power did not necessarily mean Black Power. As in the United States, many who were disillusioned looked to Africa for countries that appeared committed to progressive change. This translated to extremism in the mind-set of certain North American functionaries. "Black extremists" had a hand in the Pan-African Congress, William Ruckelshaus, the acting director of the bureau, informed the special agent in charge in Albany, New York. The event "shapes up to be a most important meeting with regard to international revolutionary Pan-Africanism which calls for unity of all people of African descent and the overthrow of 'imperialist' countries including the United States. All offices have been previously furnished background and instructions regarding the Congress."[59]

In a report on dissident activities in Ottawa, Canadian intelligence officials described an "international protest movement" that "has long seen [the] Third World as the next step" in their battle against racism and imperialism. With the Vietnam War winding down, the movement now concentrated on transnational capitalism. Canadian authorities anticipated "continuing and escalating pressure" from dissenters, especially as the energy crisis, population pressure, drought, and famine put their impress on poor countries.[60]

After reviewing a RCMP report, "General Analysis and Theoretical Orientation to the Significance of the Sixth Pan African Congress and Its Relation to the International Black Coalition," FBI director Clarence Kelley

[57] Steve Hewitt, *Spying 101: The RCMP's Secret Activities at Canadian Universities, 1917–1997* (Toronto: University of Toronto Press, 2002), 156–7, 159; Scott Rutherford, "Canada's Other Red Scare: The Anicinabe Park Occupation and Indigenous Decolonization," in *The Hidden 1970s*, 77–94.

[58] The scope of international cooperation among intelligence agencies is suggested in ALSC-C, CSIS; Airtel to SAC (Charlotte, N. C.) et al., n.d., FBI-NARA.

[59] SAC (San Francisco) to the Acting Director, March 28, 1973; memorandum re 6th Pan African Congress, Dar es Salaam, Tanzania, March 20 1973, sent to Chicago field office; Acting Director to SAC (Albany), March 22, 1973, FBI-NARA.

[60] Memorandum re Counter-Conference, Commonwealth Heads of Government Conference, August 2/10, 1973, Ottawa, July 23, 1973, ALSC-C. CSIS.

thought that the RCMP was focusing more on African affairs. The FBI's own interest in the Pan-African Congress, however, was "its potential to unify American blacks behind extremist views." The bureau intended nevertheless to continue working with the RCMP "and other cooperating foreign intelligence agencies." Kelley informed special agents that "law enforcement agencies from throughout the world" were "interested in various aspects of the SPAC [Sixth Pan-African Congress]." He ordered agents to arrange surveillance of all planning activities being held in their regions.[61]

Kelley's initiative was part of an insistence in the Nixon administration that American radicalism, including black nationalism, had alien sponsors. The CIA reported that it could find no evidence of such subversion, a conclusion the White House did not accept. FBI officials ingratiated themselves with Nixon by expanding the bureau's presence abroad to monitor any foreign cooperation with suspect U.S. groups and thereby invaded traditional CIA turf.[62]

What the FBI saw as a threatening international situation, advocates of Pan-Africanism perceived as a promising beginning. In Kingston, Jamaica, for example, 6PAC planners drew together distinguished Pan-African veterans and black nationalists from previous eras. Prime Minister Michael Manley dispatched Dudley Thompson to chair the Kingston conference, held at a government-owned hotel. Thompson, minister of state, had attended the Manchester congress in 1945. Amy Jacques Garvey, widow of Marcus Garvey and one of the congress's international sponsors, spoke to the assembly on her late husband's legacy. Roberta Sykes, an Australian aborigine, chaired a subcommittee that discussed white settler regimes in Australia, New Guinea, and the Pacific islands. Participants debated African repatriation and the feasibility of reparations for slavery. They pondered the option of petitioning the UN and the OAU on these matters. Bomani, who was also representing TANU, gave the closing address in Kingston. Tanzania was glad to host the congress, he assured listeners, but wanted it postponed until greater participation from black scientists and technicians could be had.[63]

An organizing meeting in Guyana late in 1973 piqued FBI interest because of the past association of that country with the Marxist regime of Cheddi Jagan and the U.S. role in his overthrow. The FBI placed a source at the meeting with instructions to discover any Cuban involvement in, or funding of, the congress. The bureau found no evidence that Pan-Africanists received money

[61] Hewitt, *Spying 101*, 152, 158; Director to SAC (Washington Field Office), July 19, 1973; idem to the U.S. Legation in Ottawa, January 31, 1974; idem to idem, n.d.; Director to SACs, Baltimore et al., September 10, 1973, FBI-NARA.

[62] Seymour M. Hersh, "Alien-Radical Tie Disputed by C.I.A," *New York Times*, May 25, 1973, p. 1; Ruth Reitan, *The Rise and Decline of An Alliance: Cuba and African American Leaders in the 1960s* (East Lansing: Michigan State University Press, 1999), 85.

[63] General Report of the Caribbean and South American Regional Planning Conference of the Sixth Pan African Congress, n.d.,; De Roulet, US embassy Kingston, to the Secretary of State, February 15, 1973; "Convention to Plan Pan African Congress Opens Here," *Daily Gleaner*, February 20, 1973, clipping, FBI-NARA.

from Cuba or any Warsaw Pact country, or that they ever asked for any. At a second Guyanese convocation in February 1974, the FBI learned that Fidel Castro, who had visited the country the previous December and had been well received, endorsed the congress. Guyana's simmering ethnic tensions between blacks and East Indians emerged at this meeting when an East Indian took the podium and called the Burnham government "a minority racist clique" and pleaded for black and Indian unity. He was led from the stage.[64]

Whereas the Fifth Pan-African Congress in Manchester in 1945 had been concerned chiefly with decolonization, its successor focused on neocolonialism, an emphasis that automatically raised questions about the policies and behaviors of certain black governments. In the end, these questions could not be addressed as African and Caribbean states themselves policed the congress and curtailed radical influence without overt help from the West. Independent Caribbean regimes banned NGO participation.

While a very extensive network of local, regional, and national bodies was in place, coordination remained a problem for organizers at the May 1973 North American Regional Planning Conference at Kent State University. As in the Caribbean, North American activists had some specific goals in mind. They included repeal of the Byrd amendment, the boycotting of Polaroid products and tropical produce from Portugal and its colonies, and support of the OAU and national liberation organizations in general, though debate continued about which specific fronts should be assisted. That controversy would sharpen after the "Carnation Revolution" in Portugal, which toppled the dictatorship and promised independence for the African colonies.[65]

Planning was hampered, however, by uncertainty about the presence and role of "big names" in the Black Power movement. "One notable absentee was LeRoi Jones (Imamu Baraka)," the FBI noted. "Baraka is reportedly well regarded in Tanzania and his absence from these planning meetings must occasion questions in Africa regarding the validity of the representation at these meetings." (Baraka did ultimately materialize, having been delayed.)[66] Stokely Carmichael was also missing. Ambassador Carter suggested that Carmichael thought Tanzania less revolutionary than his adopted home of Guinea. African-American elected officials, smarting from the tension between them and certain Black Power figures at the 1972 Gary conference, intended to be absent.[67]

---

[64] Director to SAC (Louisville), December 7, 1973; report on the Sixth Pan African Congress, February 2, 1974, FBI-NARA.

[65] General Report of the North American Regional Conference of the Sixth Pan African Congress, May 11–13, 1973.

[66] Ibid.; Director to U.S. Legation, Ottawa, September 5, 1973, FB-NARA; Baraka's reservations about the Congress are detailed in Amiri Baraka, "Some Questions about the Sixth Pan-African Congress," *Black Scholar* (October 1974): 42–6.

[67] Memorandum of conversation between Ambassador H. E. Paul Bomani and Ambassador W. Beverly Carter, May 1, 1974, SDCF. On Carmichael, see also Washington Field Office to Director, July 12, 1973, FBI-NARA.

Money problems also plagued organizers. Faulted by the Ghanaian ambassador to the United States for their lack of fund-raising acumen, they had trouble securing backing for the congress.[68] Some funding came from the Tanzanian government and the World Council of Churches, but continuing financial woes, conflicts with OAU member states, and ideological divisions in North America led to delays in selecting the U.S. delegation and repeated postponements of the congress, which was originally scheduled to occur in 1972. Further setbacks arose because of a failed coup attempt in Tanzania in April 1974, and the decision of OAU delegates, meeting in Uganda in May, to return to their homes before heading to Tanzania.[69]

C. L. R. James and Cortland Cox tracked down the prime ministers of Jamaica and Guyana at the August 1973 Commonwealth meeting in Ottawa. Both agreed to contributions of $10,000 for the Congress. Burnham also promised to solicit aid from corporations operating in Guyana. These politicians faced Black Power insurgencies at home and were now supporting 6PAC to enhance the populism with which they hoped to be associated. Shortly before the congress convened, however, Burnham and other Caribbean leaders ruled that their countries could only be represented by official delegations, not by NGOs. The OAU seconded their decision.[70]

"We Were Betrayed, Says Congress Committee," read a headline from the Port of Spain *Trinidad Express*. The Caribbean regional steering committee accused the Trinidad-born SNCC veteran Cortland Cox of acquiescing to the prohibition of popular organizations. They detected the hand of the United States behind the blow. Trinidadian activist Geddes Granger told the press that "the Pentagon, the Federal Bureau of Investigation (FBI) had worked with the Caribbean governments in ensuring that its infiltrators would get on the Dar es Salaam Committee to block black militants from the Congress." In a radio interview on Howard University's WHUR, an unnamed individual claimed that Washington was pouring money into Caribbean nations in advance of the congress. Trinidad's decision to attend only as an observer was followed by the announcement of new American aid to the Williams government, he noted. At a meeting in Barbados, Maurice Bishop, who would later head Grenada's government, asserted that the U.S. government had colluded in the NGO exclusion because it did not want the issue of multinational firms' exploitative practices in the region raised at the congress. Caribbean radicals then vowed not to attend the conference under any circumstances or any alternative auspices.[71]

---

[68] Acting Director to U.S. Legation (Ottawa), n.d.; Report on Sixth Pan African Congress, December 18, 1973, FBI-NARA.

[69] Cox interview; Acting Director to U.S. Legation (Ottawa), March 19, June 14 and June 25, 1974; SAC, Washington Field Office to the Director, April 17, 1974, ibid.

[70] Max V. Krebs to the Secretary of State, April 2, 1974, SDCF.

[71] Max V. Krebs to the Secretary of State, December 28, 1973; idem to idem, June 17, 1974; Eileen R. Donovan to the Secretary of State, June 13, 1974, SDCF. Stephen Mohammed, "We Were Betrayed, Says Congress Committee," *Trinidad Express*, June 13, 1974, clipping; transcript of radio interview with unidentified subject, n.d., in FBI-NARA.

The decision to bar NGOs was a victory for statist internationalism. The congress's outcome is widely interpreted as the renunciation of romantic racialism in favor of a Marxist-internationalist approach to African problems. The emphasis, in this writer's view, should be less on internationalism and more on the intent of African governments to domesticate popular eruptions. "Victory went, both within the ranks of the American delegation and at the Congress itself, to the 'internationalists'," Bai Kisogie commented. "But there were many, even among the 'internationalists' who felt that it was at best a pyrrhic victory." Pan-Africanism as it had been known in the past was now dead. "Was it necessary to summon a Congress to preside over the liquidation of a concept?" To Kisogie, the meeting "ended up with what amounted to a practical denial of the existence of an African world"[72] – a denial, one might add, that abetted the power of states over popular movements.

African Americans, like the national liberation movements, had a different relation to statism. The liberation movements had no state, and the one to which African Americans belonged was some psychic distance away and exerted its influence less openly. With Caribbean militants barred and some U.S. black radicals not attending, the FBI was now less inclined to consider all participants extremists. Director Kelley instructed agents to limit their investigations to those already under bureau microscopes. The FBI planned to have five informants in Dar es Salaam and keep some moles working Stateside "since they may provide vital information concerning any ongoing U.S. structure which emerges from the Congress."[73]

Once lengthy waits related to bureaucracy were resolved, the large African-American delegation faced another set of problems. A chartered plane scheduled to leave New York City on June 17 was canceled because of a $100 increase in fare. The charter arrangement had required that passengers pay in cash, and some could not afford the hike. Organizers made alternate arrangements via Zurich, but because the East African Airlines plane they chartered was small, some fifty delegates had to wait in Switzerland for connections. Another group left New York via Air India for London, whence they planned to transfer to East African Airways at additional cost. On the West Coast, a California delegate was trying to rent cars to drive people to New York to get airborne. While one can see the hidden hand of government in the transportation problems as is often alleged, they can also be attributed to the on-and-off-again itinerary and to airlines' taking advantage of inexperienced travelers. All or any of these reasons for the delays is likely.[74] Delegates were encouraged to take these difficulties in stride and to remain focused on their desire to

---

[72] Kisogie, "State Exhibitionists and Ideological Glamour," 9, 11.

[73] Director to SAC Albany, May 6, 1974; idem to SAC Cinncinati, April 23, 1974, FBI-NARA.

[74] SAC, Washington Field Office, to Director, June 7, 1974; SAC (Philadelphia) to the Director, June 13, 1974; FBI report on the Sixth Pan African Congress, June 7, 1974; FBI report, Los Angeles, June 24, 1974; SAC (NY) to the Director, June 17, 1974; idem to idem, same date; SAC (Atlanta) to the Director, June 17, 1974; Report of Special Agent David A. Hammond, July 5, 1974, FBI-NARA.

participate in a worldwide discussion among Black people. We will get there late, tired and ambiguous about our exact role within the scope of the discussions. We have to want to be there in that discussion more than we want to complain and feel sorry for ourselves. It is the nature of being oppressed to experience what we are experiencing! This means both inefficient handling of affairs as well as interference by anti-forces.[75]

The Sixth Pan-African Congress opened on June 19, 1974, on the University College of Dar es Salaam campus. Twenty-four African countries, seven national liberation organizations, and five Caribbean powers sent representatives. Delegations also arrived from Britain, Canada, New Hebrides, and, the largest, the United States. When the plane carrying most of the African Americans arrived, a special line at customs processed them carefully because of past arms importation issues involving black U.S. visitors. "The grounds around the conference center seemed to be dominated by Afro-Americans," journalist Hoyt Fuller observed, "who outnumbered all the other conferees combined.... There did not seem to be much camaraderie, and certainly there were few Afro-Americans communicating with delegates from other parts of the black world. But it is early yet."[76]

As a result of the travel delays, some of the two-hundred-member-strong delegation from North America did not arrive on June 19. Group representation was the center of controversy. Regional coordinators had tried to address the problem early by choosing ninety official delegates and allowing others to attend as observers. Once in Dar es Salaam, TANU whittled this down to ten official representatives. While African-American activists have been generally criticized for sending such a large and diverse group to Tanzania, Sylvia Hill, the principal U.S. organizer, subsequently defended their choices and the role she played in refusing to allow the number of attendees to be limited. "We felt very strongly that one of the critical agenda issues was to give people an opportunity to experience Africa, ... through their own lived experiences in order to build people-to-people ties," she explained. Familiarity with African issues should not be limited to the few. If anything, the amount of work coordinators had done in publicizing the event called for maximal participation. "For us it was a fundamental political issue of expanding access to this political forum and Tanzanian people beyond heads of organizations."[77]

The Tanzanian government, in Ambassador Carter's opinion, "pulled out all the stops" in protocol honoring the congress. Every cabinet officer attended Nyerere's keynote address, and the national legislature adjourned so that lawmakers could be present. In his opening speech on June 20, Nyerere stressed membership in nation-states and suggested that citizenship might mean more in the modern black world than race and ancestry. He acknowledged the hybrid

75 Report of Special Agent David A. Hammond, July 5, 1974, ibid.
76 Report of Special Agent Douglas A. Simpson to SAC (St. Paul), July 16, 1974; Report of Special Agent David A. Hammond, July 5, 1974, FBI-NARA. Fuller, "Notes from a Sixth-Pan-African Journal," pp. 71, 73, 74.
77 Levy, "Remembering Sixth-PAC," 43.

nature of the congress, making a careful distinction between a council of states, such as the OAU, and a conference focused on nonalignment, which was not, he asserted, the goal at Dar es Salaam.[78]

Instead, Nyerere saw the congress providing a unique framework for states and NGOs to work together to eliminate racism, promote southern African liberation, and pursue "human rights and human justice." In a wistful gesture to the nonviolent direct action that such leaders as Kenneth Kaunda, Kwame Nkrumah, and he himself had subscribed to, he said he hoped that the April revolution in Portugal would make the further pursuit of war for liberation unnecessary in the Portuguese colonies. Nyerere referred to Pan-African history, citing the accomplishments of W. E. B. Du Bois, Jomo Kenyatta, and Nkrumah. The congress was not to attack any African state even as it acknowledged the "demand that justice be done within the newly independent nations as well as in the older countries." The Tanzanian leader called for inter-African economic cooperation. Rhetoric alone would not suffice. The ideals of the congress had to be followed with concrete programs.[79]

The congress featured the presence of many of the most influential political and cultural figures of Africa and the diaspora during the epoch. Exiled poet and activist Dennis Brutus from South Africa, playwright Wole Soyinka from Nigeria, and Amiri Baraka (Leroi Jones), Haki Madhubuti (Don Lee), and Black Power veteran Mae Mallory from the United States attended. Guyana-born Ras Makonnen, an old hand in Pan-African activism, was also present.[80]

Beyond the excitement of such a cavalcade of admired international personalities lay the backstage efforts of the Tanzanians to balance both their national and Pan-African objectives with their relations with the United States and other Western powers. Tanzanians at independence were largely agriculturalists spread out over a vast landscape. The collectives called *ujamaa* villages derived from the desire to improve infrastructure and provide better services by aggregating the population. As in other developing countries, leaders faced the problem of how to empower rural people to stand up to the political domination of cities and towns. Unlike Tanzania, many states never made this effort.

Tanzanian officials coordinated the Sixth Pan-African Congress at the same time that they were accelerating the process of moving people into planned villages, a procedure not universally favored by the populace.[81] Not every Tanzanian subscribed to the state's African socialist agenda or endorsed the allocation of resources to the liberation organizations. Some thought Tanzania was taking unnecessary risks and undermining its own national interest. The

---

[78] Fuller, p. 74; President Nyerere's speech to the Sixth Pan African Congress, June 19, 1974, in FBI-NARA.

[79] Carter to the Secretary of State et al., June 20, 1974, SDCF.

[80] Fuller, pp. 70–81.

[81] "Toward Ujamaa in Tanganyika," Julius Nyerere interviewed by Suresh Ram, Dar-es-Salaam, Dec 10, 1962, in World Peace Brigade Papers, Wisconsin Historical Society, Box 2 folder 1. See also James Scott, *Seeing Like a State: How Certain Schemes to Improve the Human Condition Have Failed* (New Haven, Conn.: Yale University Press, 1998), 223–61.

government thus had to straddle a bridge between international commitments undertaken for ethical reasons and domestic statecraft. Reassuring American officials that it had not gone off the deep end formed part of this charge. Bomani met in Washington with the State Department African Affairs office to keep a cordial dialogue going while traveling through the United States to encourage interest in the Pan-African Congress. He delivered a press conference at the offices of Johnson Publications in Chicago, and editors from two of its serials, Lerone Bennett of *Ebony* and Hoyt Fuller of *Black World*, attended the congress.[82]

Tanzania unequivocally endorsed independence and black majority rule for southern Africa. It departed from the U.S. wish-list in maintaining good relations with Cuba and the Arab states and joining other Indian Ocean powers in opposing the militarization of that region. It recognized the deposed Cambodian government of Prince Norodom Sihanouk and maintained relations with North Korea. A vocal part of the Afro-Asian contingent in the UN General Assembly, it defended the antiimperialist stances often taken by the group. As U.S. Deputy Chief of Mission Gordon Beyer reported, "What looks like steamroller tactics to us is [the] only method [the] weak and poor have of protecting themselves." Dar es Salaam walked a fine line between guardedness toward the West and efforts to be seen as cooperative.[83]

Domestic politics required a similar athleticism. Nyerere had to convince a critical mass of Tanzanians of the merits of "African socialism" and internationalism. Meanwhile the Zanzibari Abdulrahman Mohamed Babu, admired by many young African Americans, languished in prison, detained for treason. Would-be guerrillas from the United States were thus irritants that complicated Dar es Salaam's balancing act.[84] Under these circumstances, Tanzania managed its multiple challenges well.

In spite of the best efforts, some clashes were unpreventable in the broader context of African politics. Sékou Touré, president of Guinea, sent a taped message that was read at the congress. The Guinean called for the creation of African raw materials cartels and warned participants of the evils of succumbing to racism. Touré identified *négritude*, which had emerged from an earlier

---

[82] Walter Bgoya, "From Tanzania to Kansas and Back Again," in *No Easy Victories*, eds. William Minter, Gail Hovey, and Charlie Cobb, Jr. (Trenton, N.J.: Africa World Press, 2007): 104; Republic of Tanzania. *Study of the Rural Development Programme: Ujamaa Villages and Rural Development Staff of Tanga, Kilimanjaro, Arusha* (Dar-es-Salaam: Ministry of Regional Administration and Rural Development, 1970). Secretary of State to the U.S. Embassy (Dar es Salaam), April 11, 1974, SDCF; "10 Here to Attend African Congress," *Chicago Tribune*, June 13, 1974, p. S5.

[83] Gordon Beyer to the Secretary of State, August 28, 1974, SDCF. On Tanzanian foreign policy in the 1970s see S. S. Mushi, "The Making of Foreign Policy in Tanzania," in *Foreign Policy of Tanzania 1961–1981: A Reader*, eds. K. Mathews and S. S. Mushi (Dar-es-Salaam: Tanzania Publishing House, 1981); Timothy C. Niblock, "Tanzanian Foreign Policy: An Analysis," in ibid., 24–33; E. J. Kisanga, "Tanzania and the Organisation of African Unity (O.A.U.)," in ibid., 97–122.

[84] Cox interview.

cultural response to imperialism, as an essentialist and racist philosophy, which he saw as akin to apartheid. A black skin did not necessarily mean virtue. To Touré, Fidel Castro and Salvador Allende were "closer to exploited blacks than certain Afro-American or African 'leaders.'" The representatives from Senegal, home of the foremost poet of *négritude*, President Léopold Senghor, denounced Touré's speech.[85]

The international finance community and the United Nations also came in for criticism. A delegate from Zaire questioned the great-power veto exercised in the Security Council, an arrangement that kept international armed force permanently in the hands of a few. He reminded listeners that when such institutions as the World Bank and the International Monetary Fund were set up, African countries were colonies and had no voice in their composition and procedures. These institutions should be "democratised."[86]

Discord between Marxists and black nationalists, an ongoing drama since the 1920s, played out at the congress on June 20, when a shouting match erupted between a group of African Americans and a representative from MPLA. The dispute involved some Americans' conviction that the rival Angolan liberation organization, UNITA, more genuinely represented the black masses. Westernized urban elites, whites, and mulattoes, they held, constituted MPLA's base. "In a burst of emotion," Hoyt Fuller reported, "the M.P.L.A. man held up his fist and shouted, 'You black Americans shout Black Power,' but our situation is not the same as yours. We're not against people because they are not Black." Fuller reported a similar dustup between the official Cuban delegation and Carlos Moore, a black Cuban who was a fervent critic of revolutionary Havana's racial practices. "Apparently a violent confrontation was narrowly averted during President Nyerere's reception on the grounds of the state house, and the Cubans lodged an official objection to Moore's presence."[87]

There were other sources of conflict. In the United States, women did much of the legwork involved in recruiting the delegates and sending them off. As in certain U.S. civil rights campaigns, where Charles Payne famously noted, "Men led but women organized," "sisters" were expected to stay in the background, this time in conformity to supposed African custom. When Nyerere expressed an interest in receiving no more than five of the leaders of the African-American delegation, Sylvia Hill recalled, "[Cornell University professor] James Turner announced the five; they were all men." Hill did not challenge the decision even though she felt that her work as the chief U.S. organizer had earned her a place at the table. Yet, "that night the [Tanzanian] ambassador came to see me and said that the president was inviting me to come to meet with him, and that I should come at nine o'clock. He said a car will come pick you up. When the men get there you will already be there." When Turner, Owusu Sadauki, Haki

[85] Lerone Bennett, Jr., "Pan-Africanism at the Crossroads," *Ebony* (September 1974), p. 156; Carter to the Secretary of State et al., June 29, 1974, SDCF.
[86] Carter to the Secretary of State et al., June 29, 1974, SDCF.
[87] Fuller, pp. 75–6, 80.

Madhubuti, and others arrived, Hill remembered, "I was on my second cup of tea with President Nyerere!"[88]

Bay Area physician and publisher Carlton Goodlett reported his dissatisfaction with the congress. He regretted the absence of any planned follow-up. The permanent secretariat originally envisioned, with its complementary information and technology centers, never materialized; nor was a second meeting scheduled, even though Jamaica and Guyana had extended invitations. Goodlett noted the absence from the congress of Charles Diggs and other black American elected officials, and the abdication of C. L. R. James and Stokely Carmichael. The U.S. delegates additionally faced "their lack of sophistication and experience in dealing with international forums, language barriers which reduced the effectiveness of their lobbying, and the emotional rhetoric by such speakers as Owusu Sadauki and Imamu Baraka rather than documented position papers on African conditions." Goodlett thought it was a mistake to exclude U.S. ambassador W. Beverly Carter, an African American, from the proceedings.[89]

Carter himself seconded Goodlett's skepticism. Aside from African ancestry, he did not see many common ties among represented countries. The "flurry of declarations condemning imperialism and capitalism" and suggestions for development did not result in "machinery to implement" economic programs. Carter dismissed much of the debate at the congress as bombast, especially calls for a socialist world order, but speculated that "it may presage more serious efforts in other international fora to give greater reality to these declarations which are fundamentally contrary to U.S. interests." There was, he believed, a chance that the Soviets, "and particularly Chinese," would approach delegates and exploit their resentments.[90]

The congress plan called for all delegations to submit their position papers to the plenary body. The U.S. delegation failed to produce a document they all agreed on as its workshop sessions broke down in debate about the primacy of race or class. Whereas other delegations had a single principal who spoke for the group, the African Americans did not. Some members of the press assumed that Lerone Bennett, the most senior figure and an international sponsor, headed the U.S. delegation, but he had been relegated to observer status. It surprised him when he was called out of the visitors' gallery to deliver an impromptu speech. Unlike others at the congress, most of the U.S. delegates represented no constituency at home, and few of their resolutions were incorporated into the final congress report. Amiri Baraka did not think that all U.S. delegates were serious. Some "just wanted to go to Tanzania to hang out," he

[88] Levy, "Remembering Sixth-PAC," 45. On some of the gender dynamics in the U.S. delegation, see Sis. Omowale, Delegate Coordinator, to All travelers to Tanzania..., n.d. in Report of Special Agent David A. Hammond, July 5, 1974, FBI-NARA.

[89] Carlton Goodlett, "Weak Performance at Pan-African Meet," *The Sun Reporter*, July 20, 1974, clipping in FBI-NARA.

[90] Carter to the Secretary of State et al., June 29, 1974, SDCF.

asserted. While important issues were being debated, certain "folks just went shopping or swimming."[91]

In the wake of the statist victory in Dar es Salaam, Tanzania strengthened its relations with other nations through conventional channels. In August 1974, Jamaica hosted a conference of forty-four countries. Amir Jamal, Babu's successor as minister for commerce and industry, saw the event as a harbinger of unity for the global South and traveled to Kingston to pave the way for a subsequent state visit by Nyerere, who proceeded from Jamaica to Trinidad and Tobago, Cuba, Guyana, and the United Kingdom.[92]

Although Charles Diggs avoided the Pan-African Congress, he briefly visited Dar es Salaam in February 1975, when he met with foreign minister Malecela. Ambassador Carter reported Malecela as telling Diggs that

when the decolonization of Africa is finally completed, and that day is now clearly near, Africans hope their brothers in America will not forget them or their land of origin. Africans hope, Malecela said, that black Americans will be willing to come back to Africa in order to share their skills with their brothers here. Africa needs these skills and it would be especially appreciated if black Americans helped.[93]

The message imparted was that Africans would determine the mode, manner, and timing of African-American assistance. Within the contours of that arrangement, groundwork was laid for the establishment of TransAfrica and for the divestment campaigns of the 1980s.

African-Americans' embrace of Africa did not always entail visions of future progress. It could yield to more mundane incentives when, for example, former heavyweight boxing champion Muhammad Ali, born Cassius Clay, regained his title in the "Rumble in the Jungle." It was not his first unconventional act. Ali's refusal of induction in 1966 profoundly shocked those whose ideas about champions rehearsed a particular conception of Americanism. The sports hero's significance was not limited to athleticism: he or she must represent an ideal and affirm conventional notions of patriotism, fair play, and respectability. Early in the twentieth century, black heavyweight champion Jack Johnson had defied the code. He spent his purses lavishly, openly conducted affairs with white women, and inadvertently triggered racial violence in many precincts where newsreels of his triumphs over white opponents were shown.[94]

Handlers counseled the succeeding Joe Louis to behave differently. Louis and such athletes as Jackie Robinson would adhere to high standards of

---

[91] Turner interview; Cynthia Jo Rich, "Americans Differ at African Congress," *Race Relations Reporter* 5 (July 15, 1974): 25–9; Baraka, "Some Questions about the Sixth Pan-African Congress," 44, 46.

[92] Gordon Beyer to the State Department, August 22, 1974; Sumner Gerard to the Secretary of State, September 23, 1974, SDCF.

[93] U.S. Embassy (Dar-es Salaam) to the Secretary of State, February 12, 1975, SDCF.

[94] Geoffrey C. Ward, *Unforgivable Blackness: The Rise and Fall of Jack Johnson* (New York: Knopf, 2004). See also Gail Bederman, *Manliness and Civilization: A Cultural History of Gender and Race in the United States, 1880–1917* (Chicago: University of Chicago, 1995), 1–10, 41–2.

gentlemanly deportment as the price of their acceptance. "For most whites, as long as black fighters do not denounce the entrenched racism of their national culture, society, and state, they qualify as 'Americans,' albeit validated only because as sports heroes they entertain and/or protect the ('white') nation," Joy James has observed. "For most blacks, as long as African-Americans triumph in the sports, commercial culture, or military arenas, they are viewed as a source of collective racial pride and 'entertainment' because their victorious battles as African Americans repudiate the myth of white superiority/black inferiority and offer a vicarious thrill."[95]

The integration of major league sports coincided with the repudiation of sociobiological racism by policy elites in the United States and Western Europe and the triumph of liberal universalism as the establishment creed. Black sports figures became simultaneously exemplars of their race and raceless representatives of the nation-state. This balancing act required both reticence and acuity, but as athletics became one of the limited avenues open to black success, and more blacks became athletes, the black "first" who did not question the status quo, deferred to whites, and willingly tolerated discrimination, became increasingly obsolete.[96]

Yet this path to freedom was not straight. The sport of boxing especially had considerable difficulty living up to bourgeois respectability. Racketeer influence and the shady pasts of such fighters as Sonny Liston meant that while such athletes pledged their allegiance to conservative national ideals and did not endorse protest and activism, they were hardly role models for youth or exemplars of the type of reputable "Negro" that the civil rights establishment wanted white Americans to accept.[97] There was no Jackie Robinson in boxing: fans either had to identify with the brash and controversial Cassius Clay or back his thuggish opponents. Many were dismayed and embarrassed by both.

Cassius Clay's name celebrated a well-meaning white man, an antislavery senator. In 1960, as the gold medalist in boxing at the Rome Olympics, Clay had played the standard role expected of black sports figures. He subsequently broke with the Joe Louis/Jackie Robinson tradition but in a manner wholly different from that of the free-living Jack Johnson. Unlike Johnson, Clay lacked interest in white women or conspicuous consumption, and he did not reserve his opinions. Clay, originally a Catholic, angered many sports enthusiasts, including some blacks, by converting to Islam and changing his name to Muhammad Ali, thus alluding not only to Islam's leading prophet and his son-in-law, but also to the founder of modern Egypt. The sports establishment saw this as transgressive. Ali expressed his repudiation of Christianity as a rejection of

[95] Joy James, *Shadowboxing: Representations of Black Feminist Politics* (New York: St. Martin's Press, 1999), 175.

[96] Damion Lamar Thomas, "'The Good Negroes': African-American Athletes and the Cultural Cold War, 1945–1968" (PhD diss., University of California, Los Angeles, 2002), pp. 35, 254–5.

[97] Randy Roberts, "The Wide World of Muhammad Ali: The Politics and Economics of Televised Boxing," in *Muhammad Ali, the People's Champ*, ed. Elliott J. Gorn (Urbana and Chicago: University of Illinois Press, 1995), 35–8.

the white supremacy that shaped that religion's history in the United States. His newly articulated views so offended the World Boxing Association that it temporarily stripped Ali of his title. As a Nation of Islam member, he refused the draft and faced federal prosecution.[98]

Muhammad Ali's dissidence and the harsh reaction to it expressed by the government, media, and many fans triggered enormous sympathy for him overseas. The visibility that his conversion – even if unorthodox – gave to Islam, combined with his sports celebrity and opposition to U.S. policies detested around the world, made him a complex symbol of resistance. In appropriating the right to be self-affirming and to hold opinions and make judgments, he challenged the construction of the black athlete as only an animal body obedient to the wishes of its coaches and handlers. For those at home who understood him, his act of uniting body and mind seemed analogous to the work of individual and collective healing that the civil rights movement promised. Abroad, his challenge to racism, violence, and intolerance, as well as the risks he had taken in mounting it, ensured his enduring popularity.[99]

The caldron of emotions that Ali stirred seems odd today, but the consternation and joy alternately expressed about his choices and behavior had everything to do with black self-assertion and repudiation of old norms to which all African Americans, not only athletes, were held. U.S. society would recognize a few talented people of color whose achievements affirmed the belief that success lay within reach of all and that failure was a matter of individual moral deficiency. Within the broader context of cultural diplomacy and cold war propaganda efforts, the prowess of "our colored athletes" and their absolute loyalty validated U.S. global power and prestige and countered the shocking newsreel footage of racial violence. Muhammad Ali's unraveling of this narrative proved so unsettling as to seem criminal.

His dissidence was not contained within a formal model of revolutionary nationalism or even orthodox religious dissent. A member of the idiosyncratic NOI, with certain eccentricities himself, Ali could not always be easily parsed. By converting to Islam and repudiating the Vietnam War, he nevertheless reached out to religious and political communities beyond the United States, bringing into focus people and issues outside the U.S. tale of global superiority. This is the role he played in the famous prizefight in Kinshasa, Zaire.

In spite of Zaire's mineral wealth, which under ethical government would have improved the welfare of citizens, Zairians found their living standard plummeting. Nationalization of vital farms and industries further enriched dictator Joseph Mobutu Sese Soko and his clique but contributed little to national

---

[98] Biographies of Muhammad Ali include, Thomas Hauser, *The Lost Legacy of Muhammad Ali* (Wilmington, Del.: SPORTClassic Books, 2005); Mike Marqusee, *Redemption Song: Muhammad Ali and the Spirit of the Sixties* (London: Verso, 1999); David Remnick, *King of the World* (New York: Vintage, 1998); Thomas Hauser, *Muhammad Ali: His Life and Times* (New York: Simon & Schuster, 1991).

[99] Gerald Early, "Muhammad Ali as a Third World Hero," *Ideas* 9 (1) (2002): 4–15.

well-being. As in other African states, the energy crisis hit the renamed Congo hard. The price of copper, a major export, collapsed in 1974. Food production was not keeping pace with population growth.[100]

What better time, then, to stage a high-profile international sports event? The 1974 heavyweight championship of the world took place on October 30, with titleholder George Foreman squaring off against challenger Muhammad Ali. Just as Louis Armstrong's visit to the Congo in October 1960 diverted attention from the country's turmoil, the "Rumble in the Jungle" momentarily eclipsed its continuing political and economic problems (see Figure 17). As for the U.S. government, "We were still viewing Zaire as a success growing out of the UN-US effort in what was then the Congo in the '60s," former Assistant Secretary of State for African Affairs Donald D. Newsom recalled years later. "We were troubled by a lot of the indications of megalomania and corruption that were coming out of Zaire," but Washington did not want any leftist movements to succeed. "Mobutu was occasionally toying with anti-American rhetoric, so we occasionally had to remind him of where his butter was spread."[101]

A three-day concert preceded the bout. The promoters recruited many top performers of the 1970s, including James Brown, B.B. King, Miriam Makeba, Manu Dibango, the Spinners, the Crusaders, and the Pointer Sisters. Some Zairians wanted more local talent, but international celebrity trumped local pride.[102] Muhammad Ali's magnanimity and charisma helped to create a feel-good atmosphere. He expressed his pleasure, like Fannie Lou Hamer, at "being in a country operated by black people." During an earlier trip to Ghana, he had noted the negative views of Africa held by too many African Americans. "I used to think Africans were savages ... we in America are the savages." He was avidly received in Zaire as he engaged in friendly banter with citizens.[103]

During the run-up to the fight, Ali repeatedly emphasized his desire to champion the oppressed in America and Africa. It was for them that he sought vindication for the loss of his title during the conflict over his religion, name, and antiwar stance. Yet a deep understanding of African politics did not inform Ali's love of the continent. The following year he had to be dissuaded from an exhibition match in South Africa. He retained a naive patriotism, asking

[100] David N. Gibbs, *The Political Economy of Third World Intervention: Mines, Money, and U. S. Policy in the Congo Crisis* (Chicago: University of Chicago Press, 1991), 192; "Implications of Worldwide Population Growth for U.S. Security and Overseas Interests," National Security Study Memorandum no. 200, NSC, December 10, 1974, pp. 60–1.

[101] Ambassador David D. Newsom interviewed by Charles Stuart Kennedy, June 17, 1991, The Foreign Affairs Oral History Collection of the Association for Diplomatic Studies and Training, LC.

[102] *When We Were Kings*, film, directed by Leon Gast, and Taylor Hackford, Gramercy Pictures, 94 minutes, U.S., 2005; Hugh Masekela with Michael Cheers, *Still Grazing: The Musical Journey of Hugh Masekela*, 277, 285.

[103] Hauser, *Muhammad Ali: His Life and Times*, 265; Marqusee, *Redemption Song*, 123.

FIGURE 17. George Foreman jousts with a wary Mobutu during the "Rumble in the Jungle." (Getty Images)

the U.S. embassy in Kinshasa to have President Ford watch the bout on closed circuit television.[104]

The "Rumble in the Jungle" rehearsed themes and sensibilities that, depending on the actors in question, simultaneously reflected sincere Pan-African affinities, USIA-style showmanship, the pursuit of profit, and the desire for international respectability. Muhammad Ali and his backers differed substantially from the NGOs that wanted to aid Tanzania. The Zaire bout shed light on a global entertainment industry that offered symbols and narratives of power

[104] U.S. Embassy (Dar- es Salaam) to the Secretary of State, February 12, 1975; idem to idem, October 15, 1974, SDCF.

and did not rely on social movements to be broadly communicated. As entertainment, it could divert insurgent ideas and energies into lucrative market outlets. The Africa of the "rumble" did not have to be a clearly delineated and contained geographic space, and it did not require sophisticated knowledge of the continent's diverse cultures and politics. Even as governments rose and fell, and wars and epidemics raged, the idealized Africa of Pan-African imaginaries lived on.

Conclusion

This study ends in 1974 with the issues of colonialism and African-American civil rights oddly unsettled, with race once again resurgent as a marker of both individual and national fates in the United States and abroad. Sovereignty and freedom were more problematic than expected. While statism retained its allure, the succeeding era was one in which transnational decisions that bypassed foreign offices reduced the power of central governments. A slackening of state control, increasingly evident after the collapse of Soviet communism, deeply marked international society and culture, and many kinds of migration (tourists, labor, refugees, technology, capital, information, images, and religious values). Contemporaries have been highly conscious of these transitions and actively attempt to mediate them in their own interests.

When black and white educators, officials, corporate leaders, and foundation representatives met in the mid-1950s to decide what to do about the growing clamor over integration and decolonization, they had already anticipated to some degree the scope of the impending changes that would overtake the world. They chose to make allies of the new insurgents. A Western victory in the cold war required the recruitment of emerging states and their most important citizens: new classes and politicized youth who would share elite values. While the goal of independence for the global South would be upheld, broader critiques of the international behavior of Western powers were disallowed or deemed subversive of world order. The U.S. policy establishment sought, at best, the invisibility of race and, at least, its neutrality. Civil rights, perceived as a domestic issue for Americans, was dissociated from antiimperialism. The Left, in contrast, strove to join African-American freedom struggles to worldwide radical movements and restore the affinities that they had often had in the past. Black nationalists, who could range widely on the Right to Left spectrum, did not accept cold war liberalism and did not have to rediscover a past association with Africa. Rapid decolonization in the early 1960s, the Congo crisis, and the Algerian war coincided with the domestic mass mobilizations of the civil rights movement and provided opportunities for activists to link issues of racial justice to overseas events while new states faced rival superpowers' determination to extend their conflicts across the globe.

"Independence did not entail the inversion of the hegemonic relationship instituted by colonialism," Ebere Nwaubani writes. "It did not, in other words, reintroduce as subjects of history peoples who as colonials had been merely its objects."[1] It did, however, provide these peoples with states and borrowed political institutions. These emphasized civic conformity in a centralized polity, and compliance with standards set by international financial and political institutions. Governments, regardless of their place on the map or the power they could command, were all invested in the preservation of the nation-state system. Whatever accusations former colonies leveled against the great powers, none was willing to give up "states' rights."

Ideological obstacles to black freedom in the United States lay rooted in American nationalism, defined as different from the experiences of other peoples, an exceptionalism that gave license to Americans to recreate their world abroad through both tutelage and conquest. While racists had always sought to prohibit blacks from participating in this aspect of national ambition, racial liberals sought black inclusion, but on terms once identified as for whites only. The new freedom would be color-blind, because to discuss color would be to reveal its racial underpinnings. African Americans might participate in evangelization and conquest, but only in advancing the goals of the white nation-state could black contributions be legitimate. In contrast, the African vista presented to Fannie Lou Hamer and others provided an alternative to white nationalism and its political agendas. The central place of blacks in a black country displaced, at least aspirationally, the marginality in which the African-American visitors to Guinea were socialized at home.

The civil rights movement did not succeed in defusing race as a national security issue or in halting the onrush of a militant transnational racial politics. Its original vocabulary had not been expansive enough to encompass the understanding that democracy could have no frontier. A broader vocabulary was soon found, one that could open new political spaces and accommodate an understanding of America's place in a world that yearned for democratic traditions and deplored the lack of statist support for them. The results were a renewed African-American foreign policy interest and the partial recovery of earlier forms of radicalism that significantly clashed with nation-state authority.

Race as an obstacle to the perfection of U.S. civil society guaranteed a place for a continuing independent outlook on foreign affairs among African Americans. This critical gaze has not always been clear and steady. At certain historical junctures, it enjoyed the weight of broad support from the larger society. At others, it was an outlaw sensibility. At times, it could not assimilate the objects of its scrutiny to its own native understanding of the world. The Nigerian civil war demonstrated how matters became complicated when whites and colonialism were not the immediate cause of conflict.

---

[1] Ebere Nwaubani, *The United States and Decolonization in West Africa, 1950–1960* (Rochester, N.Y.: University of Rochester Press, 2001), 26–7.

Black perspectives often confronted the contradictions in the United States' vision of itself. In spite of the lip service accorded by powerful nations to human rights, no minority group or individual claims could trump the supremacy of the nation-state framework. All governments have been invested in the preservation of that system. Whatever accusations former colonies leveled against the metropoles, and no matter how bitter the U.S.-USSR rivalry, the United Nations Charter itself carefully protected national sovereignty.

By the mid-1960s, colonial subjects had begun to reject the Gandhian strategies that had been successfully used in India. Nonviolence was at the height of its influence in the United States just as liberation movements on the continent were abandoning it. Yet African defection from nonviolence would in turn inspire African Americans, and especially the young, to seek militant solutions to the problems of racial injustice in the United States. An unyielding colonialism led to the embrace of revolution and armed struggle as the charms of nonviolent direct action and gradualism faded. Civil rights organizations became increasingly influenced by African viewpoints and more receptive to seeing revolutionary societies as models to emulate in the United States. During the 1956–74 era, fresh connections with groups on the European Left were established and existing ones strengthened. As neither the enactment of civil rights laws nor the beginning of independence resolved the problems of economic and political justice, urban communities in the United States began focusing on voluntarism and institution building, which became a pivotal concern of community based civil rights and Black Power organizations. In Africa Tanzania's *ujamaa* projects reflected this spirit.

The structural difference between national minorities and sovereign majorities reveals itself as a vexing problem for the African diaspora at this juncture. Heads of state seized the Sixth Pan-African Congress and prohibited the involvement of Caribbean dissidents. Black Americans' failure to speak with a unified voice revealed wider internal dissensions. Diaspora ambitions in general were undercut by African leaders' attachment to a politics that rendered black minorities marginal to the mission of African progress. "African governments harnessed their cultural ministries to support one-party rule, national cultural politics, and processes of nation building that were defined in hegemonic, localistic, and anti-intellectual terms," Bennetta Jules-Rosette observes. Pan-Africanist formulations of culture faded before the preference for nationalist particularisms. "In Africa," Simon Gikandi writes, "cultural nationalism, in the hands of the political class, had become a form of mystification; by the same token, the nation-state, once deemed to be the defender of postcolonial subjects, was now conceived as the major threat to the well being of its citizens."[2] The mantra of citizenship itself left unvoiced continuing injustices and unresolved inequalities. Ironically, the Black Power concept, already impeded by the diversity of its possible meanings, some of them highly co-optable, also evinced

---

[2] Bennetta Jules-Rosette, *Black Paris: the African Writers' Landscape* (Urbana: University of Illinois Press, 1998), 77; Simon Gikandi, "Globalization and the Claims of Postcoloniality." *South Atlantic Quarterly* 100 (3) (2001): 637.

a commitment to statism internationally that meant that diaspora minorities functioned most agreeably as lobbyists for an Africa ruled by elites.

The synchronous nature of black revolt in the United States, Canada, and the Caribbean suggests the utility of looking at a North American, rather than nationally specific, black freedom struggle. Examining black insurgency on the basis of a "moral geography" could lead to new insights about the diaspora. African-American discourses have been adopted worldwide, but their hegemony is displaced when they are mapped onto a narrative of continuous commerce within the Americas, textured by the histories of slavery, migration, imperialism, and cultural exchange.

While developing countries clung tenaciously to the trappings of nationalism, an integrated world market began undermining them. States whose leadership had been hastily cobbled together in anticipation of independence were most negatively affected. Nationalism had compelled an understanding of Africa as the nexus of complex human societies that would prevail over the colonial era's "heart of darkness" stereotypes. How appalling, then, that in the late twentieth century, thirty years of warfare, neocolonial policies, and natural disasters seem to have so effectively banished much of the painstaking revisionism. Nigeria "was a nation of enormous wealth," General Colin Powell informed Henry Louis Gates Jr. in 1995, "but ... they just tend not to be honest ... it is in their national culture." Nigeria, Powell asserted, is "going backward in time hundreds of years."[3]

The general's rather deterministic tale of declension was mirrored in other African events. Ugandans, recovering in 1999 from years of war, hoped to recoup a tourist industry that had shown great promise during the country's early years. Uganda's lakes and forests might draw the foreign capital desperately needed to rebuild its battered economy. When on March 1, 1999, Hutu guerrillas from Rwanda hacked and bludgeoned to death eight British and American tourists from a group that they had kidnapped in a forced march into the bush, that hope was suspended.[4]

Print and broadcast media, not content with reporting this debacle, waxed lurid at the deaths in the Bwindi National Park, also known as the Impenetrable Forest. The juxtaposition of jungle and tribal warfare – the gorilla and guerrilla – added to the Conradian allure. "Fist-thick vines; total undergrowth, overgrowth wherever you are. It would be impossible to patrol this entirely. And of course the Congo border is right there.... This is a very mountainous region. It's green; it's lush; it's gorgeous; but yes, indeed, somebody could hide in the jungle." Journalists, daubing a gaudy canvas in broad

---

[3] Henry Louis Gates Jr., "Powell and the Black Elite," *The New Yorker*, September 25, 1995, p. 64.
[4] "Scotland Yard Joins FBI in Uganda Killings Probe," *London Free Press*, March 6, 1999, p. A10; Paul Busharizi, "Uganda Tourists Killed," *Manchester Guardian Weekly*, March 7, 1999, p. 5; Kurt Shillinger "Slaying of Tourists Shows Anti-US Sentiment," *Boston Globe*, March 7, 1999, p. A6.

strokes, painted over deeper issues. That the Hutu guerrillas were part of a group that had killed 800,000 non-Europeans in 1994 was not the least of these. The Western press and Western governments skipped over the maimed and mutilated ghosts of that catastrophe, the worst instance of genocide since World War II. The Ugandan park ranger whom the rebels also killed was equally invisible. What was important was the white tourists' brutal deaths, proclaimed all over the world and made emblematic of what is wrong with contemporary Africa. "TOURISTS BUTCHERED IN BLOODY JUNGLE HORROR."[5]

Press accounts reflected no sense of irony in reporting on deluxe resorts in hungry countries where Westerners, enormously rich by local standards, photographed wildlife from fake huts. Africans were the villains of zoological tourism. "African Wildlife Threatened. Human Violence Nears Gorillas, Rhinos on Continent," Reuters announced. Yet, paradoxically, the end of tourism meant the loss of money for conservation and diminished opportunities to employ local people in and around conservation areas. In Central Africa, war placed additional strains on wild fauna, hunted for food and poached for profit in places where central governments exercise little effective control. Pressure on fragile polities further increased the likelihood of animal vectors introducing unpredictable microbes into human populations.[6] Civil wars and natural disasters challenged the notion of an African diaspora located outside the continent. Migration, both voluntary and forced, displaced millions of people, who were effectively noncitizens and remained noncitizens on the continent and in the states where they sought refuge.

The media condemned Africans' failings, their inability to safeguard their ecological inheritance and their populations, and the epidemiological dangers their frailty posed for the rest of the world. European states, disintegrating and recombining in the wake of the Soviet implosion, faced similar problems. These subjects, however, were spared the degradation assigned to Africa. Balkan refugees appeared on television and in print fully clothed, their leaders in bespoked suits and generously pompadoured and pomaded. The atrocities Europeans endured and inflicted were not clinically cataloged for public inspection. News from the Balkans lacked the shocking visuals and sensational rhetoric standard for the "Dark Continent," although comparable tribal fighting and ghastly crimes occurred there. Disparate reportage reveals how racial thought permits the public to become inured to the spectacle of nameless Africans with severed limbs, not in King Leopold of Belgium's rush for rubber, but in the contemporary rush for diamonds.

Local agency and intractable structural defects, not Western culpability, are assumed to explain Africa's arrested development. Its problems are received

---

[5] Deborah Orin, "Tourists Butchered in Bloody Jungle Horror," *The New York Post*, March 3, 1999, p. 5.

[6] Reuters release, "African Wildlife Threatened: Human Violence Nears Gorillas, Rhinos on Continent," April 2, 1999.

as unique. Adam Hochschild has written of how the holocaust unleashed in the Congo by Leopold escaped due condemnation in his time.[7] During the same era, the Western powers barely noticed the genocidal German campaign against the Herero people of Namibia. Reuters – without fanfare and to the vast disinterest of most of its audience – declared in a June 9, 2000, dispatch that in the final years of the twentieth century, nearly two million people died in the Congo. These grim facts suggest that decolonization cannot be treated as a fait accompli.

Journalism that can preserve moral distance can hinder initiative and impede understanding. Few observers saw, for example, the resemblance between the "disappearances" and assassinations effected by Central American death squads in the 1970s and 1980s and similar acts of terror perpetrated in the American South during the civil rights movement's "high tide of black resistance." What is it that seems inappropriate when such comparisons are made? Racist positivism, inherited from the nineteenth century, makes Latins "hot-blooded" and "anarchic" and life in the Tropics cheap. In the one instance, dubious personality traits and weak civil institutions in "banana republics" are assumed. In the other instance, while the disposability of the rural black poor might accord harmoniously with the same imagery, exposing the absence of civilized government in the Deep South during the period raises uncertainty about how deeply rooted in American life such foundational beliefs as representative democracy really are. Such doubt, however, is perceived as overdrawn and cannot be tolerated.

Decolonization left the white settler regimes of southern Africa standing. Rhodesia succumbed first, with black majority rule achieved in 1979 after a revolutionary war. The South African transition followed the assassinations of leftist leaders and the Soviet collapse, after which African National Congress leader Nelson Mandela, released from prison, would pose less of a threat. By the end of the 1970s, legislative protections were in place to guard African-Americans' civil rights, and there had been meaningful shifts in racial attitudes in white civil society.

Yet by the turn of the century, these achievements were being undercut by mass unemployment and incarceration, severe cuts in government support of education, the sometimes willful destruction of cities, and the renewal of white supremacist politics that were profoundly hostile to black aspirations. New disfranchisement laws substantially shrank the black vote. In the case *Richardson v. Ramirez* the Supreme Court invoked the Fourteenth Amendment in excluding convicted felons from voting. "Following *Richardson v. Ramirez*," Heather Ann Thompson writes, "states across the country began passing laws that disproportionately disfranchised African Americans. By the year 2000, 1.8 million African Americans had been barred from the polls because of felon disfranchisement laws," legislation that perversely flipped the "language [that]

---

[7] Adam Hochschild, *King Leopold's Ghost: A Story of Greed, Terror, and Heroism in Colonial Africa* (Boston: Houghton Mifflin, 1998).

was written into the Fourteenth Amendment to protect African-American voting rights after the Civil War."[8]

A new antifederalism and an emphasis on privatization once more reoriented black engagements with the nation-state. As the finance industry swept through the world's capitals, demolishing what were once the regulatory prerogatives of states, it loosened an avalanche of privatized institutions. These undercut the purchase that nations formerly had on social welfare and individual security. Into the maelstrom went African Americans, still bound by racial proscription.

Like the Italian Renaissance, the age of discovery, and other eras tagged for historians' convenience, the era of decolonization provides a tidy handle to describe and interpret a period marked by singular characteristics. It was a time of expanding states and international institutions, and formal endorsements of human equality. While these developments would point to a sanguine future, the closure they imply is misleading. Decolonization has instead been a process capable of reversing itself and has in the current age taken on the character of an infinite loop, leaving millions still searching for power.

---

[8] Heather Ann Thompson, "Why Mass Incarceration Matters: Rethinking Crisis, Decline, and Transformation in Postwar American History," *Journal of American History* 97:3 (December 2011): 732.

Bibliography

Primary Sources

Archival material

Canada, Library and Archives, Ottawa.
  Canadian Security Intelligence Service Records, RG 146.
Columbia University, New York.
  Andrew D. Cordier Papers.
Joint Center for Political Studies, Washington, D.C.
  Vertical File, Washington, D. C.
Library of Congress, Washington, D.C.
  John F. Kennedy Pre-presidential Papers, 1946–1960.
  Loy W. Henderson Papers.
Mary McLeod Bethune Museum and Archives, Washington, D.C.
  National Council of Negro Women Records.
Moorland Spingarn Research Center, Howard University, Washington, D.C.
  Percival L. Prattis Papers.
  Rayford W. Logan Papers.
National Archives II, College Park, Md.
  Federal Bureau of Investigation Records, Record Group 65.
  U.S. State Department Central File, Record Group 59.
Rockefeller Archive Center, Pocantico, N.Y.
  General Education Board Papers.
  John D. Rockefeller III Fund Records.
  Rockefeller Brothers Fund Records.
  Rockefeller Foundation Records.
  Social Science Research Council Records.
Schomburg Center for Research on Black Culture, New York Public Library.
  Alex Haley Papers.
  American Society of African Culture Papers.
  Benjamin Davis Papers.
  Franklin Williams Papers.
  Freedom of Information Act Materials on the Civil Rights Movement, 1958–1969,
    ed. David Garrow.

George Schuyler Papers.
Melville and Frances Herskovits Papers.
National Association of Colored Graduate Nurses Collection.
Phelps Stokes Fund Records.
Ralph Bunche Papers.
Schomburg Clipping File.
Tamiment Library, New York University, New York, N.Y.
Students for a Democratic Society (SDS) Records.
University of California Los Angeles.
Ralph J. Bunche Papers.
University of Minnesota, St. Paul, Minnesota.
Young Men's Christian Association Collection.
Wisconsin Historical Society, Madison.
Carlton Goodlett Papers.
Committee to Combat Racial Injustice Papers.
Michele Gibault Papers.
World Peace Brigade Papers.

Published government records.

Declassified Documents Reference System, Woodbridge, Conn.: Primary Source Media, 1998.
The Declassified Documents, Retrospective Collection, ed. Annabel Wile. Washington, D.C.:Carrollton Press, 1976–77.
Department of State Bulletin, serial, Washington, D.C. State Department Bureau of Public Affairs.
Documents of the National Security Council, 1947–1977, Washington, D.C.: University Publications of America, 1980.
FBI File on Malcolm X, Wilmington, Del.: Scholarly Resources, 1995.
FBI File on the Student Nonviolent Coordinating Committee, Wilmington, Del.: Scholarly Resources, 1991.
Federal Bureau of Investigation, FBI Documents Regarding Thurgood Marshall, Washington, D.C.: U.S. Dept. of Justice, 1998.
Foreign Relations of the United States, serial, Washington, D.C.: Government Printing Office.
Macmillan Cabinet Papers, 1957–1963, CD-ROM, London: Adam Matthew Publications, 1999.
Republic of Tanzania. Study of the Rural Development Programme: Ujamaa Villages and Rural Development Staff of Tanga, Kilimanjaro, Arusha. Dar-es-Salaam: Ministry of Regional Administration and Rural Development 1970.
United States Census Bureau, Demographic Trends in the 20th Century, Census 2000 Special Reports, Series CENSR-4, Washington, D.C.: U.S. Government Printing Office, 2002.
United States Department of Labor, Office of Policy Planning and Research, The Negro Family: The Case For National Action, [Moynihan Report], March 1965.
United States House of Representatives, Committee on Un-American Activities, *Guerrilla Warfare Advocates in the United States,* 90th Congress, May 6, 1968.
Federal Data Banks, Computers and the Bill of Rights, Hearings before the Subcommittee on Constitutional Rights of the Committee on the Judiciary, United

States Senate, 92nd Congress, 1st Session, February and March 1971. Washington, D.C.: Government Printing Office, 1971.

Military Surveillance, Hearings Before the Subcommittee on Constitutional Rights of the Committee on the Judiciary. United States Senate 93rd Congress 2nd Session, 1974.

U. S. Senate, Hearings Before the Select Committee to Study Governmental Operations with Respect to Intelligence Activities, 94th Cong, 1st session, 1976.

Published papers and reports.

Claude Barnett Papers, Frederick, Md.: University Publications of America, 1985.

General Education Board, Annual Report, 1956.

Martin Luther King, Jr., Papers, ed. Clayborne Carson et al., (Berkeley: University of California Press, 1992–2005).

NAACP Papers, Frederick, Md.: University Publications of America, 1982–96.

National Committee against Discrimination in Housing (NCDH) "The 1965 Capahosic Fair Housing Conference," May 26–8, 1965, New York: NCDH, 1965.

Dr. Kwame Nkrumah Digital Collection, Lincoln University, Pennsylvania.

Bayard Rustin Papers, Bethesda, Md: University Press of America, 1988.

The Papers of Adlai Stevenson, ed. Walter Johnson, Boston: Little, Brown, 1977.

Student Nonviolent Coordinating Papers, Ann Arbor, Mich.: UMI, 1994.

Mary Church Terrell Papers, Washington, D.C.: Library of Congress Photoduplication Service, 1977.

Tuskegee Clipping File, Sanford N.C.: Microfilming Corporation of America, 1981.

United States Senate, The Select Committee to Study Governmental Operations with Respect to Intelligence Activities, Foreign and Military Intelligence. Report no. 94–755, 94th Cong., 2d Sess. Washington, D.C.

Interviews.

George Ball interview, July 9, 1971, Lyndon B. Johnson Presidential Library.

Kenneth Clark interview, March 19, 1976, Columbia University Center for Oral History.

Eleanor Lansing Dulles interview, New York City Columbia University Center for Oral History.

Donald B. Easum interview, January 17, 1990, Foreign Affairs Oral History Collection, Association for Diplomatic Studies and Training, Library of Congress, Washington, D.C.

Charles Evers interview, April 3, 1974, Lyndon B. Johnson Presidential Library.

Jacob Potofsky interview, New York City, 1964; Columbia University Center for Oral History.

E. Frederick Morrow interview, New York City, January 31, 1968, Columbia University Center for Oral HistoryJohn H. Morrow interview, May 11, 1981, Phelps Stokes Fund Oral History Project on Black Chiefs of Mission, Schomburg Center for Research on Black Culture, New York Public Library.

David D. Newsom interview, June 17, 1991, Foreign Affairs Oral History Collection, Association for Diplomatic Studies and Training, Library of Congress, Washington, D.C.

Ethel L. Payne interview, October 13, 1987, Washington, D.C., Washington Press Club
    Foundation.
Maxwell Rabb interview, New York City, October 6, 1970, Columbia University Oral
    History Collection.
William Sutherland interview, by Prexy Nesbitt and Mimi Edmunds, New York City,
    July 19, 2003, *No Easy Victories* interviews, online at http://www.noeasyvictories.
    org/interviews/into1_sutherland.php.
James E. Webb interview, April 29, 1969, Lyndon B. Johnson Presidential Library.

By author.

Elombe Brath, New York City, May 16, 1994.
Courtland Cox, telephone, June 21, 2012.
Ernest Kaiser, New York City, May 13, 1994.
Charles Simmons, Detroit, August 15, 1998.
James Turner, telephone, April 2, 2012.

Newspapers consulted

Afro-American, Baltimore, Md.
Amsterdam News, New York, N.Y.
Atlanta World, Atlanta, Georgia.
Bay State Banner, Boston, Mass.
Chicago Defender, Chicago, Il.
Daily Press, Newport News, Va.
El Diario, New York, N.Y.
Los Angeles Free Press.
New York Times.
Norfolk Journal and Guide, Norfolk, Va.
Palm Beach Post, Palm Beach, Florida.
Pittsburgh Courier, Pittsburgh, Pa.
St. Petersburg Times, St. Petersburg, Florida.
Times, London, England.
Washington Post, Washington, D.C.

Selected Secondary Sources

Ahmad, Muhammad (Maxwell Stanford, Jr.) 2007. *We Will Return in the Whirlwind:
    Black Radical Organizations, 1960–1975*. Chicago: Charles Kerr.
Allitt, Patrick. 1993. *Catholic Intellectuals and Conservative Politics in America, 1950–
    1975*. Ithaca, N.Y.: Cornell University Press.
Allman, Jean. 2008. "Nuclear Imperialism and the Pan-African Struggle for Peace and
    Freedom." *Souls* 10 (2): 83–102.
Anderson, Carol. 2003. *Eyes Off the Prize: The United Nations and the African American
    Struggle for Human Rights, 1944–1955*. Cambridge: Cambridge University Press.
Anderson, Jervis. 1997. *Bayard Rustin: Troubles I've Seen: A Biography*. Berkeley:
    University of California Press.
Austin, David. 2007. "All Roads Led to Montreal: Black Power, the Caribbean, and
    the Black Radical Tradition in Canada." *Journal of African American History* 92
    (Autumn): 516–39.

Beauregard, Robert A. 2003. *Voices of Decline: The Postwar Fate of U.S. Cities*. New York: Routledge.

Bennett, Scott H. 2003. *Radical Pacifism: The War Resisters League and Gandhian Nonviolence in America, 1915–1963*. Syracuse, N.Y.: Syracuse University Press.

Borstelmann, Thomas. 1993. *Apartheid's Reluctant Uncle*. New York: Oxford University Press.

2001. *Cold War and the Color Line: American Race Relations in the Global Arena*. Cambridge, Mass.: Harvard University Press.

Brennan, Mary C. 1995. *Turning Right in the Sixties: The Conservative Capture of the GOP*. Chapel Hill: University of North Carolina Press.

Brenner, Aaron. 1996. "Rank-and-File Rebellion, 1966–1975," Ph.D. dissertation, Columbia University, New York.

Brock, Lisa. 1996. "Questioning the Diaspora: Hegemony, Black Intellectuals and Doing International History from Below." *Issue* 24 (2): 9–13.

Campbell, David. 1998. *Writing Security: United States Foreign Policy and the Politics of Identity*, rev. ed. Minneapolis: University of Minnesota Press.

Campbell, James. 1994. *Paris Interzone: Richard Wright, Lolita, Boris Vian, and Others on the Left Bank, 1946–60*. London: Secker and Warburg.

Carmichael, Stokely, with Ekwueme Michael Thelwell. 2003. *Ready for Revolution: The Life and Struggles of Stokely Carmichael (Kwame Ture)*. New York: Scribner.

Cleaver, Kathleen, ed. 2006. *Target Zero: A Life in Writing*. New York: Palgrave Macmillan.

Cohen, Lizabeth. 2003. *A Consumers' Republic: The Politics of Mass Consumption in Postwar America*. New York: Knopf.

Connelly, Matthew. 2000. "Taking Off the Cold War Lens: Visions of North-South Conflict during the Algerian War for Independence." *American Historical Review* 105 (3): 739–69.

Cowie, Jefferson. 2002. "Nixon's Class Struggle: Romancing the New-Right Worker, 1969–1973." *Labor History* 43 (3): 257–83.

Crespino, Joseph H. 2007. *In Search of Another Country: Mississippi and the Conservative Counterrevolution*. Princeton, N.J.: Princeton University Press.

Culverson, Donald R. 1999. *Contesting Apartheid: U.S. Activism, 1960–1987*. Boulder, Colo: Westview Press.

Curtin, Michael. 1995. *Redeeming the Wasteland: Television Documentary and Cold War Politics*. New Brunswick, N.J.: Rutgers University Press.

Dallek, Robert. 1998. *Flawed Giant: Lyndon Johnson and His Times, 1961–1973*. New York: Oxford University Press.

Dean, Robert D. 2001. *Imperial Brotherhood: Gender and the Making of Cold War Foreign Policy*. Amherst: University of Massachusetts Press.

D'Emilio, John. 2000. *Lost Prophet: The Life and Times of Bayard Rustin*. New York: Free Press.

DeRoche, Andrew. 2001. *Black, White, and Chrome: The United States and Zimbabwe, 1953–1998*. Trenton, N.J.: Africa World Press.

Dickerson, James. 1998. *Dixie's Dirty Secret: The True Story of How the Government, the Media, and the Mob Conspired to Combat Integration and the Vietnam Antiwar Movement*. Armonk, N.Y.: M. E. Sharpe.

Dirik, Arif. 1998. "The Third World." In *1968: The World Transformed*, eds. Carole Fink, Philipp Gassert and Detlef Junker. Washington, D. C., and Cambridge: German Historical Institute and Cambridge University Press.

Dudziak, Mary L. 2000. *Cold War Civil Rights: Race and the Image of American Democracy*. Princeton, N.J.: Princeton University Press.

Enstad, Nan. 1998. "Fashioning Political Identities: Cultural Studies and the Historical Construction of Political Subjects." *American Quarterly* 50 (4): 745–82.

Eschen, Penny Von. 2004. *Satchmo Blows Up the World*. Cambridge, Mass.: Harvard University Press.

Evans, Marvin. 2012. *Algeria: France's Undeclared War*. New York: Oxford University Press.

Fergus, Devin. *Liberalism, Black Power, and the Making of American Politics, 1965–1980*. Athens: University of Georgia Press, 2009.

Fisher, Christopher T. 2002. "'The Hopes of Man': The Cold War, Modernization Theory, and the Issue of Race in the 1960s," Ph.D. dissertation, Rutgers University.

Fraser, Cary. 1994. *Ambivalent Anti-Colonialism: The United States and the Genesis of West Indian Independence, 1940–1964*. Westport, Conn.: Greenwood Press.

    1992. "Understanding American Policy toward the Decolonization of European Empires, 1945–64." *Diplomacy & Statecraft* 3 (1): 105–25.

Frost, Jennifer. 2001. *"An Interracial Movement of the Poor": Community Organizing and the New Left in the 1960s*. New York: New York University Press.

Fry, Joseph A. 2002. *Dixie Looks Abroad: The South and U.S. Foreign Relations, 1789–1973*. Baton Rouge: Louisiana State University Press.

Gaines, Kevin. 2006. *American Africans in Ghana: Black Expatriates and the Civil Rights Era*. Chapel Hill: University of North Carolina Press.

Genet, Jean. 2004. *The Declared Enemy: Texts and Interviews*. Stanford, Calif.: Stanford University Press.

Gershenhorn, Jerry. 2009. "Not an Academic Affair': African American Scholars and the Development of African Studies Programs in the United States, 1942–1960." *Journal of African American History* 94 (Winter): 44–68.

Gibbs, David N. 1991. *The Political Economy of Third World Intervention: Mines, Money, and U.S. Policy in the Congo Crisis*. Chicago: University of Chicago Press.

Gilmore, Glenda. 2008. *Defying Dixie: The Radical Roots of Civil Rights, 1919–1950*. New York: W. W. Norton.

Glaude, Eddie S., Jr., ed. 2002. *Is It Nation Time? Contemporary Essays on Black Power and Black Nationalism*. Chicago: University of Chicago Press.

Gleijeses, Piero. 2002. *Conflicting Missions: Havana, Washington, and Africa, 1959–1976*. Chapel Hill: University of North Carolina Press.

    1978. *The Dominican Crisis*. Baltimore: Johns Hopkins Press.

Gore, Dayo F., Jeanne Theoharis, and Komozi Woodard, eds. 2009. *Radical Women in the Black Freedom Struggle*. New York: New York University Press.

Gosse, Van. 1998. "The African-American Press Greets the Cuban Revolution." In *Between Race and Empire: African-Americans and Cubans before the Cuban Revolution*, eds. L. Brock and D. C. Fuertes. Philadelphia: Temple University Press.

    2000. "We Are All Highly Adventurous". In *Cold War Constructions: The Political Culture of United States Imperialism, 1945–1966*, ed. C. G. Appy. Amherst: University of Massachusetts Press.

    1993. *Where the Boys Are: Cuba, Cold War America, and the Making of a New Left*. London and New York: Verso.

Guevara, Ernesto. 2000. The *African Dream: The Diaries of the Revolutionary War in the Congo*. London: Harvill Press.

Guinier, Lani, and Gerald Torres. 2002. *The Miner's Canary: Enlisting Race, Resisting Power, Transforming Democracy.* Cambridge, Mass., & London: Harvard University Press.

Guyer, Jane. 1996. *African Studies in the United States: A Perspective.* n. p.: African Studies Association Press.

Hall, James C. 2001. *Mercy, Mercy Me: African American Culture and the American Sixties.* New York: Oxford University Press.

Hall, Michael R. 2000. *Sugar and Power in the Dominican Republic: Eisenhower, Kennedy and the Trujillos.* Westport, Conn.: Greenwood Press.

Hall, Simon. 2003. "The Response of the Moderate Wing of the Civil Rights Movement to the War in Vietnam." *The Historical Journal* 46 (3): 669–701.

Harper, Philip Brian. 1996. *Are We Not Men? Masculine Anxiety and the Problem of African-American Identity.* New York: Oxford University Press.

Hecht, Gabrielle. 1998. *The Radiance of France: Nuclear Power and National Identity after World War II.* Cambridge, Mass.: MIT Presses.

2002. "Rupture-Talk in the Nuclear Age: Conjugating Colonial Power in Africa." *Social Studies of Science* 32 (5–6): 691–727.

Height, Dorothy. 2003. *Open Wide the Freedom Gates.* New York: Public Affairs.

Henry, Charles P., ed. 2000. *Foreign Policy and the Black National Interest.* Albany, N.Y.: SUNY Press.

Hewitt, Steve. 2002. *Spying 101: The RCMP's Secret Activities at Canadian Universities, 1917–1997.* Toronto: University of Toronto Press.

Hoffnung-Garskof, Jesse. 2004. "'Yankee Go Home...and Take Me with You!': Imperialism and International Migration in Santo Domingo, Dominican Republic, 1961–1966." *Canadian Journal of Latin American and Caribbean Studies* 29 (57–8): 39–65.

Hohle, Randolph. 2009. "The Rise of the New South Governmentality: Competing Southern Revitalization Projects and Police Responses to the Black Civil Rights Movement 1961–1965." *Journal of Historical Sociology* 22 (December): 497–527.

Höhn, Maria, and Martin Klimke. 2010. *A Breath of Freedom: The Civil Rights Struggle, African American GIs, and Germany.* New York: Palgrave Macmillan.

Holland, Deborah J. 2002. "Steward of World Peace, Keeper of Fair Play: the American Hydrogen Bomb and Civil Rights, 1945–1954." Ph.D. dissertation, Northwestern University, Evanston, Ill.

Horne, Gerald. 2008. *The End of Empires: African Americans and India.* Philadelphia: Temple University Press.

2001. *From the Barrel of a Gun: The U. S. and the War against Zimbabwe, 1965–1980.* Chapel Hill: University of North Carolina Press.

2009. *Mau Mau in Harlem? The U.S. and the Liberation of Kenya.* New York: Palgrave Macmillan.

Houser, George M. 1990. "Freedom's Struggle Crosses Oceans and Mountains: Martin Luther King, Jr. and the Liberation Struggles in Africa and America." In *We Shall Overcome: Martin Luther King, Jr. and the Black Freedom Struggle*, eds. P. J. Albert and R. Hoffman. New York: Pantheon Books and the United States Capitol Historical Society.

Howard, David. 2001. *Coloring the Nation: Race and Ethnicity in the Dominican Republic.* Boulder, Colo.: Lynne Rienner.

Iton, Richard. 2008. *In Search of the Black Fantastic: Politics and Popular Culture in the Post-Civil Rights Era.* New York: Oxford University Press.

Jackson, Lawrence P. 2011. *The Indignant Generation: A Narrative History of African American Writers and Critics, 1934–1960*. Princeton, N.J.: Princeton University Press.

Jacobson, Matthew Frye. 2006. *Roots Too: White Ethnic Revival in Post-Civil Rights America*. Cambridge, Mass.: Harvard University Press.

James, Joy. 1999. *Shadowboxing: Representations of Black Feminist Politics*. New York: St. Martin's Press.

James, Winston. 1998. *Holding Aloft the Banner of Ethiopia Caribbean Radicalism in Early Twentieth-Century America*. New York: Verso.

Jeffreys-Jones, Rhodri. 2007. *The FBI: A History*. New Haven, Conn.: Yale University Press.

Jeffries, Judson L. ed. 2006. *Black Power in the Belly of the Beast*. Urbana and Chicago: University of Illinois Press.

Johnson, Cedric. 2007. *Revolutionaries to Race Leaders: Black Power and the Making of African American Politics*. Minneapolis: University of Minnesota Press.

Joseph, Peniel E., ed. 2006. *The Black Power Movement: Rethinking the Civil Rights-Black Power Era*. London and New York: Routledge.

—— 2003. "Dashikis and Democracy: Black Studies, Student Activism, and the Black Power Movement." *Journal of African American History* 88 (2): 182–204.

—— 2006. *Waiting 'Til the Midnight Hour: A Narrative History of Black Power in America*. New York: Henry Holt & Company.

Jules-Rosette, Bennetta. 1998. *Black Paris: The African Writers' Landscape*. Urbana: University of Illinois Press.

Kelley, Robin D. G. 2002. "Stormy Weather: Reconstructing Black (Inter)Nationalism in the Cold War Era." In *Is It Nation Time? Contemporary Essays on Black Power and Black Nationalism*, ed. E. S. Glaude Jr. Chicago: University of Chicago Press.

Kelley, Robin D. G., and Betsy Esch. 1999. "Black like Mao: Red China and Black Revolution." *Souls* 1 (4): 6–41.

Kotlowski, Dean. 1998. "Black Power Nixon Style: The Nixon Administration and Minority Business Enterprise." *Business History Review* 72 (3): 409–45.

Krenn, Michael L. 1999. *Black Diplomacy: African Americans and the State Department, 1945–1969*. New York: M. E. Sharpe.

Kunz, Diane B., ed. 1994. *The Diplomacy of the Crucial Decade: American Foreign Relations during the 1960s*. New York: Columbia University Press.

Latham, Michael E. 2000. *Modernization as Ideology: American Social Science and "Nation Building" In the Kennedy Era*. Chapel Hill: University of North Carolina Press.

Lauren, Paul Gordon. 1996. *Power and Prejudice: The Politics and Diplomacy of Racial Discrimination*. 2nd ed. Boulder, Colo.: Westview Press.

Layton, Azza Salama. 2000. *International Politics and Civil Rights Policies in the United States*. Cambridge: Cambridge University Press.

Lazerow, Jama, and Yohuru Williams, eds. 2006. *In Search of the Black Panther Party: New Perspectives on a Revolutionary Movement*. Durham, N.C.: Duke University Press.

Lefebvre, Jeffrey A. 1999. "Kennedy's Algerian Dilemma: Containment, Alliance Politics and the 'Rebel Dialogue.'" *Middle Eastern Studies* 35 (2:1999): 61–82.

Levey, Zach. 2008. "Israel's Exit from Africa, 1973: The Road to Diplomatic Isolation." *British Journal of Middle Eastern Studies* 35 (2): 205–26.

Lewis, Rupert C. 1999. *Walter Rodney's Intellectual and Political Thought*. Detroit: Wayne State University Press.

Lewis-Colman, David M. 2008. *Race against Liberalism: Black Workers and the UAW in Detroit*. Urbana: University of Illinois Press.

Logevall, Fredrik. 1993. "The Swedish American Conflict over Vietnam." *Diplomatic History* (June): 421–46.

Lowe, Lisa, and David Lloyd, eds. 1997. *The Politics of Culture in the Shadow of Capital*. Durham, N.C.: Duke University Press.

Lubiano, Wahneema. 2002. "Standing in for the State: Black Nationalism and 'Writing' the Black Subject." In *Is It Nation Time? Contemporary Essays on Black Power and Black Nationalism*, ed. E. S. Glaude, Jr. Chicago: University of Chicago Press.

Lyons, Terrence. 1994. "Keeping Africa off the Agenda." In *Lyndon Johnson Confronts the World: American Foreign Policy, 1963–1968*, eds. W. I. Cohen and N. B. Tucker. New York: Cambridge University Press.

Macey, David. 1993. *The Lives of Michel Foucault*. London: Hutchinson.

Marable, *Malcolm X: A Life of Reinvention*. New York: Viking, 2011.

Marable, Manning, and Elizabeth Kai Hinton, eds. 2011. *The New Black History*. New York: Palgrave Macmillan.

Massie, Robert Kinloch. 1997. *Loosing the Bonds: The United States and South Africa in the Apartheid Years*. New York: Doubleday.

McAlister, Melani. 2001. *Epic Encounters: Culture, Media, and U.S. Interests in the Middle East, 1945–2000*. Berkeley: University of California Press.

1999. "One Black Allah: The Middle East in the Cultural Politics of African American Liberation, 1955–1970." *American Quarterly* 51 (3): 622–56.

McLean, Nancy. 2006, *Freedom Is Not Enough: The Opening of the American Workplace*. Cambridge, Mass.: Harvard University Press.

McNamara, Robert S. 1995. *In Retrospect*. New York: Random House.

McPherson, Alan. 2003. "Misled by Himself: What the Johnson Tapes Reveal about the Dominican Intervention of 1965." *Latin American Research Review* 38 (2): 127–46.

Meeks, Brian. 1996. *Radical Caribbean: From Black Power to Abu Bakr*. Barbados: The University Press of the West Indies.

Meriwether, James H. 2002. *Proudly We Can Be Africans: Black America and Africa, 1935–1961*. Chapel Hill: University of North Carolina Press.

2008. "'Worth a Lot of Negro Votes': Black Voters, Africa, and the 1960 Presidential Campaign." *Journal of American History* 95 (December): 737–63.

Mills, Charles W. 1997. *The Racial Contract*. Ithaca, N.Y.: Cornell University Press.

Minter, William, Gail Hovey, and Charles E. Cobb. 2007. *No Easy Victories: African Liberation and American Activists over a Half Century, 1950–2000*. Trenton, N.J.: Africa World Press.

Mkandawire, Thandika. 2002. "The Terrible Toll of Post-Colonial 'Rebel Movements' in Africa: Towards an Explanation of the Violence against the Peasantry." *The Journal of Modern African Studies* 40 (2): 181–215.

Montgomery, Mary E. 2004. "The Eyes of the World Were Watching: Ghana, Great Britain, and the United States, 1957–1966," Ph.D. dissertation, University of Maryland, College Park.

Morgan, Eric J. 2006. "The World Is Watching: Polaroid and South Africa." *Enterprise & Society* 7 (September): 520–49.

Moya Pons, Frank. 1998. *The Dominican Republic: A National History*. Princeton, N. J.: Markus Wiener.

Mullen, Bill V. 2004. *Afro-Orientalism*. Durham, N.C.: Duke University Press.

Mullen, Bill V., and James Smethurst, eds. 2003. *Left of the Color Line: Race, Radicalism, and Twentieth-Century Literature*. Chapel Hill: University of North Carolina Press.

Namikas, Lise A. 2002. "Battleground Africa: The Cold War and the Congo Crisis, 1960–1965," Ph.D. dissertation, University of Southern California, Los Angeles.

Nesbitt, Francis Njubi. 2004. *Race for Sanctions: African Americans against Apartheid, 1946–1964*. Bloomington: Indiana University Press.

Ogbar, Jeffrey. 2004. *Black Power: Radical Politics and African American Identity*. Baltimore: Johns Hopkins University Press.

Omi, Michael, and Howard Winant. 1994. *Racial Formation in the United States*. New York: Routledge.

Ongiri, Amy Bugo. 2009. "Prisoner of Love: Affiliation, Sexuality, and the Black Panther Party." *Journal of African American History* 94 (Winter): 69–86.

Palmer, Bryan D. 2003. "Rethinking the Historiography of United States Communism." *American Communist History* 22 (2): 139–73.

Perry, Kennetta Hammond. 2012. "'Little Rock' in Britain: Jim Crow's Transatlantic Topographies." *Journal of British Studies* 51 (January): 155–77.

Plummer, Brenda Gayle. 2008. "Peace Was the Glue: Europe and African American Freedom." *Souls* 10 (2): 103–22.

   1996. *Rising Wind: Black Americans and U.S. Foreign Affairs, 1935–1960*. Chapel Hill: University of North Carolina Press.

Plummer, Brenda Gayle, ed. 2003. In *Window on Freedom: Race, Civil Rights, and Foreign Affairs, 1945–1988*. Chapel Hill: University of North Carolina Press.

Posner, David Braden. 1997. "Afro-America in West German Perspective, 1945–1966." Ph.D. dissertation, Yale University.

Reed, Jr., Adolph, ed. 1999. *Stirrings in the Jug: Black Politics in the Post Segregation Era*. Minneapolis: University of Minnesota Press.

Reitan, Ruth. 1999. *The Rise and Decline of An Alliance: Cuba and African American Leaders in the 1960s*. East Lansing: Michigan State University Press.

Richards, Yevette. 2000. *Maida Springer, Pan-Africanist and International Labor Leader*. Pittsburgh: University of Pittsburgh Press.

Robinson, Cedric J. 1983. *Black Marxism: The Making of the Black Radical Tradition*. London: Zed Press.

   1998. "Blaxploitation and the Misrepresentation of Liberation." *Race & Class* 40 (July–September): 1–12.

Robinson, Dean E. 2001. *Black Nationalism in American Politics and Thought*. New York: Cambridge University Press.

Robinson, Randall. 1998. *Defending the Spirit: A Black Life in America*. New York: Dutton.

Rojas, Fabio. 2007. *From Black Power to Black Studies: How a Radical Social Movement Became an Academic Discipline*. Baltimore: The Johns Hopkins Press.

Romano, Renée. 2000. "No Diplomatic Immunity: African Diplomats, the State Department, and Civil Rights, 1961–1964." *Journal of American History* 87 (September): 546–79.

Rosenberg, Jonathan. 2006. *How Far the Promised Land? World Affairs and the American Civil Rights Movement from the First World War to Vietnam*. Princeton, N.J.: Princeton University Press.

Ross, Andrew. 2005. "Mao Zedong's Impact on Cultural Politics in the West." *Cultural Politics* 1 (March): 5–22.

Saunders, Frances Stonor. 1999. *The Cultural Cold War: The CIA and the World of Arts and Letters*. New York: New Press.

Schatzburg, Michael G. 1991. *Mobutu or Chaos: the United States and Zaire, 1960–1990*. Millburn, N.J.: University Press of America.

Scott, Carl-Gustaf. 2001. "Swedish Sanctuary of American Deserters during the Vietnam War: A Facet of Social Democratic Domestic Politics." *Scandinavian Journal of History* 26 (2): 123–42.

Scott, James. 1998. *Seeing like a State: How Certain Schemes to Improve the Human Condition Have Failed*. New Haven, Conn.: Yale University Press.

Singh, Nikhil Pal. 2004. *Black Is a Country: Race and Democracy beyond Civil Rights*. Cambridge, Mass.: Harvard University Press.

1998. "Culture/Wars: Recoding Empire in an Age of Democracy." *American Quarterly* 50 (13): 471–522.

Skrentny, John David. 1998. "The Effect of the Cold War on African-American Civil Rights: America and the World Audience, 1964–1968." *Theory and Society* 27 (2): 237–85.

Smethurst, James. 2005. *The Black Arts Movement: Literary Nationalism in the 1960s and 1970s*. Chapel Hill: University of North Carolina Press.

Smith, Jennifer B. 1999. *An International History of the Black Panther Party*. New York: Garland.

Springer, Kimberly. 2005. *Living for the Revolution: Black Feminist Organizations, 1968–1980*. Durham, N.C.: Duke University Press.

Steger, Manfred B. 2008. *The Rise of the Global Imaginary: Political Ideologies from the French Revolution to the Global War on Terror*. New York: Oxford University Press.

Stovall, Tyler. 2000. "The Fire This Time: Black Expatriates and the Algerian War." *Yale French Studies*, No. 98: 182–200.

Strange, Susan. 1996. *The Retreat of the State: The Diffusion of Power in the World Economy*. Cambridge: Cambridge University Press.

Street, Joe. 2008. "Malcolm X, Smethwick, and the Influence of the African American Freedom Struggle on British Race Relations in the 1960s." *Journal of Black Studies* 38 (6): 932–95.

Sugrue, Thomas J. 1996. *The Origins of the Urban Crisis: Race and Inequality in Postwar Detroit*. Princeton, N.J.: Princeton University Press.

Suri, Jeremi. 2002. *Power and Protest: Global Revolution and the Rise of Detente*. Cambridge, Mass.: Harvard University Press.

Sutherland, William, and Matt Meyer. 2000. *Guns and Gandhi in Africa*. Trenton, N.J.: Africa World Press.

Tate, Greg, ed. 2003. *Everything but the Burden: What White People Are Taking from Black Culture*. New York: Broadway Books, Random House, 2003.

Thomas, Damion Lamar. 2002. "'The Good Negroes': African-American Athletes and the Cultural Cold War, 1945–1968," Ph.D. dissertation, University of California, Los Angeles.

Thompson, Heather Ann. 2011. "Why Mass Incarceration Matters: Rethinking Crisis, Decline, and Transformation in Postwar American History." *Journal of American History* 97 (3): 703–34.

Vitalis, Robert. 2002. "Black Gold, White Crude: Race and the Making of the World Oil Frontier." *Diplomatic History* 26 (2): 187–213.

2000. "The Graceful and Generous Liberal Gesture: Making Racism Invisible in American International Relations." *Millennium: Journal of International Studies* 29 (2): 331–56.

Wacquant, Loic. 2002. "From Slavery to Mass Incarceration: Rethinking the 'Race Question' in the US." *New Left Review* 13 (January–February): 41–60.

Wall, Irwin M. 2001. *France, the United States, and the Algerian War*. Berkeley: University of California Press.

Ward, Stephen Michael. 2002. "'Ours Too Was a Struggle for a Better World:' Activist Intellectuals and the Radical Promise of the Black Power Movement, 1962–1972," Ph.D. dissertation, University of Texas, Austin.

Weissman, Stephen R. 2010. "An Extraordinary Rendition." *Intelligence and National Security* 25 (April): 198–222.

West, Michael O., William G. Martin, and Fanon Che Wilkins, eds. 2009. *From Toussaint to Tupac: The Black International since the Age of Revolution*. Chapel Hill: University of North Carolina Press.

Westad, Odd Arne. 2006. *The Global Cold War*. Cambridge: Cambridge University Press.

White, Evan. 2003. "Kwame Nkrumah: Cold War Modernity, Pan-African Ideology and the Geopolitics of Development." *Geopolitics* 8 (2): 99–124.

Wilkins, Fanon Che. 2001. "'In the Belly of the Beast': Black Power, Anti-imperialism, and the African Solidarity Movement, 1968–1975," Ph.D. dissertation, New York University.

2007. "SNCC and Africa before the Launching of Black Power, 1960–1965." *Journal of African American History* 92 (Winter): 468–91.

Williams, Yohuru, and Jama Lazerow, eds. 2008. *Liberated Territory: Untold Local Perspectives on the Black Panther Party*. Durham, N.C.: Duke University Press.

Williamson, Joy Ann. 2003. *Black Power on Campus: The University of Illinois, 1965–1975*. Urbana and Chicago: University of Illinois Press.

Winks, Robin. 1997. *The Blacks in Canada*. 2nd ed. Montreal: McGill-Queen's University Press.

Woodard, Komozi. 1999. *A Nation within a Nation: Amiri Baraka (LeRoi Jones) and Black Power Politics*. Chapel Hill: University of North Carolina Press.

Woods, Jeff. 2004. *Black Struggle, Red Scare: Segregation and Anti-Communism in the South, 1948–1968*. Baton Rouge: Louisiana State University Press.

Zeleza, Paul Tiyambe. 1997. "The Perpetual Crises and Solitudes of African Studies in the United States." *Africa Today* 44 (2): 193–210.

Index

9 781107 654716